Aggression In Dogs

Practical Management,

Prevention

&

Behaviour Modification

Always be kind to animals
morning, noon and night.
For animals have feelings too
and furthermore, they bite.
-John Gardner

Brenda Aloff can be reached at:
1711 Karat Road
Midland MI 48640
989.631.8217

This book available at:
Dogwise
701B Poplar
Box 2778
Wenatchee, WA 98807-2778
Orders: 1.800.776.2665
www.dogwise.com

Also by Brenda Aloff:
Positive Reinforcement - Training Dogs In The Real World
(2001). New Jersey: TFH Publications, Inc.

Aggression In Dogs

Practical Management,

Prevention

&

Behaviour Modification

Brenda Aloff

Photography by Sam Ziegenmeyer, Joanne Weber, Kathy Mazur, Amy Morris and Brenda Aloff.
Illustrations by Brenda Aloff.
Cover Design by Brenda Aloff & Joanne Weber.

ISBN 1-59196-073-8
Published by Fundcraft, Inc.
Collierville TN
1.800.259.2592

Before you work on any problem behaviours, your dog should have a physical evaluation by a veterinarian.

First Edition
First Printing, June 2002

The last digit is the print number 9 8 7 6 5 4 3 2 1

This book is dedicated to the dogs who
taught me so much I didn't want to know. Thanks, girls.
My own dogs: Jynx (final home after 4 previous owners; Smooth Fox Terrier),
Breanna (I actually purchased this one! Foxy Rascal's Breanna CD, JE),
and Maeve (final home after 4 previous owners; Why Not Legerdemain CD, TT; German Shepherd Dog).

Acknowledgments

No woman is an island and the writing of this work was not done by one person. I had much help and support. My own dogs have been great and patient (if sometimes rather violent) teachers. It would be impossible to list all of the clients and dogs that made my learning experiences possible. There are some whose involvement and dedication made this book a reality, and improved the quality markedly.

Betty Owen. Without Betty this book would never have gotten finished. She has been there for me in so many ways, not just with emotional support and encouragement. Even though she has a demanding work schedule herself, she jumped right in and spent endless hours reading and re-reading and counseling me on all the business stuff – the stuff that makes me want to dissolve into a weeping puddle of frustration. I would have despaired and scrapped this project a million times because of the business stuff if it weren't for Betty. Thank you so much, Betty.

My daughter, Abbey, and my husband, Steve, graciously covered for me in so many ways while I lived in front of the computer, planned photo shoots, littered the dining room table with illustrations (and the floor around it with my not-so-great efforts).

Lori Saxe was always there to provide me with a sounding board. She helped me frame many ideas with a clarity I would not have achieved by myself. Lori was there as I tried to figure out new software programs (this is me, who cannot work a vending machine). It was not always pretty, but she stuck with me anyway. She ended up with the huge job of doing the Final Edit. Then, to help me meet deadlines, she spent day and night helping with the input of changes. It is thanks to Lori that this text is understandable and so all of you who read it think I am literate. I may not be, but Lori is. Thank you, Lori.

There ended up being numerous editors. Larry Woodward at Dogwise provided me with much direction and his editing shaped this book in many different ways, all for the better. His support and advice has been invaluable. His initial encouragement kept me going past the original "Gee, I think I'll write a book" stage. Thanks for your support and expertise, Larry!

My friend Mary Wilmoth, who has spent hours editing the very first versions of this, and for her encouragement along the way. Then, she got suckered in again at the middle ... gullible girl. Also her endless deletion of my "passive voice" (whatever that is, but it sure bugs the hell out of her). Even though I seemed too stupid to stop including this passive voice thing in the book, all Mary's editing made the book read much smoother. Thank you, Mary!

Judy Smith did some of the editing. She wore out a couple of red pens. Her comment to me after one of the first editing run-throughs was: "Are you sure English is your native language?" I think that tells you all you need to know about the poor souls who helped with the editing. Judy did all this for me during a time when she didn't really have time to spare. Thank you, Judy.

Lonnie Olson was yet another editor. Obviously my dog training skills are far superior to my writing skills. Lonnie was one of several editors who started out at the beginning of the manuscript with tactful suggestions like: "Suggestion here" or "Please re-word for clarity" and by the end of the text was writing notes like: "Try saying it in English using sentences." I got to the point that reading the editors' sarcastic and original remarks was the only entertainment that kept me going at 2:00 AM when I was making the corrections. Thank you, Lonnie.

My current resocialization class is so awesome! These people are dedicated to making a change in their dog's behaviour and they are succeeding because of all the hard work they have put in. They spent classes enduring photo shoots. They have been willing "guinea clients" for experimentation with different techniques. Their contribution to this book is significant, because their input regarding the protocols and help in the development of the protocols is what will make your job easier when you are modifying the behaviour on your own dog. They have pushed the envelope with their dogs because I asked them to do so. Thanks for having faith in me! Big ovation for Marylu Gibbs & Misty, Lori Saxe & Data, Linda Lynch & Bailey, Dianne Stevens & Cotton, Jim Harris & Sunny. Thank you!

The photographers who made the text of the book come to life so clearly are dear friends. Joanne and her wonderful Service Dog, Willie, who accompanies her everywhere, always make any occasion more tranquil with matching sweet and patient natures. Sam brought photography equipment and dogs for me to torture with the muzzle and Halti™ photo shoots. Sam, with her great sense of humour, is an asset anytime, anywhere. With my ability to take any situation and, terrier-like, turn it into disorganized chaos, these women sorted it out and somehow managed to capture the exact images I had imagined, even though I was probably vague at times (ha!). Thanks also to Kathy Mazur and Amy Morris who clicked a couple of photos for the book as well.

The people and dogs who modeled for the photos were awesome. It is difficult enough to train a dog or set him up for an exercise without the added pressure and distraction of the photographer (minimal) and me (maximal) giving directions. Not in any kind of order (after writing this book I am heartily sick of order and organization) and all are important!

Lylenette Canfield-Stack with Jake and Pete (mini Dachshunds) and Silky and Fonzie (Chinese Shar-pei)
Marylu Gibbs and Misty (Rottweiler)
Dianne Stevens and Cotton (Coton de Tulier)
Patti Mierzwa and Salsa (Weimaraner)
Karen Breternitz and Franklin (Great Dane)
Joanne Weber and Willie (Golden Retriever)
Jim Harris and Sunny (Australian Shepherd)
Cherish DeWitt and Jack (Black Labrador Retreiver)
Marie Hopfensperger and Vinny (Smooth Fox Terrier)
Fay Reid and Maple (Golden) and Cassie (Black Labrador)
Sam Ziegenmeyer and Jamie (Wire Fox) and Ally (Yellow Labrador)
Linda Lynch and Bailey (Golden Retriever)
Pat Wenzel and Whitney and D'Art (Pembroke Welsh Corgi)
Maeve (German Shepherd Dog)
Punch (Smooth Fox Terrier)
Breanna (Smooth Fox Terrier)
Rix (Terrier-Hound mix rescue)
Rylie (Border Collie)
Olivia (Terrier-Hound mix rescue)
Lori Saxe and Data (Border Collie-Cattle Dog mix) and Cora (Corgi-All American mix)
Alicia Woodson and Amanda (Black Lab-Shepherd mix)

My sanity is preserved by the Friday Night Therapy Group. Every friday night we get together, train dogs and then solve all world and personal problems (read: bitch session) and discuss dog training, dog breeding, dog nutrition, dog health, dog people we like, dog people who irritate us, dogs ... dogs ... dogs. The regulars (some of them for going on 8 years now...): Amy Morris, Janea Little, Lylenette Canfield-Stack, Marie Hopfensperger, Judy Smith, Karen Breternitz, Lori Saxe, Alicia Woodson. Thank you, ladies, for the comic relief! The support (always welcome) and criticism (not really welcome but appreciated and it did make the book better) show how much you care.

If there are any errors or omissions, they are mine alone, and cannot be placed at the doorstep of anyone else!

Table of Contents

Section I...
Understanding & Managing Aggression in Dogs

Understanding and Managing Aggression in Dogs 21

Aggression – The Most Misunderstood Survival Trait 25

Is Dog Aggression Ever OK? 26

Appropriate vs. Inappropriate Behaviour 26

Canine Social Systems 30

Factors That Influence Aggressive Behaviour 34

Learned Behaviour 34
Genetics 35
Hormones 36
Social Development Periods 37
Stress and Fear 39
Physiological Factors 40
Resiliency and Trauma 41

How Dogs Learn to Avoid Aggression 43

Section II...Dog Communication Systems

Learning to Interpret the Signals – Dog Communication Systems 47

Why is This Important? 48
Dog Signals Provide Information 49

Dog Signals & Stress 51

How Do I Recognize Stress in My Dog? 52

Displacement Behaviours & Calming Signals 53

Displacement Activities 54
Calming Signals 54
How do I Tell if My Dog is Signaling 55

Distance Increasing Signals 60

Table of Contents

Distance Decreasing Signals 66

Tails – The Other End… 70

Interpreting Intent through Observation – Signal Clusters 72

The Role of Play Behaviour 80

Indications that Dogs are in Play Mode 82
Signs of Trouble Ahead 83
Choosing Playmates 83
Puppy Play-Groups 84
Play and the "Older" Dog 85

Dog Parks 89

Section III…Pathways of Aggression

Classifications 93

Vacuum Activity 94
Normal vs. Abnormal 94

Specific Types of Aggression 96

Lack of Socialization – Intraspecies 96
Lack of Socialization – Interspecies 97
Excessive Breed Tendencies or the Lack of These 97
Human Selection for Aggression in Dogs 98
Control Conflict Aggression 99
Fear Aggression 101
Idiopathic Aggression 102
Dog-to-Dog Aggression 102
Learned Aggression 103
Maternal Aggression 103
Neophobia 104
Pain-Related Aggression 104
Play Aggression 105
Possessive Aggression 106
Possessive Aggression – Food Related 107
Predatory Aggression 107
Protective Aggression 109

Table of Contents

Redirected Aggression 111
Territorial Aggression 112
Using Classification as an Accurate Descriptor 113
Summary For Classification of Problem Aggression 113

Stuff that drives your dog crazy 116
Entrapment 116
Frustration 116
Arousal Levels 117
Conflict 119
The Classic Scenario: Fight vs. Flight 120

Section IV..Laws of Learning

The Laws of Learning – Education for Everyone! 125
Classical Conditioning 125
Operant Conditioning 127
Overview for Teaching a Behaviour 129
Carved in Stone – Laws Of Learning 129
Primary Reinforcement 130
Reward Mark 130
For Optimum Communication You Must Also Install a No Reward Mark 131
Canines as Scientists, or: How Does the Dog Pick Out a Pattern? 132
Steps To Success 137

Tools 140
Extinction 140
Systematic Desensitization 142
Flooding 143
Differential Reinforcement Schedules 145
Counter-Conditioning 146

Section V...A Chat About Equipment

The Basics – Collars & Head Collars 153
Martingale Collar 154

Table of Contents

Head Collars 154
Acclimating Your Dog to a Head Collar 160
Leads 171
Maintenance 171

Section VI...Management & Damage Control

Implementing a Scheduled Feed 175

Relationships – Teaching Dogs That Humans Are Relevant! 177
Provide Structure – Help for Pushy or Anxious Dogs! 178

Games People & Dogs Play 180
Games Dogs Play with other Dogs 181
Games that people should play with Dogs 182

!!Quiet!! 186

The Way Owners Promote Aggression 188
Lack of Supervision 188
Lack of Structure 189
Lack of Knowledge 189
Lack of Management 189
Lack of Exercise 190
Inadvertent Reinforcement of Fearful Behaviour 190

On A Walk And Approached By Loose Dogs 191

Section VII...Hi Ho! Hi Ho! It's Planning Before Off to Work We Go

Dogs Make Lots Of Mistakes – So Do You! 197
Timing 198
Approximations 198

Rules 199

Table of Contents

Already Got A Problem vs. Prevention 201
The Relevance Of Observation 203
Getting Started 203

Sudden Environmental Contrast (SEC) 205

The Master Plan 207
Mental Gymnastics 207
Human Behaviour Changes 209
The Plan 210
Jeez, That Was A Lot Of Work – Now What? 211
Problem Solving – Hi Ho, Hi Ho, It's Off To Work We Go 212

Section VIII...The Fix - Protocols

The RM/NRM and Release Cue 217
Determine Positive Reinforcers for Training. 217
Before You Install the RM: 218
To Install the RM: 219
The NRM 220
The Final Polish – The End-Working Cue or Release Cue 221

Name Recognition 224

Eye-contact & Involvement 225
Using Eye Contact as an Anchor 225
Challenge List 242
Maintenance of Behaviour 244
When Do I Correct? 244
Secrets Of Success 247

The Zen Sit & Down Stay 248
What To Have Ready: 249
Acquisition: Manufacture a Sitting Behaviour 249
Placing a Behaviour on a Verbal Cue. 250
Acquisition - Manufacture a Down Behaviour 250

Cease & Desist! 263
Acquisition 265

Table of Contents

Keep In Mind 266
Adding The Cue 266
Over-correction: doggy push-ups 270

The "Twos" Game 275
Game Rules 276
To End this Game 277

Common Sense is Just Not That Common...Taking Advantage of Calming Signals 278
Fear and a Controlled Retreat 279
As a regular agenda 280
Central Theme 281

Training a Polite Greeting 284
Opportunity Training 285
The Cold Shoulder 286
Raise Criteria 286
DRI - Teach Sit to Greet 286
Raise Criteria 287
Challenges 287

Targeting 289
Extrapolating the Exercise 291
Prior History of Aggression or Dogs with Extreme Fear 292

Wait at the Door 294

Territory Entry and Appropriate Greeting Behaviours 296

Handling & Restraint - Desensitization to Being Touched 301
Using TTouch to Enhance Trust 302
Restraint 304
Desensitization to Having the Collar, Head and Neck Touched 305
Collar Touches 308
Sitting and Standing Restraint Exercises 310
Muzzle Grabs 311
Settle 313

Yielding & Husbandry Behaviours 318
The Following Challenges Can be Added to this Basic Behaviour 320
Advanced Husbandry Behaviour - Nail Clipping 321

Being Brave Is Better 324

Table of Contents

Help for the "Cautious" Dog and Human Approaches 324
Secrets for Success 325
Body Postures 325
Basic Protocol 326
Acclimating the Dog to Bizarre Human Behaviour 328

Resource Guarding (Garden Variety Possessive Aggression) 332
Food Bowl Exercises: The Food Be With You 334
Object Guarding: One Species' Trash is Another Species' Treasure 337
Location Guarding: Green Eggs and Ham 340

Dog to Dog Approaches 342
Approaches 343
Raising Criteria: Person-to-Person Approaches 346
Dog to Dog Approaches 349
Dog approaches from behind 349
The Fine Art of Butt-Sniffing 349
In Closing... 350

Leash Aggression 353

Advanced work with Dog-to-Dog Approaches 359
Preparations 362

Aggression Directed Toward A Canine Housemate 369
Why Are They Fighting? 369
Anatomy of a Dog Fight 370
Management 373
Protocols for Housemate Aggression 374
How Trainers Thwart Their Own Progress 376
Summary 379

There Are NO "Recipes" To Modify Aggression 381

Appendices

Case History Examples 385
Learned Aggression, Territorial Aggression. 386
Play Aggression. 388

Table of Contents

Learned Aggression, Territorial Aggression, Breed Tendencies 390
Possessive Aggression, Protective Aggression, Learned Aggression. 391
Predatory Aggression. 394
Territorial Aggression, Learned Aggression, Fear-based Aggression. 396
Fear Based Aggression, Learned Aggression, Generalized Anxiety. 397
Abnormal Behaviour. 400
Control Conflict Aggression, Possessive Aggression, Abnormal Behaviour. 402

Glossary 407

Resources 415

Suggested Reading and Viewing Material 416

Seminars – and Thanks 416

References 417

Index 419

About The Author 425

List of Illustrations and Photographs

Acknowledgments 6

.... 6

Contrast Between Assertive & Yielding Postures 32

Stress 52

Sniffing 56

Look-Away 57

Lip-Licking 57

Blinking 57

Yawning 58

Scratching 58

Shaking 59

Distance Increasing Signals 60

Distance Increasing Signals-Extreme 62

Distance Increasing Signals-Warning 63

Distance Increasing Signals-Territorial Barking 64

Distance Decreasing Signals – Submissive Roll 67

Distance Decreasing Signals – Appeasing Facial Expression 68

Distance Decreasing Signals – Paw Lift 68

Distance Decreasing Signals – Neutral But Friendly 69

Normal Tail 71

Tucked Tail 71

Dervish – Signal Clusters 73

Distance Decreasing Signals – Friendly 74

Distance Increasing Signals – Guarding, Extreme 75

Defensive 76

Defensive & Uncertain, Extreme 77

Offensive & Assertive 78

Play Bow 81

Role Playing Games 87

Friendly Approaches 88

List of Illustrations and Photographs

Necessary Tools 131
Inappropriate collars 153
Martingale Collars 154
Safety Modifications 155
Halti Head Collars 156
1 of 2 Holding The Dog To Put On The Halti 157
Step 1: Fitting the Halti 158
2 of 2 Holding The Dog To Put On The Halti 158
1 of 2 Fitting the Halti 158
2 of 2 Fitting the Halti 159
A Minor Skirmish Because the Head Collar Feels Foreign 161
Teaching Ally to "Give" To The Pressure Of The Head Collar 162
Yes! 163
Teaching Ally To Move & Keep The Leash Loose 164
Back Up... 165
...And Pivot into Heel position. 165
Sit Correction With Head Collar For the Dog Who KNOWS Sit 166
Down Correction For The Dog That KNOWS Down - Photo 1 of 2 167
Down Correction Photo 2 of 2 168
Acclimating Jamie to a Muzzle 170
Using Squeeze Cheese 171
Muzzles 172
Installing a RM 219
Back-Away 227
Move-Into 228
Approximation #1: Obtain Voluntary Attention 230
Approximation #2: Manufacture Direct Eye Contact 232
Make A Choice 234
Using Body Posture As A Cue 235
Premack Principle 236

List of Illustrations and Photographs

Front Position 238
Moving Attention at Heel 241
Person Offers Food 243
Challenge: Treats On The Chair 245
Moving Attention: Advanced Challenge 246
Nose to Toes is the Ticket! 251
Fold Back Down 253
Tie-back 258
Challenges: Stays 261
Moving By & Resisting Temptation 269
Involvement & Leave It Combined 271
Increasing Control With Desist - Challenges 272
Calling Past Food 272
Using Prey Objects To Teach "Switching" # 1 of 4 273
Using Prey Objects To Teach "Switching" # 2 of 4 273
Using Prey Objects To Teach "Switching" # 3 of 4 274
Using Prey Objects To Teach "Switching" # 4 of 4 274
Calming Signal In Response To Another Dog's Stress 282
Calming Signal 282
Manufactured Calming Signal 283
Touching the Target 290
Following the Target 290
Troubleshooting 291
Target Your Hand 292
"Friend" Cue - Using Targeting as a Greeting Behaviour 293
Territory Entry & Greeting 1 of 3 298
Territory Entry & Greeting 2 of 3 299
Territory Entry & Greeting 3 of 3 300
Assess-a-Hand 306
Collar Touches 309

List of Illustrations and Photographs

Advanced Collar Touches 309
Basic Sit Restraint 310
Exam By Others - Sit Restraint 312
Settle - Hand Position 315
Settle 315
Big Hugs Are Part Of Husbandry Work 316
How to do the Nail-Hold 322
Acclimating Salsa To Bizarre Human Behaviour 330
Down Near Food Bowl 335
Food Bowl Work 336
Using the Assess-a-Hand 336
Typical "Guarding" Posture 338
Alerting 344
Dog Approaches #1 of 2 347
Dog Approaches #2 of 2 348
The Fine Art Of Butt-Sniffing 351
Tight Leash Approaches #1 of 4 356
Tight Leash Approaches #2 of 4 357
Tight Leash Approaches #3 of 4 357
Tight Leash Approaches #4 of 4 358
Advanced Dog Approaches Near Leashed Dogs 361
Dog Approaches & Threshold Distances 363
Advanced Dog Approaches Near "Loose" Dogs 364
Advanced On-Leash Approaches #1 of 2 366
Advanced On-Leash Approaches #2 of 2 367

UNDERSTANDING AND MANAGING AGGRESSION IN DOGS

A Positive Approach

Introduction

How to deal with aggression in dogs is a controversial subject. There is probably no issue more divisive among dog trainers today. Over time, however, there has been a growing acceptance of the idea that a dog presenting with aggressive behavior is best treated using positive training and management techniques rather than the coercive, forceful methods favored in the past.

This book is based on the notion that many dogs display aggression because they are "uneducated." This is a dog who, for whatever reason, never learned how to communicate in an appropriate and effective manner to humans and/or other dogs. This animal learned that aggression can be an effective tool to gain social distance or gain access to valuable resources. These animals, in general, respond very well to a protocol designed to help them access new ways of behaving in social situations. My field experience has taught me that these dogs are best worked with using the positive methods outlined in this book.

By contrast, some dogs display aggression because of physiological and/or chemical imbalances, essentially suffering from what in a human would be called a "personality disorder." These animals are classified as "abnormal." For an abnormal dog, the training and management protocols laid out in this book may be inappropriate or dangerous. If you have any doubts about your dog, or you are afraid of your dog, it is imperative that you seek specialized help from a Behaviour Consultant or Veterinary Behaviourist. I will outline how to work with these professionals in cases where a dog is showing aggression due to such physiological abnormalities.

If your dog Already Has A Problem, or you are seeing behaviour that causes you concern, you will want to educate yourself about the items listed below. Make no mistake about it, modifying your dog's behaviour will require a serious commitment on your part. *Preventing* aggression in your otherwise healthy dog also requires a significant level of commitment from you, the owner.

To minimize the chances of aggression problems developing, AND to modify behaviour in the dog who is already presenting with aggression, you will want to know:

- What aggression is and how it has been used by dogs through the history of the species as a survival trait.
- Factors that influence aggression in dogs.
- The meaning of yielding and assertive behaviours and how to recognize them.
- The importance of socializing your puppy or dog, and what that really entails.
- The signals dogs use to communicate with other dogs and with humans.
- How to manage the environment to reduce tendencies toward aggressive behaviour.
- How to change your dog's behaviour.

The chances of raising an aggressive dog are reduced when the dog learns proper behaviour and his owners use the right training and management techniques.

Because I have lived with dogs who have aggression problems, I find it easy to empathize with the stress this places on a family and the guilt that can accompany this stress. Dealing with an aggressive dog places owners in a situation they are ill-prepared for and forces upon them decisions they don't know how to make. Pet owners often ask, "Did I do something wrong?" And the answer often is "Yes," despite their best intentions. The owners didn't try to get it wrong; mistakes were made out of a simple lack of education. What is past is past, however. I always emphasize "How We Are Going To Deal With This NOW" and focus on future interactions. The past is used only as a history to help with the education process.

In this text I don't only discuss philosophy. I have laid out step-by-step instructions, real Nuts-and-Bolts, Roll-Up-Your-Sleeves stuff that is field proven in modifying aggressive behaviour in dogs.

Good Luck! We all need a helping hand sometimes. By learning the concepts and techniques in this book, you will be in a better position to overcome and prevent aggression problems, for your sake and that of your dog - whose life may depend on it!

Section I

Understanding and Managing Aggression In Dogs

A Positive Approach

1

AGGRESSION - THE MOST MISUNDERSTOOD SURVIVAL TRAIT

An academic definition of aggression would be: With consideration for context and normal species patterns, aggression is behaviour or behaviour patterns that are used to resolve conflicts, due to threat or challenge, that are ultimately solved by either contest or deference. What this means, fundamentally, is that aggression is an adaptation that dogs use to aid them in the "Survival of the Fittest" game. It is used as a means to gain control over important resources or to gain personal space. Aggression is one of many social behaviours dogs use to *communicate information* to other dogs, humans, and any other species with which they come into contact.

We often misunderstand dog aggression because we fail to realize that dogs relate to humans and other species just as they would another dog unless *we* teach them differently. A dog is genetically prepared to behave only as a dog. Dog language is the only language that dogs are familiar with, and it is the only language they come "hard-wired" with to communicate. If you are raised in America and speak English and you go to another country where German is the prevalent language, you are initially going to have trouble even asking where the bathroom is. Unfortunately, this is a problem many of our dogs have too! The difference is, dogs sometimes die because of such minor communication problems.

This book is devoted to teaching you and your dog how to operate as a team. The emphasis is on educating your dog to better communicate, thus reducing the need for aggressive or defensive behaviour to resolve conflict.

The target group is the uneducated dog. By raising your awareness of the dog's efforts to communicate with you and by learning how to communicate (effectively modify behaviour) with a dog presenting with aggression, you will know how to prevent aggression in the general dog population.

The onus is on us, the humans, to educate our dogs about appropriate behaviour with people and to learn the language that dogs come equipped with. Normal and common human mannerisms may be naturally misconstrued by a dog. As a greeting ceremony, we humans habitually obtain direct eye contact, advance into personal space with a hand extended, and show our teeth in a smile. How do you think a dog might interpret that behaviour? Consider: What do direct eye contact and bared teeth mean in Dog World? If we cannot be sensitive to dog language and understand its implications, then we are likely to make matters worse for the aggressive dog, as well as inadvertently promote aggression in dogs.

2

IS DOG AGGRESSION EVER OK?

Appropriate vs. Inappropriate Behaviour

Think carefully about the words "appropriate" and "in context." There are certainly occasions where you might view aggression as appropriate and in context. If someone attacked you and your dog growled, snapped, or even bit to force the intruder to flee, everyone would be very impressed with your dog's courage. On the other hand, if the same dog bites a child, you may find yourself in court and your dog in a shelter on Death Row. You are setting an unrealistic standard if you believe a dog should never bite, no matter what the circumstances. How about if the animal is being tortured? Or if her very life is in danger? How else can dogs convey to humans that they feel threatened to the extent that their life is at risk?

It is feasible that an aggressive move by a dog is reasonable and appropriate given the context. Dogs who present with aggression aren't "mean" and wicked creatures. It is not a matter of "this is a good dog, she loves me, she would never bite" versus "only bad dogs are mean and bite." This stigma is a manifestation of the unrealistic views uneducated people have about dogs. This doesn't mean you get to make excuses for marginal, risky or dangerous behaviour. The point I wish to make is that you need to understand the species for what it is, and then go about the task of educating the dog and yourself. All dogs are a combination of desired and undesired traits, just as you and I are.

Given the above, one can define normal behaviour as "Appropriate When In Context." In other words, as the way a majority of healthy dogs with a similar experience and education would react in the same situation.

I see a fair amount of same-sex dog aggression in my Fox Terriers. This is not at all unusual for the breed. My males will square off, posture and escalate aggression over miniscule breaches of etiquette and lack of regard for personal space, such as an accidental bump or jostle from one of the other boys, unless I intervene. But they all are extremely tolerant of bitches and pups of both sexes. They will allow even adolescent males all kinds of leeway, and are very playful, taking a benevolent role with the younger generation. The same male Smooth Fox Terrier who will allow a puppy to pull on his ears is ready and willing to be immediately reactive and unfriendly to any intact male, known or unknown, threatening or not. All that is required is the olfactory stimulation of testosterone, accompanied by any remotely challenging body language or more than a glance of eye contact. The Terriers, as a group, are well known among their aficionados to have a tendency toward being "dog hot." Standing outside (or inside!) the Terrier ring at a breed show is different than standing outside the Golden Retriever ring, for sure! The above described reactivity level and willingness to escalate aggressive behaviour is well within a normal range of behaviour for this breed. This same reactivity level and willingness to escalate aggression at the drop of a hat would not be normal or in context for a Golden Retriever or a Cavalier King Charles Spaniel.

Police and Protection dogs are very carefully trained to exhibit aggressive behaviours in response to different situations, and on cue. These animals are educated about exactly when humans feel aggression is desirable and are trained to respond appropriately to cues and context. The dogs are placed in various situations, and carefully taught when aggression is in context and when it is not. It is not left to chance. The dogs are taught to judge carefully and methodically, keeping in mind that dogs are not, and never will be, humans and do not see the situation as a human would. Then the aggressive behaviour is placed under stimulus control; that is, it is put on cue by the handler. What is appropriate aggression for these dogs is quite different from that of the average pet dog, because their job is very different. However, even Police and Protection dogs are constantly under strict control. No dog, pet or trained protector, can be expected to make human judgment calls – if he makes the wrong choice with his teeth, the results can be disastrous.

By contrast, inappropriate aggression occurs when there is no actual threat to the animal, and the animal's past experience should have established the situation as non-threatening. Consider: would a normal dog (that is, the majority of dogs) have learned an alternative behaviour to use in this circumstance? If so, this makes the aggressive display inappropriate because the "normal" or "average" or "majority of" dogs would have figured out that it is not required in this context. Out-of-context aggression is different: The aggressive display just doesn't "belong" here, and the dog is exhibiting inappropriate display (language) for the situation, either from lack of education or misinterpretation of the situation.

The following case histories give you examples of some out-of-context and inappropriate behaviour.

Table 1: Case History #1

Heaven On Arf Behaviour & Training Center

Labrador Retriever-Siberian. Male. Castrated.
DOB: Oct 1996

Note: So you know a bit about his background, I began work with this dog in May of 1998, at about 18 months of age.

Past Medical History: Unremarkable medical history, normal physical at last veterinarian visit.

Environmental and Social History: Puppy separated from mother at 2-3 weeks old. Dog taken by rescue society personnel and re-homed. Current owner is my client. The rescue personnel and the client have done some socialization with the dog. The clients are very dedicated and competent individuals.
Presenting issues: A history of inappropriate agonistic display (note for the reader: a term ethologists use to discuss the body language that surrounds conflict resolution in canines) toward dogs and people, and is beginning to escalate in aggression as he reaches social maturity (age 24 months). Dog is also having severe symptoms of separation anxiety: hyper-salivation, vocalization, attempting to get out of the crate to the point of injury.

While doing enrichment exercises with this dog, we brought a person he didn't know into his visual range. When this person reached a distance of about 10 feet, this dog began to scratch the earth. The context in which this behaviour is commonly used is after urination or defecation. I have also seen this used as a "challenge." When this behaviour is combined with a direct stare, as it was currently being used, aggressive display would be the correct interpretation. Because I had interacted with this dog enough to be familiar with his particular body language, it was apparent to me, by his relaxed facial features and the way he was holding his tail, that he wished to greet this person. Janea, my approaching "helper," was interpreting aggression and halted her approach. At my encouragement, Janea continued her approach to the dog. As she reached him, and he continued scratching, I signaled the dog with a No Reward Mark (note for the reader: a NRM is a previously established cue that notifies the dog to offer another behaviour) and requested a Sit. The dog happily complied and was excited about interacting with this new person. He never intended aggression. This is out-of-context behaviour. The language itself was okay in another context, but didn't suit this situation at all! This dog is hard-wired with the correct dog "moves," but because he was deprived of normal early interaction with mother and littermates, he doesn't always access the correct behaviour for the circumstances.

Discussion Re: Case History #1

The excerpt from Case History #1 (see Table 1) clearly illustrates out-of-context behaviour.

After this one time, neither I nor the clients observed this behaviour in this animal again. He just needed the correct behaviour pointed out to him. I think of it as the same kind of situation that a person might encounter when she goes to her first really fancy restaurant. Which fork to use? As soon as it is pointed out, it is easy to access the correct fork – but until education occurs, it's a mystery!

As a further note, just to illustrate how a dog who accesses incorrect language can really get into trouble, thus perpetrating the cycle of aggression, think for a moment about what would have happened if this dog had used this behaviour to greet another dog. Another dog would have most certainly interpreted this as aggression! Now, depending on how reactive the second dog is, there is a distinct possibility of a bad experience, on top of inappropriate communication, when the approaching dog reacts!

Table 2: Case History #2

Heaven On Arf Behaviour and Training Center

German Shepherd Dog. Male. Castrated.
Dog is approximately 3 years old at date of visit.

Past Medical History: Unremarkable medical history, normal physical at last vet visit.

Environmental and Social History: Client obtained puppy from reputable breeder at approximately 8 weeks old. The clients have encouraged guarding behaviour in the dog. They took the puppy to two group classes, using traditional training methods (choke collar). The dog did very well in classes and was social with the other dogs and people, although the classes did not have "play-group" interaction, so the dogs were always near their owners and on leash and were collar corrected for approaching other humans or dogs.

Presenting issues: Escalating aggression, with both family members (except the wife) and strangers who are at the clients' home. The owners became alarmed at their lack of control over the dog's behaviour because he has bitten family members, as well as a delivery person.

Incident:
This occurred when the dog was approximately 2 years old. The wife was reading in the reclining chair in the living room and the dog was lying along side the chair. She fell asleep. The husband walked into the living room from the hallway and passed by the dog and the wife in the chair from a distance of approximately 3 – 4 feet. The dog raised his head and stared at the husband as he walked by. The husband spoke to the dog (said his name in a friendly manner and some other friendly words). The dog then rose up, lunged at the husband as he passed by, and bit him in the back of the leg, resulting in slight punctures and bruising at the site of injury.

Discussion Re: Case History #2

Case History #2 (see Table 2) is an example of Inappropriate response to a situation the dog should have learned was non-threatening.

This is clearly an inappropriate response to this circumstance. The husband is a family member, and was being non-threatening. The dog's past experience should have clearly identified this as a non-threatening situation.

3

CANINE SOCIAL SYSTEMS

Traditionally, much of dog behaviour has been neatly pigeon-holed into the categories of dominant or submissive. These words have been over-used and misused such that they mean something entirely differently to different groups of people, almost to the point of being entirely useless. Many people (including dog trainers) use "dominance" as the excuse for every misbehaviour, not taking into account whether the dog is properly trained or not! To the scientist and ethologist, dominance is defined as: *priority access to a preferred resource.* It doesn't necessarily describe an attitude, belief or approach an animal has.

Using dominance as the "reason" your dog does not come when you call it or doesn't sit when you request a sit is excuse-making. There are technical reasons why your dog complies to a cue or reacts to the environment. Regardless of your philosophy, behaviour is governed by the Laws of Learning. Dominance is only one tiny facet of behaviour, not the all-consuming trait it is often portrayed to be. If a training technique is working, it is following the principles of learning. A shortcoming of using dominance as a "reason" for behaviour is that it does not direct you toward a solution the way that learning theory does.

To understand aggression, knowledge about canine social systems is handy. Historically, our dogs were scavengers and social predators. Social animals live in groups as a survival mechanism. For animals with the ability to kill each other, but who have a system of social cooperation, a set of behaviors evolved to insure they do not injure each other when settling differences. In terms of group dynamics, Rank Order is just one of *many* social traits that evolved as effective mechanisms to keep canine social systems functioning smoothly with a minimum of violence and risk of physical injury.

The process of Rank Ordering does not produce a rigid linear hierarchy, unbending and unyielding, so much as it is indicative of an individual's need *at that point in time*. The Rank Order within a social group or pack is *dynamic* (ever changing) and *highly dependent on context.* For instance, if you are very hungry it may be much more important to get that food item than it is to get a toy, so you may easily give up the toy but assert yourself for the food.

A Resource is defined as anything that is important to that particular animal at that particular time. Therefore, a Resource could be something obvious and tangible, such as food, or more abstract and individual, like personal space. How fiercely your dog guards a resource depends on How Important This Resource Is To Him Right This Minute. If an animal is successful with guarding behaviour, he will choose to access the behaviour again. In some circumstances this guarding behaviour becomes a habitual response cued by the environment.

What is important to remember about dogs using "status" as a means to gain access to resources is that if the resource or "need" changes, so may the comparative status of an individual. I hesitate to use words like "alpha" because this is another word that is bandied about so much that its definition is blurred. However, in a social group, there is often an individual who gains access to a preferred resource more times than not. For example, if my terrier bitch, Breanna, doesn't want a bone to chew on and another dog comes over, she may allow the other dog to "take" the bone away from her. BUT, if she wants this bone, she can send the other dog away with a look. I have seen her "allow" another dog to retain possession of a piece of food or bone when it was not important to her OR if it was obviously more important to the other dog than to her. I have also observed occasions when she has lurked and stared at another dog who had something she didn't want (such as a toy; she prefers live game...) and persevered until the other dog nervously left the item. She would walk up to the item, sniff it, maybe move it 6 inches, then walk away and allow the other dog to have it back. Basically, "If I want it, I can have it. If I don't want it, you can have it!"

The mistake many pet owners make is that they do not appreciate dog social systems for what they are. The owner makes mistakes in interpreting dog language or, most often, is not even aware the dog is communicating. Because of this, the dog learns she can have priority access – and this is the conception of a behaviour problem that could have been avoided. Pet owners are not necessarily aware of the resources that are important to dogs (eating and sleeping areas, toys or people). So they allow the dog to learn to guard these resources, often thinking it is a "cute" behaviour in that tiny puppy. The same behaviour is NOT so cute in a large adult dog. Another common error is that the owner does not recognize the guarding behaviours as guarding behaviour, and do not realize that this will grow into behaviour that will put the puppy at risk as an adult.

The other great mistake is made by the owner who is so paranoid, every move the dog makes is seen as some sort of status-seeking behaviour. The whole "don't let your dog go through the door before you because he is dominating you" ideology. I mean, really. I don't allow my dogs to go through the door until I tell them they can do so, but it is a safety issue; I dislike being dislodged off my feet by dogs shoving me aside in their excitement to get into the yard. If a dog runs through the door ahead of me, I wouldn't assume he has sinister intentions and is trying to "pull one over on me." I think he just wants to go outside and is taking the direct route.

So often there is a simple explanation for your dog's behaviour – she is doing it because she wants to or simply because she has learned that she can. No evil intentions or sinister overtones. You don't need to keep your dog constantly groveling, you just need to make it clear that the games are played by your rules. For instance, if I want a dog in bed with me, I invite her up. If I choose not to have my feet lain on all night, I can crate the dog or tell her to go sleep in the living room. But it is my choice! If I want to allow my dogs to sit near me while I eat lunch and do cute stuff for food (Begging at the table!), I can do so. If I want a quiet family dinner with no dogs lurking and drooling, I put them in the other room on a Down-Stay while we eat. My choice! This is how you communicate to your dog that you are going to be establishing the rules, and she is not.

Ritualized Behaviour Patterns are a chain of behaviours recognized amongst members of a species to have a specific meaning. Dogs use these to help determine, without resorting to violence, who gives in and who prevails in situations where conflict might occur. If social animals had no other way to resolve conflicts over resources, access to them would be regulated by aggression and fear or the species would have killed itself off long ago. Ritualized Behaviour Patterns make for clear communication. This keeps stress levels lowered. This promotes beneficial social behaviour, because stressed animals tend to be more reactive from the accompanying chemical changes in the central nervous system. To avoid these unpleasant consequences, social animals rely on an elegant solution – ritualized behavior patterns. These patterns take two basic forms in Conflict Resolution: a dog is either Assertive or Yielding.

Assertive behaviors could be described as:

- "I gain access at this time."
- A measure of authority in a given context.
- One member asserting herself over another.
- Self-confidence in a given context.
- "This is really important to me right now."
- Accepting Authority.

Yielding behaviors could be described as:

- "I give in this time."
- A measure of compromise.
- One member capitulating to another.
- Possibly (but not always) insecurity in a given context.
- "This is more important to you than to me right now, and I am willing to acknowledge that."
- Giving Authority.

This is an example between two extremes of body language. There are many "hues" in between these two illustrations.

Contrast Between Assertive & Yielding Postures

Remember when you are observing dog language that there will be breed variation. A Beagle with floppy ears pricked up at an alert position will obviously never look like German Shepherd dog with it's ears pricked up in an alert position.

To learn to recognize dog language, all you have to do is be observant. Watch your dog, observe the topography of the behaviour, then look at the context and the events that followed. That is how you begin to make connections between what the dog "looks" like (behavioural topography) and what the dog's intentions are when she "looks" like that! Keep a notebook to assist you with this effort. That is a good beginning!

Why are these behaviour sets useful in social groups? Assertive and Yielding behaviors help dogs establish a peaceful coexistence in their group. This is an energy-efficient coexistence, and, therefore, the best way to survive. The obvious advantage of ritualized behavior patterns is that a stable social order is maintained with a minimum of violence and physical injury to the group members. Confrontations can be reduced to reminders, which are often of an extremely subtle nature. This is effective survival – emphasis is placed on cooperative living. A human example might be a warning look you give your teenager when she is sitting at the dining room table, and she has the chair tipped back on only two legs. I have only to glance pointedly at my daughter and she will lower her chair. Compliance with my wishes is not due to physical beatings, but is a learned behavior. In the past, such acts have met with mild verbal disapproval by yours truly, as well as verbal approval for appropriate behaviour. The verbal reminder and social disapproval have been faded to only a glance. Dogs operate just as subtly.

In Summary

It is useful to understand how dogs interact with their own species because dogs will attempt to use the same communication techniques with humans as they do with dogs. Dogs do not start out "bilingual." This is a skill we must help them develop, as we develop our own skills for understanding dog language.

Humans miss many dog communication signals through unawareness, ignorance and a lack of sensory ability or different perception of information obtained from the environment. For instance, dogs use many olfactory communication signals – humans just don't have the nose for it.

Dogs "negotiate" all the time, using their own native language, including assertive and yielding behaviours. A dog will cease trying to use negotiation as a means of conflict resolution and will access other behaviour (fight or flight) because:

- Ritualized Behaviour Patterns, the dog's Native Language, are not recognized or were not learned because the dog never got a chance to use them.
- Native Language has been "lost" because the dog has been punished for using calming signals, increasing the probability that aggression will be used.

Occasionally, even dogs who are using Ritualized Behaviour Patterns correctly will still resort to a physical altercation, if a resource or space conflict becomes strong enough because of that individual's current need or past experience.

Recognize that context has much stronger implications in aggression than the traditional ideas of dominance and submission. Much of dog behaviour that humans label "aggression" is a symptom of the dog Guarding Valuable Resources. Dog behavior is dictated by what is the most important resource right this minute. This paradigm is more direct and is much closer to how the dog perceives the situation. This paradigm is less emotional and anthropomorphic, two items that only "muddy the waters" of an effective prevention or behavior modification program.

4 FACTORS THAT INFLUENCE AGGRESSIVE BEHAVIOUR

Dogs developed assertive and aggressive behaviours to assure their success as social, family-oriented, pack animals. In addition, several other factors are known to influence aggression in dogs. These include:

- Learned Behaviour
- Genetics
- Hormones
- Social Development Periods
- Stress and Fear
- Physiological Factors
- Resiliency and Trauma

Learned Behaviour

Dogs use behaviour as an experiment. So, your dog will do "something" and then she will see what the results are. Given the information your dog obtains, she will base future decisions on which behaviours were most effective (gained her what she wanted) in that context. Dogs are very flexible inventive creatures, discarding, adding and changing behaviour as required.

The classic example used to illustrate learned aggression is the mail-carrier. She comes to the house daily, distributes the mail, and then leaves the area. The mail-carrier would do this whether your dog made a fuss or not! But from the dog's point of view, the situation is very different. As the dog watches from a house window, a non-family member approaches territory. The dog barks an alarm. The intruder leaves. The dog assumes that his barking generated the mail-carrier-leaving response. This happens day after day. The dog's display escalates, and the dog is also being allowed a Daily Practice Session, which has the effect of strengthening this behaviour. The dog may even begin to generalize this display to people who are just walking by on the sidewalk. Then the delivery person actually enters territory. The delivery person thinks she is just going to deliver a package, after first having you sign for it – but from the dog's point of view, the intruder is not only behaving abnormally (barking has always chased these intruders away before!) by not leaving the territory immediately, but the delivery person is advancing onto territory right through the front door! So the dog escalates his display of "you don't belong here" and the delivery person, who is waiting for you to sign the package, then turns to the dog and gives him friendly eye contact. What the dog perceives is: direct eye contact = direct threat. Not only is this person not leaving, the dog's usual display is ineffective. Now the dog is really feeling defensive and more concerned. The delivery person reaches out to give a friendly pat – and the dog bites her.

There are also the mis-associations that occur. The dog starts out friendly to other dogs and humans, and so whenever he sees another dog or person on the sidewalk, he rushes to meet them. The owner, not liking to be dragged down the street, punishes the dog with a good hard collar correction on a choke chain or a tug on the pinch collar. The dog, whose behaviour is making perfect sense to him, does not associate the punishment with his natural greeting behaviour, but instead begins to see approaching dogs or humans as a *predictor of punishment.* Therefore, the dog begins to become defensive at the sight of another person or dog. This cycle of frustration at not being able to greet, coupled with the fact that the dog is feeling defensive, can culminate in a bite – sometimes to the owner (redirected aggression) and sometimes to the hapless dog or person that the dog is finally allowed to interact with. In the education, management and protocol sections of this book, I supply you with tools to deal with both of these situations. In a very abbreviated fashion the answer to both of these problems is to make the appearance of the mail-carrier and the approaching dogs a *predictor of reinforcement* – given by you. This way the dog is allowed to develop appropriate judgment about approaching persons. This technique has the added advantage of teaching your dog to look to you for advice.

GENETICS

Understanding inherited breed traits helps you reach an educated conclusion about an individual dog's behaviour. This same understanding may aid in determining whether a dog's behaviour should be judged as abnormal or not. Dogs have been selectively bred for hundreds of years for specific traits that modern owners have now decided are "problem behaviours." Yes, your Sheltie barks and nips at the heels of running children – they are herding. Yes, your Smooth Fox Terrier is impulsive and predacious – meaning that keeping pocket pets or cats in your household is probably not a good idea! What might be normal behaviour for one breed could possibly be classified as abnormal in another. Chasing in a Sheltie probably means the dog just wishes to "move the sheep" around. Chasing in a Terrier may be just the beginning a prey sequence, and may be more likely to terminate with a harder bite and shake, as opposed to a nip.

A very basic prey sequence consists of the following list of loosely chronological behaviours:

- Eye
- Stalk
- Chase
- Bite (Shake)
- Bite (Hold)
- Dissect

We can see some breeds will have been selected to interrupt or terminate this sequence. For instance, it is fervently hoped that our Border Collies will interrupt at a Chase Sequence, whereas your basic terrier was not selected for an interrupted prey sequence. Just chasing the game was not helpful on the 19th century (and prior) farms, as merely chasing will not rid the farm of rodents. The Border Collie was expected to herd, not harm, the livestock. In earlier times, dogs acting outside the expected hard-wired behaviour patterns were quickly removed from the gene pool.

When considering genetics and a particular breed's specific work, look at the guardian breeds. Remember, our ancestors did not have leisure time to devote to dog training – the goal was to breed animals having a natural tendency toward behavioural traits that would be desirable in a certain line of work. This behaviour was expected and *respected.* People didn't assume dogs would be friendly. For instance, what traits would you select to make a good guard dog? One trait I would choose for my guard dog would be a natural tendency to be very suspicious: "If it is different, it must be dangerous." Many individual dogs have this trait to some degree, but it is marked in the guarding dogs. Another enhanced trait is territoriality: "You are different, therefore you don't belong here." Also enhanced is possessive behaviour: "This is mine!" For instance, the Rottweilers who drove the cattle to market also had the job of wearing the money received in a bag around their neck for the trip home. "This is mine" protected the farmer's earnings.

Not only is there a vast array of traits and characteristics and personalities between breeds, but within a specific breed as well. Any breed, after all, is made up of individuals who will display a range of characteristics. Even though breeders aim for certain favored traits, there will still be a wide range of outcomes, including dogs who show a low or lack of breed tendency and those who display excessive breed tendencies.

We must acknowledge that genetics play a role in the behaviour you see displayed by your dog. All too often, however, breed type is used as an excuse for aggressive behaviour and thus is not managed or corrected by the owner. Whatever genetic background a dog has, inappropriate, out-of-context aggression is never normal or acceptable for any breed. So, while it is recognized that certain herding or guarding breeds are "reserved" and often not immediately friendly with strangers, that kind of behaviour is far removed from inappropriately "resource guarding" an item or owner from a non-existent threat.

In summary, while there are genetic factors to be aware of, use the information you know about the breed, as well as about the individual, to alert you to areas where your dog may need more education. Don't just use the breed as an excuse to keep you from making the effort to prevent or solve aggressive behaviour problems. *All dogs* need to be exposed to many different stimuli to make them safe and to enhance their judgment and reduce their stress level, thereby *raising their bite threshold and lowering their reactivity levels.*

HORMONES

Hormones are produced by various organs in the body, are transported to another organ and, once there, stimulate the second organ to function or respond to their presence by chemical activity. Hormones can influence thought patterns and stimulate the brain in a variety of ways. I will restrict my discussion of hormones to the effect they might have on defensive or aggressive behaviours.

Hormones can play a significant role in aggression. Testosterone, for instance, acts as a type of behaviour modulator that makes reactions more intense. The intact male dog will react more quickly to stimuli, with more intensity and for a longer duration. Statistically, castration has decreased aggression in 62% of cases where male dogs have been displaying aggressive tendencies toward other dogs, particularly other male dogs (Overall, 1997). On an anecdotal level, based on my own field experience, aggression toward humans can also be decreased significantly by castration in a majority of cases. Statistics tell us that the majority of serious dog bites are done by the intact male dog over two-years of age.

Maternal aggression is the reaction of a female dog who has whelped puppies and is nervous about any changes that occur in the environment, causing over-reaction. There is a direct correlation between hormonal levels and maternal aggression.

Intact bitches who are living together and coming into heat may be inspired by the change in their estrogen and progesterone levels to begin quite nasty displays and fights. I have also found that spayed bitches may become very reactive around each other if you have a bitch that is intact and coming into heat. Amongst experienced dog people bitch fights are infamous. My own experience backs this up. Once two bitches decide they dislike each other and begin violent fighting, it may prove impossible in some of these cases to reconcile the bitches to co-existing together. I, as well as many of my clients, have obtained excellent results reducing aggression in bitches by spaying.

Many of the hormonal effects on aggression are allayed to a great degree merely by altering the dog – that is, castration (removal of the testicles) for males and spaying (ovariohysterectomy) for females. Good results can be garnered by altering the dog, no matter the age. However, it is much to your advantage to do the procedure as early as possible, because then there are many habits that simply will not develop, such as excessive territorial marking in males and females, and many sexual behaviours that humans find unsavory: licking a bitch's urine, teeth chattering and mounting, to mention just a few. (Remember though, not all mounting is sexual behaviour – it can also be rank-ordering behaviour.) The sooner altering takes place, the less you will have to deal with the residual habits formed by intact animals.

You should not hesitate to alter your dogs. Scientific studies have shown that normal female and male dogs were unaffected behaviourally by early spay or castration procedures (as early as 12-16 weeks) in any detrimental way. Many veterinarians prefer to wait until the dogs are 6 months of age to minimize surgical risks, and also for the simple fact that the animal is larger and easier to work on. In fact, there are well-known benefits involved with neutering which we do not need to hash over here. For many reasons, both behaviourally and health-wise, please spay or castrate your dog!

If your dog is presenting with aggression in any way, passing those tendencies along to offspring is irresponsible and places generations of animals at risk.

Social Development Periods

Dogs experience developmental periods during which they are more adaptive toward and/or sensitive to novel stimuli. If a dog is isolated and is not exposed to a wide variety of experiences during critical social periods, behavioural problems such as aggression are more likely to occur.

According to Scott & Fuller (1965) in their Bar Harbor, Maine, studies, dogs go through critical developmental periods during the first 20 weeks of life:

- Weeks 3-8: learn to interact dog-to-dog.
- Weeks 5-12: learn to interact with humans.
- Weeks 10-20: learn by exploring novel environments.

These studies show that if a dog is not exposed to certain stimuli during the relevant time frames then there is a higher risk of developing behaviour problems that are connected with specific development periods. For example, puppies who don't see humans until they are 16 weeks old may never develop proper dog-human relationships. Puppies who leave their mother prior to 7 weeks old and are hand-raised will probably not interact normally with dogs, nor have normal dog-human relationships. Especially crucial in the 5-8 week time frame is the bite-inhibition a pup learns from his mother and littermates. This is when the puppy is learning the language that will allow her to be unafraid of and communicate effectively with her own species. This ability will also affect the dog's overall self-confidence levels, therefore her interactions with her environment and humans, as well. Keeping puppies with mother and littermates during this stage of development will encourage a lifetime of normal behaviour patterns.

People place puppies at younger ages either because of total ignorance of the species they are breeding, or because they are lazy; the puppies are a lot more work for the human care-takers beginning at 5 and 6 weeks of age, particularly if they are kenneled in the house or garage.

In an ideal world, separating a puppy from its mother and littermates permanently would not occur before 7 ½ to 8 weeks of age, with my personal preference being 8 – 9 weeks. The exception is, if the puppy is 7 weeks old, and is not getting exposure to a lot of different experiences where he is, he might as well be with you IF you are going to provide a variety of experiences for the puppy. If you are careful or fortunate enough to be purchasing a puppy from one of those stellar breeders who are not just warehousing the puppies, but are, in fact, socializing, training and housebreaking – it is just fine to leave those pups with mum and breeder until they are 12 weeks old. In short, lack of exposure to certain stimuli at critical times places a dog at high risk for developing behaviour problems that are complex, deep-seated, and difficult to deal with.

A good rule for breeders is one that was shared with me by my friend and long-time breeder, Carol Wainwright: The Rule of Sevens. By the time a puppy is seven weeks old he should have been exposed to the following situations (and any others you can think of!):

- Been in 7 different locations (obviously they need to be safe and offer no risk of disease to pup)
- Eaten from 7 different kinds of containers
- Met AT LEAST 7 different people (including safe, gentle children)
- Ridden AT LEAST 7 miles in a car (or more)
- Been in a crate at least 7 times (more is better!)
- Played with 7 different kinds of toys
- Been exposed to AT LEAST 7 different contexts: for example, had their picture taken, exposed to learning simple behaviours like Sit, etc.
- Been played with or taken somewhere alone, without mom or littermates, 7 different times

Dogs genetically prone to developing an especially reserved personality, and the potentially escalating aggression patterns that can result from this natural reticence, should be extensively socialized and exposed to novel stimuli steadily from 8 weeks to 24 months of age. Then a protocol for continuing education at intervals throughout the dog's life as a preventative measure should be instituted. The guarding, flock guardian breeds and terriers are prime candidates here. Also included would be the working herding breeds (such as Border Collies and Australian Shepherds), which tend toward territorial and anxiety-based aggression.

In fact, the most important step you can take towards preventing aggression in dogs is to *extensively socialize regardless of breed or personality type.* That's the safest way to move forward! Dogs will tell the experienced handler how much socialization they need, but since not all handlers have the same experience level, be safe rather than sorry. Expose your dog to everything you can think of, and continue to do so throughout your dog's life, most intensively from 8 weeks to 24 months of age.

The general knowledge seems to be that puppy kindergarten is "socializing" your dog. Indeed, this is true; but it is just a start! Dogs need to be exposed to novel stimuli of all kinds, some more than others – and for a much more extensive time-frame than a six or eight-week puppy class. The bold puppy will be naturally more tolerant and less frightened of novel situations. The more cautious the puppy, the more he requires this exposure. The slightly cautious puppy may be easier to handle on a daily basis than the fearless puppy. The cautious puppy will just get into less mischief because avoidance is his natural response to novel stimuli, whilst the bold puppy will have a natural response of "what is that?"

When choosing a pet it is very important to know yourself well and how much effort you are willing to put into training and social experiences. The very cautious and the extremely bold puppies are the dogs most likely to bite as adults. Both require the most extensive training. Both have a higher tendency toward risky behaviour as adults. The cautious dogs are very unforgiving of training errors. The bold dogs are very good at getting their owners to comply by wearing them down, like water on rocks.

Dogs who do not have extensive exposure to novel stimuli are at much higher risk for development of behaviour problems (anxiety AND aggression) as adults. It is clear that puppy kindergarten is important and an excellent beginning. Based on the dogs I have observed, both my own and thousands of boarding dogs and training dogs, it is just as clear that training and exposure to a variety of people and dogs should continue through 24 months of age. Alternatively, if you have a good place to take dog classes, where the methodology is humane and based on positive reinforcement, take a puppy k class, then plan on repeating some sort of class every 2 to 3 months, at the very least.

At my training center, we offer classes for puppies where socialization with other dogs and people is stressed and very basic obedience is started, such as Sit, Down, Come and Leave It. Then people can move into a "Beyond the Basics" class with a variety of activities, including obedience, agility and scentwork, such as tracking. Compatible dogs may play in these classes, but the emphasis is on working around other dogs and being mannerly, peaceful and resisting the distraction of the other dogs. Off-leash safe dogs can move into an agility class, or take repeats of the above. At the age of 9-12 months or older, less socially appropriate dogs move into a "Re-socialization" class. In this class, we emphasize proper dog-to-dog approaches and good manners around other dogs and people. This class is specifically for dogs who are presenting with cautious, dicey or aggressive behaviour.

A guideline for classes with the express intent of getting your dog around other dogs and people, and to practice compliance to cues even though she is distracted and/or excited, is:

- Puppy k at 8-12 weeks of age.
- Repeat the puppy class or take a beginner class at 5-6 months.
- Repeat the beginner class or seek out an agility or obedience class that emphasizes manners at 9-12 months of age.
- Take some sort of class when your dog is 18 months old.
- Take some sort of class when your dog is 24 months old.

This is a minimum program. I prefer that people train continuously, but most people take off a month or two in between, and that seems to work just fine for the majority of dogs. In between classes, people can use their training skills and continue to take the dog out and about for a variety of experiences.

If you take a couple of classes, then take your dog home and live quietly with him, you may not have any trouble at all, mostly because this dog is never placed in any situation to test his coping skills. But those are precisely the dogs who are at higher risk for developing problems, simply because they have not practiced their coping skills in a variety of contexts.

Creating social puppies who grow into social, well-adapted dogs is less risky merely because of the smaller size of puppies. Also, puppies have wide open social windows and do not have a whole list of well-established stimuli that they have associated with fear. Older dogs can be socialized, but it is definitely more time consuming and the safety factor is compromised.

It is important to understand that it is easier to socialize puppies, but that *training* can be done at any age! Dogs are always capable of learning, just like you are. You don't stop learning at age 25 or 40 or even at age 80! So it is with our dogs, who learn new behaviours at any age.

It is best to introduce puppies to a variety of circumstances because then you greatly reduce or eliminate the factors that make a dog at risk for anxiety and/or aggression later on.

If you are looking at an older "multiple-home" dog, though, don't be discouraged. (A multiple-home dog is one who has been in more homes than the birth home and the original placement home. These dogs have often been in bad situations, been at a shelter or dog pound, bounced from home to home, and so on.) The vast majority of dogs *can* be rehabilitated with behaviour modification. The lovely thing about older dogs is that the problems, if they are going to be there, are observable; and a stable older dog is very much a WYSIWYG[1] proposition. I have worked with both puppies and older multiple-home dogs, and cannot say I have a great preference. Both have made excellent working dogs and great pets for me and my family and for many of my clients as well. Older dogs are superior choices for families with young children for many reasons, not the least of which is: what family with a toddler and an infant in diapers and working parents has time to devote to training a puppy as well?

Stress and Fear

Stress and fear are the Big Ones – the prime causes of aggression. Both factors will always have a profound and significant effect on aggression. While these are grouped together, and are often seen in tandem, they are two separate and distinct categories.

1. What You See Is What You Get

Stress stems directly from an inability to cope with whatever the current situation may be. For myriad reasons, the dog lacks the skills to contend with whatever the existing circumstances are. Aggression is merely a symptom indicating how stressed the dog is being made by the environment.

Stress is like an allergic person's reaction to the environment. If you have hay fever, you will probably be able to tolerate some allergens. When you really have trouble is when you are exposed to several allergens over too short a period of time for your body to cope. The result is an allergy attack. This is a classic case of "The Straw That Broke the Camel's Back." Given a number of stressors in a short time, just about any dog may behave aggressively. Given enough stress over a long period of time, a dog may develop a brittle, over-reactive temperament.

Stress and fear are similar in that both encompass a physiological change in the body, as well as psychological responses to a situation. Fear specifically activates defensive behaviour patterns, which prepare the animal for flight or fight responses. Stress is the precursor to fear, making the dog more susceptible to a fearful response because of a lack of confidence in his ability to cope with the current situation.

If exposed to fear and stress-inducing stimuli for extensive periods of time, it is possible for the body to get so far out of the normal range, chemically and behaviourally, that the body finds it difficult or impossible to return to its normal emotional state and behaviour patterns. Long-term exposure to stress and fear is frequently the root of pathological behaviour patterns, which may manifest as frank displays of aggression.

If conflict arises between two dogs, and one dog becomes stressed, the preferred option a normal dog attempts is yielding and/or appeasement behaviours to "turn off" the aggression. Yielding is just one way a dog signals non-aggressive intent. If the encounter becomes more intense, the dog may try an escalation of submissive display. If this strategy does not "work," the stressed animal may become fearful. If this display does not end the confrontation, flight may be attempted. This fearful state may also occur if the other dog does not have sophisticated language skills, and is not responding properly to the request of the stressed animal by "backing off."

If flight is not an option, the fearful dog enters into a defensive mode, where aggression becomes a viable tool for the dog. Of course, at this point, the stressed animal (who became the fearful animal) is not using a "display" or Ritualized Behaviour Pattern to attempt conflict resolution. He is merely in a reactive state and appears desperate to just escape the situation, using any means to do so.

The problem is that the RESPONSE of the other dog to this reactive state is a reactive state of his own – and now you have a dog fight. In this scenario, the "other" dog could have halted the escalation of the stressed dog's behaviour at any time, merely by responding in a calming way, or by leaving the stressed dog entirely alone.

The good news is that you can raise your dog's bite-threshold by teaching her how to cope in stressful and fearful situations. We will review how to do this later in the book in detail. Suffice it to say here that manufacturing appropriate behaviour in different contexts, desensitization programs, and counter-conditioning programs all aid in giving a dog the self confidence required to choose non-aggressive behaviour instead of aggressive behaviour. These procedures or protocols give your dog information about alternative paths of behaviour, and about your approval of those alternative paths!

Physiological Factors

Let's make it simple. Think of the brain as being divided into two sections. Any neurosurgeon will think this is *very* simplistic. But for our purposes, it will do.

The Limbic system is where primitive reactions reside – strong, overwhelming emotions such as fear, lust, grief and rage are initiated and centered here. Think about this as being the Lizard-Brain. Then you have the polar opposite – the Pre-Frontal Cortex, where higher-order learning and thoughtful action take place. This is the Einstein-Brain. When your dog is in the midst of an aggressive event, where do you think his actions originate?

The Lizard-brain and the Einstein-brain do not pull as a double team. If one is "Leading," the other is "Following." One strategy to provide the dog with is a Switching Mechanism. This gives your dog a way to Switch over from her Lizard-brain, where she is merely reacting to her environment in a Knee-Jerk Reaction Way, to her Einstein-brain, where she can begin to problem solve and access alternative behaviours. The protocol for self-relaxation exercises – The Zen Sit & Down covered later – provides an excellent switching mechanism.

Physiological changes are inexorably connected to an emotional state and physical postures. This is a chemical issue, originating in the endocrine and central nervous systems. To illustrate this, think about the following context. One might encourage a person who is emotionally very upset to "Sit down and take ten deep breaths." If you are very upset and you take this advice, you will notice that you actually do feel much calmer and better able to cope with the current situation. This action provides a "switch" to get the person to turn down the over-reactive emotional Lizard-brain state and return to a rational "thoughtful action" state. This is exactly the function you are invoking in your dog when you ask him to "Remain Seated and Be Calm," or to "Look and Anchor," as described in the protocol section.

Some dogs cannot make this switch because pathology is present. In this case, I strongly recommend specialized help. Consult with an experienced person who will know if pharmacotherapy, in addition to behaviour modification, is a viable and wise option. It should be noted that pharmacotherapy for aggression is a relatively new and sometimes unpredictable approach. This requires the close monitoring of an extremely dedicated and educated owner with the help of a behaviour specialist and a veterinarian.

Resiliency and Trauma

Some dogs are very brittle – they respond with fear or aggression to small stimuli across a wide variety of situations. Brittle dogs do not "rebound" well. That is, once stressed, the recovery time is slow. Other dogs are very resilient and can tolerate a lot of frustration and provocative stimuli without becoming aggressive or fearful. What makes some dogs more resilient? Resiliency comes, in part, from inborn chemical factors of the dog, making some individuals just more likely to be temperamentally resilient.

The sum of the dog's past learning experiences is a huge contributor to resiliency. Dogs who are socialized well and early to a lot of dogs, novel experiences, and a wide array of humans, develop resiliency to stress. Dogs who have a sound temperament and a preponderance of pleasant social interactions will not be overly affected even by a traumatic event. My dog, Punch, for example, was very well-socialized and had years of good experiences with other dogs when she enticed Maeve into a contest one day, and was injured grievously. Punch, to this day, becomes pushy and provocative around Maeve (it's the terrier in her, she cannot help it), but she is still fine with other dogs, even other German Shepherd Dogs. Resilient, sophisticated dogs discriminate well between specific stimuli.

On the other hand, dogs who have poor early socialization can be put off balance by even a single trauma and quickly generalize aggressive or reactive behaviour to all other dogs (or people, if that was the source of the trauma).

Dogs who are cautious as puppies tend to be less resilient as adults. If owners recognize this early on and make huge efforts to socialize the dog, it helps compensate for the dog's natural tendency.

Similarly, an early history of multiple traumas, as can be found with some multiple-home dogs, can produce a brittle dog. These dogs easily generalize conflicting experiences and respond to all novel or provocative stimuli with reactivity, and do not discriminate which stimuli are actually benign. "I'll get you BEFORE you make me uncomfortable" becomes the modus operandi.

Creating a resilient dog is best done early, with a great deal of positive exposure to novel people, environments, and other dogs.

Working with a dog who is already brittle involves teaching the dog to substitute new, better behaviours for aggressive or fearful responses, as well as teaching him to recognize neutral and non-threatening stimuli. Also important is training him to understand dog language, thereby enabling him to discriminate calming signals from distance-increasing signals. Then, teach him that, if he encounters distance-increasing signals, he can keep himself out of trouble by using calming signals and remaining non-reactive.

5

HOW DOGS LEARN TO AVOID AGGRESSION

Based on what has been covered so far, we can state that aggression occurs in otherwise healthy dogs (dogs who are not suffering from a chemical abnormality or some other physiological abnormality, or what we might call in people a "personality disorder") for a number of possible reasons:

- Due to a lack of education and/or socialization when young, the dog never learned the "language" skills necessary to avoid aggressive behaviour by using communication.
- Due to a lack of continuing exposure to novel stimuli, the dog becomes fearful of "new" or unfamiliar stimuli.
- Incorrect use of punishers caused the dog to learn that approaching dogs and humans are a Predictor of Punishment, without learning that his Behaviour is what is making the handler cross. What happens is that an undesired association was made: The other dog or person's approach heralds a "dangerous" event (the punisher the dog receives).
- The humans who interact with the dog fail to understand the dog's language and place the dog in a position where he feels he has no alternative but to resort to aggression because of personal space violations or other unintended threats.
- If past aggression by the dog resulted in access to a desired resource or personal space, then, in the dog's mind, "the behaviour made sense" and the dog received reinforcement for using aggression. That is, as a direct result of aggressive behaviour, the dog achieved a goal. Unless something changes, the dog will continue to use aggression as long as the end result is reinforcing to him.
- The dog, again due to lack of experience, misinterprets human or dog language as a threat.
- The dog is placed in situations or contexts that encourage aggression, or the dog learns aggression from a dog she lives with or has a lot of contact with.

Normal dogs with adequate early experiences, including opportunities to interact with dogs and humans, understand and use signals that allow them to avoid aggressive behaviour. These signals are your canine's natural language and dogs are very intuitive about it. By contrast, dogs who lack early experience, are not well educated, or have experienced trauma may have "lost" their native language, or, more accurately, no longer believe that language "works." It is our responsibility to help our dogs regain their language, to the degree that we can. In short, humans need to learn some dog language, just as dogs need to learn some human language, so that we can all interact with optimum understanding. Learning your dog's language and teaching your dog human language are what training is all about. Establishing a Communication System IS training. Remember: *If you have to say it in a sentence, your dog will never get it*, because dogs do not use the same language we do.

Normal, experienced dogs are fluent and sophisticated in their own language and have learned a wide variety of ritualized behaviour patterns to avoid aggression amongst themselves. As dog owners, we would do well to learn how they communicate in this way. For example, I use my Basset Hound, Fletcher, to socialize rambunctious puppies, adolescents and, on some occasions, older uneducated dogs. It is common knowledge at my kennel: "Fletcher runs the nursery." It is incredible to watch Fletcher work. I have seen him, on occasion after occasion, keep the peace amongst a group of puppies. If the play becomes too rough in his estimation, or one of the pups begins to look frightened, Fletcher ambles over and lets out a huge "Woof," or steps directly and physically, but neutrally, into the midst of the confrontation. Startled, the pups will pause. In many instances, I have seen him direct 3 puppies to 3 different areas with just a glance. At a distance of 4 or 5 feet from each other, they will sit quietly, carefully looking away from each other. When Fletcher turns and walks away, the pups resume their play, more gently this time, lest Uncle Fletcher has to speak to them again! Woe unto the puppy who makes another puppy squeak! That indiscretion is dealt with quickly and succinctly, usually with a body slam. I have never seen Fletcher put a tooth on a puppy. He just uses his excellent communication skills and his authority. If only I had **his** skills! Then I could call myself a dog trainer!

In the next Section, you will learn more about your dog's native language. You will learn to observe dogs with a specific purpose in mind: to make observations of the dog's native language so you can come to a better understanding of what the dog's intentions are. You will learn about Ritualized Behaviour Patterns, specifically, those that might precede a display of aggression, and those that are pertinent because they are **not** used as a display of aggression. The goal of these observations is to learn your dog's native language so that you can better modify your dog's behaviour, prevent aggression, and assure yourself that you are not inadvertently raising an aggressive dog.

Section II

Dog Communication Systems

6

LEARNING TO INTERPRET THE SIGNALS - DOG COMMUNICATION SYSTEMS

Have you ever read "To Build A Fire," by Jack London? It is a story about a man who was a keen observer, but who had never learned to interpret the significance of what he observed.

This story begins with a man who lives in the far north. He goes outside and notices the extreme cold. He observes signs of dangerous conditions, such as that, when he spits, the spittle freezes and "cracks" immediately, even before it hits the ground. Instead of recognizing and placing merit on his observations, he makes an unnecessary trek into the wilderness. During the short, routine journey, he gets wet. Even though he has with him all the materials he needs to build a fire, he is unable to do so because his wet hands are rendered useless by the cold. Because he did not place significance on his observations, and did not come to the correct conclusion that the conditions were too harsh for travel, he freezes to death.

This is an appropriate sentiment to begin a discussion about dogs and their own Native Language. During the interviewing process, it is apparent to me that my clients have noticed and remembered many mannerisms their dog has displayed. However, these behaviour patterns have either been misinterpreted by the humans (filtered through a belief system rife with anthropomorphism), or the signals have not been meaningful (and are therefore ignored) because the humans didn't know what the dog was trying to communicate. If only they had understood at the time what the dog was actually telling them! Many of my clients don't bring these observations up until I ask them pointed questions about how the dog "looked." Because the humans didn't understand what they were seeing, they weren't able to "interpret the significance" of the signals they had observed.

Dogs make endless effort to communicate with humans. Lack of awareness and misinterpretation occur between us because dogs do not understand our language intuitively, and we do not understand theirs. Dogs will "talk" to humans just like they talk to other dogs. Ironically, humans are making exactly the same moves, talking to dogs in human spoken language. Since dogs do not have the necessary physiological characteristics to acquire human spoken language, the onus is on us, the humans, to learn dog language and open the lines of communication.

As you proceed through this text, you will learn about Communication Tools that you can teach your dog. These Tools will enable you to open additional lines of communication and increase the rapport between you and your dog.

Bees communicate by "dancing." Bee dancing involves geometric patterns like spirals and figure 8's that are used to convey information to other bees. Sure, dogs bark, but most of their communication is done silently, through "dog dancing." Dogs are excellent observers of prey animals and of each other, and body language takes precedence over spoken language.

Why is This Important?

Before you begin to train, it is important that you understand what your dog is trying to tell you, and recognize the effort she is making to communicate. Knowing what dogs are saying to you and to each other is invaluable. With an aggressive dog, it can mean the difference between a dog you have to euthanize and one you can work with. This is so because, in modifying behaviour with these animals, it is imperative to interrupt or prevent undesired behaviour cycles and to detect stress levels *early*. In order to do this, you need to be able to "read" your dog so that your training efforts are not Too Little, Too Late. Bad in romance, bad in dog training!

Observing and interpreting dog language is how you ultimately:

1. Predict what the dog might do next, so you can avert or manage the behaviour effectively.
2. Apply the proper training and management techniques before the behaviour escalates into aggression. Once the behaviour evolves into a display of lunging and barking and snapping or biting, your "Training Moment" is long gone. Now, rather than taking a proactive step to solve a problem, you can only practice "Damage Control." Damage Control will provide you with adrenaline rushes, but it will provide no behaviour modification for your dog.

Your dog doesn't "express" his emotions as much as he "lives" them. It is crucial that you understand that your dog does not have a "Hidden Agenda." By that I mean: if your dog is thinking about something, you will see it expressed in the topography of his body language. It will be observable. For instance, if your dog walks in the kitchen and begins to air-scent, is he thinking about that pot roast on the counter? You betcha! If a stranger enters your home and your dog growls at that person, he IS thinking about gaining some physical distance between himself and the perceived threat.

In order to manage and modify aggressive behaviour efficiently, you need to gain expertise in recognizing the topography of behaviour so you can ascertain the dog's emotional state. This helps you decide what your next action will be. To avoid clouding the issue with emotional overtones and moral judgment, think of aggression as being one possible strategy to gain or insure exclusive access to a Resource (food, toy, couch). Then you can use observable behaviour as a guide to modify behavioural topography and its accompanying emotional states.

Recall that much of a dog's language can be divided into Assertive behaviours and Yielding behaviours. Assertive behaviours are ritualized patterns used to gain resources, social or physical distance and, if unheeded, often lead to aggression. Yielding behaviours are signals that are the opposite of aggressive. These signals are used to appease another dog or human, and appear via lowered body posture or a submissive roll. These behaviors are Ritualized Patterns that are used to inhibit aggression. These yielding behaviors are used specifically to **initiate** behavior among dogs that is incompatible with aggression. A common appeasement behaviour, like rolling over on the back and urinating, may be used to diffuse socially tense situations.

Try to ascertain what signals your dog is using in various contexts. Also ask yourself whether your dog is an effective communicator. Some dogs who are poorly socialized are not fluent in their native language and will misuse or delete signals. It is also possible that people have misconceptions about the language dogs use and misinterpret what they see. Assertive behaviours are usually associated with "dominant" dogs but are, in fact, often used by dogs who are extremely insecure or under-socialized. Perhaps because of lack of experience, a dog feels threatened, even when there is no real threat. A dog may just be under-educated and misinterpret the other dogs' signals. Social tension and anxiety also occur because a dog is corrected harshly around other dogs or is corrected for using calming signals (body language dogs use with other dogs to signal non-aggressive intent – discussed at length in a later section). This dog sees other dogs, no matter how they are "talking," as a Predictor Of Punishment.

Selective breeding has, in some instances, made communication between dogs more difficult. In some cases, selective breeding has altered the physical and visual signals that a dog is capable of giving. Floppy ears, lots of fluffy coat, docking of tails and ears all render dogs unable to communicate as effectively. These same physical features may unintentionally send the wrong message to another dog. For instance, raised hackles can signal escalating aggression. The uneducated dog who has never seen a "fluffy" dog may well be alarmed the first time she does so. The natural state of the long hair standing up on the neck and back may be mistaken for a piloerector reflex. You can see why some breeds seem to be naturally threatening to other dogs without even trying. Humans don't own the market on communication problems among their own species!

In summary: There are many known signals that dogs use to communicate. The better you understand these signals and what they say about a dog's intent, the better equipped you will be to modify the animal's behaviour.

When you identify the dog's body language and understand what emotion it could be originating from, this gives you important clues about the dog's current emotional state. The dog's emotional state gives, in turn, clues about how reactive the dog may currently be. At the same time, it is important to keep a non-judgmental point of view. If a dog has just snapped at you, it is a bit difficult not to take it personally, I'll grant you that! But this attitude will not modify the dog's behaviour. It takes a Plan to do that. Don't worry! As you advance through this book, I will explain how to develop a plan.

Dog Signals Provide Information

To work safely with an aggressive dog, it is necessary to recognize the entire range of dog emotions. A relaxed body posture, indicating a relaxed, non-reactive state, gives you information about how "safe" the dog is at this moment, as well as what kind of feedback you should give the dog. A stressed body posture tells you the dog is becoming more reactive, therefore less "safe." Again you must make a decision about intervention and feedback. Displays of frank aggression indicate a dog who is extremely "unsafe." You must make a decision about how to best protect yourself and others who may be in danger, and note the precipitating event as a "trigger."

Thus, it is impossible to work with aggression until you can recognize the early signs and read the dog's body language. How can we communicate with each other if there is insufficient knowledge of the other species? If you cannot read the information the dog is displaying, then you won't be giving appropriate feedback. Then you are only reacting to the current situation and practicing damage control, not actually modifying behaviour.

It is easy to recognize frank displays of aggression, such as bared teeth, growling, or lunging and biting. By the time you are observing *these* behaviours, you are Behind The Power Curve. The aggression has escalated so far that your opportunity to teach the dog anything is long past. At this point, whomever the aggression is directed at, whether a human or another dog, is also reacting, thereby providing the aggressor with even more reason to continue escalating the aggressive behaviour. In addition, the possibility that the aggressive behaviour is reinforcing in this situation, and therefore ever more likely to occur again, is high. Positive Reinforcement promotes a behaviour being repeated in the future because the dog found it rewarding or profitable in the past. For instance, if your dog growls at you when you reach for her brand new rawhide bone, and you withdraw your hand, the dog is positively reinforced for growling. Don't get me wrong, withdrawing your hand in this situation is wise, because then you will be able to use your fingers to dial the phone to get help, or to turn the pages of this book, and therefore eventually modify the behaviour of the dog. Nonetheless, the dog has still been reinforced for the undesirable behaviour, *because it worked.* The dog retained the bone and you gave her social distance.

You cannot intervene and persuade the dog to use different behaviour patterns until you can accurately interpret the signals the dog is using. Since it is imperative with an intervention program to get in way **ahead of** an agonistic display, **before** your dog begins a specific behaviour chain, you must be able to identify that moment at which you can most effectively step in with guidance.

Your goal is to anticipate the aggressive event by:

1. identifying the environmental triggers, and
2. identifying the signals your dog is displaying early enough for you to intervene effectively.

Now that you understand the importance of using dog signals in your prevention and behaviour modification efforts, the following chapters in this section are devoted to helping you identify dog signals.

7

DOG SIGNALS & STRESS

I think of Dog Signals as falling into five categories. In addition to stress-related topography, there are types of intentional Signals that dogs use specifically for Conflict Resolution:

1. Stress-related topography (observable behaviour, behaviour sequence, or physical reaction) is that which is primarily reflexive – the physiological symptoms of stress.
2. Displacement Signals are behaviours done "in place of" something else, and are specifically out-of-context. The dog may be using a familiar activity to "comfort" herself. These signals indicate to others that the dog is feeling stressed.
3. Calming Signals are used as a way to avoid threats and to communicate a wish to prevent confrontation. The dog uses these signals both to calm himself and to communicate to others nearby that he wishes them to remain calm also. These signs indicate that the dog using them has an awareness of personal space infringement (either his own or the other dog's), and he wishes to communicate his own non-aggressive intent or good will.
4. Distance Increasing Signals (from your dog's point of view), which say, "Please move out of my personal space," or perhaps, "Move right on out of my territory." Maybe even, "Move right on out of my life."
5. Distance Decreasing Signals are an invitation from a dog to approach. A Yielding behaviour would be one type of Distance Decreasing Signal. A Yielding behaviour is something the dog accesses to appease or to turn off or prevent aggression in another dog or human. Another Distance Decreasing Signal would be a play bow or a paw-lift, both of which are friendly overtures inviting one to "come hither."

Recognition of all of these signals, as well as an ability to recognize stress-related topography, will aid you in understanding dog language. Attempting to modify behaviour when you don't know what your observations mean can lead to tragic errors when treating aggression.

In summary, you must be able to differentiate between:

- A calm relaxed dog
- A stressed dog
- A dog displaying displacement behaviours
- A dog who is making the effort to be non-threatening
- A dog who is escalating aggressive display

The more knowledge you have about display, the better the decisions you will make. It is important for the dog to be able to trust you and feel understood. It is important for you to make the right decision about which consequences are appropriate for the circumstances: should you support the dog, supply reinforcement, redirect the dog, or punish the behaviour? Correctly interpreting display will also improve your timing of consequences and intervention.

I will begin with learning to recognize Stress-related behaviours and Displacement and Calming Signals because they are often the *first indication apparent to humans* that a dog is feeling a bit uncomfortable.

How Do I Recognize Stress in My Dog?

Stress comes from an inability to cope with the current situation. Aggressive or defensive behaviour is a symptom. The environment, the situation, or sometimes the owner is the true source of the stress.

It is important to recognize the overt signs of stress, because, at this point, our dogs are telling us that they are in a reactive state. The chemical changes discussed earlier are already on the rise. This may be one of the first indications you have from your dog that a problem could escalate.

Signs of stress include:

- Sweaty paw prints
- Vocalization – whining, growling or frantic barking
- Dilated pupil (the physiological response to an adrenaline "dump")
- White rim on eyes
- Flaring whiskers
- Body tension (stiff, rigid appearance and movements; slow movements)
- Muscle ridge around mouth
- Muscle ridge around eyes
- Dog uninterested in food
- Excessive or frantic activity level
- Increased or decreased activity level
- Shallow breathing
- Rapid breathing or panting with the corner of the mouth drawn back and facial tension
- Holding breath (often a precursor to a bite)
- Excessive, sudden hair loss or exfoliation (dander appearing on the surface of the coat)
- Hypersalivation (drooling)
- Freezing – a dog holding **very** still with a rigid body
- Increased heart rate and respiration
- Flight reactions
- Fight reactions
- Any behaviour you have never seen before may be an indication of stress

Photo by Joanne Weber

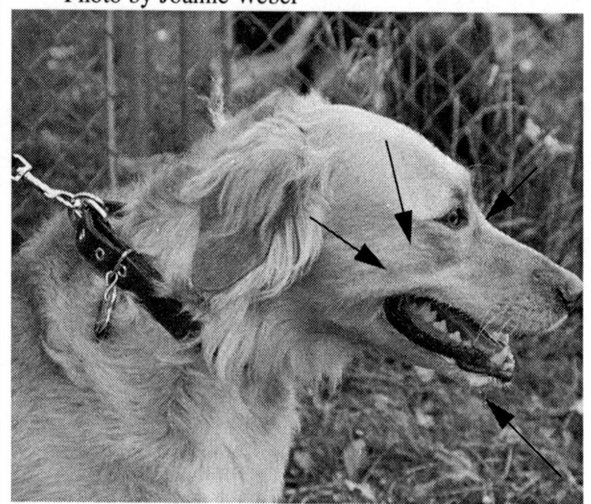

Bailey exhibits signs of stress. There is evidence of hypersalivation (foam on the bottom lip; just prior to taking the photo some large strings of saliva dripped to the ground...). The lips are pulled way back, and there is a ridge evident above the lips near the back of the lips. There is also tension in the face, resulting in ridges around the eyes (in this photo they are most obvious below the eyes).

Stress

8

DISPLACEMENT BEHAVIOURS & CALMING SIGNALS

Calming Signals are studied extensively by Turid Rugaas. (Her book, *On Talking Terms with Dogs: Calming Signals*, is a must-read.) They are used *specifically* and *deliberately* by a dog to "calm" down others in the environment. This implies that the dog is aware of personal space (his own and others) and is making an intentional endeavor to communicate with others.

There are two related definitions of displacement behaviour in the literature. For behaviourists, a displacement activity, technically, is simply a stress-induced behaviour used because the animal doesn't have any other behaviour to "access" in response to the current situation. Many behaviourists use this to refer to a purely reflexive response.

At a seminar I attended, Turid Rugaas used the term a bit more broadly. Displacement behaviours are used to "distract" the other dog (or person) by using a totally out-of-context behaviour to divert the other dog's attention – rather like a tap on the shoulder and a "Hey, did you notice this really interesting smell?" in order to divert the other dog's attention momentarily. It allows a "time-out" from the current activity. You can qualify the definition for your own use – just make a note of whether you observe the dog behaving reflexively or whether the behaviour appears to be deliberate. Is the dog using the behaviour to comfort herself? Or to communicate with others in the environment?

Displacement and Calming Signals are often used for the same purpose by the dog; both may indicate stress caused by invasion of personal space past that dog's comfort zone in this particular context, and a wish to avoid aggression. The big distinction between them is the function they currently serve for the dog.

It is important to note that the same signal can be used to convey more than one meaning. Just as some of our words have more than one meaning, so can dog signals. The English word that sounds like "to" can mean: "Are you going TO the store?" or "I am going, TOO or "I have TWO of those." A list of displacement signals might include some of the same behaviours that a dog would use as calming signals. Whether it is a displacement or a calming signal, specifically, would be ascertained by determining the function the behaviour is serving for the dog at that time or in that context.

Displacement and Calming Signals are therefore used by dogs to:

- Signal non-aggressive intent
- Indicate stress

- Calm other dogs, a kind of "sit down and take 10 deep breaths and you'll feel better"
- Serve as familiar "comfortable" behaviour that alleviates a dog's feelings of insecurity

Displacement Activities

Some common displacement activities are:

- Marking territory
- Increased activity level (fooling around – the equivalent of nervous, inappropriate laughter in humans)
- Scratching
- Yawning
- Shaking
- Sniffing
- Looking in a direction away from the threat

A dog exhibits displacement behaviours to distract himself from an unfamiliar or unpleasant situation, particularly when he is unable to cope. Some of these behaviours are used to demonstrate non-aggressive intent, such as yawning and the other signals also used as calming signals.

A displacement behaviour may have different effects on group dynamics, sometimes working to distract other dogs, depending on its presentation. Some of these behaviours, such as marking territory or increased activity levels, will agitate other dogs rather than calm them down.

For instance, Marking territory can surface as a sign of extreme insecurity, and therefore might be used as a displacement activity by a stressed dog. Marking territory can also be a sign of status-related behaviour and escalate aggression amongst two dogs, particularly making males more volatile (although I have also seen this have a similar effect on my fox terrier bitches). The quintessential "pissing contest," if you will. In the second case, the behaviour is not a displacement behaviour nor is it a calming signal. Particularly if the dog is staring at the other dog as he lifts his leg, and then walks off a bit to see what the other dog does, this is a pretty clear Distance Increasing signal.

Calming Signals

Dogs use Calming Signals to communicate non-aggressive intent. These signals are used with others who are an unknown entity, with a known entity in potentially volatile situations, and in play situations where the play is beginning to make an dog feel uncomfortable with the direction the play is going. If a dog uses a calming signal, she is looking to see a calming signal being returned as reassurance from the other dog or person.

Dog use the following signals both to indicate stress or a personal space violation, while at the same time to communicate: "I'm friendly – I mean you no harm." Or perhaps, "You look really nervous, I am not threatening you. Return me a signal so I understand you are not threatening me."

There are some signals that transfer well to people. That is, there are some signals of non-aggressive intent that humans can make use of to reassure or communicate more effectively with dogs. The next time your dog is nervous, try looking away and yawning. Many dogs will show visible signs of relaxation instantaneously. It is truly amazing! This indicates that a calming signal can also be used to convey to a second or third party "Don't worry, it is a safe environment."

Another signal that can be used effectively is Lip-Licking. A very easy and a subtle way to signal your dog to relax is to look at your dog, averting your eyes slightly, and licking your lips a few times.

Other Calming Signals include:

- Sniffing
- Yawning
- Looking Away
- Scratching
- Lip-licking
- Nose-licking
- Paw lift
- Moving slowly in an arc on approach
- Sitting or lying down
- Blinking

- Slow careful movements
- Shaking
- Sneezing

How do I Tell if My Dog is Signaling

or just doing regular stuff?

Of course, these are all behaviours that dogs display under many circumstances. For instance, a dog will lick his lips to get food off them, and scratch when he has an itch.

So, how do you distinguish between just regular, normal, old sniffing or yawning and use of these same behaviours as a Signal? Look for Out-Of-Context use of these behaviours. Then you can suspect that they are being displayed by the dog as a specific communication in an attempt to calm dogs (or humans) in the vicinity who are making her feel uneasy, uncomfortable, worried, stressed or threatened. The situation or the company may be unfamiliar to your dog. The unfamiliar makes many of us feel a bit uncomfortable until we establish we are Safe In This Context.

For example: In-Context sniffing is what dogs do in the kitchen when you are cooking. My dogs are well accustomed to the fact that humans drop stuff on the floor all the time. It is not unusual for one of the dogs to go and sniff the kitchen floor periodically, "Just Checking." An example of Out-of-Context sniffing is when my dog is playing with another dog whom she doesn't know very well. Suddenly, in the middle of a wrestling or chase game, one of the dogs stops and begins sniffing the ground. This is one way the dog communicates to his playmate, "You are playing too rough and make me feel uncomfortable. Tone it down, please."

Sometimes your dog is looking away from you to look at something else. This is In-Context. If you are cross with him, or scolding him, and he makes it a point to "look away," your dog is using a signal to communicate non-aggressive intent to you and is asking you to calm down and communicate non-aggressive intent back to him. Sometimes when you lean over a dog you don't know, or reach for him, he will look away. This is another example of a dog who is telling you, "I am non-threatening at this moment. Give me a sign that you are not threatening me."

A dog might also use Calming Signals because she senses that another dog in the vicinity is worried. So, Dog #1 could use a Calming Signal to reassure Dog #2 that the environment is safe.

One way to make use of the communication efforts your dog is using is in the training environment. As I became aware of efforts my dog made to communicate with me, and began to understand those communications, my new knowledge validated what I already decided: I do not correct dogs in a Group Sit or Down situation, by using punishers such as yelling or collar corrections, for behaviour such as sniffing. Instead I have gotten excellent results by allowing the dog to use calming signals and keep applying positive reinforcement to the desired behaviour. Soon the dog will gain enough confidence in this situation to not have to resort to the use of calming signals. Keep in mind, it might be the actions of the dog or handler near her that is making your dog nervous enough to have to "calm" the situation down. Many times dogs are also trying to calm their own handlers!

If you adopt my training philosophy, you may decide, as I have, that you do not wish to watch or have your dog around training situations where a lot of physical punishment is taking place. I find this situation needlessly stressful for my dog and for me. At times I have been looked at as being decidedly eccentric when I have refused to participate in group Stay exercises where loud or harsh corrections are doled out. If in a group class, I ask, "Is anyone going to be using loud corrections or leash corrections with their dog?" If so, I opt to not participate at all. Though some may treat you like you're an oddball, others will understand. The big benefit here, of course, is that my dog is appreciative! If I am in a Fun Match or Show'n'Go, I keep a close eye out and, if I see someone going out to correct, I go stand near my dog to offer support and feed her for maintaining position in the face of this "challenge."

I am not necessarily saying that all of these corrections are cruel. I am saying that I do not believe that stress makes a solid Sit or Down Stay.

Punch was breaking her stays because she had become wary of people coming up to dogs next to her and correcting them. When I made this event a predictor of reinforcement for her, she soon got to the point that, instead of becoming worried and shifting position, lying down, standing, or moving in this situation, she would herald the approach of other handlers to their dogs, eagerly looking to me for her cookie when the dog next to her got corrected.

Try calming signals on a dog you know before you try them with an unknown dog. Watch the dog's reaction closely. Usually you see some of the tension go out of the dog's face, and then the eyes blink in response. Sometimes you can see the dilated pupil, or a once-stressed eye with white showing, begin to return to a more normal and relaxed state. The tail may begin to wag in a friendly or tentative manner. Some of the tension will begin to drain out of the dog's body.

Use caution with animals you don't know – always! Some reactive animals, because of past experiences, interpret any human behaviour that is not familiar as "dangerous."

Once you begin to observe behaviour and realize that the dog is not just making random movements, but that the behaviour you see is purposeful, you have opened a whole new door of communication. That feels good!

Now that I have discussed this matter with words, let's look at a series of illustrations. These help you to better remember these all-important signals.

Sniffing

Sniffing

Sniffing is a frequently used Calming Signal. An example of this would be the first time I put Maeve, my GSD bitch with known aggression issues, out with one of my fox terriers, Dervish, who was an intact male at the time. They began innocently enough, loose in one of my fenced play areas. All was going well. Then Dervish began to run and Maeve chased. Still going great. They made about five or six circuits of the 70 x 100 area and then Maeve's body language and demeanor began to subtly change and she began to exhibit behaviour that was making Dervish feel uncomfortable – she was shifting into prey drive. Dervish, who had extensive social experience, noticed this "change" just before I did, which is what actually alerted me to watch more closely. He lowered his tail slightly, glanced back a couple of times, then, before I even had time to intervene, abruptly skidded to a halt and began to sniff the ground very intently. Maeve slowed down, trotted over, shook once, the glaze left her eyes, and I could see Maeve my dog returning. She sniffed the ground also, and from that moment on I have never seen her treat Dervish as if he were prey. Dervish plainly communicated to her, by being non-reactive and using sophisticated communication skills, that he was "one of us." "Tone it down, girlie! This isn't the real thing!" I have seen my dogs and client's dogs use some pretty amazing language to diffuse potentially dangerous situations.

Look-Away

Look-Away

Turning away is often accompanied by lip-licking. It is definitely a polite and friendly gesture. This is a great behaviour for humans to use when approaching dogs who are unsure. If a dog is polite enough to give you a "look-away," you should respond in kind. When approaching timid dogs, *you* should initiate this. If you approach a dog you don't know, it is wise to begin with a look away and work up to direct eye contact to see how the dog receives it. Remember, in a dog's native language, immediate direct eye contact is rude and considered challenge or threat behaviour. Once you are aware of, and begin to look for, relaxed, confident eye contact, you will be surprised at how few dogs give it in a truly comfortable manner without specifically being taught to do so. In fact, many dogs you meet, until they know you a bit, refuse to meet your eyes. I do not use direct eye contact in a threatening way with my dogs, nor do I ever "stare them down." This is not the kind of relationship I wish to foster. Teach your dog that direct eye contact from humans is friendly and non-threatening I do not use eye contact in a punishing way.

Lip Licking

Lip licking is very frequently used, often combined with looking away and blinking.

Lip-Licking

Blinking

Blinking eyes, or blinking frequently or with exaggeration, is a signal of friendly intent.

It is very difficult to draw a blinking dog in one frame. But I'm sure you get the picture!

Blinking

Watch your dog's facial expression and eyes when he is relaxed and you are petting him. Often you will notice the muscles above the eyes moving slightly. You will see the eyebrows shift back and forth, just a small movement. Or he may slightly shift his glance back and forth. Shifting eyes and moving eyebrows indicate the same emotional state as blinking.

Yawning

Yawning is another frequently seen Calming behaviour. Yawning also "translates" well – try a Look-Away and a Yawn the next time your dog appears stressed. Watch her relax. Some dogs get very excited that you finally "understood" what they have been trying to tell you!

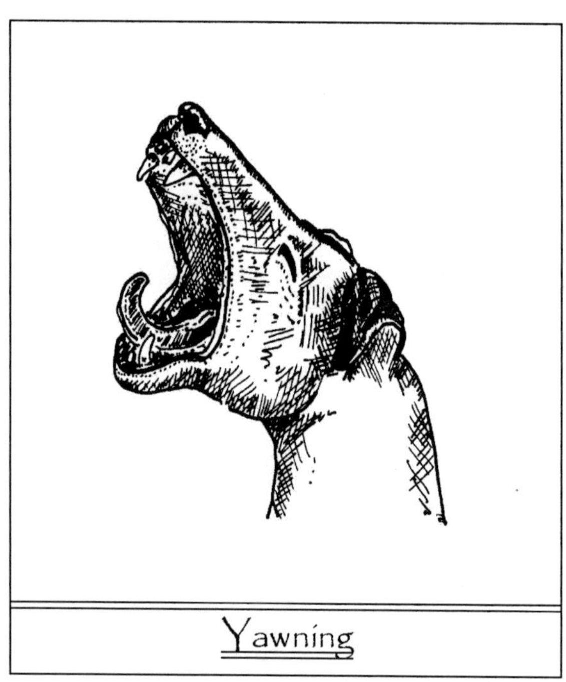

Yawning

Early on in my work with aggressive dogs, I was boarding and training a young Rottweiler male with known aggression. After working with him, I decided to turn him into a kennel run with Fletcher, my super-sophisticated-with-social-skills Basset Hound. As the young dog raced toward Fletcher, snarling, my heart was in my mouth. Just as I was chastising myself for being a bloody idiot, Fletcher looked at the young dog and did not panic. He casually sat down, looked away and yawned. The two-year-old Rottweiler skidded to a quick halt with a puzzled look on his face. He pulled a reference booklet out of his back pocket and frantically began to search for: "What to do when other dog does not become overreactive." Anthropomorphic musings aside, which are included here merely for entertainment purposes, Fletcher's use of calming signals effectively and immediately diffused a volatile and potentially deadly situation. The young Rottie followed Fletcher around like a baby puppy for the rest of the week, respectfully minding his manners. This was one of many dramatic social interactions I have seen dogs use to stem violence.

Scratching

Scratching

This is out-of-context, remember. Sometimes your dog really does have an itch!

Let's say, the dog is sitting in a group of dogs on a stay. The dog doesn't know the dogs on either side of him, and doesn't feel comfortable. In addition, the dog has been corrected for breaking ... or ... the dog on his left is nervous because his owner is in the process of returning to correct....Suddenly, your dog stands up and begins to scratch. Or maybe even remains sitting and scratches. This is your dog telling you that he is stressed.

Breanna has scratched on the Halt in the middle of a Figure 8 at an Obedience Trial. It was the stress of watching me be nervous! She was trying to tell me to calm down and asking me to return to my normal demeanor! It is difficult for me to feel good about correcting my dog for *my* unusual behaviour!

Shaking

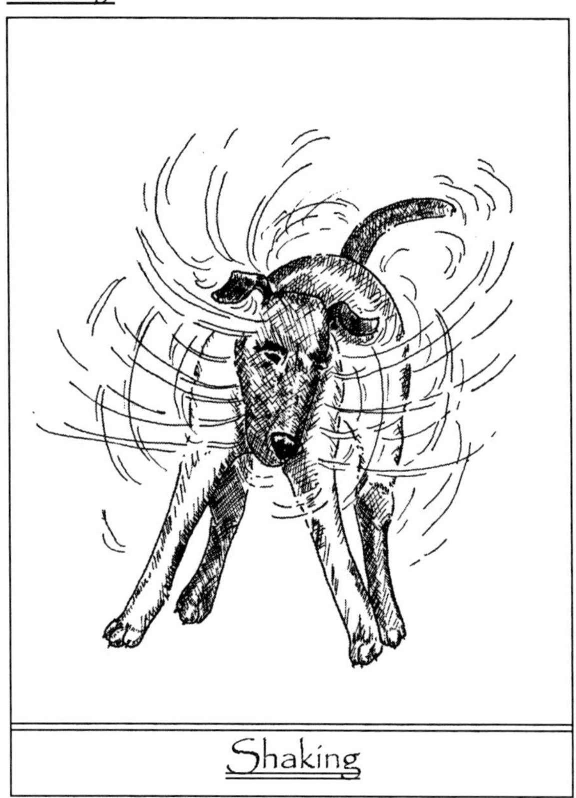

Shaking

Shaking is very interesting. Often when I see two dogs approach each other, the moment gets a bit tense as the dogs enter each other's personal space. Then the dogs may both signal non-threatening intent. Then you often see one or both shake. Turid Rugaas' explanation for this is wonderful – she calls it "Shaking off Stress." How descriptive!

Learning a new language, be it French or "Dog," requires practice and time. A good way to learn about body language is to visit your local animal shelter or humane society. Working as a Veterinary Nurse or at a Boarding Kennel can increase your skills. Volunteering at your local Humane Society or Dog Shelter will expose you to many dogs who are untrained and under stress. Talk to dog people and watch dogs. Communicate with your own dog. Your relationship will grow and prosper.

9

DISTANCE INCREASING SIGNALS

TO MINIMIZE CONTACT AND INTERACTION

Distance Increasing Signals are designed to gain social distance. Assertive, threatening, and aggressive behaviours all fall into this category. Understanding these signals will save you from being on the receiving end of a bite. In the context of a behaviour modification program, it is imperative to be able to intervene before the behavioural sequence advances very far.

Distance Increasing Signals include:

- Staring.
- Snarling. (Lips are lifted vertically. The line formed by the lips is short.)
- Ears erect or flat.
- Tension in the body or face.
- Stance. (Particularly changes in head/neck position, either raised or lowered.)
- Piloerection.
- Urination and Ground-Scratching; Marking territory.
- Tail straight or arched over back.
- Wagging just the tip of the tail, or wagging in a short, sharp arc with the tail held "up" over the back as much as the structure of the dog will allow.
- Stalking.
- Brief "Look away" at a very tense moment.

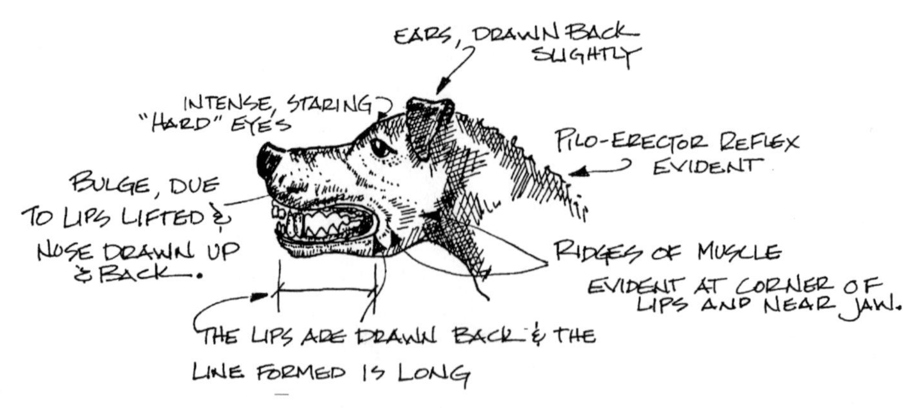

Distance Increasing Signals

While dog in the previous illustration looks fearsome, and certainly *will* bite, his facial expression can give us a lot of information about his emotional state.
Let's make a list:

- Eyes
  Intense.
  Staring.
- Ears
  Are not straight forward, but are drawn back slightly.
- Muzzle
  The tip of the nose is drawn up and back. This, combined with the "lip-lift," makes for a slight bulge in the area where the whiskers are.
- Mouth
  Drawn Back – the lips look "long."
  Teeth Showing.
  Ridges of muscle are evident at the corner of the lips, and another ridge near the jaw.
  Lips are drawn back far enough to show not only the incisors and canines, but also the molars.
- The piloerector reflex is evident on the neck (the hair is standing up).

But what does all this mean? This dog is in more conflict about the outcome of the situation than you might think. The lips drawn back indicate a defensive state. A dog in a defensive state will very likely halt his attack if you carefully move out of his territory or personal space before he becomes extremely reactive. (This is in contrast to the dog who is observing you as "prey." A dog who is treating you as a prey object will continue to pursue and or follow you for a longer distance, and may even move in to nip at you to see if he can get you to move so he can have a satisfying chase. In this state, dogs tend to be quieter and have a stalking body position, although this is not always true. Think of Border Collies moving sheep: the lowered stance, silence, intensity.)

The piloerector reflex validates this. A piloerector reflex is most often evident when a dog feels uneasy or uncomfortable, and is due to a lack of, rather than an excess of, self confidence. It is also displayed by dogs who have been "startled."

When emotions change, our body changes chemically. Actually, of course, the chemical change internally *precedes* the external "observable" behaviour. By the time a dog is exhibiting this much emotional discomfort, she is already under the influence of a significant "chemical dump" of components like adrenaline and other neurotransmitters. These chemicals prepare the body internally for a Fight or Flight response. When in extreme states, dogs are not "thinking" so much as "reacting."

Remember, in the discussion that follows, I am not just meeting a dog on the street but modifying behaviour, and therefore have some control over the situation. If meeting a dog on the street – remain non-threatening, but leave the situation as soon as possible from a lateral position – DON'T RUN, DON'T face the dog, DON'T turn your back on the dog! Prevent presentation of a frontal body position and favor a *sideways body position*. Keep your arms folded across your chest, not dangling. Avoid direct eye contact, but keep the dog in your peripheral vision.

When *working with* a dog who is using threatening body language I suggest you diffuse this situation rather than escalate the tension. The tricky part, of course, is diffusing the situation without actively providing some sort of Reinforcing Consequences for the dog's current behaviour.

Make sure to display non-threatening body language: Keep your body sideways to the dog. Be calm – no sudden moves! If in doubt, stand still and see if that calms the dog. Remain still and *breathing* until the dog relaxes a bit, then you can try to move calmly away. Keep your eyes and face averted and keep the dog in your peripheral vision. Move away laterally, and slowly, as soon as you can, trying a few steps while monitoring the dog's reaction so you can pause again.

Once you see the dog relax somewhat, you can try to ask for a behaviour you can reinforce, such as "Sit." This is useful only if the animal knows Sit, of course! So, do ask for a *known* behaviour.

Sit is known by most dogs so it is a good cue to try. If you have practiced Sit with this dog and reinforced it in the past, you are in a much better strategic position.

You may have to wait for some time for the dog to calm down before you even attempt another approach or any sort of communication. If this is the dog you see on your initial approach – you are already in very big trouble! The best move is for you to get out of the situation safely and regroup! You will need some way to control the situation and the dog so no one gets bitten!

The best bet is don't *ever* let a situation get this far out of control! Manage the circumstances in such a way that the animal is not made this uncomfortable. Refer to the protocol "Zen Sit and Down" for help with a Be-Seated and Remain Calm exercise, so you are able to provide a "Switch" to help change the dog's emotional state from "Fight/Flight" back to a more relaxed and normal state.

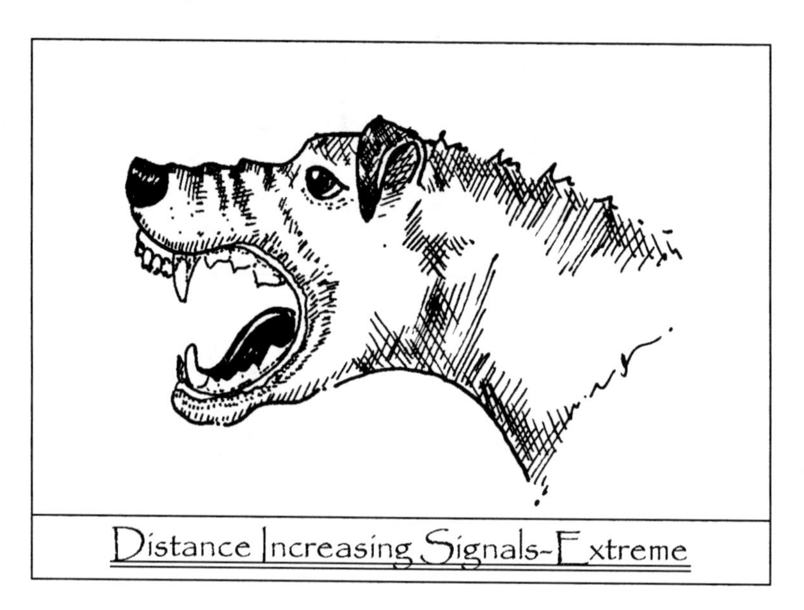

Distance Increasing Signals-Extreme

If you compare this dog's facial expression to the ones previous, you will see some subtle differences:

- Eyes
  Intense, Staring, Not blinking.
- Ears
  Forward.
- Mouth
  Lips are lifted extensively exposing the gums, and drawn back, yet still somewhat "C" shaped.
  There are wrinkles on the foreface.
  Ridges of muscle are evident at the corner of the lips and near the jaw.
  Lips are raised in the front far enough to wrinkle the nose up.
  Lips drawn back far enough to show just the incisors and canines.
- This dog is in an extreme state. He is also defensive and in great conflict. Reasoning with him will be a fruitless endeavor until he "chemically" calms down.
- Pay particular attention to how far the lips are lifted as opposed to drawn back. The "longer" the lips appear, the less self confidence the dog is displaying.

It is important NOT to move any closer into this dog's body space! Continue to breathe; dogs are very sensitive to breathing patterns. Look away and lick your lips. Lower your shoulders and look non-threatening. Remain still. If the dog relaxes somewhat, you could try backing away very slowly (remember to breathe!) from the dog, with your head and eyes averted, licking lips, your hands still and up over your stomach if possible. Move slowly away until you are in a position to close a door between the two of you or find safe sanctuary in whatever fashion is the most expedient.

Again, if you have ignored the signals the dog has given you until you are at this display, you are in serious trouble. Manage the dog and the Setting Events (situation) better so you never see this face directed at you!

Distance Increasing Signals-Warning

Go ahead! Make a list for yourself. This is a Shepherd-mix I saw one day at the Animal Shelter, so you can assume that the eyes are "Shepherd-shaped," as are the ears. The general overall carriage is that of a Shepherd as well. Different is the rather lighter bone structure on the head, and also the more slender and upright neck.

List observations about:

- Eyes
- Ears
- Mouth and Lips

The obvious answer is, of course, don't approach. This dog looks quite willing to escalate display, perhaps explosively. Note, in particular, that the dog does not look intimidated; she has a "Don't come any closer, I am willing to do something about it" look. In fact, moving much closer than 3' to this dog's cage caused an immediately escalated warning, then an explosive quiet lunge. A hint that tips you off to what may happen after the initial display: note the lips are "c" shaped. That usually means more serious business. For further discussion about this "c" shape vs. elongated lips, see the chapter: "Interpreting Intent Through Observation – Signal Clusters."

Distance Increasing Signals- Territorial Barking

This is my Shepherd Maeve, in what I would call her "Defensive Barking" mode. This display is meant as a warning to those encroaching on territorial boundaries. Notice it is a "big" display, with a lot of drama. This is intended to make you notice and go away.

It may or may not be accompanied by piloerector reflex, depending on how "startled" the dog feels.

I would stop my approach if I were you! This dog is willing to escalate aggression, but is making a pretty clear effort to warn you off. This is a signal that the animal would allow you to move along peacefully, in most instances – as long as moving along means "not coming any closer in any way and you are increasing distance between the two of us immediately."

Overt aggressive displays are designed to avoid aggression. Remember that! This may help you to, instead of taking aggression "personally," see aggression in a more non-confrontational manner. Allowing emotion to override logic does not get you where you want to go. This clinical approach has been very helpful to me when I am classifying and modifying aggressive behaviour, because then I am proactive and thoughtful in my method rather than reactive and making the situation worse.

65 Distance Increasing Signals

10

DISTANCE DECREASING SIGNALS

TO INVITE INTERACTION

Understanding when your dog tells you she wishes to interact normally is important, because then you can give her social approval for behaving in an appropriate manner. You send your dog a very confusing message if you misinterpret these signals and punish her for using them, or overreact because you are afraid she might be aggressive. (If your dog has had aggressive incidents in the past, you are understandably a bit gun-shy about allowing her to "go too far," lest she have another incident.) This is one of the ways people effectively destroy the dog's native language. Many people are nervous about letting their dogs interact with other dogs because they think the dogs might become aggressive. Also, people often do not know what they are looking at when dogs are interacting, and they misinterpret play as fighting or escalating aggression as play. People allow marginal behaviour, mistaking it for play, and fail to intervene when it would be a good thing to do. Whether your dog is approaching other dogs or people, you need to know what your dog is telling you about how she feels about the current situation. This gives you the opportunity to provide proper feedback so that the dog learns appropriate behaviour in any given context.

The following is a list of Distance Decreasing Signals:

- Forequarters lower than rear-quarters (play-bow, greeting or yielding display).
- Avoidance of eye contact.
- Submissive grin. (Lips are pulled back horizontally. The lips look "longer.")
- Ears slightly lowered, drawn back or drawn so that the pinna is held out to the side of the head.
- Lowering of body.
- Wagging tail.
- Flicking the tongue.
- Lip licking.
- Raising forepaw.
- Rolling over.
- Urinating while rolling over or on back.
- Lifting the rear leg when a human touches the dog near the flank, or when another dog sniffs this area to reveal the inguinal (groin) area. Often the dog will stretch the rear leg out behind her so the "sniffer" has an easier time of it.

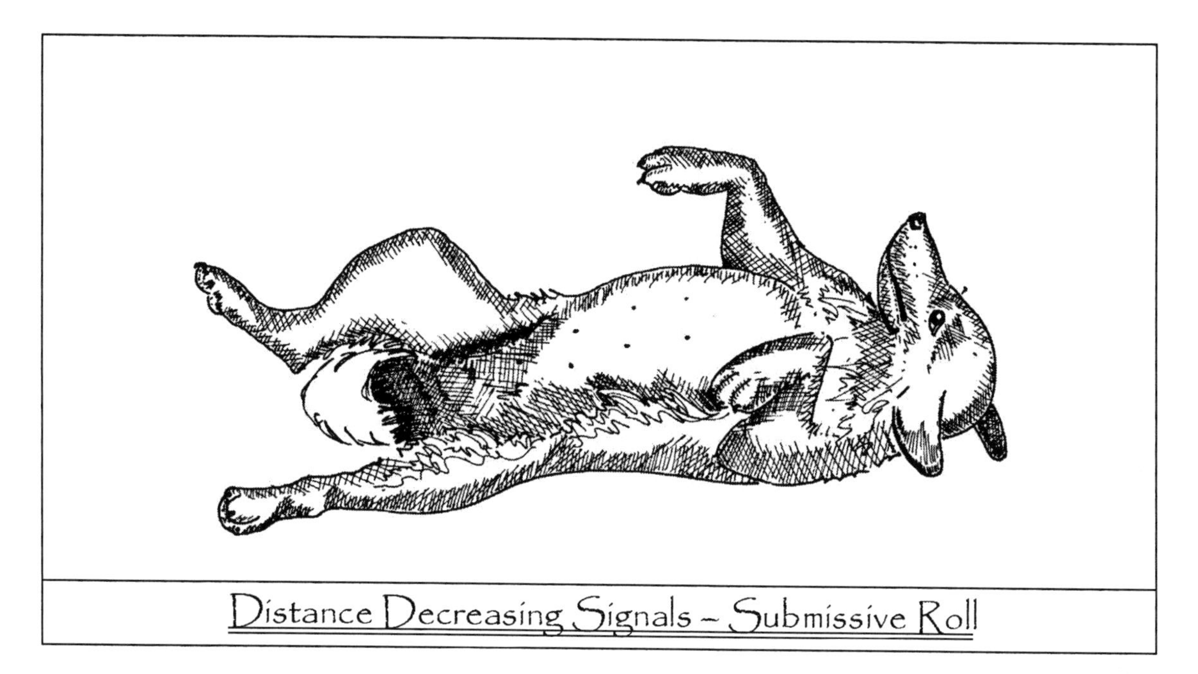

Distance Decreasing Signals – Submissive Roll

This dog is displaying a passive yielding posture:
- Ears are flattened.
- Lips are drawn back (but no teeth showing).
- The eyes are squinting or elongated and blinking.
- The tail is tucked between the hind legs.

This dog may be asking for a tummy rub, or simply telling you how much she respects you.

This posture may (or may not) be accompanied by urine dribbling. Punishment is definitely contraindicated (a medical term indicating the inadvisability of using a protocol or medication) in this case! You will only increase the submissive urination. Instead, use positive methods to teach the dog to greet by sitting.

A dog in a submissive posture should never be punished. Punishing this animal will only make the dog feel more anxious in your presence. In addition, you teach the dog that you ignore attempts to communicate with you.

I have seen dogs with fear and anxiety who assume a submissive-passive posture and then lift their lip in a snarl, or snap at you as you reach for them. Why would an animal do this? There are various reasons, but here are a few of the most common:

- Some dogs do not trust you to respect submissive body language. Perhaps past experience taught them that this posture, which normally "turns off" dog aggression, does not always work with people. For example, a dog jumps on a person. The person becomes angry and shouts at the dog. Then the dog rolls over in a submissive posture and urinates. The person then gets angry because the dog has urinated on the floor, and administers further correction. This scenario is all about humans communicating very ineffectively with dogs, and I can tell you the dog received all the wrong messages from this human.
- Some dogs just seem to get confused and don't know which signals they are giving, as though they never learned the "correct words" (body language) to use.
- Others exhibit this posture in submission, but perceive your "reach" toward them as a further escalating threat. Now the dog has placed herself in a position of limited flight option, so you get a defensive reaction.
- Other dogs learn that you cannot move them easily from this position, so this position combined with a snap prevents you from removing them from an area they want to remain in, or prevents you from placing them in an area they don't want to be in.

So, it is possible that once a dog tried this passive submissive posture to no avail, and all flight options are exhausted (in the dog's paradigm, she is "cornered"), the dog may switch into defensive behaviours.

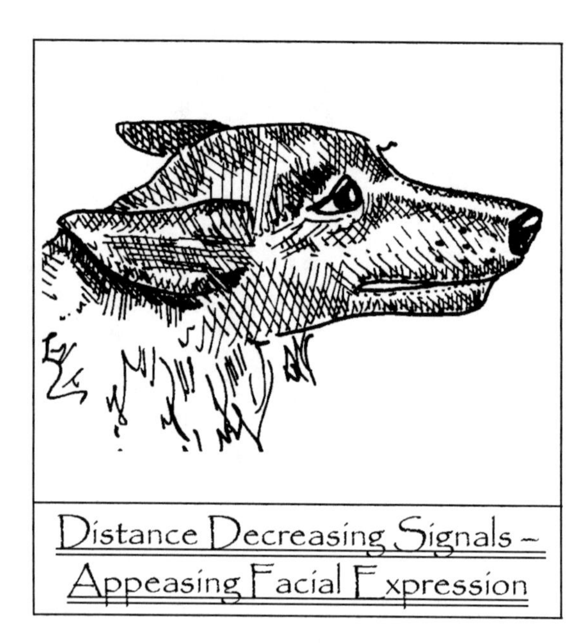

Distance Decreasing Signals – Appeasing Facial Expression

Friendly Approach Behaviours

- This is the same facial expression, only right-side-up, as it were. Notice the "long" lips. A dog who is displaying friendly, yielding behaviour will approach you in a placating manner. The tail will probably be held low and the back or rump area may be slightly curved.
- The tail may be wagging at the tip, or the whole tail may be moving. The tail motion will most likely be in a sweeping manner, either a gentle sway or in a faster, larger sweeping motion.
- The dog may try some pacifying behaviours, such as pawing or licking at the dog or person they are directing the behaviour toward. If it is a dog, this animal would be nudging the other dog's muzzle or licking at the other dog's muzzle or lips.
- Many dogs exhibiting a friendly greeting display do what I call Pretzel Maneuvers. They curl their body or bend in the middle of the body in an exaggerated fashion, wiggling and waggling both ends, with their nose practically touching their tail! Vinny, the Smooth Fox Terrier of a friend, will wiggle with so much delight when greeting human friends that he bends his body in a "C."

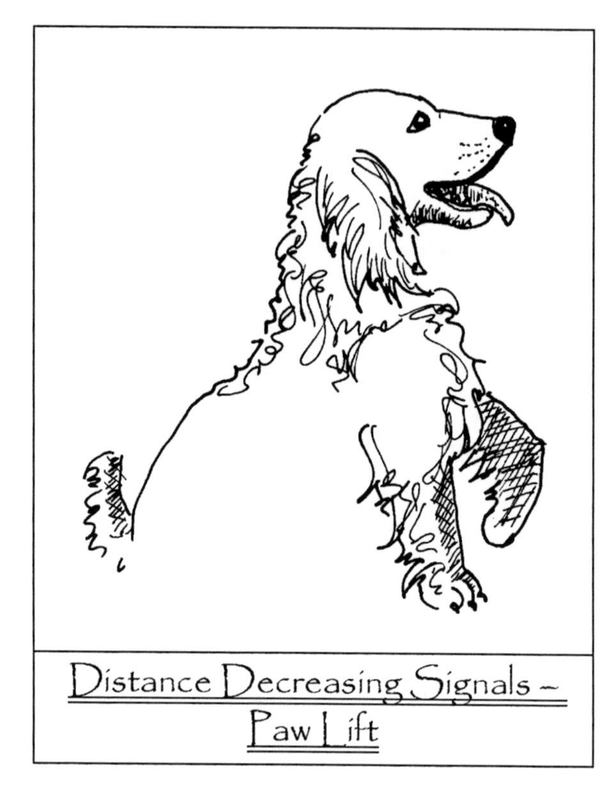

Distance Decreasing Signals – Paw Lift

This dog is displaying relaxed and friendly behaviour:

- Wide open mouth, lips covering or partially covering the teeth.
- No evidence of muscle ridges at the corners of the lips or across the top of the nose.
- Ears in a forward and relaxed position.
- Eyes open and blinking.
- The paw lift is a submissive gesture, to signal care-seeking behaviour.

Go ahead and pet – you'll both benefit!

This dog in "Neutral But Friendly" below, has a friendly and relaxed demeanor.

- The lips look "long." (This becomes more apparent to you as you compare the pictures later of dogs who are displaying overt aggression.)
- The lips are relaxed. There are no ridges of muscle evident over the nose or at the corners of the lips. The ears are held forward,

the eyes are open and shaped "normally" for this dog. The dog is blinking.
- The tail may be held straight out behind the dog, up over the dog's back, or just hanging down. It may be still or wagging in wide sweeps.
- There is no tension held in the dog's face.

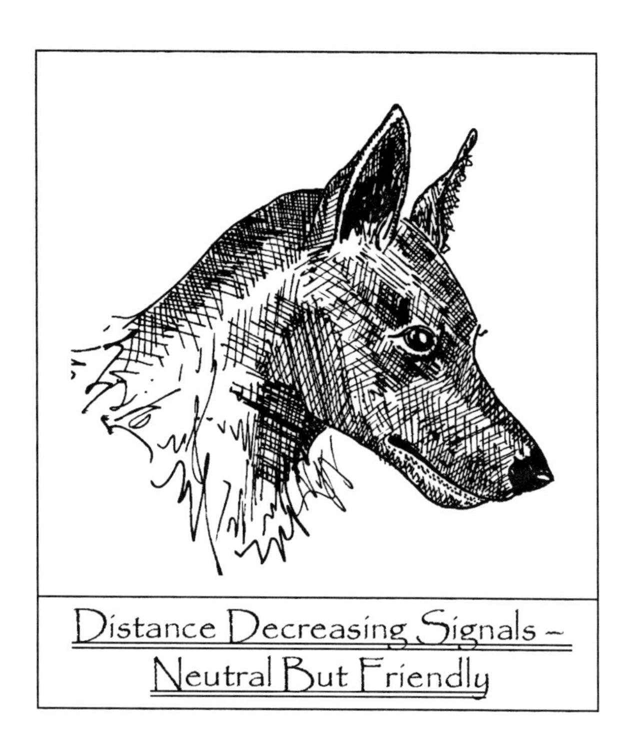

Distance Decreasing Signals – Neutral But Friendly

Wondering about subtle displays that indicate a dog who is not amenable to your approach? Take the neutral facial and body expression and look for the following characteristics: A more intense or staring eye contact. Ears held more tensely forward and a still tail in combination with A Stare would be plenty to halt *my* approach. A dog in a neutral posture may still be making a decision about whether he will welcome your approach or not! Keep an eye on any changes the dog makes in his signals and especially pay attention to any body tension as your distance decreases.

Observe very closely any pupil changes. Pupil changes are often one of the first visual signs that a dog is in conflict about the situation. So, in absence of any light changes, if you see abrupt pupil changes, you might want to reassess your approach.

It is always safest and smartest to allow a dog to approach you, instead of you violating her personal space.

11

TAILS - THE OTHER END...

Tails can be very tricky! First you need to know about how the particular dog you are observing carries his tail naturally, when he is in a relaxed state. That requires observation. After you have worked with many dogs, you can make an educated guess if you don't have time to observe the animal. Knowing your breeds is a big help here. So is a basic knowledge of skeletal structure.

Different breeds have different tail sets. This has to do with how the skeleton is put together and the angle at which the tail connects to the spinal cord. A Siberian or a Pug has a tail that curls over the back. So does the Keeshond. A Kees who is feeling a little submissive might just uncurl his tail a bit, whereas the same level of emotion in a Sheltie would have the Sheltie, with her naturally lower tail carriage, tucking her tail between her legs. The Italian Greyhound normally tucks his tail between his legs as a learned behaviour. That is what IG's are encouraged to do when they are shown in the breed ring.

Please remember that a wagging tail only means that the dog wishes to interact. Look closely for other signals so you can ascertain HOW the dog wishes to interact with you!

Remember to look for "clusters" of signals. Each signal may be a "word," but the various signals combined will make the "sentence." Check the overall body posture and demeanor: look for tension, then look at details. Is the tail still, wagging, over the back, tucked or at half mast? If at half mast, or low – is it normal for that breed or dog? Is there tension in the face, can you see teeth, is there any vocalization? Keep a close watch on pupil size. Sudden changes in pupil size are always a warning that "something" is happening, in the dog's estimation. Dilated pupils are an indication that there is stress present (assuming there is no light change to account for the pupil reaction). Is the dog giving you any overt signals of threatening or non-threatening intent? Looking at the "pieces" of the puzzle, then assembling them logically, enables you to recognize and understand what your dog is trying to tell you! Observation and experience will give you information about the big picture.

This Fox Terrier in the illustration below is feeling friendly and curious. The paw lift is a Distance Decreasing Signal. It may indicate a little bit of uncertainty on the dog's part, a care-seeking type behaviour, or may just be a friendly overture.

Normal Tail

This posture is characteristic, in particular, of many Smooths I have observed in the Breed Ring as they look at the judge or at their Handler in anticipation of a squeaky toy or treat being tossed their way.

Notice the tail, held perpendicular to the top-line. This is normal tail carriage for a Foxy.

Tucked Tail

I rarely see one of my Smooths tuck his tail all the way between his legs. I see this "tea-cup handle" tail position on submissive Fox Terriers who are extremely uncertain. Interestingly, I have also seen a similar tail on dogs who are concentrating on a task really hard. Punch will often lie chewing on a bone, no other dogs or people anywhere around her, and wear this tail.

A tail that is lower than that individual's NORMAL carriage is indicative of uncertainty. This is why it is very important to know anatomy and breed descriptions. A vast knowledge of the species cannot be emphasized enough. Assumption of knowledge is not enough. Humans make many mistakes because they "assume" that a dog is behaving this way or that way based on anthropomorphism.

Particularly if you work with aggression, which has some inherent danger in and of itself, avail yourself of all the knowledge of the species you can. As you do, make sure you take a clinical viewpoint. This is why ethologists are so important to us. I am careful to read their work paying close attention to the observations. Then I run that information through my own belief system and conclude what it means. For instance, in my field experience, based on observation, without trying to place any emotional value on the dog's posture, I see my dogs chewing on a bone with a tucked tail. I don't necessarily believe that this means they are feeling "submissive" or "uncertain." I think they may be concentrating very hard on the task at hand and wish to communicate to others nearby that they are not feeling defensive.

I have observed a similar tail posture on dogs learning a new obedience task. The rest of the dog looks active and lively, but the tail carriage is slightly lowered, and perhaps the ears also. If I look at the dog's face, it has a look of concentration. The body is not tense. Having observed this on dogs I know well, therefore knowing that they were not punished while learning obedience exercises, upholds my hypothesis. My conclusion is that a tucked tail may indicate a high level of concentration, or a dog who is uncertain, or a dog who is worried.

Tails are an important part of dog communication systems, and are used in combination with other signals.

12

INTERPRETING INTENT THROUGH OBSERVATION - SIGNAL CLUSTERS

When you observe dog body language, remember that the dog is the "native speaker." You are learning from the dog and you are not a "native speaker." Native Speaker is a significant concept – it implies that all who are native speakers of that particular language will intuitively understand very subtle nuances. Human languages are split up into "Formal" and "Informal." If a person whose native language is French begins to learn English, he begins with Formal English. If we used the word "cool" as slang – "Wow, this dress is very cool" – it is confusing to the non-native speaker. The non-native speaker might feel the dress and be puzzled by the fact that its temperature was not moderately icy. I find my sixteen-year-old daughter and her friends' conversations extremely interesting – phrases such as "I'm down with that" mean that they are in agreement with each other, and the words "You Go, Girl!" with specific facial and hand gestures mean they really like something. (Sometimes it takes even us old native speakers a moment to catch up with the young native speakers!) The point is that, because of physical differences and vastly different sensory messages (dogs have great noses, their vision is different, and so on), it is impossible for humans to totally duplicate dog language, just as dogs don't have the means to speak as we do. What we *can* do is observe, and use what we observe, to understand dogs. Then, we use this knowledge to communicate with dogs to the greatest extent possible.

I think of each "signal" as a separate word, and the combination of signals as a sentence. If I said to you "bookcase," but nothing else, you would know the object I was referring to, but not much else. If I include the word "bookcase" in a sentence, the precision of my meaning increases and misunderstanding decreases: "I really love my antique bookcase," or "Please dust the bookcase for me." The word "bookcase," alone, leaves you standing there bewildered (and perhaps wondering about my mental prowess!), whereas a complete sentence brings precision to the communication. So it is with dog language. You can't look just at the wagging tail – that merely means the dog wishes to interact. It is the smile or the snarl at the other end of the dog that gives you additional information about whether you might want to pet this dog.

In the following "Signal Clusters" illustration, Dervish's tail is slightly lowered. If you didn't know this particular dog well, that might not be apparent to you. I know Dervish, and he customarily carries his tail straight up or very slightly curved over his back. Always look for signal clusters, rather than just one signal, to tell you the dog's emotional state.

When observing dogs, it is important to note that not all dogs will, in a story-book fashion, progress from one stage of communication into the next. There is a lot of variation in normal ritualized behaviour patterns amongst canines.

Dervish – Signal Clusters

Let's make a list of some of the obvious "signals" in the illustration above:

- Foreleg lifted
- Ears drawn down and back
- Head and neck lowered
- Body lowered and crouching
- Eyes narrowed and blinking

While the dog is still directing his attention toward me, and is looking at me, he has averted his eyes, and is not staring directly into my eyes, but is focusing on an area somewhere around my chin. He is squinting and blinking.

He has paused in this position, and is maintaining a crouched position and holding still.

Take a guess. What could this posture indicate? Is the dog curious? Startled? Angry? Is he likely to move into your body space and bite?

In fact, this is the position Dervish assumes when he is feeling very chastised! This posture indicates many yielding behaviours.

In a like situation, when my German Shepherd Dog feels similarly chastised, her body language is vastly different. She would be lying on the ground, or crawling on the ground toward me, tail lowered and tucked between her legs. It might take her a few approaches, even once the situation was well over, to stop offering some sort of appeasement behaviour, such as lowered ears.

I give you this contrast because, just as people may show individual body language for a given emotion, so do dogs. For instance, if you really hurt someone's feelings, she might begin to cry. In the exact same situation, another person might turn and walk away from you. The same circumstances might cause another person to become angry and yell at you (aggression).

Look carefully at context. For instance, if I was playing a fetching game with my dog, and he ran to me, dropped the ball, play bowed, grabbed my hand with his teeth, then barked at me – I would not call that aggressive or dominant behaviour!

Now, consider the same basic behaviour, same basic situation: I am reaching for a toy my dog is playing with, and the dog runs up to me and drops the ball. There is a split second of stillness, then the dog grabs my hand with his teeth, and holds my hand firmly, but not painfully. The hold lasts a very short time, maybe two or three seconds. There is no vocalization. There is obvious and pointed direct eye contact.

Both of these situations require training! The first one I would classify as a training problem – the dog is over exuberant and playing way too rough. In the second situation, there are obvious overtones of assertive behaviour, and Resource Guarding behaviour as well. The second situation requires an immediate assessment and a Behavioural Protocol. It is marginal (risky) behaviour – not a big deal in and of itself, but definitely moving in an undesired direction.

The moral of this story is: Look for Signal Clusters and Look Closely at the Context. Sometimes you have to make connections, such as: The play bow in the first example is a signal for non-aggressive intent, which was followed by the dog "holding your hand with his teeth." I'm not saying I wouldn't reprimand this behaviour (by halting the game and then resuming play with MY rules), but the dog's intent was plainly non-aggressive. The message in the second situation is clear (because of the *entire sequence* of signals) – a correction administered to the human for invading the dog's personal space.

In the following illustrations, notice how Signal Clusters indicate the emotional state of the dog.

This little Smoothie wants to play ball! He is displaying a toothy, relaxed grin! His ears are forward in anticipation of the game and his tail is wagging in a large arc. He is especially pleased because it's you, his special friend, and has even lifted his upper lip to show his upper canines in a slight "submissive grin." His eyes are open, but he is blinking and not staring with a "hard" eye. There are no ridges of tension in his jaw or the corners of his lips. Play Ball!

Distance Decreasing Signals – Friendly

This Smoothie does *not* want to play ball!

The wagging tail is only indicative of a wish to interact and does not always indicate friendliness. The rest of the body posture gives you details as to how the dog considers the interaction.

Here, the tail is held up and is wagging in a short, sharp motion. Many ethologists, for clarity, term this Flagging instead of Wagging.

The jaw shows ridges of muscle evident at the corners of the lips.

The neck is lowered at just slightly above the shoulder height, and the head is lowered and extended (held sort of parallel to the ground), or "pushed forward." This is very typical of a stationary guarding posture.

This is a self confident animal, at a step past the initial warning of body tension and staring.

Distance Increasing Signals – Guarding, Extreme

Location	Observation
Eyes	Staring Intense
Ears	Upright
Lips	Lifted Drawn back slightly
Tail	Still or Flagging (short, sharp motion)
Head Position	Extended forward Lowered
Neck Position	Lowered

This dog is not as self confident and assured as the dog in the previous Figure. Either the dog has been startled and unexpectedly approached, or the dog is feeling insecure about maintaining a resource. The main indication of this is the slight piloerector reflex on the neck only.

In spite of all that, the dog has decided to "hold his ground." An audible growl would most likely accompany this posture, as the dog "warns you off."

Defensive

Location	Observation
Eyes	Staring Intense
Ears	Upright
Lips	Lifted just enough to bulge the muzzle out slightly in the whisker area, but not enough to wrinkle the nose on the top. Ridges of muscle evident at the corner of the lips, and another ridge near the jaw. Lips drawn back far enough to show just the incisors and canines.
Tail	Still or Flagging (short, sharp motion) Raised
Head Position	Extended forward Lowered
Neck Position	Lowered Piloerector Reflex evident

The tail is tucked. In many breeds the tail is tucked tightly between the legs at this point.

The piloerector reflex extends along the neck, down the back and right up to the tail. I have seen some dogs whose tail even looked like a bottle brush, just like a halloween cat!

He is growling loudly.

This dog is scared to death. If you asked the dog, his perception is that his very life is in danger. This dog is physically cornered, or else his perception is that he is cornered, and has no flight option.

Defensive & Uncertain, Extreme

Location	Observation
Eyes	Staring Intense
Ears	Drawn back slightly Flattened slightly
Lips	Lifted just enough to bulge the muzzle out slightly in the whisker area, but not enough to wrinkle the nose on the top. Ridges of muscle evident at the corner of the lips, and another ridge near the jaw. Lips drawn back far enough to show just the incisors and canines.
Tail	Lowered or tucked
Head Position	Extended forward Lowered
Neck Position	Lowered Piloerector Reflex evident and extensive

Offensive & Assertive

Not only does this Smoothie not want to play ball with you, she is absolutely sure that you won't be taking the ball under any circumstances. She is secure in her position and she is certain you understand yours. If you do not, she will be quite happy to make it clear to you. She may be silent or growling very low. You might only be able to discern vocalization if you were silly enough to touch her ribs and feel the vibration. As you reach the distance the dog has determined is "critical," she will bite you.

Location	Observation
Eyes	Staring Intense, hard
Ears	Upright and straining forward
Lips	Lifted Curled ("C" shaped) Drawn back

Location	Observation
Muzzle	Wrinkled Ridges of muscle evident at the corner of the lips, and another ridge near the jaw. Lips are raised in the front far enough to wrinkle the nose up extremely. Lips drawn back far enough to show the incisors and canines.
Tail	Still or Flagging (short, sharp motion) Raised or extended right up over the back
Head Position	Extended forward
Neck Position	Raised

A short anecdote about this face. In my boarding kennel, we had an intact male Great Pyrenees, Gent, visiting. He was very protective of me, and we handled him accordingly. He was no light-duty animal, weighing in at about 140 pounds. Jynx, one of my little Fox Terrier bitches, was in the kennel, and, as was her wont to do, she was running around, making sure that no one had dropped any crumbs of food along the front of the kennels. As Jynx approached the front of Gent's kennel, Gent slowly stood up and let out that low warning growl that makes the hair on the back of my neck stand up. I was right behind Jynx and getting ready to "rescue" her. (They couldn't get at each other through the kennel; physically they were both "safe." However, I don't need dogs fence-fighting in the kennel!) Jynx totally ignored Gent's warning, and just continued to rummage for a small bit of biscuit that had fallen near the edge of his kennel. (In defense, we were in the process of sweeping up after feeding.) As I was on my way across the room, Gent growled again, and bared his teeth, his bulk towering over tiny 14-inch Jynx. Jynx paused for perhaps one second, got very still, then glanced up at Gent as if she had just noticed him, and showed him this face as she made a single, short, almost inaudible growling vocalization. She didn't even stand all the way up, she was down on her front elbows reaching for this elusive cookie. Gent stopped dead, turned around, and lay down quietly in the back of his kennel, his back to Jynx, his face carefully averted. Jynxie went back to rummaging and got her biscuit. I gave another to Gent and called Jynxie to her kennel. The incident was over before I could even count to 10. Just goes to show you that the old saying is true: "It's not the size of the dog in the fight, it's the size of the fight in the dog."

13

THE ROLE OF PLAY BEHAVIOUR

One important vehicle from which puppies learn about displays and native language is engaging in play behaviour with other dogs. Thus they learn when a situation is truly threatening and when it is not. Playing with several dogs allows them the opportunity to learn that not all dogs have the same exact display and signals, which is how a dog becomes sophisticated with native language. This makes for a dog who does not get into trouble; in fact, it is hard to get this dog into trouble because he does not overreact to other dogs. Therefore, allowing a puppy to play with other dogs is a way to prevent aggressive behaviour later on in life. Understanding play behaviour, and how it relates to aggression, will help you become a more proactive trainer who can assess a dog's behaviour and head trouble off at an early stage.

Common play behaviour in dogs includes many of the same behaviours you would see in a "for real" physical confrontation. Play with littermates is how dogs learn when and how to use appropriate display to resolve conflicts and avoid aggression. Dogs in play are practicing their fluency in language so they can become good communicators and avoid aggression. One of the best things you can do for your dog is to make sure she is playing with dogs who use sophisticated, or at least normal, language. Dogs will learn by mimicry – copying the behaviour of conspecifics. A dog who is fluent and sophisticated in his own language can teach your dog to be polite, social, and confident!

A Play Behaviour List might include the following:
- Stalk, Chase
- Bared teeth
- Ambush
- T Position (head over the shoulders of the other dog)
- Shoulder/hip slams
- Circling and pushing
- Boxing or sparring
- Attacking
- Mounting with or without pelvic thrust
- Biting littermates' face/head/neck area
- Ears very erect or very flattened
- Growling vocalizations

The same list may be used for agonistic behaviour signals. How does a dog know the difference? One way is through the use of displays that have a non-aggressive intent. If a dog "Play Bows," it seems to mean, "The behaviour that follows this is not 'real' aggression, there is no intent to harm." If the play gets too rough, or escalates into a situation that one member finds uncomfortable, you will see the

The classic "I am playing, I am non-aggressive, I want to be your friend" Play Bow. Depending on context, this might also Signal "I acknowledge your Rank." The lowered ears and slightly lowered tail show me that this dog is signaling submission, at least temporarily, until she has gathered more information about the person or dog she is engaging with. The other possibility is that she is intentionally appearing to be submissive to encourage a timid dog to interact with her.

Play Bow

"uncomfortable" animal use calming signals (some specific out-of-context behaviours), such as sniffing, to signal non-aggression. These can be used as an invitation for the other dog to send a calming signal back as reassurance that "this is still play."

When I visited Wolf Park to observe the wolves, I was fascinated by the fact that, to the handlers there, a similar behaviour to the one above is often referred to as a "Prey Bow." The wolves will use this behaviour in front of large prey animals (e.g., bison) to "test" them and see if it will "move" the prey or cause some other response. Once the prey animal is moving, the wolf can better assess whether this is a good target animal. The prey animal will often face the wolf and wait for the wolf to move away. Then the wolf adopts a crouch similar to that observed in Border Collies when they are eyeing and moving sheep. Obviously, in a good Border Collie, the prey sequence has been truncated, whereas it has not been in the wolf!

My own dogs acknowledge *me,* as well as each other, with a specific, modified Play-Bow-type stretch. Sometimes they stretch with the fore quarters lowered, sometimes with the hind quarters stretched out behind them. Sometimes they do both. It is a way of saying "hello." This is a friendly and relaxed greeting generally used with *known* dogs and people.

When dogs are play bowing to each other, they have often given prior signals to let the other dog know that they are interested in initiating a prey game. Game and play are the key words here. If a dog is going to immediately make an unfriendly overture to another dog, I have never seen one use a play bow to do so. I have, however, seen my bitch Breanna USE a play bow specifically to intervene and dissipate the aggressive display of two of my boys when they were "facing off" – a posture that quickly escalates into a violent interaction. Those boys were facing each other with hard eye contact and on tiptoe, and were just getting ready to shove each other with shoulders, no doubt to be quickly followed by grabbing each other with teeth. Breanna dashed in between them and play-bowed once to each boy. I was amazed to observe those boys immediately break eye-contact, shake (the stress off), and walk away in two separate directions. Breanna ran up to each boy separately and gave him a little lick and a friendly body wiggle and then went back and lay down in the dining room where she had been. Her behaviour caused all tension to evaporate, and we all had a lovely, peaceful afternoon.

Consider the following scenario: two dogs approach, play bow, and commence play. After a few minutes, the play escalates, and becomes increasingly rough. Concurrent with this heightened intensity of behaviour, one of the dogs suddenly breaks off play and begins to sniff the ground. This sniffing behaviour is "Out-Of-Context" here, a calming signal, specifically used to communicate non-aggressive intent. You will likely see the play stop and become, at least temporarily, calmer. If the rough play continues to escalate, even with one member obviously signaling non-aggressive intent, separate these two dogs, at least for a few minutes of "calm down" time. There is no need for one dog to practice being terrified and one dog to practice being overbearing or aggressive. I don't know that I would ask them to play together again; it very much depends on the individuals and their histories.

It is imperative to know the difference between dogs who are playing and dogs who are Posturing. "Posturing" is a term I use to define that subtle moment when play behaviour, or other "approach" behaviour, begins to become something else: any behaviour that indicates more reactivity. Pushy or overbearing behaviour, or more body tension, indicates a dog who is no longer "playing," but is beginning to feel crowded, threatened or insecure. Insecurity can be acted out as Assertive behaviours or Yielding behaviours, depending on the individual.

Think about it for a moment – secure people don't run about telling everyone how "secure" they are. They are not wondering if they can cope. A certain type of insecure human personality will often come on a bit too strong, in an effort to compensate for the feeling that they cannot cope effectively with the situation. *Dogs who are not good communicators use gestures that are "too big."* Instead of just walking up with an arced approach and sniffing, they will rush up and fling themselves on the ground, writhing and squirming at the other dog's feet. My dogs greet such an animal with the attitude: "You can just say hello, you don't have to overdo it!"

Other "too big" greeting behaviour is evident when a dog approaches and pushes the other dog with her chest or puts her feet on the other dog's shoulders. Two sophisticated dogs will approach using some form of arc and calmly sniff each other. A secure, self-confident dog tends to be relatively understated in her dealings with other dogs. Dogs in play who are both remaining in "play mode," and are comfortable, will stay relaxed with each other over personal space.

Keep in mind the following descriptions are "typical," but by no means complete, and in a slightly different context might mean something different. They will give you somewhere to begin as you are learning from your own observations. I have watched thousands of canids at play and have witnessed many altercations, from mild snipes to severe fights that would have culminated in death, had I not been there to intervene. Yet I learn something new from each group of dogs I see together.

Indications that Dogs are in Play Mode

- If something else catches the dog's attention, he will look away from the other dogs, look at what caught his interest, then resume play. It is possible to test this by making a noise or commotion, running and clapping, walking in between the two dogs, or some other activity that might cause them to look around and see what else is going on in the environment. If they are difficult to interrupt, I would make it a POINT to do so. Reward the dogs for being interrupted, then allow them to resume play, watching them carefully for "too intense" behaviour.

- You will customarily see the dogs changing "roles," switching from prey to predator. You will also see dogs who switch positions while "wrestling" – one is on top playing the aggressor, while the other dog is on the bottom. No matter the role or position, the dogs should exchange roles occasionally, whether chasing or wrestling.
- The dogs will both display relaxed facial expressions. If you can look at their eyes, the pupils are neither excessively dilated nor pin-pointed; they are normal for the amount of light in the environment. The dog's lips will be most likely to be drawn back toward their ears, rather than in the "C" shape that is illustrated in the "Distance Increasing Signals" chapter.
- Dogs in play can be quite noisy, although there is a lot of variability in noise level in dog play. A dog fight can be noisy also, but the timbre of the sound is different. When observing dogs playing and interacting, be alert to ANY changes in sound. Did the vocalizations just become much louder? Are they changing from one kind of vocalization to another? Is it suddenly very quiet? Any changes in sound may herald a change in the interaction between the dogs, so pay attention to these, and be ready to interrupt play.
- If one dog hurts the other by biting too roughly, Dog #2 can yip or squeal a little and easily interrupt the dog who is being a bit too rough. It often happens very fluidly, just as if two humans were interacting and one of them plainly said, "Ouch! Be careful!" The play may hardly be interrupted.

Signs of Trouble Ahead

- One dog cannot interrupt the other dog's advances easily (e.g., yielding attempts are not working), and becomes frightened. When dogs wrestle, this might be indicated by a more frantic struggle, with the aggressor holding on and not allowing the other dog up, even though that dog is beginning to show distress.
- There is facial tension, flaring whiskers, and/or sudden pupil dilation.
- One dog is ignoring calming signals that the other is giving.
- One dog is chasing and the "chasee" begins to display signs of alarm, such as lowering the tail and looking back in a worried manner, while the "chaser" begins to look more and more intent.
- It is not easy to interrupt the dogs' play, or get them to at least glance in your direction, with a loud startle noise or by yelling one dog's name in a pleasant tone of voice. If this IS the case, then you should intervene and make a decision about whether to allow the dogs to continue to interact.

Choosing Playmates

While we are discussing play behaviours, I would like to re-emphasize how important it is to carefully choose your puppy's playmates. Just as you would choose nice children with nice manners and appropriate social skills to play with your children, ideally so would you choose appropriate puppies and dogs to teach your pet good language skills. Older dogs who are calm and non-reactive, or playful while keeping their social skills intact, are great choices, as are puppies who have similar activity preferences.

Before you allow your puppy or dog to play with another dog, test drive the possible playmate. Ask the dog's owner some questions:

- Has your dog played with other dogs or puppies before?
- Was your dog okay with the other dogs?
- When your dog was playing with these other dogs, how old was your dog? (Remember how significant this can be. As a 6-month or 9-month-old pup, this dog may have approached other dogs totally differently than he does now as a 5-year-old adult.)
- How does your dog approach dogs he doesn't know?

If your dog is an older dog, and you are introducing her to another older dog, you might want the dogs to meet initially in a neutral area (neither dog's home territory). It is wise to leave the leashes on so you can get hold of the dogs if an altercation develops. Have a hose or bucket of water handy (many minor altercations can be broken up by using cold water tossed or sprayed on the dogs). If there is any doubt at all, have both dogs muzzled so everyone can remain safe if the situation deteriorates. *It is easier to remove muzzles and leashes if the dogs get along with each other than it is to remove the stitches that may result if they are not.*

For older dogs, especially if you are unsure of your dog or the other dog, opposite sex playmates are a good rule, although not a hard and fast one. Many dogs of the same sex will be amenable to each other, but serious fights rarely develop between males and females. The doozies are the same-sex fights. It is the male-to-male brawls and the notorious "bitch fights" that can be quite fierce, particularly if the parties involved are sexually intact.

From the older dog who does NOT want to play, your pup can learn not to bother those who do not wish to be bothered. This correction can look quite alarming to the uninitiated, but it is valuable for an uppity puppy to learn that he can't just irritate everyone into playing. An older dog may pin your puppy by holding him with her body and feet and vocalizing with growls. Sometimes until the puppy screeches and urinates. As long as the older dog is not biting hard or biting and shaking, this is a viable correction. After such a correction, there should never be a puncture wound. What you see afterwards from a puppy who has learned from his experience is an immediate apology. This is directed toward the older dog in the form of muzzle licking, lowered body posture and ear carriage accompanied by a lowered and wagging tail. Then you might see the older dog initiate play with the upstart or just walk away from the puppy. Once an adult has pinned a puppy, a glance is usually enough to tone the youngster down.

I do not allow frequent, excessive corrections to puppies by other dogs. If the older dog is pinning the puppy immediately without first "asking" the puppy to go away with some lesser displays, that is inappropriate behaviour by the older dog. (Remember "asking" might be an extremely subtle behaviour, such as pointedly ignoring or avoiding the puppy.) If the older dog is *constantly* correcting the pup at random, I also discourage that.

Puppy Play-Groups

Having several puppies together is a wonderful experience for them, such as happens at a puppy play session or a puppy k class. Here, several puppies, 6 months and younger, can interact in a totally juvenile manner, and the risk is small because the puppies are small. In our classes, we mix puppies of like tendencies. That is, we split the groups into 2 categories:

- The Chess Players: The quieter, cautious pups who are not physically "rough" with each other and prefer chasing or just walking around together, with some mild wrestling and gentle body contact.
- The Graffiti Painters: Those puppies who you just know would paint the town red if given the opportunity. The boisterous, rough and tumble puppies, the ones who were born to play Australian Football or rugby. Watch your knees when supervising this group!

Some rules for puppy play-groups: At first, NO toys or food on the floor. To be safe, this is a good rule for any group of dogs or puppies who don't know each other well. If all is going well, you can put SEVERAL TOYS out on the floor. I make sure there are 2 or 3 of each KIND of toy: 2 or 3 tennis balls, 2 or 3 fuzzy toys, 2 or 3 rope toys, etc., with the number of toys exceeding the number of puppies. NEVER use any food, raw bones, or other high-value, volatile food-related items. Save Buster Cubes™ and other high value toys for individual play and omit them from group play. For my dog, Zasu, the Wiggly-Giggly Ball™ is taboo in a group; she immediately begins object-guarding behaviours.

Several times during the play, interrupt by calling the pups. Have the puppies drag a leash initially – that way you can back up the Recall (come-when-called behaviour). Keep the leash on until the Recall is reliable. In classes at Heaven On Arf, we have owners call their own pup, get hold of the leash, back out of the play group with their puppy, and feed him a treat. Once the puppy looks at the owner, he is released back into the play group. This way you are teaching your puppy to come when called, reinforcing him with food AND the "life reward" of returning to play (so coming when called does not always precede "the fun's all over").

No "humping" allowed – that is, no mounting another puppy from the front, side or rear, accompanied by pelvic thrusting. This is not always a sexual behaviour, remember; it can be a Rank Ordering maneuver. Often the dogs who are using this are a bit insecure. It doesn't matter whether the behaviour of that individual is rooted in pushy or insecure emotions; I do not wish to promote this behaviour in any way. Mounting puppies are removed from the "mountee" puppy with mild verbal disapproval ("I don't like that!") together with a hand on the collar or leash just sufficient to remove them from the body of the other dog, and then allowed to return to play. It might take 3 or 4 such corrections, but the puppy gets the picture: "humping" is not appropriate social behaviour in any company! If he continues to do this after being removed 3 or 4 times, give the "mounter" a time-out in a crate or away the play area for one or, at most, two minutes, then return him to play. Another alternative to the crate time-out is to take the "mounter" outside for a five minute walk, then bring him back in to try his social skills again.

If pups are timid, make sure they are not further terrified by the antics of their playmates. Encourage the other pups to play in another area (run off shouting and clapping to another part of the room to lure the puppies into a different area), and allow the scared pup to sit near his NEUTRAL, QUIET owner. This owner is not to "coddle" and sympathize with the puppy, but will remain a neutral support system for the pup. Do not allow these pups to hide under chairs, etc. Usually by the end of the second or third play session, they are at least running around the other pups on the periphery of the action and are beginning to join in and play. If it is a small dog running with big dogs, I encourage the owner to pick up the dog, but remain "in the fray," sitting in a chair with the puppy on her lap and giving the pup appropriate feedback for non-reactive or non-frightened behaviour.

Some tiny toy pups are truly at risk playing with big, rough dogs or pups. Don't coddle them, but do find them gentler playmates or playmates their own size. Puppies shouldn't have to be HURT in the name of socialization.

Some puppies are really keen to play, and others more hesitant. This is all within a normal range of behaviour. What is not within a normal range of behaviour is excessive, serious "adult" aggression in very young dogs, or frenzied biting. You need the help of a behaviour consultant for dogs showing these behaviours. Another "flag" for risky behaviour as an adult is the puppy who runs and hides and, 8 or 10 weeks later, is still just as terrified as he was the first night of puppy class (given that the puppy is being offered appropriate playmates who are not too intimidating).

Play and the "Older" Dog

As a dog reaches that crucial 12-to-24 month age range, you typically see much less juvenile behaviour and more "serious" rank ordering and adult behaviour. Territory may become more important by this age, as do other resources, such as owners, toys or food. Running dogs this age together becomes more volatile and riskier, the primary reason to get your younger *puppy*, whose social window is wide open, into several canine social situations.

Some dogs retain playful, juvenile puppy behaviour well into adulthood. This is a wonderful attitude for a domestic dog and just comes naturally for some. If you have a dog like this, great. What is more common, though, is that dogs in this age group are now no longer interested in playing Chutes and Ladders™ and Go Fish, and have other things on their mind.

This is usually the age at which my own dogs are placed into play situations with great discretion. I have some older terrier bitches and Maeve, my shepherd bitch (who came to me as an 18 month old with many problems, including aggression), who have selected dogs they like and can associate with. I do not expect them to "play nice" with everyone they meet, and, indeed, past experience has taught me that Breanna and Maeve do not play well with others.

I see other older dogs who do not look like they are enjoying play, although they are not in the least aggressive. They just no longer want to play puppy games anymore. The older dog often does not want to have the goofy puppies body-slamming him. Many older dogs in groups of dogs they don't know look slightly uncomfortable. I find this normal and acceptable, although aggressive behaviour, biting, fighting, and over-reacting are NOT in any way acceptable.

It is unreasonable to expect ALL dogs to ALWAYS get along with EVERY dog they meet. I don't expect this from myself, certainly, and am able to avoid people I don't want to be around most of the time. I think it is wise to give our dogs the same option.

At the same time, even my nasty girls are not allowed to "act out" their status concerns, nor bully other dogs. I have modified behaviour in my dogs to be safe under many circumstances, even if another dog rushes up to them and is bouncing around. This is a situation that neither Breanna nor Maeve thinks is acceptable, and which has a tendency to make them wish dearly to reach out and chomp the idiot dog doing the bouncing. But the behaviour modification I have done with them renders them safe in my presence. If you are going to have your dog out in public, she must have a minimum of manners. Part of that is, if another dog rushes up, you need to at least have time to get the other dog out of her face before she decides to take matters into her own hands – or teeth. So, your dog must be willing to turn to you, before turning on the other dog, at least long enough for you to withdraw with her.

Management is still my most effective (and safest!) tool. Maeve and Breanna do not run loose with unknown dogs. Period.

Play should be fun for your dog, but not ALL situations that you might think are fun for your dog are, in fact, fun. To some extent, it is "all right," and even prudent, to allow your dog to tell you what situations she finds fun and which make her uncomfortable, and for you to make allowances for this. This is not an excuse to NOT socialize your dog, but, as she becomes older, it is realistic that she may take exception to specific circumstances or dogs.

Play can begin as play and escalate into an aggressive event. If there is going to be a change from Play to Posture, there is a subtle difference, initially, in body tension as the dogs approach. Then, as the interaction continues, rough behaviour escalates. The Posturing Dog begins to ignore signals of discomfort from the other dog.

What begins as Posturing can also relax into Play, as indicated by a dog's willingness to recognize and acknowledge violations of body space and allow the other dog personal space. Play gives dogs a chance to practice using language skills. This experimentation with signals gives them information about how to get into and stay out of trouble!

When two dogs are interacting, watch both dogs very carefully. I prefer to work with one dog who is very stable, has sophisticated language skills, and whom I know well. I bring the "problem" dog in and observe my "control" dog very carefully. If the problem dog is making my control dog uneasy, I step in quickly to provide a time-out. This technique requires a very high level of expertise. However, one can gain a lot of diagnostic information about the problem dog this way, as well as teaching the problem dog to be less reactive. In this situation you would, of course, prioritize safety. That means muzzles, leashes, dragging long-lines – whatever it takes to reduce risk and prevent injury to either animal and to humans.

Even in normal play situations, if a dog is making another dog uncomfortable to a marked degree, or one dog is not responding correctly to calming signals, step in and give the dog feedback about his behaviour in the form of a time-out or Cool Down. How else is appropriate behaviour taught? In some situations it is neither appropriate nor safe to allow dogs to "settle their own differences." If I allowed Maeve and Breanna do this, I would definitely have dead dogs. Should puppies be allowed to harass older, perhaps physically weaker or sore dogs? Absolutely not. Should adolescent dogs be allowed to be too rough with tiny puppies? Again, No.

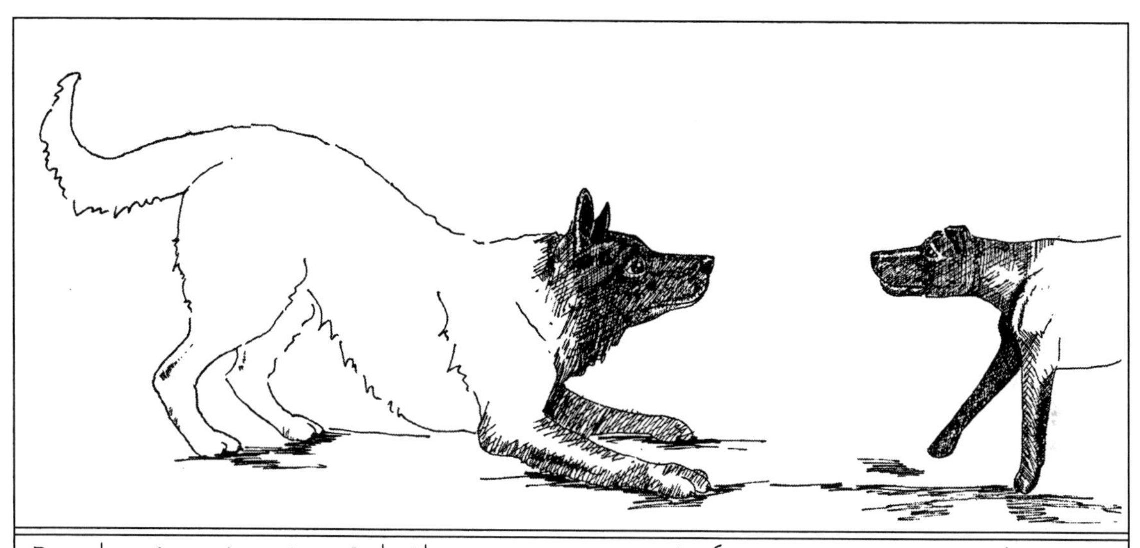

Dogs love to participate in Role Playing Games. Instead of Dungeons & Dragons™, they often play Prey & Predator. Here, Maeve and Dervish, who are old friends (and are therefore comfortable and familiar with each other's language) are engaging in play. Maeve has volunteered to be Prey, and Dervish has assumed a Predator role. He is in the Eye and Stalk sequence: head and neck lowered, very intense stare, and exaggerated, slow movements.

Next Dervish will leap at Maeve. While Dervish is in mid-air, Maeve may choose flight, or she may roll over in a submissive playful gesture, and they will play, as I call it, Mouth Jive Games, where they "fence" using their faces with an open mouth.

Then they will trade, and Dervish will be prey and Maeve will chase and "hunt" Dervish down. Dogs who get along will switch roles frequently. This willingness to "trade" roles is one way to determine that the current relationship between dogs is compatible, healthy and non-combative. Often the more assertive animal will volunteer to be prey first, perhaps to give the more timid or reserved animal the self-confidence to join in play.

Role Playing Games

We monitor our own species like this all the time. It is how we teach our own children good people skills. It is easy to give kids feedback because we both speak the same native language – human! In order to provide this service for our dogs we must first avail ourselves of as much of the dog's native language as we can. For dogs who do not have good communication skills with humans or dogs, you must offer them some assistance. If you do not give feedback to the dog at the earliest moment that inappropriate behaviour begins, you have lost a valuable opportunity to help your dog.

The tendency of someone who is not very experienced is to interfere too little ("they can settle it") or too much (interrupting to the point that the dogs become frustrated and irritable, and therefore more likely to begin an altercation). Education about dog social systems and how dogs communicate will help you learn when to separate dogs, and even how to tell which dogs you don't even want to try together! Experience will polish your skills so that you can increase a dog's social skills with some well-timed feedback.

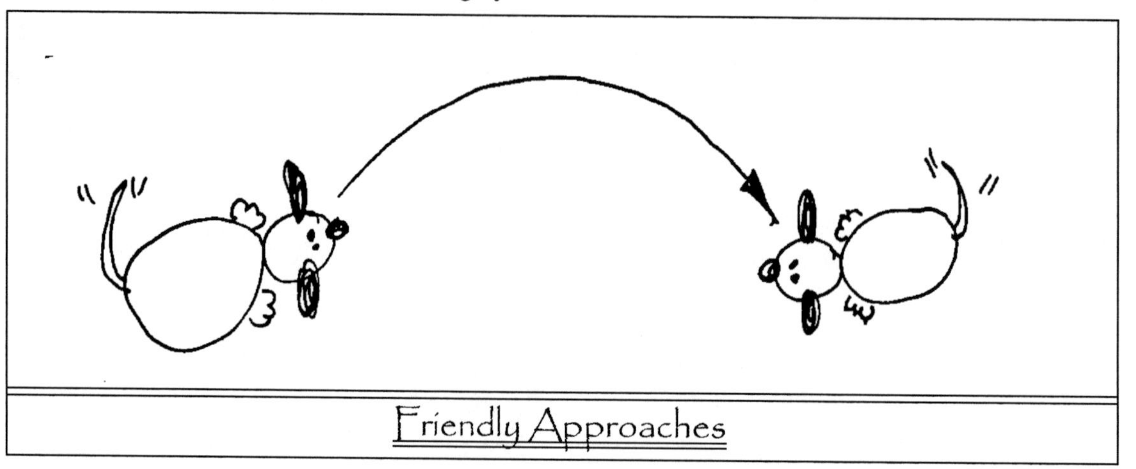

Friendly Approaches

All dogs like to participate in a greeting ceremony. When two friendly dogs greet, they commonly move toward each other on an arcing path, not a direct path. Then they may sniff the inguinal area, the genitals, and muzzles, usually in that order, though not necessarily.

You may then see the dogs entering into a discussion over Rank. However, they may just begin to play by exhibiting an obvious play-bow to display non-aggressive intent. Often the more submissive animal will signal using blinking eyes, paw lifts, nuzzling behaviours, with the ears slightly lowered. The more assertive animal will signal non-aggression by glancing away from the other dog with slightly squinting eyes (using an eye movement only, not moving the head), drawing the ears back slightly and, perhaps, with a slight or exaggerated head turn away from the other dog.

You can take advantage of this knowledge. When meeting a new dog, don't face her head on. Turn so your side is presented to the dog. Don't make eye contact. Allow the dog to approach you. Don't reach for the dog until you are certain that the dog feels comfortable with you. If you do reach, do so slowly and with your palm facing away from the dog and the back of your hand turned toward the dog.

The best way to make friends with shy or recalcitrant dogs is to ignore them and allow them to initiate approaches. Soon you can't get them out of your pocket! If they do not follow this path, they are giving you very valuable information! Take Heed!

When your dog is greeting another dog, or even just meeting one on the sidewalk, allow him the room and opportunity to arc. If your dog does not arc on his own, you can teach him how by helping him to arc with your own path of travel and body language. Encourage the behaviour by gently directing his eye contact to you for a moment and then allowing him to greet the other dog from the shoulder or side, instead of directly from a frontal position. Make an arc in your own path if you are not stopping, and keep your dog's attention on you. A head collar, which is discussed extensively in the "A Chat About Equipment" section, may be necessary to achieve this the first few times, until your dog "gets the idea." (Detailed discussion about training dogs how to approach each other can be found in the chapters: "Dog-to-Dog Approaches," "Leash Aggression," and "Advanced Work with Dog-to-Dog Approaches.")

14

DOG PARKS

Dog Parks are theoretically a wonderful idea. But are they the right choice for you and your dog? I have ambivalent feelings about Dog Parks. Personally, I would never take my own dogs to a dog park. My worry is that, even if my dogs are safe and well-socialized, how do I know about everyone else's dog? In my own case, as I have mentioned previously, a couple of my dogs play well with some family members, but are uninterested in expanding their social horizons, and I am okay with that. I don't expect my dogs to play with every dog they meet, nor do I wish them to. I, however, live and work where I can easily socialize my own dogs with many other appropriate dogs (they go to dog class with me 5 or 6 nights a week, so there are plenty of opportunities to play with appropriate others). I have friends with dogs and we can mix and match play groups. For people who do not have this luxury, there are still many options. I encourage my clients who go to puppy class together to exchange phone numbers and meet outside class so their dogs can continue to socialize after class is finished. Keep your eye out for other people with dogs, and if the people AND the dog are nice, arrange to meet up for a Dog Play Session, or start out by going for a walk together and see how that goes. Advertise in your local newspaper that you wish to begin a dog play group.

My biggest concern with Dog Parks is that dogs will learn inappropriate language and behaviour from dogs who are rude and unsophisticated with uneducated owners. Should I place my dog in a situation where she has to "defend herself?" Letting dogs "work it out on their own" does not appeal to me, unless I am *certain* that the dogs involved have the social skills to do so peaceably.

On the other hand, for dogs who are never going to get off-leash runs or interact with other dogs in any other way, I guess it is the lesser of two evils. I have several clients who love going to the dog park here in town, and feel it has been beneficial. But all of them have also had some an incident come up that has made them acutely uncomfortable. There have been dog fights and injuries. There are owners who are NOT aware of the fact that their dog is a bully, let alone taking any action to teach their dog better manners. This places your dog in the situation of having to deal defensively with a bully and be terrified by him. What do you think dogs learn from such encounters?

Adolescent dogs constantly push the envelope on the tolerance of other dogs. Watch the interaction between dogs closely so your adolescent is not torturing some older dog or frightening a pup. Similarly, ensure that your older dog or pup is not placed in situations that cause her to be overwhelmed and scared.

Also watch for victimization – aggression or mobbing by one or more dogs toward a "scapegoat" dog. If a dog is appropriate and using calming signals, and others are ignoring this, the interaction should be interrupted. After a couple minutes of cool down or time-out (dogs on leashes and sitting or downing), you can loose the dogs again to interact. If the aggression was overt or excessive, or one dog was terrified and defensive, you may choose to not loose the dogs together again. This is a judgment call. Was the snapping actually appropriate? Did the actions of one dog cause the other dog to escalate his aggression, or did that dog "get the message" and move out of personal space, as requested? If any overt, continuing aggression occurs between dogs, it is time to separate those dogs and make decisions about whether they ought to be placed in a situation to interact freely. Dogs should also be separated if there is any arousal between them sufficient that the dogs were difficult to interrupt or they caused any damage to each other.

One tendency of groups of dogs who get to know each other and who play together regularly is to "pack up." When a "new" dog enters Established Territory, the "gang" will attempt to disperse the new arrival. Sometimes the new arrival will be readily accepted, but if he is not, the situation can result in canine and human injury. All this means is that new dogs should be carefully and systematically introduced into established groups, and that may not be under your control at a public dog park.

Dog Parks look to me like going to a cocktail party where you know few, if any, people. If you are a normal person, and reasonably sober, you will naturally feel some discomfort around a bunch of people you don't know well. Contrast this with the feeling of getting together with a bunch of people you have known for years. You are comfortable and relaxed.

I have clients who have changed their residence so their dog can have bigger yards and adopted a second dog so that their dog has company. Obviously, this is not a choice for everyone. Solutions for exercise and socialization are individual and depend on many factors, such as finances, mobility of the handlers, and work schedules. You must decide your own priorities and financial limitations.

A solution many of my clients have come up with, instead of going to the Dog Park, is to create their own play groups. They meet regularly at each other's houses in a safe fenced yard, or at an alternative fenced area. This has worked extremely well, is safe and predictable, and the dogs get to enjoy the companionship of old friends.

In summary, while I don't think Dog Parks are always a bad thing, I have seen my clients and their pets placed in situations that were not good socialization experiences. Be cautious. Friends of mine who are veterinary technicians have told me about many dogs who come to the clinic to be stitched up after a "play session" at the dog park. Assess the situation carefully before you put your dog in it. Go watch your local dog park, without your dog the first two or three times, and make sure you like what you see before you toss your dog in there.

Section III

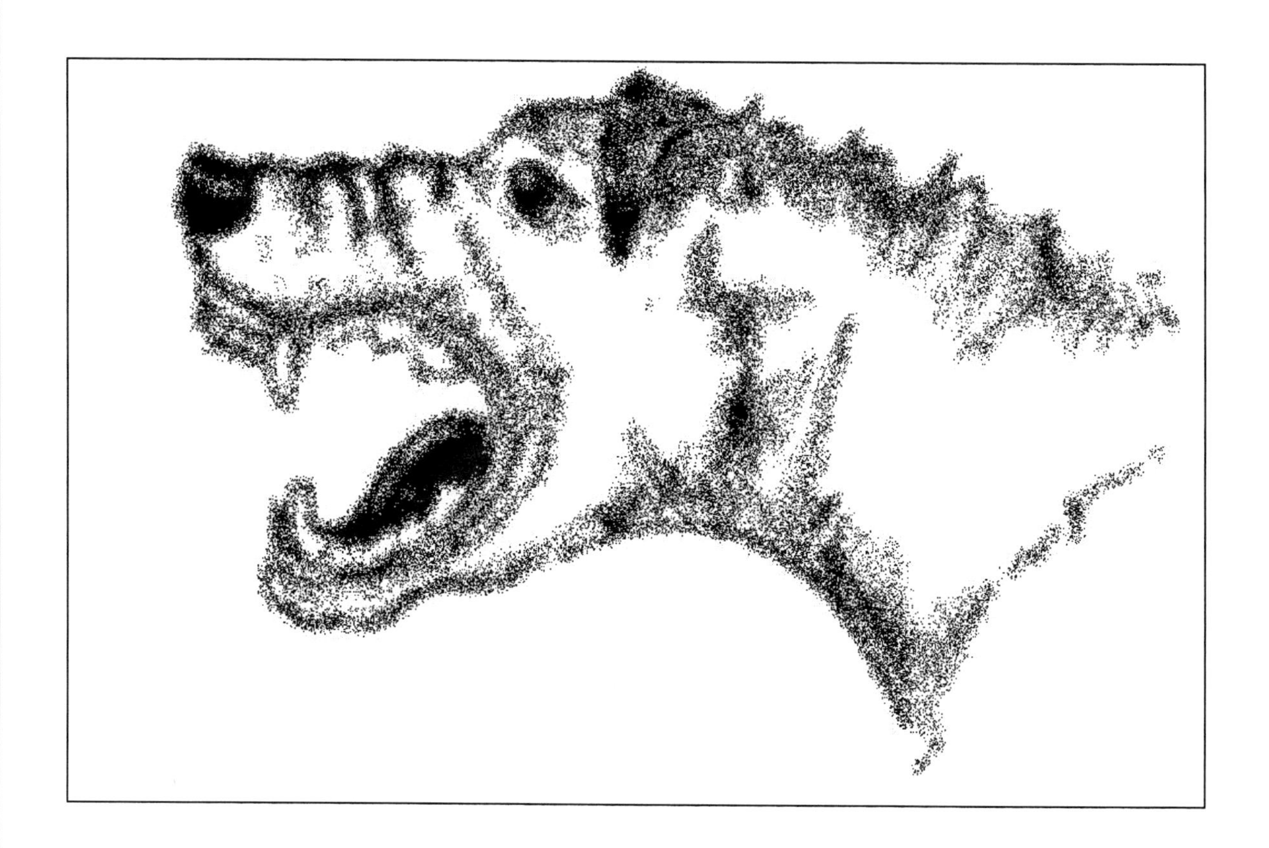

Pathways of Aggression

15

CLASSIFICATIONS

Labels are detrimental to modifying behaviour if you use them to characterize the animal or allow them to limit your thinking. Labels can follow an individual long after they have outlived their usefulness. Labels themselves do not solve a problem and may cloud the real issues. For instance, knowing I have PMS does not necessarily put me in a better mood. Or, consider the new co-worker whom you have not yet met. Another co-worker approaches you and says, "So-and-so says the new girl is lazy." The new co-worker has just been "labeled." Others may now have preconceptions about this person, before they even meet her, based on their own interpretation of the "label." Later, you might find out that the new co-worker is recovering from an illness and therefore wasn't working at her full capacity when this comment was made. And what exactly does "lazy" mean? One person may interpret this word differently than another.

Classifying behaviour can serve a purpose, as long as those classifications are used thoughtfully and accurately and are not overused. If the classification is used as a short way to describe observable behaviour, then it may expedite your thinking and note-taking. The danger is that people have a tendency to generalize a dog's entire life experience using one quick description, and that is inappropriate.

Following is a brief description of different classifications of aggression. This helps when communicating with other people, but only if the person you are talking to has attached the same significance or definition to the classification that you have. It is difficult to determine a classification for behaviour from a quick description of the behaviour by someone else. When working with an aggressive dog, I often withhold a final decision about classification until I have placed the dog on a protocol and followed the behaviour carefully for 30 to 60 days. Observing how the dog responds to an individual protocol helps me classify a specific set of behaviours accurately and points me toward which protocols to emphasize or do next.

The following list provides you with descriptions that do not just "label" your dog, but allow you to communicate clearly with others about your dog's behaviour. I base this classification system primarily on two resources: *Clinical Behavioral Medicine For Small Animals*, by Karen Overall, MA., V.M.D., Ph.D. (1997) and *A Diagnostic Classification of Problem Behavior In Dogs And Cats*, by J. S. J. Odendaal, BSc, MRCVS, DVSc, DPhil (1997). I have used these two resources for years and they are excellent.

This chapter is not intended to teach you to diagnose, but rather to be a brief overview of some classifications of aggression that I find useful. Classifying the behaviour may point you toward the appropriate protocols. It may only be of use because it provides "shorthand" for your note-taking. At first glance, you might not be able to classify the behaviour accurately at all!

Before you get into the descriptions of the individual classifications, let's discuss a couple of subjects that will affect the classification.

Vacuum Activity

Vacuum Activity is a response in the absence of the stimulus that usually produces it. If the animal does not have a response or coping mechanism for a particular context, a "vacuum" is created. The dog will "fill" this vacuum with an activity that is often inappropriate. Aggression is one of those responses a dog may fall back on if he is stressed or frustrated and does not have a previously conditioned behaviour to fill the void.

Another example is the dog who is a "spinner." The dog chases his tail, sometimes even injuring himself in the process. This becomes an obsessive, uncontrollable response. The "spinning" may have started out as a response to frustration For example, the dog is crated and other dogs are running by. This is a common occurrence in any kennel or shelter. The dog's frustration level builds day after day. He is prevented from interacting as he wishes. In frustration, he begins to spin. Soon, this spinning behaviour generalizes, and every time the dog begins to feel a little "fired up" or anxious about *anything* – feeding time, say – he will begin to spin. Soon the spinning behaviour occurs with little or no external stimuli.

Normal vs. Abnormal

One aspect of classifying behaviour involves determining whether the dog is "normal" or "abnormal." This may not be something that an inexperienced person (or many experienced dog trainers) can determine. Much of what people consider "problem" behaviours are just normal-old-dog-behaviours that are undesirable or dangerous in a particular context. Just because it is normal that dogs love to raid the litter box and eat cat feces does not make this a trait that people are thrilled about.

A general definition of "normal" is a spectrum of behaviour that is exhibited by the vast majority of dogs, or at least by most dogs of a given breed (normal for that breed). More specifically, a normal dog has behaviours that are within the range of typical dogs and also has a typical ability to learn new behaviours and habituate to new environments. Normal dogs, by virtue of both their genetics and their socialization, are, most importantly, *chemically* normal – their brain chemistry is such that, though they may have some undesirable behaviours, they will be able to learn new, better behaviours at a reasonable rate.

Abnormal dogs, on the other hand, may be exhibiting atypical behaviour, extremely exaggerated behaviour, or misplaced or non-adaptive behaviour. The abnormal dog is also less able to modify his behaviour than the typical dog, usually because of a chemical imbalance that interferes with learning, as, for example, occurs in dogs with seizure disorders, extreme separation anxiety, or panic attacks (where stimuli provoke a response beyond the dog's control). Abnormal dogs do not process information like other dogs do – they are "wired" differently and do not learn like normal dogs, so you will see a slow or erratic learning curve with a lot of spontaneous recovery of the undesirable behaviour.

A normal dog habituates to novel stimuli quickly. A normal dog learns new behaviours relatively quickly. With repetition, the new, installed behaviours are readily retained. The dog's behaviour changes long-term and becomes more reliable over time. (Remember, when I am discussing "relatively quickly" here, I am speaking of a steady increase of reliability over a time frame of three months to a year or two.) One indication that abnormality is present is when a dog learns a new behaviour, but there is (even when the client is doing everything correctly) a high incidence of spontaneous recovery. With these dogs, the spontaneous recovery is frequent. When spontaneous recovery does occur, the target behaviour retains intensity such that there is not much difference between the original intensity and that which is observed after much training has taken place.

In a normal dog, spontaneous recovery is there, but over time it is seen less frequently, occurs with less intensity and is more easily interrupted.

Abnormal dogs have chemical imbalances. This chemical interference may affect the degree to which the animal can exhibit impulse control. The neuro-chemical flood the animal experiences is beyond his control, such as is experienced in panic attacks, and interferes with learning. This prevents the animal from progressing forward in the protocols and responding to the environment and to learned cues. This places us in a whole new ball game: now we are discussing life-long management that never ceases, protocols that will have to ALWAYS be in place and, perhaps, medication.

Deciding what pharmacologicals are used or, indeed, whether any should be used at all, belongs in the realm of veterinary medicine.

Determining whether a dog is normal or abnormal is relevant to the prognosis. *Prognosis* has to do with predicting the final outcome – the practitioner is making a prediction based on her experience and statistics. What are the chances that this animal will display the new appropriate behaviour across a wide range of circumstances? What are the chances that the dog's behaviour will improve steadily with continued training with less and less spontaneous recovery? Clinicians have a rating system for prognosis: Excellent, Good, Fair, Guarded and Poor. Abnormal dogs, because their learning is impeded, have less favorable prognoses.

Do not assume that, because the dog's behaviour is unusual or very undesirable, the dog has a chemical imbalance and cannot learn normally! Many undesirable behaviours are just *extreme behaviours*, and occur in chemically normal dogs. For example, many dogs have undesirable behaviour, such as aggression, simply because they have learned that such behaviour works for them in their household (i.e., agonistic displays gain them some sort of resource or comfort zone). I have seen dogs who are behaving in a very alarming fashion respond in a gratifying manner to the proper protocol. A crucial part of determining whether the dog is normal is to get started with the protocols and see how it goes!

Ascertaining and interpreting whether a dog is abnormal is NOT for the neophyte. However, armed with observation, education, and the protocols in this book, you can make amazing improvement in your dog's behaviour. At the same time, you will be learning how to gather relevant information as you go along so that you can make the maximum impact on the dog's behaviour problems. The bottom line with the abnormality question is: the dog will either be capable of helping you change his behaviour or he will not, and beginning the work will provide you with endless information about the dog you are working with and how much "help" the dog will be capable of.

SPECIFIC TYPES OF AGGRESSION

Many of these kinds of aggression occur in the absolutely normal dog; it is the intensity and persistence with which the behaviour is exhibited that may transcend the normal and become maladaptive, disordered, or abnormal behaviour.

The following is a list of types of aggression. This is distinct from the "normal" vs. "abnormal" distinction discussed above. Classifications of aggression are often distinguished by the aggression's *cause* (e.g., lack of socialization) and by *clusters of similar situations* that elicit aggressive behaviours (such as with resource guarding). Understanding the types of aggression may assist the trainer in predicting the environments that will trigger reactive or agonistic behaviour, or in preventing these types of behaviours from further developing in puppies.

Unless otherwise noted, all of these classifications of behaviour may be used to describe aggression toward another dog (dog-to-dog aggression), toward a person (dog-to-human), or toward a third species (dog-to-cat, for example). Some dogs will have strong tendencies to be aggressive toward only some targets; for instance, they may be aggressive toward other dogs in a wide variety of situations, but never toward people. Other dogs may show some types of aggression toward dogs, and other types toward people, or they may be aggressive toward everything and everyone in a few situations (such as when guarding their food).

In addition to identifying some of the causes and triggers of aggression, pay attention to the *targets* of your dog's aggression.

Table 1: Classifications

Classifications
Developmental Stages – Lack of Socialization, Interspecies
Developmental Stages – Lack of Socialization, Intraspecies
Excessive Breed Tendencies, or Lack of These
Human Selection for Aggression in Dogs
Control Conflict Aggression
Dog-to-Dog Aggression (see also Developmental Stages, Lack of Socialization)
Fear Aggression
Idiopathic Aggression
Learned Aggression
Maternal Aggression
Neophobia
Pain-Related Aggression
Play Aggression
Possessive Aggression
Possessive Aggression – Food Related
Predatory Aggression
Protective Aggression
Redirected Aggression
Territorial Aggression

The following classifications are subsets of: Developmental Stages.

Lack of Socialization – Intraspecies

Lack of experience with a dog's own species leads to fearful behaviour, and, possibly, defensive aggression directed toward its own species in a general, blanket manner (not directed only to specific dogs, such as would be normal for a dog who is determining rank order, engaging in same sex aggression, etc.). These dogs also have difficulty communicating effectively with their own species; that is, they do not develop appropriate dog language.

This is commonly seen in dogs who are removed from their mother and littermates at 2 to 6 weeks of age. Puppies should not be removed from mother and littermates and placed in their new homes until at least 7 weeks of age; for the smaller breeds (terriers, toys), it is best to leave them until 8 to 12 weeks, provided the breeder is supplying the pups with environmentally enriching experiences. This behaviour is also evident in dogs who are never taken out for environmental enrichment experiences after they are brought home at 8 weeks old.

For a variety of reasons, dogs classified in this category never learned good dog language skills. They do not process what other dogs are telling them correctly, nor are they able to communicate effectively with other dogs.

Unsophisticated dogs tend to use language that is way too "big" for the context. I can remember introducing "unsophisticated" dogs to my basset, Fletcher, who was one of the most sophisticated "speakers" I have ever met. Inevitably, the unsophisticated dog would dash up to Fletcher and fling herself all over him, writhe on the ground, grovel and urinate; or would rush toward him with a hackles-up, stiff-legged approach, ready to rumble. You could nearly hear Fletch say, "Geez, you could just have walked up quietly and exchanged a nice, calm butt sniff."

Generally, these dogs use defensive behaviour as their first tool in social communication. For instance, if a group of dogs rushes up and overwhelms this type of dog, instead of doing the sophisticated thing and sitting or lying down (a calming signal), she immediately resorts to using relatively extreme defensive behaviour the moment her flight options are limited. For some of these dogs, the flight option isn't even considered – when they see other dogs, they immediately begin rank-ordering or defensive displays, neither of which are appropriate within the first second of meeting another animal.

Lack of Socialization – Inter-Species

Lack of experience with a wide variety of humans leaves many dogs fearful (therefore opening the door for aggression) toward humans wearing hats, walking with crutches, or even of different races than they have been exposed to. For some animals, *any human* that they do not know well is suspect and is treated with extreme caution or fear.

It is very important that your dog be exposed to the widest variety of humans possible. It is just as crucial that your dog is taught normal human mannerisms: eye contact is harmless; reaching for him isn't a threatening gesture; being restrained by humans is not a life-or-death situation; and other actions that humans commonly do are benign.

For these dogs, any human, other than those well-known, is immediately considered a threat, as is any body language people exhibit that the dog is not familiar with.

This category has the easy solution: education should provide the "fix," provided the dog is able to habituate (has normal adaptive behaviour).

The following classifications are subsets of: Variations in Breed Temperament.

Excessive Breed Tendencies or the Lack of These

Selective breeding created dogs who were bred for a specific original purpose. In so doing, we created our own monsters, if you will.

The highest percentage of purebred dogs will fall in a middle range for these traits. Because of genetic variation, however, there are individuals who possess either a lack of these breed-specific traits or excessive breed tendencies. This only becomes a problem, of course, when it violates the expectations of the humans who own the dog.

Because your dog is of a particular breed is NOT a valid reason for dangerous behaviour. It is

NOT okay for your guarding-breed dog to snarl and growl at men who approach you because "the breed is just like that." People who use the breed as an excuse for lack of socialization and lack of education for their dog are a major source of dog problems. When owners do this, a dog is trapped in a destructive behavioural path by the owner's excuse-making. If the dog has a problem, admit it, get over it, and get to work on it.

As an example, some German Shepherd Dogs exhibit a dramatic degree of display and reactivity, with use of "excessive force," to evict an intruder. Or the dog prevents non-threatening persons from normal approaches. Or the GSD guards one family member from another for no apparent reason. These constitute normal shepherd traits, but carried to undesirable excess. This dog is a liability because of the zeal and lack of judgment exhibited.

The polar opposite would be a GSD who displayed absolutely no guarding behaviour at all, no matter the circumstances and training. This would prove to be a disappointment if the dog were obtained as a civil protection dog or a dog to be trained in Schutzhund work.

Common Behavioural Rule-Outs:

- Learned behaviour
- Lack of education
- Poor training
- Lack of exposure to novel stimuli
- Lack of exposure to other dogs and/or people

Human Selection for Aggression in Dogs

Some breeds have been specifically selected for high intensity, frequency, and duration of aggression with low thresholds for stimulation of defensive or guarding behaviours.

These traits also occur in breeding programs where the owners carelessly bred undesirable-temperamented dogs because they have desirable physical traits.

Additional major players that contribute to this classification (as well as many other temperament and health problems):

- Breeders who breed because of high demand for a breed merely so they can make a buck.
- Pet people who breed because "I have a dog and you have a bitch, and let's do puppies," without proper knowledge of bloodlines and genetic screening.
- Commercial breeders who breed for puppy mills (which are commonly licensed by the USDA).

Obviously, we are discussing heritable traits here, so it might be difficult to classify this unless you had extensive knowledge of the pedigree of the dog you are dealing with.

There is a strain of pointers that were bred specifically by research personnel to exhibit fearful and nervous behaviours so that anxiety and fear could be better understood. This is an example of breeding for a specific, inherited trait. Some breeders choose, for a reason, to breed specifically for certain "types" of aggression. This might be useful for particular types of jobs. People using Flock Guardians to protect sheep from wolf, coyote, and free-ranging dog kills want a dog who will exhibit Territorial Aggression. If a breeder is breeding intentionally for specific traits so the dog can perform a useful job, AND the breeder places the dogs appropriately and understands what he is doing, breeding for specific traits is a good thing.

The following classifications are subsets of: Variations in Ethogram.

The following are behaviours that stem from "hard-wired" behaviour (fixed action patterns or instinctive behaviour). Agonistic display is behaviour that would be used for defense, rank-ordering or conflict resolution within the same species. I think if we were able to ask dogs, they would not consider these "problem" behaviours, but would tell you that they are doing what comes naturally to them.

Very few humans wish to live in a dog pack using dog rules to run their homes. Most of my clients expect the dogs to exhibit dog behaviour and they know their dogs will bark at people coming into the house, but they wish the dog to be quiet when cued to do so. Jumping is NOT okay when there are toddlers, guests or elderly people visiting your home. People expect dogs to learn not to urinate and defecate in the house, bite the mail-carrier, and so on. Barking, eliminating, jumping to greet, biting, and many other behaviours are naturally occurring and well within the range of normal dog behaviour. However, humans consider these behaviours problems when they cannot teach the dog to curb his natural tendencies in order to cohabitate with people.

Therefore, these are considered "Problem Behaviours" by humans when the behaviours occur more (or less) intensely or often than they expected. Changing these is primarily a matter of education and teaching the dog impulse control.

If agonistic behaviour is excessive, it can be interpreted as "how the animal is temperamented" (genetic), learned, or a deviation from normal behaviour strategies. The big decision in my point of view is this: Is the dog behaving on a continuum of normal behaviour, although inconveniently for this client, OR is the dog exhibiting behaviour that is particularly deviant from the norm in frequency (increased or decreased behaviour patterns) or intensity (extreme behaviour patterns)? Does the dog become aroused inordinately (exceeding reasonable limits) and is the behaviour of an unusually high intensity? Is the dog able to return to a calmer state in a reasonable time? High intensity of a behaviour can pass normal thresholds and result in unusual behaviour (e.g., extreme anxiety may cause a dog to exhibit self-injurious behaviour). Extreme frustration may result in explosive redirected aggression.

Control Conflict Aggression

Some practitioners use this term to refer to human-dog interactions only, and I adhere to this. Others use this term to refer to dog-to-dog interactions as well, but I prefer to classify that as some form of dog-to-dog aggression, using a good description of the triggers and function the behaviour is serving for the animal.

I prefer the term "control conflict aggression" to "dominance aggression" because of the misleading quality of the term "dominance."

The animal who discretely fits into this category is indeed abnormal. These animals are *obsessive* about rank order, and seem to think of almost nothing else. This classification is very frightening because the animal is in conflict with known humans over an intangible item: control of the environment. It occasionally appears as if the animal is entering into conflict over a location or food, but the behaviour will be exhibited over a wide band of contexts.

The dogs classified under this heading are constantly on the lookout for some "slight" to their authority or status – control freaks to the nth degree – and are ready to do battle over it each and every time. Their immediate response to most social situations is to use aggression or assertive behaviour (intensely, seriously assertive, not just physically a little pushy) to maintain status. They do not seem to have any other mechanisms for conflict resolution. These animals tend toward an inability to learn normal social tolerance on a reliable basis, even with behaviour modification.

This behaviour stems from a dog being maladaptive and insecure and who is struggling to cope with this innate insecurity.

Topography

- These animals are very intolerant to being touched, and become irritable very easily when being touched or if a human tries to physically control them, even in minor ways, such as blocking the dog's passage in a room.
- This dog may offer little or no warning and the triggers may be inconsistently displayed and broad, due to the accumulation of the dog's irritation level.

- Touch and restraint, however, will be a common thread that causes response. What may vary here is the intensity of the response. Even if the dog begins with a low-level response, she will quickly escalate the behaviour if you do not heed the warnings issued.
- The triggers often occur under very low stimulus levels, due to the fact that these dogs have no capacity to cope with even low levels of frustration.
- The dog may often exhibit playful or affectionate behaviour, then become reactive when his "victim" responds. For example, the dog comes up and nudges you to be patted and might be quite insistent that you do so. Then once the dog has successfully solicited this attention, and you pet him, he "warns" you with a growl or snap to stop.
- Minimal touching and stimulation can evoke an out-of-context response.

As an example: The following dog was a Rottweiler-mix, bitch, spayed, approximately 36 months of age. Her owner was sleeping on the sofa and the dog was lying on the floor next to the sofa. The dog was awake, and the wife was sitting in the chair near the dog. The husband shifted in his sleep and his arm and hand touched the dog on the shoulders. The wife said the dog stiffened briefly, looked directly at the sleeping husband, then bit the man immediately with no further display, and without acting startled. The man received 4 puncture wounds with some tearing and bruising. The bitch had a history of being intolerant of being moved and touched.

Common Antecedent Stimuli (Triggers)

- Being touched
- Being moved
- Physical control

Common Behavioural Rule-Outs

- Make sure the dog is educated correctly about human body language and being touched, and isn't just a bit "touch sensitive" because they have had *bad experience* with human touch or *lack of experience* with human touch. (See the protocol for "Handling & Restraint.")
- Learned Aggression
- Possessive Aggression
- Territorial Aggression
- Fear Aggression
- Pain-related Aggression

I am quite irritated with the over-use of this category. It seems that every misstep a dog makes is attributed to the dog having a "dominance" problem by the unenlightened, and, if the dog bites, attributing the incident to "dominance" aggression. This also goes for dogs who do not like to be touched and who have not specifically and systematically been taught about human touch and about being restrained. This classification is only to be used as a very specific description of a dog who is *incapable of normal social interaction.*

Owners can promote this behaviour in a dog, or create a dog who mimics this behaviour, by placing the dog in situations where he is always granted success. Not placing limits on the dog's behaviour and allowing him to exhibit endless pushiness encourages him to use physical force to obtain resources. If you are wiping your dog's feet and he growls at you, so you never wipe his feet again because "he just doesn't like that," you are contributing to this behaviour.

If the dog is endlessly and immediately indulged, he never learns to deal with any frustration and is never allowed to develop any patience when he doesn't receive immediate gratification. When this occurs over a long period of time – from puppyhood until 18-24 months of age (a time when dogs are prone to being more assertive because of social development periods) – you have created a monster. An animal who has never been thwarted never learns to deal with frustration, creating low thresholds for frustration. This causes the dog to be reactive when he is placed in a frustrating situation. In short, lack of structure (not teaching the dog to deal with daily life) will destroy the dog. This doesn't mean you have to be inhumane or Attilla the Hun. It just means you should institute and follow house rules and make sure you can handle and restrain your dog. (See protocols for "Handling and Restraint" and "Yielding.")

Fear Aggression

This classification depends on the intensity of the aggressive behaviour and the context in which it occurs. It is normal for dogs to bite if they are extremely frightened. However, some dogs have such a low threshold for fear that they become defensive and bite even when the threat is negligible or non-existent.

Fear-based aggression is often accompanied by urination and defecation while the dog is behaving in a defensive manner.

I have reiterated in this book that fear and stress often result in aggressive behaviour as a symptom of the underlying anxiety. A dog may display aggression in conjunction with overt fearful behaviours, such as avoidance, or escape behaviours, or physiological changes in the body that are related to the sympathetic branch of the autonomic nervous system. If a dog is presenting in this manner, Fear Aggression is a reasonable classification.

Without getting too complex, I will give you a brief definition of the sympathetic branch of the autonomic nervous system. If you are interested in this topic, refer to any text on physiology. These will give you details about specific body systems and the chemical changes that take place. *Clinical Behavioral Medicine for Small Animals* (Overall, 1997) has information on this subject.

The *sympathetic branch of the autonomic nervous system* helps to control several reflexes. When the dog is aroused, stressed, or frightened, this system is stimulated. There are responses the body has to this stimulation, some of which are observable. When you see one or more of these responses, you know that the sympathetic nervous system is activated and that the related chemical changes are taking place. You may note one or more of the following:

- The pupils become dilated.
- The sweat glands become activated and sweating occurs. In a dog, this may mean his nose suddenly begins to drip or he leaves damp paw prints or begins to pant.
- The heart rate and force of contraction increase (the pounding heart you feel when you are startled).
- The bronchi in the lungs dilate and the blood vessels in the lungs are mildly constricted, resulting in shallow, rapid breathing patterns.
- The guts will temporarily have decreased peristalsis (motility). When peristalsis resumes, it may do so intensely, causing loss of bowel control.
- Piloerector muscles become active (the hair stands up).
- The dog loses control of his bladder or bowels.

Topography

- Aggression is accompanied by overt signs of sympathetic nervous system responses.
- You might observe shaking and trembling, or fearful looking behaviour exhibited immediately after the aggressive display, or mixed in with the display.
- The dog may sneak up behind you and bite, then run away. (Differentiate this from herding behaviour and from predatory behaviour.)
- This type of aggression is often directed toward humans, because in the past people have used inappropriate punishment, excessive force, or punished the dog when he was already in a fearful state. People often use punishers with poor timing and the dog becomes confused. The dog quickly associates not understanding what humans want (confusion) with punishment. Now the fearful aggressive behaviour is easily triggered if any human looks even the least bit threatening, or the human displays a behaviour the dog doesn't understand or has not seen.
- This dog will exhibit avoidance behaviours as a first choice, but if cornered will quickly resort to defensive behaviour.

Common Behavioural Rule-Outs

- Possessive Aggression (which may look very fearful in nature, depending on the dog's past experiences).

IDIOPATHIC AGGRESSION

Idiopathic means "for no reason." Although many people call and tell me the dog "suddenly lunged across the room and bit for no reason," the reality is that as soon as I begin taking a case history, I find that, not only did the dog have a valid reason (a reason that at least falls within the confines of what I have seen before in other dogs), the dog was warning them that this was going to occur for some time.

Idiopathic behaviour is sometimes referred to as "Rage Syndrome" or "Springer Rage Syndrome." This label is incorrect. This is a fine example of a discrete diagnosis being erroneously used as a "label." Rage is a very anthropomorphic term and not applicable here. Also, there is a high incidence of resource guarding behaviours in many breeds, Springer Spaniels among them. I have had many people call me and say their instructor or veterinarian told them their English Springer has "Springer Rage." When I begin to investigate I discover it is garden-variety resource guarding behaviour.

There is a version of this diagnosis that is valid. This would be *excepting* those dogs who are displaying seizure-related disease, with aggression as a symptom of the mental storm that is occurring. To definitively diagnose this behaviour, an extensive physical work-up is required from a veterinarian. All other neurological functions must be checked to rule out pathology. This must be accurately diagnosed by a team consisting of a behaviour specialist, the owner of the dog, and a veterinarian (preferably a neurological specialist).

Topography:

- Extreme force and violence.
- Extremely unpredictable. The dog is CALMLY lying in your lap one moment and the next moment is intensely attacking you. The key word here is "calm," not to be confused with "still." Dogs will often be still for a moment before they launch a frontal assault when they are guarding an object. That moment of stillness is a warning – "the calm before the storm" – not a true relaxed emotional state.
- May attack humans, dogs or inanimate objects.
- Usually does not show aggressive tendencies at other times.
- May look confused with glazed eyes (sympathetic nervous system response) just prior to attack.
- 1-3 years of age.

There is documented prevalence in English Springer Spaniels, American Cocker Spaniels and St. Bernards.

Be careful with this classification. This is not a "catch-all" description for aggression; this classification is often misused when there is a lack of knowledge by the practitioner who is confused about how to categorize the behavior of the patient.

Common Behavioural Rule-Outs

- Possessive Aggression
- Control Conflict Aggression
- Redirected Aggression
- Predatory Aggression

DOG-TO-DOG AGGRESSION

Remember that dog-to-dog aggression can occur under a wide variety of circumstances, as discussed at the beginning of this chapter. Therefore, do your homework, and do not immediately resort to this classification just because your dog growls at another dog. There are many reasons this would happen, many of them perfectly normal in aspect.

Dog-to-Dog Aggression is a very generalized category to designate dogs who are socially not just inept, but who are *actively* "looking for" trouble with other dogs. Aggression is a consistent response to other dogs, and this dog will use aggression, ignoring signals from other dogs. The aggression occurs in absence of threat behaviour from the other dog; in fact, the other dog may be socially appropriate in every way, and this dog will still use aggression. These dogs may start out just being pushy as youngsters, but, by the time they are adults, their response to another dog is simply an all-out attack as soon as they get close enough to get hold of the other dog.

If you have an older dog in the household who behaves this way and you bring home a puppy, the behaviour will very likely be perpetuated. The younger dog will quickly learn this behaviour from the older dog.

It is best to use or rule out the other categories prior to depending on this classification because this classification is easy to overuse.

An example of this classification is an 18 month old GSD castrated male I worked with. He approached a female dog on leash. She was using lovely greeting behaviours. He walked up to her, and, instead of responding to her signals or even trying any alternatives, he grabbed her by the back of the neck and began to shake her. The dogs were quickly separated. His customary response to other dogs is to use aggression, right out of the gate. This response is consistent with dogs he meets, and is exhibited as lunging, barking and growling whenever he sees another dog at a distance.

Learned Aggression

As soon as an animal learns that aggression leads to a successful outcome, aggression is readily accessed. There is almost always a learned component to aggression – so I tend to use this category discretely for dogs who appear to have "just stumbled on" this behaviour pattern, discovered "it works" and are exploiting[1] that fact.

1. Exploit is being used literally as "to employ to the greatest possible advantage" (*The American Heritage Dictionary of The English Language, 1976*), not meant to imply that the dog is deliberately pondering about a strategy.

With this classification, you are making an educated guess, so you are trying to extrapolate: for some animals this behaviour would never be accessed under normal conditions, but because the dog is placed under an extraordinary amount of stress, the behaviour is accessed and found to be successful. A dog who is a stray may not have had tendencies toward food aggression if he were well fed in a home, for example, but on the streets he learns to fight over food because it is scarce.

When using learned aggression as one classification, 99% of the time there is an additional classification used to describe the specific triggers: Fear aggression, Possessive aggression, etc. When I use this classification, I describe its extent – for example: possessive aggression, *strong learned component* (from existing family dog).

If a fearful animal becomes desperate enough to snap at someone reaching toward her and that person recoils, then the person just taught the dog: "If you become uncomfortable you can relieve your discomfort by using defensive behaviour." I am not saying do not draw back if a dog takes a snap at you, but don't be foolish enough to *continue* reaching toward an animal who is uncomfortable and telling you so with body tension, which may be accompanied by a quick warning glance. You are only allowing the dog to practice aggression. The next time a similar situation occurs, the dog may choose not to remain uncomfortable for the five minutes it took her to snap the first time, and may access the snapping behaviour in 3 minutes. The next time it may be 5 seconds. Then the dog may begin to generalize this defensive behaviour to ANY situation where she begins to feel the least bit frightened.

Maternal Aggression

Hormonal changes or inherited temperament tendencies may cause a new mother to launch intense attacks on strangers (dog or human) who approach her puppies.

Topography

- The behaviour depends on the hormonal state of the bitch. The symptoms will abate as her hormonal state changes.
- Will display defensive behaviour when a person or animal approaches puppies, most intensely when puppies are younger.
- Protects toys and bedding from people and dogs while nesting prior to birth.
- Some bitches will guard toys quite aggressively, even in false pregnancy.
- If the bitch feels like she is under chronic threat, she may eat her toys or her puppies.

NEOPHOBIA

These dogs react to EVERY new situation, location, or object with behaviour that ranges from cautious to terrified. The dog will exhibit intense avoidance behaviours, verging on and sometimes extending into panic. It is as if these dogs have no "rebound" or ability to adapt to anything unfamiliar to them. This is definitely an abnormality because the lack of ability to habituate is at the root of this classification. The ability to change and adapt, to habituate to new contexts, is basic to successful survival skills. Dogs unable to habituate are clearly maladaptive in some way.

In extreme cases, the dog will become so fearful that he develops phobias – sudden and unreasonable fears. Sometimes the fear begins to occur in absence of the original stimuli.

This classification is relevant only to our discussion because aggression can be a symptom of the way this dog copes with fear.

This behaviour may be caused by isolation during crucial developmental stages, but also has a strong inherited component.

PAIN-RELATED AGGRESSION

Grading pain in an animal who cannot speak is difficult at best. Some animals are incredibly stoical and some just the opposite. When I take my little Smooth Foxies in for vaccinations, they stand there wagging their tail the entire time – they don't notice anything except the cookie they get afterwards. My Border Collie, on the other hand, is ridiculous about such matters, whining, looking pitiful in general, and limping after an antibiotic shot in the leg. However, when she is working, I swear you could cut her legs off and she would hobble along happily, ignoring the inconvenience. So pain is variable and subjective, not just among different individuals, but even within the same animal.

Therefore, use this category specifically for the dog who uses "more than necessary force" to indicate that what you are doing is hurting him. This is a rather bizarre classification in my reckoning. Because we don't really know how much pain this animal is in, how can we determine when the animal is protesting too intensely? This becomes a subjective "call" on the part of the practitioner and depends on the experience that practitioner has had with animals.

Any animal who is injured may become defensive or bite if you attempt to approach, especially if you are manipulating her body and it increases the pain. Use safe behaviour when you are working with injured animals.

Some animals show aggression when they *anticipate* pain – this is certainly a reasonable description of pain-related aggression. The best guideline to use here is: Does the animal access intense aggression immediately? Or does the dog warn you, then, if you persist, escalate the behaviour quickly and intensely?

Pain-related aggression is very understandable behaviour. I remember being in an emergency room myself, being stitched up after a dog bite. The injury was on a finger and very deep, near the bone and a bunch of little ligaments. The intern was probing and poking and cleaning the wound before the local anesthetic took effect. I asked her to stop and she didn't. I quite clearly recall informing her that if she continued much more I would be compelled to hurt her. Now, normally I just do not speak to people that way, but I was ready to back it up with action.

Topography

- If a dog is old and therefore more frail, arthritic, recovering from an injury, or a variety of other tangible reasons, and people bump or children play roughly with the dog, the dog becomes defensive. Easy to see why! The association between human approach and pain can trigger a response even BEFORE the dog is hurt.
- This response can quickly become fear aggression.

Common Behavioural Rule-Outs

- Control-Conflict Aggression.
- The dog was never habituated correctly to human body language and being touched. (See protocol for "Handling and Restraint.")

PLAY AGGRESSION

These dogs begin interacting with others by exhibiting obvious play behaviours. However, once a certain threshold of stimulation is exceeded, the dog's behaviour begins to escalate rapidly into intense threatening actions. A human analogy might be someone who begins playing Monopoly and then leaps up, turns the table over, and begins to slap you. Play stimulates the dog to the extent that she becomes over-aroused, given the context; she will begin to display threat behaviour or snap at and bite the other dog, ignoring clear signals from the other dog that would normally truncate the play.

Another permutation of Play Aggression is the dog who doesn't *precede* play behaviour with play signals. So, even though Dog #1 starts out intending to play, his lack of communication is easily interpreted by other dogs as threat behaviour. This may elicit defensive behaviour from Dog #2. From this, Dog #1 surmises that other dogs are unpredictable and, on subsequent meetings with dogs, becomes defensive.

Dogs in this category do not have normal social patterns nor appropriate social responses to other dogs. To fall into this category, the dog must consistently display an intent to harm[1] in circumstances where normally dogs would display play behaviours without losing sight of the fact that it is "play." Basically, I am talking once again about high intensity of behaviour that is triggered under low thresholds.

Aggression may also be directed toward humans who are playing with the dog, once certain stimulation thresholds have been exceeded in the dog.

The difficulty here is differentiating Play Aggression from what is merely rough play. Play Aggression may be a natural tendency in the individual. Rough play may also be a natural tendency, but is often taught to dogs by humans who encourage this when the dog is a puppy, or by allowing your puppy to play with dogs who are rough and do not back off when requested by other dogs to do so, forcing your dog to become defensive. Playmates who are "too rough" can also teach your dog that signals "don't work" to turn off aggression in other dogs.

"Rough Play" could be used as a descriptor of just that: dogs who are just being physically too rough and are ignoring the discomfort communicated to them via calming signals. Understand that Rough Play can escalate into Play Aggression. When the rough play is seen in very young dogs, there is increased risk for the dog to develop escalated behaviour – Play Aggression – as they mature.

Topography

- Arousal-related aggression which is caused by over-stimulation.
- Dogs who do not use distance decreasing signals.

1. Do not misinterpret "intent to harm" in this sentence. I do not mean to imply by "intent" that the dog is coming into this situation thinking, "Hey, I'm going to hurt this other dog," because surely this is not the case. This has more to do with dogs who reach a level of excitement or stimulation and then lose control of their behaviour. This is a chemical issue.

- Dogs who consistently ignore the calming signals of other dogs and continue to harass and frighten the other dog.
- Dogs who, when the dog they are playing with becomes frightened, become more stimulated, continue to escalate behaviour, and threaten or bite the playmate.
- May begin with play behaviour but change to more serious displays as the play continues.
- When playing with humans, the dog does not quickly learn to differentiate between toy and human flesh. Grabs at human hands and clothing, may cause minor (not requiring stitches) tearing in skin and clothing.

Common Behavioural Rule-Outs

- Rough Play (which is marginal behaviour).
- Possessive Aggression – if toys are involved with the event when the dogs are playing, then my first inclination might be to lean toward some form of resource guarding or possessive aggression. If a human is in the area with the dogs and the fights seem to consistently occur around the human, or are sparked by another dog approaching the human, then some form of resource guarding is a possibility.
- Predatory Aggression.

My terriers are prone to play aggression, as well as something that starts off looking like play aggression then quickly converts to predatory drift.

A big cause of Play Aggression is failure in education. This dog did not have the opportunity to learn about limits on his behaviour and bite inhibition. Removing pups from littermates too early contributes to this problem. Not providing adequate opportunities to interact with normal members of their own species will always contribute to this problem. Also, dogs who are easily aroused because of their own natural tendencies, or breeds that tend toward extreme predatory behaviour, are prone to exhibiting play aggression.

POSSESSIVE AGGRESSION

For a lengthy discussion of possessive aggression, refer to the Resource Guarding Protocol, "Give Me That, It's Mine."

The dog will actively and consistently use agonistic display and confrontational behaviour to obtain or retain a valued object. The resource importance is:
- defined by the dog
- not related to status issues.

Topography:

- Very typical guarding postures indicated by a lowered head and neck and stillness on approach. The dog may warn. You may see a lot of display or the dog may become reactive after only very subtle warning (split-second stillness and slightly lowered head).
- The response is highly contextual. That is, the aggression only occurs in the presence of a valued object or location.
- The dog can look defensive or assertive. My own dogs who have had possessive aggression have taken on a defensive posture with humans (lowered tail, lowered head, defensive postures) and vary between defensive and assertive postures with other dogs. Plainly, both kinds of postures could be used with humans or animals.
- This dog has difficulty, perhaps from a very young age, with relinquishing toys or objects. I have seen serious, not-kidding defense behaviours in my terrier babies as early as eight weeks of age. I am not picking on breeds here, just relating experiences I have had. I have also seen guarding behaviours in Corgi and Rottweiler puppies by twelve weeks, and in very young Australian Shepherds and Border Collies. This is a discrete behaviour that differs from the normal "sorting it out" stuff that one commonly sees in youngsters, so you would have to have done a lot of "dog-watching" to pick this up.

Common Antecedent Stimuli

- Easily and inadvertently triggered by a non-threatening or innocent approach toward the valued object or location, as well as by reaching for the desirable object.

Possessive aggression can be exhibited toward other dogs or to humans (or other animals, such as house cats).

Possessive Aggression – Food Related

All the stuff about possessive aggression holds true, except that the presentation of the behaviour occurs only in the presence of food or other edible items, such as raw-hides, soup bones, etc.

These dogs typically guard a food bowl (which may generalize into guarding the location where the food bowl is kept) or special food treats such as pig ears.

As a child I was cautioned about approaching a dog when it was eating. Good advice for your children and you, too – if you do not *know* the dog is safe, do not *assume* the dog is safe.

This is a bone-chilling category. If the dog does not have good bite inhibition and there are toddlers present, it is indeed a recipe for disaster. If someone drops food on the floor accidentally, and a child reaches for the food at the same time the dog does ... it can be very bad.

I had someone phone me about their beagle mix who was guarding his food bowl. They had small children in the home. I cautioned them about this behaviour and the possible dangers and urged them to get immediate help. The family was very busy, and decided not to spend the money and time "right now." I heard via a mutual acquaintance a few weeks later that one of the children had a birthday party, some food fell on the floor, and the child and the dog went for the dropped cake simultaneously. The dog ended up dead after this encounter and the child needed stitches to close facial wounds.

Predatory Aggression

Hunting is normal behaviour for dogs. Selective breeding has given us a wide array of predatory behaviours. In some breeds, prey behaviour has been reduced for the most part to scenting and retrieving. In others it has been honed to retain chase, eye and stalk behaviours, but truncated to remove bite, kill and dissect behaviours (herding breeds).

A Predatory Sequence includes some or all of the these behaviours in chronological order:

- Scan
- Eye
- Grab-bite
- Shake
- Hold
- Kill-bite
- Dissect

My own jolly little Smooths have been selected to harass fox out of their dens, a job they are admirably suited for: small size, large teeth, high pain tolerance, and tenacity like you wouldn't believe. Also with this package comes very low arousal thresholds to produce extreme behaviour. Very handy for drawing fox out of the den. The deal is, if you know and understand breed tendencies, you can be prepared to live with it and train for the eventuality. You can monitor arousal levels at a young age and teach the dog how to Switch and Anchor. (For protocols, refer to the Level I protocol, "Eye Contact and Involvement").

For dogs who are to be used for any original purpose (excepting breeds like the toy, non-sporting and drafting breeds), a high degree of predatory behaviour specific to that breed is desirable.

When your dog chases a ball or a Frisbee, or she runs around shaking a fuzzy toy, her actions are based in predatory behaviour. People find these traits desirable and acceptable. About half of my own dogs absolutely adore dissecting fuzzy toys and will persist until the squeaky thing is out of the toy and silent. Predation can be expressed in a variety of ways: chasing bikers or joggers, chasing a ball, and carrying a fuzzy toy are all forms of predation.

Killing livestock is not acceptable. And yet both killing sheep and killing a fuzzy toy are on the continuum of predatory behaviour.

Because dogs are domestic animals, selecting human children or adults as targets for predation by exhibiting stalking or other predatory-type behaviours is abnormal. Let me clarify this: I am not discussing the stalking your Border Collie does when you are playing with a toy. I am discussing dogs who are seriously looking at toddlers or infants as "wounded" because of the way they are moving and are intensively honing in on them. It appears as though, in the face of certain stimuli, the dog is unable to distinguish the difference between inappropriate and appropriate prey and unable to exert control over his behaviour.

There is much discussion whether predatory behaviour should even be considered "aggressive" behaviour, with some merit. Predatory behaviour is very "deep" behaviour, rooted-in-the-brain-stem stuff. My point of view is that predatory behaviour is not aggression – but that may just be a battle over semantics, because the resulting damage is the same whether you call it aggression or not. Teeth are involved, even though it is not over conflict resolution specifically. I have seen dogs treat other dogs as prey. The resulting bites and damage are the same as with the dog that is guarding territory or resource guarding an object.

Topography

- Predatory aggression is quiet aggression, not the normal snarling, growling kind of stuff that is preceded by stiff-legged posturing. Prey behaviours can include intense stares, quiet approaches, body-lowering, tail-twitching, salivating, stalking. Dogs in prey mode will silently and quickly approach their target. One fierce, very hard, full-mouth bite accompanied by shaking the selected target is a common indicator of predatory behaviour. The dog is focused so intently on his prey that interrupting the behaviour is *extremely* difficult.
- The behaviour may involve any of the predatory sequence behaviours, and proceed in a chronological order, although an individual behaviour within the sequence may be "skipped."
- There will be no warning vocalizations before the dog leaps on grabs and shakes the "prey."
- The dog may stalk other animals, infants, toddlers, persons who look disabled (limping or uncoordinated gait), or cyclists, just to mention a few of the more common predatory "targets."

Common Antecedent Stimuli

- Quick movement.
- Jerky movement.
- Another animal frightened or struggling.
- Limping or injury in a conspecific.
- Uncoordinated movements of children/adults.
- Animals that have already been targeted or established by the dog as "prey," such as cats.

Common Behavioural Rule-Outs

- Territorial Aggression.
  Often forms of territorial aggression are misclassified as prey behaviour, such as a dog chasing a jogger or skate-boarder down the sidewalk. Ask: What function is the behaviour serving for the dog? Does he chase intensely, never giving up or does he chase only until the biker is off territory?
- Redirected Aggression.

Predatory Drift can occur dog-to-dog. In this case, under normal circumstances, the dogs would coexist just fine, but certain stimuli trigger a limbic response where one dog begins to see the other dog as prey. This is prevalent in the terrier breeds and is also seen in herding breeds, particularly the herding/guarding types, such as Malinois or GSD's.

Some dogs "shift" into predatory mode when they are playing and the play reaches a certain intensity. Chase games can quickly become not a game but serious business for such animals. At this point these dogs begin to treat the other dog as "prey" and not as a member of their own species.

The most dramatic example of this I saw is the very first time I turned Maeve, my rescue GSD, loose with one of my terriers. Understandably nervous given her history, I did a lot of work with the two dogs in extremely controlled circumstances. If she were to remain here with us among the living, it was essential to determine that she was capable of some normal relationships with her own species. The day came when I decided to give it a try. So I took Dervish, raised by me from a puppy and extensively socialized, and Maeve out to the 70 x 100 play-yard. I often walked them together on leash and they were frequently loose in the house together. However, I well know that turning dogs loose in a large area is a whole different experience for them. Dervish play-bowed and immediately initiated a chase game. Maeve tore off after him as Dervish raced around the yard at full throttle. As Maeve chased him, after a couple of minutes, I could see some very subtle and scary changes occur in her demeanor. She became more intensely focused on Dervish. She became silent and quit panting. Her body was sliding low over the ground. Very subtly she appeared to me as if she shed her coat of civilization as she ran. Dervish noticed this about the same time I did, glancing back at her and slowing his pace. An attempt of mine to verbally interrupt Maeve's chase behaviour resulted in absolutely no response; in her aroused emotional state she seemed incapable of processing the fact that I was requesting a known behaviour. Terrified of what would happen next, I started toward the dogs in an attempt to physically intervene. Dervish, however, had the situation well in hand. As Maeve reached him (at this point I was practically having an out-of-body experience), he stopped dead and began to sniff the ground. I watched, amazed, as Maeve stopped just short of reaching out and grabbing him, shook her head then her body. I stood right there and watched her pupils return to normal and the glaze go out of her eyes as she sniffed the ground next to him. This entire episode occurred in approximately 5 to 8 seconds, but had the surreal feeling of the timelessness when a situation is out of your control. After this experience with Dervish's sophisticated use of his native language, Maeve, even when in similar situations, never displayed that behaviour again with a playmate. Dervish somehow taught her that he was not prey, and that play behaviour did not have to become prey behaviour.

Note here that Maeve's behaviour is indeed "predatory aggression," not "play aggression," because getting over-stimulated by the rough play is not what occurred in this incident. She was literally seeing Dervish as prey until he interrupted the sequence. From this episode it is apparent that she is not misreading dog language; she understands it well.

Do not count on calming signals, however, to always interrupt a dog's predatory sequence. While I have seen this strategy of using calming signals work, I have also seen instances where it did not.

Protective Aggression

A third-party approach will provoke an aggressive response, even though the approaching party is clearly not threatening. This would be a consistent response to third-party approaches, or at least a predominant response.

Topography

- Low-threshold stimuli provoke an agonistic display with intent to prevent the third party from approaching the individual the dog is "guarding."
- Constant scanning of the environment.
- Intense Alerting behaviour directed toward a third party. This resembles quiet stalking behaviour, but the dog will keep an upright body posture, rather than a lowered body posture. She may lower the head and neck slightly or raise the head and neck slightly. The movement of the dog will become more "economical," taking on a gliding appearance.
- Barking and vocalization when a third party approaches.
- Lunging toward third party in an attempt to drive it away.

- The dog will keep herself between the "protectee" and the "approacher."
- The agonistic behaviour will increase as the third party gets closer. Or, even more dangerous and business-like, the dog quietly waits in a watchful, guarding posture as the third party approaches.
- If you remove the person the dog is guarding, the behaviour immediately ceases. This can be very dramatic. I was working with a three-year-old male GSD and his female owner. The female owner was very passive. The dog was very intense and fierce and serious in his display when I would approach. We muzzled the dog, and I would approach and have the owner hand me the leash and walk away. It was, admittedly, tricky to get hold of the dog without injury to myself, but the muzzle made it possible. As soon as the owner was out of sight, the dog would immediately turn to me all wagging tail and friendly face. I could remove the muzzle and work the dog as long as the owner was not present.

Common Behavioural Rule-Outs

- Territorial Aggression
- Possessive Aggression
- Fear Aggression

This is quite disagreeable behaviour, and is inadvertently caused by the handler in many cases. The dog is given consent to "possess" the handler, because, for this dog, the innate tendencies to guard are present, but may not show up until social maturity, thereby catching the owner by surprise. The handler allows this behaviour to develop when it is not made clear to the dog that the handler is going to be in control of who approaches. If the handler does not make this clear to the dog, the dog will take tremulous or *neutral* feedback from the handler as "permission" to begin guarding. (Sometimes the handler is tremulous because of the dog's reactive behaviour, but the dog doesn't know that! They think the nervous behaviour of the handler is caused by the approach of the third party.) Some of these dogs, on some level, are free-lancing, making a decision to possess and guard you just as they would with a piece of slimy rawhide.

To determine "where" the behaviour is coming from, you must figure out if the dog is guarding, or if she is misinterpreting the body language of the third party. Understanding which is going on will help you determine the function the behaviour is serving for the dog, which in turn points you to appropriate protocols. For prevention, this is one reason it is important to educate dogs about all sorts of human behaviour and approaches – so the dog learns to correctly interpret friendly vs. unfriendly approaches.

It is also important to distinguish this classification from *Protective Behaviour*, where your dog is defending a family member from an *actual threat*, and has shown appropriate judgment in the past distinguishing threat vs. non-threat behaviour in the approaching party.

Protective aggression is most often directed toward a non-family member, this "Third Party" being an essential component and differentiating this from Possessive aggression. In some cases, Protective aggression is directed toward a family member because the dog interprets the family member as "threatening" another family member.

Protective Aggression is defensive behaviour that is exhibited in absence of a threat and involves a Third Party.

People foster this behaviour and create their own monsters when they encourage puppies to "protect" them from a family member in play. The dog does not know the difference and, as an adult, might take this job very seriously indeed. The dog who misinterprets the intent of the third party, because the third party is "pretending" to be threatening, is at high risk for developing Protective Aggression. It is easy to see how messing with the dog in this manner, just as a lark, and without the proper training and controls, causes trouble.

Also promoting this behaviour is the owner who is very passive and inadvertently "allows" the dog to partake of guarding behaviour by remaining neutral or helpless. This confirms the dog's belief that this person needs someone to guard her, or, at the very least, on a behavioural level, leads the dog to believe that his current "guarding" behaviour is condoned by the owner.

Often people don't even realize that the dog is exhibiting subtle guarding behaviour, and so they don't do anything about it until the dog, *taking the person's non-reaction as permission*, begins to exhibit more intense displays.

The dog may also feel that the owner is "backing him up" by remaining passive or neutral.

Redirected Aggression

Redirected aggression is aggression that is consistently directed toward a third party when the dog is interrupted or prevented from directing the agonistic behaviour toward the original target.

The dog, when excited or aroused, no matter the original cause, will turn and "unload" the aggression onto the closest or most available target.

Topography:

- The third party is a necessary component in addition to an "original cause." The original cause may be a dog, person, squirrel OR situation – dogs in an aroused state at a door or fence, for example.
- The third party is someone (human or animal) who was not involved in the original context or circumstance. The third party was standing by innocently or approaches after the frustration has begun.
- Occurs frequently between dogs in the home. This may or may not be further complicated by status-related issues between the dogs. (See the chapter, "Aggression Toward a Canine Housemate," for more on this.)
- Once focused on the third party, the dog may resolutely hunt the third party down.

Common Antecedent Stimuli

- Provoked by frustration and over-stimulation, and maintained by rehearsal.
- Occurs when the dog is already in high-arousal mode.
- Often occurs in locations where dogs are liable to come into contact with each other because of restricted space (e.g., two dogs at the door in a foyer; two dogs running along a fence barking at the neighbor's cat).

Redirected Aggression often occurs between dogs in the same home, just because many opportunities present themselves for the behavior. For example, when the doorbell rings, dogs may be frustrated because they cannot get at the guest and unload on each other. They may also redirect their aggression onto each other just because they are fired up from the situation. This may or may not be further complicated by two of the dogs having status-related conflicts. My dogs, Jynx and Breanna, out of 8 dogs, would always choose each other to unload on at the door – that was not a "random" choice of a third party, so, knowing their history, I would classify that as redirected aggression as a symptom of status-related conflict.

Redirected Aggression is not accidental aggression such as the type that occurs when a person reaches in between two fighting dogs and gets bitten. With an accidental bite like this, the dog may not even be aware of what he is biting. Redirected Aggression is more deliberate. For example, my husband Steve once broke up a fight between my dogs Sport and Dervish. Steve had to use a little shoe leather, and once he broke Dervish's hold on Sport, Dervish turned around, gave Steve a warning snarl, and quite purposefully lunged at Steve. Overstimulation and frustration caused Dervish to "unload" on Steve. Normally Dervish is a reasonably nice dog, and very affectionate with his people.

Dogs are especially vulnerable to Redirected Aggression at territory entry areas, which are already highly charged. So, look for this with dogs at the door, running a fence, and at a gate. It also commonly occurs when walking two dogs on leash. The dogs see a squirrel. They both get excited and begin lunging and barking at the target. Frustrated by an inability to reach the original target, one dog attacks the other.

Common Behavioural Rule-outs:

Redirected Aggression pretty much always looks like itself, but may be more fully described by adding additional descriptors or classifications to *help define the trigger or function* of the aggression, if discernible. The redirected aggression may be motivated, mixed in with, or complicated by predation, territorial behaviour, or status-related conflicts. For example, I was lure-coursing with Breanna and was holding her, waiting for our turn. When the dog in the heat prior to ours was released from the starting box, Bree stared intensely and briefly struggled to follow. I reassured her, "Bree, wait, it's your turn next." Definitely NOT reassured by this information, she looked at me, whined and keened at the lure one more time, and sunk her teeth into my arm. This was redirected aggression, with a predatory component (her predatory arousal and frustration were being "unloaded" onto my arm).

TERRITORIAL AGGRESSION

Establishing and defending territory are basic behaviours in the majority of species.

A boundary (determined by the dog) will be actively defended against all parties that the dog decides are intruders. Most people say they wish a dog to defend territorial boundaries, but when a lawsuit results, they might change their mind.

Many breeds were bred to have a degree of territorial aggression. Many dogs express this merely as "watch-dog" behaviour; that is, the dog will bark to raise an alarm that territory has been invaded. In your average Labrador or Golden, this means that, once the people are in the door, they get the licking treatment. For the guarding breeds, an intruder remains an intruder, and these dogs aren't kidding. Many of the herding breeds have territorial tendencies and are willing to back it up. I have met many Australian Shepherds and Belgian herding dogs (Tervurens, Malinois) that are territorial. The Flock Guardians (Kuvasz, Komondors, etc.) are bred specifically for territorial behaviour. German Shepherd Dogs were bred to be a "living fence." A person would establish the boundary for the dog, then: nothing goes out and nothing comes in. Family members (those the dog is familiar with) are to be herded back into the territory and intruders are expelled by whatever force required.

Territorial aggression in particular becomes a problem for dogs who are unsupervised and *allowed to practice* the behaviour frequently, unchecked by their humans. This also becomes a problem for dogs who take the job overly seriously when people are entering territory, such as through your front door. If the owners of the dog have not made it very clear to the dog, through training, that *humans* are making the decisions about who enters the house, then the dog will certainly make those choices.

Topography

- Alarm barking.
- Very demonstrative and "Big" warning behaviours exhibited. These behaviours intensify as the distance between the dog and "intruder" decreases.
- The dog is defending a territory IN SPITE of cues that the approaching person or dog is not threatening.
- Defense of a specific area.
- Usually defending a familiar area. This area may have visible boundaries like a fence. The area may have invisible boundaries like an electronic fencing system. The area may be arbitrarily established by the dog and "maintained" by the dog via patrolling and scent marking (urine, feces, anal gland secretions, and scratching the ground are a few ways dogs leave scent markers).
- The dog defends the area or uses agonistic display (that can escalate over time into a bite) against unknown or "invaders."
- The area defended may be permanent, like a yard, or mobile, such as a car.
- The area defended may be established over a long period of time or the dog may decide that he owns the "territory" after being in it briefly. As an example, an intact male dog is being walked on leash. He is in the area five minutes, marks a few bushes and feels as if he has established a territory and begins to defend the area.

Common Behavioural Rule-Outs

- Frustration behaviours such as those related to fence-fighting.
- Learned Aggression. (Some dogs will "learn" this behaviour from other dogs they are living with. They might not have these tendencies, but mimic the behaviour of their housemate.)
- Fear Aggression.

USING CLASSIFICATION AS AN ACCURATE DESCRIPTOR

When specifying a classification for aggression, use as many as necessary to correctly describe what is happening. For instance, if dog-to-dog aggression is occurring between your dog and a dog you meet on the street at random, is the display directed towards ALL approaching dogs? Some? Loose dogs only? Dogs on leash with people? Does the aggression occur only if the other dog approaches your dog's yard? Or only if the dog approaches you, and only if your dog is on a leash?

The following is a classification for a dog who is guarding chew toys from the other household dog, but not from people, and it is not known whether the dog will guard the toys from people the dog doesn't know: Resource Guarding (fuzzy toys and rawhides specifically, to date), directed toward canine housemate only; known human family members excluded; strange humans unknown. The more specifically you categorize, the more informative the classification is.

As you see, the above is not really dog-to-dog aggression because the incident is isolated and involves an object.

SUMMARY FOR CLASSIFICATION OF PROBLEM AGGRESSION

I am of two minds when it comes to classification. In the hands of experienced dog trainers, it is a useful tool. Classification can help predict the variety of circumstances where one might see the undesirable behaviour. For example, determining that a dog is classified as having "possessive aggression, food-related," tells us the dog guards it food aggressively. Since any behaviour is at risk for generalization (a tendency that is greatly wished for when training desired behaviours!), the trainer can predict that the dog *may* also be at risk to guard its toys, its crate and even its owner as favored possessions. Thus, the proactive owner does a protocol for Resource Guarding in general, as well as working on the known specific context. By doing so, other related problem aggression is prevented or minimized. At the very least, a lot of information is garnered about the dog's behaviour when one determines the classification. Now the owner has a much better shot at predicting under which circumstances the undesired behaviour will surface. This information increases the probability of success for owner and the dog through training and management.

However, classification can have its drawbacks. "Classifying" too quickly with insufficient information, or *labeling*, can lead the trainer and owner to close their minds to possibilities. Labeling leads to not being imaginative and experimental in the training protocol. It can send one down the wrong protocol path altogether. It can lead to not seeing *detail* as one tries to fit every behaviour into a narrow description, whether it belongs there or not. (Is the dog aggressively guarding me from other dogs because it guards its possessions and is resource guarding? Or is the dog, instead, displaying protective aggression, or just aggression the dog learned was effective to get something it wanted?) Labeling the dog as a "resource guarder" may obscure the specific, fine detail in this particular dog's repertoire, making it harder to modify his behaviour.

Another problem with classification is that much of the dog's behaviour is not so easily pigeonholed as we would like! Often the dog is presenting with aggression that falls into several different categories, or it is difficult to determine exactly what function the aggression is serving for the dog, which makes actual classification difficult to do. It may be more helpful, if these lines are blurry, to *concentrate on what reinforc-*

ers are sustaining and/or perpetrating the behaviour.

Another great area to attack are the triggers that cause the behaviour. Sometimes, after you work on these specifically, and you get a few layers peeled away, the function the aggression is serving becomes clear. At that point you can come to better conclusions about classification and future protocols. For example, a dog is presenting with assertive, self-confident aggressive display. At first glance, this might look like control-complex aggression. But as you learn about the case history and work the dog, it becomes apparent that the dog was not ever systematically taught about human body language and was not taught basic husbandry behaviour (Handling & Restraint). The aggression probably started out as a defensive behaviour, rooted in fear. But, as the dog gained success in keeping feared advances away, the aggression took on an on-the-offensive air.

In short, classifying the behaviour, understanding the function the behaviour is serving for the dog, knowing the dog's prior history – all are pieces to the puzzle. The more pieces you have, the quicker you can put the puzzle together. All will help you predict future circumstances under which reactive behaviour might occur. All will help you plan a good behaviour modification protocol. All will help in "tweaking" the protocol to fit the individual dog.

All that said, I would advise folks not to spend a great deal of time agonizing over specific classifications, worrying that you don't know prior history, or mourning the fact that you can't put your finger on the original function the behaviour was serving for the dog. Some of those answers may be buried deeply in the dog's unknown past or there may be several "layers" of undesired habits that overlay the "core" behaviour by the time you get your hands on the dog.

The less experienced you are with a wide variety of dogs (and therefore what constitutes normal dog behaviour and typical breed behaviour) the more this holds true! *Emphasize "getting the job done."* Ultimately, with behavioural modification, what counts is the successful long-term change of the undesired behaviour. Focus on working through the protocols, on your dog's observable behaviour, on eliminating the reinforcing circumstances that are sustaining the behaviour, and on the triggers that elicit the behaviour!

To accurately classify aggression one must:

- Have good knowledge of breed tendencies. At the same time do not be tempted to immediately label an animal just because he is of a certain breed – let each animal tell you the extent to which he exhibits breed tendencies. I was at my human physician's office for a routine visit, and at the end of the visit he wondered if he could ask me some questions about his girlfriend's dog. I inquired as to the breed, and he said it was a two-year-old male Rottweiler. Immediately I was thinking aggression issues, because of the breed, gender and age of the animal. (Jumping to conclusions and labeling ... "Try Again" for me!) His question actually was an anthropomorphic, but very considerate, thoughtful one: Did the dog see him as an intruder in the household? Doing the clinically correct thing, I inquired about the appearance of the dog's behaviour toward him: Was the dog friendly with him? Did the dog allow him to pet him and would the dog play fetch games? Had the dog ever growled or approached him in a tense or stiff manner, any pilo-erector reflex, dilated pupils, stiff slow movements? The answer was that the dog slobbered all over him all the time, followed him around and was friendly and gentle. Obviously the dog was not presenting with any kind of aggression at all.
- Have seen a vast number of dogs to determine what constitutes a "normal" (vs. abnormal) continuum of behaviour.
- Refer to a veterinarian for physical rule-outs and for diagnostics of pathophysiological diseases.

Many clients who bring dogs with aggression problems do not have the above, excepting a vet to take the dog to for physical rule-outs. They are quite short in the experience department. Yet they still wish to work with their dog. True, they have consulted with me, but when I give them a classification of the aggression it doesn't really tell them what to do. What does make sense to them, and starts teaching them to problem solve effectively when I am not there to help them, is:

- understanding dog language so they can be proactive;
- identifying triggers and modifying behaviour surrounding those;
- identifying what is reinforcing, thus maintaining, the behaviour.

This places the dog's inappropriate behaviour into a realm that they can work with. Observable behaviour is behaviour that can be modified. Identifying triggers is something they have already done. Understanding dog language and how dogs learn gives them the tools they can use to modify the dog's behaviour.

The bottom line is: the owner of the dog is the one faced with the "grunt work" of doing the protocols and managing the dog's environment on a daily basis. Because of all the rescue work I have done with dogs who have unknown histories, I learned that: If a behaviour is observable, it is modifiable. To begin the work, I need only to:

- Know what undesirable behaviour I want to change.
- Identify the circumstances under which the behaviour manifests.
- Have a desirable behaviour I wish the dog to exhibit in place of the undesirable behaviour.

Even if all you can do at this time is list the events and triggers, you are off to an excellent start. You can begin to immediately modify the behaviour surrounding each trigger. The next step is to be proactive to the nth degree so the animal is not allowed to practice behaviour that is undesirable. Every time you teach your dog a new behaviour to use to cope with a trigger that causes her to be in an aroused, stressed, or defensive state, you have "padded" that context for the dog. If you install several behaviours, you have increased the safety level of this animal quite a lot, as she can then access several "other" behaviours prior to reaching the "I-use-teeth" behaviours.

Classification can serve a purpose in the overview of the problem, as long as you do not allow the process of classifying the behaviour to stymie the effort you spend on the details of "fixing" the problem. This is a help to those of you who are on the front lines working with people who have problem dogs. Classification aids you in coming to a prognosis and in adding or expanding protocols.

In the real world, the classification and the protocol process are intertwined, and not necessarily easily made into a rigid chronological course. You may do a bit of one, then a bit of the other, which gives you ever more information about the dog you are working with. Each bit of information provides you with arrows pointing the direction to go next.

Let us separate Diagnostics from Classification. Diagnosing (requiring a veterinarian) whether a dog is chemically abnormal is useful in some cases. It will tell the owner if supplemental pharmacological treatment to aid training will be of use, and will also prepare the owner for a longer, more difficult training process. Pharmacological intervention is not a "magic pill." If that were the case, none of us would be inventing and implementing these long, and sometimes difficult, behaviour modification programs. Pharmacological intervention is just one more tool, and is only applicable in some cases.

16

This chapter discusses Chronic Environmental Stressors. These are chronic problems with training technique and/or the environment your dog lives in. These are traps that you want to be aware of as a trainer. Aggression is often a symptom of one or more of these specific stressors.

Entrapment

Entrapment transpires when you ask for or encourage the dog to behave in a certain way, and then the behaviour is punished when it does occur. The best example of this I can think of is, unfortunately, also one of the most frequently observed ways that humans train a dog to come when called. The dog is called, and the response is tardy (the dog does not come immediately). Eventually, when the dog does come to the owner, the dog is punished for not responding immediately. This is confusing for the dog, who finally did come when called (albeit not with the quick response desired) and then was punished for doing so.

The dog does not "get" from this sequence that Coming When Called is a good thing. She entirely misses the whole "tardy was being punished" because of the poor timing of the punishment.

If this happens, the tardy response must be worked on as a separate exercise to convey to the dog that a timely response is part of the exercise.

Frustration

Frustration results when the dog is prevented from fulfilling a desire or accomplishing a purpose. Frustration causes a dog to become aroused and over-reactive. Extreme frustration may certainly result in the aggression being redirected from the original source of arousal to whatever or whomever is next to the dog at the time.

Barriers, like leashes and fences, are a huge source of frustration for dogs. Being thwarted by a human who is physically restraining the dog, such as by holding her by the collar, is a source of frustration. Barriers, leashes and humans are all a part of daily life for a domestic dog and are requisite for keeping your dog safe. Therefore, a dog needs to develop coping mechanisms to deal with frustration, because surely your dog will encounter this on a daily basis.

Uncontrollable and unpredictable anxiety and frustration, where the dog cannot alter the environmental factors, causes maladaptive behaviour. We see the symptoms of this: obsessive compulsive behaviour, panic attacks such as occur with separation anxiety, and aggression.

Many dogs are already placed in situations, by living with humans, where they are under-stimulated and under-exercised, which can lead to being easily frustrated as they are already biologically "under siege."

Another contributing factor to frustration lies with how people live with dogs. Dogs who live with little structure are simply not provided with opportunities to learn how to cope with frustration in an acceptable manner. People have a tendency to allow dogs to live a life free of structure, in part, due to these reasons:

- The owners are over-indulgent (they love their dog and this is how they express this emotion).
- The owners are passive by nature and the dog may be naturally "pushy."
- The owners are too lazy to provide the animal with consistent rules.
- The vast majority of dog-owners do not understand about how important structure is for their dog. Therefore they are not providing consistent rules just because it has never occurred to them to do so.
- People are uneducated about how to provide structure for the dog in such a way that makes sense to the dog and "feels" humane to the owner.

A dog can get frustrated if he lives in a house where he feels "under attack." Perhaps another dog in the house is constantly controlling or aggressive toward him, or he is often "teased" by human members of the family. Such confrontation can lead to tremendous stress and frustration and to a defensive-aggressive reaction.

Frustration is a main component of redirected aggression. Frustration can lead to extreme arousal levels very quickly, particularly if the dog is displaying predatory behaviour and is prevented from obtaining the prey object.

Very small amounts of frustration can actually improve learning. I use this when I am teaching a retrieve. At first, I will reinforce the dog for small bumps to the dumbbell with her nose. Once I have reinforced a few of these in a row, I withhold reinforcement. In frustration, the dog will escalate the behaviour and give a harder bump to the dumbbell. "Hey, I've been getting a cookie (results) for this! Didn't you notice!" I reinforce this, and then reinforce only the harder "bumps." Then I withhold reinforcement again, and if I juggle my reinforcement schedule properly between reinforcement, extinction, and frustration, eventually, just like clockwork, the dog will escalate the behaviour until she takes a tentative "bite" at the dumbbell.[1] The frustration remains controllable by the dog, therefore it never reaches a point where the dog needs to be overly concerned or aroused.

Make the distinction between chronic or intense frustration, which is the real "trap" to avoid, not the small frustrations that inevitably occur or are valuable during normal socialization and learning.

Arousal Levels

All dogs get "fired up" over something. There are two components to observe when you are evaluating high states of arousal:

- Some dogs become aroused very easily (reactive under low stimuli).
- Some dogs have extremely slow recovery – they take a long time to return to a calm, rational state.

Both are indicative of dogs who are going to present or are already presenting with aggression.

My Basset would lift his head, see the family cat, and lay his head back down and continue snoozing. My terriers, when the same cat crosses the yard twenty times a day, explode off the sofa and hit the bay window with enough force to make it shake. Screaming and leaping, they love to get themselves worked up over this cat. The adrena-

1. Of course, what you are literally reinforcing in this particular case are the "extinction bursts." Instead of allowing them to peter off into nothingness, you "catch" the extinction burst and reinforce it.

line rush is fun! Obviously the Basset is not as prone to this addiction. The terriers, however, need to work on lowering their reactivity level on cue from me. It is important that I can interrupt their display and have them come to me even when they are in this excited state.

Commonly high arousal levels occur because humans allow them to occur, thus inadvertently reinforcing them. Sometimes humans encourage these because they think it is cute in the puppy. This same level of arousal in a sixty or seventy pound adult (or even a twenty pound adult), with an adult dog's attitude, may be quite another matter.

A dog doesn't start out as an eight week old puppy attacking people at the door and hospitalizing them. The pup is allowed to run to the door and behave wildly. Soon the doorbell itself causes the cascade of chemical reactions that is observable as high arousal. The dog practices this behaviour frequently (rehearsal) and the owners are even delighted because the dog is barking an alarm and behaving "protectively." The stage is now set for the dog, as he reaches social maturity, to start becoming serious, and possibly dangerous, about territory entry.

When the dog begins to alarm the owners with excessive, well-rehearsed displays, they begin to restrain the dog at the door by holding the collar as they answer the door. Now, as the hapless guest enters and the dog growls, the owners drag the dog backwards as she continues to look at the intruders and warn them against further approach. Frustration builds. In many homes, the owners are even reassuring the dog as they restrain her and she snarls and lunges at visitors. The dog takes all of this as approval for her current behaviour, as well as associating this emotional state of frustration with guests entering territory.

Of course, not all dogs bite in this instance. Friendly dogs just become ever more frenzied in their greeting behaviour until the owners feel as if they are running the gauntlet every time they answer the door (not to mention the poor guest who is mobbed, slobbered on, and knocked off balance by the exuberance of the inappropriate greeting).

Obviously, the best time to intervene here is when the dog is a puppy. Teach the dog right from the start how to reduce his arousal level when someone comes to the door and give him alternative greeting bahaviors to practice. (See protocols: "Training a Polite Greeting" and "Territory Entry.")

The most common action that occurs at doors and *other situations of high arousal* is that the owner constantly PHYSICALLY restrains the dog by the collar, as the dog lunges forward (because the handler doesn't know how else to control the dog). In addition to the physical restraint, the handler adds one of these two ingredients, or worse yet, alternates between both:

- The owner scolds the dog and admonishes her to "calm down."
- The owner reassures the dog to "calm down, it's okay."

The dog then becomes frustrated and acts out the frustration in one of two ways, depending on both her nature and her history:

- The restraint and the scolding by the owners to "calm down" adds anxiety to the mix, resulting in an ever-more-frenzied reaction. The dog becomes a whirling dervish at the door in the effort to greet the guest. The anxiety increases the dog's physical activity often resulting in more punishment, which increases the anxiety ... you get the idea. This is called a punishment cycle. OR the dog becomes so frustrated and anxious that she begins to display aggressive behaviours toward the person entering or redirecting aggression toward the person holding her back, the one who is "preventing her from taking care of this 'problem'."
- The restraint and reassurance of the owner to "calm down, it's okay," sounds like reinforcement to the dog, thus strengthening and validating whatever emotional state the dog is currently in. This means the super-friendly dog is beside himself, perhaps urinating in excitement, but at the very least in a state of greeting frenzy. This may feel to the

> guests exactly like a shark feeding frenzy, as they are assaulted with joyful body slams and happy little claws. The dog who is already figuring that this intruder doesn't belong has this feeling heightened by the owner cooing "it's all right, honey, they won't hurt you." You might as well be saying "Go ahead honey, tear up our nice visitor. Mommy/Daddy likes that."

The above examples are just a few of many concerning high arousal levels and the huge effect they exert on a dog's behaviour. The gist of all this is: Arousal levels have a terrific impact on the dog's perception of the situation and the way the dog handles that situation. When your dog is going down the path of arousal, what begins as a trickle may soon become a tidal wave. Obviously, then, teaching the dog switching exercises and anchoring exercises becomes very important. These give the dog ways to regulate arousal levels and alternative behaviours to cope with situations that stir him up. These are discussed at length in the Level I Protocols.

The degree to which you can modify the dog's arousal levels (and behaviour) and how much self-control the dog develops are dependent on the big two: nature and nurture. Depending on the individual's basic temperamental make-up, the dog may learn to exert amazing control over herself, remaining calm in a situation that previously had her climbing the walls. Depending on your skill and commitment, and how much you are willing to manipulate the environment (management), you may gain 90-99% behaviour change in the dog.

Sometimes it is not a question of "how" fired-up the dog gets, but "what she does" when she gets fired-up. Whenever I watch Flyball I am amazed. The potential is very high at this activity for redirected aggression or predatory drift to occur. The dogs are in a high state of arousal. Prey behaviours have been encouraged. Yet there are relatively few incidents because the dogs have been trained to focus on a specific prey object. If the handlers get a dog who is displaying aggressive tendencies and does not readily respond to the training, they replace the dog on the team.

I have dogs at home that just would not ever be safe under those circumstances no matter how much training and/or behaviour modification that I did, just as I have dogs at home that would be perfectly safe in that context with very little training. Some dogs are just not temperamentally prepared to handle this level of arousal without becoming a slave to predatory or aggressive behaviour. As soon as your dog ceases to respond to known cues, she is entering this emotional state and is Hanging Up The Phone.

Conflict

Conflict can occur in varying degrees and, of course, not all permutations of conflict will cause an organism to behave in a maladaptive way. You are in conflict several times a day under normal circumstances. Do you have a burrito or sweet and sour chicken for lunch? Do you paint your living room blue or taupe? These situations result in small hesitations regarding your decision.

When conflict is inescapable and it has been learned that making a "wrong" decision can have severe emotionally or physically painful consequences, then we have the makings of stress, anxiety and aggression.

Conflict can create havoc in a life. If the conflict is severe and chronic, a maladaptive response will often develop in an attempt to cope with it.

Types of conflict include:

Approach/Avoidance

> occurs "...when the behavioral goal is both attractive and aversive" (Lindsay, 2000, p. 346).

Dogs wish to approach and interact with people, but do so by jumping. Then people step on the dog's back toes, kick him, knee him, or hold and pinch the dog's paws. Depending on the amount of pain or trauma this causes the individual dog, now we have a dog that wishes to approach and is highly motivated socially to do so, but is afraid to approach because of past experiences. Ambivalence is not a pleasant emotion! This is not always the cause of, but can lead to, behaviour such as submissive urination (not to be confused with excitement urination), defensiveness, or avoidance.

Avoidance/Avoidance

> "occurs when behavioral alternatives are both in some way aversive, something akin to being placed 'between a rock and a hard place'" (Lindsay, 2000, p. 346).

This immediately brings to mind those persons who, in the name of "proofing" their dogs, place the dog on a sit stay and then put a leash on the dog and have someone pull the dog off the sit stay so they can punish the dog for "breaking" the sit. The dog is in a stressed internal state because, if he resists the pull, he is still being punished for staying by the pulling that is occurring. The experienced dog also knows he has been told to Stay and is perhaps nervous about moving because of past harsh physical correction for moving. If he does not resist the pull and gets up, he will be punished. If he resists the pull, he will be yanked on until he gets up so the handler can administer a correction. Lose-lose proposition for the dog.

As an aside, you can use the above technique, but by slightly altering the consequences, help the dog to understand that resisting pressure on a stay will earn them reinforcement. Instead of punishing if the dog breaks, just neutrally replace him in a Sit. Give a very small pressure, not so much that the dog moves, and quickly give the dog a treat for remaining in place BEFORE he moves. Gradually increase the pressure on the collar, reinforcing for appropriate behaviour each time you increase the pressure. Now instead of conflict, you have promoted understanding.

Approach/Approach

> "occurs when two behavioral alternatives are nearly equally attractive and difficult to choose between" (Lindsay, 2000, p. 346).

This type of conflict appears to be the least evil of the three categories. We are actually utilizing this when we do a move-away exercise as described in the protocol entitled "Cease & Desist." By distancing the dog from one desirable item, we decrease the availability/desirability of that item and, just by proximity, increase the availability/desirability of the handler. The distance helps to make the decision easier, actually removing the conflict for the dog.

The Classic Scenario: Fight vs. Flight

The first two options commonly accessed when in an aroused state are flight or fight-related behaviours. Some dogs avoid trouble, while others, faced with similar stimuli, get embroiled in aggressive confrontations. Why does one dog choose to fight in potentially aggressive situations, while another chooses flight?

The two big reasons are:
- he can't leave.
- he thinks he can't leave.

A dog displays active defensive behaviour because he doesn't think he has any choice. Once this occurs a few times (or, in some instances, there is one-trial learning) the response becomes *habit* – the behaviour the dog accesses FIRST when presented with a particular stimulus.

Examples:
- The dog is physically restrained in some way that prevents him from using flight. Leashes, fences, corners – all of these are everywhere, and are necessary for keeping our domestic dogs safe from harm, but can contribute to frustration, thus encouraging aggressive encounters.
- The dog tries flight, but it does not make the environment safer. The option that remains is "fight."
- The dog is of a fearful nature, and is more likely to present with defensive behaviours than flight because of innate or inherited tendencies.

- The dog is of an assertive nature and has had success with confrontation.
- The dog has learned to fight. Flight is no longer accessed as a first option because it has a history of not working to alleviate the situation. The dog has learned that a defensive or confrontational display does gain relief. Basically, avoidance hasn't worked, but confrontation or defense has.

Dogs universally come with low impulse control and prefer instant gratification and direct access to resources. (Are humans so different? Impulse control is learned behaviour, no matter the species.) If you do not intentionally teach impulse control, how can you be sure it will be there as part of the dog's behavioural repertoire? Low impulse control generalizes into an inability to cope with frustration, a state that domestic dogs must deal with on a daily basis. Dogs need to learn to cope with the frustration of not being able to chase the paperboy or reach the squirrels or take the food off the counter, or of being restrained by humans – the list is endless. The majority of dog owners leave this all important concept to chance, mostly because they do not understand how impulse control permeates the way the dog handles each and every event in daily life.

Obviously, it just comes easier for some individual dogs to cope with stressors present in the environment, but if you don't "test" this ability with training, how do you know how your dog will behave when "under fire?"

Section IV

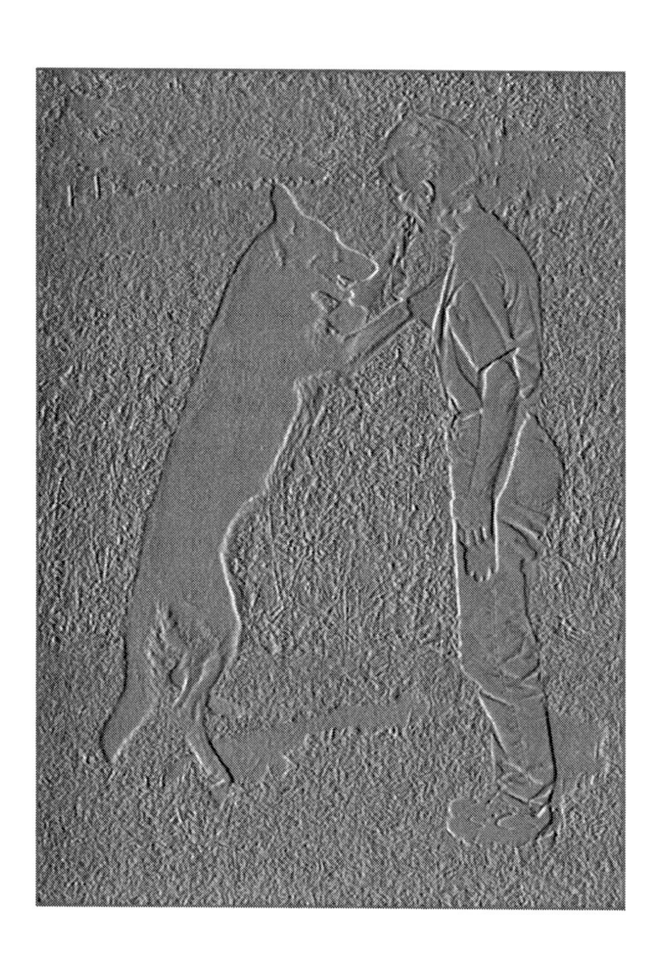

Laws Of Learning

It's all about Teamwork

17

THE LAWS OF LEARNING – EDUCATION FOR EVERYONE!

The protocol for any behaviour is based on The Laws of Learning, so a working knowledge of how the dog learns and how to best establish a communication system with the dog is *required.* This is explained in greater detail in my book *Positive Reinforcement: Dog Training in the Real World* (2001). There are also many helpful books on this topic listed as suggested reading in an appendix of this very book in your hand.

Learning occurs through experience and involves making judgments about current and future behaviour based on what was experienced in the past.

Animals learn primarily by *association.* These associations will occur whether you are consciously training your dog or not. The dog is making associations (picking up patterns of events) all the time. "Learning" a behaviour involves making an association (learning a pattern): a certain stimulus will predict the occurrence of another stimulus. (A stimulus is an event that motivates a response from your dog, or an event that she "notices.") From the dog's point of view:

- I hear "Sit."
- I assume a certain position.
- I receive a cookie.

Classical Conditioning

Classical conditioning involves an animal making an association between a neutral (unknown or unnoticed) event and a meaningful event (one that already elicits a response from the animal). The most common example of this is of a dog making an association between a bell ringing and his food appearing. After the bell (the neutral – unknown or previously unnoticed – stimulus) is *paired* with the food (known, meaningful stimulus), the dog *associates* hearing the bell with getting food. We know that the dog makes this association because he salivates when he hears the bell in absence of the food. This salivation is the *proof* that classical conditioning has taken place.

Classical conditioning involves specific elements. The bell, the food, and the salivation in the above example all have technical names. The *Unconditioned Stimulus* is the known, meaningful stimulus – in the example, it is the food. The *Unconditioned Response* is an unlearned, automatic response that comes "hardwired" in the individual and is not based on the individual's experience. It is a reflexive, instinctual response that occurs across the whole species. Examples, in humans, include sweating under stress or squinching up your face when lemon juice is squirted on your tongue – stuff that happens without you thinking about it. (This is significant because it means that the response is strong and not under conscious control.) In the above example, the Unconditioned Response is the dog's salivation when the food is presented. So, the meaningful Unconditioned Stimulus (food) produces the automatic Unconditioned Response (salivation).

The new, neutral stimulus is called the *Conditioned Stimulus* (you are *conditioning*, or teaching, the animal to associate it with the Unconditioned Stimulus). In the example, the Conditioned Stimulus is the bell. It has no meaning to the dog until he learns to associate it with food. You know that this association has been made because the dog salivates in response to the bell alone, just as he does to food. Thus, salivation is the *Conditioned Response*; the Conditioned Response and the Unconditioned Response are always *exactly the same response*.

So, there are four crucial elements here, just to summarize (stick with me here!):

- The Unconditioned Stimulus (UCS) – meaningful event (e.g., food)
- The Unconditioned Response (UCR) – automatic response to UCS (e.g., salivation)
- The Conditioned Stimulus (CS) – neutral event (e.g., bell)
- The Conditioned Response (CR) – same response as the UCR, but now given to the CS, too

The learning occurs when the dog associates the UCS with the CS. This happens because the UCS and the CS are *paired close together in time* (ideally within about half a second). That is, over and over, the bell is rung just before the food is presented. Because these events repeatedly occur close together, the dog learns to associate them. He picks out the pattern: bell means food is coming. The formerly neutral CS takes on meaning.

More formally, the training would look like this:

1. Feed the dog, which evokes a salivation response. This salivation response occurs in a hungry dog with no prior training. This food is the UCS, because the dog reacts to it consistently with no prior conditioning.
2. Now add the CS. Ring a bell just prior to presenting the food to the dog. This is the CS, because it *currently* has no meaning for the dog.
3. After this pattern has been repeated a few times, the animal learns that the CS (the bell) predicts the arrival of the food.
4. Once this learning occurs, the bell evokes a salivation response (conditioned response), even in the absence of the food.

There are many examples of classical conditioning that you can identify on a daily basis, and most of them are quite a bit more complex than the simple example above. Most responses observed in the real world are a complex mix of classical and operant conditioning (see next section). Before bed, my dogs all get a cookie. When they see me go into the bathroom to brush my teeth just before bed, they all gather around the dog cookie jar in anticipation. My teeth-brushing behaviour has come to predict cookies for my dogs. Several events have come to predict an end result – teeth brushing predicts cookies which causes the dogs to exhibit reflexive behaviours such as drooling in anticipation of the cookies.

Another example is the walk. Most dogs respond to their owner picking up a leash by getting all excited. This is because they have learned that your leash-picking-up behaviour predicts a walk. Again – picking up leash predicts walk which causes an increase in certain reflexive behaviours, such as respiration, because the dog becomes excited. A certain emotional state becomes associated with the simple gesture of picking up the leash.

You will learn to use classical conditioning to *change your dog's emotional state* by using a technique called Counter-Conditioning. If your dog responds in a fearful, nervous or aggressive manner to a given, predictable stimulus (trigger), it is possible to change the dog's paradigm about this event, person or context. Obviously, for the dog who is reacting in this manner, this event (stimulus) is currently associated with unpleasant consequences. This event has, in short, come to predict that unpleasant stuff happens to the dog in this context. For example, if you are walking your dog and every time she sees another dog she is given a collar correction and told "NO," the appearance of another dog has come to predict unpleasant consequences for your dog. When she sees another dog, she feels pain or is subjected to social disapproval. *The appearance of another dog has come to be a predictor of punishment.*

You can take this event or context and, over time, pair this now unpleasant event (the appearance of another dog) with looking at you and receiving a cookie, social approval, or a game, or all three. Eventually, your dog will see another dog and, instead of expecting the worst, she will eagerly look at you and engage with you, because the other dog has now become a predictor of reinforcement. In this manner, you are not just training your dog, you are *changing her motivation* to behave in a certain way. This in itself changes the dog's behaviour. She no longer is worried about the other dog, so she does not have to behave in a defensive manner. This is beyond damage control or management – this is the magic of behaviour modification.

The lovely thing is that you can observe reflexive behaviours in your dog that will tell you if the correct association is taking place. When your dog sees another dog and becomes aroused, you can see it in your dog's behaviour. His pupils may dilate, his tail may raise, and he may look very alert and still for a moment, then his flanks fall and rise more rapidly (indicating increased respiration), or he might begin to pant heavily. When you can walk by another dog after a protocol has been implemented, and your dog ignores the other dog or looks at the other dog with no change in his respiration, you know that you have altered your dog's paradigm. He is now more relaxed when other dogs approach.

This may take many many repetitions, and you will probably see spontaneous recovery of the old, undesired behaviour from time to time. As more time passes and you get in more repetitions of the desirable behaviour (paired with reinforcement):

- This sudden "outburst" of the old undesired behaviour (spontaneous recovery) will become weaker.
- There will be more time in between the incidences of spontaneous recovery.
- The duration of the old undesired behaviour will diminish.

Operant Conditioning

The theory of Operant Conditioning is based on Thorndike's Law of Effect, which states that future behaviour is based on consequences. Behaviour that is followed by a pleasant outcome is likely to be repeated. Behaviour that is followed by an unpleasant outcome will decrease.

Operant Conditioning recognizes this very simple fact and capitalizes on it. You will learn to use operant conditioning to manipulate consequences so that you can influence future behaviour.

Operant Conditioning acknowledges the animal's contribution to the learning process. The behaviour involved is voluntary or *offered* behaviour. The trainer *selects* desired responses and helps the animal to remember the behaviour as significant by manipulating the consequences.

This means closely controlling the environment so that the consequences are presented to your dog in a way that you can "drive" her *toward* a desired behaviour and *away from* an undesired behaviour.

What if the animal is not offering a desired response? Ah! There is a solution for that too! You:

- Reinforce a response that is "close" to what you are looking for and *shape* it toward the desired response, and/or
- Control the environment so you can manufacture reinforceable behaviour.

As an example, shaping a Recall would involve choosing behaviours that "approximated," or were close to, the end goal of having your dog come to you when cued with "Come." You would reinforce the following behaviours, raising criteria gradually:

1. First, whenever the dog stays near you.
2. Then, any time you move away from the dog and she follows.
3. *When the dog is already moving toward you,* say "Come" and feed her when she gets to you.
4. When the dog is moving away from you, begin to *run in the opposite direction or move away* from the dog and, *as she turns toward you,* use your cue, "Come," and feed her when she gets to you.
5. Finally, when the dog is moving away from you, use your cue, "Come," and feed her when she gets to you.

In real life, Classical Conditioning and Operant Conditioning are often intricately intertwined, as in the following example.

The object is to take the current behaviour and shape a desired response by providing relevant feedback through consequences. *Management* helps to both prevent rehearsal of the undesired behaviour and manufacture reinforceable behaviour. *Shaping*, an integral part of OC (operant conditioning), is the gradual raising of criteria. Just as you start with general math and work your way towards quantum physics, so must information be presented to the dog in small packages that can easily be assimilated. This means also that the dog gets lots of opportunities for reinforcement for appropriate behaviour, encouraging her to "do it your way" without adding fuel to the fire of reactivity and frustration. Classical Conditioning will occur as you change the dog's emotional response: pairing pleasant stuff, like treats, with previously arousing situations, so she associates the context with a relaxed and happy emotional state.

Let's say your dog is growling at people coming to the door and lunging at them. In designing a protocol for this dog, the first consideration is safety and preventing rehearsal of the behaviour. This means you must first practice management. If the doorbell rings, you must get your dog on leash. This protects your guest and your dog. The leash will also allow you gently guide the dog into a Sit if she does not respond to a verbal cue and prevents rehearsal of lunging. It will keep the dog near you and make the situation more controllable. Until you have *reliable* verbal control you MUST HAVE physical control.

The opportunity provided by management allows you to manipulate the consequences – that is OC. By teaching the dog to Sit instead of lunge, you are shaping observable behaviour from one form into another. (In other, less dangerous instances, the dog would be allowed more "room" to offer behaviour.)

By pairing appropriate behaviour (sitting quietly) with treats, and discouraging or controlling inappropriate behaviour (jumping, growling), the dog will learn to Sit and pay attention to you when guests come.

It is in teaching the dog to change her paradigm about people entering territory where the magic of behaviour modification occurs. Changing the consequences and providing the dog with feedback helps her to perceive this old context in a new and different way. As she gets rewarded for being calm when guests come, the arrival of guests becomes associated with pleasure and the calmness becomes an emotional habit. You genuinely change the emotional and sympathetic nervous system response. This is Classical Conditioning.

There are specific protocols included in this book to handle the above situation; I lead you through the process step-by-step in "Wait at the Door" and "Territory Entry and Appropriate Greeting Behaviours."

A Communication System

A specific communication system provides the essential tool you will use to change the behaviour of your dog. Behaviour Modification programs are based on using food and activities your dog finds fun, or items your dog wants, as aids in creating a working communication system between the two of you. You will take advantage of these items by pairing them with words and phrases that you wish the dog to respond to (cues). Reinforcers will also be used by pairing them with events to change the way the dog thinks about certain situations. You will manipulate events and behaviours by using classical and operant conditioning. Your goal is to actually change the way your dog "thinks" about a particular context. In addition to this, you will teach your dog to exhibit impulse control and *to* "think" instead of just react.

This information must be presented to your dog in a deliberate, thoughtful manner, and in a specific syntax, or your results will be disappointing. The laws of learning hold the key to this specific and madly successful communication system. When information is presented to your dog in a way that she *understands* it, she will be cooperative.

Some people do not like to use food treats. Maybe they haven't had the desired results in the past because they have not been using the food with precise timing and delivery. A less charitable reason is that some people like to "have power" over a creature who must accept the situation. For others, the behaviour change of having to carry treats is one that they must become accustomed to. Think carefully about why you wouldn't use food to train, and let me remind you that, while we are involved in retraining you as well, the dog's behaviour is the important subject here. Think of food as a tool, just like the collar, or the leash, or your voice. When you are hanging drywall, you can certainly do the job with a hammer and nails, but screws and a power driver not only finish the task more quickly, they do a superior job that is longer lasting as well. Just as in all other tasks, when training an animal, it is much easier if you have the *right* tools *and* use them correctly.

Overview for Teaching a Behaviour

The end result of training is to have a dog who responds predictably and reliably to cues. Stimulus Control means you can elicit a behaviour in the presence of a specific cue. It also means you can predict duration, frequency, and intensity of that behaviour. In its most basic sense, Stimulus Control means you can begin and end a behaviour on cue.

The following steps are required for teaching behaviour and getting behaviour under stimulus control:

1. The first component required is reinforceable (desirable) behaviour. Your job is to obtain voluntary behaviour. Or Manufacture Appropriate Behaviour using positive techniques and a non-threatening manner. Or choose behaviour the dog is offering to reinforce.
2. Use Management and Feedback to communicate what the desired behaviour is to the dog.
3. Use Shaping to mold the behaviour in small, easily understood steps. Build the behaviour by raising criteria.
4. Add a cue. This may be verbal or a signal. Sometimes it is best for the cue to be environmental (for example, the dog sees another dog and, without a cue from the handler, looks directly at the handler for advice).
5. Begin Challenges: Increase the level of difficulty to build reliability, fine-tune behaviour, and teach better coping mechanisms.

Now, just as your head is spinning and you are wondering how to do those five simple steps, relax and read on!

Carved in Stone – Laws Of Learning

Rely on Your ABC's

- A= Antecedent
- B= Behaviour
- C= Consequence

Behaviour is learned by associating the Antecedent (stuff that happens before a behaviour) and the Consequences (the stuff that happens after a behaviour) with the Behaviour in question.

If you want behaviour(s) to be learned, there are 3 Requirements that must be met for understanding to occur:

1. The *Antecedent* must be consistent and concise.

   You and your dog must both understand which *cue* belongs with which behaviour. You must both identify the cue as being THE CUE. When I ask people what cue gets their dog to lie down, many think that their dog has identified a verbal "Down" as the cue. But they don't actually get the behaviour from their dog unless they say "Down" *and* point at the floor. If you were able to ask both participants, the human would identify the cue as the word "Down," whereas my bet is that the dog interprets the word as extraneous and identifies the cue as the Pointing Finger.
2. The *Consequence* must be appropriate for the dog and the context, and must be on the correct Reinforcement Schedule.
3. The *Timing* must be precise: For optimum learning to occur, the Consequence (Reinforcement or Aversive) must be applied during the behaviour or within ½ second.

Above all, dog training involves communication. Manipulating Consequences is a big part of this communication. Consequences come in two flavors:

- Reinforcement, which increases behaviour.
- Punishment, which decreases behaviour.

Reinforcement is heavily relied upon because it creates stable, reliable behaviour without enhancing fear, defense, unpredictable avoidance responses, and other fall-out that is associated with punishers.

How to Establish Communication with any dog is discussed next.

Primary Reinforcement

- The scientific and technical definition of *Primary Reinforcement* is: Required for Survival.
- Required for Survival List: Food, Water, Air, Sex. You will, of course, need to make your own choices, but, from this list, my choice in training is to rely on Food.
- Training Treats are TINY! They should be about ½ the size of your little fingernail, or about the size of one tiny piece of dog kibble!
- Training treats need to be easily and instantly consumed. They need to be something your dog loves.
- Note: The Real "T" Word in training is Timing!

Primary Reinforcement is the way to initially open up communication lines. You don't have to teach the animal that this means "good" – the animal knows this already. Primary Reinforcement gives us a Common Ground to Plant Communication In! It provides a non-confrontational way to establish that you and the dog are in alignment, not at odds. Yo baby! Now we're on a roll!

Reward Mark

How Do You Stop Using Food? More Ways to Communicate Effectively

- Also known as: Conditioned Reinforcer, Secondary Reinforcer, Bridge, Event Mark

Food is used as a Tool to open up lines of communication. Once you have some "vocabulary" in common with your dog, you can begin to use your Reward Mark in lieu of food on some occasions, and, later on in training, on most occasions. The Reward Mark (RM) is a word or other signal (like a clicker) that you have presented contingently with a Primary Reinforcer until it becomes meaningful to your dog. The RM becomes a predictor of Reinforcement and *Marks* the event as "remember this – we'll need it again."

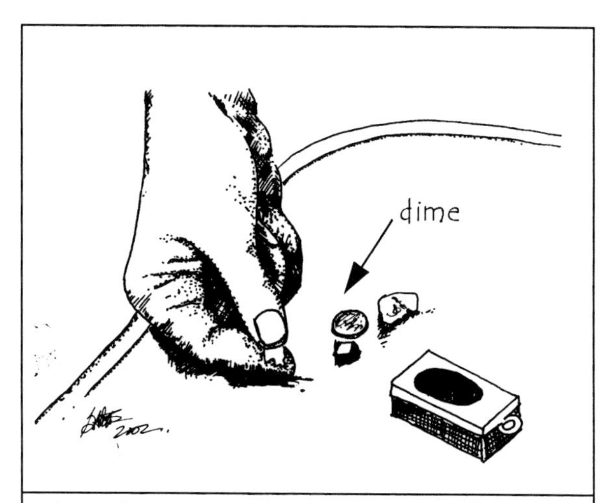

This is how you hold a treat most of the time, between your finger and thumb, to maintain control of the delivery of the food to the dog. The treats themselves are TINY! About the size of a dime, or much smaller for the smaller dogs. The clicker is used as a Reward Mark.

Necessary Tools

How Do You Install It?

NOTE: There is a specific protocol to teach you how to install the Reward Mark. (Refer to "The RM /NRM & Release Cue protocol.) Consider this a short course.

- Associate a word or signal (like the word "Yes" or a clicker) with a treat.
- After your RM (Reward Mark) is netting a strong response from the dog, you may begin to replace the delivery of the RM/Treat combination with only the RM on some occasions. A RM will need to occasionally be paired with food to keep it strong and valuable.
- A RM means "Yes, I really like that Behaviour and I want to see it again!"
- A RM is a predictor of Reinforcement.

For Optimum Communication You Must Also Install a No Reward Mark

This is technically a Conditioned Aversive, or, as some writers express it, an Extinction cue, although we are battling semantics here a bit. Suffice it to say: A No Reward Mark comes to mean "That Behaviour will get no cookies from me right now! I am looking for something else." You will, in essence, play a game of Hot and Cold[1] with your dog's behaviour using a RM (Reward Mark) and a NRM (No Reward Mark) to give your dog quick, precise and deliberate *information.* The NRM is a word that you use to signal to the dog that you wish to see a behaviour *other* than the one that has just been offered. A good NRM to use is "Try Again." My clients come up with excellent words like "Sorry" or "Not Yet." The NRM should be delivered in a *neutral and non-judgmental tone of voice.*

The NRM is used to provide information to the animal. The NRM is not a physical punishment nor should it ever be associated with any sort of physical punisher or severe social disapproval, such as a scolding tone of voice. Your dog does not have to cower, lower its ears or "look guilty" in order to receive information. Once your dog understands the NRM as information, following the use of a NRM, you will see your dog offer you a different behaviour (it may be very subtle) instead of the behaviour that you have just rejected.

I have heard some trainers state they do not use a NRM because their dogs are "too soft." If you are using your RM/NRM *as an information system,* this will not occur. Dogs who understand this system well respond to the NRM by working harder and offering other behaviour to "win" a RM; they don't shut down. When used properly, a NRM means Keep Trying. Dogs who are "cross-over" dogs (started with punishment-based techniques, then switched over to positive methods) may have a tough time with this at first because, for these dogs, making an incorrect decision or error has been dangerous in the past and has been associated with physical correction. The biggest problem with the "cross-over" dog is that, when you give her a NRM, she tends to shut

1. The child's game where an object is hidden and you direct another person toward finding it by using only the words "Hot" or "Cold."

down or stop offering behaviour. However, after a few months, particularly if the handler reinforces the dog for "trying" a few times, these dogs will come round.

It took my GSD bitch about 9 months to begin offering behaviour, but she also has trauma injuries to her back due to physical correction from a previous owner. Making incorrect decisions for her, with some of her prior owners, was very dangerous and painful indeed. The biggest challenge, then, with cross-over dogs is that you have to do a lot of manufacturing of behaviour.

Some dogs, once they understand a NRM well, do look disappointed, but they also continue to offer other behaviours in an effort to guess the right one. It's like watching the contestants on "Jeopardy!" When they get a wrong answer they look disappointed, too! Nevertheless, they continue to work for the prize, as will your dog, as you gain sophistication in communicating with each other.

A NRM does *not* take the place of "No," which in my house means "Don't ever do that again under any circumstances." Reserve NO for those times in which it is applicable. (Like counter-surfing. That is a "No" behaviour.)

How Do You Install It?

NOTE: There is a specific protocol on how to install the NRM. Consider this a short course, and use the protocol "The RM/NRM & Release Cue" to help you teach the NRM to your dog step-by-step.

- You can install a NRM "on the fly." I just begin using the NRM word as I am working the dog, to indicate to her that the behaviour she just gave me will not be reinforced because I want some other behaviour.
- Over the period of a few days, the dog starts to figure out that when she hears "Try Again," no food is forthcoming. In short, this word is a predictor of No Reinforcement for your current behaviour! Try Again
- You can also install the NRM deliberately, which may increase your dog's learning curve.

Here is an example of using the RM/NRM system to work with your dog. You have reinforced several sits and downs, but the dog is still making errors occasionally:

- If you ask for a Sit and get a down, say "Try Again."
- Pause for about ½ to one second. Then try asking again for the behaviour you wanted: "Sit."
- If the dog doesn't move, or looks confused, after another "Try Again," repeat the command and then try to "help" the dog with a lure or a hand signal. Another great strategy is to change your location by moving a couple of steps and repeat the cue again.
- When you get the correct behaviour, in this case a sit, say "Yes," then deliver the food treat.

In competition training, the Retrieve on Flat is a place one might use a NRM. If your dog runs out to retrieve the dumbbell, but then gets distracted and starts back without the dumbbell, say "Try Again," pause ½ second, and repeat your retrieve cue: "Get It." If the dog turns around and gets the dumbbell, say "Yes!" as she picks it up.

Try using the NRM for growling at an approaching person. "Try Again" as you redirect the dog's behaviour into a Sit and Relax behaviour or a Down or a Move Away (see protocols). Then, when the dog responds to the obedience command: "Yes!" and deliver a treat.

Canines as Scientists, or: How Does the Dog Pick Out a Pattern?

Your dog, without the benefit of Human Spoken Language, is maneuvering through her environment, trying to decide which behaviour patterns are to her best advantage. **Dogs use their behaviour as an experiment.** Just like you do. Your dog will perform some action and see what the results are. (How Scientific!) This enables your dog to make decisions about future behaviour. Strategies that do not work are quickly abandoned and successful strategies are accessed again.

How can we help our dogs choose behaviour patterns that we approve of? Is there a quick way? Yes! By correct use of *Reinforcement Schedules.*

Your dog "Picks Out The Pattern" by way of Reinforcement Schedules. There are two categories of Reinforcement Schedules, which in the technical literature is further broken down into subsets.

For our purposes, we can define the Reinforcement Schedules as follows:

A *Fixed Schedule* means that Reinforcement occurs consistently and predictably. The Fixed Schedule is used when a dog is first learning a behaviour. To teach your dog to Sit you would provide a primary reinforcement (food) each and every time your dog sat. This promotes the "sitting" behaviour so it will be repeated. It provides the dog with reliable feedback about which behaviour is currently desired. A Fixed Schedule makes a behaviour *consistent.*

A *Variable Schedule* means that Reinforcement occurs unpredictably. It is used to Maintain behaviour. (Once a behaviour is occurring consistently, you begin to reinforce occasionally instead of every time.) A Variable Schedule helps to make the behaviour *strong* and teaches your dog to be *persistent.* A Variable Schedule teaches your dog to remain on task. A Variable Schedule makes a behaviour resistant to extinction.

To understand Reinforcement Schedules well, it is also necessary to know about the different Stages that predictably occur when a dog is learning a task. Any behaviour will go through various stages of development.

Acquisition and Fixed Reinforcement Schedules

The first Learning Stage is Acquisition. The dog is learning a behaviour and needs to complete two essential tasks:

- Make a connection between the Behaviour and the Consequence.
- Make a connection between the Cue and the Behaviour.

This is why when you are teaching your dog a new task you: *Get the behaviour first. Then add the cue.* This is the proper order because dogs learn primarily from humans by association and experimentation. You cannot name the baby until it arrives, and you cannot name a behaviour that does not yet exist or have relevance for the dog. Once a behaviour is available (obtainable because it is offered or can be manufactured) you can begin the association that a particular "word" or cue belongs with a certain position or emotional state.

For the dog who does not know Sit, if that dog is standing while I am saying "Sit, Sit, Sit," just exactly what behaviour is this dog associating with the word "Sit?" He is associating the behaviour of standing (or jumping around or sniffing or whatever he is currently doing) with "Sit." The best way to teach a behaviour is to lure or manufacture (get) the behaviour somehow. To manufacture a Sit, a treat held over the dog's head is effective. Once you know you can manufacture the sitting behaviour, just as your dog begins to sit, you can begin to teach him the word that will become the cue to place his bottom on the floor. Just as those hind legs begin to bend, say "Sit." When your dog is sitting, use your RM and deliver a tasty treat. After several repetitions of this, your dog will begin to associate the word Sit with the behaviour of *beginning* to Sit and *remaining* in a Sit.

Manufacturing behaviour is all about obtaining voluntary behaviour. Do not place or force your dog into position. When the behaviour is voluntary, your dog learns to OFFER behaviour. Otherwise, you are teaching your dog to be passive and to force you to constantly remind, restrain, and bully her into "behaving." If you do your dog's "homework" for her, then how will she have the skills to pass the "test?" With proper feedback, you are placing responsibility on your dog to make decisions. This gives you the opportunity to provide meaningful information back to her. In this manner your dog learns a very important lesson: her behaviour has consequences.

BIG HINT: Don't add the cue until you have the Behaviour! This move will save you and your dog endless frustration with Missed Associations.

In the Acquisition Stage, it is important to provide consistent information to your dog, so the pattern (what behaviour has which kind of consequences and what cue is attached with this behaviour) is easy to establish. Contingency is one of those six dollar words that means two events "touched" (or, how quickly and reliably one event followed the prior event). Contingency is a big issue when animals are trying to establish a relationship between two events. If the events are not presented close together time, the pattern is difficult to establish, thus slowing the learning curve considerably. Indeed, if the timing is poor enough, the connection is not made at all.

When in the Acquisition Stage of a behaviour, use a Fixed Reinforcement Schedule:

1 Behaviour = 1 Cookie

To show why you need a Fixed Reinforcement Schedule initially, take the following quiz.

Pick out the Pattern:

Table 1: Pick out the Pattern. In 12 minutes, 6 Events occur at 2 minute intervals.

Trial #1	Trial #2	Trial #3	Trial #4	Trial #5	Trial # 6
Bell Rings	Bell Rings	Bell Rings	Bell Rings	Bell Rings	Bell Rings
½ second Pause	½ second Pause	½ second Pause	½ second Pause	½ second Pause	½ second Pause
I hand you an M&M™ candy	I hand you an M&M™ candy	I hand you an M&M™ candy	I hand you an M&M™ candy	I hand you an M&M™ candy	I hand you an M&M™ candy

Concerning Table 1: If you guessed that every time you hear the bell ring, you get an M&M, you are correct! Learning to associate the bell ringing with getting an M&M is easy because, on a consistent and predictable basis, there was a direct connection (contingency) between the bell and the M&M.

Table 2: Pick out the Pattern. In 12 minutes 6 Events occur at 2 minute intervals.

Trial #1	Trial #2	Trial #3	Trial #4	Trial #5	Trial # 6
Bell Rings		Bell Rings	Bell Rings	Bell Rings	
½ second Pause				½ second Pause	
I hand you an M&M™ candy	I hand you an M&M™ candy			I hand you an M&M™ candy	I hand you an M&M™ candy

Concerning Table 2: In this Session, no clear pattern is apparent. Yet many of our training sessions or interactions look just like this and have similar relevance for our dog. A pattern might become apparent over 100 Trials. You can readily see that for the best and quickest understanding in the fewest number of trials, FR-1 (Fixed Ratio Schedule, with 1 Behaviour = 1 cookie – the pattern in Table 1) is superior for *establishing a pattern.*

The Consequences must be consistent in the Acquisition Stage so your dog can figure out exactly which behaviour it is that you are applying R+ (Positive Reinforcement) to.

In the Acquisition Stage, your dog establishes the relationship between:

- Behaviour and Consequence (e.g., Sit = Cookie).
- Cue and Behaviour. You have added your cue or "Start This Behaviour Now" command (e.g., "Sit" means: assume a certain physical position).

Once these relationships have been established and the dog no longer needs any "prompting" with treats or hand cues and his butt hits the ground when you say "Sit," your dog has succeeded in making the A-B-C connection. Antecedent – Behaviour – Consequence. "Sit" = Sit position = cookie.

Now that this relationship has been well established, it is time to move the animal onto a Maintenance Schedule.

Maintaining Behaviour and Variable Reinforcement Schedules

To best maintain behaviour and strengthen the response, a Variable Reinforcement Schedule is used.

How can I create a Variable Reinforcement Schedule?

- You ask for two or three or more behaviours before you deliver a treat, although you may choose to use a RM frequently for behaviour you like. In short, you are asking for more behaviours from the dog, for less and less primary (food) reinforcement. (FYI: this is an example of a **variable interval schedule.**)
- You become unpredictable about when food treats are given (**variable interval**).
- Use dog kibble sometimes and pieces of cheese or other special treats sometimes (**reinforcement variety**).
- Use one treat sometimes. For Really Good Efforts or First Correct Efforts give your dog several treats (**variable ratio**).
- Use food sometimes, petting sometimes, and games sometimes as Reinforcers (**reinforcement variety**).**Intermittent Reinforcement**[1] can also be used. This means you apply food treats only to "best efforts."

A Variable Schedule, if executed properly, causes your dog to be ever more committed to responding consistently to your cue. Your dog will become more intense and persistent about working because the dog will "gamble." The dog will "take a chance" that reinforcement will occur *at some point, IF she continues to work.* The same principle keeps the gambler sitting at the gaming table. Your dog, however, knows it's a SURE DEAL if she remains on task.

Let's say that I request a Sit. My dog complies, with the attitude, *I sat. I bet I get a cookie!* I say "Yes," and request another behaviour (without delivering a food treat). I request Down. My dog complies with the attitude, *I better hurry and down. I didn't get the cookie last time, so I must be real close to a cookie!* I say "Yes," and request Stand. My dog complies with the attitude, *I need to watch closely so I don't miss an opportunity for R+.* I say "Yes" and request Roll Over. My dog complies and I say "Yes!" and deliver a food treat. My dog has the attitude: *All Right! I knew that cookie was on its way. I knew I was getting closer and closer to my reward! I know that if I persist and keep working I get what I want!*

Variable Reinforcement Schedules make behaviour more intense, stronger and resistant to extinction. They teach your dog to remain on the job, overcome adversity, and remain focused and working. Your dog learns to persist and win a reward for his efforts.

---

1. Intermittent Reinforcement is also known as Selective Reinforcement or DRE (Differential Reinforcement of Excellent Behaviour). For extensive discussion of differential reinforcement schedules, see the "Tools" chapter of this book.

Don't be surprised by this fact: when you *initially* place a behaviour on a Variable Schedule, it is common to see variable behaviour. As you persist, you will see the behaviour move consistently toward a steadily improving, much stronger response over several Trials.

When I first place the known behaviour of Sit on a variable schedule I will get:
- A % of Correct, but average, responses to Sit
- A % of Slow responses to the cue
- A % of "No" Sits
- A % of Perfect, prompt, "Best Ever" Sits

Over time, with persistence on your part and use of a Variable Schedule (especially, in this case, use of Selective Reinforcement – DRE), the percentage of correct responses will increase, and so will the "Best Ever" responses, while the "Slows" and "Nos" get weeded out because *those behaviours do not get reinforced.* Dogs don't waste their time on doing stuff that doesn't get a pay-off. (Not any different than you and me!)

How to Weed?

- Use a RM for all correct responses ("Yes" or a Clicker).
- Use a RM and deliver a food treat for some correct responses ("Yes" + a cookie).
- Use a NRM for all incorrect responses ("Try Again").
- Have a Street Party and provide Hazard Pay (big or special treats) for "Best Ever" responses and for first time learning breakthrough responses (First Correct Efforts).

As an example: My dog knows how to sit on command, but her response is sometimes slow. I want a prompt response to my command.
- I use a RM for all correct responses.
- No Sits get a NRM and I calmly re-place or re-cue for the Sit behaviour.
- Any Quicker-Than-Average Sits get a RM and 3 or 4 treats delivered individually, each with its own RM (e.g., Yes-cookie; Yes-cookie; Yes-cookie; Yes-cookie).

  As an alternative, I can use an extra-special treat – something I don't use often, like cheddar cheese or little pieces of steak. This is *Hazard Pay* – above average reward for above average effort.
- I stop reinforcing any of the slower responses, verbally or otherwise, and "notice" only the NEW criteria – quicker Sits.

  The first 3 or 4 Excellent Responses get Hazard Pay. Then I place this Excellent Response on a variable schedule.

For best results, to *Maintain* known behaviour, be unpredictable. My advice is that you also remain generous. If an exercise is difficult for your dog, don't be stingy with attention and treats. *Do* apply your attention and treats to appropriate behaviour!

These are just the basics of the Laws of Learning. Great books to help you learn more about training this way are: *Dog Training – The Gentle Modern Method* (Weston, 1990); *Don't Shoot The Dog* (Pryor, 1984); *The Culture Clash* (Donaldson, 1996); *How Dogs Learn* (Burch and Bailey, 1999); and *Positive Reinforcement – Dog Training in the Real World* (Aloff, 2001).

How Do I Know When to Use What Schedule?

1. Acquisition – Fixed Schedule

- Learning new concepts.
- Making the ABC connection (Antecedent-Behaviour-Consequence).

2. Fluency – Variable Schedule

Once the dog has made the A to B to C connection, you use a Variable Schedule. As your dog enters a stage of Fluency, you will observe:
- Increased rate of responding.
- More automatic responses.
- More consistent responses.

As you continue to reinforce known behaviours on a Variable Schedule, you will be advancing their strength.

3. Generalizing Behaviour

Generalizing behaviour means that you will be teaching your dog to provide consistent behaviour under a variety of conditions.

- Fixed Schedule when first introducing any new circumstance, then moving to a Variable Schedule as your dog gains confidence and proficiency in that particular situation.

By use of different Challenges[1], you explain to your dog exactly what this exercise means.

4. Maintenance – Variable Schedule

- Constantly check to see that skills remain sharp.
- Part of maintenance includes reviews. A Review might consist of a quick run through of the steps you used to originally teach the behaviour.

Steps To Success

- Have a Plan! Define the Task and have a clear vision of what you are asking your dog to do. Outline the steps you are going to use to get there.
- Limit New Skills. Work on one Skill at a time. When you are shaping a behaviour, you are working on one of three aspects: *Frequency, Duration* or *Intensity*. When you are working on a new step in an exercise or a new skill level, temporarily relax your old standards until you have the new skill taught. For example, if you are working on Stay exercises, work duration first. Stay very near your dog, and work up to 15 seconds. Then move one step away and reduce the time. Work the time up to the old level of duration from the new distance, and take another step back. Reduce the time as you increase the distance, working the time back up to the previous level.
- Are there any Prerequisites? Is your dog ready to learn this task? Before you can run you must learn to walk. Before your dog can "Stay" she must learn Sit or Down. "Stay" begins with one second, then two, then several, then a minute, then more.
- Successive Approximation, or Shaping, is very important. Your success rate will depend heavily on your ability to reduce an exercise into Baby Steps, for easy, quick learning curves, and to control frustration. Use these Baby Steps to raise criteria until you attain your Terminal Response.
- Experienced trainers expect the dog to give a lot of incorrect responses. This is an integral part of the learning experience for the one doing the learning. Allow a certain amount of experimentation and, at the same time, provide a clear path to the correct behaviour while placing roadblocks to incorrect behaviours.

  Note: If working with a dog who has aggression problems or who is over-reactive, you must be careful to keep the dog and others safe. Experimentation will be appropriate in controlled settings with many of the behaviours you teach your dog – but *not* in the case of aggressive behaviours specifically. That means that rehearsing aggression will not be allowed, and a roadblock *will always* be placed in front of that behaviour (using techniques that I explain to you as we go along).

  In other cases, for example when learning eye contact, allow the dog some incorrect responses in order to practice learning skills and to provide the dog with valuable information.
- If you have to explain it in a sentence or by using words your dog will never get it! Your dog is not a mind reader, either, even though she is a keen observer of body language. Help your dog succeed by using consistent cues.

---

1. A Challenge is an activity which helps to clarify the parameters of a behaviour for your dog. Challenges often take the form of adding distractions. In this situation, *help your dog to succeed.* As your dog learns to remain in a sit even when company comes in the front door, he is learning that sit means sit no matter what the situation is. The exercises in the "The Fix...Protocols" section of this book include examples of Challenges.

- Do not assume learning! We often assume learning where there is still only coincidence!
- Short, fun sessions spread over several days will net you better results than long, tiring drills. I work my dogs in very short bursts of just a few minutes at a time. Some dogs tolerate longer sessions, some do not. On a personal level, yours truly does not tolerate long sessions well, either! Integrate training into daily interactions.
- "No" isn't helpful! Use a positive directive, like "Leave It" or "Sit," to direct your dog toward appropriate behaviour. Then you have manufactured appropriate behaviour that you can apply R+ to. That is our goal! Give your dog information! About what to DO, not just what to avoid doing.
- If the key to Real Estate Sales is Location, Location, Location, the key to good training is Management, Management, Management! Control the situations and circumstances to the best of your ability. Be proactive by being alert to problems that could develop. Then make moves to prevent those problems. Practice safe procedures, such as keeping your dog on leash or in a fenced area when appropriate. Teach your dog new behaviours in a non-distracting environment where she feels "safe." Then move on to Challenges to increase your dog's understanding. These are just some ways to use Management as your main ally!
- Use the KISS Method of Training: Keep your talking and body language to a minimum and Keep It Simple, Simon! Do not get into conversations with your dog. Avoid phrases like: "Please, if you do this High Jump in Competition I will give you everything you want, forever," or "If you get into the trash again, you are down the road!" I know these phrases are uttered out of a wish to communicate with your dog in the way *you* understand best (spoken language), but they muddy the water of clear communication between human and canine. Make it a point to practice in front of a mirror so you can see your body language. Sure, tell your dog all your troubles, and all about your day – but save it for when you are cuddled up on the sofa together, not when you are training!
- Have the Vision – then Keep it! Keep your *Window of Expectation* narrow. If the dog isn't getting the exercise, go ahead and break the exercise down into smaller baby steps. Of course, in the beginning, be less demanding. And use successive approximation to make the exercises reasonable for the dog to learn. But do not reinforce low standards, nor allow your dog to practice behaviour you find inappropriate.
- Be flexible. Assess your data and make changes to your training program as you go along. Plans for your next session are based on results of the last session.
- Be a good record keeper. If you do not write down and keep a notebook on your training sessions, how will you know when you are making progress? We often fail to R+ progress in ourselves as well as our dogs, because we aren't aware we are making progress. Take notes!
- Provide appropriate consequences. Stop your dog from going down the wrong path with a NRM (No Reward Mark) and manufacture appropriate behaviour so you can apply R+. Occasionally, a well timed "NO," if warranted, followed by a positive directive, "Sit," is just the thing. Sometimes Management is the only answer. Use judgment and learn from your mistakes!
- Begin each training session with a quick review. Introduce new items or higher criteria. End with some behaviour your dog enjoys, or a game.

Before We Go Any Further:

If everyone who has contact with the dog is not going to participate in the behaviour modification protocols, neither must they interfere with the efforts being made by those doing the work. In instances of aggressive behaviour, the cooperation of all whom the dog comes into contact with will be requisite, particularly that of family members. In my experience, the trend with my clients is: unless the entire family is in concert, the results are going to be much less than ideal. In fact, the situation may not be workable at all. Dealing with the problem of the dog is enough;

one does not need conflict, infighting, and inconsistency amongst the family members as well. It is important that all family members and others with whom the dog is in constant contact are handling the dog appropriately and consistently. All for one and one for all is the motto!

You and your dog will make mistakes and errors in judgment. This will require patience with yourself and family members, as well as with your dog. However, if you continue to work consistently, you will net results.

Important Concept: Many people seem to misinterpret Positive Reinforcement Training to mean "permissive" training. Nothing could be further from the truth. Management, prevention and using food properly (as a tool to aid the learning process), are all important to your success.

Permissiveness and *inconsistent behaviour* on the part of the humans involved have no place in behaviour modification. If they are used, the results netted will reflect that!

Undesired responses are recognized. Often a NRM is used as information in lieu of a physical punisher. This way the dog gets INFORMATION about undesired behaviour. Positive Reinforcement as a technique promotes "work ethic" in the dog.

A dog with a "work ethic" is one who understands the Behaviour = Consequence connection. This dog understands that she can control the environment to a great degree by exhibiting desired behaviours, and it is to her benefit to do so. It also brings home the point that *you* are an integral part of the equation. *You* are the one who provides opportunities for R+ and consequences.

Working with a dog who includes you in the equation is ideal!

The alternative is working with a dog who has developed a strategy of subtracting you from the equation every chance she gets, because she considers you "in the way" of her access to the environment. Dogs also avoid working and "shut you out" because of confusion and/or fear. The dog has been punished and doesn't really understand exactly "why."

You are not being "permissive" by using positive reinforcement – as long as you are consistently reinforcing only the behaviours you want to see! You are not being permissive by avoiding or decreasing the use of punishment. The goal is to provide the dog with clear information so she can behave in a way you approve of and will be eager to work.

18

TOOLS

This chapter consists of the most common techniques used in a behaviour modification program. For more detailed information, refer to books specifically about Behaviour Modification, where you will find oodles of terminology and charts and graphs and history about Learning Theory. This volume is not intended to take the place of books that deal specifically with learning theory and the principles of behaviour modification. Knowledge is power, so I would encourage you to read the books listed in the Recommended Reading appendix of this book.

EXTINCTION

If a behaviour is being exhibited, it is being fueled by reinforcement. Sometimes the environment itself is reinforcing the dog. For example, if your dog jumps a bunny rabbit in the front yard, he will quite likely give chase and have a grand time doing so!

Extinction is a technique you can utilize in any behaviour modification program. Extinction occurs when all reward or *reinforcement is removed for exhibiting a specific behaviour.* When the reinforcement ceases to occur, so does the behaviour that it was sustaining.

Often reinforcement is occurring inadvertently, and is provided by the owner. Below are a few examples of how this can happen:

- The owner is unintentionally reinforcing undesired behaviour. An example is: reassuring the fearful dog.
- The owner is not *actively* participating in the dog's learning experiences and is not training the dog *specific* behaviours in certain contexts. This is an example of the owner not being proactive. Instead, the owner allows the dog to "train itself," and then assumes the dog will make all the correct decisions. For example, I never assume that my dogs will just "take it for granted" that human eye contact is friendly. Many dogs do not. I prepare all my dogs and all the rescue dogs I send on to homes by doing eye-contact exercises to the extent necessary for each dog, such as the ones described in the "Eye-Contact and Involvement" protocol in this book.
- The owner is not managing the dog's environment, and the dog is learning that he can "reinforce himself" by partaking of the environment, handily excluding the human from the equation. If the dog is allowed to run off leash without proper training, the dog quickly learns that he does not have to come when called if he prefers to chase a jogger down the street. A long line or drag line on the dog in the yard and at the park for several months will allow the handler to keep the dog safe AND to curtail the dog's activities, giving the handler a chance to teach the dog desirable behaviour in an *assortment* of

contexts, and to build a reinforcement history for desired behaviour.

- The owner does not recognize the canine body language that precedes risky behaviour. Because the owner does not intercede, the dog interprets the handler's inaction as neutral feedback (permission to proceed) or approval for his current behaviour. Therefore, the dog escalates the behaviour until it develops into a form the handler finally identifies as aggression. By this time, it is likely that the dog "gets results" from using the escalated form of behaviour.

If you are going to be a post, the dog will seek feedback from the environment.

- The handler notices marginal behaviour but does not identify it as *risky* behaviour. Because the handler does not intervene, the dog continues to rehearse undesirable behaviour on a low level. The handler does not try to intervene until the behaviour is extreme or excessive, by which time the dog has built up an extensive reinforcement history for undesired behaviour.
- Perhaps the behaviour is encouraged on a low level because the owner finds the behaviour flattering or amusing. The owner does not recognize that *for the dog* this is serious business.
- The handler does not recognize the marginal behaviour at all. The dog continues to rehearse undesirable behaviour. The handler doesn't notice until the behaviour is extreme or excessive.

To use extinction, first figure out what reinforcer is maintaining the behaviour. Then manage the setting events or environment so that the animal is prevented from being reinforced for that behaviour. You must prove to the dog that this behaviour No Longer Works:

1. Prevent the reinforcement from occurring.
2. Remove the reinforcing circumstances from the environment.
3. Through awareness and your own self-discipline, stop inadvertently reinforcing behaviour.

Ninety-eight percent of my clients with puppies are concerned and harassed by their puppies masquerading as crocodiles by biting hands, feet, and clothing with needle-sharp teeth. In my house, I don't worry about puppy biting. Not because my puppies don't do this, but because I do not notice it. By actively Not Noticing, I utilize extinction to perform its special kind of magic.

To speed the process of extinguishing a behaviour, management techniques (such as, for puppy biting, not waving your hands around the dog's face all the time!) are critical to success. In addition, I take advantage of operant conditioning by Noticing and heavily reinforcing desired human-dog interactions. Removing social interaction by placing the over-stimulated puppy in a crate with a bone to chew on and immediately ceasing play if I feel puppy teeth on my skin are two more educational aids. Using the protocol in the "Handling & Restraint" chapter takes care of the rest of this troublesome, but normal, puppy behaviour.

The key remains the process of extinction – removing reinforcement for undesired puppy-crocodile-behaviour. Over time, as other, desirable behaviours are reinforced, the puppy abandons puppy-biting as a strategy to gain attention. In this manner, puppy-biting just fades away – it becomes extinct.

If you are going to use extinction to get rid of a behaviour, you will need the patience to wait it out. For a while, the dog may intensify the undesired behaviour, making it seem, at first, like the technique is failing. But hang in there – you are probably just observing a learning phenomenon called an Extinction Burst, as discussed next. This is a normal part of the extinction process, and, if you can get through it, you will be well on your way to extinguishing the unwanted behaviour.

Extinction Burst

When a behaviour has a history of reinforcement and the reinforcement contingency is suddenly removed, it is very frustrating for the individual involved. The individual was expecting a certain outcome and that outcome did not take place. The first reaction to this interruption in predictability is an escalation of the behaviour. "Hey! This has always worked before, perhaps I just need to add a little more of it!" Usually dogs will try repeating the undesired behaviour a few times, then they will become markedly more vigorous and intense in their display of the behaviour. This is the juncture at which most people decide that the dog is not going to give in and they capitulate to the dog's demands in some way. If this is what happens, then that person has just reinforced an intense version of the behaviour they were trying to get rid of in the first place! So, if you begin an extinction technique, you *must* hold out until the dog figures out that escalation of the behaviour is a dead end and will no longer be reinforced. At that point, the behaviour does not really disappear, as much as it is no longer used because it "just doesn't work anymore." This is like discarding an old garden hose that got leaky, but instead of tossing it in the trash, you hang it in a dark, shadowy corner of an outbuilding. It is still on the premises, just not in regular use.

It is vital to install a desired behaviour to take the place of the undesired behaviour in the context. At the very least, reinforce "absence of" the undesired behaviour to promote keeping the undesired behaviour unaccessed and tucked away in deep storage.

Spontaneous Recovery

The other common phenomenon associated with extinction is Spontaneous Recovery. That means that you haven't seen this old behaviour for a while; then, under specific circumstances, the undesired behaviour re-emerges. If the behaviour has been extinct for a period of time, spontaneous recovery will be short-lived, and the behaviour will show less intensity and be of shorter duration. If you do see spontaneous recovery, the best way to handle it is the way you got rid of the behaviour in the first place. If that was through extinction, then you will have to put into place the circumstances that brought about the extinction in the first place. If that was through some other technique or protocol, then do a review of that. The behaviour will disappear again, this time maybe for good!

Extinction is a great way to get rid of undesired behaviour. When this technique is effective, it brings about a modification in the behaviour of the dog with the least amount of wear and tear on the dog. Extinction works because the dog learns that the target behaviour (the behaviour you were trying to get rid of) is no longer gaining him a desired outcome. The behaviour no longer works. Dogs don't waste much time doing stuff that doesn't work!

Systematic Desensitization

Desensitization is all about slowly and *systematically* exposing your dog to a given set of stimuli in such a way that the dog begins to feel that this context is "safe" instead of "dangerous." This technique requires excellent observation skills. It is imperative that the internal state of the dog changes from sending messages that promote the dog being aroused or fearful to remaining in a calm internal state. Remember: observable behaviour is what gives you information about the dog's internal state.

Any desensitization program is built around very gradual exposure to stimuli that the dog finds disturbing, at a level that is so low, there is no exhibition of the undesired behaviour. Systematic desensitization depends on controlled exposure to the original stimulus by increasing the intensity level of the stimulus in such a way that the dog is slowly conditioned to accept that which he originally found to be stressful, fear-inducing or anxiety-producing.

The goal is for the dog to view a context with a new, relaxed and confident attitude.

Desensitization can be a life-saver, and for most dogs presenting with aggression, desensitization is going to be a big part of what you do, because the majority of aggression is an expression of fear- or anxiety-based behaviour.

The pitfall of desensitization is that the setting events must be very carefully controlled UNTIL

THE DOG HAS COMPLETED this attitude change. If you are executing a careful program for a dog with noise phobia, and the dog is doing well, but two weeks into the program you have an uncontrolled event occur (the neighbors set off a bunch of fireworks), you will be right back at square one again.

Let's say you are working with a dog who is afraid of having his collar touched, and has bitten you because you have grabbed him by the collar. You have been carefully desensitizing the dog to this and are up to being able to touch the dog's collar. The dog is even eagerly looking forward to having you touch his neck, cheek and collar for tasty treats. The UPS person comes to the door and you have placed the dog in his crate. However! You have not properly latched the crate because you were in a hurry, the dog pushes on the crate door and unexpectedly dashes toward the door you are holding wide open for the UPS person. As the dog dashes by you, you manage to grab the collar and prevent the dog from running into the street. The dog panics and bites you. This does not mean that your desensitization program has failed or is doomed to failure. It merely means that you will be starting back at the beginning of your desensitization program again. The dog was placed in a context in which his skill set just didn't have the advanced tools this situation demanded.

Once completed, desensitization can "hold up" quite well, even if some events occur that the dog was not desensitized to specifically. My own Maeve, once constantly on the alert and scanning when we were in a crowd, went to a huge benched show last year to go into the obedience ring. She has been shown, but never at such a large, chaotic, stress-inducing area such as Cobo Hall in Detroit. She handled it like a pro, showing much less stress than I expected, even when an incident I could have never predicted came up. She was unflappable, even when a hapless spectator walked right up to her and grabbed the toy she was holding in her mouth before I could react. (Having grown up with a variety of pets and livestock, the naivete of the general public never ceases to amaze me, although you would think I would learn.) This guy didn't realize how risky his behaviour was; he just assumed he was going to play with the dog, without even asking permission from me. Maeve showed remarkable judgment. She was not about to give her toy to this bozo. She managed to hold on to the toy and, dragging the guy with it, to look at me for advice at the same time. The look on her face was not benevolent; she obviously felt this guy was really over-stepping his boundary! This is a dog who has great potential for possessive and protective aggression, and this person was violating both of those, plus her personal space. However, under fire, she behaved admirably! My careful exposure of her to the situations I had placed her in, and the constantly positive associations I had provided, really did hold up when placed to the test. I am grateful! This episode proves that you cannot prepare for every single eventuality. Always, the setting events supply you with a curve ball!

When using Desensitization, the rate of progression is governed entirely by the dog's ability to *habituate* to the context. Some dogs will make rapid progress and others slower, but the dog determines that speed. The success of using desensitization will depend upon your ability to design a stimulus gradient that raises criteria in a controlled fashion and on your ability to read the dog. If you never stress the dog at all, you will never move forward; if you stress the dog too much you will have to begin over and you may do some lasting damage.

FLOODING

Flooding is used primarily to reduce fearful behaviour. Whereas desensitization requires that the dog is NOT exposed to intense versions of the fear-producing stimulus, flooding requires the opposite. When you use flooding to modify behaviour, the objective is to elicit the fearful behaviour, and then wait for the dog to "stop responding" to the fear-inducing stimulus.

Flooding is a very tricky technique to use properly and can do damage to the dog's psyche if not executed properly. Using flooding techniques with a dog who has shown overt aggression to you or others in the past is not advised. Executing a flooding exercise can be very difficult to watch, also. In some cases, for the animal to "stop responding" requires that they are mentally and physically exhausted.

Flooding involves continuous exposure to the stimulus until the dog habituates. The term "habituate" has a discrete meaning in this context: that the dog has ceased to react to the stimulus. This means that the sympathetic nervous system is in a normal chemical state. The respiration is normal, the heart-rate is normal. The least criteria is the animal is relatively relaxed and accepting of the situation.

Once you have placed the dog in the presence of the fear-inducing context, you must continue the exposure until the dog calms down. This means the context does not change until the dog exhibits calm behaviour. In addition, the dog may not leave the area until he has habituated to the context. Once the dog is calm, lavish reinforcement is in order.

Dogs discover that, when they are afraid of something, if they avoid it and retreat from the area then they feel "relief" and safety. This feeling of relief is very powerful, and it maintains fearful and avoidant behaviour. Flooding techniques depend on the dog learning that avoidance does not work, but remaining in the context and being calm does work. If you think about this carefully, it is easy to see the numerous pitfalls that can occur while carrying out a flooding program.

The Flooding experience will have to be repeated a few times to have a lasting effect. Flooding may work best for fears that are not too intense. If the setting events cause your dog to "hang up the phone" and try to leave the area in a manner that causes her injury (going through a plate glass window or damaging herself trying to get out of a crate), then this is not a technique to use. If your dog becomes defensive or exhibits aggression when her flight behaviours are restricted, then you are obviously placing yourself and others in danger during the flooding process.

If you are going to use flooding on a low-level fear behaviour, your primary objective is to keep everyone around the dog safe (including you!) and to keep the dog safe while still preventing her from leaving the context. This may mean head-collars, collars, leashes, crates, and muzzles. Initial use of a stimulus that is less intense or muted or at a greater distance presents the stress in more tolerable packages.

An example is a dog who is afraid of people wearing hats. The dog, when on leash, will try to dash away, and ceases to respond to known cues when a person with a hat on enters the room. If loose, the dog runs and hides under the bed. If the person wearing the hat approaches the dog and he cannot get away, he begins to growl and back away from the person as far as he can. If cornered, the dog will snap at the hatted-one. The owner is certain the dog would bite if pushed.

To use a flooding technique, the dog would be placed in a room so that any flight behaviour is prevented. A hatted person will walk up near the dog and remain there until the dog no longer reacts to her. At first, the handler has the dog on a leash and head-collar.

The following example uses flooding. Each step uses a stimulus that is initially less intense.

1. A person wearing a hat enters the room and stands near the door. This person makes sure she looks away from the dog and doesn't stare at the dog. (It is okay, and probably smart, to keep the dog in peripheral vision!) This hatted person stands still until the dog is calm. Once the dog is calm, deliver reinforcement and the hatted one leaves the room.
2. A hatted person enters the room and walks a bit nearer to the dog. No matter what the dog does, the hatted person does not respond.
3. The hatted person walks up to the dog.
4. The hatted person tosses treats to the dog.
5. The hatted person pets the dog.

It is essential during the protocol, that you do not move on to the next step until the dog is calm each time. This indicates habituation to the present stressor.

In this situation, the handler should obviously prevent any lunging, snarling, or other displays of overt aggression from occurring. If these displays do occur, then you are using the wrong program as you are placing the helper in danger. If there is any doubt about this, make sure your dog is muzzled prior to beginning. If overt display occurs, move the dog away from the hatted helper, using a strategic retreat (refer to the "Being Brave Is Better" protocol for approximations). As soon as the dog is calm, the helper should leave the room. You now embark on a desensitization program with this dog instead.

Summary

Flooding differs from desensitization in the level of response from the dog. With a desensitization program, you will be very careful to *avoid* presenting stimuli that evoke a strong response in the dog. With flooding, we place the dog in a situation that *does evoke a response* and then allow him to habituate each time.

DIFFERENTIAL REINFORCEMENT SCHEDULES

Differential Reinforcement Schedules are used to increase the probability that a specific behaviour will be accessed by the dog. Manipulating reinforcement is how you raise the odds that one behaviour will be accessed over another. There are different classes of reinforcement schedules. *Fixed Schedules* occur predictably within a time frame (every two minutes) or after a fixed number of behaviours have occurred (1 behaviour = 1 cookie). *Variable reinforcement* occurs unpredictably. *Differential reinforcement* implies that you are Choosing a Particular Behaviour to reinforce. There is terminology to describe specific kinds of differential reinforcement schedules. I use a mnemonic to remember these by: AEIO (all the vowels but U).

DRA

Differential Reinforcement of Alternate Behaviour. DRA is when you choose a desired, ALTERNATIVE behaviour to reinforce. This gives your dog a new task to focus on in lieu of an undesired behaviour. This will discourage the undesired behaviour from presenting itself.

An example is having the dog walk to the door and lying down near you, instead of barking, when the doorbell rings. The dog theoretically could bark and lie down, but giving the dog an alternative task to focus on will most likely eliminate the barking.

DRE

Differential Reinforcement of Excellent Behaviour. This refers to selecting only the very best examples of the behaviour you are working on for reinforcement. You will be looking for extra commitment, willingness, a calmer attitude, a really quick response, and the like.

As an example: ceasing to reinforce slow responses to "Down" and reinforcing only immediate responses to the cue.

DRI

Differential Reinforcement of Incompatible Behaviour. DRI entails reinforcing a behaviour that is totally incompatible with the undesired behaviour. Think about reinforcing a polar opposite, such as Sitting vs. Jumping: if the dog is sitting, he cannot be jumping.

DRO

Differential Reinforcement of Other Behaviours. DRO is probably best described as reinforcing absence of a particular behaviour. When using DRO you will reinforce any behaviour except the undesired behaviour. I use this technique when I am having no luck getting a behaviour that is incompatible, or with a dog who does not have many known cues, or with a dog who is just not displaying much behaviour other than the undesirable behaviour. If you are working on diminishing barking in the crate, you could encourage and reinforce any behaviour in the crate OTHER than barking. You could feed silence, chewing on a toy, lying down quietly, or any "other" behaviour.

An example of using Differential Reinforcement is given below. This would be classified as DRI, because looking at the owner and lunging away from the owner are mutually incompatible.

Your dog lunges at other dogs when you are walking. This defines the undesired behaviour. You would prefer that, when your dog sees another dog on your walk, he looks at you.

To break this down:

- Antecedent: the other dog approaches.
- Current Behaviour – Undesired: your dog lunges and barks.
- Goal Behaviour – Desired: your dog walks quietly beside you and looks at you.

The new task will be taught and practiced in a situation that is non-distracting and does not provoke the undesired response. This new behaviour will be generously reinforced. Once the dog is performing the new task easily in non-distracting surroundings, you will raise criteria and practice the behaviour under two or three more challenging situations, but still not the really intense, arousing situation of "another dog on a walk." So, you might practice this in your own yard. Have a person approach while you Reward Mark & Feed the dog. Next, a known dog that your dog really likes could be used as an approach dog as a further challenge. You will be specifically reinforcing non-reactive and attentive (to you) behaviour. (For further discussion on how to obtain this, see Level I Protocols.) Once you get solid attention at these stages, you are ready to try your regular walking route again.

The real trick is to make the new task SO REINFORCING in the old context that the new behaviour is "chosen" over the old behaviour. So, for this first walk, you will have a treat that is of very high value to your dog. As soon as YOU see the other dog approaching, you are going to immediately remind your dog of the new behaviour you want him to use. Use your cues, your prompts, and your prayers – whatever it takes to get the desired behaviour, then pull out all the stops when you reinforce. This first correct effort MUST net a huge reward for your dog. The moment you can get your dog to look at you in lieu of lunging, plop down an entire can of tuna fish and heap on lavish praise. The First Correct Effort that is made memorable is very likely to be accessed next time in favor of other behaviour, because it worked so great for the dog!

As time goes on, you will need to use less and less reinforcement to maintain this behaviour as looking at you becomes the dog's habit, or *first accessed behaviour,* in this context. The new behaviour displaces the old behaviour.

Differential Reinforcement is the process of teaching your dog to use a desired behaviour in place of an undesired behaviour, even though the circumstances or setting events presented are the same.

Differential Reinforcement is a very powerful way to modify behaviour. It will work only if you can make the new behaviour MORE reinforcing than the old behaviour. This is sometimes difficult, but you can do this because you will control the setting events and stack the deck in your favor to bring this about.

Counter-Conditioning

A lot of what I see people defining as counter-conditioning is actually differential reinforcement, which is specifically concerned with operant or voluntary behaviour. To really understand counter-conditioning, it is necessary to have a grip on classical conditioning, because counter-conditioning is closely related to classical (respondent) conditioning. Both involve conditioning that is specifically related to changes that are "reflexive" in nature (or, related to an emotional state).

Counter-conditioning occurs when a previously classical-conditioned response is replaced with a new classically-conditioned response. This concerns an emotional level or state, and changes that are specifically occurring on a respondent (reflexive) level.

Classical Conditioning

Classical conditioning involves the animal learning an association between two stimuli. In the Pavlovian example that many people are familiar with, two stimuli become associated just by being repeatedly presented close together in time, and will elicit the same *reflexive* response.

A dog naturally salivates when presented with food. If a bell and food are repeatedly paired, the dog will eventually salivate when she hears only the bell, even when the food is not around.

This response is reflexive, or automatic. It can be an automatic physical response, such as salivating, sweating, yelping, or changes in the digestive system or blood vessels. Such responses generally involve the autonomic nervous system – *fast, innate, unlearned reactions that control basic bodily functions.* The response can also be an automatic basic emotional response, such as fear or a sense of relief. Note, here, that we are talking about, again, innate, unlearned basic "lizard-brain" emotions that just pop up automatically.

Most responses are clusters of basic emotional reactions and physical reactions. The dog, for example, may have a number of automatic responses to entering a Safe Situation: physical responses such as relaxation of tense muscles, slower respiration, and reduced heart rate, as well as emotional responses such as a feeling of comfort and relaxation. If the dog starts associating YOU with Safe Situations, then she may have this cluster of automatic responses when she sees YOU. This is called trust.

For a more detailed discussion of classical conditioning, see the section in this book called "Laws of Learning." Excellent discussions are also contained in *Learning* (Catania, 1992) and *Behaviour Modification: What It Is and How To Do It* (Martin and Pear, 1996).

Back to Counter-Conditioning

Classical conditioning elicits *involuntary* responses from the animal. These responses are reflexive, like drooling or increased respiration. (Some texts will use the term "respondent" instead of classical. The terms are interchangeable.)

Operant conditioning involves learned *voluntary* behaviour. The animal is "thoughtfully" responding rather than reflexively responding. The significance for those interested in behaviour is: Where is the observable behaviour originating from?

It is apparent when we look at behaviour that is occurring in the Real World that both operant and classical conditioning are included within a behavioural sequence.

There are also two components to our emotions, a classical or "respondent" component and an operant component. The autonomic nervous system is involved in breathing, digestion, heartbeat and glandular functions. "Autonomic responses occur as unconditioned reactions to stimuli, and such responses can be visible as blushing, trembling, and crying." (Martin and Pear, 1996, pp. 196-197). Even though Martin and Pear are discussing human reactions in this sentence, the same application is true for animals as well, with differences in the external (observable) behaviour. These physiological reactions are closely linked to certain EMOTIONS, such as embarrassment, fear, or grief. How you handle the emotions you feel reflexively depends on learned behaviour. When you "feel" a certain emotion, what voluntary "action" do you take?

How fear is displayed, other than the reflexive physiological responses, depends on what coping mechanisms the individual has learned to use. Some individuals tend toward a certain direction – fight or flight. But learning and environment have much influence on what the individual does about the fear-producing stimuli. Is avoidance the first choice? It is if it has worked well for the dog in the past. Is defense the first choice? It is if the dog has successfully used defense to gain relief and distance from frightening objects in the past.

Using these principles to modify behaviour involves changing the way the dog "feels." We monitor this by observing what emotions the dog exhibits (because we cannot ask him how he feels) in a certain situation.

If an outgoing puppy has not had extensive experience around small children he approaches the child joyfully, with no fear. The toddler promptly grabs the dog by the ear and will not let go. As the puppy screeches in fear, the toddler involuntarily tightens his grip. The puppy, frightened, bites the child. Every adult in the vicinity begins to yell, not even necessarily at the puppy. The puppy, thoroughly unnerved by this experience, may now develop a fear of children, particularly if he has not had any prior pleasant experiences with children and if no pleasant experiences follow this one.

Now the puppy has made a direct connection between children, pain, and fear. The puppy may be afraid of children who are friendly and gentle, and react with fear or anxiety merely at the sight of a child on the street.

The goal is to replace the emotion of "fear" with a feeling of calm benevolence. Counter-conditioning is one tool to use. To achieve this feat we will find a small child who is gentle and controllable. Take the puppy on leash near the child and feed the puppy some really tasty stuff, or take the pup's favorite toy and play near the child. The idea is to get the puppy to associate the child with "good" feelings as opposed to fearful feelings.

Gradually the child would be allowed to come closer and then to interact with the pup, while the puppy associates the interaction with treats, games, social approval, and NO fear. So while you do everything you possibly can to REDUCE the fear, you will do everything you can to INCREASE feelings of security and fun in the presence of the child. This will create a dog who does not need to behave fearfully or defensively near children because he is comfortable around children. This is true counter-conditioning: changing the way the dog *feels* about this set of conditions changes the way the dog *acts* around them. Calm, comfortable, and self-confident is the dog, as opposed to fearful and defensively biting. This is because you have worked to promote a calm, relaxed emotional state around children.

Later on in this book I discuss using "switching" exercises. These use both operant and classical conditioning to associate a *physical position* (such as sitting) with a *certain emotional state* (being calm and relaxed). See the protocol for "Zen Sit and Down."

Conclusions:

Some of the techniques in this chapter concentrate on changing the internal chemical state of the animal, which will be reflected in the external, observable behaviour. This works on a very primitive, limbic level, and involves principles of classical (respondent) conditioning. This is imperative for changing the way the animal perceives and feels about the situation.

In changing the dog's perceptions, the dog's behaviour is modified both directly and indirectly – directly, because high-arousal behaviour, such as a defensive display, is reduced; indirectly, because the dog is more receptive to learning and adopting new behaviours because he feels "safe" enough to do so.

This adorable collection of techniques provides the means to teach the animal to respond to previously arousing or fear-provoking situations by "switching" from a state of high arousal to a calm chemical state. In other words, the dog is learning to switch from knee-jerk reactions using his Lizard-brain to thoughtful actions and higher-order learning using his Einstein-brain.

Using both classical and operant conditioning is the path toward stable, lasting behaviour changes that generalize best.

There will be an occasion to use every tool here if you are modifying the behaviour of a dog who is already presenting with aggression.

It is just as valuable to use these principles when teaching your dog how to develop coping behaviours that will prevent aggression. The more experiences your dog has that he feels comfortable with and “good” about, the less the chances are that the dog will develop risky behaviour in the future.

Section V

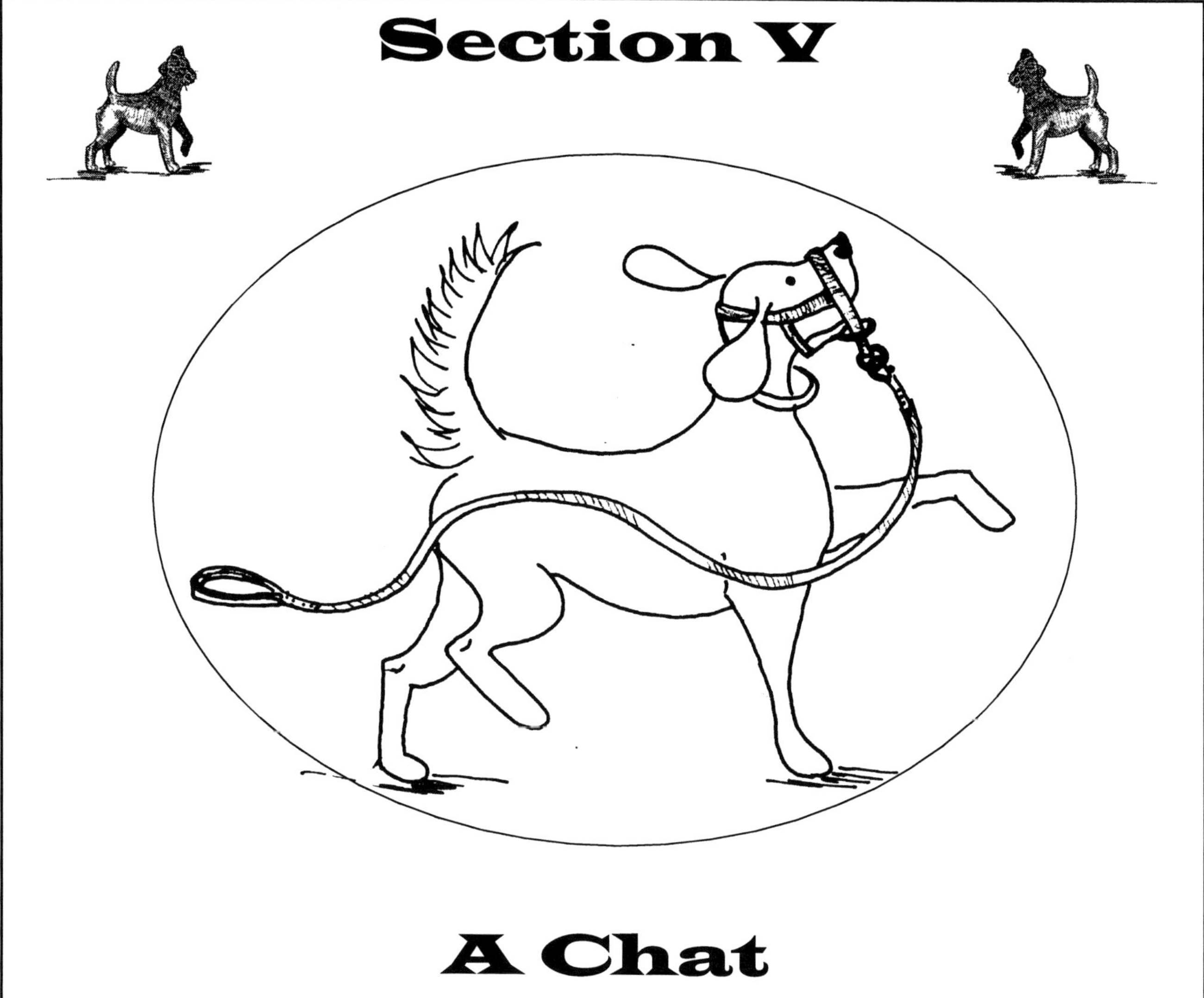

A Chat About Equipment

19

THE BASICS – COLLARS & HEAD COLLARS

Neither a pinch collar nor a chain choke collar (often identified by the euphemism "training collar") is appropriate equipment for these protocols. Both of these collars rely on positive punishment (a physical punisher that is applied to the dog) and implied discipline to control the dog – therefore on *avoidance* to obtain behaviour. In the case of the choke collar, the damage done to the dog's esophagus by bending it time and time again over the years is detrimental. The pinch collar can cause considerable pain, and this is disadvantageous to our protocol because of the associations made: the other dog or person approaching causes pain, therefore the dog resents and fears the approach of the third party all the more. For dogs who direct aggression toward the handler, this may truly endanger the handler. Knowledge of the Laws of Learning and Dog Language show that pain is NOT the optimum method for changing a dog's behaviour or way of thinking. (If you are having trouble with this concept, don't take just my word for it, do some research, beginning with *Coercion and Its Fallout* by Murray Sidman (1989).)

Photo by Sam Ziegenmeyer

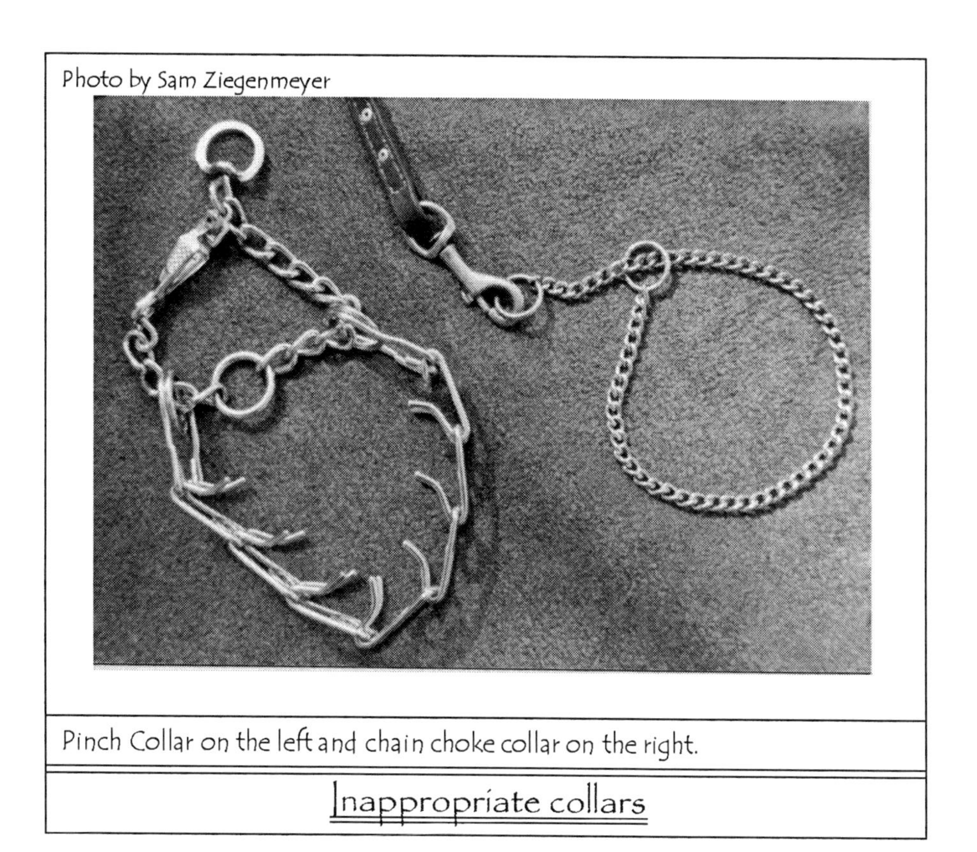

Pinch Collar on the left and chain choke collar on the right.

Inappropriate collars

Aggression is not the after effect of "behaviour." Behaviour is the observable end product of a chemical state. Have you ever braked your car suddenly to avoid an accident? Your body gives you a nice healthy adrenaline dump in response to your perception of the dangerous situation. If your dog becomes so reactive over another dog or person, to the extent that he is incapable of listening to you, he is in an aroused chemical state. His Lizard Brain has decided a Fight or Flight response is required. If the dog is already in a highly aroused chemical state and then his air supply is shut off with a choke collar, or pain is inflicted with a pinch collar, you are not doing anything to help this animal to calm down! A choke or pinch collar contributes to the arousal level by increasing the adrenaline level.

I prefer to use equipment that will contain the dog, manage the dog's behaviour, and ultimately contribute to the behaviour modification protocol.

Martingale collars do not continue to tighten indefinitely as a choke collar does, yet they will not allow your dog to slip out of the collar and get loose.

Martingale Collars

MARTINGALE COLLAR

Your dog should be fitted with a martingale collar, or some other type of "limited-slip" collar.

HEAD COLLARS

Next, a head collar is requisite for an aggressive dog. You will use this special collar to keep your dog under control and to minimize danger to yourself and others.

Head collars are very much like the halter used to control a large animal such as an equine or a bovine. You would never attempt to lead a very large, strong animal by draping something round his neck or shoulders – the strongest part of the animal!

One advantage of a head collar is that it is difficult for the animal to drag you toward the destination of her choice, because the leverage and physics are on your side. So your shoulders and hands are spared a lot of wear and tear.

The more important advantage, from a viewpoint of behaviour modification, is that the handler can exert control over what the animal looks at. This is so important because, if a dog is looking at something (another dog, a human, a squirrel), that is what he is thinking about. If what he is looking at is getting him excited, this arousal level can lead to aggressive behaviour in some dogs.

With a regular collar, you can back up and pull on it, but the dog is not prevented from looking at the object that is maintaining his arousal level. Even if you are dragging the dog in the opposite direction of whatever the current Dog Magnet is, the dog is still able to maintain its aroused state because it is continuing to look at and over-react to the magnet. Until you break the eye contact toward what your dog is fixated on, you do not have any effect on what he is thinking. *If the dog is looking at "it," he is still thinking about "it."*

With a head collar, you control what the dog is looking at. This, then, is the first step in a series of approximations that will be used to gain control of the dog's behaviour. A head collar is a form of doggy mind control.

Head collars are an absolute life-saver, and it is the job of all of us who are educated to inform the general public that these are not muzzles, do not harm the dog, and are, in fact, much more humane than the generally accepted choke collars. It is ironic that if you are at an AKC show or trial, a head collar is not allowed to lead your dog on the show grounds, yet a choke collar is. This is indicative of the lag in current information and public perception about collars.

A head collar is used by all dogs who come to me with aggression problems. I prefer the Halti™ to other head collars I have used to date. The cheek pieces assure a good fit for most dogs and keep the head collar in place. With a Halti, I can keep the dog's mouth shut if I absolutely need to. (For dogs with very short snouts, a Gentle Leader™ or snoot loop may be the better option.)

There are a couple of equipment modifications I do to maximize safety and control when using a Halti.

It is possible that a dog could slip a Halti off. I pay really close attention when I am working with a dog, and have never had one slip off. You can add a small piece of narrow rope with snaps to attach the Halti to the collar. Then the leash snaps to the Halti. Or, you can clip the leash both to the Halti and the ring on the collar. Now if the dog slips the Halti, you do not have a loose dog.

I advise my clients to use either a safety-pin or to put a stitch in the double fabric on the crown of the Halti once it is adjusted properly for their dog. The nylon occasionally slips insidiously, and allows the Halti to loosen up without the handler being aware of it. The safety-pin or stitch prevents the slippery nylon from sliding. This way the Halti to is prevented from loosening up and allowing the dog to slip out of it when tension is placed on the leash.

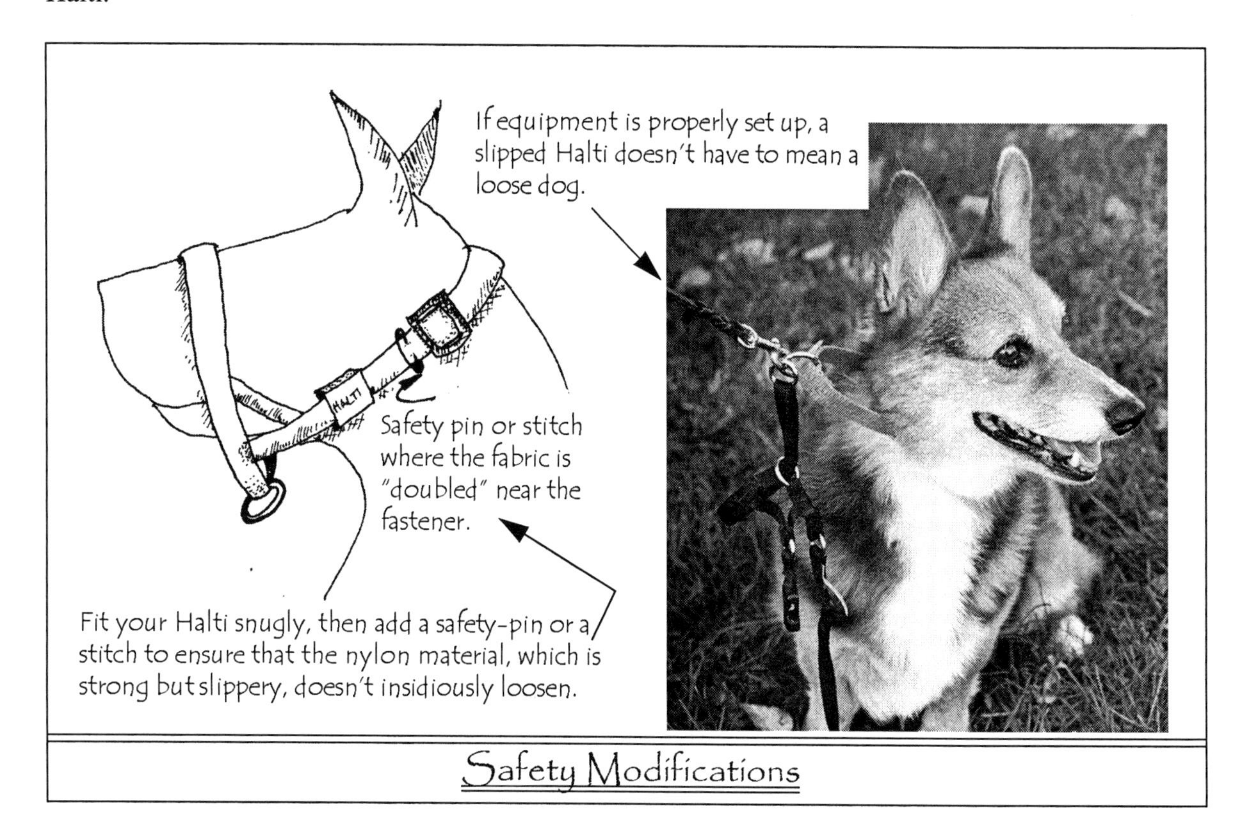

Safety Modifications

Brenda Aloff

These dogs are wearing Halti head-collars that have been safely fitted. Misty (above) has a separate strap that connects her head-collar to her collar. I prefer this because then the cavesson (nose-band) of the Halti can swing freely, tightening and loosening as intended. Data (below) has his head-collar connected to his martingale collar using just the leash snap. This is fine as long as the martingale collar fits the dog so that the "handle" on the martingale collar allows the cavesson on the Halti to loosen and tighten without interference.

Halti Head Collars

20

FITTING THE HALTI

To use the Halti, first place it on the dog, then give him a treat. Make a fuss over how gorgeous he looks with his new "jewelry." You may then remove it as soon as the dog is not pawing at it. You may have to manufacture this behaviour – by a constant feed or by holding the dog's head up so he can't paw at it.

The fit of the Halti is very important. If it is not correctly fitted, the dog will get loose at an inopportune time, or the nose band will not be placed for optimum control. What I like best about Halti head-collars is the cheek-pieces that are thick and rigid enough to keep the cavesson in place properly (just like the halter you would use on a horse). The head-collars that are just a nose-loop connected to a collar do not, in my opinion, afford the control and leverage that the Halti does. If necessary (and you can't be tremulous about it!!!), I have successfully prevented dogs from biting me while wearing a Halti. In similar situations, the nose-loop/collar varieties have not performed as well.

Halti Photo Essay by Sam Ziegenmeyer.

If your dog is safe to handle, this is the easiest way to put a head collar on a dog who wishes to back away from you as you are putting it on. Here, my knees gently hold Ally in the flank area and prevent backward movement. My hand under the dog's chin prevents forward movement.

If your dog resents it (snaps or growls) when you try this, or you are concerned she will, you can stand next to the dog and have a leash on her regular collar to help control movement. Position the dog so that if she backs up, she will back into a corner. Do not stand in front of the dog and reach toward her to put on the head collar – the majority of dogs will back away in alarm. Stand by the dog's left shoulder and stand on the leash. Holding the head collar in your left hand, slide the nose band over the dog's nose, use your right hand to keep it on her and then buckle the collar behind the dog's ears. It may take several days to acclimate your dog to the Halti.

1 of 2 Holding The Dog To Put On The Halti

Put the cavesson (nose-band) over the dog's nose...

2 of 2 Holding The Dog To Put On The Halti

Then, snap it behind the ears, taking care to not get the dog's hair tangled in the clasp.

Make sure the Halti is VERY snugly fitted behind the dog's ears, or she will rub her head on your legs or the ground, or paw at the Halti a few times, and it will come right off. This is a result of it not being fitted properly to the dog – a mechanical error on the part of the handler!

1 of 2 Fitting the Halti

Immediately reward with treats if the dog will accept them from you and hasn't already thrown herself to the ground in an effort to remove this thing that feels so odd.

2 of 2 Fitting the Halti

21

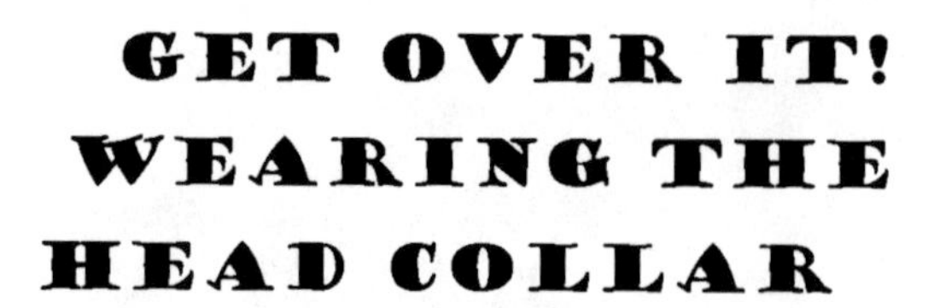

GET OVER IT! WEARING THE HEAD COLLAR

It would always be my preference to introduce a dog to a head collar slowly and using TTouch™, thereby reducing stress for the animal. (Refer to "Handling & Restraint" protocol, as well as any of Linda Tellington-Jones' TTouch books.)

Sometimes, to work with a dog safely or to avoid the owners being dragged around and hurt, I introduce a Halti to the dog in one session. Often, by the time the owners bring the dog to me, they are quite desperate and frustrated with the dog. My preference would be to take longer, but sometimes, when that is just not possible, I use the "quick" technique outlined here.

It may be a big stretch for the owner to believe that we are going to train the dog without a choke collar. Or perhaps part of the family sees the sense in this, but another family member (read: spouse) is not in agreement and thinks that taking the dog to a "dog shrink" is idiotic in the first place. So I need to do something to get the dog under control quickly and safely. Once the people see some results, they will be more willing to accept the rest of the program. Being that it is not a perfect world, and I generally need to act posthaste, this quick method is very effective and humane, as I am allowing the dog to make all the decisions about the correction. If possible, take your time introducing the Halti. Even if you are forced into using the quick method, still do some short, sweet stuff: Put the Halti on and let the dog eat, then remove it. Put the Halti on and give the dog several tasty treats, then take the Halti off. If you have the luxury of time: over several sessions put the Halti on until the dog stops fussing, then feed the absence of fussing, then remove it. Take the dog for several walks while wearing the Halti, but do not have a leash attached to the Halti, only to the dog's collar. After a week or two of this, you can introduce the dog to using a leash with the Halti.

Acclimating Your Dog to a Head Collar

You may allow the dog to paw at the Halti a little bit, just enough so she realizes on her own that the Halti does not come off this way. In order to maintain this belief for the dog, you have to intervene and not let the dog dig at it too much. Once she decides this strategy does not work, she will abandon it and begin the process of getting accustomed to wearing the Halti in a relaxed manner.

You can put the Halti on, feed a treat, and take it off. Repeat this several times.

Photo essay by Sam Ziegenmeyer

It is pretty normal for the dog to attempt to remove the head collar. Many owners find this much more distressing than the dog does. If you allow the dog a brief period (maybe 10-60 seconds) of experimentation so she figures out that this is not coming off, then reinforce her for appropriate behaviour, she will quickly come round. Some dogs are very amusing about this. My little Fox Terrier, Punch, responded by backing in circles for a bit. I laughed at her which perpetuated the behaviour, so watch out what you giggle at, or notice by "feeling so sorry" for the dog. Giggling and "noticing" a behaviour will reinforce, therefore encourage, exactly the behaviour that you wish to get rid of. Honestly, it's not like you are hurting them. The pawing is a natural reaction to: "What in the world is this thing? It feels bizarre!". I find that once I get the owners over it, the dog quickly comes round.

If I have my druthers, I do prefer to introduce the dog to the head collar as gently and slowly as possible, but at some point the dog (and owners!) just need to get over it!

A Minor Skirmish Because the Head Collar Feels Foreign

Put the Halti on the dog, and then feed her a meal. As soon as the meal is finished, remove the Halti.

Once the dog has had the Halti on a few times, you can begin to teach her what it is for.

1. Place the Halti on the dog, with the Martingale collar.

2. Put a leash on the Halti, and a leash on the Martingale collar.

You will NEVER "pop" or jerk a dog with a Halti. Always gentle, steady pressure will be used.

The first thing to teach the dog is that she can "control" the pressure of the head collar by "giving in" to it. To teach this: Place your hand on your upper thigh to anchor the leash. Now back up until there is a *slight* pressure on the Halti.

The dog will most likely protest this, and move backwards to pull even harder on the Halti. Entice the dog toward you with voice and treats.

If one or two quiet requests and enticing treats do not net you an immediate response, then just be still and quiet and plan to out-wait her. You tried to help the dog. If the dog is not open to help from you right this moment, just wait quietly and patiently. This is not a "teachable moment."

Some things just need to be figured out by the individual in her own way. (Remember all the great advice your parents gave you that you should have followed and didn't? You just had to learn it on your own. This lesson does teach: heed the good advice given!) If you wait, then, for the dog to move forward ever so slightly, or just to lessen pressure on the leash, jump right in there with a RM and cookies. This is how you provide the dog with information she can use. The general tendency, at this point, is for the dog to start attending to the other information you are giving her, and to begin accepting your advice. That translates into her making a conscious effort into keeping the leash loose and watching you.

Hand is anchored on thigh.

As soon as the dog learns to "give-in" to the pressure exerted by the head collar, she will be able to easily control the correction received. I anchor my hand on my thigh – I am NOT pulling on the dog, the dog has chosen to pull on me. As soon as she takes one step, or even leans forward slightly, the pressure will abate, the punishment will cease, and your dog will learn two very humane, yet valuable, lessons: 1. I can control what happens to me by behaving in a certain way. 2. My handler can help me out of a difficulty if I include her in the equation.

Teaching Ally to "Give" To The Pressure Of The Head Collar

The moment the dog lessens the pressure or, better yet, takes an actual step toward you, thereby relieving the pressure on the Halti, Mark It & Feed It.

Repeat this a few times, giving a treat for each step as it is taken toward you.

Most dogs quickly learn that the best bet is to keep the Halti loose by not pulling back against it. Now you are ready to take a little walk. You have the two leashes on the dog so that she can be aided by both the collar and the Halti if you need them. Teach the dog to respond quickly to the collar itself by giving a *gentle, steady* pressure on the collar. If the dog doesn't respond to this by slowing or turning toward you, you can back up that request with a steady, gentle pressure on the Halti, causing the dog's head to turn toward you. Mark It & Feed It.

Have lots of good treats available and be very generous with your praise, approval and treats for these first lessons with the Halti.

Ally gets MANY rewards – relief from the head collar and a tasty treat and social approval. This insure that future decisions about resistance are much easier for her to make! Good timing is key to success. It is imperative that absence of resistance (the dog isn't pulling), is reinforced by keeping the leash loose so the dog may remain comfortable.

Yes!

In Summary.

Keep a neutral tone, and take your time acclimating the dog to the Halti. Most dogs respond similarly to the first time you put a regular collar on them. They scratch and shake and try to get rid of it. It feels different and funny. But with time and patience, they all learn to wear a Halti. It may take a couple of weeks of gentle, short lessons. I often joke with my clients and tell them it is just like learning to wear a wedding ring; in some ways it is a mental exercise more than a physical exercise....

Do NOT put the Halti on and immediately correct. Do not expect a miracle. This is merely one more tool you are going to use. Training, training, training is always the real answer to problem behaviours.

Be very careful to keep the leash loose on the Halti, unless you are specifically using it to convey information to the dog. If your dog is walking nicely or moving toward you and you are maintaining a tight leash on the Halti, you are, in effect, punishing your dog for the appropriate behaviour. This constant tight leash eventually teaches the dog to pull on the Halti, just as the same tight leash taught him to pull on the collar.

Caution: Never leave a Halti on an unattended dog. The head collar is used to work with the dog, so you can manufacture reinforceable behaviour. *Never tie a dog with a head collar.* A Halti is not meant to be used for this purpose. It is dangerous!

Now back away from the dog. As long as the dog follows and remains oriented toward me, the head collar will remain comfortable and the leash loose. For this reason, you need to make certain that you keep your hand still. You may choose to hook your thumb in your pocket to ensure that if any pulling is done, it is being done by the dog.

Now that the dog is keeping the leash loose and looking at me, I have limitless opportunities to reinforce this desired behaviour.

Teaching Ally To Move & Keep The Leash Loose

The next step is to back up, Mark & Feed the behaviour; then...

Back Up...

...Pivot into Heel position.

Soon Ally is walking normally and quite happily by my side. This entire session was photographed in "real time," and took about ten minutes (sometimes we had to stop and wait for the photographer to position herself, etc.). Sam, the photographer, brought Ally because I told her I needed a dog who hadn't worn a head collar and would for sure throw a little fit.

...And Pivot into Heel position.

22

NON-COMPLIANCE, KNOWN BEHAVIOUR AND CORRECT USE OF THE HEAD COLLAR

A Halti may be used *GENTLY* (NO JERKING) to enforce a request when your dog is so reactive that she is not functioning very well. The Halti may be used in this particular manner (described below) only for KNOWN behaviours with an *extensive* reinforcement history. A Halti is not to be used to *teach* these behaviours (we use positive reinforcement for that); it is used to manufacture KNOWN behaviours under circumstances where your dog is becoming reactive and ceasing to listen to you.

If you request a Sit and receive non-compliance from a dog who is fluent with the behaviour, a GENTLE upward tension on the head collar for non-compliance is acceptable. I am very carefully judging the amount of tension exerted. NO JERKING!!!

The pressure should be slightly uncomfortable, not painful. The motion used should always be a steady pressure, NEVER sudden or jerking.

IMMEDIATELY release the tension on the head collar the MOMENT the dog begins to comply. This is essential for providing adequate information to the dog.

Sit Correction With Head Collar For the Dog Who KNOWS Sit

To use the Halti to back up a request for a Sit that was not heeded by your dog, *gently* pull straight up and *maintain* slight pressure on the Halti until the dog Sits. Immediately administer your RM, IMMEDIATELY loosen the leash, and deliver a tasty treat the first couple of times. After that, you may put this behaviour on a variable schedule, reinforcing only if the dog Sits without requiring the Halti prompt.

The Down prompt with the Halti is straight down until the dog complies. For a Down, it is often best to stand on the leash so your hands are not around the dog's face, which merely causes her to attempt to "change the subject" by writhing around and biting at your hands. Hands waving around the dog's face also add unnecessary confusion to your cue system.

CAUTION: If your dog has been explosively aggressive, or growled at you, use extreme caution. It is certainly feasible for the dog to suddenly lunge toward you and take a bite at you during this exercise. If you think this might be even a remote possibility, have a muzzle on the dog, as well as the Halti, before you attempt to use this technique. Never do this with a dog you do not have an extensive reinforcement history with. ALWAYS be proactive and safe.

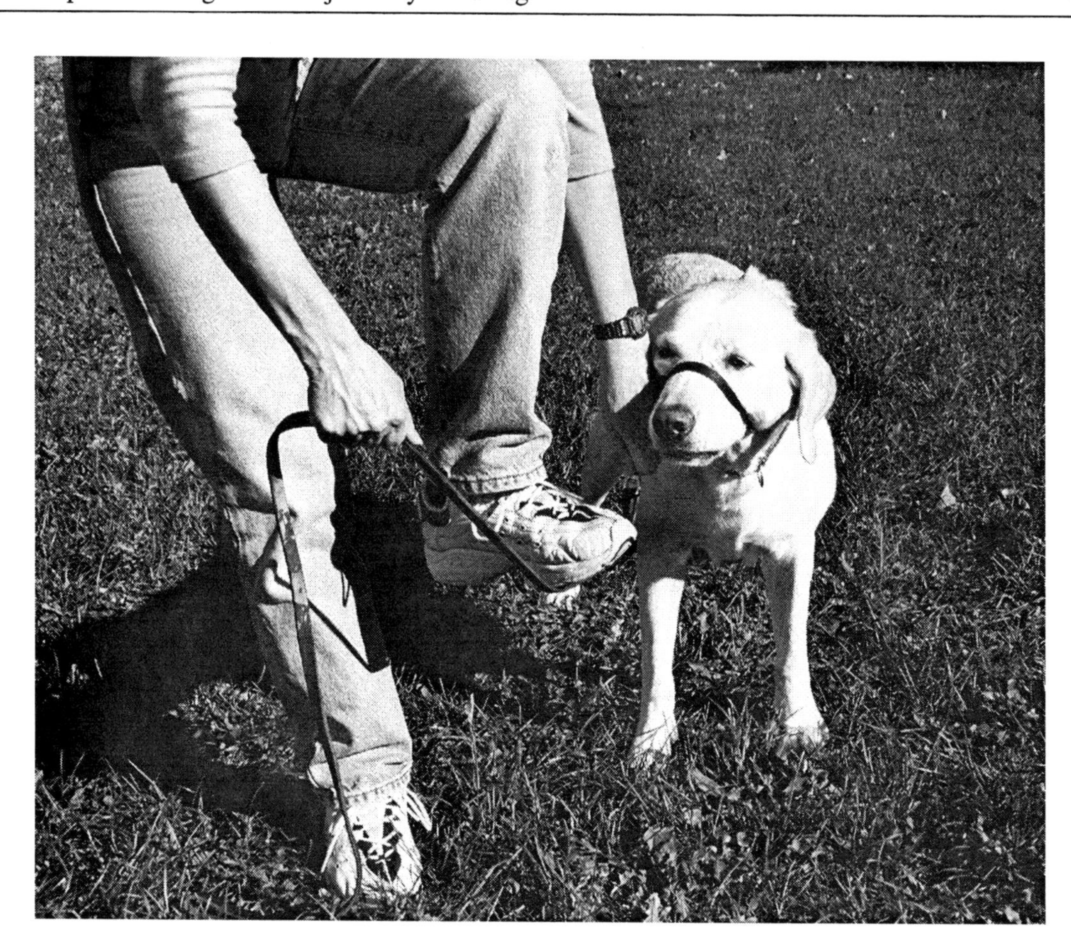

This is pretty much the most severe correction that I use, with the exception of doggy-push-ups. DO NOT jerk the dog to the ground. Again it is a *gentle, steady* tension straight down, maintained until the dog complies.

Down Correction For The Dog That KNOWS Down - Photo 1 of 2

While it is necessary to have your hands next to the dog's face during the first portion of this correction, as soon as you have the snap under your foot, get your hands away from the dog's face, and allow her to figure out again that resistance is just not going to work. As soon as the dog is lying quietly, Mark It & Feed It.

Down Correction Photo 2 of 2

23

MUZZLES & MISC. EQUIPMENT NOTES

A muzzle is necessary equipment for the safety of the handler, other people, and other dogs used as "helpers." For dogs who have growled or snapped at someone already, muzzles are required equipment for many situations, particularly when training a behaviour you are unsure of how your dog will respond to. Safety of all concerned should always be paramount when you are working with an animal who has shown any tendency to become irritable, or has growled or snapped at someone.

Nylon muzzles are lightweight, reasonably comfortable for the dog, and strong. The muzzle should fit tightly enough so the dog cannot get his mouth over anything even as small as a finger! However, do fit the muzzle so you can squish a soft treat in your dog's mouth, or he can open his mouth far enough to get a little lick of squeeze cheese or peanut butter off your finger or, preferably, a spoon, while he is wearing the muzzle.

I recommend you habituate your dog to a muzzle whether you think it is needed now or not. That way, the dog is already accustomed to the muzzle and it can be used immediately when it would make the task safer. If you never need it, fine. So you took a few minutes to prepare for an event that didn't arise. Use this opportunity to count your blessings!

Teaching your dog to accept something she is not enthused about is also an excellent exercise for both human and dog. Humans learn some pragmatism, dogs learn compliance, and both learn the very important lesson of "Get Over It." You are also building trust in your dog: "No matter what I, your handler, introduce to you, you can trust me, I will not hurt you."

Human behaviour regarding muzzles is very interesting. People act like a muzzle makes a dog a pariah. The owner with the muzzled dog is often treated with suspicious side-long glances and comments that are obviously due to ignorance on the part of the speaker. These are the owners who should be commended! It means they are aware of their dog, aware that the dog has risky behaviour and that they are keeping everyone around them (including their own dog!) safe. It serves as a lovely non-verbal warning to approaching people that this dog doesn't welcome warm and fuzzy physical greetings from unknown persons and dogs.

Many people have a perception that muzzles are "cruel." Is it more cruel to muzzle the dog, therefore allowing the animal many more opportunities for mental stimulation and training, or to kill the dog because it finally bites someone? Veterinarians and groomers hesitate to use a muzzle because their clients become so emotional over it, therefore taking unnecessary risk. Really folks, what is better? The dog wearing a muzzle for ten minutes or a horrid experience for everyone involved, possibly culminating in injury?

computer art (Adobe Photoshop) based on photo by Sam Ziegenmeyer.

Do not expect your dog to love a muzzle immediately. At first he won't.

If your attitude is cheery, yet determined, when you introduce your dog to the muzzle, the dog will soon accept it. Here, Jamie is handling the new jewelry just fine. If you act like this is some sort of punisher, your dog will respond accordingly. Also, it is important to put the muzzle on daily for a while.

You can get your dog to accept the muzzle with the use of great treats that they can lick and don't require much chewing. If your dog can chew a treat, they can chew a finger off someone. If the dog requires a muzzle the whole idea is that they cannot get hold of things to bite them. Squeeze cheese and peanut butter are great treats for this exercise. Once a dog habituates to a muzzle, they are quite casual about wearing it.

Acclimating Jamie to a Muzzle

It seems people would rather allow a dog's nails to reach uncomfortable and arthritis-producing lengths rather than muzzle the dog and clip the nails. Amazing. Perhaps my own pragmatic attitude comes from years of handling livestock and rescue animals that need husbandry work done for physical well-being. Getting myself hurt over these tasks is ridiculous and certainly will not help the animal!

I remember a person who approached me at a clinic I was conducting. She had a large-breed guarding dog. She asked that I work the dog, but she was worried about him coming into the building because he was aggressive toward other dogs. I asked her to describe "aggressive" and she was not very forthcoming, but, after some questioning, described a reactive, sometimes explosive dog. She was clearly uneasy about handling her dog in this circumstance. I asked her if the dog was friendly with humans, and if he would allow me to approach him and handle him enough to work him, so I could help her take him into the building. She replied that he was "pretty friendly with most people." I must admit that didn't inspire confidence! Risk needs to be minimized if I am going to help the dog. Dog bites do not aid the dog in living a long, happy life, they hurt, and can cause permanent damage to the recipient. I replied I would happily work the dog and help her get him into the building, but she would need to have the dog muzzled and wearing a head-collar to keep myself and others safe. She quite huffily informed me, "He doesn't like muzzles and head-collars. They upset him so much." I gently reiterated to her that I needed to keep myself and others safe, so he would need to wear them before I could safely work with him. I watched, in open-mouthed amazement, as she turned on her heel and promptly walked away. Now this was asking a lot: that I would take a dog who is questionable with other dogs and people, and not allow me to protect my own safety and that of other innocent bystanders.

Photo by Sam Ziegenmeyer.

Squeeze cheese has the added advantage of keeping your fingers at a distance from the dog's mouth. I like this when I don't know the animal or he has already taken a snap at me.

Jamie is a real peach and was probably wondering how he drew the short straw for this photo series. However, you can see that, although he had his "why are you doing this?" ears on, he quickly accepted the entire ordeal. The attitude of the handler is ALL IMPORTANT. Be pragmatic, calm and determined, and you will go a long way in animal training.

Using Squeeze Cheese

If a dog becomes reactive toward another dog, then redirects the aggression toward me or his owner, and someone gets bitten, is there a winner here? Not! With proper equipment to keep everyone safe, it might be possible to teach this dog to be less reactive. But if an owner cannot bear to make the dog a bit uncomfortable in this process, the process won't happen. If your own emotions are more important to you than the dog's overall well being, then you will have to accept whatever the dog will give you. However, don't expect that others should have to have their own safety, or that of their dog, compromised so that your dog isn't made uncomfortable.

Take a realistic look at your own attitudes and make a sensible choice, based on what is best in the long run.

LEADS

A leather lead is important because it does not slip through or burn hands like a nylon leash might. My second choice would be a cotton lead. Leashes should be periodically checked for fraying or wear around the stitching.

MAINTENANCE

Check your muzzle, Halti, leash, and collar for excessive wear or weaknesses on a regular basis. Equipment breakage can have tragic consequences when working with an aggressive dog, not only in what the dog learns from the experience, but also in safety. Make sure all of your equipment is in tip-top shape each time you get it out to use it, particularly before you are going to do work that you have not attempted before, or when what you are going to do may be challenging for the dog. A broken leash or collar at an inopportune moment may mean the emergency room for you or others and euthanasia for your dog. Do not risk anyone receiving a bite.

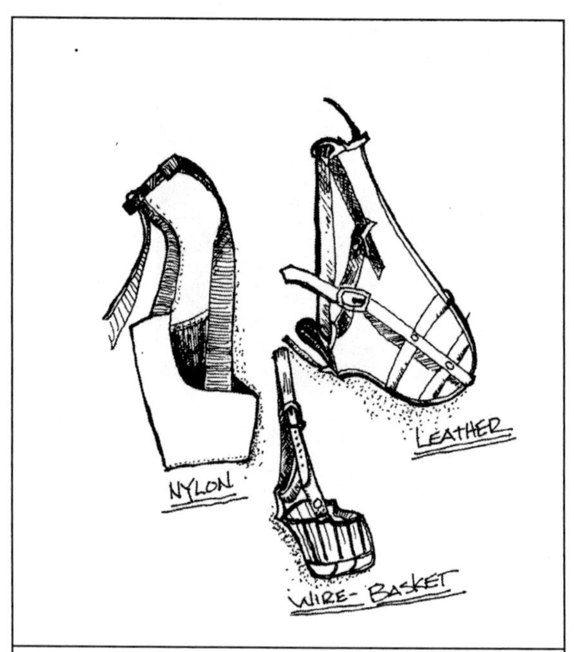

On the left is a nylon muzzle. In the middle is a basket muzzle. Basket muzzles are nice because the dog can open his mouth to pant better, but if a large dog lunges at you and hits you with the wire basket, it will leave quite an interesting bruise! The leather muzzle on the right is quite comfy also. I usually use the nylon muzzles; they are cheap, comfortable and strong.

Muzzles

Management & Damage Control

24

IMPLEMENTING A SCHEDULED FEED

A scheduled feed is a grand idea. If your dog is ever ill, the first thing your veterinarian will ask is: "When and how much did your dog eat last?" If all you ever do is fill the food bowl when it is empty, you are not keeping track of intake. Also, kibble left out all the time is constantly exposed to the air and therefore is deteriorating and losing nutritional value, attracting bugs, and other icky stuff.

One thing I consider to be neglect on the owner's part is the overweight or obese dog. Many of these dogs are free-fed. All that fat is difficult to drag around and puts unnecessary strain on the dog's muscular, skeletal and organ systems. You are shortening your dog's life and contributing to health problems in her old age (and increasing your health-care bill!) by allowing your dog to be fat.

I ask you, if you have children in the house, do you keep a constantly groaning buffet always available for them? NO! Meals are served at meal-times, and snacks may even be available, but not constantly. We have scheduled meals for our children and for ourselves.

For successful training, a scheduled feed is essential. For the vast majority of dogs, everything in life is free, free, free. Toys are scattered all over the floor, love and affection are available on demand, and there is always food around. It is no surprise that many dogs do not find humans relevant enough to respond to their cues. When your dog sees you in control of food – The Primary Resource – she knows you are powerful and Relevant! This is a perfect way to show your dog "Who is *Really* In Charge Here" (that's you, in case you were wondering!) in a very non-confrontational way. When you ask your dog to work for her meal, you are teaching her that:

- You are relevant.
- Obeying cues is a great way to earn food!
- Appropriate behaviour MATTERS.

My sweet Miss Breanna, who in her youth, decided that many KNOWN obedience behaviours were totally optional and sometimes removed from her current job description, learned differently when I cleverly utilized a scheduled feed. Most notably, she began performing a retrievc, which she always thought was stupid. The rule became, "You don't get the dumbbell, you don't get dinner." The first time I got the dumbbell out at dinner, she pointedly ignored my request to "Get it." She glanced at the dumbbell, rolled her eyes at me and pranced off to bounce and leap around the food bowl placed on the counter-top. I promptly took her prepared dinner, put it back in the fridge and walked away. About 5 minutes later, I got out dinner and the dumbbell, set up, and asked for a retrieve. When she refused, I just put the dinner away again. After about six of those trials, Breanna decided that retrieving was FUN! To polish her broad jump, her drop-on-recall – you name it, if it wasn't hunting (a-never-asked-for-but-always-offered activity) – the behaviour became dependent upon meals. Once Breanna (and subsequent dogs) figured out this puzzle, the response rate to my cues increased exponentially. Then, responding appropriately to known cues also became a HABIT! Not bad!

Here is how a Scheduled Feed is done:

1. For adult dogs, divide the dog's daily ration into two portions. For puppies, three or four portions are required.
2. Place the first portion in a bowl and place it on the kitchen counter, dining room table, or other inaccessible, but visible, location.
3. Ask your dog for a Sit, a Down (any KNOWN behaviour) or a sequence of known behaviours.
4. When you get an appropriate response, give your dog her meal. If she eats in her crate, take her and her food to the crate.
5. Remove any unfinished portion in 10 to 15 minutes.
6. If your dog has inhaled her food in 3.2 seconds, that is normal dog behaviour.
7. Repeat this for each meal.

If you are changing your dog from a free-choice to a scheduled feed, expect her not to eat the portion right away. After all, she is used to being catered to! Stick to your guns! Within a couple of days you will have a dog that understands the concept of a scheduled feed, and is looking at you differently – like you matter!

If your dog is fat and untrained, or if she is especially resistant to compliance, reserve 50-75% of her daily ration of dog kibble for training. There is nothing that says a dog has to eat a whole bowl of food at once – you can hand it out a bit at a time for good behaviour. Reduce your healthy adult dog's meals accordingly when you add the calorie intake of treats to training.

You will find your dog much more motivated to work for treats or even her daily kibble with a scheduled feed!

If your dog is ALWAYS crazy for food, then, by golly, YOU have a very trainable dog! Lucky you.

25

RELATIONSHIPS – TEACHING DOGS THAT HUMANS ARE RELEVANT!

This program works well to provide structure for dogs with anxiety problems. It is a deference program as well, and is excellent for the dog who does not believe that humans are relevant!

I have put "my own twist" and philosophy on this, but this general program was written about by William Campbell (1975) many years ago. It has a timeless wisdom that all should heed!

The *vast* majority of dogs who are categorized as "dominant" actually have anxiety, or are merely uneducated or untrained. They have never been systematically taught to accept or trust human touch. The lovely thing about this protocol is that it has little potential for exacerbating any problems, and it has a great capacity to do good things for any human-dog relationship.

Our domestic dogs are forever dependent on us for food, water, access to the outdoors, love and affection, as well as for discipline and order in their lives. Yet very few humans take advantage of the multitude of training opportunities this provides.

Most of us have been well trained by our dogs to attend to them whenever they demand it. Because dogs tell us they want to go out, they want a drink, they want a treat, they want a pat, and we comply without first requiring something from the dog (any desirable behaviour: Involvement, Sit, Roll-over, whatever), it is not apparent to dogs that humans are relevant. It is really not surprising that dogs do not consider humans relevant. What is more surprising is that more dogs don't become pushy! For the insecure dog, many of our interactions lead the dog to believe there are no boundaries – making their world look even more uncertain. Many dogs become overly demanding in an effort to define the boundaries and figure out the rules.

We love our pets; they are part of our family. It is so easy and fun to spoil them! I spoil my dogs, too – but I also provide structured obedience (it doesn't require nearly as much as you might think!) and "House Rules" which must be followed. Having rules and knowing that they must be followed is important to your canine friend. It makes Spot feel secure and loved, just as it does for human children and adults. Before you can "enforce" the rules, your dog must be taught what the rules are. *IT IS NOT FAIR TO CORRECT FOR A LESSON NOT YET LEARNED.*

Our dogs do not have the instincts, background, or judgment to deal with much that they encounter living in a human society. Dogs should not and do not have the judgment to decide: who sits where in the house, who gets to walk in the yard or be admitted into the home, whether they should run in the road, and other such matters. We must be the "guide" of our Family Group and make decisions for our pet's physical and mental safety, and for the well-being of our visitors and family, too!

Provide Structure – Help for Pushy or Anxious Dogs!

If your canine friend falls into this category, you are certainly not alone! Most behavioral problems exist because of a lack of or poor communication between canine and human. As soon as you learn that there are effective ways to let your dog know what you want, he learns how to earn your praise and approval. Being the one that doles out the reinforcement makes you relevant and makes it clear that you have the authority to provide consequences. Understanding that **Consequences are Contingent On Behaviour** makes your dog understand the relevance of your commands.

Helping the anxiety-ridden dog, or changing a demanding or non-compliant dog into one who accepts your wishes, involves following a protocol that is easy to describe, but which requires commitment and self-discipline from you.

The formula is easy: Each time your dog asks you to do something (e.g., petting, taking out, feeding), you ask him to do something for you.

The scenario looks like this:
1. Spot approaches you and nudges you.
2. You respond by saying, "Spot, Sit."
3. As soon as Spot sits, you may pet to your heart's content.
4. Before you feed dinner, ask Spot for a "Down."
5. Before you allow Spot to go out the door, "Sit" and "Look at me."

A good follower needs to function for the leader. Because your dog is living in a "human" environment, he must be a good follower. Things run much more smoothly this way! To have a good follower, you must be a good leader. Your dog also needs your approval and praise. It is a "paycheck" for work well done. And companionship is very likely why you got your dog in the first place. You should be enjoying each other, not in constant confrontation!

In summary, whenever you are approached by Spot for attention, you must ask him to Sit or do something else. Then go ahead and praise or pet. Do avoid prolonged petting and attention at first (for about 2 weeks). Prolonged "fussing" over the dog will slow down your progress considerably and cause backsliding. Use obedience for other circumstances also. Ask for a Sit or Down or a trick before you: feed dinner, pet your dog at any time, let your dog out, let your dog in, leave for a walk and during walkies, and before you throw a toy.

Integrate requesting a Sit or Down or other behaviours into daily life and **every interaction** that you can with your dog. The advantage to this, is that you are able to do several Training Shorts throughout the day – each one taking about 5-10 seconds. *Repetition is the secret to having reliable behaviour on cue.* Each time a behaviour is performed, that behaviour is strengthened. As a by-product your dog is forming a habit of compliance. Yes!

When you stick to this "program," you will find a new dog in the house within a week or two. Not only is he more interested in your opinion, he will also be more relaxed. He is no longer having to make decisions that he is incapable of making. Plus there is the added benefit of getting "good" attention and praise from you. The benefits for you should be obvious: you get an even better friend because you are cooperating with each other. The relationship is enhanced because the tension caused by the question "What are the Rules?" is resolved!

You may see a few days of withdrawal, confusion and "pouting" behaviours. This is certainly within a normal range of response. Remember, you have just changed the rules, and initially your dog may be very puzzled – his routine has changed. Why this sudden backslide? Spot has worked so very hard to *train you*, and you were responding so well!

This program works wonderfully to provide structure and security for anxious dogs and to provide boundaries for pushy dogs.

In fact, this program works well for any dog. The *real* reason the program works: It makes **Consequences Contingent On Behaviour**. The issue is really not so much "Who is Boss?" with dogs, but "What's in it for me right now?" Dogs, like humans, are looking for structure, patterns and predictability so they can know the rules and, therefore, work within the framcwork.

For those of you who are interested, this program is utilizing the Premack Principle (after David Premack). This states that a high probability behaviour (something the dog wants to do, such as dash out the door) can be used to reinforce a low probability behaviour (something the dog might not otherwise do voluntarily, like sit prior to the "dashing").

26

GAMES PEOPLE & DOGS PLAY

Games are one of the essential reasons we get our dogs, whether we are aware of it or not. Many people would say companionship, but games are an integral part of companionship. Games and play are how people and dogs learn to interact socially. There are many games you can play with your dog to enhance your relationship and to get to be a kid again yourself. The mental and physical health advantages of play for both of you are endless!

Play and games are how dogs naturally learn to interact with each other (particularly as puppies). Games are a way to teach dogs how to interact with humans also. Most dog games center around chase (prey) and possession. Games can be used to teach your dog that people ARE NOT dogs and do not wish to play in the same manner as dogs (such as, rolling each other around in the dirt and biting and body-slamming).

Good experiences with play will prevent aggression. For dogs who are presenting with aggression or marginal behaviour, play is important, because you can practice teaching the dog appropriate behaviour with humans by selecting your games thoughtfully.

Many times the way people play with their puppies promotes behaviour that will be interpreted as aggression in an adult dog. If dogs are allowed to play possession games and "win" them all the time, this sends the message that using teeth to maintain possession is okay. When the dog gets tired or annoyed with you during play and uses defense to get you to stop, you are teaching defense behaviours. If you drive the dog into a highly aroused state, then continue to "push" her with rough play, she may be frightened and resort to defense to back you off. You lose your temper and punish the dog, and an unpleasant cycle of events has begun.

No puppy or dog should be *slapped around the face, head or mouth in play.* Do not offer your hand or arm for the dog to bite or grab in play. Only appropriate games should be played, providing relationship-building exercises where the dog is reinforced for showing considerate behaviour to humans.

Any time dog teeth come into contact with human skin, interrupt the game without delay! Depending on the situation, one of several techniques may be used:

1. If your dog gets rough and possessive or constantly tries to get you to chase her, then keep a leash on the dog to prevent Human-Chases-Dog games. Keep plenty of treats handy to teach your dog that giving up toys and coming to humans with her toys is to her advantage.
2. If you are working with a pup who wants to play and she is grabbing your hand instead of the toy, immediately stop the game and pointedly ignore the pup for a moment. (Stand up, look up toward the ceiling and cross your arms). You

may then re-engage the dog in similar play and see if she has gotten the message. You may need to repeat this one or several times, depending on the individual, for them to get the message.

Do not engage in the kind of rough play in which you are shoving, pushing and rolling around with the dogs and encouraging them to body-slam you. Also taboo are those games that seem to highly amuse humans: aggravating the dog intentionally until the dog becomes reactive (poking at the dog, slapping at his face, etc.). Inevitably these are the same people in the family who complain the dog will not listen to them. This play also gives dogs the clear message: humans are a target for rough play and it is okay to get aroused, aggravated and be very physical with them.

People should not play with their dogs by rough housing and chasing. Rough housing tells Spot that it's OK to be rough with people, and he will inevitably frighten or hurt a child or non-dog oriented adult. Chasing games are not fun for you at 6:00 a.m. just before leaving for work in the freezing rain, or when Spot has your panties in his mouth when guests are over.

Keep your dog and others SAFE! Educate your dog about safe and appropriate play behaviour from Day One.

Games Dogs Play with Other Dogs

These generally fall into one of the following categories: prey and chasing games, possession games (which may quickly escalate into intense or serious "This is MINE and I am not kidding" behaviour), or mock fighting.

In chasing or prey games, one dog is the "predator" and one is the "prey." The dogs may trade positions with no apparent rhyme or reason, but that is part of the game. When the "prey" is caught, she may be rolled to the ground, grabbed by the neck, and a mock battle may ensue. My dogs seem very fond of chewing on each other's feet, face, and ears or stalking and pouncing. The strategies are wonderful to watch. One will attempt to cut corners and "head 'em off at the pass" in an attempt to catch the other.

If the "Hunter" becomes too boisterous with the "Hunted," it's time for parental intervention. Sometimes smaller or younger dogs become frightened if the other players become too rough. Once frightened, the dog behaves like real prey. Call both dogs to you or get hold of one of them to stop the activity and give both a little break. A Social Time-Out in the form of crating or a Down-Stay is a good way to implement a break.

Mock Fighting

Think of Tweedle Dum and Tweedle Dee! Lots of "fake" posturing and wrestling. Dogs are very fond of "mouth games" and growl and chew on each other's faces. One dog will pin the other to the ground and, with flashing teeth and lots of noise and action, they will mouth each other. You will notice that all well-socialized dogs involved will very carefully inhibit their bite. After all, if they bite too hard no one will play with them!

General fun is being had by all as long as the dogs are inhibiting their bites. No one appears frightened and trying desperately to get away with tucked tail. No one is yelping. The dogs exchange roles.

Warning Signs: One dog constantly mounting all the other animals. This is often a sign of insecurity. A bully is in the making unless this behaviour is curtailed so that other, more desirable modes of interaction can be developed.

The same applies to those dogs who greet by running up and placing their paws on the shoulders or backs of other dogs. My own Breanna is famous for this and it's just about as playful as someone coming up and shoving you instead of shaking your hand. Not cute! Or friendly!

If both dogs begin to "spar," where they are standing on their hind feet and "boxing" with each other, with lots of eye contact, there may be trouble. As long as one dog clearly submits, with the eyes looking away, ears back and head lowered, all is well. Friendship and play will commence.

Games That People Should Play With Dogs

The Best Games reinforce the qualities you want your dog to exhibit with people in general. There are lots of them, and I bet you'll come up with even more once you get into the spirit of it all. Most everybody has little "personal" games they play, kind of like a private joke. Breanna "smiles" in the morning when I allow her on the bed for her morning tummy rub, and Punch likes to jump into laundry baskets (my husband taught her that, if she does this, she will get a cookie). Zasu and Rylie love to chase tennis balls. Zasu, a Smooth Fox Terrier, also likes to pounce and bark at everything – rakes leaning against the side of the kennel, water running out of the hose, balls, and a variety of other stationary and moving objects. Rylie, a Border Collie, likes to stare intently at tennis balls as much as she likes to chase them.

The games below are used to teach Sit, Down, Give or Drop-It and other cues. Yet another example of using "daily life" or Premack's Principle to gain reliable response to cues.

Hide 'n' Seek

1. Have a helper hold the dog while you show the dog a cookie or toy and get him all excited.
2. Go out of his sight – just around the corner at first.
3. Call the dog and have the helper let him go.
4. Time for a street party when he finds you!

Alternative:

1. When you are out for a walk and puppy is ignoring you a bit, duck behind a tree, bush, etc.
2. Peek and see if puppy notices you aren't there.
3. If he does, and starts looking for you – great!
4. If he doesn't, attract his attention by calling his name, or suddenly running off while calling his name.
5. Play-time when he finds you!

You might want your dog to be on a long line for this game initially. Playing this game with a very independent dog may backfire on you, as it has on me with my terriers on an occasion or two...so make darn sure that you provide a safe situation before you play this game by using a fenced area or a long line. My advice is that puppies drag a long line for about the first twelve months of life to promote good habits.

Fetch

Fetch games are always taught with two or three of the SAME article. Refer to the Protocol, "Twos," for additional discussion on this topic.

1. Without shoving the toy in your dog's face, get her all enthused about the article.
2. Throw it, at first just a short distance.
3. As she puts her mouth on the object and picks it up, say her name, clap your hands, move away from her.
4. Show her the toy you have in your hand, to bring her back toward you.
5. When she brings the toy she has to you, don't focus on the toy, but *focus on her* with social approval (verbal "oohs & ahhs" and pats).
6. You can encourage her to drop the toy she has at your feet, or after five seconds or so. Put your hand on the toy and say "Give," and then encourage her to give the toy to you.

   Alternatively, begin playing with the toy you have until she becomes interested and curious and drops the toy she has to investigate.
7. As soon as your dog drops or gives you the toy, immediately throw it or one of the identical toys you have retained, so your dog can be immediately rewarded for giving up possession of the toy.
8. Quit playing while the dog is still very eager. Usually two to three Retrieves the first few times you play this game is plenty. Don't be tempted, because you and the dog are having fun, to continue this game until the dog becomes bored and wanders off. Over several sessions increase the number of repetitions as the dog gains enthusiasm and lengthens her attention span.

9. A great way to end this game is to trade a cookie for the ball (or toy). Then you retain possession of all the fetch toys.

Once your dog is dropping the toy or willingly giving it to you on request, you may just use one toy for this game. But it is helpful to begin with the multiple toys so your dog understands that "giving something up" will actually "get" him something.

Caution: This game is appropriate ONLY if your dog has not tried to "guard" items from you in the past. This is indicated by your dog exhibiting a guarding posture, growling, snapping, or biting you when you walk by, or try to take, items.

If your dog has shown possessive aggression, please proceed with extreme caution, and initially, use lots of high value treats to encourage the dog to relinquish the toy she is currently in possession of. These dogs need to be on leash so you can prevent rehearsal of running off with things, causing you to chase them down, which could end with a bout of defensive behaviour.

Refer to the protocols: "Cease & Desist" and "Resource Guarding" for further discussion of possessive aggression and other possessive behaviours.

Beat the Clock

This game teaches your dog to listen to you even when she is excited. It is a game that can be played for both short or long periods of time, so it is versatile enough to be played daily and on the spur of the moment.

1. Your dog is on leash for the initial stages of the game, and off leash when she is reliable.
2. Begin play; as dog gets excited, give a command she knows well.
3. The goal is an immediate response.
4. As soon as the dog offers the requested behaviour, *immediately* begin enthusiastic play again.

Be quiet or use a NRM when the dog resists. Then you can try repeating the cue one more time. If your dog is off leash at this stage and you are not getting quick response, place a leash on the dog to limit movement and to assist you in obtaining the desired response from your dog.

The leash is not to correct the dog, but to limit her movement so you can obtain a correct response by whatever means is appropriate for this dog's skill level.

Let the dog learn that she controls the game – the quicker she responds to you the quicker the play starts up again. If she does not comply, the game will stop.

Find It!

1. Begin with your dog's favorite toy or cookie.
2. Show the item to your dog, then place it a short distance away and say, "Find it."
3. When this step is mastered, hide It under something.
4. You can begin hiding It in other rooms.
5. You can teach a dog to systematically search a room.

Shell Game

If your dog guards food or toys, consider the use of an Assess-a-Hand™ in lieu of your own precious digits to see if this will be a safe game to play with your dog. If she reacts favorably, this can be a great game to teach the dog restraint and to practice "trades" of a sort. (For more information about the Assess-a-Hand refer to the protocol, "Handling and Restraint.") If your dog tends toward possessive behaviour, she needs to complete all of the Foundation and Level I protocols and "Cease & Desist" and "Resource Guarding" protocols before attempting this game again. Possessive behaviour includes sudden stillness as you reach for the toy, growling, lunging, or snapping.

2. Put your dog on a Stay.
3. Place a cookie under one of three bowls or baskets.
4. Release your dog with "Find it."

5. Spot will use her nose to locate the cookie and overturn the basket to claim her prize.
6. You can help if she seems confused by showing her the proper basket and overturning it for her.

Tug Games

This is a favorite game of many dogs, and one that many trainers discourage. This is a judgment call – I think that it is an excellent game and play this game with all my dogs. This game can easily go awry, but like all games, if rules are instituted and followed, a good time can be had by all. Tug games can teach many valuable lessons to your dog if handled suitably. Restraint, calming down when she is excited, allowing the owner to limit and control arousal levels – this game can teach all these things. Tugging provides your dog with an outlet for pulling, shaking and running: all activities the vast majority of the canine population loves to do.

Caution: For a dog who is already presenting with aggression, this is NOT an appropriate game. If your dog has exhibited possessive behaviour or if she has bitten you or threatened to bite you in the past, this is NOT an appropriate game. For some dogs, this game will never be appropriate.

As always, proceed with safety first and foremost in your mind. Don't take chances; if your dog makes you uncomfortable with this game, or this game is too rough for you because of the amount of pulling the dog is doing on your shoulders, don't play it!

I do not allow anyone other than myself to play this game with my dogs. I want to give the dog an outlet for prey behaviour, but I do not wish to promote rough play with random people. The whole idea is that this game PROMOTE the control I have over my dog, not to allow the dog to be rough.

Some Rules for Tug Games

I enforce fairly gentle tugging by my dogs, and they pick up on this quickly.

- Tug games are initiated by human invitation ONLY.
- The arousal level of the dog is controlled by interrupting the game periodically, requesting an "out" of the toy. You may need to use a treat to gain compliance.
- If the dog "outs" (gives up the toy), she may have one of two possible rewards – a treat or you may simply request a Sit, Down or other cued behaviour, and, as a reinforcement for compliance, you may offer the toy and resume the tugging game.
- If your dog ignores your signal, make sure you have a leash on her so you can Ruin The Fun by limiting her movement.
- If you feel teeth on human skin, immediately gain possession of the toy and put it away. The game ends if an "out" signal is ignored, or the dog becomes too rough or unmanageable.
- If you are unable to maintain control of this game, DO NOT PLAY. It will teach all the behaviours you want to avoid.
- NEVER EVER should children be allowed to play tug games with dogs. Children do not have the requisite judgment and it is way too easy for them to be overpowered by the dog.

Trouble-shooting for Tug Games

If you get into trouble and the dog refuses to give the object back, or you are concerned by your dog's behaviour, gaining possession of the object becomes a priority. The first times you play this game, the dog should be on leash. To re-gain possession of the item may become a waiting game. Don't try to take the toy if it appears as if it is dangerous to do so, but also do not allow the dog to take off and enjoy the toy by himself. Keep the dog on leash and just start walking around. Wait until the dog becomes interested in something else or becomes bored and drops the toy. Perhaps a whole handful of string cheese tossed on the ground will convince the dog to drop the item. DO NOT reach for the toy at this time. Merely move away from it with the dog, and encourage her to come with you using food to do so. Then you can move the dog out of the area, away from the toy. This allows you to tie the dog back or take the dog out of the area entirely, and you can go back without the dog to get the item. Now do all the Foundation and Level I protocols. Study all protocols that are relevant to Resource Guarding and gaining control of your dog's impulse control and handleability. Protocols that will be helpful: "Handling & Restraint," "Resource Guarding."

Roy Hunter has written some excellent books on games, you can play with your dog, many of them scenting games, which are very fun. There is an excellent video called "Take a Bow ... Wow," that shows how to teach many great tricks. Tricks are based on learning and cooperation, so teach as many tricks as you possibly can. These materials are available through Dogwise. (Their Web address is www.dogwise.com.)

Playing games with the dog will strengthen the relationship in many ways. If properly used, games further prevention of aggression. Playing appropriate, carefully chosen games with the dog already showing aggression helps to get the dog and handler on a different wavelength and educate this dog about how to properly behave with humans in a more relaxed way. People tend to be more relaxed when they teach tricks as opposed to "obedience" lessons. When owners are not so uptight, it is good for the relationship.

27

Why discuss barking in a book about aggression? Barking itself is not necessarily aggression, but barking is an indication of arousal. A dog can keep himself in a chemically reactive state by continuing to bark. Let's face it, when dogs are calm and relaxed, they are not barking. Barking can cause other dogs in the area to become reactive as well, escalating the probability that defensive or redirected aggression will occur.

A dog who begins to approach another dog and is barking directly at the other dog is certainly indicating that this encounter may not be a peaceful one. If the second dog reciprocates with vocalization, the chances that this will be a peaceful encounter just took a very big nose-dive. Same goes for person approaches. If a dog is barking, she is not at peace.

People expect dogs to bark, and nobody minds that they do when it is appropriate (such as, temporarily, when someone comes to the door); what all of us *would* like is that our dogs be still when we ask them to do so. One of the best ways to teach your dog to be quiet on cue is to place both the barking and the silence on cue. Your dog already does both, you just don't have stimulus control provided by YOU. Both behaviours are currently on cue from the environment only, or from some internal stimulus from the dog herself. Blessed Silence already exists, you just need to install a cue for it and then reinforce the heck out of it.

Begin by placing barking on cue. When you see your dog get ready to bark, give him a verbal cue, "Speak," and then reinforce this. At first, you will most likely see an increase in offered barking behaviour, but be patient. Soon you will be able to turn that behaviour on and off at will. Now that you can cue barking, you can practice switching from barking to silence.

Like barking, quiet behaviour is also naturally occurring! When your dog is already being quiet, go up to him and give a different, VERY OBVIOUS hand signal or a sudden verbal cue (like "Quiet!"). I use both. I tap the dog's head firmly with my fingers and follow that by a "Quiet" word. Then I have both at my disposal and can use one or the other as the situation dictates. After you give your new cue for silence, immediately Mark It & Feed It. Do this several times. Your dog will be puzzled at first, and will probably have absolutely no clue about what he is being reinforced for, but he will still eagerly eat the cookies you are handing out!

Now you can either cue the dog to bark, or wait until he barks at something. Allow one or two barks (don't let him really get going!) and give him his "Quiet" cue. Initially, especially if your dog is kind of excited because he is barking at something in particular, you might have to use the head tap to surprise him out of barking. Once you give the head tap, and he, in surprise, looks up at you and ceases barking for a second, you must very promptly Mark It & Feed It. At first, have several treats handy, because you will give a slow, steady constant feed for the silent behaviour, while continuing to repeat your cue, as long as the dog is quiet. This is so he can associate the new cue with his silent behaviour.

If the head tap alone does not work, you can try a squirt of water in the dog's face, then repeat the original cue again, always reinforcing the silent behaviour immediately, no matter how you get it! Act VERY serious as you give him the water squirt, but not raving and angry.

Caution: For some dogs the water squirted in the face is reinforcing. My little terrier, Zoomer, begins to leap around and bark furiously when she sees a water bottle because for her this is a great game! So, for some dogs, the water squirting will work immediately, and for others it will not work at all.

If the head tap AND the water do not work, try a loud startle noise in the following sequence:

1. Give the cue you are attempting to install: "Quiet!"
2. A loud startle noise (a wooden spoon hit against a pan works pretty well, two pans slapped together better, and an air horn will stop almost anyone in his tracks, including your neighbors...).
3. Repeat if required.
4. Reinforce the quiet behaviour.

For really determined barkers, an air horn is very effective to back up your cue of "Quiet." Do remember to reinforce the quiet behaviour. Your dog may be alarmed at the air horn and behave in a frightened manner. Do not validate the frightened behaviour. DO encourage him to come over near you, then ask for a Sit, say "Quiet" again, and reinforce it. Soon your dog will understand that, if he complies, the air horn does not sound.

The air horn, other noise, or water is meant to startle the dog out of his barking frenzy, into a quieter state. It is not a punishment. It is meant to get the dog out of a reactive state, and to manufacture Quiet Behaviour, so you can use Positive Reinforcement.

Again, be sure to be serious and CALM when using these startle techniques, not angry or punitive.

As with other exercises, it is prerequisite that the target behaviour be practiced in a controlled setting first. Only after the dog has at least some fluency in the behaviour is it appropriate to Challenge the dog by raising criteria and placing the dog in situations with increasing difficulty (those that typically elicit barking).

If a situation comes up that the dog would normally be barking his fool head off, and the dog barks a couple of times then is silent, Jackpot! Or if the dog is silent in a context in which he is normally barking, again, heavily reinforce the absence of barking. It is important that First Correct efforts are generously reinforced. Notice the really good decisions your dog makes!

In this manner, you will, over a week or two, gain control over the dog's behaviour. You will no longer reinforce barking behaviour, nor cue for it unless you want to practice quiet behaviour. Instead you will continue to reinforce the quiet behaviour and never, ever reinforce the barking behaviour. This is an extremely effective way to manufacture a dog who is quiet on cue and who offers quiet behaviour voluntarily.

28

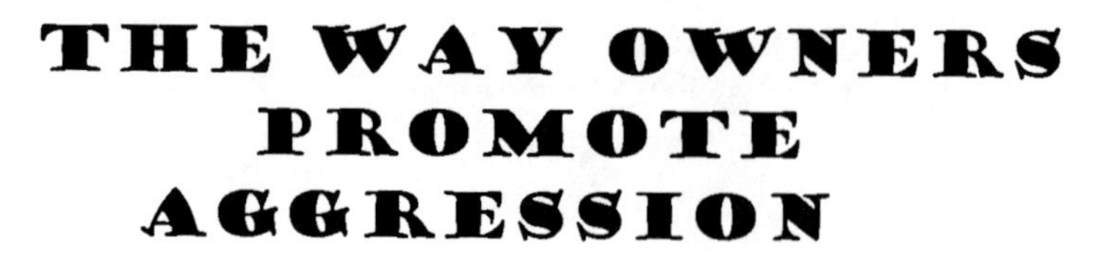

In a dog's environment, there are several factors that promote aggression. Owners, unknowingly, promote aggression in many ways. If you become aware of the contexts or environmental cues that promote aggression, you can prevent them from occurring.

Lack of Supervision

Leaving unattended dogs tied-out or enclosed in electronic fencing systems unquestionably promotes aggression. The dogs are on territory and are allowed to bark, lunge and snarl at passers-by. It is the exact same circumstance that occurs with the mail-carrier: the dog thinks that his escalation of barking and lunging is what causes the passing people and dogs to continue on their way. Every time this happens, your dog is practicing unsavory habits: deciding who is allowed on his territory, and using agonistic displays to move the "intruders" away from his territory.

Some dogs don't really take this territorial stuff seriously. But do you know that about your unsupervised dog? If you are not there to observe behaviour, your dog, unbeknownst to you, may be rehearsing risky behaviour that will escalate. Maybe you will never get into trouble with your dog. However, if your dog is in this circumstance frequently, don't be surprised the day that someone decides to come closer (the dog would interpret this behaviour as ignoring a clear communication to leave the area) and an unpleasant event occurs.

Electronic fence systems may keep your dog in, but they do not keep your dog safe from other dogs wandering in. It also means that neighborhood children have more access to your dog than is safe.

Points to remember! All dogs should be supervised around children always.

Leaving your dog within a fence, visible or electronic, and leaving for work allows your dog to develop and rehearse undesirable and dangerous behaviour patterns.

Daily practice of inappropriate behaviour (unsupervised within fences or tie-outs) will promote aggression that becomes unmanageable.

Lack of Structure

People don't realize how very important it is to place limits on their dog's behaviour. This helps your dog to learn to effectively cope with the kinds of frustration that daily life with humans imposes on dogs. Learning lessons like:

- Everything you see isn't available for the taking.
- You will be crated even when you don't want to be sometimes.
- People are going to restrain you physically (such as on a leash, or holding by the collar).
- Sometimes you need to lie down and be quiet...

and many other structure-related events are part of being a pet.

This is very closely related to supervision, but has a slightly different twist. Part of teaching your dog about structure will involve having the dog "work" for what he "gets." Also, teaching your dog that he has to do things sometimes that he would rather not do is a vital part of providing the dog with structure.

The advantage to teaching your dog about structure and rules is that your relationship with your dog becomes much more cooperative. This is a lesson quickly assimilated by your dog, and the benefits are life-long.

Lack of structure promotes insecurity in your dog.

For more discussion on this topic refer to the chapter titled "Relationships: A Program for Teaching Dogs that Humans are Relevant."

Lack of Knowledge

All people who come to me with aggressive dogs have one characteristic in common: they do not understand the dog's native language. The lack of communication and the miscommunication that result are unfortunate in the extreme. Good communication between dogs and humans is a primary ingredient for success in both prevention of aggression and modification of the behaviour of dogs who are already presenting with aggression. (Refer to Section II "Dog Communication Systems" in this book. See also the appendices for further reading.)

Very few people have much of an understanding of dogs as a species. To make up for this, people tend to anthropomorphize – filter the dog's behaviour through a "human" point of view. This process is rife with assumptions instead of facts. I will reiterate a sentiment many dog writers before me have used: dogs are not little people in fur suits.

Lack of Management

Dogs are allowed way too much freedom and allowed to make too many decisions without the owner giving them timely feedback. Dogs are allowed too much freedom before they have been trained and have formed good habits. "Lack of Management" is totally avoidable.

When you get a puppy, the care for the first six months of the dog's life is considerable and time consuming. When you get an older dog (24 months or older), the dog will settle in more quickly, but the first thirty to sixty days will still be time-consuming. A lot of this time involves establishing rules and setting limits on behaviour (structure) – in short: Management.

Good management is directly related to planning ahead. Setting the dog up to succeed, and then reinforcing the desired behaviour, is far easier than using training techniques, that lead to failure and create problems that must be fixed later.

People and events around your dog need to be managed, too. Do not practice Rough Play, nor allow your dog to be placed in a situation where he is being teased. Children, and an astonishing number of adults, do not have good judgment in this arena. Teasing is when someone annoys and pesters the dog who is physically trapped and cannot get away or is forced to use defensive behaviour to get away. Poking at the dog, constantly offering food or a toy, and not allowing the dog to ever be able to gain possession of it, may frustrate the dog to a point of frenzy. Children poking the dog through a fence, or family members unkindly prodding the dog until he retaliates – all of these constitute harassment.

Allowing dogs to bark constantly at passers-by or when people come to the door can promote aggression dogs of a certain temperament. Allowing the environment to train your dog guarantees that your dog learns undesirable behaviours at the same time they are learning to leave you out of the equation.

An excellent booklet on this topic is *Management Magic* by Leslie Nelson and Gail Pivar (1997).

Lack of Exercise

Puppies need tremendous amounts of exercise and stimulation *each day.* Do not underestimate this, or you will be regretful at some point. See the chapter titled "Games People and Dogs Play" for suggestions. Add walking the dog to your list of "things to do." Find areas where your dog can safely be turned off leash – fenced yards are an absolute godsend.

It gets easier to provide adequate exercise as your dog gets older. He will recharge slower for one thing. Also, as you gain control over the dog's behaviour, it is easier to get the dog exercised and keep him safe while doing so.

If you cannot find any areas to turn your dog totally loose, attach a 40-foot drag line to the dog so he can get greater amounts of exercise and you can still control the dog and keep him safe.

Inadvertent Reinforcement of Fearful Behaviour

If your dog is displaying fearful behaviour, it raises the possibility that defensive behaviour, which will be exhibited as aggression, will follow.

It is a common human reaction to comfort and reassure an animal who is unsure of the circumstances or is frightened. When this occurs, the handler validates the dog's current fearful state. The dog interprets the handler's reassurance as approval of how he is behaving "right now." The handler, in this instance, is actually conditioning the dog to remain in a fearful state and to behave in a fearful manner. Fear is the first step toward some form of defensive aggression.

Not all cautious or fearful dogs will definitely display defensive aggression in the future, but it does raise the odds. See the protocol: "Being Brave Is Better" for specific information regarding handling fear responses.

Fearful behaviour is also promoted by not getting a wide variety of experiences on a regular basis as a puppy, adolescent and young adult dog.

In General:

- Stop inadvertently reinforcing aggression.
- Stop inadvertently reinforcing fearful behaviour.
- Stop punishing aggression – show the dog *what you want and how to behave* using the protocols in this book, or any other technique that works, but don't just randomly punish aggressive behaviour. Punishment always has "fallout." That is you may punish a behaviour you didn't intend to decrease, or you may promote aggression because of missed associations. Your dog may become distrustful of you. Punishment can contribute to arousal and anxiety levels, pushing them ever higher.
- Reinforce appropriate behaviour whenever you see it.
- Be aware and proactive.
- Do not assume that your dog, at social maturity (18-24 months of age) and beyond, is going to be friendly with every dog he meets. Introduce adult dogs under controlled settings whenever possible so that you can monitor the situation. Remember that many adult dogs have different agenda than puppies do.

29

ON A WALK AND APPROACHED BY LOOSE DOGS

Dogs running around loose without supervision are a common problem, particularly for my clients who live in town.

Quite often loose dogs will rush up with the intent of being unfriendly. Or, the loose dog may be too friendly and overwhelming to your dog who is either ready to tie you up so he can go play, or wanting to kill this idiot who is rushing up so rudely into his personal space. I don't have any great answers for this hornet's nest, but it does help to have tons of cookies with you. Often you can distract your own dog by moving away from this dog and reinforcing him for doing so. It is imperative that you get in a position where you can prevent prolonged, hard eye contact between the two dogs, because this certainly means that things are going badly.

In truly desperate situations, I have been known to pick up my small dogs. If this is your only option, do so slowly and carefully. Do not snatch up your dog. The act of lifting up a dog in the presence of another who is in an aroused state is **very** provocative, and may cause the dog left on the ground to jump up and bite. Make sure your dog's tail and feet are tucked up and not available as fodder for the snapping jaws. Watch your own hands and face also.

I have been in the situation with my German Shepherd bitch of having a dog intrude into our personal space and leap all over her. Maeve, who is not always friendly to other dogs and certainly doesn't like RUDE dogs rushing up because of protective aggression, does not take kindly to this. After much behaviour modification, she no longer immediately becomes dangerously reactive in this situation. The behaviour modification certainly made a difference, *but just as important is my bargain with her*: "If you do not react to this, I will handle it for you so you don't have to." Her judgment in this area has improved immensely, but I still cannot be cavalier about it!

I have handled this in the following fashion. But do keep in mind that, if you choose to do this, you are placing yourself at some risk for a dog bite, or at the least some buffeting and scratches from the intruder dog. You are also placing yourself at risk from your own dog, depending on the amount of control you have over him. My immediate concern is that I maintain enough control over the situation to prevent dogs from getting connected to one another by biting, because then injury will become certain. Once the animals have hold of each other, it is always bad. Therefore, I get my dog BEHIND me and I keep blocking the other dog from her by keeping my body between the two dogs. You can see the inherent danger here if the other dog is not friendly. At least this way I can manage to keep the two dogs apart, and can be yelling for the other dog's owner to come and get his dog if he is around. The entire time, maneuver yourself out of this area. Citronella spray or an air horn may help to repel the intruder dog.

If the intruder dog is on home territory, chances are that, as soon as you get a certain distance from that dog's "boundaries," she will just leave you alone. In extreme cases, when MY dog is the concern and the intruder dog is just dumb and friendly, I have successfully prevented my own dog from causing damage by doing the following, which must be practiced many times OUTSIDE this context to habituate the dog to it.

As the Intruder Dog approaches, I "hug" my own dog with my right hand round her body, just behind the front legs, and contain her head with my left hand round her muzzle, and hold her head over my left shoulder. I then lift my large dog's front-end off the ground and contain her that way. Your dog may not be totally thrilled with this situation, so be forewarned that you might be placing yourself in a risky spot. Then our socially inept, but friendly, dog will usually just sniff and wag and bounce around for a minute, find you totally uninteresting, and leave. You can just let your dog down and continue on your merry way, the "merry way" having been somewhat marred by this rather unsettling incident. The key is that the incident was "just unsettling" and you prevented it from entering a financial arena with vet bills or litigation. If the approaching dog is challenging or aggressive rather than friendly this hold will not work, as it will only hold your dog still for the oncoming attack.

Many times you can get the other dog to leave by ignoring him. Being unfriendly, yelling, etc., may just cause the intruder to become more aroused instead of less so, although you can give it a try. If shooing the intruder dog away doesn't work on the first or second try, it's not going to. Then your "shooing" efforts are counter-productive, causing your dog and the approaching dog to become ever more aroused.

The best defense is to make yourself and your dog appear as uninteresting as possible. This means getting your dog to look at you, and moving away from the other dog as calmly as possible. Move your dog away at a moderate pace because a fast pace may encourage the intruder to chase you. By the way, I would not turn MY back on the other dog, but would face my dog and the intruder, while encouraging my own dog to come to me, turning her back on the other dog. This avoids the potentially dangerous eye contact between the dogs.

Remember, I know nothing about this intruder dog. If my dog is not happy about the situation, I don't want eye contact because I don't want my dog to "start" anything. Even if my dog IS friendly, I don't know how volatile the intruder is. Avoiding eye contact between the two dogs is the best way to keep a lid on the situation, at least until I can assess the intent of the intruder.

It is important in these situations to know that your own dog is "handleable," as you might have to take hold of her collar or pick her up while she is in an excitable state. There are exercises in this book that will, upon completion, ensure that your dog is accustomed to being handled. (Refer to protocols for "Handling & Restraint" and "Yielding.")

Defensive Tools

You can try taking an air horn with you on walks. This may serve to get rid of the other dog, but keep in mind you will also be alerting everyone in the neighborhood (may be a good thing, may be a bad thing) and deafening yourself and your dog. If the noise ends up being associated with the approaching dog, your dog may find this unnerving such that she becomes fearful of dog approaches. This situation depends a great deal on your individual dog's temperament and whether she tends toward noise sensitivities. A good strategy is to go on the walk without your dog once or twice and use the air horn on the dog(s) who are a chronic problem on your route. If you are fortunate, the dog will associate you with the air horn and avoid you when she sees you coming. Then, when your dog is with you, have the air horn handy. Just showing the intruder dog the air horn may cause her to move away. You may attract considerable and undesirable attention from humans in the area with this technique, particularly from the owner of the dog in question. Whether this is a risk worth taking is your judgment call.

Where it is legal, you might consider pepper spray to ward off unwanted loose dogs. Be cautious with this because it is very easy to spray yourself and/or your own dog. A friend of mine was walking her dog when two loose dogs charged up to her and began to lunge and snarl. She tried telling them to "git" and moved away, but the dogs continued to follow and escalate their agonistic display. She finally resorted to spraying the intruding dogs with a pepper spray. The dogs dispersed. Finally, at this point, the owner finally entered the scene and began to yell and advance threateningly toward her. So she sprayed him too, then left the area. She gets my vote!

Citronella spray may have some effect in lieu of pepper spray.

The "Defendabrella" idea was passed along to me by an acquaintance who attended a Patricia McConnell, Ph.D. seminar and related the following idea to me. The protocol below is designed by me, so any errors are mine alone.

You can desensitize your dog to an umbrella, and then carry one with you when walking. Use it to discourage loose dogs from approaching you by opening the umbrella suddenly when they get close to you and your dog.

If the intruder dog is being nasty, sometimes you can startle him away with the umbrella. It is possible the umbrella could be used as a "sacrifice" if the situation becomes truly alarming. Yes, you will abandon your umbrella, but, with any luck at all, you and your dog will leave safely.

Before using this technique, make sure your own dog is not alarmed by your opening the umbrella suddenly while you are standing beside her! This involves first opening the umbrella from quite a distance and giving her cookies every time she remains calm. Then gradually decrease the distance until you are standing right beside her and she is comfortable with this activity. More precisely:

1. Have the umbrella lying around, both open and closed, while your dog is eating a meal.
2. Carry the umbrella on your walks, both open and closed. It is not really necessary to use tons of treats here unless your dog is very intimidated by the umbrella.
3. With your dog held by a friend, or tied from a distance (start at 10' and see if it is okay with your dog or too close; then adjust your distances accordingly), very slowly and carefully open the umbrella. Your dog will get treats for being calm about this.
4. Working at a pace the dog is non-reactive to, gradually step closer and closer, until you are holding the dog yourself, or are standing right next to her and opening up the umbrella.
5. Now go back out to your original threshold distance, and open the umbrella suddenly.
6. From the same distance open it and wave it around.
7. Now work your way back up to your dog, at a pace the dog is non-reactive to, until you can be walking along with her, stop, and open the umbrella and wave it around. Copious treats for this.
8. Once your dog is walking while you carry the umbrella, don't forget to add opening the umbrella, waving it around and yelling "Go Home, Get Back" as you might if another dog approached you when you were walking. Give your dog plenty of treats for not being intimidated by your rather bizarre behaviour!
9. Now you are ready to use this as a way to cope with loose dogs on your walk.

If you already know there are dogs on your route who are intimidating or a nuisance, take a walk on that route without your dog, but WITH your umbrella. That way you can see if your defense strategy will work on those dogs who are being bothersome.

If you have leash laws in your neighborhood or county, you can always ask your local animal control office to help. Some may be of great help, others are so overwhelmed with the daily workload that they may be of little help to you.

You can also try negotiating with the people whose dogs are running about loose. Again, this may not be well received, so you will have to make a judgment call about what will work best in your own particular situation.

Caution: The use of an air horn or a "Defendabrella" both require judgment about whether it is worth the risk of causing problems with your own dog in order to get the other dog away from you. In some cases it may be well worth the risk!

Electronic Containment Systems

Dogs behind "invisible" electronic fences get lots of practice charging their boundaries and using defensive behaviours to frighten "intruders" away. Again, calling on these owners may be useful, or it may not. I have had clients who were terrified to walk their dogs down their own street because of dogs fiercely charging invisible fences. The dogs stay in their boundaries, but my clients were still very wary, and their dogs were terrified also. The following technique may be frowned upon by the dog's owner, but it worked well for some of my clients. We took extra hot dogs with us and tossed a handful in the electronically-fenced dog's yard. After a couple of days, the "contained" dogs were looking forward to the hot dogs with wagging tails, and their demeanor would change as we were recognized on approach. You have to get close enough to toss the food inside the dog's boundaries, unfortunately, and that means dragging your dog closer to this dog who is terrifying her. It isn't necessarily pretty, but it can work. Some dogs just become more defensive and fearful behind their invisible fence, and escalate their display as you approach. Also, if a dog's owner sees you doing this, he might be understandably alarmed. Then, however, you might have an opportunity to discuss the real issue here – their own dog's behaviour and lack of supervision – and negotiate a solution. Depends on how reasonable the human is.

Avoidance

All this said, avoidance of loose dogs may be a valid choice, and always is the safest choice. You can choose to walk an alternate route if there is a chronic problem with your current route.

Section VII

Hi Ho! Hi Ho! It's *Planning* Before Off to Work We Go

30

DOGS MAKE LOTS OF MISTAKES - SO DO YOU!

It is important to anticipate errors that the dog might make in real life so we can simulate them in practice and help the dog learn the decisions we want her to make. If the dog has never seen the particular situation before and makes a judgement call and it is the wrong one – who is really to blame here?

Presenting the dog with Challenges, and then giving her information and feedback about the decisions she makes, is how you will educate your dog about how to make appropriate decisions in a given context. This is the way you shape behaviour in the direction you wish it to go.

Do not venture into a situation just praying your dog is going to "get it all right," just because she does it at home. Inevitably, there will be something that the dog does not see at home. But if you have done your homework, placed the dog under varying situations, and taught the dog how to cope with stress, you will have a much better chance of success. The better you do your "proofing," the fewer glitches you will have to discover.

It is easy to be emotional, but this will not aid your efforts. I deal with this by getting very clinical. I write out the description of the Target Behaviour (the behaviour I wish to change). I include: past locations, environments, my cues, etc. Then I write out the description of the Terminal Response (the behaviour I want to see). Now I share with myself ideas about how I might alter the situation so I can get my Terminal Response. This is the way I handle "taking it personally." I find that if I am really focusing on just the behaviour and how I am going to modify it, I am much more level-headed. It is so very easy to get a "tempest in a teapot" going. Get a grip and use your logic to override your emotions! I will walk you through this procedure in the chapter "Master Plan."

Some additional hints:

- Use consistent Antecedents (cues).
- Food is not a substitute for a good relationship; it is merely one of the tools you use to teach, just like a collar or a leash is used.
- Don't bribe or threaten. Reinforcement is the paycheck for a job well done. That means the criteria have been met!
- Be proactive and decisive. If you have thought about how you are going to handle a situation when it all goes to hell-in-a-hand-basket (rest assured, at some point it will), you will be prepared to do something other than stand helplessly by, feeling your frustration escalate.

TIMING

Timing is everything! I cannot over-emphasize the importance of timing. It is so important to be focused on your dog, yet remain aware of the environment around you. If you are really paying attention to your dog's behaviour, your timing will improve.

Inevitably, many clients I work with are either *not noticing appropriate behaviour that they should be reinforcing, or their timing is too late or non-existent.*

Just as detrimental is early reinforcement. What most commonly happens is that the person "cheer leads" or "bribes" the dog in an effort to get appropriate behaviour. This unintentionally reinforces that very behaviour he wishes to reduce or delete.

I see cheerleading and bribery often when people are doing Heel work. The dog is lagging behind, and the handler, in an effort to get the dog to speed up, encourages her with, "C'mon, let's go!" and then feeds the dog, or uses food to encourage the dog to speed up. Whenever this is done, the slow behaviour is validated and reinforced.

The other reason for "too early" timing is that the handler is failing to raise criteria. That is, he is reinforcing the correct behaviour, but too soon – not waiting for duration or commitment to the behaviour. For instance, when you first begin shaping a behaviour you can accept any step in the right direction. The first few times you say "Sit," you will quickly Mark & Feed the behaviour the very moment the dog's bottom hits terra firma. However, if this is what you continue to Mark & Feed, you will never get an actual sit-and-remain-seated behaviour. In other words, the dog will never learn to COMMIT to a Sit. The dog will, understandably, think the cue means, "when I sit, I get a treat and then I can get back up." In order to GET duration, you must reinforce it. As soon as you have a dog who will sit for you with a verbal or hand signal, raise criteria by gradually delaying the food treat for greater periods of time, and increasing distance. When the dog has a rudimentary understanding of the cue, begin to raise criteria to improve the behavior by reinforcing not JUST the behavior itself, but the dog's COMMITMENT to the behaviour.

APPROXIMATIONS

One category of common dog training errors concerns approximations.

The criterion is too low: the trainer does not raise criteria, because he is afraid of failure or he gets stuck and doesn't know the next step. To avoid being caught in this trap, have a plan and know your next step.

Also remember what your last step was, so when you need to lower criteria you will be able to do so.

Another common approximation-related error is the criteria are too high: the trainer does not break the goal behaviour down into tiny enough approximations.

Because these errors are common, I have provided you with step-by-step instructions in this "The Fix – Protocols" section. If an approximation is too high, and the dog is failing to meet criteria, you must find intermediate steps between the approximations I have provided. I have broken these protocols down into fairly small approximations, but for some dogs the steps may still be too big. Or you may misinterpret or try to jump ahead. If the lesson is not going well and the dog fails, begin problem-solving by checking your timing first and your approximations second. This may require a videotaping of your training sessions so you can pinpoint where you are going astray.

31

OR: IF YOU DO THIS YOUR LIFE WILL BE EASIER!

Before training:

Always always don your Humour Hat and Zip up your Patience Suit!!

Train once or twice a day for five to fifteen minutes at a time,

for "formal" training sessions. Better yet, make every interaction with your dog count! *Daily life is the best way to train!*

Never ever train if you are in a foul temper!

This is unavoidable on days when you are crabby and you must still handle your dog. In this case, fake it! Pretend you are NOT crabby. Crabby people are not using their normal excellent judgment. I have set my own training programs back a month at a time by acting (or rather more accurately, reacting) out of temper.

Make your cues count.

If you cannot enforce it or manage the environment so that it goes your way, don't let the words pass your lips! You are teaching your dog to disobey if you nag impotently at him. Technically, what occurs in this situation is that you are desensitizing the dog to the cue you are using. You are teaching your dog that response to a given stimulus is optional. A cue is a "heads up" for your dog: signalling a potential chance for the dog to earn reinforcement.

If you do not have verbal control, you must have physical control.

This means long lines, fences, collars, leashes, head collars – whatever it takes to keep the situation under YOUR control. Remember, the object here is not to PHYSICALLY RESTRAIN the dog. The goal is to MANUFACTURE reinforceable behaviour.

If your dog is unsure, don't correct – reteach the exercise.

Do not just mindlessly correct!! As discussed in the "Laws of Learning" chapter, going back to kindergarten with a behaviour is not failure in any way. It is a necessary part of the learning process. Review is good. Repetition is required for learning to take place. During the process of generalizing a behaviour, you will be required to *lower and raise criteria many times* as the situation and the dog's learning curve dictates.

If you must correct, do not call the dog to you and then administer the correction or be cross. *Go to the dog* to correct behaviour. Every time your dog comes to you, love and praise him, even if his response is tardy. Work on the tardy response separately, but when your dog comes to you – it is always good! The great example here is of people who have not taught a proper recall, or who have not properly generalized the behaviour. Then when the dog disobeys, and doesn't come right away, they become cross and angry. They call several times. Then when the dog DOES come, he gets "what-for." Not fair, and very detrimental to your training.

Don't call the dog and then do something he hates ...

like baths or nail clipping. Go get your dog, or call him to you, then play and give a treat. While still holding on to him or placing him on leash so you have that necessary physical control, lead him to the grooming area and bathe, clip nails, place in crate, etc.

Approximations are all important.

Each behaviour must be broken down into small bits. This provides information in a way that is easily assimilated by the dog. It is the classic tale of the tortoise and the hare – slow and steady will win this race!

By breaking the behaviour into easily attainable steps and then raising the criteria, your dog will be a willing worker because:

- She understands what you want.
- She gets a lot of success, so instead of getting discouraged, your dog feels confident. Success begets success!
- Aggression is reduced because you, the handler, are also getting reinforced by the success of the dog. Therefore, your frustration level is reduced, and you are placing less social pressure on your dog. This translates into a reduced aggression level in the handler, which, in turn, means the dog doesn't have to feel defensive or anxious.

Approximations build a good foundation for the terminal response or end goal behaviour. Like building a good house – the foundation is firmly anchored making for a stronger home.

32

ALREADY GOT A PROBLEM VS. PREVENTION

The Foundation Behaviours and the Level I Behaviours in the chapters that follow will give your dog the tools to *learn how to learn.* They will teach your dog to look to you for direction. This is a package deal: your dog will be counting on YOU for precise information. Since you are the one who is in the driver's seat, *you* are the one responsible for a navigation plan. This doesn't mean the dog is "just along for the ride," though. You will find that your dog has constant input and provides feedback for you as well. Your dog's job is to pay attention. Good training feels like good conversation – it is a sharing experience.

IMPORTANT: You may be working on several protocols simultaneously. It is not necessary to do one, finish it to completion, then begin the next. There are pre-requisites designated for you if they are required to begin a protocol. For example: Today in your 15 minute formal training session, you are planning to work on:

- Involvement
- Cease & Desist
- Sit & Down Stays

During the day, around the house, you may have several opportunities to do 10- to 60-second training sessions:

- Your dog needs to go outside, so before you open the door you will request a "Look" behaviour.
- You decide to have a cup of tea and, while the water is warming up in the teapot, you have plenty of time to call the dog and do a Sit or Down Stay for one minute. OR you could do several "down" trials where you are specifically working on a quick response to the verbal cue. ("Down – Yes!" Move 2 steps. "Down – Yes!" And so on.)

These are just a couple of examples. You will need to do your own planning of how to organize your time. Just remember that *the more you integrate these exercises* (particularly the Foundation and Level I behaviours) *into your dog's daily living experience, the quicker you will see a change in the dog's overall conduct.*

My approach to aggression has been shaped by the dogs I have lived with and many of my clients' dogs and the involvement that I have had working with them. I have read endlessly and talked endlessly to other people with dogs. The exercises that have worked well for me, and for the clients who make the commitment to persevere, are catalogued in the Protocols in this section.

I use the same protocols to prevent aggression that I do with the dog who is already presenting with aggression. This is because the crux of the matter is education. A naive dog is a naive dog – and what she needs is education. Either the dog never received the opportunity to be educated or the education was, for some reason, not understood by the dog. Or her education did not consist of positive experiences that allowed her to learn appropriate behaviour, but instead encouraged defensive or confrontational behaviour.

The protocols that follow will prevent defensive and confrontational behaviours from developing in your puppy or dog. All dogs can benefit from these exercises. All relationships will be enhanced and become more trusting. For dogs who are presenting with cautious or defensive behaviour, or who are beginning to show other alarming signs of aggression, the following exercises will help you to explain to your dog how to maneuver around in the world: peaceably. You will change your dog's paradigm about how she views the world in order to modify her behaviour. This is what behaviour modification is all about: not merely suppressing behaviour, but actually changing the way your dog perceives a given context. You will be teaching work ethic and impulse control. You and your dog will learn to be a team and communicate effectively with each other.

I wish to reiterate here that some dogs are abnormal or have a disorder. For these dogs, you will observe much more spontaneous recovery. The old habits will be much more difficult to eradicate because of abnormal learning patterns. New behaviours will be much more difficult to install for the same reason. If you are following the protocols to the letter, and are still really struggling and not making much progress after 4 or 5 months of work, you might want to seek specialized help. Your animal may not be exhibiting misbehaviour or lack of education – he may actually not be processing the information you are giving him in a "normal" way. Just as you teach a dyslexic child to read differently than you would a "normal" child, these abnormal dogs may need extra help. In some cases medication may be appropriate to lower anxiety levels in order to facilitate learning. Beware of using psychopharmacology without a good behaviour modification plan. This is a fruitless endeavor.

This said, the great difference between prevention vs. rehabilitation is in HOW I proceed with the protocols. With an animal who is already presenting with behaviour that is causing concern, it is important to move ahead with safety as the primary consideration. With older dogs who are dog hot, thinking that they may be able to run in the dog park after a couple of weeks of work is unrealistic. Overall, the work will proceed at a slower pace, because you are overcoming prior reinforcement history for undesired behaviour and installing desired behaviour.

Doing prevention work with your young puppy is, comparatively, a breeze. Her window of acceptance for new experiences is wide open. You are not battling old habits that must be overcome, as well as installing new responses. The size of a puppy is of great benefit also. The jaws are not as strong, the teeth, while razor sharp, are not as big and damaging. The danger level in exposing puppies to other puppies or stable older dogs is practically nil because of the social development stage and the smaller size.

This does not mean that an older dog cannot make incredible changes in her behaviour. I have personally rehabilitated dogs with some very amazing results, and also watched the magic worked by my clients on their dogs using the behaviour modification protocols outlined. It requires a lot of work and a lot of commitment. It means changing your own behaviour patterns. But the results are well worth it. When Maeve came to me 3 years ago, never would I have believed that she would be the dog she is today. If I don't tell people that she has had some *very* serious episodes of aggressive behaviour in the past, they would never know it. Strange dogs can run up into her face and she no longer overreacts. She looks to me for help when she becomes aroused instead of just handling each irritation with her teeth. Just when I thought she had come as far as she was going to, I'll be darned if she didn't make yet another behavioural breakthrough and start treating people like she liked them instead of merely tolerating them because I was present. When I started with Breanna, never did I think she would be safe enough to do out-of-sight stays with other dogs. And yet, at an obedience trial, when a Shar-Pei mounted her during the group exercises, she held herself together and did not tear this untrained animal limb from limb. Because Breanna had been reinforced in this group-stay situation repeatedly for not reacting, by golly, she didn't. (The major problem that day was more one of human-to-human aggression – me maintaining my temper and not tearing the Shar-Pei's owner limb from limb for not properly training her dog.) When you see your training and behaviour modification holding together under fire, it is an amazing accomplishment.

To summarize: If you are working with a puppy, you can pretty much move ahead as quickly as the pup will allow you to do so, emphasizing a huge variety of new experiences. For dogs that are presenting with marginal or risky behaviour already, you will need to move forward much more slowly and carefully, keeping the safety of you and others in the forefront.

The meeting of the minds that will occur between you and your dog will increase your understanding of not just dog behaviour, but human behaviour, specifically your own! The changes in your relationship will be wonderful. You will become a team.

The Relevance Of Observation

Remember the relevance of observation and the importance of the following equation:
chemical state (the internal state) = behaviour (the external state).

Observation of the behaviour, the dog's external state, is how you gather information about the dog's chemical, internal state. This provides you with valuable information about the function the aggression may be serving for the animal. Knowing this helps you to select the most relevant protocol and maximizes the potential of the protocol you will be using. For example, if a dog is indicating a fearful state you might wish to proceed slowly, and concentrate on increasing the dog's self-confidence levels in this context – if he is not afraid, he won't feel defensive. If, on the other hand, the dog indicates self-confident body language and is using aggression because it has worked in the past to gain him resources, you may wish to embark upon a different path to explain to this animal that "aggression will not gain you resources." This does not mean you will confront the animal. It does mean you will have to place the animal in situations that change his paradigm about when resources are available to him and when they are not.

During the process of doing the protocols, you will find out much information about your dog.

1. Is the dog exhibiting normal learning patterns?
2. Is the dog adaptable?
3. How quickly does the dog rebound from stressful situations?
4. If this is a dog who is presenting with aggression, what will the prognosis be? (Excellent, good, fair, guarded, poor, unresolved.) What will be the prognosis for a high percentage of improvement?
5. Does your dog have potential for reactive or risky behaviour? If the dog is NOT presenting with aggression, these protocols will indicate the probability of potential for aggressive behaviour and under what circumstances. This information places you in the position of being able to minimize this potential.

Getting Started

Whether you are preventing problems or modifying behaviour that is already occurring, the following protocols are the key to success.

The protocols begin with Foundation Behaviour – the essential step of establishing a communication system. Next, the Level I work focuses on teaching your dog about impulse control and including you in the decision-making process.

The Foundation and Level I work is crucial. All of the work is based on these and once completed, you will be amazed at the change in your dog, the enhanced communication, and the compliance to your cues.

The protocols address ever more specific and difficult learning tasks as you advance. Begin the Foundation and Level I protocols immediately. Next begin the Handling and Restraint work.

Before moving on to the more specific work, you will need a navigation plan. The chapter "The Master Plan" will provide you with tools to develop a plan.

33

SUDDEN ENVIRONMENTAL CONTRAST (SEC)

Sudden Environmental Contrast concerns changes in the environment. A change that might not be significant to a person may be very provocative to a dog, such as another dog or person at a distance or someone entering a room.

SEC can provoke great arousal in dogs, and is a primary source of aggressive defensive behaviour. If you have a dog who is already presenting with intense arousal that shifts to aggression or predatory behaviour, you must be vigilant about any changes that arise in the environment.

Your dog might be happy and relaxed at dog class UNTIL another dog runs up within twelve inches and barks and play bows. Even though this dog is inviting play, if your dog is startled or irritated by this, she might react defensively. This is an example of a sudden change in the environment. Another common SEC is a door opening and someone new entering territory. Let's say you are at a dog class, and you and three other people are peacefully working your dogs. A fourth person and dog enter. Two of the three dogs "on territory" startle and begin to bark. The third dog follows suit and also becomes aroused. It is easy to see how these situations can quickly escalate into one that is not "friendly."

If your dog becomes reactive in situations like this, a good way to handle it is to consider this context a "Leave It" exercise. Your job is to be **proactive** and, as soon as you see or sense someone entering the area, whether your dog has become reactive yet or not:

- Request a "Look" behaviour, and if that is not enough...
- Quickly use a "Leave It" and back or move away from the person coming in the door until your dog orients toward you.
- Supply lavish reinforcement for maintaining involvement with you instead of "giving in" to the environment.

Preventing extreme arousal in situations of SEC is handled the same way. Early on in training, use any SEC as a cue to look at you. Your dog learns to look at the cause of the SEC, then immediately "check-in" with you by looking at *you* instead of reacting to the environment.

Now that you know to look for SEC and to be ready to react quickly when SEC presents itself, you are armed for success!

- Develop habits that help you to control the environment and to maintain control of the dog. Cues such as "Look," "Leave-it," and "Come" will be a big help.

(Refer to the "Eye-Contact & Involvement" and "Cease & Desist" protocols.)

- You must also remain calm or, at the very least, THINKING. You cannot change your dog's paradigm of the situation and teach him to control himself if you are in a panic and just "reacting reflexively" instead of reacting thoughtfully your own self.

Being proactive is the Name of This Game! Teach your dog that SEC is not a circumstance that demands arousal and reaction.

- If you meet an unknown dog or person unexpectedly, do all you can to diminish the situation and keep it diffused. Use a Move-Away exercise (see the "Cease & Desist" protocol) to get your dog to orient toward you, and reinforce all movement toward you and attention that the dog gives to you. Distance is the best "diffuser" in these situations, if distance is an available option.
- As other dogs or people are approaching, BEFORE your dog becomes aroused, distract him, then reinforce him for staying near and paying attention to you. Initially, you might need to use a constant feed to accomplish this.
- If you meet an unknown dog out of the blue, IF THE OTHER DOG IS MERELY CURIOUS and your dog is dog-friendly and merely curious also, loosen your leash suddenly (but don't drop it!) and then move AWAY from your dog while saying a "Good bye" or "Let's Go" type of cue. As you reach the limit of the leash, your dog will feel it, and, if she is not already moving toward you, she should respond quickly to the light pressure on the collar once you have completed the Foundation and Level I protocols. REMEMBER: This exercise must only be undertaken with *friendly* dogs, and may not be effective at all until your dog has completed the Level I protocol exercises, so that your moving away from her provokes a strong following response.
- Reinforce your dog heavily for ignoring the environment and interacting with you until or unless you grant him permission to partake of the environment. (See the "Cease & Desist" protocol.)

A great prevention strategy is to reinforce (RM or RM & treat) each successful pass by humans or dogs or cars, etc. If your dog is concentrating on you and what you two are doing, she will not be so worried about or focused on what is happening in the environment. If you are proactive, you can easily promote the dog remaining committed to you rather than defaulting to the environment each time there is a small change. Building trust and communication between you and your dog is what the protocols in this book are all about.

34

THE MASTER PLAN

Okay, you now know a lot about aggression. Why it makes sense to the dog. What intrinsic and extrinsic factors are contributing to the behaviour. The kinds of environments that foster aggression. The events and actions that maintain it. What aggression looks like.

So what?! You still have not fixed a darn thing!

We shall remedy that posthaste. Roll up your sleeves! This is where you go to work. Before you begin, you will make a navigation plan to support you through the stormy seas ahead until you sail into the calm harbor of behaviour modification. This plan will change and grow as you progress, so be open to this as you advance.

This section is meant to be used as a general guide, not as a definitive street map. Each Case History will be unique, and so will the family dynamics and environmental considerations for each animal. For instance, if there are children in the house, the dog who is resource-guarding food would be handled with much more caution and much less tolerance for error.

The first portion of this chapter applies more to dogs who "already have a problem." People who are doing preventative work may not require some of mental gymnastics listed below, but it will still be interesting reading!

What I discuss next is how to go about making this navigation plan – your own individual master plan.

Your handler attitude and expectations are all important as you are going through the learning process with your dog.

MENTAL GYMNASTICS

Preparing Yourself for Undertaking The Task.

Behaviour modification is not an exact science. The protocols themselves may need "tweaking" along the way. The order you do the protocols in may change, although you will ALWAYS complete the Foundation and Level I work and the Handling & Restraint protocol first. If one problem is becoming more serious and requires attention, take care of that. Then return to the work that got interrupted. As you move through the protocols with your dog, you may discover that the problem is not what you originally thought it was, but something else. Just keep working and you will improve. Pay attention to the details, but keep an eye on the big picture at the same time.

When you are listing goals and expectations, be realistic. Consider other family members (pets and people). I myself have made agonizing decisions because "the needs of the many outweigh the needs of the few." (Trekkies should recognize that phrase....) If one animal is making everyone else miserable or is dangerous to them, and behaviour management and modification is not netting you the results you need in order to co-habitate, then you may have some tough decisions to make. On the other hand, with management, so many behaviour problems are made tolerable. So, don't overlook major management strategies for controlling aggression. Management goes hand-in-hand with the behaviour modification protocols, but is easily neglected or resisted by owners.

Owner attitude is all-important and closely related to outcome. *Commitment, persistence and consistency* on your part all contribute to success. But you may not be the only family member involved. For the best possible outcome, your family must be in it with you also. You might need to call a family meeting to make sure you are all in accord and that you have the cooperation of the others as you go through the protocols. You may discover that changing the ideas and behaviour of the family members becomes as irritating as the dog's behaviour was in the first place. Or, maybe not. Maybe your family will find themselves in concert. Good for you! Your prognosis just made a little leap in the right direction!

You are already on the short list for failure, and may be placing yourself or others (including your dog) at risk for physical harm, if:

- You think that the dog is dominant and that is the issue, so, therefore, you need to place the dog in a provocative situation until he becomes aggressive and then "take him down."
- You have a "Sink Or Swim" attitude. You think that dogs can just settle altercations on their own and "they just need to learn how to handle themselves." While this may be true in some cases, in most others it is quite emphatically not so. Few people can distinguish these cases.
- You suffer from "Deer Caught In The Headlights" syndrome. You feel panicky when the dog exhibits reactive behaviour; you "lose your head" and cannot think clearly. The fact is, in training, you may have some hair-raising experiences. The important thing is to keep your head during the crisis. You can have your nervous break-down later.

  The cure for this particular problem is knowing what to do – once you have a clear plan, you won't need to panic.
- You think that confrontation is the way to "teach the dog a lesson." If you meet aggression with aggression, and the dog chooses to continue escalating her aggression, what is your big plan now? One of the dogs I worked with comes immediately to mind. He was about 120 pounds (no fat I might add), a 2-year-old intact male Rottweiler who had been allowed to raise himself in the back yard with no limits ever set on his behaviour. To feed him, the family would lure him into a large chain-link kennel and then throw the food from six feet away, because if they got any closer he would lunge at them and savage the fence. Well, I wasn't certain I could win a direct confrontation with this boy. Actually, I was quite certain I would not win. Several months later, after a lot of work, management and an extensive reinforcement history, he would do a Sit Stay while fed. If I scolded him he would crawl on the ground in abasement. This authority was gained with management and positive reinforcement. But that first day I was a very long way from gaining anything but personal injury from confrontation.

  The point here is that confrontation may teach the dog the wrong lesson entirely: that he CAN win. It may not be possible for you to "win" a confrontation at all.
- You suffer under the delusion of one of the several Lassie myths:
  - Dogs are sweet and innocent creatures that really don't want to hurt anybody.
  - You think YOU won't get hurt because you are "good with animals" and "dogs

always love you" and the dog will just respond to your own kind nature.

- You make constant excuses for your dog's behaviour. Pick one: You think that dogs are "just like that" or "my dog REALLY wouldn't actually HURT anyone" or "this is just how (fill in the breed) are" or "he didn't really mean to bite."

Well, now that I have pretty much alienated every human being on the planet with this list, and you are all good and p----d at me, remember that you are reading this book to get results. The attitudes above will not get you the results you desire.

You will set yourself, your family and your dog up to get those desired results if you:

- Are, above all, Observant.
- Are Proactive.
- Are Confident. As you gain skills and have small successes with the protocols and learn how to manipulate the environment, this will come, even if you don't feel that way right this minute. (Right this minute you may be feeling a bit overwhelmed with information.)
- Are Cautious. Be safe. Safety is always Priority Number 1. Better Safe than Sorry may sound trite, but it is all too true when handling aggressive dogs.
- Have the ability to remain in control of your own emotions, or at least your own actions, even though you have just gotten a large adrenal dump because your dog did something alarming.
- Are aware of your own body language and can control your body language to help your dog, even if you are "under fire." (You may, of course, have your nervous breakdown later, as I do. Just schedule it for after the incident, not during.)
- Do not let your ego get in the way. If you get in over your head, extricate yourself from the situation as safely as possible, and know when to stop or back down. You may "lose face," but you'll be in one piece, and in a position to continue the behaviour modification program. I have, on many an occasion, used calming signals and blatantly "submissive" body language and saved my own sweet little self.
- Realize that Knowledge is Power. You have an understanding of the species and its body language. You have an understanding of classical and operant conditioning, and know how to set up a communication system with the animal.

Human Behaviour Changes

Are You Ready? •

- Are you willing to change your own behaviour and interactions with the dog? It is surprising to me how many people come for help, then refuse it because, in the end, it is easier to stay with the old attitudes and undesirable habits. These folks, after additional altercations and, in many cases, injury to themselves or others, often euthanize the animal.
- Are you willing to embrace long-term management as part of your life? Aggression is serious stuff. To keep the dog and others safe, it is necessary to make some long-term changes in the way you manage your dog's daily life. Make no mistake about the fact that your lifestyle will be altered as well.
- Do you understand that, if your dog is presenting with aggression, particularly if she has a bite history, you have a problem that may involve the legal system someday? BE INFORMED. Different states have different laws, and the laws may be in flux. Contact an attorney and your insurance company if you have questions in this arena. In a court of law ignorance is not a valid defense.
- Do you understand that long-term protocols and constant review of those protocols is a requirement?
- Are you willing to adjust your lifestyle to accommodate the management and protocols that are required to modify your dog's behaviour? I have a lovely, heated kennel and office combination. This makes it possible to keep the dogs I have. One group spends time in the house, then the other group. During the day they can all be kept safely separate in the kennel when I am not in attendance. I have them all to the point where my "special" ones are not explosively

reactive with each other even though they detest each other. (Breanna and Maeve in particular). They can be loose together if I am standing there watching. They can all sit and have cookies together. People can even knock on the door and they can get excited and run into each other with no mishaps. I have visual barriers up so they cannot see each other when kenneled and unsupervised, because that situation promotes aggression. But the tension of constantly being around each other is alleviated by the way I *manage the daily life* of these animals. Not everyone has that luxury. What kind of adjustments are you able and willing to make?

All right. The reality check is over.

Whew....Those are all tough questions, some of them with no great answers. The bright side is that you can make a difference if you give it a good try. For some dogs this is life or death. Now, on to our master plan.

The Plan

The first step is a rather general Case History. You will think in a systematic manner about the environment your dog lives in and his daily routine. Some answers you give to these questions may, in fact, not even be relevant. On the other hand, there might be some red flags as you go along, too. At this point it can be difficult to determine what is relevant. Like a detective just beginning a case, you need to gather all possible information so you can figure out what IS relevant.

Personal History and Daily Environment

- List people in the house, with gender and age.
- List pets in the house, with gender and age.
- Does the dog have specific problems with anyone above? What? Favorites? Whom?
- Any changes in the household? List them.
- How old was your pet when acquired?
- How long have you had this pet?
- Why did you get your dog?
- Where did you get your dog?
- Where do you live? (Busy street near a school with a Herding, Terrier or Guarding Breed? You leave him loose in the yard unsupervised? And he barks, you say? Rural setting? Many visitors?)
- Describe a typical day for your dog: when you feed, when he goes out, etc.
- Does your pet get sufficient exercise?
- Is your pet contained in a fenced yard? On a tie-out? Walked on leash? Outside unleashed and supervised? Unleashed and unsupervised? (If the last one, you need immediately to change your ways.)
- List any health issues, present or past, even if minor.
- List any training done by you, or group or private classes taught by others. How did it go?
- What formal training do you use on a daily basis? Grade the following as VERY Reliable (95% or better compliance), Sort of Reliable (better than 50%), Unreliable (less than 50%): Sit, Lie Down, Stay, Walk on loose leash, Leave It, Drop It, Retrieve.

Functional & Task Analysis

Now that you have thought about the dog's general environment, it is time to get down to more specific details concerning the Target Behaviour(s). The first step to problem-solving is to identify the problem itself.

Make a list like the one below. List each troubling behaviour separately (the Target Behaviour). Then decide on a Desired Behaviour that will work better in place of the problem behaviour.

Table 1: Hit List

Target Behaviour	Desired Behaviour
Uncontrollable barking and agitation when the doorbell rings.	One or two barks, then the dog immediately quiets and becomes calm when I say "Quiet."
Dog alerts and lunges at other dogs.	Dog looks at me for advice.

For each item on the Hit List, use a separate sheet of paper and answer the following questions:

- How long has the target behaviour been occurring?
- At what age was the target behaviour first observed?
- Has the frequency of the target behaviour increased since first observed?
- Has the intensity of the target behaviour increased since first observed?
- Is the behaviour predictable? (If the behaviour is extremely unpredictable proceed with MUCH caution and use all tools available for safety, such as muzzles. You may wish to seek the help of a behaviour consultant if the behaviour is very violent and very unpredictable.)
- Can you interrupt the behaviour verbally?
- How difficult is it to interrupt the behaviour?
- List ways you have attempted to interrupt the behaviour and the results of each.
- Do you think you may have contributed to the problem? List how.
- List what you have done to correct this problem to date.
- Describe the extent of each of the following. Does the behaviour result in:
  - display?
  - threatening behaviour?
  - inhibited bites? (You felt the dog's teeth, but no marks or bruises were left.)
  - injury? Describe the location and extent of any marks, bruises, punctures, tears, etc. that occurred from the dog's teeth on human skin (to help determine bite inhibition). You may also note any damage done by claws, but note that the damage was not from teeth.
- Expectations: How much improvement to make the target behaviour acceptable to you and your family? (Remember, be realistic. And flexible.) You might misjudge this at this point and find out, once the behaviour begins to improve, that you can live with less improvement than you originally thought. Conversely, you may discover that the 50% improvement you thought would be okay is just not working out.)

Setting Events

Setting Events are the "stage" on which the Target Behaviour is played out. The Setting Events tell the story of each incident. This is valuable information which ultimately becomes the primary tool to determine which protocols will be used. It will provide a list of "triggers" or precursors of the behaviour so you can be proactive and know which kinds of situations you need to manage. It will tell you what frustrates your dog and causes conflict and arousal.

For each incident list:

- Approximate Date.
- Location.
- Who was present.
- What was happening just before this incident occurred?
- What your dog looked like *just before* this incident occurred. Describe: Eyes, Ears, Tail, other body posture.
- A description of the incident itself.
- What the dog looked like *during* this incident.
- What happened immediately after the incident. Was the dog punished or contained? If so, how?
- What your dog looked like just after this incident occurred.
- Anything else about this incident that you noticed?

Jeez, That Was A Lot Of Work – Now What?

From these three pieces, the Daily Environment, the Hit List, and the Setting Events, a pattern will begin to emerge. You are able to see, perhaps for the first time, some of the connections between the three. From this systematic analysis, you are now able to think about the incidents more clinically, and more clearly.

These worksheets allow you to evaluate the contexts in which the aggression occurs. This allows you to avoid or to be ready for these instances, and also to "set-up" the environment carefully so you can show the dog how you want her to behave (manufacture reinforceable behaviour). It gives you the opportunity to reinforce desirable behaviour.

You will also derive from the worksheets:

- A list of precursors or triggers for the behaviour. This is crucial. Note or number the triggers from most to least likely to cause arousal in your dog.
- Determine a threshold for tolerance (distance). This allows you to begin your work with this in mind and improve safety and chances of success.
- A list of body language observed.

The Setting Events sheet will tell you which is the earliest observable behaviour you recognize that indicates the dog is even becoming marginally reactive? (It is at this Earliest Observable Behaviour that you should intervene or interrupt behaviour.)

From your lists, you may also be closer to determining Classification of the dog's behaviour, if that is not already apparent to you.

The information provided from these lists will also help to choose which protocols to complete.

Information provided by the lists will identify the consequences that are providing reinforcement for the behaviour. This is VERY valuable information, since this tells us a lot about the function the behaviour is serving for the animal.

As indicated by the lists, you should now have quite a bit of organized information to go on. You will use these lists to create practice sessions.

ALWAYS complete the Foundation and Level I protocols first. Those are the exercises that all of the rest of the work is based on. A communication system, impulse control, and attentiveness to the handler are requisite for results. Most importantly, those protocols help to forge a working relationship between you and your dog built on trust, whether preventing or "fixing." As you complete those protocols you will learn a lot about your dog that will aid you when you are making judgments about future protocols. As you practice the Foundation and Level I protocols, you will gain handler skill and build a Working Relationship with your dog. That will sure come in handy when you are raising criteria and placing yourself and your dog in more exciting, distracting, or arousing situations! Your dog will gain skills during those protocols that will assist in the more difficult work that you will be asking of her later.

Next, begin work on the protocols that address specific triggers your dog responds to.

Problem Solving – Hi Ho, Hi Ho, It's Off To Work We Go

To effectively problem solve, the first step is to ACCURATELY identify the *problem*. Then you can go on to figuring out how you are going to *solve* it.

Identify the PROBLEM:

1. Refer to your *Hit List* for behaviours that are targeted for modification.
2. Peruse the *Personal History & Daily Environment* to see exactly where and when the dog is rehearsing undesired behaviour. If you are going to modify behaviour, first and foremost you must prevent rehearsal of the undesired behaviour.
3. Refer to the *Setting Events* worksheets. How could you have been proactive and prevented the occurrence? How could you change the Setting Events to TEACH instead of practicing damage control?

Begin to problem SOLVE:

4. List all the triggers from the *Setting Events* and add any others you have noticed in "daily life."
5. List any risky or marginal behaviour. Prevent this or be prepared to intervene before the behaviour increases in intensity. The earlier you can intervene in the behaviour cycle, the better your chances of making a behaviour change.
6. List all observable behaviour and use of native language. You can use your *Setting Events* worksheets to get you started. Then begin noticing occurrences of use in daily

life. List them as well. This gives you clues about when you can intervene. Interruption and re-direction of a behaviour must be done way BEFORE lunging and barking or high-arousal so your dog can learn to identify this "feeling" and learn to access the desired behaviour in lieu of the reactive behaviour.

7. Begin the Foundation and Level I protocols no matter what your dog's problems are. This is true for prevention work as well.
8. Simultaneously work on the Handling & Restraint protocol. This work cannot be emphasized enough. Being able to handle an animal, restrain him and gaining his trust makes the dog safe.
9. According to the specific triggers, choose a protocol that addresses that trigger.
10. Tweak your protocol as required to suit the individual dog. The dog will help you out here – you just have to watch and interpret the *observable behaviour.*

Table 2: Triggers

Triggers
Knocking on the door
Ringing the doorbell
Guests entering the home
Newsboy delivering paper, even though he doesn't knock or ring – he is just on the porch

REMEMBER:

- Behaviour modification is not an exact science. There will be "tweaking" along the way.
- List realistic goals and expectations.
- Leave behind "coulda, shoulda, why didn't I" – discard these attitudes and move on.
- Owner attitude is all-important and closely related to outcome.
- Safety is always the first priority.

Table 3: Body Language

Body Language
Behaviour is often very sudden and it is difficult to "get in ahead of it."
Dog goes from "just hanging out" to running towards the door barking.
Vocalization – barking.
Occasional pilo-erector reflex.
Occasional barking.

Table 4: Example of a Master Plan

The Target Behaviour is Uncontrollable Barking at the door.	The desired behaviour is a dog that is Quiet on cue. Further, it would be ideal if the dog greeted guest calmly.
Foundation Protocols	Provides a communication system.
Level I Protocols	Provides control, teamwork, attention, impulse control and gives us a list of alternative, desired behaviours to use in place of barking and reactivity.
Handling & Restraint	Teaches trust, makes the dog safe to interrupt and handle when aroused.
Refer to Management & Damage Control: Equipment	A head collar will make the dog more easily controlled initially. Later you will be able to control the dog off leash.

Table 4: Example of a Master Plan

Refer to Management & Damage Control: Relationships	Makes you relevant, increases the dog's awareness of behaviour/consequence connection.
Refer to Management & Damage Control: Quiet	Teaches dog to cease barking on cue.
Wait at the Door	Reduces the habit of arousal. Provides practice for you to control the setting events and the dog's behaviour, and puts the dog in the habit of deferring to you in a location previously associated with high arousal.
Training a Polite Greeting	Teaches self-restraint and desired greeting behaviour.
Territory Entry and Appropriate Greeting Behaviours	Teaches the dog to remain calm, follow direction and defer responsibility to you.

Whether you are doing a prevention program (GOOD FOR YOU!) or you are modifying behaviour in a dog who is already presenting with over reactivity, you will have gained a greater understanding of the problem and of your dog. If you already have a problem, my heart is with you! I, too have lived with dogs who are "problem children." These experiences have given me an entirely different perspective on the species! Also, quite a few stitches and hair-raising adventures. It is a better perspective overall – one that is realistic and appreciates the species, and the individuals in it, to a much greater degree.

I understand, in a "been there-done that way," the heart-wrenching decisions that sometimes must be made. The guilt. Wondering what you did or didn't do that contributed to the problem. Wanting desperately not to repeat any mistakes. I understand how it feels to love a dog and feel responsible for her welfare. I know what it feels like to want to work with a dog that everyone is telling you is a lost cause, and wondering if you are crazy or unrealistic to try.

I must admit that I am ten times the trainer from working with these dogs. I pay attention, for one thing! I have much empathy for dogs who are trapped in a destructive stimulus-response cycle, or dogs who are anxiety-ridden and defensive.

The Laws of Learning, management, behaviour modification, positive reinforcement, the dog's native language – these hold the answers. The more you understand how animals learn and about the species you are working with, the more efficient you will become. While it is a hard lesson to learn that you "cannot save 'em all," you will certainly increase the number you can save.

Working with "difficult dogs" has made my own efforts toward prevention of such behaviour in my puppies and rescue dogs more intense. It is our responsibility to make well-informed decisions about these dogs so we can do what is best for them (and for us and our other human and canine family members).

I want to ensure that my dogs are well-educated and safe to be around. I no longer assume that *any* dog will be safe, nor do I leave it to chance. Being proactive is the key to success!

Section VIII

The Fix

Protocols

35

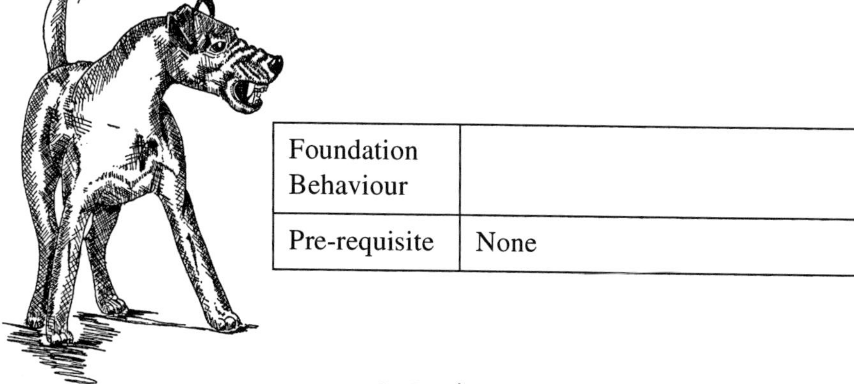

Foundation Behaviour	
Pre-requisite	None

ESTABLISHING A COMMUNICATION SYSTEM

THE RM/NRM AND RELEASE CUE

Goal	Establish a way to communicate with the dog.
What it teaches	The dog understands that a RM/NRM (Reward Mark/No Reward Mark) gives him information. The dog understands when he is on "your time" and working vs. "on his own time."
Practical Application	Dogs and humans come equipped with their own unique and SEPARATE language. If we want to be able to train a dog, we must first communicate with him in a manner he can understand.

This protocol, of all the protocols in this book, is ESSENTIAL. It is so important that you "get" this concept and incorporate it into daily life with your dog. If you cannot quickly and precisely communicate information to your dog, how the heck are you going to teach him anything? All the work that follows is based on this RM/NRM communication system.

DETERMINE POSITIVE REINFORCERS FOR TRAINING.

To get started, you will need to make a list of things that are rewarding for your dog. This list will provide you with Primary Reinforcers (technical definition:

required for survival. For our purposes: Food). In addition, you will have several options for Auxiliary Reinforcers (other stuff your dog likes to do, but that don't qualify as a Primary). These are what you will use to reward your dog for the behaviour you want, and, just as important, to PROVIDE INFORMATION to him about what you want.

What should you use to reinforce desired behaviour? Highly desired items make the best rewards. This means, on familiar territory, such as at home, you may use your dog's regular dog food to reinforce behaviour. When in new or more distracting situations you will need to use Hazard Pay. Hazard Pay consists of super special treats like string cheese, chicken or a brief game with a favored toy.

"Life Rewards" are very salient (noticeable and meaningful) and make excellent reinforcers. An example may be opening a door to let your dog out if she Sits first. Life Rewards are just another name for using Premack Principle. You will allow the dog access to something the dog likes to do in return for the dog doing a requested behaviour for you first. For an extended discussion on this topic, refer to the "Relationships" chapter.

For now, look at life through your dog's eyes. What does he like? What does he beg to do? What does he beg to eat? (If this answer is everything, all the time – you have a *very* trainable dog. It makes it real easy to Get His Number, and food is so incredibly easy to control.) What is your dog doing when he looks relaxed and happy? Contented? What activities does he avoid? When you are touching him, what sort of touching makes him move away? For which touches does he move closer to you and look euphoric?

You must use a variety of reinforcers to maintain behaviour the most efficiently.

To Do. Make a list of things your dog likes. Try to include at least three items in each category:

- What are your dog's favorite items to play with?
- What activities would your dog rather do than anything else in the world?
- What kind of physical contact does your dog like the best? (Cuddling? Belly rub? Scratching behind the ears?)
- What are his favorite games or activities?
- How does your dog get your attention when he wants it?
- What are his favorite treats?

All righty then! Now you have a list ready and waiting to choose from when you need a reinforcer. Tag some of the most desired reinforcers to reserve for use as Hazard Pay.

Before You Install the RM:

Now that you have a good idea about items you can use as reinforcers, decide on a word or signal. This word or signal will be used as a RM (Reward Mark).

One of the most important functions of the RM is that it serves as a memory aid. What is learning anyway? Remembering to do a certain behaviour at a certain time or on a particular cue. The RM tells the animal: out of the millions of behaviours you do today *remember this*, we'll need it later.

The RM MARKS the DESIRED behaviour the INSTANT it occurs.

What to use as a RM

Clickers make an excellent Reward Mark. Because the Clicker is a unique sound in the dog's environment, it is very salient for the dog.

Some ideas for verbal RM's are, "Yes," "Wow," "Good." Just make it short and sweet and keep it *consistent.*

It is entirely possible to use a verbal RM or a clicker at different times. My own dogs know and understand both a verbal RM and the Clicker used as a RM. The Clicker is extremely handy and installs behaviour more quickly when initially teaching a specific Behaviour. A Clicker also has the benefit of making you very aware of what Behaviour you are Marking for the dog. On the other hand, you always have your voice handy, so on those occasions you don't have a Clicker with you, or you are past installing the behaviour, your voice will work as a perfect RM.

- You may install both a clicker and a verbal RM if you wish. Just do so during different training sessions.

To Install the RM:

Choose your RM (Reward Mark). If it is a verbal, have your lips primed. If a clicker have the clicker handy and know how to make it "click."

Get 30 or 40 tasty treats ready, in a bait bag or fanny pack. Then:

1. RM (either a "click" or your verbal "Yes").
2. Pause approximately ½ second.
3. Deliver the food Treat.
4. Repeat steps 1 through 3 four or five times.
5. Walk or back up a couple of steps; by now it is usually pretty hard to get rid of the dog! Make the sound of your Reward Mark. Quickly deliver the food Treat.
6. Repeat the above step fifteen to twenty-five more times.

While installing the RM do not ask for any particular behaviour.

Essential Concept:

Your RM does not mean Good Dog. The magic is that the RM PREDICTS a pleasant event for your dog, and becomes ASSOCIATED with the pleasant event so it can be used to provide INFORMATION.

A RM/NRM system provides the dog with valuable and concise information about his current Behaviour.

The "Click" or spoken RM, "Yes,"....................is immediately followed by a tasty treat.

Installing a RM

Pop Quiz

- After about 20 or 30 repetitions, just stand still for a minute or so, either standing on a leash or with the dog in a safe fenced area or room. Allow the dog to become slightly bored or distracted, until he looks away from you or maybe even wanders off a step or two.
- When he does, make the sound of your RM.
- Does the dog immediately look your way and/ or come back over to you? When this occurs, the dog is beginning to understand that the RM is a predictor of Reinforcement. He has a pretty good idea that there is a connection between these two events (the RM is followed by the treat) and he is on his way to understanding the significance of the RM.
- You may begin to use your RM to provide your dog with pertinent information.
- If your dog does not orient toward you immediately, repeat the RM/Treat sequence ten or more times, then repeat the Pop Quiz.

Essential Concept

Remember your RM is NOT an attention-getter. Using your RM in this way will backfire on you, because then you are technically reinforcing the dog for inattention. In the Pop Quiz, you are using the RM in this way merely as a method to ascertain if the RM is meaningful to your dog yet! Once the RM is correctly installed, you would NEVER use it in this way. Why? *Because once your dog understands the use of the RM, whatever behaviour he is currently doing when he hears the RM becomes the reinforced behaviour.* That means the dog will repeat whatever behaviour was just marked. At this very beginning stage, we are using the RM incorrectly, if you will, in order to obtain information about the dog's current skill level.

Practice Using Your RM

Now is a good time to practice using your RM so you, the handler, become proficient. Use a behaviour your dog already knows. Most dogs know Sit, so, for our example we will use Sit.

- Give your cue for Sit. The moment the dog's bottom hits the ground:
- RM
- Deliver the treat immediately following the RM.
- Now cue for the Sit and wait for a count of 2 until you Mark It & Feed It. This is a brief lesson in how you begin to achieve duration with a behaviour.

THE NRM

Pre-requisite: You can teach this as soon as your dog understands the RM.

The RM and NRM (No Reward Mark) are used to give the dog INFORMATION, not to "praise or punish" him. Therefore, when using your NRM, keep your tone of voice very neutral. A NRM does not mean "NO." Reserve your nasty, growly tone of voice, and the word "NO," for behaviour that you never want to see again, like counter surfing.

To the dog, there is no "Right" and "Wrong" in training. There is only Behaviour that "works" and Behaviour that "does not work!" The sooner you get your hands round this concept, the better your communication efforts with your dog will be and the better your results.

What to Use as a NRM

Some ideas for a NRM: "Try Again," "Sorry," "Try Again," "Not Yet."

To Install the NRM "On The Fly

The NRM can easily be installed "on the Fly." Begin using this word, the NRM, as you are working the dog to indicate to him that the Behaviour just offered is not going to receive reinforcement. (For example, if you cue "Sit," and your dog just stands there, give the NRM, "Try Again.") Over a week or so, your dog will come to recognize that this verbal signal never predicts reinforcement and always predicts the absence of reinforcement.

The "Quick" Alternative Method to Install a NRM

1. Place your dog on leash and stand on it to prevent her from leaving you.
2. Enclose a piece of food in your hand, between your finger and thumb so the dog cannot get it from you. You may want to place your dog in a Sit position, but it is not necessary to do so.
3. Hold the treat near the dog's nose.
4. As the dog reaches for the treat…
5. Use your NRM, "Try Again," and quickly remove the treat by moving your hand straight away from the dog, or by pulling your hand up and resting it on your shoulder. You want the dog to think that reaching for the treat Chases It Away. (As a bonus, your dog is also learning a very important lesson: If You Are Patient Good Things Will Come To You. This conveys to the dog that Impulse Control WORKS.)
6. After you have done this a few times, your dog should be remaining seated and have stopped lunging. If lunging and grabbing food is a habit for your dog, it may take more than a few repetitions, or you may choose to stand on the leash so your dog doesn't knock you down or jump all over you.
7. Once the dog has stopped lunging and reaching for the treat, you may say "Yes" and deliver the treat. One way your dog will indicate to you that he does not intend to reach for the treat is by turning his head slightly. This certainly would warrant a Mark It & Feed It. If the dog gets up and begins to walk away, he is indicating that he does not intend to grab the food. Call the dog and back up a step to get her to remain with you. Mark It & Feed It. You don't want the dog to think that the NRM means to go away!

Essential Concepts

In this manner the dog will learn that the NRM precedes removal of the food, and will contrast that with the RM, which predicts delivery of the food.

This exercise also teaches your dog that lunging, grabbing behaviours DO NOT ever get him a treat, and that food is not available, no matter how close it is to his nose, until he hears "Yes."

When your dog responds to the NRM by offering you some other behaviour – and it may be subtle! – you are on your way to having established a great working communication system. The dog is experimenting – working to discover what gets you to give him a RM. It is amazing what can be accomplished, now that you and your dog are "talking!"

Caution: If your dog has ever been aggressive with you, particularly over food treats, do not install this exercise in this manner, or you may get into trouble!

The question then becomes: "How do I install a NRM? If you are worried, refer to "To Install the NRM On The Fly," and use that technique. It is effective, it just takes a little longer.

If you are the least bit uncertain, you could try using the above technique with your dog muzzled. Use squeeze cheese or peanut butter on a spoon so your digits are not near the dog's mouth. If, during the teaching of a NRM, your dog lunges at you, snarling, is growling and warning you, or is using stiff body movements or stalking movements, I advise you to get help from a behaviour specialist immediately. An extreme reaction such as this indicates very serious marginal behaviour that need the input and experience of a professional.

The Final Polish – The End-Working Cue or Release Cue

First let us define the term "Release." Release does not mean that the dog is then encouraged to jump around and be crazy. It merely means, "you are not working right now." As soon as I use a Release cue my dog waits expectantly for the next exercise. If it is not forthcoming, then she will go do her own thing.

Stimulus control implies that we both *begin* AND *end* the behaviour on a cue. The "begin working" cue is the command itself, such as "Sit." The "end working" cue is the Release word. Dogs who are taught in this manner become very sophisticated students. They will use the RM itself as a continuation cue – not only does the RM come to mean, "Remember This Behaviour, we will need it later," it also tells the dog, "You are on the right track – Keep Working!"

Personally, I find that using the RM as a "keep going" cue and having an additional Release cue allows training to be less interrupted and to flow more smoothly than if you allow the RM, itself, to "end" the behaviour.

Clicker Purists use the "click" to end the behaviour. (For an informative short course about that technique, a good video is *Clicker Magic* by Karen Pryor (1997). A good book is *Click! For Success* by Lana Mitchell (1997).)

You may use the RM either way, just be consistent. You cannot use the RM as a continuation cue one day and a release cue the next. Decide how you are going to work, and be consistent with how you use it.

Good words to use for your Release cue: "All Done" or "That'll do."

A Release cue is necessary for the dog to understand when he is working (on your time) and when he is technically not working (on his own time). This is important because otherwise the dog will constantly "guess" about when he is done working. We see this often exhibited in Stay work. The dog is told to "stay" but if anything distracts him, like a door opening, the dog allows the environment to release him. If taught a clear Release cue, the dog no longer has to guess. You will tell him when he is "clocked in" and working vs. "clocked out" and on his own time.

Common Errors

A Release cue does not mean you release the dog, and play a big game with a bunch of excitement and leaping about. A common misunderstanding is exhibited by people working on a Stay exercise. When they are done with the Stay, they get their dogs up and immediately play a game. What is really being reinforced here? Being released! If you want to reinforce the stay, the reinforcement must occur DURING the behaviour. Also, Stays should always be a "calm" behaviour, and so that is the emotion you wish to promote all "around" the behaviour.

I am not saying "don't play games with your dog," I am saying that you will get superior results if you use games properly – as a consequence. Therefore, if I was heeling with the dog and getting great work, I might say, "Yes," then pull out a ball or toy and encourage the dog to begin to interact with me, with a "C'mon and play," or "Get It," cue. In this fashion I use a game as the consequence (positive reinforcement) for good behaviour! BUT I would NOT say, "Yes," then give my release cue, "All done," then start a game. I want to make sure the dog is understanding that the game is a consequence for "good work" if I am using the game as a training tool. The proper syntax is that reinforcement occur during or immediately after the behaviour. This is followed by the Release cue to signal "clocked-out" to the dog.

Now is a good time to practice using your new excellent communication system (RM/NRM) so you become proficient. Use a behaviour your dog already knows. Most dogs know Sit, so for our example we will use Sit.

Give your cue for Sit.

If the dog sits:

- RM.
- Deliver the treat immediately following the RM.
- Release your dog by using some sort of Release Cue. I use "All Done" or "That'll do" with my own dogs.

If the dog does not sit:

- "Try Again" (or whatever you have chosen as your NRM).
- Repeat the cue "Sit."

- Prompt the dog for the Sit (hold the treat over his head or use whatever means you used to teach the Sit).
- When the dog sits, Mark It & Feed It.
- Release cue.

36

Foundation Behaviour	
Pre-requisite	None

NAME RECOGNITION

Goal	Your dog will look at you under any circumstance when you say her name.
What it teaches	To orient toward you when the dog hears her name.
Practical Application	If your dog will look at you, the chances she will follow the cue you are giving her is increased immeasurably. Good Name Recognition is a great way to get the dog's attention in any circumstance. Also, it is not always clear to a dog when we are talking to her. Saying her name helps her to know that you are requesting compliance to a cue.

- Say the Dog's name.
- Mark It & Feed It.
- Repeat the above steps twenty to thirty times.
- Place the Behaviour on aVariable Schedule. (One way to use a Variable Schedule is to vary the number of times the dog offers the behaviour before she gets a treat. For more on Variable Schedules, refer back to "The Laws of Learning" chapter.)

Once your dog has these Foundation Behaviours (RM/NRM Communication System & Name Recognition) installed, you have the Foundation of a beautiful relationship! Whether you are living with this dog, in which case your relationship will be much more complex, or you are a trainer who needs to establish what I term a Working Relationship, you have just embarked on a wonderful journey.

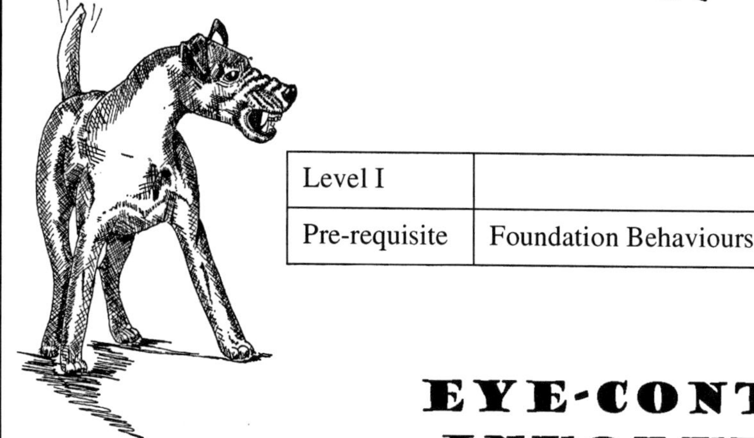

Level I	
Pre-requisite	Foundation Behaviours

EYE-CONTACT & INVOLVEMENT

Goal	The dog will attend to and remain involved with the handler, ignoring other dogs, food, pigeons, people, etc.
What it teaches	The handler is the most important thing in the environment.
Practical Application	In daily life, we ask a dog to resist paying attention to many activities and distractions that are going on around her. Some of these activities hold much more interest for the dog than the work we are requesting. This exercise is all about teaching the dog to remain on task, even though distractions are going on around her.

Using Eye Contact as an Anchor

For dogs who are already presenting with over-reactivity or aggression, this exercise becomes much more than just an "attention" exercise. This behaviour becomes an *Anchor* for the dog. For instance, when Maeve, my GSD, is in a situation that is causing her conflict or arousal, since learning this Involvement exercise, she stares not just into my eyes, but almost into my very soul. She has learned to use this eye contact to "Anchor" her emotions and to lock her focus onto me, which is the perfect response I have reinforced umpty-million times. Maeve now uses this Anchoring behaviour to keep herself in a calm emotional, and therefore chemical, state. I encourage all my dogs to pay attention, but for dogs who have a tendency to become over-reactive to the environment, this exercise serves as a lifesaver (perhaps literally in some instances!). I can tell when Maeve really needs the calming effect of the anchor. As she becomes intense about something in the environment, instead of directing this intensity outward, she uses the eye-contact between her and me as a life-line, much as a drowning person uses a buoy hooked to a line.

At first, some dogs misinterpret eye contact, and take it to mean a direct threat or challenge, and will respond accordingly. Work very carefully and safely until you determine how your particular dog is going to react to this training exercise. If your dog shows overt aggression with this exercise (stalking, lunging, growling, barking, or biting), get help from a qualified person ASAP. If in doubt, try this while the dog is muzzled. In addition, you may also wish to tie the dog back, so if he lunges at you, you can get to safety. If your dog responds adversely to direct eye contact from a known person that he is friendly with, you need IMMEDIATE help.

Because eye contact may be perceived as threatening, it may elicit fearful or even defensive behaviour. Your dog may just exhibit mild avoidance by being unwilling, initially, to really LOOK into your eyes calmly. Be patient with these dogs and, at first, accept glances at your chin or nose, and "shape" the behaviour towards looking deeply and with concentration into your eyes.

Another strategy with dogs who are uneasy about direct eye contact is to make sure you are not "staring" at them. Blink rapidly, shift your eyes so you are looking into their eyes, then quickly shift your eyes sideways and then back again. This will convey non-threatening intent to dogs. After they have received cookies for allowing and tolerating this sort of eye contact, you can begin to raise criteria and leave your eyes on theirs for longer periods of time.

For the dog who has shown aggression, you need to get real serious about Involvement work, and do quick reviews all the time, throughout the dog's life. Once the dog is accepting eye contact well from "friends," it is time to ask strangers to try. This exercise requires the right "stranger," for sure: someone who can follow directions quickly and will not overreact to a dog who may lunge, bark or growl. It is *imperative* that all are kept safe, so a muzzle, tie-back, head-collar and a martingale collar that the dog cannot slip out of are very important. Safety must be paramount. Just because a dog has "been doing well" doesn't mean that each time you introduce someone new, the dog will not react. However, when you do get to that point, you have made significant progress!

If You Don't Have Attention, You Don't Have Anything! If you are not giving as well as receiving attention, you don't have teamwork. This exercise is very much about YOU and your ability to concentrate and remain on task. You need to be attending to your dog, too! This is a communication loop!

I actually prefer the term "Involvement" to the catchwords commonly used here, like Attention or Focus. For our purposes, this exercise is not only about attention per se, although attention is an integral component and by-product of this work. Involvement better conveys Team Effort, and that the Communication Loop is working.

Strategies for Inattention

Before you begin, remember that it is pretty reasonable (indeed normal!) for your dog to react to a Sudden Environmental Change that is startling to him. He probably will always glance toward whatever is startling, but it should be a glance, not a change of Involvement from you to the distraction. Significant to you is the Recovery Time. How long did your dog look at whatever was distracting him? If your dog says, "Hey! What's That?!" with a glance that lasts a second or a fraction thereof, it is an entirely different matter than when your dog says, "Oh....cool...I really need to see this close up and personal" and begins to move toward the distraction, forsaking you entirely.

Strategies for your dog on those occasions when he is succumbing to distraction in the environment:

- Wait it out. This is my favorite and the best option. However, if your dog is becoming reactive in response to a person or dog approaching use one of the other techniques outlined below, as you do not wish your dog to rehearse reactive behaviour.
- Back away from the distraction, until your dog turns and looks at you.
- Move between your dog and the distraction.

Silky (the Shar-pei), alerts on, and pulls toward, the other dog.

Photo Essay by Sam Ziegenmeyer.

Lylenette backs up, and Silky disengages from the environment and engages with her handler.

- Move into the dog, **carefully**. Do not be rough or abrupt; this is an attention-getting device for the dog who is totally ignoring you, not a punisher. I shuffle my feet so that I do not accidentally step on tender toes. I might bump the dog **gently** with my knees. This is a gentle "tap" meaning, "Hello, anybody home?!" – not a hard bump or a tackle! *CAUTION:* If your dog has shown aggressive reactions to being touched, do NOT use this technique!
- When your dog moves away from you, move or back away in the opposite direction he is headed. He will be attracted by your motion and follow. This is not an excuse to administer any sort of jerk or collar correction. Move away and firmly, but without jerking, take the dog with you.

Photo by Joanne Weber.

Caution: practice, at first, in calm circumstances and be aware of possible redirected aggression when in arousing circumstances.

The handler Moves Into her dog to diffuse the situation, show the dog that the handler is aware of the environmental change, and direct the dog's attention back toward the handler.

Move-Into

- Continue moving, with frequent changes of direction, until your dog attends to you. By attending, I mean that the dog finally looks at you, perhaps in annoyance, perhaps in frustration but, at last, he DOES look at you! These first few times your dog may not look right up into your eyes, but indicating toward you (his head is oriented in YOUR direction for a change) is a reinforceable approximation for up to five or six trials in the Acquisition Stage. Then work on shaping the "Look" at your face.

Verbal chatter, verbal nagging and leash corrections merely irritate or confuse your dog, and soon he is looking everywhere but at you. *You* become a nag, and a boring nag at that! This is because punishment makes for really excellent discrimination skills, and the apparent irritation here is YOU! You are preventing your dog from having access to the exciting environment, therefore *you become the item to avoid.*

You want your dog's paradigm (belief system) to be that YOU are The Way and The Light to all the good stuff! So, manufacture attention without verbal nagging and leash corrections, and then raise your criteria to voluntary attention. Soon your dog and you will be working partners, rather than partners in conflict.

You may wish to begin these exercises by kneeling with your dog on the floor. If you choose to begin with kneeling, you are adding an additional step to the exercise. This step is applicable for dogs who are short.

CAUTION: Kneeling in front of a dog who has shown aggression prior to this, so you can practice looking into his eyes, is a very bad idea, as you are then in a very vulnerable position. Eye contact is very volatile for these animals and it requires very small approximations (steps) to teach them that eye contact is non-threatening.

Working with your dog on a table is another viable option for short dogs. The table also works great for super-wiggly large dogs to limit movement and direct attention to the business at hand.

As soon as possible, maybe after 4 or 5 trials, and quite likely within the same session, you should be standing, not kneeling, with your dog. Dogs who were started on a table should be moved to the floor.

These strategies help the dog become captivated with you, rather than spending all his energies evading you. When you use harsher methods than these to achieve attention from your dog, it is like using a serrated steak knife to do surgery. You may still get the job done, but not only is the elegance factor way down, the wear and tear on your dog and the relationship is way up. In fact, considering the way dogs learn, you are extremely likely to do harm to your training and to your relationship, because your dog will associate the punishment with you, causing more avoidance behaviour. Worse yet, the punishment will be associated not with inattention, but with the other person or dog distracting him. This will slow your behavioural protocol, and may increase the dog's aggressive and reactive behaviour.

My personal goal with this work is that the dog is not just looking at me to avoid punishment, but actively thinking about what he can do for me.

ACQUISITION

Prepare And Plan

The following list of training tips will help you begin this protocol.

- It is easiest to begin training in an environment that is free from major distractions and is familiar to your dog. This way he will be able to concentrate best during the acquisition stage.
- Remember that training treats are tiny! If you are doing competition work specifically, you may choose to use a food that you can "store" in your mouth and then spit at the dog. Only in dog training can you find these disgusting habits cheerfully accepted by others!
- You will need to have a cue word lurking in the wings until you are ready to use it. Commonly used cues for this behaviour are: "Look," "Watch," "Ready." *Remember*: To eliminate the possibility of Missed Associations, DO NOT use your cue word for attention until you have the behaviour established. Remember! You cannot name the baby (behaviour) until it arrives (is observable)!
- Just so we are on the same wavelength: Your cue of "Ready" is not so much "Watch Me!" as it is a predictor of reinforcement. "Ready" comes to mean: Opportunities for reinforcement are now available. Do not underestimate the power of Opportunity for Reinforcement. This is a very potent tool, and when your dog realizes that you are the Master of Ceremonies, he will begin to endow you with the respect and attention that you have been craving!
- As well as a cue word to begin the behaviour, you will also need to have a clear Release cue so your dog knows when he is working. The end goal is Stimulus control. Stimulus control implies that the handler can begin and end the behaviour on cue.
- Remember: Baby Steps, Baby Steps, Baby Steps to Success. That's what Approximations are all about: Baby Steps. Train using small, easily understood steps. Approximations channel the dog in the right direction.
- The fact that you can teach your dog that a word or cue means that Opportunities for reinforcement are now available is at the heart of Positive Reinforcement Training methods. Any cue from you becomes a signal to your dog that Opportunities For reinforcement are now available! Very exciting! That is also why a No Reward Mark becomes so powerful – it indicates that No Opportunities For reinforcement Are Currently Available! Disappointing! At the same time, the dog comes to understand that both the RM and NRM are valuable information and the way to success.

APPROXIMATION #1

Opportunity Training

Once you have the preliminary planning in hand, it is now time to achieve and enhance your Target Behaviour. Each dog will progress differently, depending on how much he seeks out your company and human interaction on his own. Some dogs just naturally want to hang around you, and gaze into your eyes immediately. Others need to work up the "bravery" to look you right in the eye. Some dogs, like my first Smooth Fox terrier, Breanna, are horribly independent and are distracted by the noise of a gossamer butterfly wing outside the window, and come with virtually NO impulse control. Obviously, there will be much variability with these lessons, as dictated by your dog's personality and natural attention span. However, ALL dogs will benefit from this protocol and will respond amazingly quickly if you are applying good judgment with your approximations and your timing. I have spelled out the approximations, which leaves you to decide only when to advance to the next approximation and to time your reinforcement properly.

Click! followed by treat when Cora "checks in" with her handler, Lori.

Photo Essay by Joanne Weber.

Stand on the leash until the dog orients toward you. Wait patiently and quietly – this exercise is designed to obtain voluntary attention, not prompted attention.

Approximation #1: Obtain Voluntary Attention

The primary goal of this first approximation consists merely of getting your dog to stay voluntarily in YOUR vicinity.

- The best place to begin is by reinforcing all attention the dog gives you voluntarily. If your dog seeks out your company, social interaction and treats are in order. For a very self-sufficient dog (read: one not particularly interested in what you're doing from moment to moment), you may begin with applying reinforcement ("Yes" and treat) to just being near you and hanging around.

Begin with your dog on leash. Gradually transfer the behaviour of orienting toward you to off-leash when it is reasonable to do so, only in controlled, appropriate environments. Take into account the dog's safety and how much you can control the environment.

- Move backwards or laterally away from the dog.

  When on leash, don't jerk your dog toward you as you move away. You want your dog to respond either to a gentle pressure from the collar or merely to the motion of you moving away. Notice and reinforce all of these:

- Intention behaviour: as soon as your dog begins to turn his head toward you, Mark the behaviour, then Feed It when the dog gets to you. Ditto for the items below.
- Your dog moves toward you.
- Your dog stays near you.

If you are working outside, or the first several times you are working in any new area: Begin with your dog on a leash or long line. Do not hold the leash or line in your hand. Your object is not to "hold" your dog near you, but for him to wish to voluntarily remain near you. On the other hand, you must keep your dog safe. If your leash is in your hands, you may be tempted to use it. Therefore, step on the leash or tie your dog to a ground stake or a tree. You can fasten the leash around your waist, but please use good judgment about your size, the dog's strength, and the health of your back. If available, work initially in a fenced area, where you can also step on the leash.

Staking back the dog works well if you are small and the dog is large and difficult for you to control, and you are concerned that you will be tipped arse over applecart if you are standing on the leash when the dog takes a mad lunge at a chipmunk. Choose a stake or tie-back that will be sufficient to hold the dog should she lunge. Dogs are strong creatures, so do not underestimate the force generated by a dog lunging at the end of a tie.

APPROXIMATION #2

Manufacture Direct Eye Contact

For dogs who are extremely nervous about this whole "eye contact" thing:

When your dog is in a relaxed frame of mind, and in a familiar, safe setting, look him directly in the eye just for a split second. Then quickly slide your eyes sideways so you are looking away from or past the dog. Lick your lips (a calming signal). Repeat. RM & deliver a treat while your dog allows the brief glance of eye contact.

Gradually you will begin to prolong the eye contact before you do the eye-slide. Continue delivering treats for appropriate behaviour. The goal is a dog who begins to meet your gaze with a steady *relaxed* gaze of his own.

Now that you are assured that the dog will ACCEPT eye-contact, you may proceed with safety.

With your dog sitting or standing in front of you:

1. Hold a piece of food in your hand (left or right, doesn't matter), with the food held between your finger and thumb and your hands at your sides or held quietly near your chest.
2. Show the dog the piece of food by placing it in front of his cute little nose.
3. Quite rapidly, but smoothly and calmly, move the piece of food to your nose. As the dog's eyes meet yours...
4. Mark It & Feed It.
5. Repeat this sequence four or five times.
6. Move a few steps (a new location!) and repeat #1 through #5. Do this ten or fifteen times. End your session when the dog is doing well. Quit while you are ahead!

Over the next sessions, move to a different room or area. Repeat Steps #1 through #6. Quit each time on a "good" trial.

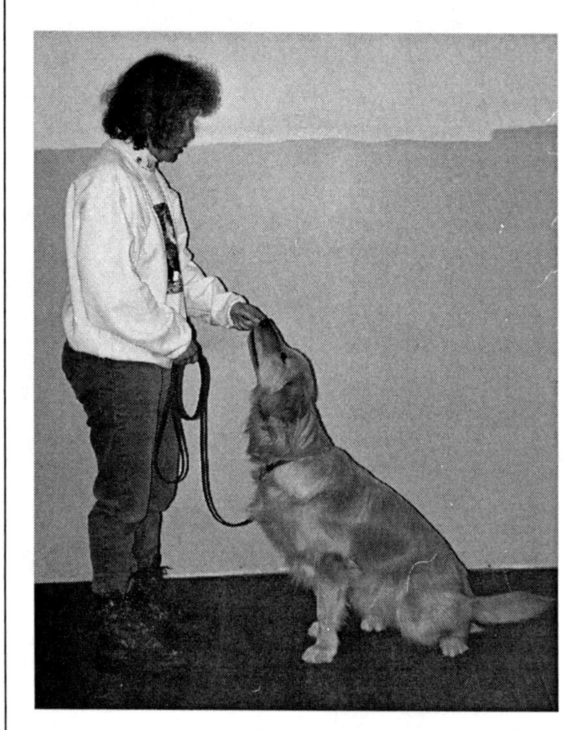

Food to your dog's nose, then, smoothly...to your nose – "YES"...

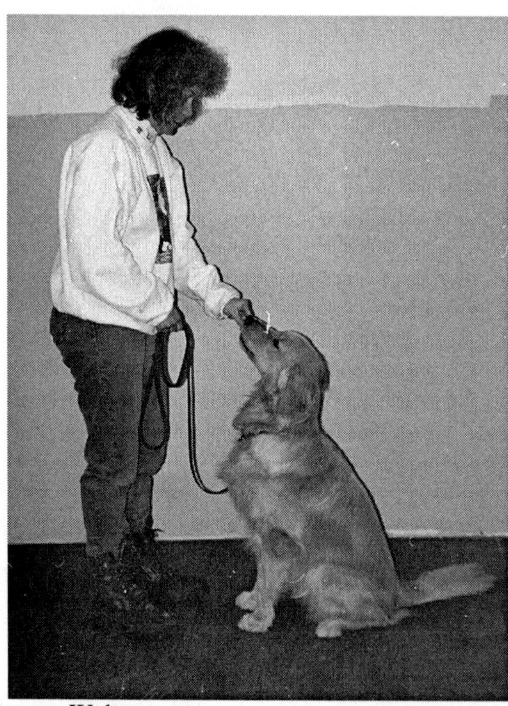

...Then deliver the reinforcer to the dog.

Photo Essay by Joanne Weber.

Approximation #2: Manufacture Direct Eye Contact

Approximation #3

Making a Distinct Choice – Voluntary Eye Contact

As you will have observed, the most likely item your dog is really looking at, in these initial steps, is not you so much as the food. (But now he is at least close enough for you to commence training him!) Well, it is time to improve on that!

Whether the dog is sitting or standing does not matter at this stage, but I prefer him not lying down. Initially you are looking for (no pun intended) any attention or eye contact directed toward you. At first, just quick glances are fine. Soon you will have the desired response: your dog will look into your eyes with an intensity that indicates he is making a conscious decision to use you as a target for his attention.

1. Have a leash on your dog with the other end on the floor under your foot.
2. Stand still and quiet, with your arms at your sides, the food enclosed in your fist.
3. Your dog may bark, whine, sneeze, nudge, paw, look at the hand with the food, leap, and try many other cute tricks. Remain neutral and still. Wait.
4. If your dog tries to leave, make sure you are stepping on the long line or leash and don't allow him to take off into the wild blue yonder. But put up with everything else, ignoring all the other annoying AND cute behaviours. This means standing quiet and still and looking at your dog in a friendly, but calm, fashion.
5. Suddenly, your dog, probably in frustration, will glance up at your face. (Hey! You! Give me the Food Already!) Immediately Mark It & Feed It. He must be looking up (at the very least) and preferably at your eyes (Excellent!) to get the treat. Initially accept even very short glances as successful efforts to Mark & Feed, and be quick with your RM.

In this manner you will harden your dog's resolve to keep working and pay attention even at this early stage. This is a very handy behaviour! This work can be done even with very young puppies, at 7 or 8 weeks old, if you take their totally-tiny attention span into account.

In summary, this particular approximation requires that you play a patience game, with the goal of having your dog voluntarily look at you. Prompts and reminders are counterproductive after you have done three or so Trials. It is time for the dog "to do his own homework." You cannot do it for him. Wait for the desired behaviour and allow your dog to problem solve! Allowing your dog to problem solve aids in memory recall, and also eliminates much experimentation with behaviour later, because your dog will have figured it out at this juncture. Sooner or later your dog will look at you. As this behaviour builds a reinforcement history, your dog will look at you ever more often, giving you further opportunities to apply reinforcement to the desired behaviour.

Approximation #4

Elaborate on the "Choice" Thing

1. Show your dog the food enclosed in your hand – but don't let him have it.
2. Move the hand with the treat so you have it held out at shoulder height, with your arm extended and the food visible.
3. The instant your dog looks at you and away from the treat, Mark It & Feed It.

Don't expect instant results! Very likely you will see much of the same behaviour that you did with the first part of this exercise! At some point it will occur to your dog to look at you instead of at the food. Now you are on your way....

In this approximation, your dog will have to make a decision that is very obvious to you about what she is going to look at.

Remember: wait quietly! No chattering – you want your dog to problem solve. When the dog figures out for himself that eye contact is not only his very own original idea, but also yields treats ... he is hooked!

The intention here is to reinforce the dog for making a CONSCIOUS DECISION to look AWAY from the food and look at YOU. The real lesson you are teaching here is that Access to reinforcers is not the direct line that it might seem to be. The line travels from the dog, through you, THEN to the reinforcement. This is very valuable knowledge for your dog to possess. If you can get your dog to buy into the fact that the goods are available through his own CALM and INVOLVED behaviour, you have made a great step forward in The Big R (The Relationship), as well as a giant step forward in compliance and deference to your requests.

APPROXIMATION #5

Increasing the Threshold

Stop reinforcing Swipes (quick glances) and look for that commitment to look into your eyes for longer and longer periods of time. When you release your dog with a Release Signal ("Done," "Free," "Kisses," whatever your release word is), and your dog chooses to continue working with you, rather than gazing around, looking away from you or running off to the end of the leash, certainly apply reinforcement to that! When you do you are reinforcing remaining on task.

It is a great and satisfying feeling when your dog takes a treat, and then says to you, "I choose to give up the environment and stay here with you and work." This is the beginning of a Work Ethic, which is an installed behaviour for most dogs and humans, not something they just "come with."

Your dog must be calm and still in order to maintain eye contact. As a by product of practicing eye contact, you are also reinforcing this calm and focused, involved behaviour.

At this point you have a dog who is receiving a treat around every 3-5 seconds. Work that threshold up to 20 or more seconds of eye contact between treats.

In summary, you are raising criteria from glances to the dog making a commitment to gaze into your eyes. Not your chin or ears or chest. But a conscious decision to make your eyes a target for eye contact.

Remember, the goal here is to have voluntary involvement. When the dog has made the association that you are a predictor of reinforcement, and that being near you provides great Opportunities for Reinforcement, you have made a big step forward in your ability to elicit desired behaviour. (By extension, that means he will be looking to you more often for advice about his next move!) Yes! This is your first real step toward lowering your dog's reactivity level and having him look to you for advice about "How do I handle this situation?"

APPROXIMATION #6

Adding the Cue

Bringing a behaviour under stimulus control dictates that you first have The Behaviour. So don't be in a big hurry to add that cue! Using a cue too soon, before your dog has a reasonably good understanding of what the behaviour is about, always results in problems later. The more reliable the behaviour, and the closer it is to the Terminal Response before you add the cue, the more reliable and consistent of topography (what the response looks like) the ultimate outcome will be.

Photo Essay by Amy Morris.

This particular Body Posture means Remain In Heel and Keep Your Eyes On Me! I begin with a stationary position and reinforce that many times before I begin Moving Attention work. Moving Attention is multi-tasking and requires much more skill and concentration from the dog.

Using Body Posture As A Cue

If you add a cue too early, you will be effectively *adding it to a variety of behaviours.* Thus, it becomes more probable that, instead of one, consistent response, you will get any one of a number of responses the dog has associated the cue with. In addition, if you use the cue before the dog understands the behaviour, you will "water down" the response; the dog will acknowledge the cue only if it is convenient, because it has not been established exactly when a response is required.

When we speak about a cue, most people assume we mean a verbal cue. But your dog does not, and you should learn this from your dog!

- The cue may be verbal, the one you chose in your planning stage.
- The cue may be a certain posture.
  The posture cue may apply more to competition dogs. For instance, when I stand straight and look ahead, with my left hand held in front at my waist, my dogs run over, get into heel position and get "Involved."
- The cue may be contextual. For example, when your dog dashes out the back door, he rushes to the fence to look for squirrels. Or, "Oh, the Obedience Ring – that means pay attention."

I use several cues for Involvement. One is a verbal "Look." One is formal Heel position, one is formal Front position.

I also use an informal "check in" cue with my dogs, which means to orient toward me for a moment. I would use this when we are walking informally. I wish my dogs to "check back" with me every half-minute or so. When I cue, "This way," it means to turn and move toward me and pay attention until I issue another cue or release them.

The Premack Principle is a very valuable concept. Using it in daily life makes it clear to the dog that consequences are based on behaviour. Here, the handler has the dog Sit and make Eye Contact before the dog is allowed to go out the door into the safe fenced yard. When the dog does as the handler requests, she gets what she wants – outside.

Premack Principle

I have taught my Shepherd bitch, who came to me with some rather alarming aggression issues, to default ALWAYS to me. ANYTIME she sees anything in the environment that is interesting to her, her habit now is to glance at it (person, dog, rabbits, deer) and then to immediately look at me for information about what "we" are to do about it.

When you have attention that is beyond just a glance and is approaching 5 to 10 seconds of intense eye contact, you may begin using your cue word. However! If you are looking for "competition style" attention, you must give the dog a Release cue before the eye contact shifts away. Remember about the stimulus control thing. If you do not have a clear on/off switch, you are teaching the dog that there is no clear distinction about "when to work" and "when not to work." This is very confusing for your dog. As you increase criteria, you will wait longer and longer before you give the Release cue.

Don't whine. It is very very irritating when people whine, beg, wheedle or nag using their Attention Word. If you take a look at dogs, you will see that they also find it irritating, intimidating and certainly not engaging! If you are using your Attention Word, and your dog is consistently looking away from you, take a look in the mirror.

If you feel you are not nagging, whining, or begging, there are one or more technical reasons why you are not getting compliance: Competing Reinforcers (the dog finds the environment more rewarding than you); Ratio Strain (too Thin a Reinforcement Schedule too soon, or you are not being generous enough at this stage); Lack of Generalization (the dog hasn't been in enough different situations using the new behaviour yet). Time for the human part of the team to do a bit of problem-solving!

APPROXIMATION #7

Introduce Premack

Premack behaviours are named after the guy who did the initial work on studying what would happen if you use a high probability behaviour to reinforce a low probability behaviour. In other words, use an activity your dog likes to reinforce him for compliance to a cue. Ian Dunbar calls these "life rewards." This technique is very potent, so think about how you are going to apply this technique with your dog.

If you want to teach your dog that you are relevant, put Eye Contact into every context. This is the key to making every interaction with your dog "count." More effective than drilling your dog on obedience, or working with him formally 30 minutes a day, are the Ten Second Training Sessions.

My dog wants to go outside? Give me Sit and Eye Contact and I will open the door. Want to be out of your crate? Want to get on my lap? On the sofa? Want some pats or scratches? Give me Involvement and then I will allow you access to what you want. Using Premack's Principle makes this game relevant to everyday life for your dog.

This technique encourages your dog to notice something in the environment that interests him and, instead of doing the direct access thing (leaving you and going to the distraction), to look at you for input. Through classical conditioning and associative learning, the distraction becomes an antecedent cue to Involve himself with you! Hot dog!!!

APPROXIMATION #8

2 Behaviours – Sitting and Looking

For those who are going to do competition, a Front with Involvement is a specific position: the dog must be sitting straight and within a certain distance of your toes. It is not the intent of this text to cover competition work, but it is worth a quick mention for those of you who are Preventing Aggression and considering competition. If you are curious about that, peruse manuals such as *Clicker Training For Obedience* by Morgan Spector. If you are using this exercise with a dog who is not being groomed for competition obedience, the details of the position are not crucial. If your dog has aggression problems, competition may not be an appropriate goal at this time; however, by the time that you complete all the protocols, competition may be within your reach. The big plus is you will be able to teach competition behaviours lots quicker because your dog knows how to learn and you will have super attention.

Photo Essay by Amy Morris.

This Front is great for any purpose and qualifies as a competition Front as well. Note the handler's arms are at her sides. She is not prompting or bribing the dog or begging her to pay attention. At first, just a second of attention is reinforced (Mark It & Feed It). Add duration to the behaviour a second or two at a time.

Front Position

- You may have to place your dog into the sit. This is fine. Some dogs just end up sitting in front of you because it is the easiest place to play this game.
- Some dogs are made quite uncomfortable if you are bending over them at all, and shorter dogs will find it easiest to sit back a bit in order to see your face. Again, unless you are working on competition obedience, the exact positioning of the dog is much less crucial than the eye contact itself. If the dog is uncomfortable about personal space, you will have to Shape him into sitting closer to you over a couple of sessions.
- Each time you change position (e.g., Heel to Front) getting Involvement from your dog is a whole new task. A change in position is a change in context, so you may see spontaneous recovery of poor attention.
- Seek to prolong the eye contact and get the dog to commit to paying attention to you. The look you are working to achieve will have the intensity that indicates that your dog is making a conscious decision to make you a target for Involvement.

Keep in mind that a quick glance in the direction of something that startles the dog (a noise or movement) is a very different event than glancing, maintaining the look at the distraction, and then deserting you to move toward it.

Troubleshooting

If your dog looks away during the sit, for more than a glance, even if he is looking back to you, he is making a choice. Be patient in this Acquisition Stage, try waiting it out. You are further ahead if you let the dog figure this puzzle out and voluntarily give you the all-important Involvement. (Remember the earlier discussion about the benefits of the dog doing his own "homework" and problem solving.)

Review Sessions are not unusual when you change the setting or context of a behaviour, and should be expected.

If the dog is not looking at you, say the dog's name to catch his attention, or move in a direction opposite where the dog is looking. When the dog turns to locate you, he must see you looking like fun, with a RM, a big smile, and, the first few times, a cookie as well.

If prompting is required to get more than a glance from your dog, use as little prompting as possible. If you have to prompt more than once or twice, you need to go back and do a Review Session (review the first steps again with your dog to remind him what the appropriate behaviour is).

If you are getting NO attention, crate the dog for five or ten minutes, then try again. (My attitude is, "If you won't play with me, you don't get to play at all.")

APPROXIMATION #9

The Role of the NRM

Most people are ready to introduce the NRM for non-attention after two to five attention sessions. (A SESSION would consist of approximately 3 to 10 Trials. A TRIAL begins with your cue and ends with your release word.) The goal of each Session is to add 2 to 5 seconds to the dog's attention span, thereby removing him from the Attention Deficit crowd and placing him into the whiz-bang class that has 15 to 30 seconds of constant attention.

REMEMBER! A NRM is NOT used to obtain your dog's attention – what is reinforced in this exercise is voluntary attention that is in the process of being placed "On Demand." So, if you are finding yourself using a NRM more than a few times: resist opening your mouth, go back to the earlier sequences, and review the material with your dog. With every single exercise you may have to lower and raise criteria and do reviews throughout. Don't get too wigged out about this; it is the natural process of learning.

APPROXIMATION #10

Pivot from Front to Heel

1. Begin with your dog in a Sit and step into Front position. The leash is still under your foot if your dog has a tendency to wander, or needs to be kept safe. One treat is enclosed in your left hand. You can "store" the additional treats in your right hand, or in a fanny pack or bait bag.
2. When your dog looks up at you, you can Mark It & Feed It. With a treat in line with your dog's nose, slowly pivot to a Heel position. If his attention wavers while you are pivoting, Freeze. Wait. When your dog looks back at you, Mark It & Feed It and continue with your Pivot. Initially, when you are conditioning the attention, wait for the dog and keep applying reinforcement to the attention you get. You'll get more. That's one of the Rules. Whatever is Reinforced will certainly be repeated.

Your dog's head may stay tilted towards you if she is sitting in heel position, but I do not demand that my dog contort himself into an uncomfortable or stylized position. You can tell if he is oriented toward you and paying attention to where you are. This is all you need.

If you move and your dog doesn't even notice you moved, then obviously he isn't paying much attention, is he? The stationary position that you are working on in this Approximation is the one that your dog will eventually adopt when you are moving. Breanna, my Smoothie, habitually heels with her nose just slightly tilted toward my pant leg. She can keep track of me there and still be looking where she is going. Maeve, my Shepherd, likes to heel looking straight ahead, then turning her head towards me, then looking ahead again. I find this quite acceptable, even for competition purposes. My Border Collie puppy likes to turn her face right toward me and look up. Punch, one of my other Smooths, does vertical Heeling: she leaps and looks. So, I do allow each dog to bring some of her own "style" and personality into this exercise and to remain comfortable while she is working.

Approximation #11

Stationary Heel Position – Teaching A Station

Initially you will "step into" or pivot into heel position, because obviously your dog doesn't really know where this Station is yet. That is all teaching a Heel position is. It is just teaching your dog to go to a Station or Location on cue, maintain position with that Location when it moves, and remain in Location until released.

1. The leash is under your foot, or passed behind your body and held in your right hand, with the dog on your left. One treat is enclosed in your left hand, between your finger and thumb. You can "store" the additional treats in your right hand, or in a fanny pack or bait bag.
2. Once you have the dog's attention: Request a Sit, then you step into Heel position.

   Note: In the following steps I am using "Look" as a cue for Involvement and "Heel" as a cue that combines a physical location in space AND attention. Thus, the dog comes to associate a specific station or location with the word "Heel." I am using a known cue of "Look" to help the dog to understand a new cue of "Heel."
3. If your dog's attention is still on you, you may add your verbal cue, "Look," Mark It & Feed It.
4. You will also introduce the new cue of "Heel." Deliver a treat when your dog is in the appropriate position.
5. I alternate using both cues of "Look" and "Heel." Gradually use more cues of "Heel" than "Look," until "Look" is faded out. The treat delivery will have a very specific location, such that the treat is placed where you want your dog's visual reference point for heeling to be. For most dogs this will be somewhere on your pant seam, at a height varying considerably depending on the height of your dog.
6. Begin to wait longer and longer between the "Look" or "Heel" verbal cue and the RM. The RM would be accompanied each and every time with delivery of a training treat at this stage. BUT you will introduce a Variable Schedule because you will be waiting for ever more duration of the behaviour, a second or two at a time....
7. Now, add a more "formal" posture, making sure you aren't all twisted sideways watching your dog. With your dog sitting in Heel, look out ahead of you, as if you were walking (but don't move yet!), and reinforce your dog for remaining in Heel position. *This is still a stationary exercise at this point.*

After you release your dog, remember to give him a play break and then begin another Trial. Do 3-10 Trials per session. You can do 2 or 3 sessions a day if you like.

When *moving* in Heel position you will be (or should be) watching where you are going. To prepare for that a mirror is a useful tool to check the dog's position, or you can glance down and use your peripheral vision. If you are constantly turned sideways looking at the dog, it can actually cause lagging behaviour, and is very uncomfortable!

If you are doing this work correctly, attending to your wishes is evolving in a very natural way.

Approximation #12

Stationary Challenges

It is not required that you have your dog moving in Heel with attention before you introduce some

Challenges. You can choose some of the stationary Challenge exercises from the "Challenge List" at the end of this chapter. You can work on some of these, and work on teaching Moving Attention during the same Training Session. For example:

15 Minute Training Session
Work on Stationary Attention – up to 30 seconds.
Work on Heeling "Starts" (as in Approximation #13).
Challenge: Stationary Attention with food on the floor 3 feet away.
Quit while you are ahead! End with a successful behaviour.

APPROXIMATION #13

Moving Attention and Beyond

You have a lot of automatic attention by this time. If you don't, review the approximations and repeat the exercises until you do.

Introduce Heeling Starts. Say, "Ready," or "Look," to cue your dog that a work session is beginning. Say "Heel." With both feet still together, lean forward very slightly, just as you naturally would to begin walking. Take one step, and give the dog a cookie. Work up to two steps, ten steps and more.

You really do not need to "drill" this behaviour. If you get up from the sofa during a commercial, you can Heel your dog to the kitchen and give him a cookie for doing the behavior.

Photo by Kathy Mazur.

Moving Attention at Heel

APPROXIMATION #14

Challenges (Adding Distraction)

Why Challenge? The main objective of Attention Training is to prepare your dog to be dependable about remaining Involved with YOU. When you add Challenges, you are not trying to see if you can "GET" the dog nor are you looking for opportunities to correct the dog. *Adding challenges to the exercise is to build confidence and to clarify the exercise for the dog.*

Practice your Challenges from various Working Positions: a Sit at Heel position, a Sit in Front position, and with your dog moving as well as stationary. Believe it or not, it takes different skills to have stationary and moving attention!

Up to now you have been asking your dog to "Look" longer to get the treat. By this point in the training program, you are no longer giving a constant feed under familiar circumstances the dog. However, Challenges add distracting circumstances and when you first do this, you will likely need to temporarily go back to Kindergarten. With each new Challenge you begin with a constant feed, then move to a Variable Reinforcement Schedule. This is the process that gradually hardens the dog's resolve to Resist the Distraction and Win the Prize.

Warning! Danger, Will Robinson, Danger! This Sequence is where people often go wrong. How? The human forgets that the dog must have some time to assimilate a change of circumstances. Remember that you will have a few Trials in "new" settings where you must relax your time requirements considerably. This way the dog generalizes the behaviour much more quickly.

- Select a distraction from the upcoming Challenge Lists and use your reinforcers generously.

If your dog resists looking at the distraction at all: give a bonus – several pieces of food delivered in the following manner: RM/treat; RM/treat; RM/treat, and so on. Add a little extra social approval as well.

Strategies for the Inattentive Dog

If your dog looks at the Challenge and does more than glance at it for 1 or 2 seconds: Use a NRM. If you need to use the NRM more than twice – time for a Review Session.

If your dog glances at the "Challenge," then looks back at you:
1. Mark It & Feed It.

2. Initially accept a glance, but after one or two Trials, immediately raise criteria so that the dog is remaining on task for a count of 2-3. Make sure the dog is committed to gazing at you instead of gazing around at the environment.

Other great strategies for the inattentive dog:
- Move-Away from the distraction until your dog looks at you or looks toward you.
- Back-Away.
- Move-Into the dog.

Challenge List

Try the following exercises first with your usual bait bag as part of your wardrobe. Then try each challenge with no food in your hand and remove your bait bag from your person. You may place the treats in your mouth, on a nearby table, or in a training bag (you know, the bag with all your training stuff in it) on a chair. This way you can store food on or near you without being obvious about it.

- At any time during this process, when you get an Excellent response or a First Correct Effort provide Hazard Pay or a Jackpot. Don't be tempted to repeat an exercise until your dog gets it wrong – learn to quit while you are ahead!
- You are to become silent for longer periods of time, giving the dog less frequent verbal feedback. This will harden the dog's resolve to hang in there and continue to pay attention, even though it may be more difficult to do so. This is also a "confidence builder" in that your dog will be reinforced heavily for making correct decisions all by herself without constant prompting, continuous cheerleading, or reminders from you.
- Assume a handler position of Heel or Front. A second person now comes up at a distance of three to four feet. Have this assistant work gradually closer, one step at a time, hardening each response (getting a consistent response over a number of trials: such as three Excellent responses in a row, or 8 out of 10) before you move on to the next approximation. Eventually, this person will be standing next to the dog. Eventually the helper will follow the dog while he is Heeling. If your dog looks away: NRM. If you need to NRM more than once: Review Session. For a Review Session, you will back up to a previous approximation (step) where the dog was succeeding, and then advance forward again. This means the assistant temporarily increases the distance and gradually re-approaches.
- Toss or drop a piece of food. (Pay attention – step on the food or move away if the dog goes for or looks at the food).

Photo essay by Joanne Weber.

When first beginning the Offering Food Challenge, the helper will tempt the dog by holding out a treat. As soon as the dog looks at the helper, the helper should immediately look less enticing by standing up straight or moving slightly away from the dog. In the first trials, the handler might prompt the dog with a reminder, "Look," such as Lori is doing here. As soon as the dog turns back to the handler, Mark It & Feed It.

As this exercise advances, the handler waits quietly with no prompting until the dog looks back at her voluntarily. This is followed the first couple of times by a jackpot, and perhaps, to make the moment extra special (therefore MEMORABLE), a little street party.

The next step would be to have the "food temptress" move closer to the dog to offer the food. Notice in this photo the helper is not all that close, about 3 feet away from the dog.

Person Offers Food

- Place food on a chair, allowing your dog to see you doing this. Walk near the chair and ask for Sit and Involvement.
- Work backwards from the dog one step at a time, until you are six feet away during the distraction, returning to the heel position before releasing.
- Have an assistant walk by and toss food.
- Have a person talk while walking at a distance of more than five feet.
- Have a person bounce a ball or gently swing an umbrella at a distance of five or more feet.
- Have a person offer food in a neutral way. If the dog "goes for" the treat, the helper removes the food and turns his back on the dog.
- Have a Person approach the dog and stroke it.

Initially you will want to do this in steps as follows:

1. Provide a constant feed for the dog as the helper lightly touches dog.

2. The helper touches the dog and if he resists distraction, then provide the RM and treat.
3. If the dog loses attention, NRM. Wait for your dog's attention to come back to you and then begin another Trial. If a simple NRM is not effective, try another technique from the "Strategies for the Inattentive Dog," section in this chapter, above.

The helper is not allowed to use the dog's name or a strict voice – have the helper be very subtle, at least initially. Later he may begin to approach the dog more as a person on the street would.

The moment the dog begins to respond to the Distraction, your helper must cease attention and pointedly ignore the dog. This is done by having the helper look up toward the ceiling or sky, and fold his arms across his chest, so that the dog gets the picture that this person is not reinforcing in any way, shape or form. For the timid dog, the looking away will tell her that this person is not threatening. For the dog who is nervous about direct eye contact, ditto.

Caution: Dogs who have problems with people approaching may not be ready for this just yet. If this is the case, complete the "Being Brave Is Better" protocol.

Maintenance of Behaviour

Place Involvement behaviour on a Maintenance, or Variable Reinforcement, Schedule. That is, you will use your RM frequently, but you will use a RM & Primary reinforcer (food) on only some occasions. After a while, the response becomes a habit and is integrated into the dog's Behavioural Repertoire. Each time you introduce a new Challenge, you will have to temporarily use a fixed schedule, then you will move the behaviour onto a variable schedule.

When your dog has completed this exercise, it is exciting to know that he will voluntarily choose to attend to what is important to the handler instead of what is important to the dog.

I provide primary reinforcement (food) for this behaviour throughout the life of the dog. You will have the dog on a very thin schedule after several months, and won't need to use frequent reinforcement any longer. Don't be afraid to go back to kindergarten as necessary.

When Do I Correct?

After you have presented the dog with many Challenges, and he has proven to you that he understands this concept, only then is it fair to correct. Correction coming at this stage, when the dog is on a Variable Reinforcement Schedule, will serve only to give the dog information.

The word "Correction" is defined by many as a collar or leash correction (a sharp jerk to the leash) given to a dog wearing a choke collar. I want to make sure that you do not misinterpret what "correction" means to me, so we don't have a war over semantics. "Correction" to me is NOT a leash correction. Most often it is removing my person (therefore, Opportunities for Reinforcement go way down). I move in the opposite direction of the distraction so distance can diminish the value of that Reinforcer while enhancing my own Reinforcement value. (Refer to the "Cease & Desist" Protocol for additional details on the Move-Away.)

Just so you have a clear picture, a correction might be one of the following:

- A good attention-getter for the distracted dog is a little tap right on the top of his cute little head. This is a tiny tap meaning "Where are you?" – not a hard thump of irritation!

- Move off in the opposite direction. Physics dictates that when this occurs the dog will come to the end of the leash, and as you continue to back up, the dog will face you. This is not a "jerk" to the dog, but a gentle, firm message: "You are with me." As soon as he is oriented toward you, give him a big "Yes" or a click. *You need to look like the fun playmate here and be jolly.*

Photo essay by Joanne Weber.
Amanda looks longingly at the cheese placed on the chair...but quickly transfers her attention back to her handler voluntarily (without prompting)...
...and willingly walks away from a "sure thing" to go to her handler.
Challenge: Treats On The Chair

Now, the part of this correction that will CHANGE THE DOG'S BEHAVAVIOUR: Continue to move backwards to encourage the dog toward you. When the dog catches up with you, Mark It & Feed It. In subsequent incidents, begin to wait for 3-5 seconds or more of attention before you Mark It & Feed It. This maneuver is intended to surprise the dog and therefore encourage her to keep better track of you – not as a means of physical punishment.

Photo by Joanne Weber.

These dogs have learned how to resist various temptations and remain involved with the handler in lieu of the environment. There is a plate with food, toys, and a bait bag full of cheese on the floor.

These results were NOT obtained with collar corrections or nagging. They were obtained by giving the dog clear feedback and by managing the environment so that the dogs were successful only if they remained attentive to the handler. This is not beginning, but advanced work.

Moving Attention: Advanced Challenge

- If your dog is boisterous and a leaping maniac and simply WILL NOT attend to you: Crate the dog for five or ten minutes. If he doesn't want to play your game, he won't be allowed to play any game. If your dog is timid, this is what he has been longing for, so you give the timid dog a little break, by taking him for a walk or asking him to lie down for a minute so he can decompress. Then you can return to work.
- Sometimes the dog is looking right at you, but he is not here with you! If your dog is gazing at you but is obviously dreaming of the sandy beaches of Tahiti, his attention is waning or gone, tap his head (gently – this is a wake-up call). Then do a Review Session, consisting of easy and familiar Baby Steps, working quickly up to his current skill level.
- You can try a Down Stay for a couple of minutes, then resume work on the Involvement.
- Review the "Strategies for Inattention" section in this chapter. The MoveAway, BackAway or Move Into are all effective.

Remember: If you have to prompt for attention more than once or twice, it is time for a Review

Session! Do it right now, don't wait another minute. This is a temporary process: quick review for the dog, utilizing the first steps you used to get attention. (Refer to Approximations #1 - #4).

IMPORTANT!! The biggest mistake you can make is to correct or frown or act irritated when your dog is looking at you. Why? Obviously, this would be applying an Aversive to the Desired Behaviour. Big Error. Don't do it.

Secrets Of Success

- Timing is all important here!
- Look pleasant. Smile! Or at least don't frown and look crabby when you are doing this stuff. What a turn-off!
- If the food is dropped by accident and you cannot prevent the dog from getting the treat, just tell the dog, "Get It." You might as well look omnipotent here. If you do not tell the dog to "Get It," prevent him from getting it. Step on it or quickly back away, taking your dog with you. With any luck at all, learning to Hoover the floor is not what you are teaching. With practice you will develop enough skill to not drop the treats all over the dog's head. If you do a few times, so what? The learning curve will be a bit slower. Once you gain confidence and dexterity your dog will be gazing at you constantly and you will be delivering reinforcement on a proper schedule with adroitness!
- Delivery of the treat is always upwards (the dog looking up) and with the dog moving into your space. Don't chase your dog down to give him the cookie, make him come to you. That's the whole point here, right? Remember: Organisms will gravitate to placement of reinforcement. All that means is that the dog will return to the location he receives reinforcement.
- From this point forward, when you ask the dog to work, pay attention and don't be gazing around, yourself. Get in there, get the Involvement, do the exercise and then give a clear release signal.

The minute the dog is in Heel position is a signal that it is time to go to work and attention is a must. If you have the dog in heel position *you* must be as Involved as you want him to be.

This doesn't necessarily mean staring at the dog's face when you are walking. It means you are attentive, aware of and *involved* with your dog. You can look ahead and still see your dog in your peripheral vision. You can even be attentive and aware of the environment and your dog if you are talking to someone else. Multi-tasking takes practice! But you can do it!

Level I	
Pre-requisite	Foundation Behaviours

SELF-RELAXATION EXERCISES

THE ZEN SIT & DOWN STAY

Goal	The dog will Sit or Down on a verbal command and/or a hand signal and will remain there until released. The dog will remain relaxed and committed to the Sit or Down.
What it teaches	Self-restraint (impulse control). A means to calm down and relax. To use the Sit and Down as calming signals. To Switch from an aroused to a relaxed emotional state.
Practical Application	Sit and Down are excellent ways to take your dog out of Drive and into Neutral for a minute, or for ten minutes, or for extended periods of time (more than fifteen minutes). Sit and Down can keep your dog out of trouble and prevent her from being in the way or from bothering someone who doesn't want to pay attention to the dog right at that moment. This exercise is all about teaching your dog to place herself in an internal state that doesn't necessarily reflect the external stimuli around her. Basically, you are teaching the dog that she does not have to mirror the chaos in her environment. A Sit or Down, since they are themselves Calming Signals, can be used to calm other dogs in the area. This can keep the environment more controlled. These two behaviours are key components of taking a dog into public places when you wish her to be still while you are otherwise occupied.

Concepts for the dog to learn:

- Length of Time to Stay
- Distance
- Resisting Distraction
- Remaining Relaxed

This behavioural protocol is one of the essential steps required for the prevention of aggression or the rehabilitation of your dog. You are looking for something extra here once you have the Sit behaviour. You are looking specifically for **Sit and Be Calm**. These are not obedience exercises, although your dog will be more obedient when you have mastered them. The objective is to get the dog to Sit, and, while in that posture, remain calm and be receptive about changing her paradigm toward the situation. Stressed or anxious dogs literally cannot learn more appropriate behaviour, and certainly cannot associate the current situation with being fun and relaxing. A reactive, stressed, or untrained dog is so involved with her current emotional state and the physiological changes that go with it that she cannot possibly concentrate on new information. The **stressed** dog is telling you that she is already overwhelmed by her present predicament.

There may be similarities in some obedience exercises you have done in the past and this protocol. Even so, there are also differences, so please attend to the exercises and execute them as directed. If you do not follow the protocol exactly, it cannot help your dog.

Using a Sit or Down as a Switching Exercise.

Switching from an aroused state to a calm, relaxed state On Demand is definitely a learned behaviour, and a very handy one to cultivate in your dog! Remember, you are always concerned with the emotional state of the dog, which is the external, observable indication of his internal chemical state.

- Dogs learn by being successful. Please follow the steps carefully. By doing so you will not teach bad habits and you will also progress very quickly, making the activity fun for you and the dog, avoiding frustration at the same time.
- Use your Sit! Every chance you get. Before you throw a toy. Before you feed Spot dinner. Before you pet Spot or play with her. Dogs learn the relevance of specific behaviours when they practice them in daily life.

Once you can elicit the Sit you can begin the Sit-Stay. The Sit itself does not have to be on a verbal cue to begin the Sit-Stay.

What To Have Ready:

- Have training treats, and have your dog on a leash. The leash should be under your foot, at a length of 4' or 5'. This is long enough so the dog can move about, but short enough that you can prevent her from wandering off.
- A RM (verbal or clicker). Remember: A Reward Mark is very significant to your dog, as it gives her information. Precise information is the name of the game.
- A NRM (No Reward Mark), such as "Try Again" or "Not Yet," to signal to the dog that you don't want the behaviour she is currently offering. Do not use "No." "No" is the most overused word in communication between people and dogs.
- Do NOT deliver the food treat if the dog is not Sitting. Initially the food treat is offered EVERY TIME the Sit is accomplished. Once your dog will sit when cued to do so in at least 3 different locations or situations, then the food treat will be offered occasionally.
- Remember! Training treats are tiny, small little tidbits. About 1/2 the size of your little finger nail.
- The treats must be something your dog likes and will work for.
- You will begin with a Fixed Schedule, then move to a Variable Reinforcement Schedule.

Acquisition: Manufacture a Sitting Behaviour

Do NOT say "Sit" at this point. Your dog does not know what Sit means, therefore, if she is leaping about or staring off into space and you are chanting "Sit, Sit, Sit," guess what behaviour your dog is associating Sit with? Duh. For now, you are merely eliciting the desired physical position.

- Holding the treat between your finger and thumb, show the dog the treat by holding it near her nose.
- At a steady speed, not super-quick or jerky, raise the treat directly above the dog's head and back slightly toward her tail.
- Timing is crucial! The first couple of trials, especially, the moment your dog's bottom hits the ground Mark It & Feed It.

Placing a Behaviour on a Verbal Cue.

- Once the Sit is easily obtained with a lure/hand signal, you will add the verbal cue. The syntax is as follows:
- Say "Sit" in a pleasant tone of voice.
- Pause (about ½ second).
- Present the old cue (hand signal) as a "helper" or prompt.
- Pause (about ½ second).
- Mark it & Feed It.

You can also take advantage of "Opportunity Training" in the following manner. As soon as you can predict the dog will approach you and offer the Sit: as you see the dog beginning to sit, say "Sit" and Mark the behaviour with "Yes" and deliver the food treat.

Using either one or both of these techniques, you will soon have Sit on a verbal cue.

Pop Quiz

Once you have repeated the above Approximation 10 or 20 times, you may do a Pop Quiz to see if the dog understands the new cue.

- Say "Sit" in a pleasant tone of voice.
- Pause (about 5-10 seconds).
- Assess the behaviour (did the dog sit?). If she did, Mark It & Feed It.

If this is a *First Correct Effort*, have a Street Party! That means a delivery of several pieces of food. I do this as follows "Yes-treat, yes-treat, yes-treat, yes-treat, yes-treat," so that the reinforcement is "drawn out" and emphasized and the dog isn't just inhaling a bunch of treats all at once instead of just one at a time. If I am using a clicker, I click the first one and then just feed the treats one at a time, but quickly one after the other - the old "machine gun" delivery.

- If the dog does NOT sit, give the dog a NRM.
- Cue the Sit again with your verbal "Sit."
- Give the helper prompt.
- Provide appropriate consequences.

If your dog has not yet made the "connection" between the verbal cue and the behaviour, as indicated by the results of the pop quiz, proceed as follows.

- Repeat 10 to 20 trials of the behaviour using the steps as outlined in "Placing a Behaviour on a Verbal Cue."
- Repeat your pop quiz.

Acquisition - Manufacture a Down Behaviour

The exact same approximations apply to the Down as to the Sit for all the distance and increasing time thresholds, as well as placing the behaviour on a verbal cue. All that really differs is the initial lure movement to manufacture the Behaviour.

If this is a dog who will never see the competition ring, it is often easiest to begin with the dog in a Sit. For competition dogs, I recommend beginning Down work from a standing position and teaching a "Fold-Back" Down.

Teaching Down from a Sit

- Hold the food at the dog's nose and get her interested in it.

  Hold the treat firmly between your thumb and finger, so the dog cannot take the treat before you are ready to give it to her.
- Slowly lower the food.
- Initially R+ the head ducking, the first step to lying down.

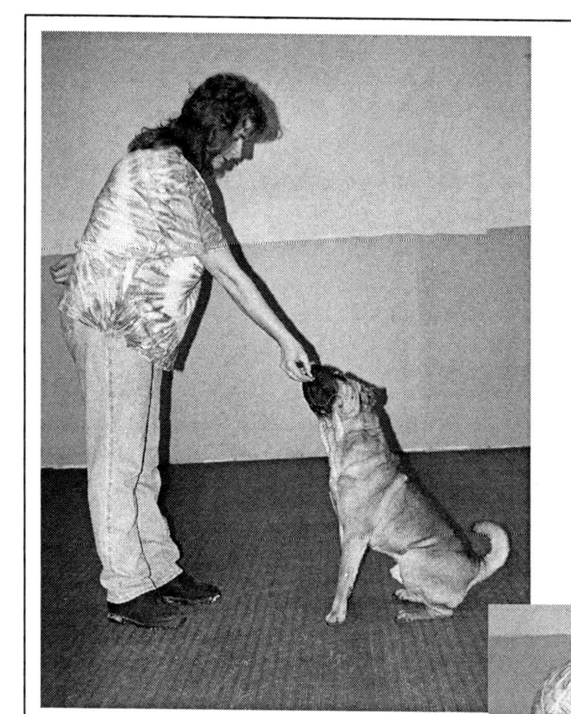

Photo Essay by Joanne Weber.

Get your dog interested in the treat you have in your hand...

...then pull his head straight down toward his toes with the lure. Some dogs need to be reinforced at this point, just for the head-ducking behaviour.

Each time, you will ask the dog to duck his head a bit lower and remain there a second or so longer.

At the point your hand is resting on the floor between or just in front of the dog's toes, and the dog is remaining in an awkward position for a few seconds, the vast majority of dogs just lie down, as it is more comfortable to do so to get at the treat. At that exact moment the dog folds to the floor and his elbows touch, Mark & Feed the behaviour.

Nose to Toes is the Ticket!

- Mark & Feed when the dog's head reaches her knees.
- Mark & Feed when the dog's head reaches her toes.
- Use the lure to encourage your dog to stretch her neck down to the floor and out just a bit.
- Keep moving the lure just a bit farther each time.
- Move the lure to your "new" distance then HOLD the lure STILL. Wait and see if it occurs to the dog to lie down.

The hand motion used with the lure is all important:

The Rule is: Nose to Toes and out.

- That is: hold the treat at the dog's nose.
- Lower it to her toes.
- Slowly move the treat straight out in front of the dog. Most people try to move the treat too quickly, causing the dog to give up.

If the dog is sitting, and, as she lowers her head her little bottom pops up...

- Remove the food treat by hiding it behind your back and issue a NRM.
- Then begin another Trial. That is, begin with a Sit, then produce the lure again and give it another try!

  After just a few tries, the dog will collapse into a down, because it is more comfortable for her to do so.
- Once those elbows hit the ground, keep a constant feed going initially for 5 or 6 seconds.
- Move a few steps and try again.
- When the dog has gone down once, you should no longer apply reinforcement to the head ducking.

Teaching a Fold-Back Down

Follow the same steps as above for the Down. All that differs is the hand motion of the lure. With your dog in a *standing position*:

- Hold a treat between your finger and thumb.
- Lower your hand slightly (to about the bottom of your dog's chest initially) and sort of lightly shove the treat right into her chest.
- Initially you will reinforce just the head ducking motion.
- To raise criteria, lower your hand a bit each time, while at the same time keeping the dog interested and nibbling at the treat without actually giving it to her. As you lower your hand, you will also increase the amount of time you keep the dog in that position before you deliver the treat to her.
- Once you are below the dog's chest, you can begin to place the treat under the dog's chest and between her front legs. As she moves to get it, she will begin to do a kind of "bowing" motion. You can reinforce this behaviour a couple of times, then:
- Increase the time requirement again. This is quite an uncomfortable position to maintain for long, and most dogs actually begin to lie down to get the treat because it is more comfortable.

I won't fool you, teaching a Fold Back Down may require quite a bit of "lure manipulation." You will really have to hang in there and fiddle with it, until you get exactly the right lure position for the dog to do the behaviour. When you hit it right, you will know because the dog will tell you by her response: she will literally fold effortlessly backwards into the Down position. I don't know how to describe it well, but after you've succeeded once you will get the "feel" for the correct hand position.

Once the Down is easily obtained with a hand signal, you will add the verbal cue. (Refer to the section "Placing A Behaviour On AVerbal Cue" in this chapter.)

Use your Down! Every chance you get. Before you feed Spot dinner. Before you pet Spot or play with her. Dogs learn the relevance of obedience when they practice it in daily life.

Once you can elicit the Down you can immediately begin work on a Down-Stay.

APPROXIMATION #1

Begin the Stay Work

Solving Stay problems requires predictability of success for your dog. The first stays are in Distraction-Free locations. If your dog is not sitting eagerly 100% of the time, you can still begin Stay work, which will, in fact, increase your

Photo Essay by Joanne Weber.

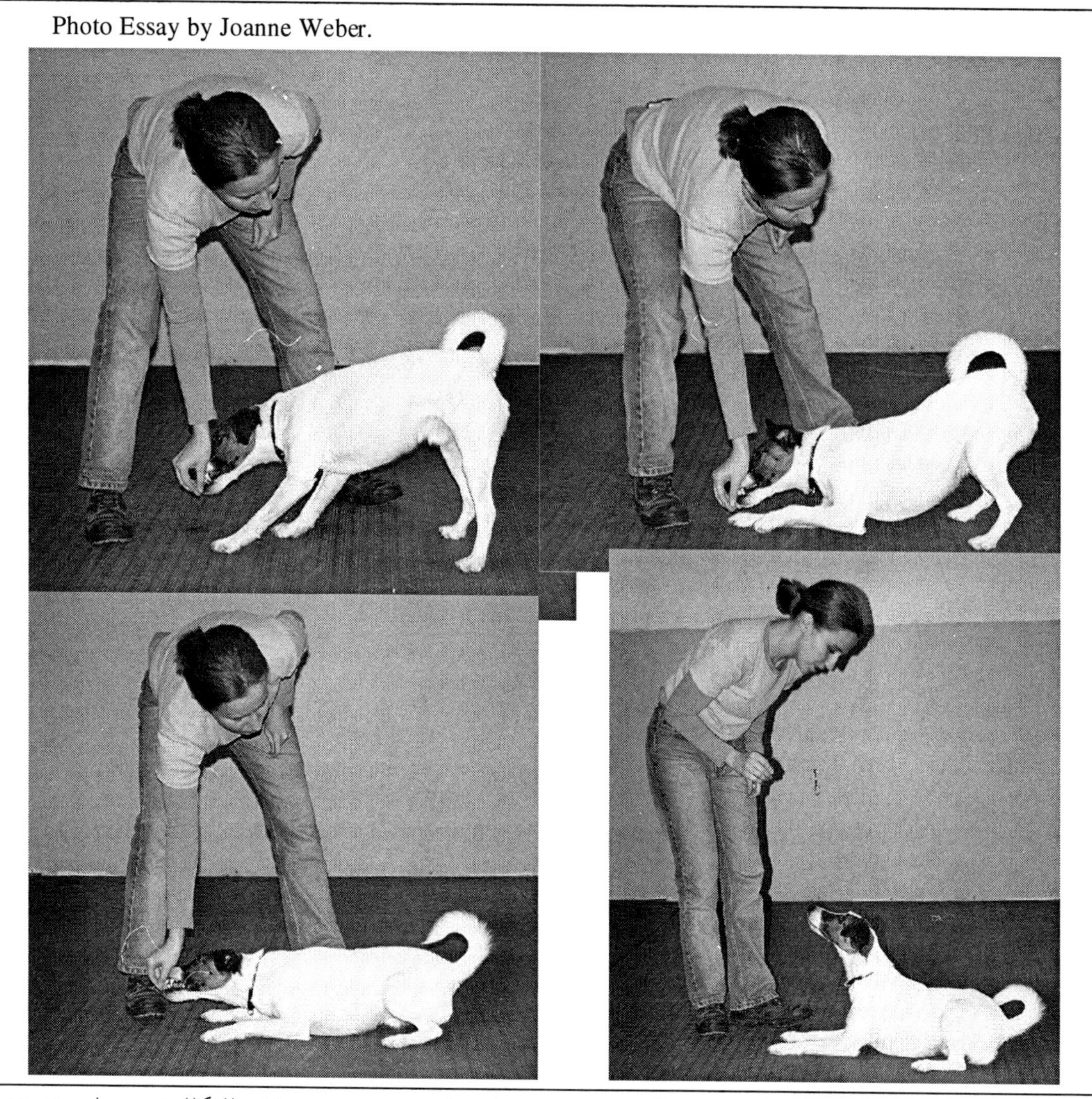

Notice how skillfully Marie positions her lure to manufacture the Fold-Back Down. The movement is always down and "into" the dog.

Fold Back Down

dog's understanding of the Sit cue. I begin Stay work almost immediately, as soon as I can manufacture a sitting behaviour. If the dog I am working with will remain seated, or OFFERS to remain seated longer than a second, I will immediately reinforce that "I am continuing to work" behaviour from the dog. Also, you don't have to wait until the dog is on a verbal cue of "Sit" to begin reinforcing "continue to Sit."

Limited Holds

If your dog is slowly lowering herself into a sit when you are first teaching the STAY, do not get into a struggle over the quickness of the SIT. Consider them two different exercises to be strung together later. Just get the Sit, by lure or lifting very slightly on the collar, work your Stays, and note that you need to work on a quick Sit in a separate session by utilizing a Limited Hold.

A Limited Hold means that, if you are cueing for a behaviour, such as "Sit," and it is taking 3-seconds for the animal to actually lower her behind to the ground and you want instant response, you need to stop reinforcing 3-second Sits. Begin by reinforcing only those Sits that occur within two seconds, then one second.

- Once your dog is sitting, keep a steady but slow and controlled stream of food flowing so that this puzzle is very easy for your dog to solve. As you progress over the next few days, stretch out the amount of time that you withhold the reinforcement. The dog is clear on this exercise when she demonstrates patience no matter how much you move the food or how long you make her wait for it. Work up to two or three minutes.

You will be *right in front of your* dog for these exercises. Each step in Tables 1, 2 and 3 is intended to be repeated two or three times. If you can do two or three in a row successfully, move to the next step. If, after any more than three tries, you still can't do the next step, back up a step and repeat that one two or three more times. Quit when the dog is doing well. To begin the next session, start one step back from where you left off.

Table 1: Stays & Reinforcement Schedules

Time	Possible Reinforcement Schedule Just as An Example
Count to 1. Then...	Mark It & Feed It (e.g., "Yes" – deliver treat) Tip: Allow the dog time to eat her treat – just a second usually is all she takes. **When she is done** she will look up at you. This means she is ready physically (she has swallowed the treat) and mentally to go back to work. At that point you may remind her: "Stay" or "Sit" or "Down," whatever you feel appropriate. When a cue is used in this manner, it is called a **reminder antecedent**. Here, use of the reminder antecedent: begins the next Trial.
2	Mark It & Feed It
3	Mark It & Feed It
5	Mark It & Feed It
7	RM ("Yes" only - NO treat). You are beginning a variable schedule here. It is best to move an animal onto the variable schedule as quickly as possible. This teaches her to "wait for gratification" and strengthens the behaviour at the same time! Wow! Two-for-the-price-of-one! You are teaching your dog to "continue" the behaviour while giving her a "you are on the right road" indication. I use a clicker or a verbal RM the same way - as a "you've got it - keep going" signal. To END the behaviour, I use a "that'll do" or "all done" cue. Therefore, my dogs continue a behaviour until I end the behaviour with "that'll do" OR until I request another behaviour (For instance, a Recall would end a Sit behaviour).
9	Mark It & Feed It
4	Mark It & Feed It
10	RM

Table 1: Stays & Reinforcement Schedules

3	Mark It & Feed It
8	RM
14	Mark It & Feed It
7	RM
3	Mark It & Feed It
12	Mark It & Feed It
15	Mark It & Feed It
7	RM
18	Mark It & Feed It
3	RM
15	Mark It & Feed It
7	Mark It & Feed It
20	Mark It & Feed It
5	RM
20	Mark It & Feed It

The previous table is designed to give you an idea of how to proceed. Work up to 2 to 3 minutes. I find that once a 30 second Stay is reached, the time threshold can be increased by 5 to 10 seconds at a time with most dogs.

APPROXIMATION #2

Take your Dog out of Drive and Place her in Neutral

Caution: This approximation involves using toys. If your dog exhibits possessive aggression over toys (i.e., your dog has threatened you by staring without blinking; growling; snarling; or snapping when you have attempted to take a toy from her), just jump around and get her a little revved up, then ask for the Sit or Down and deliver a food treat. Forget about using toys, at least in the initial stages of teaching them this game.

If your dog does have possession problems refer to the protocols: "Resource Guarding" and "Twos."

Sit When Excited

- Leap around and/or encourage your dog to play with a toy and get your dog excited.

Until you are assured of a correct response, you will do this work with your dog dragging a leash or long line. *Until you have verbal control you must have physical control.*

- When the dog is excited and bouncing around, cue for the Sit.

If you are using a toy, in the beginning stages, remove the toy from the dog's vision by putting it behind your back. Just prior to presenting the "Sit" or "Down" cue. Later on the dog should heed your verbal cue even when the toy is still providing visual stimulation.

When you put the toy behind your back, if the dog just runs around behind you, hold the toy out of the dog's reach, get hold of the leash (or long line) and encourage her to Sit and quit leaping by placing the leash under your foot at a length sufficient to allow the dog to Sit, but not so long that she can continue to leap with abandon.

- As soon as the dog Sits, Mark It & Feed It and/or toss a toy.
- Play a minute with the toy if you are using one, otherwise just bounce around with her for a minute. Then do another Sit.
- Repeat 3 to 5 times. Then consider the session finished.

The first few times your dog does not respond, remove the visual stimuli of the toy by holding it behind your back. Then help her out with a food lure and your hand signal, in addition to your verbal cue. If she repeatedly is ignoring your cue after one or two sessions, implement the following "Draw the Line In The Sand" measures.

For non-compliance to your *known* Sit cue, you may lift the collar VERY GENTLY straight up, with NO jerking and NO emotion. This is all about supplying information to your dog and showing your dog what will and will not work as behaviour strategies.

- Maintain a *slight pressure* on the dog's neck, regardless of what the dog does, until you get the correct response. In short, ignore all temper tantrums and other inappropriate responses.
- Immediately loosen the collar (but be ready to tighten it again!) the moment your dog acquiesces into a Sit.

Caution: If your dog becomes reactive with restraint or is aggressive if you hold her collar, refer to "Handling and Restraint" protocol. Discontinue this game until you can safely perform a "collar grab."

Down When Excited

Proceed as above, using a Down instead of a Sit.

For non-compliance, once the dog understands Down and has performed the Down behaviour without flaw in several different situations:

- To "help" the dog understand the exercise use a food lure several times. Then, lose the lure, but still "help" with the hand signal.

Step On The Snap for Non-Compliant Dogs

The following correction should be prepared for before using it in this particular context. Practice this Step-On-The-Snap under less exciting circumstances. Once you begin this correction, you must Wait It Out. If your dog pitches a fit and you allow her up, she has just learned that temper tantrums work. So DO NOT start this unless you are going to stick it out and finish the job.

For the dog who is still non-compliant:

- Neutrally place the leash (close to the snap) under your foot.
- Stand up with the leash under the ball of your foot, with the other end held taut by your hand, and wait for your dog to lie down.
- Expect a bit of a struggle. If your dog is afraid, you did not introduce this correction to her properly. She may just be upset because strategies that have worked for her in the past are no longer working. This is a disappointment. After all, what dogs want is immediate gratification and to do whatever they want whenever they want. I don't see this as much different than my own attitude, quite frankly....But, I, too, have had to learn impulse control!
- Remain quiet and neutral; do not touch or speak to your dog.
- Mark It & Feed It when your dog is quiet and calm.

After I have done this Rev'em up and Sit or Down game a few times, the dog receives no cookies if I must help. If she gives me the behaviour on a verbal cue the first time, she gets really wonderful stuff – tuna fish or tortelini or cheese. Make it worth her while, especially with *First Correct Efforts*. This is tough, to switch back and forth between excited and calm, but a necessary addition to your dog's behavioural repertoire.

Approximation #3

Distance Work

Now it's time for the dog to learn that STAY means *"I'll be right back."*

Your dog will only be calm, and maintain a calm attitude, on Stays if her paradigm is: "My calm, patient behaviour is what causes my handler to return." Therefore, it is imperative that you *remain close in distance* throughout this stage of the Stay. Don't try to add more than a step or two of distance. Also, returning to your dog while she is still calm will net you the excellent results you want. This means, go slow, and build the behaviour systematically and deliberately. The rule is always: *Time before Distance*.

Remember that the primary goal of this activity is to help the dog gain self confidence. You are going to use this as one of your "Switch" activities. That is, when the dog is in a reactive state, you may choose to use a Sit-Stay to help the dog to regain her self-control. Therefore: NO harsh corrections, no yelling, no being cross. Be patient, neutral and business-like when you replace the dog in position if she has moved, and calmly reassuring when delivering food treats. Use your RM/NRM system for information. Move slowly, calmly and confidently yourself when delivering food treats. If you need to move quickly to prevent the dog leaving the area, do so, but not frantically. It is possible to be quick and alert, yet not nervous.

It is very important that you catch *intention behaviour* with Stay training. That is: watch your dog's body language very closely. Before she moves she will often fidget and shift her feet; or give any one of a number of calming signals, such as licking her lips or sniffing. I do not recommend correcting your dog for using calming signals, but you can reduce sniffing merely by reinforcing not sniffing. If your dog is fidgeting or using calming signals even before you leave her, she is not ready for you to step very far away!

In fact, your dog will learn the fastest if you catch the "break" **before** it occurs (while she is still "thinking" about getting up). It is best if you can catch this Intention Behaviour of getting up and hit it with a NRM. Then remind your dog which behaviour she is supposed to be doing. If the dog begins to get up, give a NRM and if the dog remembers to remain Seated – Mark and Feed It. If the dog begins to get up and remembers **on her own** to Stay – Mark It & Feed It. These are very important concepts for the dog. Watch for muscle tension that is an indication that the dog is going to get up. Shifting, lifting front feet, muscles tightening in the haunches or shoulders may all tell you that the dog is thinking about moving.

Remember that what you are beginning to reinforce here is COMMITMENT to the behaviour. If you see any "I am getting ready to move" intention behaviour, you are still close to the dog and can step in and apply a RM/treat BEFORE the dog moves. You might try a NRM on fidgeting, and then repeating Sit. If that works, great, certainly put cookies on that!

If your dog breaks the Sit because YOU didn't catch the intention behaviour soon enough, don't say anything. Just take your dog *gently* by the collar and return her to the exact location and position you left her in.

This is where you will handle an anxious dog one way and the not-paying-attention dog another.

For the anxious dog: Cue her to Sit or prompt her with a hand signal and then, if you do not get an immediate response, you may use the slight upward pressure on the dog's collar. The idea is to make the dog slightly uncomfortable (but not acutely uncomfortable!). I want my dogs to understand that, when I request a reasonable behaviour, I do expect to get it! But I do not want to increase the dog's anxiety.

If the dog is just not paying attention, you can tend to be a little tougher, by which I mean, you are "more neutral" and less friendly. With this dog, do not cue or help the dog to Sit, merely guide her gently back to where she was and obtain the Sit behaviour with a slight upward pressure on the collar. You don't need to jerk, just make her a bit uncomfortable and wait for her to fold her rear legs and Sit (and, of course, we are using a flat or martingale collar, never a choke or pinch for this work!).

I often tie dogs back when I first begin distance work. That way if they get up and are tempted to exit the area without me, they are prevented from doing so. I can approach them and collect them back into a Sit very efficiently and calmly.

Photo by Joanne Weber.

Tie-back

Leave the leash to drag on the ground, putting an extra leash on the dog if you have tied her back. This is to prevent the occurrence of you grabbing the dog's collar, the dog feeling frightened or resentful of this and taking a snap at you. Because of past corrections, many dogs are understandably very sensitive about being grabbed by the collar. If the dog does get up, you can then get hold of the leash to gather her gently back into a Sit.

Caution: If you think your dog might bite at you if you take her by the collar, be sure to muzzle her for this exercise. Before you even begin this portion of this exercise with a dog who might growl or snap at you, you will need to have the "Collar Grab" and "Handleability" exercises completed. (Refer to "Handling and Restraint" and "Yielding" protocols.) You can work your Sit and Down, just don't use any method of correction until you have completed the above mentioned exercises.

Remember:

- Catch any "breaks" with a No Reward Mark, then take the dog back to the location and place her back into a Sit using a steady upward pressure on the collar. You don't need to jerk, just make her a tiny bit uncomfortable and wait her out. She will get tired of being uncomfortable and comply.
- Don't chatter and talk at the dog. This just muddies the water.
- As you move around, or increase distance, you can remind "Stay" (or "Sit" or "Down") as long as your dog is Still Getting It Right. This helps the dog to know she is on the right track. Remember: A command repeated in this context is called a *Reminder Antecedent.*
- In fact, your dog will learn the fastest if you catch the "break" *before* it occurs (while she is still "thinking" about getting up). It is best to catch this Intention Behaviour of getting up and hit it with a NRM. If the dog begins to get up, you give a NRM, and the dog

remembers to remain Seated – Mark and Feed It.

- If the dog begins to get up and remembers *on her own* to Stay – Mark It & Feed It. In fact, I jackpot the first half a dozen occurrences. This is a very big step in understanding for your dog.

Table 2: Add Motion

What You Do:	Possible Reinforce-ment Schedule
Now you will begin to move around. You are raising criteria by adding motion or distance: One step left and return	MI & FI (Mark It & Feed It)
One step right and return	RM (Reward Mark)
One step back and return	MI & FI
Two steps left	RM
Two steps right	MI & FI
Two steps back	RM - Stop and play a game
Three steps right	MI & FI
Three steps left	MI & FI
Three steps back	RM
Count 10 in front of the dog	RM - Game
Two steps right, count 10	MI & FI
Two steps left, count 10	RM
Two steps back, count 10	RM
Five steps right	MI & FI
Five steps back	RM
Five steps left	MI & FI
One step back, about face	MI & FI
Two steps back, about face	MI & FI
Three steps back, about face	RM
Count 20	MI & FI
Ten steps right	RM – Game
Ten steps left	RM – Game
Ten steps back, about face	RM
Count 10	RM
Ten steps right, count 20	MI & FI
Ten steps back, count 20, about face	RM
Count 30	MI & FI
Ten steps right, count 30	MI & FI
Ten steps left, count 30	MI & FI
Ten steps back, count 40	RM-Game
Count 15	RM
Fifteen steps back, count 15	RM
Ten steps right, count 30	MI & FI
Count 60	MI & FI

Table 2: Add Motion

Another big step in understanding occurs as you begin doing the circle work described in Table 3, those first times you pass behind the dog. When your dog allows you to do this without getting up or turning around, she is truly beginning to learn the exercise calmly. Watching her come to understand your cues is exciting and gratifying, especially when you can see activity, inattention or anxiety being converted into calm involvement with you.

When your dog can do all of the above calmly, it's time to harden the behavior. Each time you expose your dog to a new challenge it is important to be near your dog, just as in the Acquisition Stage. This gives your dog some familiar ground to build confidence.

Table 3: Add Circles

Walk around the dog in a small circle.	MI & FI at the first quarter of the circle
Walk around the dog in a small circle.	MI & FI at the second quarter of the circle
Walk around the dog in a small circle.	MI & FI at the third quarter of the circle
Walk around the dog in a small circle.	MI & FI at the full circle
Walk around dog in two small circles.	Reminder Antecedent (Stay) twice, RM three times, Cookie 2 times
Make the circle bigger, disappearing out of sight for just one second.	MI & FI
Step out of sight, appear after count of 2, remind dog "Stay", and disappear again for count of 3.	RM MI & FI

Important: Do not make your dog Sit-Stay for long periods of time. If you need to be somewhere for longer than five or six minutes, use a Down.

APPROXIMATION #4

Sit or Down With Challenges

At this point your dog understands the basic Sit or Down and Stay well enough. Now you are ready to begin with distraction or Challenge work.

Troubleshooting:

- If your dog breaks the Stay, remember to watch closely for intention behaviour. It is your fault that it got so far out of control that your dog got up. But!!! Of course this will happen, so when she does break the stay, the first couple of times, remind her to Sit.
- If the dog breaks the stay that third time, do the neutral gentle lift on the collar to remind her that you intended a "remain in place" behaviour.
- If your dog breaks the stay after 2 of those kinds of corrections, you have advanced too quickly for this animal. Repeat the Approximation where you know your dog feels confident enough to stay put. When you have done 10 reps, with at least 8 of them being in the Good category, advance to this step again.
- On those occasions when your dog breaks, you can begin to replace your dog **neutrally** back into the Sit, ONLY if you are certain she understands this phase of the exercise. Do this by taking her by the collar and physically guiding her into the Sit. No jerking her around, but don't be friendly either. Be Neutral.

How do you know if you should Help or Draw A Line In The Sand? Ask yourself the following:

- How many times has your dog done this particular exercise?
- How many times has your dog been in these particular circumstances?
- Did your dog make ANY effort to comply with this known command? Don't punish "trying."
- Are you certain your dog has a true understanding, and that this is truly "willful misbehaviour?"

Challenge List

1. Place your dog in a Sit with a leash on her and begin by holding the lead. Allow the lead to drop to the ground. Bend over and pick it up.
2. Gently pet your dog as she remains in a Sit or Down.

3. Have a familiar person pet your dog as she remains seated or lying down. You may have to gently distract at first, with you being very close and providing a slow constant feed to help your dog succeed.
4. Take your dog to at least 5 different locations. Expect that you will have to "go back to kindergarten" initially as you move to each new location or context. You will find that, as you work in more and more different locations, you can quickly escalate the steps until you are getting good stays in new locations almost at once.
5. Clap your hands.
6. Turn in a circle.
7. Have someone knock at the door. (This is a toughie!)
8. Have your dog remain in a stay as you toss food on the floor in front of her. (The food at first 6 feet away, gradually moved closer.)

Photo by Joanne Weber.

A variety of dogs are working at different levels. Vinny does a Stand Stay, Cora does a Sit with attention at Lori's side. Amanda's owner is behind her and purposely not looking at her; Faye stands next to Maple while she does a Down. Jake the dachshund does an out-of-sight stay, as his handler has left the room, as does Jack the Black Labrador. Obviously, if your dog is dog hot, or has a tendency to resource guard food or toys, this situation would not be appropriate until you are absolutely, positively certain that the exercise can be carried to completion safely. Vinny, the Smooth Fox Terrier DOES have possessive aggression tendencies, and Marie has spent years carefully monitoring and modifying his behaviour. This work allows her to safely do exercises like this.

Because all of these handlers have systematically and religiously worked attention and "Leave It" exercises, their dogs remain involved with them even in the face of multiple Challenges.

Challenges: Stays

When working your dog, please keep safety for your dog and others uppermost in your mind. Have a leash or thirty foot line on your dog so traffic or getting lost are not a concern. Use a tie-back for safety if you are working in an unenclosed area.

Remember to be **twice** as reinforcing in your new locations! Be fair. Give your dog the benefit of the doubt if you haven't done your Repetitions. However, once your dog has been in the context a few times, insist upon compliance. Neutrally – not angrily.

If your dog has shown any aggression in the past, you need to be doubly certain that your equipment is not worn or ill-fitting so that your dog will not get away from you. Also, for this dog, a thirty-foot line may be out of the question initially, unless you can absolutely guarantee the safety of others in the vicinity (e.g., you are behind a fence alone and the dog is on a line).

The above protocol is a requirement to claim that you have a reliable Sit or Down. It is important to continue work on Stays. Because Stays are so unnatural for your dog (no dog, under normal circumstances, sees something she is interested in, then Sits or Downs to observe it from a distance!), you will need to practice them frequently. The more you integrate your Stays into every day life, and in as many possible circumstances as you can, the better the response will be.

The trap that people fall into is that they use the Sit before the dog goes out the door and at feeding time. But they never, out of the clear blue, walk up to the dog, request a Sit or Down and Stay. If your dog is sniffing in the yard, could you walk near her (at a distance of maybe three or four feet) and, in a normal tone, request a Sit, signal for a Stay, and have it correctly performed on the first cue? The key is to use the Sit and Down in as many contexts as possible, and to use them in situations where the dog may not be expecting you to walk over and give the cue.

39

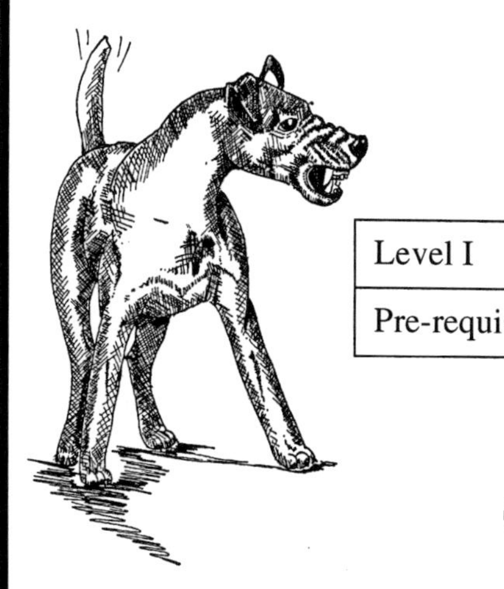

Level I	
Pre-requisite	Foundation Behaviours

CEASE & DESIST!

LEAVE IT & QUIT THINKING ABOUT IT!

Goal	The dog will walk away from or cease approaching other dogs, food, pigeons, people....in short, any distraction or article that is unavailable to the dog at that time or in that particular context. The dog defaults to the Handler instead of the Environment.
What it teaches	This exercise teaches your dog to exhibit self-control, to relinquish both the environment and the impulsive actions that come naturally to him.
Practical Application	In daily life we ask a dog to walk away from numerous "fun" items and activities, either because it is not appropriate for the dog to indulge at this time, or because the activity itself may be dangerous to the dog or others. "Leave It" allows us to communicate to the dog: "This is not available to you right now." Being able to communicate this information in a non-punitive manner gives you a great public image and is very satisfying on a personal level. It also reduces frustration and aggression. Leave It gives the dog the correct idea about "who is in charge here" without having to resort to harsh, repeated, and fruitless physical correction. When the dog will respond to a verbal "Leave It," even handlers who cannot physically correct the dog have control.

The environment is very exciting and is always in direct competition with you for your dog's attention. Technically, this is an issue of Competing Reinforcers. If your dog learns that he can "help himself" to the environment, you will always be on the short end of the stick when you need compliance of a Behaviour.

Dogs do not change behaviour to accommodate human morals, or because humans think that an activity is "wrong." If punishment is your primary tool, the dog quickly learns what is safe vs. dangerous (punishment makes dogs excellent discriminators) and learns to exploit the situation and the environment, bypassing you to the greatest extent possible. One way a dog might do this is with: "If I don't get close enough to my handler, I cannot be punished."

It is requisite that you understand how the dog interprets safe vs. dangerous: "Safe" means that, the dog gets what she wants from the situation. The method by which she obtained results is then catalogued as a "safe" behaviour. "Dangerous" means that efforts were curtailed by avoidance; that is, the dog was frightened or threatened to the extent that she ceased doing something.

"Punishment makes dogs excellent discriminators" translates into real life as: when a dog is punished, she associates any one of a number of environmental factors with the punishment (the location, the punisher, the approaching dog or person, the punisher (that's you), either instead of, or in addition to, the behaviour itself. For instance, counter-surfing is SAFE when humans are not around and DANGEROUS when they are. This is how confusion between the species develops. What humans would like to think when we punish the dog for counter-surfing is that the dog will then understand that counter-surfing is BAD. Nonsense! The dog places no moral value on behaviour. The dog learns, with just a couple of trials, the exact circumstances in which a behaviour "works" vs. those circumstances in which a behaviour "doesn't work."

Daily life with humans quickly teaches a dog that the handler is powerless under many circumstances and that he can take advantage of those situations. Humans inadvertently promote this lesson by lack of management, especially detrimental with the young dog or the dog who has behavioural problems. Although dogs do not have morals, you can teach your dog a work ethic, so that she behaves as a responsible citizen. Underneath all the applied veneer of learned "work ethic," they are still dogs, so we teach them: When I ask you to do something, it is in your own best interest to do so.

Your goal is to get your dog to believe you when you tell him, "It's unavailable, it will never be available, you may as well just quit thinking about it." Do not lie to your dog by allowing him to get an item that you tell him is unavailable. If you are slow (Bad, BAD trainer), and allow the dog to obtain the food when you have told him "Leave It," you have just told your dog, "This is optional. If you are quicker than I am, then you can have it." Essentially, in this case, you have taught the dog a great game called If I am Quicker than You and Sneakier, I Can Have It.

If your dog has ever been even slightly aggressive toward *you*, proceed with great caution. You may need to use a muzzle, Halti, collar and leash. If you are really frightened of your dog under these circumstances, do not do this exercise before seeking outside help!

Choosing the Handler over the Environment

For best results, work each approximation of this exercise in two different fashions:

1. Use the verbal "Leave It" cue. Then prevent the dog from access to the food by one of the following two methods:

- Do a Move-Away or Back-Away, as outlined below in Approximations #2 and #3.
- Cover up the food with your foot or hand.

> The reason to do the exercise with a verbal cue is because you want the dog to have a verbal cue in place in case you need to use it.

2. Do NOT use any verbal cue. Then prevent the dog from access to the food by one of the following two methods:

- Say nothing but just do the Move-Away or Back-Away as outlined in Approximation #2 and #3.

- Cover up the food with your foot or hand without saying a word.

> The reason to NOT use a verbal cue is because eventually the ideal response is for the dog to see something in the environment that he Alerts on and immediately to look at you for advice. "Alerting" is a specific response that precedes arousal. Your dog is Alerting anytime she becomes interested in or looks at anything in the surrounding environment for more than a count of 2.

Defaulting to the environment is one of the main reasons a dog becomes a "problem dog" and certainly one of the prime reasons that dogs learn that aggression works. The vast majority of dog handlers, including those who are experienced, allow their dogs to DEFAULT TO THE ENVIRONMENT. That is, the dog is allowed to partake of the environment and learns to "reinforce himself" at will. The dog responds to, and becomes overreactive to, the environment, and it is not until then that the handler tries to step in and become Part of The Loop. As far as the dog is concerned, by that point the handler is merely an interference.

With dogs who are presenting with aggression already, defaulting to the environment is not a safe option. The dog has already shown you what happens when this is allowed - he makes poor decisions! If your dog is attending to you and understands that you are always in The Loop, he is DEFAULTING TO THE HANDLER.

This is your goal: *the dog who defaults to the handler.* The savvy handler has placed herself in the catbird seat by convincing the dog that the handler is The Way and The Light - the liason by which the dog is allowed to access the environment with permission. If that permission is not granted by the handler, there will still be something "in it" for the dog.

Magnets

Dog Magnets are anything your dog is currently attracted to. For training purposes I often use food as a Magnet. Other Magnets you encounter out in the Real World are other dogs, people, squirrels, candy wrappers, animal excrement (ah, those discerning palates), and other disgusting "delicacies."

Acquisition

You may begin with Leave It as a stationary exercise. Your dog may be standing. THIS IS NOT A STAY EXERCISE! DO NOT tell your dog to "Stay." Instead be very quick to prevent your dog from getting the object you have told him to leave, by covering it with your hand or foot.

1. Show the dog the food.
2. Place food on the ground in front of the dog.
3. Say "Leave It."
4. Cover the food when dog dives for it. Be quick!
5. Let your dog bark, fuss, paw, nose, etc. Don't say anything!
6. When the dog backs up, puzzled, uncover food and say "Leave It."
7. When the dog indicates he is not going to dive for or grab the food by one or more of these:

- Looking away from the food
- Turning his head slightly
- Backing up
- Looking at the handler
- Looking patient

Mark that Behaviour (or combination of Behaviours) and Feed It.

> The dog is NEVER allowed to get the "Leave It" item. When you are finished with a trial, you will pick it up off the floor. At that point, you put it back in your bait bag to be used as a future treat.

When you are teaching "Leave It," do not allow *yourself* to be distracted. Concentrate hard by looking directly at the food. Don't worry what the dog's tail or feet are doing; focus on his cute little nose. If that nose or the eyes move in the direction of the food "magnet," cover the food quickly with your hand. Do not strike the dog, yell "No," nor prevent the dog from trying for the food treat. "Trying for it" is how you are given the opportunity to provide feedback by covering the food with your hand to communicate, "This is unavailable." This trial-and-error-learning is how the dog internalizes the lesson.

Keep In Mind

Dogs need to understand that the presence of children, people, dogs, food, toys, and other desirable items does not mean that these items are automatically available for partaking. We help the dog understand this by teaching him that reinforcement is available from the handler for resisting temptation. This becomes a very powerful exercise and is a strong bonding exercise. The dog learns that the handler is the Way And The Light to reinforcement and to all good things in life, not someone who is IN THE WAY and PREVENTING all the good stuff.

It also hammers home the fact that Consequences are contingent on Behaviour, and that the dog must perform in a certain manner to obtain reinforcement. Life is not a free ride.

The dog's belief system becomes:

- It is reinforcing to substitute my handler's agenda for my own.
- Behaviour that is Cued by the handler has the greatest possibility of reinforcement.
- It is in my own best interest to relinquish objects in my possession or objects I wish to possess, when so instructed by my handler.
- My handler, rather than the environment, is the way to the good stuff.
- Direct access is not always the way to reinforcement.

Adding The Cue

This is where you add the verbal cue if you haven't done so already, at the point when the dog is performing pretty reliably (80-90% correct response ratio).

Do not repeat the cue. In future, you want the equation to be:
1 Cue = Immediate Response

I may repeat a Cue twice for one or two trials, particularly in the Acquisition Stage, but I quickly move to the above 1Cue = Immediate Response equation. Otherwise, I am teaching the dog: Don't worry, you don't have to pay attention, I'll just keep repeating the cue for you.

However, keep in mind that, for all dogs, especially dogs who are doing service work OR dogs who have been reactive or aggressive, the best outcome is having the object itself to be the cue to pay more attention to the handler.

Approximation 1

Challenge the dog by placing the food ever closer to him.

Approximation 2

In Motion Leave It: Back Away, Pass-by or Move-Away-From It

We want our dogs to give up many Resources on a daily basis. We need to teach our dog that it is in his best interest to do so. By using this exercise, you also will be making yourself more valuable, because you are going to have a tasty treat ready for your dog as soon as he indicates he is leaving the magnet for you. The "magnet" was inaccessible, but you are not!

This translates into: Orient toward me whenever you see something you are interested in. If your dog will look at you whenever he sees something he wants or is uncertain about, you then have that split second to intervene. The act of looking toward or orienting toward you tells you that your dog is paying attention to your opinion. You are operating as a team and are in concert with each other. The dog, by looking at you, is deliberately telling you, "I am including you in my decision-making process."

Once the stationary "Leave It" behaviour is well established, introduce "Pass-by It." Pass-bys further challenge the dog and establish that "This item is unavailable to you at this time."

Do Not Under Any Circumstances take your eyes off the dog! Watch his body language closely, so you do not lie to the dog and tell him that he can play the I-Am-Quicker-Than-You game. Strategically place yourself in a position where you can ALWAYS have control over your dog's ability to get to the doggy magnet.

1. Begin with the dog on leash.
2. Allow the dog to watch food being placed on the floor. You may tie the dog back and have him watch you place the food, or have someone else place the food for you while the dog watches. If you are really clever you can hold the dog back yourself and still place the food, but this is a bit riskier. The food should be placed approximately 10 feet away from you. Or, taking the leash length into consideration, just out of reach of a dog who is at the end of his leash.
3. As the dog is focused on this great treat, make sure you do not jerk or pop or correct the dog with the leash, and do not talk to your dog.
4. Begin to back away from the food treat. CONTINUE TO BACK UP, increasing the distance between your dog and the "magnet." This action will place slight tension on the leash. There will be a distance at which the dog decides: It is too far, I cannot get it. (For some dogs, this may be a considerable distance the first few trials!) At some point, the dog will turn away from the food in some manner, or else orient toward you, or glance toward you, just because of the motion involved in your backing away.
5. AT THE MOMENT your dog glances at you, use a RM, "Yes!" Speed up your backward motion, and as the dog moves toward you Mark It and Feed It.
6. If your dog just isn't getting it, use a head collar to gain control of where the dog looks – thereby manufacturing reinforceable Behaviour.

Repeat the following trial as many times as needed:

- As soon as the previous trial is completed, begin to approach the food treat again.
- As the dog begins to strain and leap for the goodie, back up.
- Mark & Feed orientation away from the goodie.

As you go along, you will discover that each time you turn back to the food treat, the dog is paying less and less attention to "it" (access to "it" is not the sure thing the dog originally thought) and more and more attention to you. You are teaching that pulling toward an enticing object "doesn't work," but orienting toward and including the handler "always works."

Once your dog has mastered looking at you by responding to your Back-Away motion, you can begin to do this same exercise by continuing to walk by the magnet, or move laterally away from the magnet.

These In-Motion-Leave-It exercises are going to be used over and over, until it is your dog's HABIT to see something in the environment that interests or arouses him and his *immediate response is to look to you.* It is handy because it is super easy for YOU to do, and it is all you need to remember to do as your FIRST behaviour whenever your dog is distracted or becoming reactive.

APPROXIMATION 3

Look-At-Me & Leave It

Raise the above criteria to include looking at you before you deliver the food reward.

- The new rule is: If you have to Back Away from the magnet to get your dog to orient toward you (i.e., you are providing "help"), RM ONLY (no treat) as the dog orients toward you.
- If the dog voluntarily displays appropriate behaviour, then Mark It & Feed It, and the occasional Street Party. (Extra social approval, love, kisses, hugs, pats, a quick game. Whatever constitutes a quick little party for your dog.)

Your goal is to get the dog to the point where he is readily walking PAST this great food treat and all around it without even glancing at it. If at any point the dog glances at the goodie, Back-Away or Move-Away from it. Any direction is fine, whatever makes the most sense contextually. Most dogs tend to start focusing heavily on the handler by staring at the handler's face, but this is not required, just that the dog orient *away from* the Magnet.

After several trials, you will be able to walk toward a Magnet, and the item that previously made your dog strain at the leash will become a cue to glance at the Magnet and then immediately look to you, the handler.

Remember! Practice both ways: Using a verbal cue so you have a verbal cue waiting in the wings if you need it, and just as often or more often by using the slight pressure on the leash as your cue to "Leave It." If you do enough repetitions, just your body language of pausing or shifting your weight to begin moving backwards will be a cue for the dog.

After several trials (with some dogs, 6 trials and with some dogs, 200 trials), you will see your dog begin to respond *to your body language* of moving away or backing away from the object of his attraction. I often don't even get a chance to take a step backwards. As soon as my dogs sense my shift of weight and pause to begin backing up, they orient toward me. You know you have achieved your end goal when you see your dog begin to look at the magnet, then quickly glance at you for approval or pointedly ignore the magnet. Obviously reinforce this effort with verbal and social approval and the occasional food treat.

This is the goal of this work. Leash pressure is no longer required. Changes in the environment have become a cue to look to the handler for advice.

Approximation 4

Challenge the dog further. Now ask the dog to resist the temptation of a moving object. This is much tougher for the dog because motion naturally attracts his attention.

1. As you walk along, toss a piece of food off to the side.
2. Expect lunging from the dog, so toss the food well out of reach of the dog.
3. Move away from the tossed food.
4. Mark & Feed indication away from the food.

Approximation 5

Challenges: Change the distraction

This will require a list of distracting items for each individual dog, although you may find that many of the same Challenges work for each dog. Depending on the individual dog, objects encountered in his daily work, and his "I gotta have thats," create a list that will Challenge the dog. As you progress in this exercise, you will see the dog begin to walk by things that in the past he just couldn't resist!

Consider the following list and screen it with your dog and her particular bugaboos in mind. Only use those Challenges that can be completed safely. Modify this list as required, but a partial list of Challenges might be:

- People
- People with food
- People offering food
- People with dogs
- Loose dogs
- People with toys (squeaky)
- People playing with dogs & toys
- People tossing balls
- Pigeons in cages

Approximation 6

Place the behaviour on a Variable Reinforcement Schedule to maintain behaviour. That is, you will use your RM frequently, but you will use a RM & Food Treat on only some occasions. You will find that, after a while, the response is a habit and is integrated into the dog's Behavioural Repertoire.

Petey remains involved with his handler even though there are tasty treats temptingly near.

Initially you would feed the behaviour after each success, IN POSITION, as shown. Because dogs gravitate to Placement Of Reinforcement, feeding your dog in the desired position will furnish consistency of that position. After the dog understands the exercise and it is "easy" for him to do, use a variable schedule.

Remember: Acquisition=Fixed Schedule.
Maintenance=Variable Schedule.

If your dog does glance at the treats, quickly back away until your dog orients toward you, as Petey and Lylenette demonstrate here.

Mark & Feed that behaviour, then try again.

When your dog has completed this exercise, it is exciting to know that he will choose, voluntarily, to attend to what is important to the handler vs. what is important to him.

Over-Correction: Doggy Push-Ups

Technically this method would fall into the category of "over-correction." This is a form of punishment. A human equivalent would be to have to perform extra, unpleasant chores as a consequence for rude or unwanted behaviour. Like writing on the chalkboard 200 times, "I won't spit on the teacher." Or in the military, where the sergeant barks out, "Drop and give me 20!"

Caution: If your dog has ever shown any aggression toward you (snapped or growled at you), this is a risky form of correction for you to use. In your case, it is inappropriate unless your dog is muzzled and you can ensure that you are safe and will not be bitten. Think, too, about the lesson that will be taught. Unless you have the ability to neutrally outlast any behaviour your dog will toss at you, don't use this correction.

Only after you have presented the dog with *many* Challenges, and he has proven to you that he understands this concept *in the current context,* is it fair to correct. Just so there is no question about that, ask yourself a couple of questions. Has the dog done the behaviour, overall, 100 times with an 80-90% correct ratio? Has the dog been in this same context before, and been shown HOW you wish him to behave under these circumstances? Only once those criteria have been met is this punishment applicable. Correction before this stage would be a review of "Leave It." Once this is a well-known behaviour that is second nature to the dog, and the dog chooses to be unruly or to ignore you outright, it is okay to make the dog a bit physically uncomfortable as well, in the form of enforced doggy push-ups.

This is an example of a situation that could warrant this correction. When you have had the dog in the same (or a similar) situation numerous times, and each time you have patiently backed away from the distraction, administered positive reinforcement for coming to and looking at you, and the dog has performed correctly the last several times in this environment. Then, he fails to exhibit the desired behaviour.

Let's say your dog gets defensive when other dogs walk by in a crowded area, such as you might encounter going into dog class. The last six times, you have arrived early and worked outside the door, where your dog does not feel trapped or uneasy. Each time a dog entered class and your dog looked at the other dog, you did a Move-Away or Back-Away and fed your dog for looking toward you. Next, you entered class late, and fed your dog for entering the building peacefully a couple of times. Then you came early, entered class and chose an area away from the "crush" of the doorway, and fed your dog for looking at you every time a dog entered the building. Then for six more classes you entered as the other students did, providing heavy reinforcement for non-reaction and using a Back-Away for undesired responses such as growling or lunging at the other dogs. The last four times your dog has been wonderful, voluntarily looking at you. A couple of dogs have even bumped your dog slightly as they passed b,y and your dog still remained Involved with you. This time, however, as you are entering class, your dog Alerts on another dog and begins to get stiff-legged. My first choice is to do a Move Away or Back Away,. If the behaviour occurs again:

1. Grasp the leash close to your dog's collar or head-collar.
2. Do an enforced "Sit" by placing a steady upward pressure on the dog's collar or head collar. This *slight* physical correction is administered whether the dog is complying or not. Remember, this is supposed to be an UNPLEASANT experience so your dog begins to understand that there may be more severe consequences for his behaviour than merely withholding reinforcement. You don't want to hurt your dog, nor should you, but disapproval should be oozing from every pore in your body. Don't shout or yell, but you may use a low, disapproving tone of voice. I do cue the dog with a verbal "Sit" just prior to applying pressure to the collar or head-collar.

Although some may view this as punishment for performing appropriately, all the dogs I have done this with "get" that the punishment is for not Ceasing current undesired behaviour. The clients who use this technique garner good results, provided that the correction is properly timed and carried out decisively, but neutrally, by the handler.

3. As soon as the dog sits, immediately:
4. Do an enforced "Down" by placing a steady pressure downward on the collar or head-collar.
5. Repeat this 3 to 5 times.
6. Immediately back away from your dog and, as soon as he orients toward you, Mark It & Feed It and lavish on the social approval.
7. Begin the pass-by or Leave It again.

- If your dog will now Desist, Mark It & Feed It and have a Street Party.
- If your dog attempts to reach the item again, remind him, "Leave It," and immediately begin the doggy push ups. This tells him why he is receiving the punishment and notifies him how he can avoid the punishment. Then try again.

I have yet to meet the dog who has completed this Foundation and Level I work who does not respond to two or three repetitions of this method of over-correction by deciding that your way is indeed the way to go. This, of course, is only true when the exercises have been executed properly and the dog has a good understanding of them.

Using Cease & Desist as an Impulse Control and Sweitching Exercise

Please be informed that the dogs in the following photos are very food-driven. This isn't a photo set-up with dogs who are lackadaisical about the food thing. The photographs were done in real time. I will grant you that the dogs were trained ahead of time! These are the kind of results the training will get for you, too!

Cease & Desist is an exercise that requires dedicated work and absolute consistency on your part. A reasonable expectation for a consistent response is six-months to one year of work. At that point the behaviour is reasonably (98%) reliable and the dog has internalized the concept well. If you have generalized the work well, the end result is excellent compliance in a variety of arousing situations off-leash.

This seems like a long time frame, but you are bucking Mother Nature and, in many cases, a strong prior reinforcement history. Also, it requires many contexts and locations for the dog to become fluent with this behaviour.

The work is well worth it. Good Cease & Desist behaviours, combined with an excellent Recall, often make the difference between a live dog and a dead dog.

Photo essay by Sam Ziegenmeyer.

Maeve maintains eye contact even though I am dropping food right over top of her.

Involvement & Leave It Combined

Whether prevention or "fixing" is your goal, this exercise is a requirement! Cease & Desist, in all of it's variations, is the bedrock of much of the rehabilitation work you will do with already-aggressive dogs. If you are doing prevention work, and your dog is being prepped for competition, this work will net awesome, intense concentration on the handler.

Photo by Sam Ziegenmeyer.

Maeve is very aware of the food scattered around her, but understands that it is unavailable to her, even though her handler is at a distance.

Increasing Control With Desist - Challenges

Photo essay by Sam Ziegenmeyer.

Maeve comes when called, arcing slightly to show me she is avoiding the pile of treats. In dogs that have a good understanding of this exercise, this is a common response.

Calling Past Food

The only thing Maeve loves as much as food are her toys - prey objects.

Using Prey Objects To Teach "Switching" # 1 of 4

As I give the toy a toss, I cue "Come" and "Heel." If I needed to give her further information, I would use a Move- or Back-Away Motion and would have the dog on leash for the first several trials. I don't use the cue "Leave It," because I *may* allow the dog to get the toy later. Maeve cannot resist a longing glance at this temptation. She is also reflexively attracted to the motion of the toy as it is tossed and turns toward it.

Using Prey Objects To Teach "Switching" # 2 of 4

Maeve maintains her Involvement with me and does not go to get the toy. After that first glance, she has not so much as looked at it.

What I am teaching her is that she may partake of the environment only with permission from me. After she chooses to work, then she will certainly get "paid" for her efforts. This is tough stuff!

Using Prey Objects To Teach "Switching" # 3 of 4

This is a very advanced SWITCHING exercise. I am going to reinforce Maeve by cueing her to go and get the toy. I am using the prey object to reinforce several different behaviours she has exhibited: attention, impulse control, and understanding that the item is available to her ONLY when cued to do so. This shows excellent discrimination about what each cue means. She remains Involved with me even though she wants the toy. She comprehends that, if she does so, she will be rewarded for her efforts. Because this dog is easily aroused and extremely predaceous, this teaches her that being calm and patient has a high probability of reinforcement. The other valuable lesson you are teaching your dog is that she can start to get into an aroused or excited state and then calm down quickly and pay attention to you.

Using Prey Objects To Teach "Switching" # 4 of 4

40

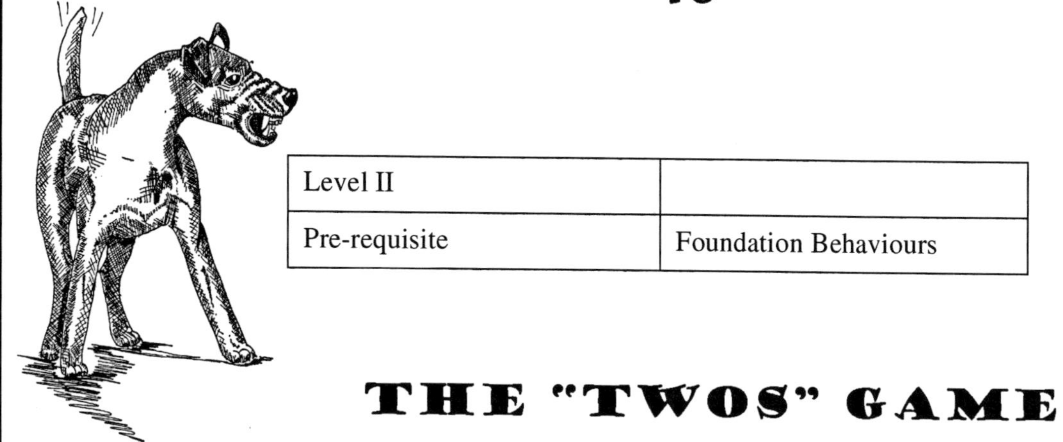

Level II	
Pre-requisite	Foundation Behaviours

THE "TWOS" GAME

PRACTICING RECALLS AND OBJECT EXCHANGES

Goal	Your dog comes when called. Your dog eagerly exchanges objects. Your dog eagerly surrenders objects.
What it teaches	With this exercise you are not only teaching the dog a wonderful recall: • When the dog is facing away from you, you are teaching her to turn quickly and orient toward you. • If your dog is possessive, you are teaching an object exchange. If your dog is young, you are promoting peaceful object exchanges. • You are preparing your dog for retrieving behaviours – the cue "get it" means there is something out there to get. • You are preparing for "send-away" type behaviours (used in competition obedience). • You are teaching a turn in place (for retrieves and send-aways).
Practical Application	The Twos Game improves your recall. It provides practice for the dog to switch from an excited, aroused state into a receptive and calm state. Most important, your dog gets opportunities to rehearse peaceful and willing object exchanges.

This game comes straight from a seminar I went to years ago that was presented by Patty Ruzzo. This is one of my all-time favorite ways to teach a dog many great skills.

Game Rules

1. Use a large visible piece of food for this game so the dog is not out there sniffing around and searching. A fingernail-sized piece of cheese or bread works well.
2. Make sure your dog sees the food in your fingers.
3. As your dog is focused on the treat, so she sees the direction it is tossed....
4. Toss the food a short distance the first couple of times, increasing the distance as the dog begins to understand the game.
5. As the dog runs after the treat, cue "Get it" (or "fetch" or whatever). This prepares the dog for a retrieve cue later on, and also gives her permission to go after the food.
6. As the dog is poised over the piece of food, opens her mouth and picks it up, and just at the moment she "gulps" it down....
7. CALL the dog. "Zasu, come."
8. Back up, if you like, to speed the dog's progress back to you, and to encourage a turn in place, and...
9. As the dog approaches you, show her the next piece of food.
10. Use the verbal cue, such as "Get It," as you toss the food.
11. REPEAT the sequence several times.
12. End the sequence with asking the dog to "Come" and "Sit." Reinforce compliant behaviour.

This game is also a great way to begin teaching puppies to retrieve. It works equally well with dogs who are reluctant to relinquish a toy once they have picked it up after you have thrown it.

This game encourages dogs to return to you gleefully, and also to give up toys. To work on retrieving behaviours and/or object exchanges, use two or three toys that are identical to one another. Otherwise the dog has a tendency to choose a favorite toy and then just retain possession of that. In place of the food above, you will use the toys. Toss one toy and as the dog is returning, show her the second toy. Do not throw the second toy until she drops the first toy. You can sometimes convince a very possessive dog to relinquish the toy for a treat and then quickly toss the second toy before she has a chance to pick up the first toy again. While she is after the second toy, pick up the first toy and continue this game of "trading" toys.

If your dog has a tendency to run off and refuses to be enticed back to you by the second toy, place her on a long line. *DO not use the line to drag her toward you.* If the dog heads in the opposite direction to retain possession, or she will not come close into you and is playing a "keep-away" game, continue backing away and moving away from the dog, and direct your own interest toward the toy YOU have. Toss it up in the air, coo at it, and keep moving away from the dog. You can walk toward the dog a bit to shorten the line, then quickly move away again. When you move away, keep the line shortened, so the dog will be cued to move toward you.

I have never seen this fail to work IF THE HANDLER is savvy enough to make exactly the right moves to attract this individual dog. Keep experimenting with your behaviour until you get her to move toward you. If she even glances your way quickly use your RM. If the second toy does not bring the dog close enough, use a food treat, trade the toy for food and then toss the toy again.

If the dog becomes focused on the food and ceases to be interested in the toy, keep enticing the dog with the toy and do NOT allow her to have another food treat until she shows interest in the toy again. Once the dog retrieves the toy back to you, she can have another cookie. This may take some experimentation on your part to figure out what will work with each dog. But it is well worth the effort, and you will learn a lot about timing and dog behaviour as you learn how to "get the dog's number."

This is the method I use with all my puppies to teach them that giving up a toy is not the trauma they all seem to think it is. Most dogs do want to play, but they just cannot get over the fact that they have to relinquish the toy in order to have you toss it again. This game helps them over that hump.

After a bit, try having the dog fetch the first toy and return to you. Then request that she drop or deliver the first toy to your hand. Then toss the first toy. You may need to use the second toy a few times just as a visual cue to reassure the dog that you are not "stealing" toys from her.

Then try using just one visible toy, tossing it, having the dog relinquish it and then tossing that toy again.

To End this Game

1. Call the dog.
2. Add a relinquish cue: "Drop it" or "Thank you."
3. Deliver a tasty treat to the dog, or several, if this is a difficult concept for her to accept.
4. You retain possession of the toy or toys and put them away.

The ending of this game is important. It is good for the dog to see you retain possession and for her to receive reinforcement for having relinquished items willingly.

Tip. The first few times the dog brings the toy back to you, make a fuss over her and do not immediately try to take the toy. Run around with the dog, allowing her to retain possession of the toy for ten or twenty seconds. Then see if you can initiate relinquishment by enticing the dog with a treat or the second toy.

41

Level II	
Pre-requisite	Foundation Behaviours

COMMON SENSE IS JUST NOT THAT COMMON...TAKING ADVANTAGE OF CALMING SIGNALS

When you see your dog using appropriate Calming Signals to communicate with other dogs, you can give him a Reward Mark. At the very least, *do not* correct him for using Calming Signals.

The use of Calming Signals or Displacement Signals provides you with a visual marker of the threshold distance at which your dog's comfort level is first being compromised. On a continuum, these signals are among the *first* observable signs that tell you the dog is aware that she is uncomfortable, with an overt attack being the *last*.

Using this information, you now have a chance to intervene BEFORE your dog becomes unduly chemically aroused – therefore, when learning can still occur with maximum effect.

Since these signals are one of the first visual signs of the dog's discomfort, they serve a twofold purpose for you, the trainer.

- They warn you that the dog feels like she has to take action to remain in equilibrium and remain "safe" within the current environment.
- By reinforcing the dog for using a "negotiation" technique instead of a "reaction" technique, you can convey to your dog that you approve of the former.

When you apply reinforcement to the Calming Signals, they will then become stronger. *Using Calming Signals will keep the dog out of trouble in the first place.* By the time the dog launches an open attack, in the form of a growl, lunge or snap, it is very difficult to redirect the dog's behaviour. Also, once an overt attack sequence is launched, if the other dog was not initially reactive, she probably will be now. So, now you have TWO reactive animals on your hands instead of one, and the dogs will begin a cycle of "one-upmanship." At the point one or both dogs escalate into lunging, barking or other agonistic display, you are merely practicing damage control.

Your teaching moments are in the past where you no longer have access to them.

The Calming Signals also serve to make your dog feel more comfortable, allowing calmness and confidence to replace an anxious state.

You may use a gentle NRM for fearful behaviour as long as you then show the dog how to obtain reinforcement. For example, if your dog is trying to back away from or leave a situation that is fear-producing for him, you might give the dog a NRM for his current "I'm outta here" behaviour. Then encourage him to stop backing away (perhaps by using his name, or moving a couple of steps and calling him). As soon as he does so, Mark It & Feed It. Then see if you can encourage him to just stand or sit there.

Cue the dog for a Sit, or ask him to shake hands or do another trick that he enjoys doing. Mark It & Feed It. Then if he will take another step toward the "scary" thing, Mark It & Feed It. If he will look at and air scent toward the scary thing without backing up again, that is reinforceable behaviour. ANY behaviour the dog does that is "bolder" than his previous behaviour, Mark It & Feed It. This places the judgment on you to determine whether the current behaviour you are observing is "better" or "worse" than the behaviour which immediately preceded it, and to provide immediate and appropriate feedback. Kind of like being fitted for new lenses at the optometrist: "Better 1 or Better 2?"

Here is another example. You are walking along the road and a child runs toward you. Your dog cringes in fear and dashes behind you, wrapping the leash around your legs. What to do? First gain more control of the setting events, calling out to the child to stop approaching: "Just a minute, wait there!" Since the current behaviour of cringing and tying you up is NOT the desired behaviour, give the dog a NRM, a neutral "Try Again." Extricate yourself from the leash, move a couple of steps away from the child, and ask the dog to orient toward you (the now-familiar Back-Away). Once the dog calms a bit, ask the child, to approach slowly while you provide the dog with a constant feed. A Sit Restraint with the dog (refer to the "Handling & Restraint" protocol) is an excellent choice for this situation; then you may allow the child to approach from the side with a cookie. Allow the dog to take a cookie from the child, if appropriate (the dog must have a gentle mouth!). Otherwise, just feed the dog yourself, and allow the child to pet the dog gently, while you continue to support the dog by holding him gently but firmly. Then ask the child to step away, move the dog away a step, and cue "Look." You have taken a potentially damaging situation and turned it into a teaching exercise for the dog. You have told the dog plainly what you do not want, what you do want, and how to DO what you want. Any calming signals used by the dog would receive a RM, and any effort to remain in place initiated by the dog and not requiring help from me would also receive generous notice and tasty treats.

Fear and a Controlled Retreat

In cases of extreme fear, it may be appropriate to ask the dog to look at you briefly, then, as reinforcement for that behaviour, Retreat from this area WITH the dog TEMPORARILY. This Retreat is executed in a very specific way. Do not just allow your dog to leave the area in a panic with you running after him. This is a planned, controlled action.

- Obtain ANY known behaviour on cue. Choose something super-easy for the dog to do.
- Reinforce that behaviour generously.
- CUE the dog that you are both leaving the area. You could use a special cue or "Come" as you begin moving away from the Scary Whatever.
- Begin your Retreat in an organized and calm manner. This doesn't necessarily mean slowly; you can move quickly, just not frantically.

If appropriate, you can then re-enter the area and see if you can get two glances, or 2 seconds of Involvement. If you are fortunate, the dog will actually begin to ANCHOR on you and use the eye-contact as a means of maintaining composure. The whole idea here is that reinforcing flight behaviour by "allowing" it will never teach your dog to access another behaviour as his First Response. He will continue to rely on flight behaviour as his "knee-jerk" response to discomfort. If you can get your dog to do ANYTHING before flight is accessed (look at you, sit briefly, anything BUT flight), and then you "help" him retreat, you have subtly but significantly changed this situation for your dog. Now, the dog has first "included you" in his behaviour pattern, has accessed (albeit with help from you) a behaviour OTHER THAN flight, and you have "helped" the dog to safety. A relationship builder!

As a Regular Agenda

Mark all successful passes by other dogs and humans on your walks. Initially this would be followed by a treat. After a bit, when your dog has formed appropriate habits in each context, you won't need to provide constant feedback to her. As the habit to pass peacefully by other dogs and humans becomes second-nature, you won't need to provide any feedback at all.

Many people make the mistake of correcting their dog when she is using Calming Signals. If this is done enough, dogs lose or inhibit many of their natural communication skills. This is very sad, because then we are rendering our dogs helpless to communicate.

Much aggression is *learned behaviour* that is unintentionally reinforced by owners. Learned aggression may also be reinforced by the environment. The classic example is of the mail-carrier. The mail-carrier approaches. The dog barks. The mail-carrier delivers the mail and leaves. The dog has no way of knowing this person was going to come and go regardless of her own behaviour. She looks at apparent cause-and-effect only: "Someone is approaching my territory – I feel uncomfortable – I sound an alarm and warn the mail-carrier to leave – and she does." Therefore, in the dog's paradigm, barking worked. After a time, this gives some dogs a sense of confidence, enough so that they escalate their behaviour to include a little nip to hurry the person along. Or they quickly escalate behaviour if other visitors do not immediately respond to their barking as the mail-carrier has in the past.

Another way owners encourage or exacerbate aggression is by punishing the dog physically when the dog becomes very reactive. This only increases the dog's arousal. Pushing the dog past levels of stress that she can tolerate, or putting her in situations that she has not been prepared for may cause her to become very frightened. When frightened, many dogs react in a defensive manner. Aggression may be the result when the dog does not know what else to do.

By building a variety of reinforceable behaviours (such as Sit, Down, Shake Hands, Stay), you will provide your dog with practical alternatives to aggression – a whole repertoire of coping skills. This means your dog will not have to resort to aggression. She will have other language and coping skills that she can access.

This also helps your dog become very self-confident in her ability to handle herself in a variety of situations.

When a dog becomes frightened and uneasy, the vast majority of humans, in an effort to comfort the dog, attempt to reassure her as they would another human. They speak in soft, sweet tones, and tell the dog "you're okay, you'll be all right." They might stroke the dog gently or pet her. All of these things that humans do to reassure the dog only serve to reinforce the fearful behaviour. You are telling the dog that "mummy loves it when you're afraid – you keep being afraid of this!"

Instead of validating the fear for the dog, ignore any behaviour that is fearful or give the dog a gentle NRM. Counteract the fear by reinforcing bold behaviour. Give the dog something to do that she knows is reinforceable behaviour, such as a Sit or Down.

Reinforce your dog heavily for ignoring the environment and interacting with you until you grant permission to her to partake of the environment. (Refer to the "Cease & Desist!" protocol for specific help.)

If the dog is concentrating on you and what you two are doing, she will not be so worried about and focused on what is happening around her. This also gives her a behaviour to "default" to if she becomes concerned. (Refer to the "Eye Contact & Involvement" protocol for specific help.)

Stress is everywhere and is a normal part of life. Present stress in a manner that is controlled and systematic. At the same time, give your dog feedback (using a RM/NRM system) to encourage development of confident coping skills.

With all the protocols in this book, *Challenges* provide you a way to:

1. Clarify the cue for the dog.
2. Clarify *exactly* the parameters of the behaviour.
3. Place the dog under "controlled" stress. It is a stressor to the dog to have to learn to generalize behaviours to a new context. Learning to ignore what is different in each context and to concentrate on doing the desired behaviour is hard work. Challenges, then, provide your dog an opportunity to develop coping mechanisms and confidence in her abilities to problem-solve in stressful situations.

Give your dog feedback (using your RM/NRM system) in a way to encourage development of self-confidence. If you are watching your dog as she enters new situations, you can tell if she is getting upset by what is going on around her. If your dog is made nervous by a context, you now know that: (1) you must give the dog feedback right now and guide her toward being less fearful, and (2) you must return to this context to help the dog habituate to it.

For animals who have a fearful reaction (and over their lifetime most dogs at some point will be afraid of something), the techniques above will help both of you approach the fearful situation with some experience with getting through it as handily as possible.

Another aid is to train your dog to touch a target stick and then a target "fist." Then you can have her target your fist during stressful situations. (Refer to the "Targeting" and "Being Brave Is Better" protocols for more help with fearful dogs.)

Central Theme

What I have been describing are Switching Exercises: teaching your dog to switch from fear or other aroused states to a calm state by practicing known behaviours that have an extensive reinforcement history. In order for this to work, you must be able to tell IMMEDIATELY when your dog is getting aroused and when she is returning to a calm state.

Basically, you are training yourself to be aware and give your dog feedback for appropriate use of native language. You are learning to speak "dog." You are teaching your dog to develop her communication skills. Increasing your dog's language skills and other coping mechanisms, will reduce the need for her to feel overwhelmed and that she must resort to defensive behaviour in order to cope.

This use of the dog's Native Language is CENTRAL in all of the work I do with aggressive dogs, and in preventing aggression.

First of all, it is a shame to destroy signals in a dog. This can produce a dog that truncates all the display, Calming Signals, growls, and other warnings, and proceeds directly to a bite.

Since the Vulcan Mind-Meld is not generally attainable between you and your dog, reading your dog's Calming Signals is the best means available to warn you that the dog is "changing" her emotional state. Dog Signals tell you what your dog is thinking about, just as surely as if she "spoke" it to you.

If you are going to effectively modify behaviour, you must "get in ahead of" extreme arousal, and this is the venue by which you do so.

Photo by Sam Ziegenmeyer.

Rylie (far right) is yawning - she is not tired! This signal is obviously a response to the chaos in the setting. She is telling me she is a bit stressed, most likely a reaction to the Golden who is exhibiting stress. This is my surmise because Rylie knows the other dogs and plays with them regularly, and they do not make her uneasy. Rylie is reassuring the Golden that it is a non-threatening situation. Notice she is looking right at the Golden as she Signals.

Calming Signal In Response To Another Dog's Stress

Photo by Joanne Weber.

These are naturally occurring calming signals. Note how both dogs are obviously NOT looking at each other. This is a great example of a "look-away." If your dog would normally become reactive in this situation, but instead gives you a calming signal, be sure to reinforce the calming signal!

Calming Signal

Photo by Joanne Weber.

If your dog does not show many calming signals, they can be manufactured! Here, Jack, the Labrador, and Sunny, the Aussie, are both encouraged to look away from the approaching dog and focus on their owners instead. The approaching dog perceives this as a look-away.

This is how you can manage or diffuse a possible confrontation by controlling your own dog's behaviour, even though there are multiple dogs present.

When you manufacture Calming Signals, you are not only controlling your own dog, but also the perceptions and reactions of other dogs.

Manufactured Calming Signal

42

Level II	
Pre-requisite	Foundation Behaviours Helpful: Sit

TRAINING A POLITE GREETING

Greeting humans and other dogs in an acceptable manner is extremely important – from the laundry and mending aspects to the public relations of dogs in general.

Dogs have a strong urge to compulsively greet everyone and everything just as they would another dog. That means that many dogs are overly enthusiastic when greeting humans. Most of our guests reinforce this horribly inappropriate behaviour by petting the dog as he leaps all over them.

Compound this with the fact that the majority of dogs are severely under-socialized with other dogs. Most live in single-dog homes so they do not get the dog interaction they would if they lived in a multiple-dog home. This contributes to inappropriate greeting behaviours with other dogs because such dogs are over-excited at finally getting to "talk to" a member of their own species.

Then there is the dog who is presenting with greeting behaviour that is alarming to the human caregivers. Sometimes this is just because the greeting is frightening in its intensity. Sometimes it is because the dog has already threatened or harmed a person or a dog. The dog may be assertive and "guarding," or territorial, or fearful and defensive. Some dogs are made fearful by owners who punish them for undesired greeting behaviours, inadvertently creating an association for the dog between Meeting Strangers (people or dogs) and Impending Punishment. A dog who is naturally of a cautious nature can quickly become defensive if she feels cornered or trapped by the newcomer.

Preventing aggression by teaching your dog how to display appropriate greeting behaviour is important for *all* dogs, but particularly those breeds At Risk for territorial aggression as adults. (Top of the list: any breed whose original purpose involved guarding flocks or territory, or terriers.) As puppies, most dogs will be friendly greeting both dogs and humans. But, as dogs reach social maturity, their social window for accepting strangers narrows. Many of the German Shepherd Dogs I have worked with are a great example of this. They come to puppy class as silly goofy little puppies, but, as they close in on 12 months of age, the owners begin to see the first tentative guarding behaviours surface. The dog begins barking a bit more intensely at the door and is less accepting of other dogs coming into the yard. This dog is telling you quite plainly that he is beginning to recognize territorial boundaries as serious business. Just as we are different people as adults than we were as toddlers, so may your dog have different greeting behaviours as he reaches social maturity. The hard-wired behaviour to defend territory kicks in at different ages in different individuals, but, somewhere between 12 to 24 months of age, you may see a change in your dog's greeting behaviour. If you have trained your dog to greet properly and continue to expose him to people and dogs in a variety of contexts through 24 months old, you will be ahead of the power curve. For the At Risk animals (because of their original purpose, or any dog who is cautious in greeting as a puppy), you will have minimized any future problems and prevented serious problems from developing. For the average dog, you will be rewarded with a dog who is welcome in any company because he is well-behaved – a dog you can be proud to take anywhere!

Dogs who are already displaying frustration (just a few steps away from aggression) when they are prevented from greeting, when they are greeting, or dogs who are extremely cautious in their greeting approaches, are waving a red flag: "I need help with my greeting behaviour!" If you do not offer your dog appropriate behaviours to access when greeting, she will make her own decisions based on dog judgment, which may differ drastically from the behaviour humans find acceptable.

Dogs who are presenting with aggression toward strangers, or who are super cautious in their greeting behaviour, need a different kind of protocol. Refer to the protocols "Being Brave Is Better," "Targeting," "Wait at the Door," and "Territory Entry and Appropriate Greeting Behaviours."

The following protocol deals primarily with the dog who is doing the over-friendly greeting, exhibiting frenetic greeting behaviour with humans, or is mildly anxious or frustrated.

Opportunity Training

So, why would a dog jump up - the number one offense in the Polite Greeting Department - in the first place? To get attention, of course. Even my most novice client gets this one right 99% of the time. So next, answer these questions: Is looking at the dog attention? Is speaking to the dog attention? Is touching the dog attention? Yes, Yes, and Yes. Even if you are screaming and pushing the dog down and away from you, to the dog, this is still attention.

The good news is that communication is the key to success. Using your RM/NRM communication system, you are taking the first step to putting a stop to muddy paw prints, tears in your clothing and the inevitable scratches that result from an enthusiastic dog.

No dog lives with his feet off the ground all of the time, because of the Gravity Thing. Therefore, your dog, even though it may not seem like it, is spending some of his time with four feet on the ground. Make sure you notice this and apply reinforcement to these occasions. Remember – when opportunity knocks, take advantage of it. It is a gift from the Training Gods. If you offend Them by not taking advantage of Opportunities offered to you, you will be punished by ever-escalating inappropriate behaviour from your dog.

Four On The Floor Rule:

Before you can expect your dog to have control, you have two small criteria to meet.

1. You must have control of yourself! If you want to stop the jumping you must be absolutely consistent! Never, ever reward, pet or reinforce your dog when he has less than four feet on the ground.
2. You must teach your dog what you consider appropriate behavior. He has to know what you want from him in order to comply.

The Cold Shoulder

The Cold Shoulder works dramatically with young puppies and adolescents, and is also effective with a pretty good percentage of the adult dog population. Again, this is primarily for the over-enthusiastic greeter.

Make certain you are removing your attention entirely! I give my clients specific instructions: Look up toward the clouds, fold your arms up over your chest (out of reach of those pesky grasping little crocodile jaws) and turn your body away from the dog. Nine out of 10 dogs take one look at this posture and, after a half-hearted try at a second or third jump, pretty much get the idea: this person doesn't look like she is interacting with me. So they put all four feet on the ground. Here's your Big Chance! Immediately say "Yes!" and deliver a tasty treat. For some dogs this is like permission to leap at your body again. Give them the Cold Shoulder treatment, interspersed with the reinforcement for the appropriate behaviour, and soon you will have a dog that makes a conscious decision about keeping the tootsies on terra firma.

Raise Criteria

Next, take this exercise one step further: Encourage the dog to jump up, using a squeaky voice, waving arms and patting your thighs and chest. Each time the dog jumps: cold shoulder. If she chooses not to jump: reinforcement and other social approval. The end goal here is for the dog to not need a verbal reminder. An environmental cue is used: the sight of a person bending over or standing near the dog ideally will be the actual "cue" to "Sit" and wait patiently for the attention to come to her.

Optional

One method of teaching your dog the proper kind of behavior is to teach him to jump on command. Ultimately you could phase out the jumping behavior by teaching the dog to jump, then never using the command. This takes quite a while, however. So, in addition to teaching the dog to jump only on command, you would also teach her the self-control she needs to not jump up when you don't want her to. Many clients skip this step, although I use it with my own dogs – I never know when I might want them to jump up, like for a swing finish in the competition obedience ring.

DRI - Teach Sit to Greet

Remember that DRI = Differential Reinforcement of Incompatible Behaviour. This means you will teach your dog a desired behaviour that is INCOMPATIBLE with jumping

First, your dog needs to know "Sit." If she is sitting and being good, she cannot be jumping and being naughty at the same time. Ultimately the goal will be to teach your dog to greet by sitting instead of jumping. You must pay attention here. Even if it's during the middle of the day and you are vacuuming and your dog walks up to you and pointedly looks at you and sits, don't ignore it! Praise each small accomplishment, especially at first.

When she is reliable with her behavior on leash, you will teach her that off-leash obedience is also required.

To teach your dog when not to jump, you will be using a "set-up." Begin with your dog on leash. The cue to be taught is "Off." Always use the same cue. The cue is not "Down." Down means to lie down. "Off" means "get off whatever you happen to be on." "Off" does not mean that you push, pull or shove the puppy off you. "Off" means that the puppy learns to voluntarily remove herself from whatever she is on. If the cue "Off" is given in a timely manner, it means "Don't get up there to begin with!"

To teach Off, as your dog is approaching you and BEFORE she gets a chance to launch herself at you, say "Off." Immediately follow this with "Sit," and reinforce appropriate behaviour.

If your dog does not sit, you need a review Back To Kindergarten session about the Sit thing. Put a leash on the dog and practice the Sit behaviour on- and off-leash. The on-leash practice is done because: *Before you have Verbal Control you must have Physical Control,* and in this case you obviously did not. The off-leash practice that follows is to ensure that your dog understands the cue without you using the leash to obtain the behaviour!

Now tie the dog back to a sturdy tree or post. Begin to approach your dog. If she begins to jump, back away from her. As soon as her feet are on the ground, begin to approach. You must be instantaneous in your response, here! Your reaction to her behaviour is what gives your dog feedback about "how to behave." When she can keep Four-On-The-Floor, you can go up, say "Off" (to associate the word with the deed), Mark It & Feed It. Then cue your dog to Sit and Mark It & Feed It. If your feedback is slick, soon Off is an offered behaviour. *Your approach becomes the cue* to keep Four-On-The-Floor and to Sit to Greet.

Once "Off" is understood with you, it is time to have a "Guinea" Guest available to meet the dog:

First practice with you approaching the guest. The dog is only allowed to greet and get pets and treats from the guest if she can do so in a controlled fashion and is offering a Sit or Four-On-The-Floor behaviour when she reaches the guest.

Once she has mastered the above, you remain stationary and have the guest approach you and your dog.

In either case the steps are similar. As you approach or the guest approaches:

- With the lead on the dog, give the cue "Off."
- Then cue for a "Sit."
- Provide Reinforcement for compliance.

Praise will then be the order of the day, followed by a cookie from the guest. Your dog must remain sitting to get any positive feedback, including petting and other attention. The leash is used just to keep her from mauling guests. A head collar of some sort, such as a Halti, might be just the ticket in this case for control.

Raise Criteria

Do not remind the dog to "Off" or "Sit." Allow the dog to make choices and then provide feedback. This is the end goal: the cue of the approaching guest = Sit to Greet.

Again, you begin with you and your dog approaching the guest. When your dog is proficient with that, the guest approaches you. In either case, the steps are as below:

1. Allow the dog to have a loose leash.
2. If the dog Sits to greet, jackpot the behaviour. A Jackpot consists of several pieces of food delivered one after the next.
3. If the dog leaps, have the guest turn away while you execute a Back-Away at the same time, without verbally warning the dog you are going to do so. The moment the dog orients toward you, reinforce him.

Challenges

Once reliable on leash, repeat the exercises off leash. It will take several repetitions for the behavior to become absolutely reliable, because the ingrained habit is already learned. Engrams are the patterns in the brain that are formed as one develops habits. You must make a new engram for your dog to follow. In the beginning, the old engram will be accessed first. With persistence and patience, the new engram will be accessed first and the desired behavior will take over.

I heard Karen Pryor say at a seminar that dogs learn very quickly when you focus all your attention on getting them to do so. And she is so right! This statement made a great impression on me. If you decide that changing your dog's behaviour is a priority, you will be consistent and dedicated about making that change come about. You will have the patience for the repetitions it takes to create new behaviour patterns. It is impossible to predict, but after 25 repetitions, and certainly after 200 to 1000 repetitions, the new behavior should be well on its way to being understood and reliable. But who's counting, right?

Your worst enemies are all those well meaning guests who encourage (whether intentionally or out of ignorance) jumping behavior. "It's OK," they say. Easy for them, their dry cleaning and mending bill can't hold a candle to yours. Their bodies aren't covered with scratches.

This is where you learn how trainable dogs are and how untrainable people are. Tell the kindly souls (who are petting and cooing while your dog is leaping) very firmly that you are training the dog, and they are only confusing him. Tell them that the dog will be disciplined anyway, because you don't want him jumping on clean visitors or children, or you when you're clean! The alternative to use here is to discipline your guests, which is the mode I choose! If an explanation to one of my own species is not working, I put the dog somewhere else, so at least my guests are not de-training for me.

If you absolutely do not have time to train with each and every guest, train with as many as you can, controlling your dog first with the leash, then off-leash. For those times you cannot train, crate your dog so she is not practicing inappropriate behaviour.

Level II Behaviour	
Pre-requisite	Foundation Behaviour: Establishing a Communication System: RM/NRM & Release cue

TARGETING

You can teach your dog to touch nearly anything with his nose. A dowel, a fist, a paper plate on the wall or floor, you name it. I begin teaching the touch command with a retractable pointer. These are designed for public presentations and can be purchased at office supply stores. I like to use a pointer because its length is so easily adjustable, and it can be handily carried it in a pocket.

Approximation #1

- Have your dog sit or stand in front of you.
- Have the target-object behind your back.
- First present the target-object (begin with a pointer) from behind your back, right up to near the dog's nose, but at a distance where he will have to reach forward ever so slightly to see what this thing is. 9.9 out of 10 dogs will immediately react by reaching toward the pointer and giving it a sniff.
- Mark It and Feed It.

Repeat this 5 to 10 times.

Approximation #2

- Present the pointer from a bit further away, so your dog has to actually take a step toward it to touch it.
- Mark It & Feed It.
- Repeat several times.

Approximation #3

- Ask the dog for multiple touches before you deliver a treat. You may say "yes" each time, but do not give a treat until you have 2 to 6 touches. Vary the number of touches you get before you deliver the treat - sometimes 2, sometimes 4, sometimes 3, sometimes 6. You get the idea - use a variable number of touches before reinforcement.

Approximation #4

- Have the dog follow the pointer around in a circle, or use it to have your dog heel or spin in a circle.

Approximation #5

Generalize behaviour by asking the dog to touch other items in other places.

The uses of target training are vast and varied. It is used in service dog work to teach dogs to close and open doors. It is used in competition obedience training to teach send-aways (or go-outs) in Utility. Target training can be used in agility to teach contacts. These are just a few ways you can utilize this training. You can teach your dog to go touch a paper plate taped to the wall, for instance, or to go to a "Station" and remain there.

Touching the Target

Troubleshooting

- If your dog is biting the pointer, give your RM JUST BEFORE the dog actually touches the pointer. Divert your dog from the pointer to the treat by removing the pointer (hold it behind your back or close to your leg so it is not such an "obvious" visual for the dog). Reinforce the dog for this behaviour a few times, then delay your RM slightly so that he is touching the pointer before you give the RM.
- If your dog is frightened of the pointer, move more slowly. Put peanut butter or squeeze cheese on the end of the pointer. Place the pointer by his food dish for a few days, or carry the pointer casually on walks or around the house, until your dog gets more habituated to its appearance and movement.
- If your dog has no interest in the pointer and simply stares at your face, you can try the peanut butter or squeeze cheese trick, as above, or crate the dog or place him on a Down Stay for a few minutes and then try again. Let the dog know that there is one game in town and this is it, so he'd best settle for this one. There is no access to any other "game" right now.

Move the pointer slowly so the dog can keep up, but quickly enough so that she doesn't run into it and stop. Ask initially for just 1 step, then 2 or 3, then more. Mark It & Feed It.

Following the Target

Your dog may experiment with different behaviours. Simply do not reinforce behaviors you do not wish to have repeated. Do not add the "Touch" or "Friend" cue until you have consistent "nose" touches.

Troubleshooting

Extrapolating the Exercise

Using Your Hand As A Target

Now that your dog will touch a pointer, you can use a part of your body as a target.

Use your own balled-up fist and teach your dog to touch your fist on cue.

Now you have two ways you can "lead" a fearful dog up to an object or person he is showing fear of. If it is a person he is uncomfortable with, have the scary person hold the target stick away from his body and you cue the dog to touch the target stick. This will get the dog to approach the scary person.

Gradually shorten the target stick. Transfer to using your fist as the "target," and then (if safe) to the other person's fist. At first, obviously, very few people you meet randomly on the street will want to take their lunch hour to help you do this, so begin this work with people you know.

Once this behaviour is installed, you can inform new people the dog meets, "Put your fist out for him to smell when you meet him."

If you wish, you can fade the fist gradually to an open hand with a treat in it. Do this by presenting your dog with a fist, and, when he sniffs it, open your fist and allow the dog to take a treat from the palm of your hand.

When you are doing this exercise:

- Don't wave your hands or the treat around, and make sure the people helping you understand this also.
- Provide clear and calm information to your dog in the form of a RM/NRM.
- Be calm yourself.
- Expect your dog to make mistakes – this is how your dog learns. Mistakes are always treated as an opportunity to provide your dog with appropriate feedback so he knows how to behave next time.

Present your hand (as a fist, the back of your hand, or your palm), just like you did the pointer. Teach your dog the "Friend" cue when she is readily targeting your hand. Here, the dog is touching with her nose, but raising a paw. If that is okay with you, fine. If you don't want the paw raise, reinforce only those touches that the dog does with the nose and without the paw raise.

Target Your Hand

Only your dog can determine how quickly he can assimilate information. Take your time. It will be worth it when you see your dog overcome his fear and approach strangers with confidence and trust and allow strangers to approach him.

Prior History of Aggression or Dogs with Extreme Fear

Obviously, not all dogs will need this targeting behaviour. Many dogs are friendly to everyone they meet. But there are also many dogs who are nervous about approaching people they don't know. The best way to encourage friendliness is to make sure your dog has contact with many people of different ages, genders, and appearances while the dog is young. Young dogs have a social window that is wide open and a natural inclination to accept new stimuli readily. For the guarding breeds especially, but for any dog who is fearful or suspicious by nature, this heavy socialization MUST be continuously practiced well through 24 months of age, and then intermittently for life.

Forcing extremely fearful dogs up to people may not work well, and may serve to frighten the dog worse. This can cause an escalation of the fearful behaviour, which can quickly disintegrate into defensive actions, such as barking. Overt displays like this are unnerving for the person your dog is meeting. If a person is nervous, and behaves oddly in response, this "odd" behaviour only makes the dog more suspicious.

If your dog has a history of biting, growling or snapping, you will need to proceed with great caution before allowing him to touch the closed fist of someone he does not know, and *it may never be an appropriate exercise to try with some dogs.* A dog with this behavior pattern will initially need to wear a muzzle to do these exercises.

How do you know if your dog is ready to advance to this particular exercise with strangers? Only after your dog is approaching people he knows (immediate family members) in a totally relaxed manner AND meets the following criteria:

- The dog responds immediately when you say his name or call him away from a person or dog, even if he is in a highly aroused state.
- He has an excellent understanding of and response to a "Leave It" cue.

For the dog with any history of aggression, once these criteria are met, practice fist-targeting with family members while the dog wears a muzzle. this should be done daily. When the dog has been perfectly reliable with approaching the familiar person and targeting in a calm, friendly manner for 12 weeks, you can proceed to doing this exercise with people outside the immediate family whom the dog knows and likes.

If, at that point, you are satisfied that your dog can meet people he does not know and be reliable, then you can raise criteria by introducing a person the dog does not know well. Of course, the dog should be muzzled these first few trips, until he proves that his behaviour modification is solid. If the dog becomes reactive it is time to do a Back-Away, most rickety-tic! If you have a dog who has already bitten someone you may choose to never raise the criteria this high because of liability concerns.

I cannot remind you enough: watch your dog's body language. Any tension or nervousness means you will need to *immediately back away from the situation*, asking for your dog to orient toward you and aborting the exercise. *Once the dog is calm,* you can make a judgment call about whether it is safe to try again, or whether you should call it a day and try again tomorrow. Once a successful greeting is achieved, Quit While You're Ahead!

Photo by Joanne Weber.

Using the command "friend" and a target behaviour, you can teach a cautious or fearful dog an alternative behaviour. You have manufactured an acceptable greeting for the dog to use instead of avoidance. A strong history of reinforcement with the target-greeting behaviour will give a cautious or fearful dog new strategies to cope with meeting people.

"Friend" Cue - Using Targeting as a Greeting Behaviour

44

Level II	
Pre-requisite	Foundation Behaviours All Level I Behaviours

WAIT AT THE DOOR

Goal	The dog will wait quietly near an open door until directed or cued to go through it. The dog will not burst out the door ahead of you. The dog will not apply 600-foot-pounds of pressure to the door to hasten its opening.
What it teaches	Self-control and safe behaviour.
Practical Application	The dog will not rush out the door in a defensive manner, or rush out an open door without permission. This keeps your dog and others safe!

ACQUISITION

Sit Near The Door

1. Take your dog near the door.
2. Cue her for a Sit or a Down.
3. Mark It & Feed It.

Work on Sit, Down and Stay in this area.

APPROXIMATION #1

1. The dog is sitting near the door on a leash. Do not hold the leash, just step on it.
2. Reach for the door knob.
3. Based on the dog's behaviour, provide Feedback as outlined below:

- Watch the dog closely. If she begins to move, even a little bit, halt your reach, immediately give her a NRM and remind her what she is supposed to be doing: "Sit." This is the way to get the BEST learning curve on the behaviour – by noticing and correcting Intention Behaviour the dog shows BEFORE she is even all the way up yet. Being proactive about giving your dog feedback about Intention Behaviour most effectively relays information to your dog about what you want.

- If your timing is slow and the dog does get up, use a NRM and replace your dog in a Sit position mechanically in the following fashion: pull up on your dog's head collar or collar *very gently* until she sits. Ignore all temper tantrums, and maintain your position. Do not say another word.

  Upon sitting, *immediately* release the pressure on the head collar or collar and Mark It. The first couple of times the dog sits, even with help, as above, give her a tasty treat as well.

  After the first couple of times, if your dog breaks the Sit, just reposition her into the Sit with no treat, only the RM. At this point, provide a treat only if she repositions herself with *no help* from you (either verbal or physical), or if she *gets it right the first time.*
- If your dog remains seated, Mark It & Feed It. Nail the first correct effort with extra recognition in the following manner. Use a calm voice and calm steady movements to help your dog remain calm and in position as you reinforce her: "Yes" - treat - no pause or slight pause. "Yes" - treat - no pause or slight pause. "Yes" - treat - no pause or slight pause. And so on.

  For first correct efforts and big achievements, deliver 6 or 7 pieces of the food individually in this manner. IMPORTANT: Do NOT get all excited yourself, and begin to jump up and down and pet the dog excitedly. You are trying to promote calm behaviour near the door, not aroused behaviour.

Approximation #2

1. The dog is sitting near door on leash. Do not hold the leash, just step on it.
2. Reach for the door knob.
3. Begin to twist the door knob.
4. Based on the dog's behaviour, provide feedback.

Approximation #3

1. The dog is sitting near door.
2. Reach for the door knob.
3. Begin to twist the door knob.
4. Open the door just a crack.
5. Based on the dog's behaviour, provide feedback. A great way to give clear feedback on this exercise, if the dog begins to move toward the door at all, is to immediately close the door. Replace the dog in a Sit and try again.

Approximation #4

1. The dog is sitting near door.
2. Reach for the door knob.
3. Begin to twist the door knob.
4. Open the door wider.
5. Based on the dog's behaviour, provide feedback.
6. Repeat the above until you can repeatedly open and close the door with no reaction from the dog.

Approximation #5

1. The leash is still on the dog.
2. Walk the dog away from the door and do something else with him for a minute. Then return to the door.
3. See if the dog automatically sits in the vicinity of the door.
4. If he does, Mark It & Feed It.
5. If not, prompt for the Sit.
6. Repeat this exercise until being near the door is an environmental cue for the dog to automatically Sit.

Approximation #6

1. The dog is still on leash. Approach the door with the dog.
2. Once the dog sits, open the door.
3. Now ask for a Sit Stay with the door open.

Practice until the opening of the door is a cue to Sit.

Level II	
Pre-requisite	Foundation Behaviours Level I Behaviours Level II Behaviour: Wait at the Door !!Quiet!!

TERRITORY ENTRY AND APPROPRIATE GREETING BEHAVIOURS

Goal	The dog will allow others to enter territory when directed to do so. The dog remains calm. The dog follows directions in the vicinity of the door.
What it teaches	Humans control territory entry. It is okay to alert humans, but then the dog understands that the humans are making the judgements.
Practical Application	The dog is not reactive around the doorway, or at least will quiet down when you ask him to, and is not in a defensive or highly aroused state.

Now that your dog is calmer in the location where others enter family territory, you can build on this behaviour. First you need to desensitize the dog to the various activities that occur around the door.

Reinforceable behaviour for each Challenge includes:
- Stopping barking initially, then after a few repetitions raise criteria to:
- Remaining quiet.
- Remaining relatively calm.
- Remaining in a Sit or Down.

If you wish your dog to alarm bark once or twice, that is fine. You can allow or even encourage a bark or two, then request "Quiet." Once you say "Quiet," make it so. That is, manufacture the Quiet behaviour and reinforce it.

Manufacturing Quiet behaviour is often easier said than done! But it is possible. Refer to the "!!Quiet!!" chapter for detailed instructions regarding stimulus control over barking.

Challenge List

- Doorbell sounds.
- Knocking sounds.
- People in the house moving toward the door.

Add your own individual activities to this list if they are not already included.

Enter Stage Left - A Real Live Person

1. Station a known person (someone the *dog* knows!) outside your door.
2. Have this person knock or ring the doorbell ONE time. It is not the time to be overzealous with stimuli yet.
3. Your dog will run to the door, probably barking like a maniac as if you had not done all this preliminary work. But don't worry, your labors are not wasted. Because of the work you have already completed, your dog will quickly catch on to what you wish him to do. He is temporarily stuck in his old behavioural "rut."

   If your dog does not fall back into his old behaviour patterns, but immediately runs to you, or runs and sits by the door, you actually do have a canine genius on your hands. Jackpot that behaviour as an excellent First Correct Effort!
4. Request "Quiet." Get it and Reinforce it.

At this point, I would caution you that the first several times you do this may not be pretty. Persevere! I suggest you practice just like there are real guests at the door. (Once there are real guests, they might be wondering why they are standing on your doorstep for 15 minutes while they hear all this noise and shuffling on the other side of the door! That's why you will practice in low-stimulus conditions first.) Call out to the guest, "Just a minute please." This, at first, is a bit of distraction and multi-tasking for YOU! So, just take it one step at a time, and don't get flustered. No wonder our dogs act like maniacs at the door - so do most humans! We drop everything we're doing and rush to the signal of the doorbell.

5. Call your dog to come to you (ha-ha) and, if he does not, go to him and put the leash on him. If you can get him to Come and Sit in this situation, at this point in the game, you are doing way above average.

To prepare for a real guest instead of this fake one, choose a place near the door and have a leash and treats handy there. You will never succeed with this unless you have your ducks in a row. Many of my clients hang the leash on the doorknob or on a closet doorknob nearby. Treats can be stored in a plastic container with a twist top and placed on a table or in the closet. I know that my own "gremlins" can open coolers, zippers, and crate doors that have latches. Tupperware™ is something they don't even consider a container. Glass containers may break, so avoid those. You don't want to create another disaster at the door.

Once your dog is good with ONE knock or doorbell ring, you can Challenge the dog by having someone knock, pause for a count of two, knock, ring, pause, knock, ring, etc. This provides a real test of the dog's self control!

Territory Entry & Greeting 1 of 3

Territory Entry & Greeting 2 of 3

Territory Entry & Greeting 3 of 3

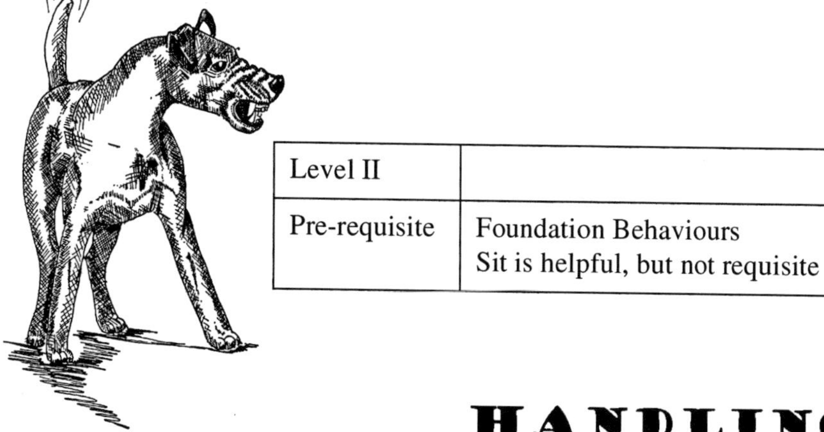

46

Level II	
Pre-requisite	Foundation Behaviours Sit is helpful, but not requisite

HANDLING & RESTRAINT - DESENSITIZATION TO BEING TOUCHED

For Additional Husbandry Behaviours, refer to the "Yielding & Husbandry Behaviours" protocol.

Goal	The dog will allow the owner to touch her anywhere, and to restrain her without aggression or undue anxiety. The dog trusts the owner.
What it teaches	Humans are safe. Part of life with humans is that restraint, physical touch, and thwarting of the dog's desire are not reasons for the dog to become anxious and/or aggressive.
Practical Application	Inevitably, the dogs who come to me with aggression problems have a lot of sensitivity about personal body space and social pressure. They do not like, are made anxious by, or flat-out become defensive by human attempts to restrain them or touch certain parts of their body. For dogs to be safe living with humans, it is necessary that they accept touch from humans. Owners should be able to touch the dog on the feet, ears, tail – everywhere. When you teach your dog that being touched and restrained is just part of every day life with humans, you are promoting good control and safety with your dog. You are relieving anxiety about touch, making for a more relaxed, comfortable and confident dog.

When discussing these exercises, it is important to know up front that restraint is never used as a punisher. The old alpha-roll stuff is NOT applicable in my paradigm under ANY circumstances. BUT, it is necessary that dogs, because they are living with us in our homes, understand very well that human touch and restraint are not threatening gestures on our part.

Therefore, approach these exercises with the idea that you are teaching your dog to trust you, even if the circumstances seem a little scary to the dog at first. This is a relationship building exercise when done properly, and increases rapport between you and your dog.

If your dog is uneasy with you simply touching him, you may need to have both the muzzle and head collar on him for these exercises. When working with a dog who has snapped at someone, it is imperative that the dog is wearing the necessary safety equipment to keep everyone safe.

I see the "You don't have the authority to touch me" behaviour most often in the multiple-home dogs who: are 24 months of age and older; are intact males; and have been on a chain or in a small kennel run their entire life. Occasionally, this behaviour is also encountered in families where the dog is very assertive and the family very passive. The humans in this situation simply don't do anything the dog "doesn't like." Therefore, the dog never develops a tolerance for the sort of frustration or irritation that can develop when a human restrains or touches him.

Using TTouch to Enhance Trust

No matter what the cause, you will begin slowly. This is a desensitization program to teach the dog to trust human touch.

There are many dog massage techniques available and Dogwise has books on these different techniques. I have obtained great results using TTouch. Linda Tellington-Jones is the author of the TTouch materials, which are often co-authored by Robyn Hood.

The best way to learn TTouch is to purchase one of the TTouch videotapes or attend a TTouch seminar. The videotapes are very informative, and my favorites come with a guidebook as well, so you have a quick reference.

Depending on your dog and how sensitive she is to touch around the head and ears, you might choose to begin with the ears. If your dog has a history of ear problems and infections, or if she dislikes to be touched around the face, you can begin with the dog standing and work on her side, around the shoulder/rib area.

To discover the "pressure" you should use when administering a TTouch, make some circles with one or two of your fingers on your own cheek. It should feel firm, but comfortable. This is a good pressure to begin with. Then you can adjust the pressure to accommodate the animal you are working on. The animal will "tell you" by her muscle tension what pressure she feels is comfortable. After you have used TTouch a few times, you will get a "feel" for the correct pressure. The only way to develop this is through practice. If a dog moves toward you, or you can feel relaxation of body tension, this is good. If she is moving away from you, you can try different pressures to see if it makes a difference. If it doesn't, go ahead and continue using TTouch with a firm, but not forceful, pressure.

Begin with your dog sitting, standing, or lying down – whichever posture she chooses. You will need to have your dog on leash so that she doesn't get up and leave in the middle of the session.

Think of the spine of the dog as being "up." Place both hands on the dog. One hand is merely to steady the dog and to let her know where both your hands are. This makes her less anxious.

The hand you are going to begin the TTouch with is resting on the dog, palm down, and with the fingers slightly curved.

You will make a circular motion with your fingers only, with a fairly firm pressure. Your palm will remain stable.

- Begin with your fingers at "6 o'clock."
- Moving your fingers to the left (so you are doing a clockwise circle), go all the way

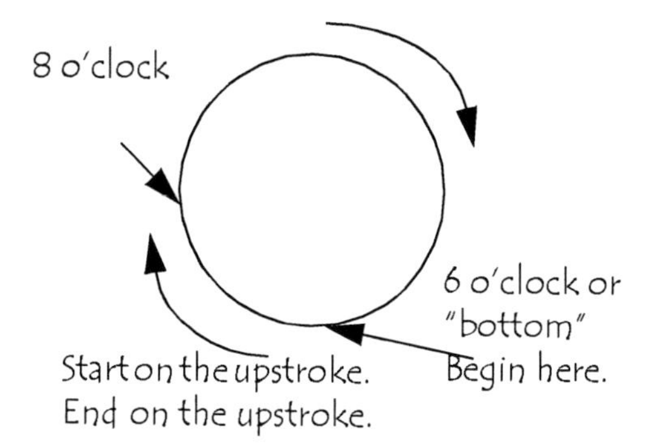

around, pass by 6 o'clock again, and stop at 8 o'clock.
- Pause.

Another way to remember this is: Rest your fingers at the bottom of the circle. Start on the upstroke and finish on the upstroke.

This is one circle. Each "touch" will consist of *one circle only*!

Pick your entire hand up off the dog and rest it in another area.

You can move to another area at random, or you can work in parallel lines across the body. As you do these circles, breathe into them, using deep relaxing breaths.

This TTouch is repeated all over the dog. At first you will want to remain in areas on the dog that she is comfortable with. This is usually on the dog's side, below the withers on the shoulder, and just in front of or on the ribs.

Then, try one circle near the dog's hindquarters (usually a more "sensitive" area). If the dog is squirmy, moves around, or tries to leave, prevent her from leaving and just continue doing circles on those areas that she is more comfortable with. When the dog feels more relaxed, you can try another circle in the sensitive area.

After one, or, for some dogs, several sessions, you are ready to see if you can work around the dog's head, ears, tail and feet. To do small areas, like the face, muzzle and legs and bottoms of the feet, you may have to use just one or two fingertips to do the circles.

After a few sessions, if you are performing the circles correctly, you will be able to feel your dog physically relax, or sag against you, as you begin your TTouch work.

I have successfully used this technique with many dogs. Once the dog is beginning to feel very relaxed with this work, she begins to let go of some of the physical tension she is holding in her body. This is a good thing! Now you may be able to use this technique in a situation where the dog would normally become anxious. Let's say you enter a room with strange dogs, like a class, and this normally makes your dog become very reactive. You might make sure that your dog is in an area where no dog can run up to her and frighten her (block yourselves off with a chair or ring-gate). You can try your TTouch and see if it helps your dog to relax. If you can get your dog to relax, even a bit, in a situation where she has been reactive, it is a big step forward in alleviating aggressive responses. It will take a lot of patience on your part, and the TTouch is only one tool in our tool-box, but every tool helps. For some dogs I have worked with, the TTouch work made a dramatic difference in their perception of the relationship they had with their humans and in the way they reacted to the environmental stress around them.

Once Maeve (my GSD who came to me with extreme aggression) learned to accept, and eventually like, TTouch, I would use it in situations that were tension-filled for her. For example, once she entered ANY territory, she figured that anyone else entering after her was trespassing. When I saw someone entering, but BEFORE she became horribly aroused, I would do a couple of circles on her shoulders, neck and head, or stroke her ears. This made a big difference in her perception of others entering the room. She was beginning to associate newcomers with relaxation.

When you are working with a reactive or defensive dog, you must be very aware of every signal the dog is providing you. At the same time, you must be mindful to what is happening in the environment. It can be difficult to do both, but with practice you will become adept at this skill. Using all of your senses can help.

To tell if Maeve was tensing up, for example, I sat with her body pressed against my knees. This way, I could feel any body tension immediately. Then I could use a TTouch or Calming Signals to help relax her.

If you have a reactive dog, you have the difficult task of radiating calmness to your dog while minutely scanning the environment for potential problems and constantly reading your dog for potential reactivity. *You cannot let your attention lag even momentarily.* This is extremely difficult to do. So give yourself a break! It really helps if you take frequent walks or "breaks" out of this situation into a more relaxing environment for a few minutes.

For instance, if you are in dog class and you or your dog are becoming too tense, go outside and walk around for a minute or two until you are both calmer. Or crate your dog and sit and socialize for a couple minutes, then, when you are refreshed, get your dog out again and continue your work.

I use TTouch endlessly with my clients' dogs and have gotten stunning results. It is an integral part of the rehabilitation process for the "already got a problem" dogs. It is equally valuable for prevention work.

RESTRAINT

This is the more difficult exercise of the touch desensitization and relationship building exercises.

I would like to discuss briefly my philosophy about alpha roll-overs, since they seem to have permeated dog training in a very big way. Very briefly: DON'T! Holding a dog down while locking eyes with her in a stare-down, or even growling at her, is recommended by some dog trainers, fellow dog-owners, and some veterinarians. *This technique is archaic and can be dangerous.* For many dogs, it creates fear which promotes defense responses that could beavoided. For other dogs, it creates aggression, anxiety or tension that may not have been there to begin with.

The best example I can think of is the client who called me because his Golden was biting when others entered territory via the front door. When I inquired if the dog had injured any guests, the client informed me that the dog was not biting the guests; she was excited to see them, but was turning on the family members and biting them! On first sight, many practitioners might jump to the conclusion of "dominance aggression." On further inquiry, I learned that these kind people, who had a great relationship with the dog in other areas, had been advised to alpha-roll the dog, hold her down, and growl and yell at her to teach her not to jump up on guests and bark at the door. This dog, who was already in a high state of arousal by greeting guests, now had two things to worry about: others entering territory AND her owners attacking her with unprovoked aggression every time guests entered. In short order, we taught her simply to go and lie on a mat when the doorbell rang. This aggression toward the owners could have been totally avoided. The training technique itself provoked a defense response and allowed the dog to practice it many times.

The premise behind the alpha-roll is that you become the alpha wolf. I think it is apparent to dogs that humans are most definitively not canids. I prefer to teach my dogs to relate to me as dog to human. I am a human, biologically and undeniably! So why not just admit it! It is as impossible for humans to emulate every nuance of a dog's body language (even though we can use some of their calming signals, as we have learned) as it is for a dog to learn and speak every nuance of our own spoken language. If someone wants to be the big alpha wolf, they'd better be greeting dogs by sniffing their butts, as well as doing the alpha-roll!

The exercise that follows, Restraint, is designed to teach dogs not that we are dominating them, but a concept that is much, much more important to the human-dog relationship: to trust humans. *Trust will replace the fear.* This is very important because, as we know, fear makes dogs reactive and unpredictable. But where there is trust, there is calmness and confidence.

In spite of how people view dogs (as "pettable" or cuddly), often dogs really do not like to have their personal body space invaded, and many dogs find human touch to be unnerving, or, at the very least, not relaxing. It is easy to tell. When you touch your dog, does he begin to leap around? Wiggle without any control? If your own body language is exciting, your dog will respond to that with leaping around. Or, does your touch make your dog sit quietly and move closer to you? Does your dog look away from you and move away from you? Or stiffen until you can feel her skin jump underneath your hand as you touch her? Of course, you know that the way you touch your dog makes a difference. The way touch has been used in the past with the dog will also make a difference in how she perceives human touch.

Some dogs come hard-wired with cuddly, I-love-to-be-touched personalities. For these dogs, accepting touch and even restraint from unfamiliar humans is not a traumatic experience. Interestingly, the majority of these seem to be the very dogs who do not have aggression problems.

Inevitably, the dogs I work with who have aggression problems also have a lot of "space and touch" resistance. The majority of Smooth Fox Terriers I have owned have pronounced opposition reflex – if I pull one way, they pull the other. If I touch them on the body with a dowel, they move into it instead of away from it. It is as if confrontational behaviour (the same behaviour that drives them to confront game) has trickled into every atom of their being. These same dogs will accept touch as long as it is their idea. But they become obviously uncomfortable (wiggly, anxious, dancing, moving away from me, or the polar opposite: head and ears down, extreme body tension) if I persist in manipulating their bodies to make them stand a certain way, such as when I hand-stack to pose them for the breed ring. These are exactly the dogs who need extensive work with being touched.

Other breeds that are often reactive about being touched, although it is expressed very differently, are the Labradors and Goldens. Their reaction when touched is often to bounce wildly around, or fling themselves to the ground and begin to wiggle violently. Sometimes this is excitement ("I love it when you touch me!") and sometimes it is most certainly anxiety about being touched and handled.

Then there are the "ambivalent dogs." When I first meet many of the Goldens and Border Collies I work with, they do the fling down and wiggle on their back thing when I reach for their collar. Then, they lift their lips and snarl or snap when the collar is touched. This mix of signals indicates just how much conflict this animal is feeling.

Note that, here, I have used specific breeds as examples for certain types of behaviour based on my own experience. Any dog, though, can be touch-sensitive, so don't assume that any dog is exempt from this! In fact, most dogs are a bit unnerved when handled, especially if they do not know you. This makes perfect sense! So, the idea is to make our dogs comfortable, trusting, and safe.

Desensitization to Having the Collar, Head and Neck Touched

Prerequisite: RM/NRM system, Some TTouch, Sit & Relax

How reactive your dog has been in the past to having moving hands around her face, head and neck will determine how safe it is to proceed with this exercise. Perhaps a muzzle is in order, and perhaps a head collar will aid you in these exercises.

If your dog becomes still, growls, or stares at you merely for placing a hand on her shoulder, head, or neck, or becomes panicked and defensive if you hang on to her collar (as in snapping and biting defensive), you may need to see a behaviour specialist before you proceed. If you have excessive trouble with this exercise, and do not make any progress, OR if your dog becomes extremely reactive and tries to bite you, it is time to seek outside help.

Proceed slowly with this exercise. It is better to make small amounts of progress than it is to fight huge battles. Remember, this exercise is designed to build trust, not a history of confrontation! If your dog is practicing calm behaviour, then she will become more calm and accepting. If she is practicing aggression, then she is perfecting confrontation.

For this exercise, Sue Sternberg's wonderful Assess-A-Hand is very useful, particularly if you are working with a dog who has snapped at you in the past. This is a realistic-looking fake hand and arm with a long reach (and no nerves!). This tool is also incredibly helpful when you are assessing dogs' temperament for re-homing and in working with dogs you don't know. (Refer to Resources for information on obtaining the Assess-A-Hand.)

If the dog snaps and you move your hand away, you have done the bright thing and saved your digits. But you have also reinforced the snapping behaviour by moving your hand away. Snapping has "worked" for the dog. Using an Assess-A-Hand, you can leave the "hand" in place, no matter the dog's reaction, with no injury to yourself. By using the Assess-A-Hand, the expected "reinforcement" did not occur. You can safely garner information about the dog and the problem this way. You will also be able to determine if there "is a problem" with a dog you do not know without risking your precious fingers.

Touching the Head, Neck and Shoulders

If you have done your TTouch work, this should proceed pretty smoothly. But because the context is different, it is still necessary to make sure the dog understands a variety of human touches,

Photo by Joanne Weber.

Assess-a-Hand

and to trust all of them. One possible approach to these exercises, is to begin by temporarily substituting the Assess-A-Hand for your own hand, gauging the dog's reaction. Once you have determined the dog is "safe," you can use your real hand.

Acquisition.

- Stand beside the dog, NOT IN FRONT OF HER. Standing at the side is less confrontational.
- Hold your hand approximately 12 inches above the dog's head.
- If the dog does not react AND remains relaxed, Mark It and Feed It.

If the dog becomes reactive, immediately issue a NRM, then ask her to Sit. Obtain the Sit and RM/treat. If the dog was sitting, you may ask the dog to come and look at you, or just follow you around the room and RM/treat that behaviour. Or ask for a favorite trick – any behaviour that you can obtain that will be reinforceable. When the dog appears to be relaxed, try again with lower criteria: Begin with your hand further above the dog's head, and perhaps slightly in front of her head. This is less threatening.

Approximation # 1

You will gradually lower your hand an inch or two at a time, until you can rest your hand gently on the dog's head with no reaction. By the time you get to that juncture, the dog should be eagerly awaiting the head touch for her treat.

- You do not have to complete this exercise in one sitting. It may require several trials spread over several days.
- Take your time.
- Always end on a successful approximation, even if it is lower than your goal for that session.
- Lower criteria if necessary.
- Raise criteria as you are able.

Approximation # 2

- You may now follow the same procedure as above, with your hand above the dog's neck.
- Follow the same procedure, except with your hand above the dog's shoulders.

Approximation # 3

The next routine involves standing in front of the dog. For dogs who do not generalize the lesson quickly, work from both sides, then work from the front. This will be apparent in the dog's level of discomfort as you work.

If moving from the side to the front is too great an approximation for your dog, you will have to move from the side to a 45 degree angle, so you are not quite in front of the dog, but not quite at her side either. Once successful in those positions, you may move to the front. If you move to the front of the dog and get any kind of reaction indicating aggression or discomfort (the dog is antsy, moving away from underneath your hand, growling, freezing, etc.), you need to work on the angled approach first.

- Standing straight up (don't bend over or loom over the dog) and in front of her, go through your approximations of holding your hand above the dog's head, and Mark & Feed for appropriate behaviour. By small approximations, just as above, gradually lower your hand until you can touch the top of the dog's head.
- Next, approximate your way down until you can touch the dog's neck.

Approximation # 4

- The next procedure involves having the dog standing or sitting about a step away from you and calling or encouraging her to come to you while you are bending over.

This is extremely stressful for many dogs. Take your time. Some dogs will be okay with coming into you, but, as soon as you begin to reach for them, they become reactive. So, pay attention to the dog's body language. In this rather vulnerable position, it is easy to take a bite to the hand or face, or be bumped hard on your nose if the dog decides to leap away.

If the dog does become reactive, lower criteria. Instead of reaching for the dog, just bend over a little, then Mark & Feed. Then bend a bit further, Mark & Feed. Then bend and move your hand slightly toward the dog, Mark & Feed. See the pattern? Just break the "reach" itself into tiny approximations.

Once the dog is comfortable with all of the above exercises, she has come a long way toward being more tolerant of a variety of "threatening" (from the dog's perception) human body postures and touches.

If your dog already is showing reactivity, anxiety, or aggression to touch, begin to work all these exercises using both a head-collar and muzzle for safety. Remove first the muzzle, then, later, the Halti ONLY when the following criteria have been met:

- The dog is not just standing and accepting touch from different people, but is, in fact, moving into people and seeking them out, longing for touch.

Some dogs may never progress safely even to minor touches from unknown people without defensive snapping and biting. In these cases, it is *at least* necessary for *all family members* to be able to safely handle the dog! There will always be situations where *somebody* has to be able to handle and restrain the dog. If you choose to keep a dog who cannot be handled by persons outside the immediate family, the dog *should be muzzled* around anyone but family members as a safety precaution. You should also consult a behaviour specialist to determine whether keeping such a dog at all is wise. A specialist will also be able to help you determine the extensive, long-term management program necessary to keep your dog alive and safe, and humans safe from her. Some dogs are safety and liability concerns for life. Let's face it, such a dog is not a candidate for re-homing, forcing you to consider euthanasia as a solution. Many decisions will need to be made about a dog who cannot be made safe.

Collar Touches

Prerequisite: Desensitization to touching the head, neck and shoulders.

For many dogs, people reaching toward them from a frontal position and grabbing their collar is entirely unnerving. Dogs have pretty good reasons for this. People grab dogs and haul and even jerk them around, or they use a collar grab before or during punishment. To the dog, this comes to mean: "If somebody comes up and grabs my collar, more often than not it is bad (even painful) news."

- Standing in front of your dog, reach quietly for the collar, but don't touch it.
- Favorable responses get the Mark It & Feed It routine.
- If your dog does not accept this readily, your immediate response would be a NRM, followed by a Sit cue or other behavior that you can reinforce. Then, go back over the prerequisite exercise again. Since this will be, in essence, a review, you should be able to go through the approximations fairly rapidly.

Minimum requirements

Gradually Approximation # until you can actually touch the collar with one of these responses:

- Good: The dog remains in position and doesn't MOVE away. A small ducking away (head movement away from your hand) is acceptable.
- Better yet: The dog is patient and neutral, but alert and waiting for the collar grab so she can have her cookie.
- Super-Stupendous: The dog is eagerly looking forward to and actively seeking your hand approaching the collar. She may lean toward you or move into you, seeking the treats she hopes you have.

When you are successful with touching the collar from both sides, the front, AND leaning over your dog, continue with the following Challenges, remembering to lower criteria and raise them again as required, with generous reinforcement:

- Quickly reach for the dog's collar.
- From a step away, step toward the dog and reach for the collar.
- From right in front of the dog, reach for the collar and give it a very slight tug.
- From a few steps away, step toward the dog and grab the collar, giving it a slight tug.

- From beside the dog, take hold of the dog's collar and pull her a couple of steps sideways.
- From in front of the dog, pull her toward you a step.

Photo essay by Joanne Weber.

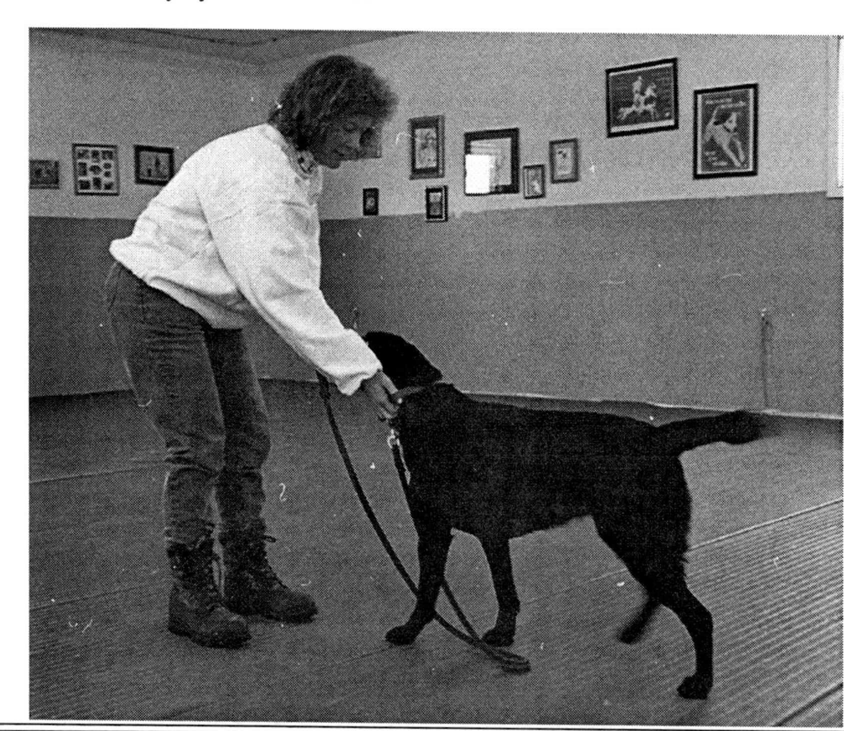

Cassie has advanced in her collar touch work to the point that she is easily guided, and this does not bother or stress her in any way. Notice she is going toward Faye willingly, even though Faye is bending over her.

Collar Touches

This is a very advanced collar "grab." Faye has taken hold of Cassie's collar and is giving it a firm tug. Notice Cassie willingly moves toward Faye in an energetic, but relaxed, way.
Even though you are giving a tug toward you, go gently at first and keep the experience jolly and fun! For timid dogs, this firm "tug" part of the exercise may not be appropriate if it is too intimidating for them.

Advanced Collar Touches

Photo Essay by Joanne Weber.

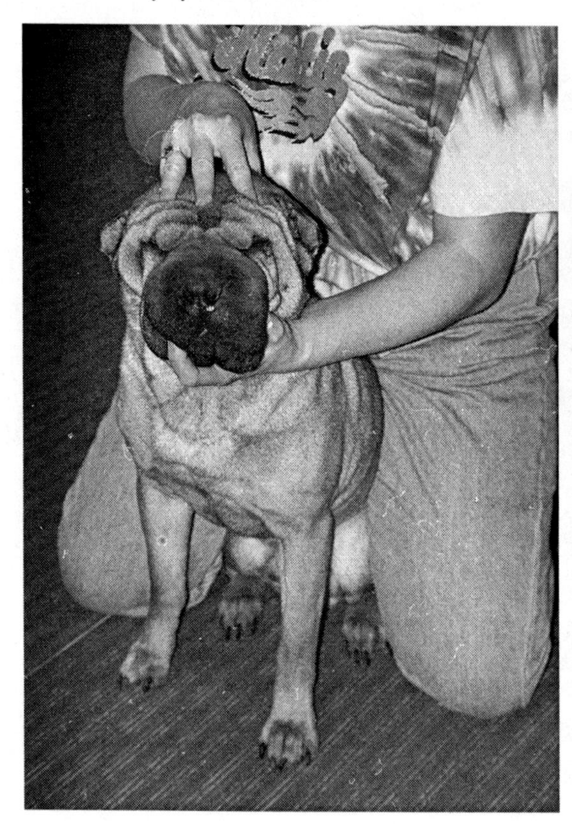

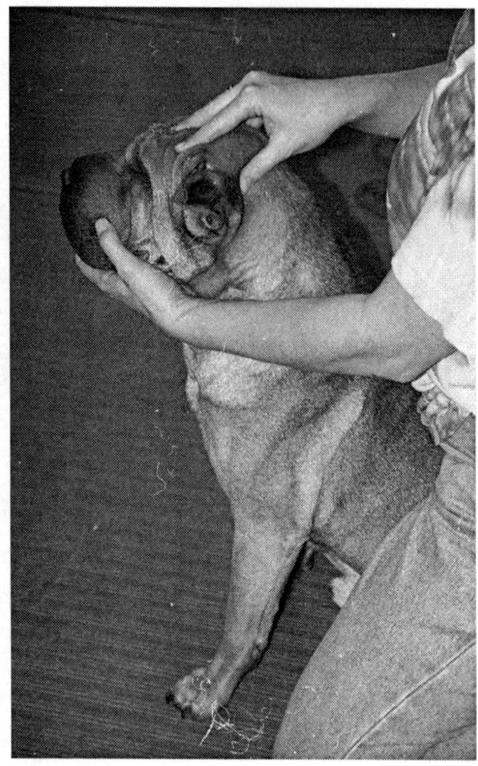

This photo shows the correct position for both participants. Note that Fonzie is resting his chin in Lylenette's hand. When the dog is voluntarily resting his chin in your hand, you can remove the hand on top of the head. If the dog begins to fuss or lifts his chin, replace the upper hand and encourage the dog to rest his chin in your lower hand again. You will be using your RM for compliance. Be silent and outlast the dog when he is fussing and struggling. You may try a NRM, but if it does not gain you an immediate response, just be quiet and outlast the dog. No scolding or reprimanding - that merely validates the dog's distress and fussing.

Lylenette is not HOLDING the dog's chin or forcing the behaviour. Her lower hand is cupped to form a comfortable "rest" for the dog's chin.

Basic Sit Restraint

Sitting and Standing Restraint Exercises

For this exercise, you will need to add one new skill: Teaching the dog to rest her chin in your hand and accept a light hold on her muzzle.

With your dog in a Sit position, stand or kneel behind her and block her from moving backwards with your knees. It will feel like you are having the dog sit on your feet and lean against your knees as if she were in a sort of chair. Place one hand under the dog's chin, with your fingers gently curled around her muzzle (NOT TIGHT and NOT HOLDING the muzzle). Your other hand is simultaneously placed with the little finger behind one ear and the thumb behind the other ear. The remaining three fingers gently rest on the area of the dog's back-skull. The occipital protuberance is the little bony ridge that you can feel at the very rear of your dog's skull. The nuchal crest is the slight depression just to the left and right of the occipital protuberance. This is the area you are targeting with your remaining three fingers. Some people prefer to have these three fingers resting just on top of the back-skull. Both will work: I prefer to target the occipital protuberance and the nuchal crest, but you don't have to be super-exact about that.

By pressing forward with the upper "back-skull" hand, gently encourage your dog to rest her chin in your lower "chin" hand voluntarily. Lighten the pressure with the upper "back-skull" hand immediately, using slight increments of lessening pressure, as soon as you feel the dog "weighting" your lower hand with her chin.

If your dog struggles or resists, remain quiet and neutral. If your dog wrestles out of your grip, just begin again, gently and neutrally, no matter how many repetitions it takes to outlast the dog. DO NOT chatter or scold! As soon as your dog does weight the "chin" hand, the reinforcement is the slight lessening of the pressure. It is also appropriate at this time to immediately do some low, calm praise of your dog, including a RM. Once the dog is weighting your lower "chin" hand calmly, you can release the pressure on the upper "back-skull" hand gradually, but completely.

Gradually lengthen the amount of time your dog will rest her chin in your hand without prompting from the hand resting on the back-skull.

Once your dog readily rests her chin in your lower hand, move on to these Challenges.

Place your dog in a Sit position and stand or kneel behind her. With one hand gently cradling the dog's chin and muzzle, and your other hand resting lightly on the dog's back-skull or on her collar, introduce the following:

- Have a person approach and pet.
- Have a person approach and examine the dog's ears. The teeth. The feet.

Now you may also do the challenges with you standing by the dog's side, and the dog resting her chin in your hand. Have a helper run his hand over the dog's head, examine her ears, pick up her feet and gently wag the dog's tail.

This exercise is handy in a million ways. You can eventually use this as a way to calm a puppy when he has "crocodile jaws" syndrome, as all puppies do (you know, when they are just snapping at everything around them playfully). You can use this if you have to medicate ears or eyes by yourself at home, or as a way to control your dog at the veterinarian's office.

This is a great position to teach the wiggly puppy to accept. Now, you can use it when children wish to approach and pet. It is particularly convenient before the puppy has a stable Sit-Stay (e.g., but you have taken the puppy to pick up the kids at school).

As a prevention tool this is excellent. All dogs should learn this, and I teach it to all attendees in my puppy classes. As a way to give the older, problem dog a "task" to do when being examined or groomed, and to teach all dogs that human restraint is "how it is," it is beneficial.

Muzzle Grabs

Grabbing and holding the muzzle is what one dog would do to administer a correction to a subordinate. To make double sure that your dog does not overreact to you examining teeth, or will not misinterpret human hands holding her face, practice grabbing the muzzle using the same steps as you used for the collar grabs. Use a muzzle when you first begin these exercises if your dog has shown any aggression toward you in the past, or if you are unsure of how she will react to this type of handling.

Once your dog will accept a light touch, you can try a light, gentle "shake" of the muzzle, followed by generous reinforcement.

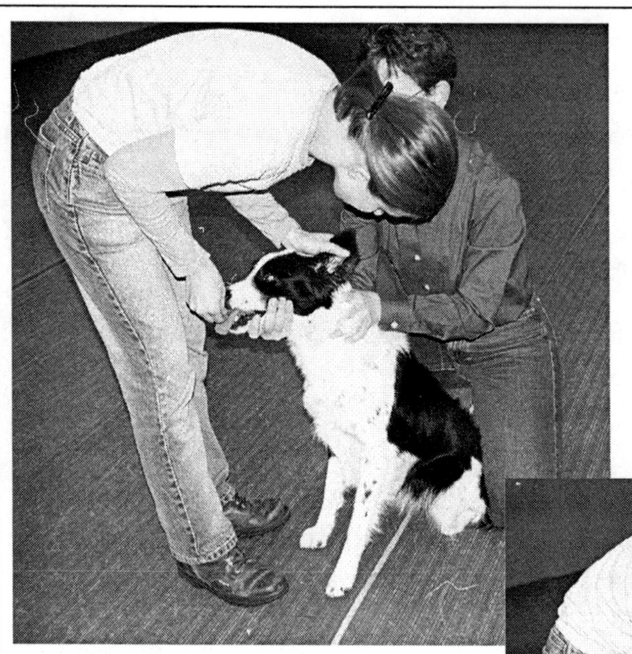

Marie examines Rylie's ear. She feeds a treat at the same time, so Rylie associates this restraint the exam, and all of this "lurking" over her by humans with Good Stuff Happening.

Marie moves to the mouth and teeth exam. Your veterinarian will be grateful that you did this work, for sure!

Now for handling the feet and checking the paws....This makes Rylie a bit anxious and she looks up at me for reassurance. I remind her to rest her chin in my lower hand with a little pressure from my "backskull" hand. I tell her she is doing just fine, and I approve of her not fussing and struggling, with a verbal "good girl."

Exam By Others - Sit Restraint

Settle

Prerequisite: Touch Desensitization, Down

A Settle position is one where the dog is calmly reclining flat on her side, with her feet stretched out before her.

Remembering that this is the ultimate restraint exercise, proceed carefully and safely. During this exercise, some dogs' first reaction is to panic. If you feel this will be traumatic for you, seek immediate help from an experienced behaviour specialist. This exercise is extremely important, and is a true trust and relationship builder if done correctly. Done incorrectly it will most certainly jeopardize your success, and in extreme cases can be dangerous.

This exercise is most easily and safely done with puppies and then continued periodically throughout their life to maintain the skill. I find this is not frequently done, and if it is, is often done as an alpha-roll-over type maneuver, which is *contra-indicated in any dog, no matter what the circumstances are*. Keep in mind that the primary reason we are doing this exercise is to teach dogs to trust humans and feel comfortable with humans restraining them.

Restraint for dogs, at some point in their lives, is inevitable. Some form of restraint is usually required in the veterinarian's office, to administer injections, or ear medicine, or to look at a hot spot. You have to restrain a dog to clip her nails – a task that is ideally done every 2 to 3 weeks. If your dog runs outside in the field and comes in with burrs knotted into her coat, you may have to flip her over and restrain her to comb and cut out the burrs. A dog who cannot be restrained cannot be physically maintained and will not be behaviourally stable and safe.

Remember that you can use your calming signals here to help relax your dog. If she is lying still, but tense and licking lips or yawning, do a glance away and yawn or a lip lick yourself. She is asking you for reassurance with her calming signal and wanting to know that you are not going to threaten or kill her. Communicate back to her that you are non-threatening and can be trusted, and that you are trying to communicate, listen, and respond to her need in return for her cooperation.

Use a muzzle and martingale collar and leash or a Halti and a leash (with the muzzle added, if required) until you have determined that you are going to be able to safely handle the dog for each approximation and exercise.

Acquisition

- Kneel on the floor. Use a nice comfy rug or comforter underneath you to save your knees. If on a hard surface, make sure there is comfy padding under your dog.
- Place your dog in a Down.
- Position yourself so that you are kneeling close to her, near her shoulder.
- Allow her to become accustomed to you kneeling and petting her from this position, and to consenting to your manipulating her over onto one hip.

  If you need to, you can have a second person feeding the dog as you physically manipulate the dog, or you can provide some treats for appropriate behaviour. I most often just use my "touch" and voice as the way to give the dog social approval for this exercise, because I don't have enough hands to hold the dog and feed her!

Approximation #1

When comfortable with the above, and with the dog in a relaxed state (your TTouch work comes in handy at this time) you are ready to advance.

- Using the least amount of force possible, with one hand on the dog's shoulder and one hand on the dog's hip, gently roll her over onto her side, so all four legs are on one side of her body, oriented away from you.

If the dog acquiesces to this with good grace – that is, by relaxing a moment and accepting a treat – she may now get up. Allow this to occur by gently and calmly removing your hands from her body and letting her get up.

If the dog is struggling or making a fuss at any time, DO NOT reassure her and tell her it is okay. Number 1: she will not believe you. She does not think it is okay if she is struggling. Number 2: the dog will interpret your reassuring gentle tone to mean: "Yes, I loooove it when you are struggling, frightened, angry, and acting like an idiot." In short, your dog will infer from your reassuring tone that this behaviour is desired by you and that you are reinforcing it.

So, what to do with the struggling dog? Remain neutral, do not allow her to get up, and if she does, insist that she lie back down near you. If she ceases struggling at any time, make sure to immediately RM and provide social approval. If you have an assistant, which is handy for this exercise, she can feed the dog while you hold, IF the dog is holding still. Any time the dog is struggling, remain quiet and neutral and outlast the dog, quickly oscillating to verbal approval for still, calmer behaviours.

When your dog is remaining calm with the above portion of this exercise, you may move to the next step.

Approximation #2

With you kneeling, and the dog laid on her side with her feet oriented away from you, place your forearm across the dog's neck, and with that hand, grasp the dog's front leg (*the leg on the "BOTTOM"*). It is imperative that you hold the leg RIGHT NEXT TO THE BODY, so that, if the dog struggles, you do not hurt her.

Simultaneously, with the other hand, grasp the dog's rear leg (*again, the one on the BOTTOM*), RIGHT NEXT TO THE BODY to avoid injuring a dog who is struggling.

When grasping the legs, make sure you are right near where the body and the leg hook together. If you hold the legs near a joint, and the dog struggles, you will twist the joint and perhaps cause injury to the dog.

Have your assistant provide a constant feed to the dog who is remaining still. Provide verbal approval as well.

As soon as you are able, as indicated by the dog's relaxed muscles, loosen up your grip on the rear leg, and see if she will accept a nice little tummy rub. If she then begins to struggle, re-grasp the rear leg and hold the dog in place.

As soon as the dog begins to tighten up and struggle, you must maintain your hold on the dog. If you allow her to get up now, you are teaching her that throwing a temper tantrum, or being extremely frightened and struggling, snapping, whining, and so on, work very well to make you let go. You are thereby inadvertently applying reinforcement to the inappropriate behaviour.

While the dog is struggling, DO NOT talk to her. Do not stare at her face. Remain neutral and calm. If she wiggles out of your hold, lay her back down and start over. You can prevent her from flinging her head around and/or biting you if you keep your forearm gently across her neck.

As soon as you can, introduce the TTouch to the dog while she is in this position. This will facilitate getting the dog to accept and trust this restraint exercise. A bit of struggling is to be expected, but do not turn this exercise into any more of a confrontation than necessary. Remember to maintain a calm, relaxed demeanor. Keep breathing. If you are holding your breath, your dog will notice and this is a red flag for a dog, telling her you are also upset and panicked.

If your dog wants to look at you during this exercise that is okay. Friendly eye contact can receive social approval. Unacceptable is: staring you down, or engaging your eye contact, then "freezing" and staring at you. If this occurs get out of the situation as calmly and safely as you can, and discontinue this exercise. If your dog behaves in this manner, you definitely need to consult with a behaviour specialist.

"Settle" Photo Essay by Joanne Weber.

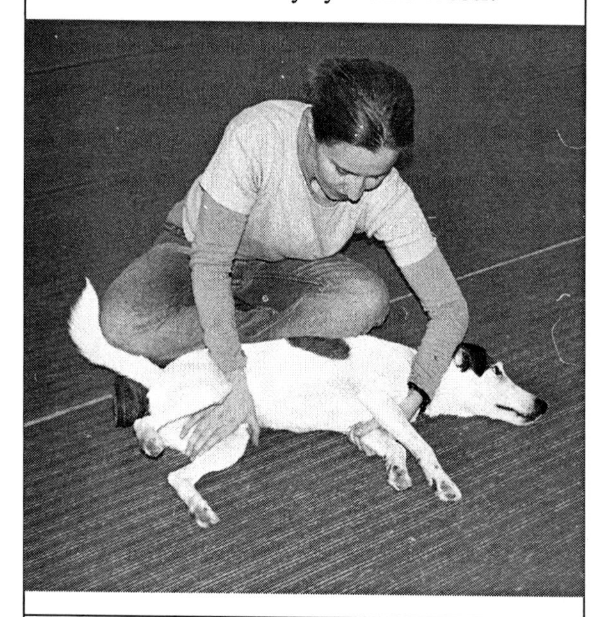

Marie grasps Vinny 's legs close to his body. Vinny has learned to relax during this exercise. It may take several repetitions of this for your dog to respond and remain relaxed. It is well worth the time spent!

Settle - Hand Position

As soon as your dog realizes that you are not going to give in to temper tantrums, AND that reinforcement and social approval are provided for calm, still behaviours, she will indeed stop struggling.

Once you begin this restraint exercise, it is all-important to "outlast" the dog. Confrontation is to be minimized, but your dog must also understand that you are not going to give up and allow her to prevail. To be successful, the dog must at least hold still in the initial stages, and actually relax in the latter stages.

Over time, dogs come to enjoy this exercise, because restraint is no longer frightening to them, and therefore is no longer a reason to be thrown into a defensive emotional state. You are showing your dog her worst possible fear, and helping her to overcome it. This is why this exercise is so important. Many aggression problems are caused by fear and the resultant over-arousal that accompanies defense states. It will be a very big step forward for your dog's comfort and safety, and for your relationship, when she trusts you enough to allow a "settle" restraint!

Approximation #3

Once your dog will accept this exercise with you, it is time to add other family members. With you holding the dog in its "settle" position, the family members can approach and feed the dog and participate in the TTouch.

This is a great way to show your dog that you are "backing up" the authority of the other family members, especially children, and that these other family members are also to be trusted. Children should NEVER be allowed to do this exercise, unless they are participating as above with parental supervision. They do not have the judgment required to determine when this is an appropriate exercise or when to let go, continue to restrain, or other decisions that need to be made on the spur of the moment. Children are also physically incapable of carrying out this exercise correctly.

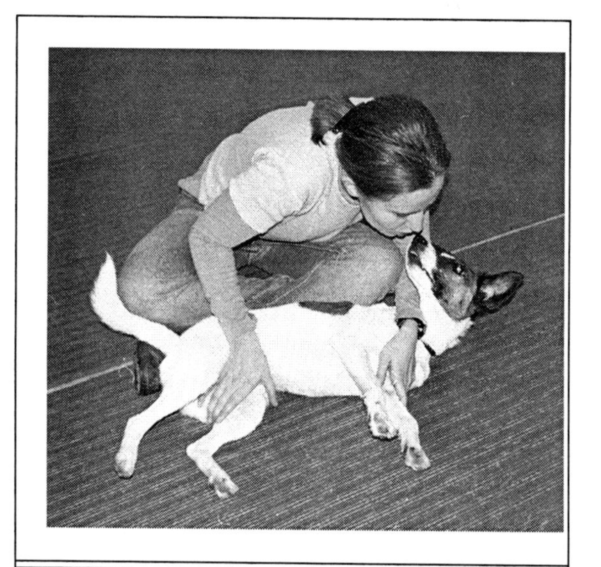

Vinny gives Marie relaxed, friendly eye contact and a little kiss.

Settle

Photo by B. Aloff.

Karen is hugging her 12 week old puppy. Franklin looks a bit alarmed, but remains relaxed and accepting. Many dogs panic or become resentful at this kind of handling, interpreting it as threat behaviour on the part of the human.

Franklin quickly figures out that this is friendly and reciprocates with a little snuggle. It is important that our dogs understand that this is normal, non-threatening human behaviour.

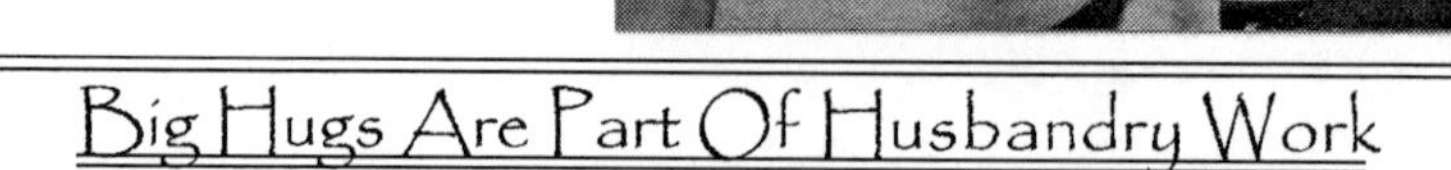

Big Hugs Are Part Of Husbandry Work

Challenges

Engage other people to help. These persons must be very level-headed and non-reactive. Instruct them to be neutral and to not stare at the dog and to touch only when you give them the sign. You must also be sure your equipment is safe and that you have control in a controlled setting with which the dog is familiar. If the dog begins to struggle, have the helper disengage for a moment, get the dog relaxed, and then try again.

As a rule of thumb, if you are doing prevention work, a muzzle may not be required. If you "already have a problem," or if your dog has shown any aggression in the past, absolutely do not take a chance. Muzzle the dog before you begin.

When you have truly achieved the ultimate restraint, your dog will acquiesce to having its mouth, face, feet and tail touched and moved by others. Once you are at this point, it is often no longer necessary to restrain the dog at all to use TTouch or to handle the dog's feet and mouth.

Maintenance

Periodically, make sure you do the actual "Settle" exercise, with the dog on his side and you holding the legs with your forearm resting on the dog's neck. Since this is human body language that many dogs find threatening, occasional reviews remind your dog that a Settle is not scary. This also insures that when you have to physically restrain the dog, you will not get any adverse reaction from her. Do the Challenges periodically, too. In a Sit Restraint or Settle position, have a helper hold the dog's feet, examine her ears, and hold her tail as a veterinarian might do.

Level II	
Pre-requisite	Foundation Behaviours All Level I Behaviours For some exercises or dogs, completion of the Handling & Restraint Protocol may be required.

YIELDING & HUSBANDRY BEHAVIOURS

Dog training is rife with Rin-Tin-Tin and Lassie Myths. My least favorite myth is that old stand-by: your dog should do what you tell her to because she loves you. (My husband loves me, but that has not yet prevented him from irritating me on numerous occasions. I am certain he has mutual feelings about this, and would say that I am extremely non-compliant myself.)

Dogs are domestic animals and they are living in my home, sleeping on my sofa, eating in my dining room (okay, I admit it: sometimes right off my plate on the table). Because of this whole domestic thing, it is required that dogs trust me enough to allow me to move them, restrain them and restrict their movement on occasion. Practicing handling and restraint exercises teaches your dog that, when you move him and restrain him, you are not going to hurt him and your intent is benign.

The exercises below compliment the "Handling & Restraint" protocol, but may be done independently of that protocol, except where noted.

These exercises are for prevention of aggression. If your dog has already shown resentment of personal space infringements, you will want to complete the "Handling & Restraint" protocol first to ensure that the following exercises will be safe for you to do. If your dog has snapped or growled at you, it is wise to make sure you are going to be able to manufacture an outcome that is reinforceable. Therefore, leashes, collars, head-collars and a muzzle are in order. You will also proceed very slowly and cautiously. Your approximations will be infinitesimal and you will reinforce all non-reactive behaviour generously.

It is important that you don't "push" the confrontational or defensive dog too much too soon, or you may get an undesirable or dangerous reaction. For that reason, with a dog who may be reactive or confrontational, it is important to make certain that you use this as a desensitization procedure – *never* press the dog into reacting. As mentioned above, for dogs who have already shown you risky or marginal behaviour, the "Handling & Restraint" protocol should be completed prior to doing this.

Some form of husbandry behaviour (yielding and restraint) should be done on a daily basis, especially when your dog is 24 months and younger. Puppies are going to want to "mouth" and flop around during these exercises, so keep your hands away from the puppy's face, or muzzle him, or hold him in such a fashion that he cannot bite at you. Ignore these antics, simultaneously keeping hold of the puppy AND keeping your hands away from his needle-sharp teeth. Yes, it is possible! The puppy will eventually calm down, providing you with the opportunity to reinforce the behaviour.

Reinforcement in these exercises will, for the most part, consist of social approval and a RM. You can quickly move to not using treats. It is difficult to give treats with many of these exercises if you are working by yourself, because both your hands will be busy holding the dog, so don't worry about that too much. These exercises are used to help the dog understand "limits" on behaviour, and they are designed to teach the dog to yield to humans when requested to do so. These are humane ways to teach the dog to trust you and that yielding to, rather than confronting, humans is a reinforcing experience. In some cases the reinforcement comes from the dog "stopping struggling," which has the direct result of you relaxing your grip and giving the dog social approval.

The exception would be for those dogs who are very timid and are convinced that, just because you wish them to move, it means that you are threatening them. For these dogs, you will wish to use a generous reinforcement schedule, using lots of treats, for a longer period of time.

Our primary goal with this protocol is to teach your dog that normal human behaviour is not threatening.

ACQUISITION

of Basic Yielding Exercise

The following exercises are used, not because you are trying to dominate your dog, or because you "need to show them who's boss," but because *your dog should have a variety of experiences to prepare him for normal human behaviour.* If someone walks by the dog at some point and accidentally touches him, or wakes him, you want your dog to just figure that is part of daily life. If no one ever disturbs the dog, the dog is much more likely to be over-reactive when it does occur.

- If your dog is lying on the floor, go out of your way to walk over to him and ask him to move. You can do this any one of a number of ways, and you should practice all of them. Use a verbal cue. As you approach the dog, very gently touch him with your toe, and, if that doesn't move him, shuffle your feet VERY GENTLY until the dog moves out of your way. When he does so, give him social approval. You can also provide a treat the first couple of times, but after that, unless you are working with a dog who is timid or confrontational, you don't need to do anything but provide a verbal or pat as approval.

With dogs or puppies you are doing *prevention* work with, you can just start as above and reinforce appropriate behaviour.

The pushy dog and the timid dog...

would be handled much the same, although the behaviour reinforced is quite different. The general idea with these dogs is to do as much of the exercise as possible WITHOUT getting a reaction.

Since you want the *pushy or confrontational* dog to eventually comply automatically, without thinking about it, constantly reinforce them for compliant, yielding behaviours. Compliant behaviour is to be reinforced frequently with this type of personality because it is this dog's natural tendency to be pushy or confrontational rather than cooperative. The majority of dogs will quickly yield and not be resentful about it. Most dogs intuitively get the whole physics thing, that two of you cannot occupy the exact same bit of the planet at the exact same time. The pushy or confrontational dog, however, seems to think that everyone else's matter must flow around them, and if it doesn't, it is a personal affront. It is quite interesting that if you make it reinforcing for this personality type to be yielding, they are more than happy to become compliant. That means that the yielding and restraint exercises, for these dogs, are not just desensitizing them to human co-habitation of space, but are also teaching them cooperation.

The *timid* dog, as you go through the steps, is reinforced for non-timid, bolder behaviour, or neutral, non-stressed behaviour while still complying. If the timid dog leaps out of your way in a frenzy and you reinforce that, you have just reinforced avoidance behaviour, which is different than yielding behaviour! So the timid dog requires a leash (so he does not resort immediately to running out of the room or other weird avoidance behaviours) and some very gentle handling. Refer to the "Being Brave Is Better" protocol for more advice on handling timid dogs in general.

You might start by walking near the timid dog from a little distance. Mark & Feed non-panicky behaviour. Then walk and stand next to the dog. Mark & Feed calm behaviour. Next walk up, Mark & Feed, then nonchalantly ask the dog to move and Mark & Feed calm, compliant behaviour.

- Periodically remove your dog from furniture, arbitrarily. If he is sleeping, wake him gently and then make him move. You may toss a treat AFTER the dog has vacated. DO NOT wave the treat around or announce that you have a treat and bribe the dog off the furniture. Quietly and calmly cue the dog to get off, and then, SURPRISE! Look at the great reward you get for compliant behaviour.

Acquisition

of Basic Husbandry Behaviours

- Go get your dog and put a leash on him. You can stand on the leash or hold it in your hand to prevent the dog from moving around too much.
- Physically keep the dog in a standing position, using the following specific method to do so: Place one hand under the dog's chin, and the other arm in front of the rear legs. This effectively prevents the dog from moving forward or from sitting. Make sure the dog is facing a direction that YOU have chosen. Initially Mark & Feed for compliance, but quickly work to a thin schedule, or just use touch and voice to reinforce the behaviour.

It is important to remember to remain neutral and quiet when the dog is fussing, and save speaking to the dog for when he is being still. A NRM may be used for undesirable behaviour or fussing. If you use a NRM a couple of times and the dog is still fussing, just be still and *outlast* the dog. Quickly notice and use your RM for compliant behaviour.

If your dog is reactive, or you think he might be, use a muzzle in the beginning stages of this exercise! If you haven't handled your dog a lot, it may frighten or frustrate him when you do not immediately let go of him while he is struggling or trying to walk forward. Your dog will quickly get over these feelings of insecurity if you remain calm and consistent and time your feedback properly.

The Following Challenges Can be Added to this Basic Behaviour

- Once the dog is standing, change the direction the dog is facing, and remain in that position for a count of five, ten or fifteen (whatever, as long as YOU choose how long), once the dog is still.
- Remove the arm that is in front of the rear legs, and wag the dog's tail for him.

- Stroke the dog from head to tail repeatedly, sometimes quite firmly (don't hurt the dog), sometimes soft.
- Lift the tail and examine the anal face. Or at least pretend to do so!
- Run your hands down the dog's legs and pick up the dog's foot. Examine the underside of the paw (dogs generally hate this).
- Practice using a towel to "wipe" the dog's feet off.
- Stroke the dog's tail from the base to the tip.
- Use a brush or comb and do a little grooming.
- Have the dog lie down, then examine and wipe her feet. Also, from a down position, brush the dog's tummy, sides, head, and any other body part you can reach.
- From a standing and lying down position, examine the dog's teeth.
- From a standing and lying down position, examine the dog's ears.

Advanced Husbandry Behaviour - Nail Clipping

Prerequisite: Sit Restraint and Settle, which are described in detail in the "Handling and Restraint" protocol.

Approximation 1

With your dog standing, sitting, or lying down on his side, pet the dog and handle him all over. When the dog accepts this calmly, you may raise criteria.

Approximation 2

Get out the nail clippers. With your dog in any position you prefer, or the one he accepts the best:

- Touch the dog's shoulder with the nail clippers.
- Mark It & Feed It.

Approximation 3

Follow the above with touching the dog on the head, the back, the tail, and the feet with the nail clippers.

Approximation 4

Pick up the dog's foot and touch the nail with the nail clippers.

Approximation 5

This step is done without the nail clippers in your hand. If the dog moves around, or rather WHEN he moves around, it is easy to cut too deeply into the nail and into the quick. "Quicking" the dog is practically a done-deal if you hold the dog's foot only, and do not stabilize the nail itself.

You are going to hold the dog's nail and foot in a specific way to minimize this from happening.

Support the dog's paw in your hand and, with your index finger and thumb, grasp the nail itself and get all the hair back away from the nail. Do this hold with one nail, Jackpot and quit for this session. A Jackpot is an extra generous helping of treats all at once. At the appropriate time, you give your RM, then plop down this super-duper special treat and more than usual of it! Instead of one or two pieces of the usual treat, set down a couple tablespoons of canned cat food, dog food or tuna fish.

The next session, try holding on to 2 or 3 nails, one at a time, of course!

In different sessions, do the exercises below:

- Work up to doing one whole foot.
- Do one nail on each foot.
- Do one foot and one nail on another foot.
- Do two feet.
- Do two feet and one nail on the third foot.

I'm sure you get the idea! Don't try to do all the feet the first session, unless your dog looks quite comfortable with the exercise.

Use a super-generous reinforcement schedule!

This is multi-tasking for you, so be patient. Initially, the dog may fuss. If you are the least bit concerned that your dog will be reactive, muzzle him. Dogs who will bite under no other circumstances may snap or bite you when you are fiddling about with touching feet and nail clipping.

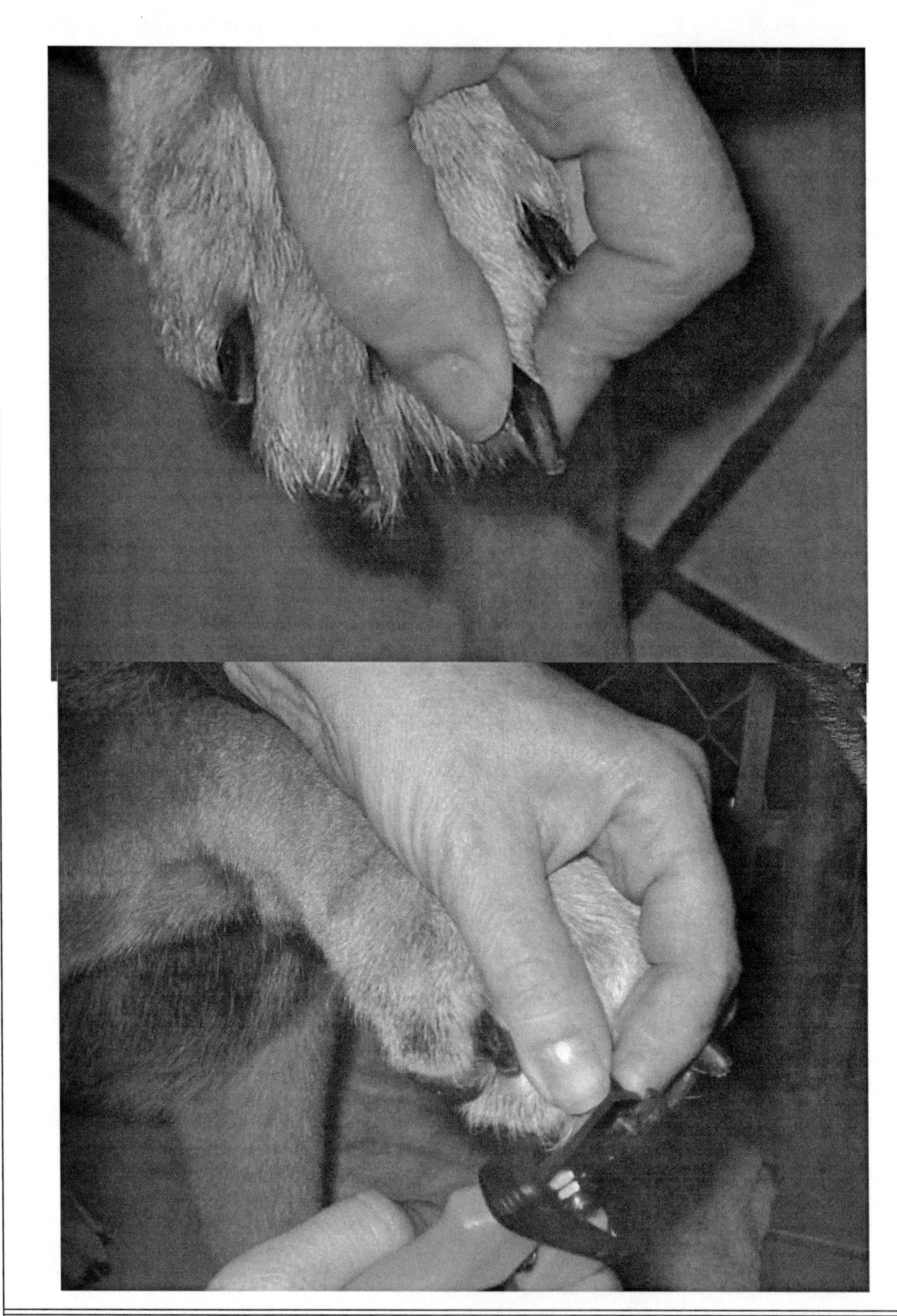

How to do the Nail-Hold

If your dog has really hairy feet and it is difficult to keep the hair away from the nail, take an old pair of nylons and poke the dog's nails through the hosiery. This will keep the hair back, so the clippers are not grabbing the hair and pulling it as the cut is made.

Once you have desensitized the dog to the nail clippers and the noises they make, and you have desensitized the dog to foot-and-nail-holding, you are ready to raise criteria.

Approximation 6

Holding the nail, touch the dog's foot with the clippers, but do not make a cut! Work with this until you can touch each nail with the clippers.

Approximation 7

Same as Approximation #6, except this time you are going to touch the first two nails with the clippers and cut just the end off the third. Stop and generously reinforce after the cut. Now you do not reinforce the dog after each nail-holding, but only after a cut is made. Only make one nail cut in this session! After you make the cut, then continue doing the nail-hold and touch exercise.

Approximation 8

Work up to some nail touches and two cuts, then three, and so on.

NOTE: You may use a second person to do a constant feed as you do the cuts and touches, if it is needed. If you are using a helper, move on to the helper feeding after only the cuts, and not after the touches.

If you never do any of this stuff, then don't be surprised if your dog becomes reactive and unreasonable when you need to. Not being able to be handled, touched, and restrained, having no history of dealing with frustration, and trying to be in control of the environment constantly – these all predispose the dog to becoming defensive and biting. In order to be even reasonably safe, these basic husbandry behaviours are necessary, and the vast majority of people leave this important lesson to chance. Then, they are shocked and puzzled when their dog eventually displays defensive behaviour or bites someone.

48

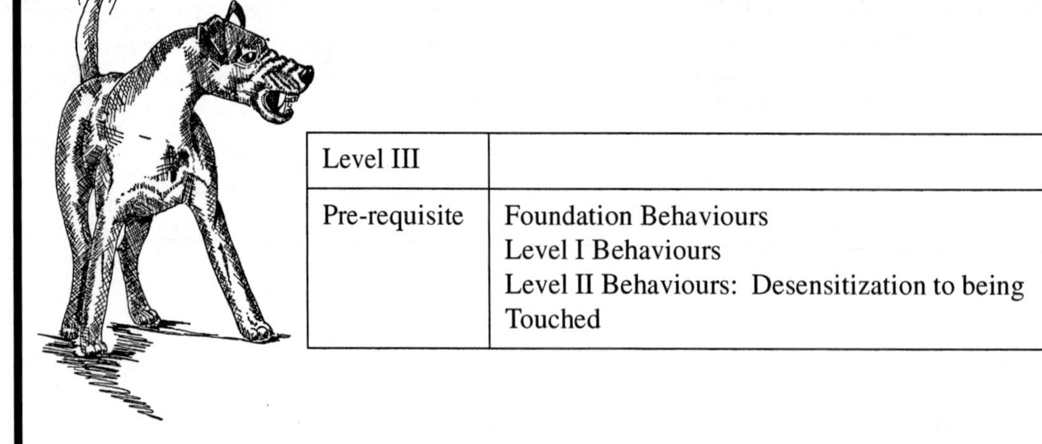

Level III	
Pre-requisite	Foundation Behaviours Level I Behaviours Level II Behaviours: Desensitization to being Touched

BEING BRAVE IS BETTER

Help for the "Cautious" Dog and Human Approaches

Fearful behaviour is extremely difficult to dispel because avoidance behaviour is powerfully reinforcing.

It is not reasonable to expect our dogs to love, or even like, every person or dog they meet, but it is not too much to expect them to learn to behave in a civil manner.

Fear is a normal and useful survival trait. Unfortunately, in some animals, fear is such a constant companion that they approach almost every experience with trepidation. This is seen usually in dogs who were not extensively socialized when young. Socializing is a broad term that encompasses a variety of experiences that all dogs should be exposed to if they are expected to co-habitate comfortably with humans. Our society has changed drastically in the last 50 years. The demands on humans have increased a good deal, and that extends to our friend, the dog, as well. To live harmoniously in today's society, we expect a lot of behaviour from our dogs that they are not genetically prepared for, such as being left alone for long periods of time. In addition to that, we expect them to be friendly, or at least accepting, to all humans that they meet.

Fear responses in the puppy are easily developed. Genetics and heredity play a big part of how the puppy or dog responds to a given situation – but so does his education about his environment. It is always a combination of these two factors that determine the end result of a dog's "temperament."

Fear behaviour will often "rush in" to fill a behavioural vacuum (a situation in which the dog does not know what to do), so have a variety of alternatives for the dog to use: Sit, Down, Shake, et al. By building a variety of reinforceable behaviours, your dog has practiced alternative coping skills and his use of them under stress is more likely. This means your dog does not have to resort to OR LEARN aggression because she has other language skills she can access.

In addition, your dog gains self-confidence by using her native language skills, so she doesn't have to be afraid she cannot "cope with" this situation. For a discussion on fear and calming signals, refer to the chapter "Common Sense Is Just Not That Common."

Knowledge gained from reading, seminars, and extensive field experience only strengthens my belief that many training techniques that are commonly used promote aggression in at least some portion of the canine population. The key here is education. Some trainers recommend using a slip or "choke" collar, and administering a collar correction (sharply jerking on the leash) for any wrong-doing. If positive reinforcement is outweighed by Positive Punishment and Negative Reinforcement, the training method should be analyzed. It is not the fault of the collar, necessarily, but the way it is being used.

If a dog is receiving punishment and he does not understand the reason for it, confusion is certainly one result. Confusion leads to frustration. From there, aggression may be just around the corner. Other results are fear and avoidance responses. Defense is a direct result of fear. If you are doing the punishing, certainly some of the fear is directed toward you. Avoidance can surface in different arenas, sometimes unpredictably.

Luckily there is a safer and more humane method to get a well-trained dog, and this method promotes mental health and a good relationship between you and your dog and between your dog and other people.

Dogs in today's society must learn to cope with a vast number of noises and novel experiences. The puppy who is socially deprived is often the animal who exhibits fearful and aggressive responses to his environment. Prevention of this is obviously the best medicine, but if you have an older dog who was a puppy who missed out on a lot, then you need to make up for lost time. If your adult dog is frightened of humans and cringes or hides behind you when someone approaches, you have a dog with "avoidance behaviour." To overcome this, you need to generate bold, non-avoidant behaviours and reinforce them. This will involve patience on your part and understanding of appropriate timing so the dog begins to understand that Being Brave is Better!

Secrets for Success

Secret #1: Do not reassure your fearful dog! None of this "It's okay, sweet-pea," while you stroke him lovingly. Since dogs do not understand the subtle nuances of the English language, and, in their human-to-dog interactions, learn primarily by association, the message the dog receives here is: "My caretaker likes the way I am behaving RIGHT NOW. Therefore, I will continue to behave fearfully because that is what is receiving reinforcement."

Secret #2: Ignore all fearful behaviour to the best of your ability. If you must do anything, control the situation physically as best you can by requesting a Sit or some other attainable behaviour. It does not matter what the behaviour is, as long as it is "gettable."

Secret #3: Apply reinforcement to any behaviour that can be perceived as:

- Moving forward
- Less fearful than the last reaction in this context
- Less fearful body language

Body Postures

Postures that might indicate that your dog is feeling stress are:

- Lip Licking (out of context)
- Pupil Dilation (out of context)
- Sniffing the ground (out of context)

Remember: any dog who is feeling stress is more likely to escalate into aggression.

Accelerated discomfort spilling over into Agonistic Display may be indicated by some of the following:

- Urination.
- Excessive Salivation.
- Slinking postures.
- Rolling over on the back and retracting the lips – here is an animal in severe conflict and quite likely to nail you.
- Lowering or tucking of the tail.
- Ears pulled back horizontally.
- Piloerection reflex (hair standing up on the back of the neck, back and perhaps extending down the tail region. Some look nearly like a cat with the bottle brush tail).
- Growling.
- Snapping.
- Head and neck slightly lowered, looking up at you out of the "tops" of the eyes.
- Any sudden stillness – this often happens just prior to a "Strike," or Lunge culminating in a bite.

For the dog who is using aggression to get out of situations that makes him feel uncomfortable or fearful, behaviour modification involves treating both the fear and the aggression.

Basic Protocol

This protocol is really only applicable if your dog has anxiety or fear-based aggression around humans. It can be used to prevent the cautious or downright fearful dog from becoming aggressive with humans.

Teach a really good Sit & Remain Calm. This is not "obedience," per se. Teach the Sit with all positives: no punishers beyond a NRM or gentle pressure on the collar; no collar corrections made by jerking. What you are applying reinforcement to is Sit & Remain Calm. Practice this Sit & Remain Calm in as many contexts as you possibly can. The goal here is not just to hold the Sit-Stay, but to Sit and Relax. How can you tell? The dog will focus on the handler and the food. He will begin to look calm, he will cease rapid, hyperactive-looking movements. His eyes will become softer, with less dilated pupils. The tension will go out of his jaw. He will begin to ignore distractions.

Make sure your dog is hungry before you begin the following exercises.

Approximation #1

In the exercises below, if your dog will not "take" the treat from the person, have the person just toss the treat on the ground and allow the dog to come get the treat. The person should not reach toward the dog as the dog is eating the treat off the ground.

1. Put the dog on a light line or leash at least 6 to 8 feet long.
2. Dogs tend to find humans less threatening if they are not facing them with the human staring them in the eye. Provide a known person with some yummies. Have the person walk ahead of you slowly, holding his arms at his sides, with a piece of food in each hand. The food must be obvious to the dog.
3. Allow your dog to catch up and take the food. The person should relinquish the food while still moving slowly away from the dog.

   The good thing here is that the dog is being reinforced only for bold forward movement. The dog made the decision to investigate rather than avoid. The human was seen as an asset rather than something to fear.
4. The "stranger" should get more food ready and do this 3 or 4 times. Then pause for a few seconds as the dog takes the food.
5. Now modify this slightly by having the stranger partially turned toward the dog.
6. Next, have the person call the dog from a few steps away. Initially, he might be squatting sideways with his eyes pointing down or away from the dog. The person should offer yummies.
7. Try this with the helper standing. As the dog approaches, let him have the yummies, then step quietly away from the dog so he doesn't feel threatened. Watch the dog carefully here: he may find any movement provocative and may lunge.

8. Do this with as many people as you can. First with known persons, then advancing to unknown persons who can follow directions.

Raise criteria with each new person, as follows:

1. Food without Touch.
2. Food Together with Touch.
3. Touch then Food.
4. Touch then Food intermittently.

Other Exercises and Management Strategies

- The key here is to make the dog feel more self-confident overall. Do 5 or 10 minutes of formal obedience using positive methods. Sit, Down, Stay, Fetch. Teach some tricks.
- Start on an Enrichment Program. Take the dog one new place every week. Take him to the vet, have the techs give the dog a yummie and go home. Any situation like this is good. The key is to build the dog's confidence in new situations so he begins to have the self-confidence to cope instead of responding fearfully.
- A TTouch program will be of great use to you. This is not a "massage" program, although a massage program will also be of benefit to you. There are books and videos available about TTouch techniques. These materials are listed in the Suggested Reading section.
- Remember: Reinforce only those movements that show the dog is moving forward and becoming bolder. Ignore any behaviour you do not like.
- Do not reach toward this dog from a frontal position. Do not reach toward him if he is cornered! Do not reach toward this animal if his perception is that there is no escape (e.g., when in a crate, under a bed or table). Call the dog to you and ask for a Sit & Remain Calm.
- Never, ever physically punish a fearful dog. Physical punishment will prove to the dog that he was right in his assumption that you meant him harm. You will validate his fearful response and promote defensive behaviour.
- While you are putting a Behavioural Protocol in place, do not put the dog in any situations where he might "Practice" aggression. Big No-No! Until the dog is ready for that situation under controlled circumstances, just keep him out of trouble.
- Do not reinforce inappropriate behaviour inadvertently by "reassuring" the dog. As far as he is concerned, this is validating his fearful emotional response.
- Warn anyone who comes into contact with the dog that the dog is in training and may be unpredictable. If in doubt, muzzle the dog – that keeps most people at a distance. This allows the dog to gain confidence without strangers constantly approaching, and relieves the handler of worrying about a bite. Do not let the muzzle make you, the handler, complacent. You are training. Keep this dog out of trouble. If the actions that precede a bite take place – even if they do not culminate in a bite because the dog couldn't open his mouth – he is still Practicing aggression.

Outside the box: How to train people to behave when they come into contact with your dog:

No direct eye contact. Have the person stand next to you or laterally to the dog, not frontally. Have the person ignore the dog, even if the dog sniffs him. If the dog does sniff him, the handler should praise the dog, the "stranger" should continue to ignore, until the dog is very confident – then approaches should be made in very small increments with the dog guiding the way.

Controlled or Strategic Retreat

Do not allow your dog to practice "flight" behaviour. If you do not prevent flight behaviour, your dog will never learn to access any other kind of behaviour as a first response. Just keep him near you, even if that involves you doing a sort of Sit Restraint exercise to give him confidence (refer to "Handling & Restraint" protocol). You may try then asking for a quick "Any Behaviour You Think He Will Do" (Sit, Shake, Look, whatever); when your dog even tries to comply with this, or actually manages to give you a quick look or sit, Mark It & Feed It (if he will take the treat). Then, you may cue the dog and do a Strategic Retreat by moving away from the scary thing with him looking at you. This technique at least allows you some semblance of control, and will actually provide structure and help to modify the current initial flight reaction into a different first response.

Once you have done a Strategic Retreat, try moving back into the "scary area" again and begin another trial. Try to remain in the area a second or two longer this time. See if you can get two different behaviours that are known and on cue.

If the dog is going to come into contact with guests in your home, the following instructions should be observed:

1. Place the dog in another room, or crate him.
2. When guests are in and things have settled down, the dog may be introduced to the guests in the following manner:
3. The dog may come out only if he is quiet in the "holding" area.
4. Place the dog on leash. Hold the leash, but try to keep the leash loose.
5. A head collar and/or a muzzle may be appropriate.
6. The dog may come into the "guest" area and Sit & Remain Calm. Or he may lie down next to you and relax.
7. School your "guests" so they agree to allow the dog to approach them, without reaching toward the dog.
8. The dog must Sit & Remain Calm. The guests must not reach out to the dog in the initial stages of training. It may be only after several visits that the dog becomes "unstressed" enough to take a treat dropped on the floor by a guest, or accept a treat from her hand.
9. Minimize any stressful behaviour by moving away yourself with the dog and asking for Sit & Remain Calm.
10. Minimize sudden movements and noises, introducing the dog to these circumstances in a gradually appreciating manner, coupling them with reinforcement.
11. If the dog approaches any visitor, canine or human, he should be requested to Sit & Remain Calm by the guest and this should be "backed up" by you if he does not immediately comply for the guest.

CAUTION: If your dog has shown any aggression toward children, you should get help from a behaviour consultant immediately. There are a couple of great books on dogs and kids. One is *Dogs & Kids: Parenting Tips* by Bardi McLennan (1993). *Your Ideal Dog* by David and Ruth Weston (1997) has a section on dogs and kids.

Interaction with small children should be very closely supervised. The dog should wear a collar, headcollar (and a muzzle if you are remotely nervous about this), and a leash. NO EXCEPTIONS. Once your dog proves to you that he is safe around children, you may relax a bit, but do not take any chances where dogs and children are concerned!

If the dog shows stress in the presence of small children, he is telling you something. Respect this. You may ask the dog to Sit & Remain Calm just for a second, then put the dog away in a room or other safe area away from the children unless you are going to be in immediate and constant supervision. If you are extremely concerned about your dog's reaction to children, place the dog "away" before the children arrive, and bring him out when things have calmed down. This is definitely a circumstance where you must "Choose Your Own Species." Prevent trouble with children by being proactive and responsible. And remember, muzzles are always better than stitches.

Acclimating the Dog to Bizarre Human Behaviour

Desensitizing the dog to garden-variety human behaviour is quite a project. In addition, we have such a wide selection of bizarre human behaviour to choose from.

Let's begin with relatively normal human behaviour that dogs might find alarming, such as eye contact, touching, and collar and muzzle grabs (see the protocols for "Involvement" and "Handling & Restraint"). Once your dog is accustomed to daily stuff, you can advance to the bizarre (but often exhibited!) human behaviour. Halloween comes once a year. It is a weird spectacle for me to watch sometimes, and I am a member of the participating species.

Acclimate your dog to the following kinds of human approaches. This follows all the normal human approaches. You may or may not have to break the approximations for each Challenge into tiny steps, depending on how your dog assimilates the information.

Sky (who suffers from personal space issues, neophobia, and is very uneasy with many human behaviours), is a mature Australian Shepherd bitch who belongs to a friend of mine. Janea loves to play all sorts of games with her dogs. In one of them, she stalks the dog, then races around with her, then lavishes hugs and kisses on the dog. The dogs love it! Except Sky, who was terrified of any sort of human behaviour she didn't see a thousand times. Janea got this dog as a puppy, and the rest of the litter is of quite a normal temperament. But Sky suffers from at least a disorder, if not downright abnormality, in the lack of her ability to adapt to changing surroundings. Janea and I are in concert on the thought that, since the dog is living with humans, within reason, she must learn to adapt to what humans behave like. Also, as long as the human is not harming the dog, it is a good exercise for the dog to learn that situations she has found to be frightening can be coped with, and in fact, are not threatening. It took Janea about a year of work, but now when Janea play-stalks Sky, she no longer flips out with displays of intense panic and avoidance behaviours. Sky has even started to enjoy this funny game and play back.

- Stalking – lean forward and advance slowly, then toss treats and/or play a game when you get near the dog. No deliberately frightening the dog during this exercise – such as yelling "Boo!" or other sudden frightening events. The stalking itself is probably terrifying enough at first! If your dog begins to display overt defense behaviour or overt aggression of any kind, stop immediately. Stalk from a further distance, practice safe behaviour, and control the setting events with leashes and muzzles. Use whatever it takes to make this a safe exercise. Stalk for one second, then throw a handful of hot dogs and continue to increase criteria from there. Some dogs immediately identify this as human play behaviour and will joyfully respond with play bows and "tail-on-fire" running behaviours.
- Run at the dog.
- Bounce around.
- Wear a variety of hats.
- Wear head-phones.

I had my GSD bitch, Maeve, about eight or nine months, and she was very good with my family, once she identified them as important to me. She would have, at that time, happily protected my daughter Abbey from a threat and had readily accepted her as a family member. (You can interpret this to mean, with a guarding dog, that anyone who bothers a resident "sheep" is in for some trouble!) I was sitting at the dining room table doing some paperwork and Maeve was lying under the table. We were both facing the staircase. Abbey came down the staircase wearing a new set of head phones. She got about half-way down the stairs when I felt electricity in the air. I glanced down at my shepherd, who was rising slowly from under the table, in a definite guarding posture, her eyes trained on Abbey. It was one of those vignettes that begins to move in slow motion because it is potentially "bad" and out of your immediate control. I knew I could not get between them quickly enough, so I prompted Abbey to speak to Maeve, while I was in the process of trying to get out of my chair and move between them. But my intervention was not even remotely necessary. The moment Abbey said "Hey, Maeve," Maeve immediately began wiggling and wagging. "Oh, it's you." Then Maeve said (yes I am indulging in a bit of anthropomorphism), "Hey, yourself – what is that thing you have on your head!?!?" Maeve has never reacted since to people wearing any kind of head phones, but obviously that was the first set she'd ever laid eyes on. Just shows you how something we feel is simple and take for granted is very alarming and puzzling for our dogs, with the vastly different sensory input they have compared to us humans.

Photo by Brenda Aloff.

Salsa is surely not enamored with this bird-woman! But because of past training, and the trust that has built up between her and her owner as they went through the process of Behaviour Modification, instead of avoidance, panic, or defensive snapping and growling, Salsa holds her ground and is well rewarded for her success. Note how calmly Patti is behaving – alert and watchful so she can give Salsa appropriate feedback, but relaxed and supportive at the same time.

Salsa originally came to see me (actually her owner Patti made the appointment...) because she was so fearful that she could not withstand the stress at Dog Shows or the exam that the judges do in the Conformation Ring, and she was exhibiting fearful avoidance and defensive behaviour.

Salsa's behaviour is quite amazing considering what we started with. She is taking a frontal advance and direct eye contact from bird-woman. After this, a mere human judge in the show ring should be a breeze! And in fact, it was. After several months of diligent work, Salsa waltzed into the Breed Ring and didn't just put up with it – she had a great time and finished her AKC Championship easily.

Garage sales are great sources of masks and other stuff. Janea (bird-woman) is holding a device that makes your voice sound like Darth Vader. Flowing clothing, carrying umbrellas, wearing hats, sounding funny, wheelchairs, walkers – all of these are excellent for this exercise. Keep the experience positive.

Acclimating Salsa To Bizarre Human Behaviour

- Wear halloween masks. I buy a variety on sale. I am fortunate; my friends Janea and Karen haunt garage sales for treasures that work well for these exercises.
- Wear flowing clothes, capes, wrap a sheet around yourself, wear different kinds of hats, silly wigs, anything you can think of.
- Carry an umbrella. Go easy with this one, dogs are very frightened of the umbrella opening suddenly. Begin at a distance and raise criteria as the dog dictates.
- Carry a dowel or a yard stick.
- Use a cane, crutches, a walker.
- Get the dog around wheelchairs.

This work is very important. Dogs are going to encounter many things as they live with humans that humans take for granted as non-alarming. In the dog's paradigm, and with his different vision, olfactory and auditory input, all of these novel items might be cause for defensive behaviour. To really know your dog is safe, and so that he trusts you when you tell him, "This will not hurt you," it is wise to expose the dog to as many different stimuli as you can come up with.

This protocol produces a truly socialized dog, one who can quickly and calmly adapt to a wide variety of novel stimuli. That's not just Socialization – that's Sophistication!

49

Level III	
Pre-requisite	Foundation Behaviours Level I Behaviours Level II Behaviour: Desensitization to being touched

RESOURCE GUARDING (GARDEN VARIETY POSSESSIVE AGGRESSION)

OR:

GIVE ME THAT – IT'S MINE!

What is "Resource Guarding?" Just what it sounds like. If the dog considers something valuable (a resource), she will guard it. For a moment, step back in time, and reduce your view of the world to that of biology and basic survival. Historically, for social predators and scavengers (such as dogs), dinner required a big expenditure of energy, and you potentially had a lot of "misses" before you "caught" dinner. It is pretty normal behaviour to guard whatever one considers to be valuable. Now, this is the dog's perception of valuable, not yours. Dogs generally don't guard money, even if it falls on the ground. But food, toys, and locations are valuable resources to a dog. As are people. Some dogs really get into guarding Kleenex™ or Q-Tips™ or other objects. Remember, the dog's perception of what is valuable is what counts here, not yours.

Resource Guarding shows up frequently in domestic dogs even though there is an endless supply of kibble and love and hundreds of generations of selective breeding. As a survival trait, you can see how it would be advantageous – Nice Guys Finish Last, and, in the wild, you suffer if you give dinner away. So Resource Guarding would be a trait selected for in The Jungle, and, obviously, much less desirable in Our Living Room. Just because guarding can be classified as relatively normal behaviour does not mean it is acceptable behaviour.

Just to show you how weird – I mean interesting – it can get, take the following anecdote. My daughter's dog is an intact male Smooth Fox Terrier. Sport adores his mummy. As males go, he is exceptionally easygoing and, as Smooth males go, he is off the chart in being "good natured" with other dogs. My point is that he is one of the most non-aggressive dogs I have ever met – of any breed. But he adores my daughter. His one shortcoming (from a human viewpoint) is Resource Guarding. He's not too possessive about food. But fuzzy toys he definitely will guard with considerable vehemence.

One day my daughter brought her violin case in and set it by the stairs. (Remember, she is valuable to him and her scent is all over this violin case.) First, he marked the violin case. Yes folks – he peed on it to show ownership. (My actions here are not what concern this discussion – basically I cleaned up after him.) About five minutes later, one of the other family dogs, a bitch who can clean his clock, walked by the violin case. Whatever boundary line Sport had decided upon had been crossed and he lunged at Punch snarling and snapping. This is one instance of what Resource Guarding can look like. Had I not happened to see him mark the case five minutes earlier, I would have had no idea what precipitated Sport's "idiopathic" reaction. As we can see here, it was not idiopathic aggression at all, but Resource Guarding. "This belongs to 'mom,' therefore, me; I am guarding it; don't go near it."

Resource Guarding can wear many faces. Be observant and figure out what the triggers are. List them. Then manage behaviour carefully to avoid the triggers whenever possible, while simultaneously setting up situations where you can manufacture and reinforce correct behaviour. My field experience bears out my belief: "Once a Resource Guarder – Always a Resource Guarder." This can be very hard-wired behaviour, and has a hereditary basis in some cases. In most instances, the behaviour can be managed and modified to acceptable levels. In houses where there are children involved, I tend to be extremely conservative, and if the behaviour cannot be managed well, I recommend placing the dog, depending on the severity and presentation of the behaviour.

Modifying behaviour in a puppy is obviously easier, if only from the standpoint that a puppy is smaller and, if he does nip or bite, you the damage will be much less. The puppy or young dog does not have the extensive and successful reinforcement history for guarding that the adult dog has.

When working with a dog who is Resource Guarding, do not pooh-pooh the gravity of the behaviour. Although the objects a dog may choose to guard (paper towels) may seem ludicrous to you, the dog is dead serious about this.

Use caution. Punishment is most definitively not the most effective way to deal with this problem. Most notably, punishment is contra-indicated because it is so difficult to time the punisher properly. Also, the dog is already in a defensive, guarding state and so anything you do to punish will increase the defensive behaviour and further muddy the waters. The dog becomes confused because you are punishing a behaviour that is so innate to him that he really does not make the connection *you* are thinking he should.

There is also the distinct possibility that punishment will make the dog more aggressive and aggressive sooner into the sequence. As an example, the dog begins aggression at a greater distance to their food bowl than previously. Aggression will get you aggression back in many cases – so then what is the dog practicing? You got it! The important thing to remember here is the goal – *a non-aggressive response about resources*. By introducing punishment, you may win that battle, but lose the war. The danger of "fallout" from the use of punishment is certain in this scenario.

High priority exercises for puppies for prevention of Resource Guarding are:

Food Bowl Exercises: The Food Be With You

Prerequisite: RM/NRM

When your dog/puppy is eating, be around. Don't just put food in the bowl and leave. Sit beside her, and pet her and put your hands in the bowl. Occasionally drop really yummy treats in as you dangle your hands in the bowl – you know, little pieces of cheese or pizza. Really Good Stuff. The idea here is to let the dog understand you aren't interested in taking her kibble and eating it yourself. Through repeated experiences, the dog will come to understand that when humans are near the food bowl, Really Good Stuff shows up for consumption.

With any dog that is unfamiliar to you in this specific situation, do not behave in a rash manner, or it is quite possible you will receive a bite. Observe the dog's body language carefully. Before a dog snaps/bites, she will warn you. There will be a "typical" guarding posture coupled with a split-second of stillness. Many dogs will crouch slightly and have a tension in their face and body. The dog's eyes will be "hard," and the pupils may be very dilated. Then, "the vorpal blade goes snickersnack"[1] – the snap or bite occurs. Sometimes a dog will growl softly or rumble deep in her chest prior to snapping.

With any animal you don't know well, or for one you do and have known to be dicey in the past, initially do any reaching toward or work around the food bowl with the Assess-a-Hand. It has saved my fingers on many happy occasions. On every occasion I have used it, this tool has, at the very least, kept my anxiety level lower!

To continue with Food Bowl training: Practice taking the food bowl away, then really sprucing up dinner. Add a little cottage cheese, yogurt, egg, or whatever. Walk up to the dish while the dog is eating and add a tasty morsel. The message you want to send is: Humans and Food Bowls in close approximation is a good predictor for Really Good Stuff.

To generalize the response, have other people repeat the exercises that you have done. The younger the puppy is when you begin this work, the better. These are also Trust and Self-Confidence Builders. To quote Jean Donaldson, "Any kind of resource guarding stems from insecurity and paranoia. The dog operates under the assumption that someone approaching her soggy raw-hide or bowlful of kibble is a major life-or-death deal" (Donaldson, 1996, p.78). I think about it like this: Dogs are going to assume that you are thinking like they are and, if it is valuable to them, then you must find it valuable, too. If you were a dog, you would covet the article and try to gain and maintain possession of it.

For older dogs or puppies who have a prior history of risky behaviour, go slowly and carefully. Wear heavy gloves or have a muzzle on the dog to begin with. Use the Assess-a-Hand.

Exercise for dogs who have a history of snapping or growling, or guarding articles from humans by assuming a "guarding" body posture:

1. To begin, this dog no longer eats from a bowl. She receives all of her kibble from your hand for doing various motivationally taught obedience exercises or tricks. Do this for 5 to 10 days.
2. Next, do the above exercises, but near the dog's food bowl – which is *empty.* Repeat for 2 to 5 days.
3. Put the dog in a Sit or Down Stay about 5 feet from the bowl. Have the dog dragging a leash. You can use an assistant who is out at the end of the leash. Put a small handful of kibble in the bowl. Release the dog to go eat the food. Follow her towards the bowl, but hang back beyond the threshold distance. Pick up the lash, and back away from the dish and call her. Place her in a Sit or Down and repeat. Each time a repetition goes well at a given distance, in the next trial, follow the dog a step closer.

1. From the poem by Lewis Carroll, *The Jabberwocky.*

Eventually you will be at the bowl with the dog.

4. Then you can begin walking or moving around near the bowl as the dog is eating. This is adding motion to the equation.
5. Next, you will increase the distance you "follow" back to the first threshold distance. Instead of remaining standing, squat down. Now you will gradually decrease distance again, over several trials, until you are squatting next to the dog's bowl. Ask the dog for a known behaviour or two near the bowl, and reinforce the dog by feeding her from your hand sometimes and by releasing her to her bowl sometimes.
6. Approach the empty bowl and the dog, put a small handful of food in, retreat. Repeat 5 to 10 times.
7. Approach the empty bowl and the dog, remove the bowl, put a handful of food in, release the dog to eat. You can do this as above with the dog on a Sit Stay (restrained from behind) or with her just standing next to the empty bowl. Decide which is most appropriate. Repeat 5 to 10 times.
8. Sit next to the empty bowl and the dog, stroke and talk to the dog while adding tasty treats to the bowl at random intervals. Keep one hand on the bowl.
9. Sit next to the bowl while the dog is eating her kibble. Remove your hand from the bowl to add the tasty treat to the bowl. Be careful. *This is a big step* for the dog; *motion* around the food bowl is very provocative.
10. Approach the bowl while the dog is eating, remove the bowl, add the yummy, replace the bowl, and repeat 5 to 10 times.
11. If you receive a "warning" at any time, back up and repeat the steps, beginning back 2 or 3 steps from where you currently are. If you cannot get close to the bowl, find the threshold distance and toss the food at the dog from that distance. Be careful – again, the motion of throwing the food at the dog could be very provocative.

Photo essay by Sam Ziegenmeyer.

D'Art has a long and illustrious history of food-bowl guarding. To work with him, Pat places D'Art in a Down-Stay at a slight distance from the food bowl. He is reinforced by having the food tossed to him from a distance. Having him tied back or held back on a leash is a necessary move for the first several sessions. Note in the "Down" picture, D'Art is giving Pat a Look-Away (calming signal).

Down Near Food Bowl

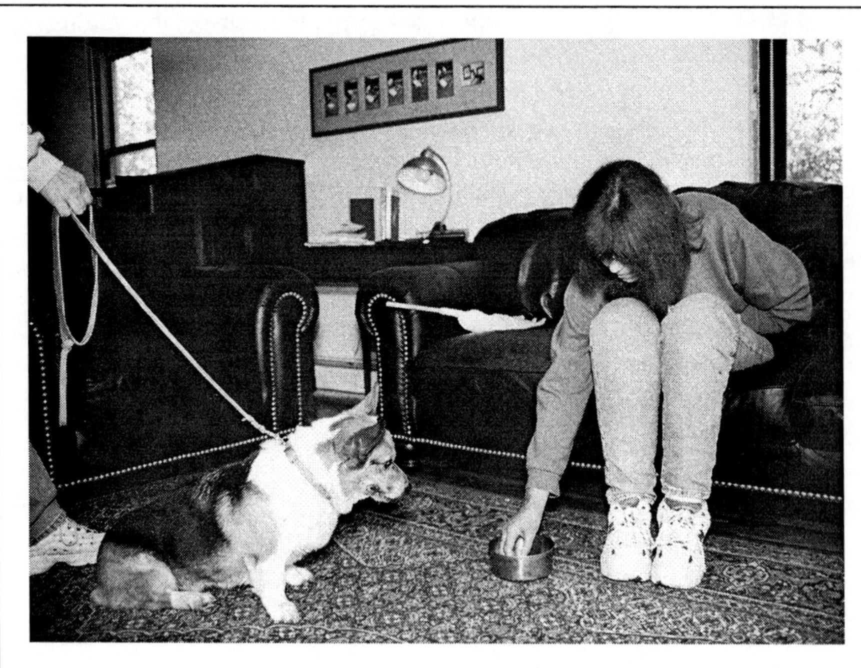

D'Art is leashed for safety. Pat places some tid-bits in the bowl, while D'Art maintains his Sit-Stay.

Food Bowl Work

Pat uses the Assess-a-Hand to reach near the bowl.

Using the Assess-a-Hand

Begin at Step #1 with another person. If you are working with children, obviously, never put them at even the slightest risk. (Have the dog tied back if required.)

If the dog is guarding the food bowl and a child is around, crate the dog to eat to ensure the children's safety. Make certain that "dropped food" on the floor does not elicit the same response as approaching the dog's food bowl. Some are general food-guarders, other specifically guard the food bowl only, and not dropped food on the kitchen floor or at the dining room table. If you are unsure, keep the dog away from the child if any food is going to be involved. If the dog and the child reach for dropped food at the same time, the results can be disastrous.

If you have a dog who ferociously guards the bowl and children are living in the home (not just visiting), I would recommend you do some very serious thinking about this arrangement and the possible ramifications.

If you get into a hole – stop digging! If you feel afraid or lack confidence – Stop! If the dog is an explosive guarder or biter or lunges toward you at any time, get the help of a qualified trainer or behaviourist. Shop carefully, check their methods, and make sure you feel comfortable where you are going with this.

Object Guarding: One Species' Trash is Another Species' Treasure

Prerequisite: Foundation Protocols, Level I "Cease & Desist."
Handy: "Sit & Down," "Come When Called."
Refer also to "Twos" protocol for further ideas.

Some dogs appear to be almost compulsive about Object Guarding. Their actions appear to be extremely reflexive and not really under their control. Others seem motivated by the fact that *you* seem so entranced with that Kleenex, Q-tip, toilet paper or hamburger wrapper. Look at the following scenario. The dog comes into the living room with a used Q-tip he has filched from the Treasure Trove. (We call it the bathroom trash.) You immediately dive on the dog, chasing him if necessary, the whole time yelling and trying to wrestle the item away from him. Does it look like you think this is a valuable item? You betcha! Is this a good attention getter? Yo! The dog has been nudging her slimy tennis ball toward you for the last hour and you are sick of tossing it across the floor and wish to find out "whodunit" in your murder mystery. So the dog appears with the used Q-tip and voila! You emerge from the depths of the sofa to play this great game with a vengeance.

You need to prepare the dog for the day that you need to take something from her. Because, trust me, that day will come! Dogs will eat all manner of junk, including excrement, Kleenex, tinfoil, and the knobs off the dryer if they can climb up and reach them. Canis is an extremely successful species and this is one of the reasons that they are. Picky Eaters don't survive all that long in The Jungle.

The goal here is to teach the dog that when humans take things, they usually give them back. And you always get this Really Tasty Treat in exchange. Therefore it is Win-Win. You win, the dog wins.

First, make sure that any object that the dog has guarded in the past is no longer available. Period. If you try to take a prized possession away before the dog is prepared with an extensive reinforcement history, you are looking at a Lose-Win scenario. That is, you lose, the dog "wins," and you set your training back seriously. That is also a great way to get bitten.

For Object Guarding, you will practice object exchanges. Begin with an object the dog is lackadaisical about and is unlikely to guard.

Establish a "Trade-Me" cue, like Drop It, Thank You, Out, or whatever you are going to use. If you have been unsuccessfully using a word already, change the cue you are using.

Approximation #1

I love Sue Sternberg's technique of walking by the dog and saying "Drop It," and then tossing down, near the dog, a tasty treat. Without pausing, continue to casually walk by.

My preference is to do this first approximation when the dog doesn't have any objects around at all. This conditions the dog to look at you and anticipate a pleasant event when he hears "Drop It." This is very much preferred to the dog shifting into a defensive state and assuming that "Drop It" is Fightin' Words.

This exercise will also help with those dogs who are not aggressive, but may be slightly possessive, grabbing kleenex and socks at will. It is also effective with those dogs who have discovered that, no matter how busy you are, they can engage you in a great chase game if they streak by with your new fifteen dollar panties from Victoria's Secret, or one of the kid's toys.

It's mine, mine, mine! Note the lowered head and neck and the looking up at you out of the top of the eyes. This is an unmistakable guarding posture.

Typical "Guarding" Posture

Approximation #2

1. Wait until the dog has an object or toss the dog an object.
2. From a distance, firmly give the "Drop It" cue.
3. Follow by dropping or tossing a treat to the dog.
4. Walk away or continue walking from the area.

Gradually make this distance less and less, until you can walk up to the dog while she has an object, shove treats toward the dog with the Assess-a-Hand (or your own if the dog has not shown aggression to you in the past) or toss the treats down.

Approximation #3

1. Give the dog the object.
2. Say "drop it" or "out" or "thank you" in a Pleasant Tone. (Whatever your "trade me" cue happens to be.)
3. Trade the object for a cookie.

Depending on the degree of possessiveness this animal exhibits, this may mean throwing an entire handful of great treats to keep the dog busy

for a bit so you can get the "object." Or, it may mean placing an extremely high-value treat like a couple of tablespoons of tuna or cat food on a plate as your Trade.
4. Return the Object.

Many of the Fox Terriers I have gotten in Rescue are fierce guarders of objects or food items. I do this protocol with all of them. Even the ones who start off lunging at me, snarling and snapping when I approach, end up being quite reasonable and very manageable. Mostly, people have taken things from the dog and frightened him in doing so, or people have hit and punished the dog over possessions, instead of teaching a peaceful trade.

Approximation #4

1. Say "Thank You" (or whatever your trade cue is), with no treat visible, while the dog has the valued object.
2. Then get the cookie from your pocket and give it to the dog.
3. Then return the Object.

The first time, do one successful exchange. Then get the heck out of Dodge. Walk away.

Work up to two, then vary between one and five exchanges consecutively and walk away. Vary the object as time passes, working toward more valuable objects. The dog's perception of valuable – not yours. Therefore, dirty underwear and icky-ear-wax-Q-tips are the Very Valuable Object.

After you have "set up" several exchanges over a period of 5 to 7 days, be prepared with cookies and try to take a chew toy that the dog has just picked up off the floor. Sometimes exchange kibble, sometimes something really special, such as cheese or steak. Vary the reward according to the value of the object.

After a while, you can trade the object for just a cookie.

The next step is to do the above with different people. Proceed with all safety measures in check here: use gloves, leashes, Halti's and muzzles to absolutely ensure the safety of your helper. The helper must also be capable of not acting panicky, nor leaping around and screaming at inopportune moments.

Next, move to "hotter" objects. That means rawhides and greasy hamburger paper. By the time you are ready to try the Really Valuable Objects, you will have to leave a Kleenex or greasy, yucky paper on the floor so the dog can get it, and then you can make the object exchange.

Believe it or not, enough repetition and correct management of the situation yields a dog who is eager to give up objects. You may create a monster – like my own little Punch, who brings me various objects to exchange for treats. She will rummage in Abbey's book bag and produce a half-eaten sandwich, but, instead of eating it or chewing up the plastic wrap, she gleefully seeks me out and relinquishes her find for a treat I provide. True, this is a sometimes irritating, but never dangerous, habit. And one I find vastly preferable to my dog biting a child or guest who ventured too near a slimy piece of rawhide. Also if you don't find it amusing (I must admit I do), you can then fade that habit by not reinforcing it.

Some of the stuff my dogs manage to bring me is quite amazing. My Bassett Hound actually brought me the vacuum once, and Breanna, who can unzip anything, fetched (or perhaps filched) me a bunch of stuff at a dog show from someone else's training bag while I was standing nearby chatting (blissfully unaware of her heathen-like behaviour). She had brought me several objects one at a time (including a dumbbell, collar, dog toy, and a bait bag), when an amused bystander finally pointed out the items at my feet.

Children should not be allowed to deal with a dog who is a known Resource Guarder. The risk is too great. It is easy to frighten children, who will then behave in a manner that is not conducive to fixing the dog's problem. If this occurs, you now have TWO problems, a scared, and maybe, injured child in addition to the dog. Children should *always be under the supervision* of adults when around dogs. If your dog guards objects and children will be around, pick up ALL the objects. Watch like a hawk. If you cannot watch like a hawk, confine the dog safely until you can.

Dogs do not generalize well. If the dog's Resource Guarding appears to stem from hard-wired behaviour, you will always be managing this problem. This means management and constant review of exchanges for the life of the dog.

Prevention is absolutely the best "cure." Beginning these exercises with each young puppy holds far less risk for humans than rehabilitating an adult with well-entrenched habits, big teeth, and strong jaws.

Don't encourage any dog to guard any objects. Make it clear that you are calling the shots in a non-confrontational way using formal obedience, tricks, and daily life. Teach that it is fun to obey and in the dog's best interest to do so. Ultimately, this is how you create an animal who voluntarily makes the "right" decisions in a human world. This is Learned Behaviour!

Location Guarding: Green Eggs and Ham

Prerequisite: Foundation Protocols; "Cease & Desist" protocol; "The Zen Sit and Down Stay," "Come When Called."

Another type of Resource Guarding is Location Guarding. The dog jumps on the sofa and prevents a person from sharing the space by using social-distancing maneuvers such as growling, snapping, and lunging. The best protection here, again, is prevention. If you are going to allow the dog on the furniture, practice getting the dog off and on the furniture. If the dog is not allowed on furniture, the dog still needs to understand about humans around sleeping areas.

Begin the dog ASAP with moving over on the floor, on the sofa, on the bed. Use placement commands and reinforce the behaviour with food treats and play. Practice by encouraging the dog up onto the chair, then using "Off," then your prompter, if required, followed by a food treat. The best thing is not to use the food itself to lure the dog off the sofa or out of the location, but to use prompts to do that. Make kissy sounds, move away from the area yourself, then provide the food treat once the dog complies. The treats can be on top of the TV or somewhere not overtly obvious, and definitely out of the dog's reach. No Self Serve!

If your dog has a history of location guarding, she must drag a leash so you can safely enforce placement or off cues until you have verbal control.

After a few repetitions of this, do a "Cold Trial." That is, wait until the dog is up on the chair and settled in. Then go over and use "Off," followed by any prompters required, followed by Really Good Stuff. Really Good Stuff needs to be variable. Food is good, but so is "Great! Lets go for Walkies" or "Yes! Frisbee" or "Wanna play ball?"

It is essential to your success that you do not bribe. Saying "Walkies" to GET the dog off the furniture is far different than saying "Off," getting compliance, and then saying "Yes! Walkies!" The first teaches the dog manipulative behaviour. The second actually modifies behaviour and teaches your dog about behaviour-consequence contingencies. Keep a handle on the training idea and remember that reinforcement follows compliance. The Technical Lingo is "ABC," as follows: 1. Antecedent (Cue/Prompt/Command); 2. Behaviour (dog gives some sort of behaviour); 3. Consequence (the ball is in your court – you decide what you will use for reinforcement).

Summary

Prevention is the best path to take. Do these exercises with your puppy, before any problems develop. If you are dealing with a known Resource Guarder, proceed cautiously with all safe-guards in place (leashes, muzzles, etc.) and, if the behaviour gets worse instead of better with your efforts, it may be time to proceed with the help of an experienced Behaviourist. Make human safety, especially for children, paramount.

Teach on and off the bed and the sofa; in and out of the car, the house, the crate. The whole Green Eggs and Ham Thing: Will you eat them in a box, will you eat them with a fox? Dogs who are raised to be happy about obeying and being cooperative are so much less likely to have aggression problems. If you think about the fact that biting is very normal dog behaviour, it gives you pause and motivation to prevent any problems from occurring down the road.

Other Smart Stuff to Do:

Another mandatory exercise is handle-ability. (Refer to protocol "Handling & Restraint.") The dog should be familiar with all sorts of touch, all over his body. TTouch and massage are both good ways to introduce touching. Make touch fun and pleasurable. Get the dog accustomed to being tightly restrained, like a child would hug him. Gradually increase the amount and length of restraint, one element at a time. Proceed safely. If you get an adverse reaction, back up and use lots of cookies. Allowing humans to handle the dog is another Self-Confidence and Trust builder. If the dog feels relaxed and comfortable in the presence of all humans, and understands that humans have rather odd body language, but are basically harmless creatures that often provide Really Good Stuff, she is much less likely to engage in guarding behaviours. The first requirement for guarding behaviour is a suspicious attitude toward the guardee – an attitude that is more difficult to maintain if she feels comfortable and non-threatened around humans.

Refer to the protocols "Twos," "Handling & Restraint," and "Yielding & Husbandry Behaviours," as well as the Foundation and Level I behaviours, for more help with Resource Guarding.

A great way to deal with guarding behaviour is also to teach a good retrieve. Retrieving and Guarding are non-compatible behaviours; they cannot exist simultaneously, assuming that part of the retrieve is the presentation. Begin with a good motivational retrieve. Keep in mind, a proper retrieve is not an overnight process and needs to be handled non-confrontationally.

50

Level III	
Pre-requisite	Foundation Behaviours Level I Behaviours: Have Fluency. Level II Behaviour: Handling & Restraint

DOG TO DOG APPROACHES

Goal	Your dog will allow other dogs to pass by and near him without reacting inappropriately with extreme play behaviour, or barking, lunging and growling, or by becoming so aroused he cannot pay attention to you.
What it teaches	Other dogs are not always available for play. They are not dangerous. It is not his business to run over and kick everybody's butt.

For these exercises, the dog is to wear a Halti. The dog should also be on his martingale collar. A muzzle is also requisite if your dog has shown ANY aggression to dogs in the past. Once it is determined the dog is well under control, non-reactive and actually relaxed, it may be okay to try the exercises without a muzzle for those dogs who must start out wearing one. However, the owner must be alert to any signs of body tension, stress or discomfort by the dog and must be able to safely move away from the other team to avoid any aggressive incidents. If your dog has shown any aggression toward other dogs in the past, it is also important, when you take the muzzle off, that the other dog you are working with is very steady and non-reactive. This is particularly crucial in the initial work. Otherwise, it is very easy to get into trouble! As your dog gains fluency, it is fine to move on to more challenging situations.

Just for a moment, let's look at expectations. Once you finish this protocol, it is still unrealistic to think you can immediately go to the dog park and let your dog go. These protocols are designed to build the relationship between you and your dog. My concern is that you understand your dog's language and that you and your dog have a communication system. It is the goal of this protocol that your dog see other dogs and immediately turn his attention to YOU.

While primarily for the dog who is already presenting with some problems, this protocol can still be used to teach your dog how to approach other dogs. Lucky you, the one who is preventing problems – you will be able to proceed quickly, and without a muzzle, to teach your dog to behave in a calm manner around other dogs.

Approaches

These are desensitization programs. Do not place your dog in circumstances beyond his current skill level, or yours. Aggression, in many cases, is merely a symptom of anxiety and fear. Only your dog can determine the rate at which he can learn new coping mechanisms to stem the underlying anxiety and fear. At the same time, while proceeding patiently, you must make sure you are raising criteria, therefore creating opportunities to reinforce ever more desirable behaviour. It is also important to know your dog and to have done enough training so that YOU make the right moves to obtain the behaviour or to apply damage control to the various difficulties that come up.

If lack of self-confidence or lack of education is at the heart of the aggression, then anxiety and fear are probably still the core causative factors.

If the relationship with your dog has been frequently marred by confrontation, then this causes concern. The protocols in this book are designed to place you and your dog in accord, so you can leave confrontation behind. This frees you up to work on the real issues at hand – the fact that your dog is "dog hot."

Whether fear, anxiety, relationship or some other concern is contributing to the problems you are facing with your dog, you must complete your "homework" before beginning this protocol. That means you have achieved fluency with all of the Foundation, Level I and the Handling and Restraint protocols. These protocols give you the tools to interrupt undesired behaviour *without exacerbating* other underlying factors that are contributing to the problem.

This means you must have excellent stimulus control with cues such as "Leave It" and "Here." Remember that success is defined by no aggressive events, and little to no reaction from your dog.

People tend to attribute aggression problems to "dominance." This is short-sighted in the extreme.

Mostly, it is just not clear to the dog that defaulting to the environment, instead of the handler, is incorrect. The dog has a deep-seated habit – defaulting to the environment and responding with knee-jerk arousal to environmental stimuli. This habit has been in place for so long that it is very difficult to interrupt when you first begin to do so. This is a relationship dilemma rather than a rank issue because the dog isn't trying to "dominate" you. She has just been allowed to practice the undesired behaviour. It is a relationship crisis because your dog, in this instance, is not including you in her decision-making process.

Many of my clients express, "My dog is so protective of me." This is their supposition about why the dog growls at approaching people or dogs. If you have not asked your dog to protect you, he is free-lancing. Free-lance protection jobs are not permitted in my household! I determine who comes and goes and who makes approaches. On the other hand, if you have not made it clear to your dog that you are making these determinations, he will quickly step in and fill your shoes. If you were in a small aircraft, and suddenly the pilot fell out of the seat, my guess is you'd probably give flying the aircraft a try, even if you didn't have a clue about driving a plane. I sure would! So it is with your dog. If you aren't manning the helm and it appears to him that someone ought to be, he will give it a whirl, even though he does not have the tools to make judgments about human social situations unless extensively trained to do so.

No matter whether aggression toward other dogs or people is a problem, or you are doing prevention work, this protocol is useful for teaching your dog to accept novel stimuli and feel good about accomplishment. Everything you do to boost your dog's self confidence will raise his bite threshold.

Photo essay by Joanne Weber.

Misty is looking at and just beginning to move toward Cotton. The rule is: If your dog is looking at something for more than 2 or 3 seconds, she is Alerting.

Marylu responds by immediately moving Misty away from Cotton and toward her, so Misty understands what she is supposed to be attending to: Marylu, always!

Note the loose leash. Misty's response is a result of Marylu merely stepping backwards. No verbal cue is necessary. This comes from endless repetition of moving away from distractions.

In the meantime, Diane asks Cotton to Sit and Look (and stop leaping) to minimize Misty's reaction. Smart, proactive handlers pay attention to the environment around them so they can diffuse arousal when possible.

This situation was set up on purpose, in this controlled manner, because Misty is quite predacious and movement makes her very reactive. This allows us to teach Misty to exhibit some self-control. Misty has been so difficult to handle that Marylu was afraid to take her on walks, concerned that Misty would knock her down and get loose. Misty, after a few months of work, has made vast improvement. She is walking with other dogs (on leash) during class and paying attention to Marylu, even when other dogs are walking by. We take the dogs in Resocialization Class out in public parks for walks, and Misty is handling all of this calmly. These are just some of the exercises that are making this behaviour modification work.

Alerting

Just For Your Information: If your dog has people aggression issues, just substitute "people" for the "dogs" in the following approximations for Determining a Threshold, Dog Approaches and Dog Approaches from Behind. Whether people or dogs, you can handle the situation in a similar manner. (You can, of course, leave out The Fine Art of Butt Sniffing for people-problems.)

To Begin: Determine a Threshold

1. First determine the threshold at which your dog reacts to other dogs. *For dogs who have shown aggression:* At what point does your dog spot another dog and *begin to exhibit* signs of body tension, nervousness or hyperactivity? Is it eight feet or thirty feet? You will start at a distance just prior to the distance at which your dog begins to react with obvious signs of growling, barking, and lunging. To begin at a distance at which some *slight* body tension and even a *slight* pilo-erector reflex is evident is acceptable.

From this distance, begin to recognize the first signs your dog uses to indicate he is On Alert." When you are working with dogs who have been over-reactive or aggressive with other dogs, it is critical that you understand the importance of Alerting, and can recognize it quickly. *Alerting* is the point at which the dog is beginning to get fired up. For dogs who are going to react inappropriately, this is a crucial moment. *If you do not respond to this Alerting behaviour in your dog, he will ASSUME that you approve of what he is doing and will "back him up."* If you do not notice an Alerting Event and let it slide by, you are, in your dog's paradigm, directly giving him permission to follow through with his current thoughts and become more reactive. If you are going to modify this dog's behaviour, when the dog Alerts is the optimum time to intervene. Remember: Once past this stage and into a stage of more intense reaction (lunging, barking, snarling, growling), you are merely practicing damage control and are not modifying behaviour at all (at least, not in the direction you want to be going!).

At the first signs of Alerting, you will use your Move Away from it exercise. (See "Alerting" photo.) Just move away or, better yet, in the Acquisition Stage of Learning, Back Away from the dog your dog is alerting on. Don't dawdle; move backwards quickly, but smoothly. When you do this Back Away, remain neutral. (I know easier said than done, but it is possible. So do it.) Emotionality or anger on your part will merely validate your dog's point of view that other dogs ARE bad news and always cause trouble. Correcting your dog or yelling at him will exacerbate this behaviour, again by validating your dog's current paradigm that every time another dog appears, you become upset, nervous, and occasionally attack him.

THE MOMENT your dog turns toward you, use a RM. Continue to back up two or three more steps, using verbal encouragement to keep your dog moving toward you. As your dog reaches you, Mark It & Feed It. Deliver a Jackpot for First Correct Efforts. After the first couple of correct efforts at one threshold distance, Mark It & Feed It, then resume work by decreasing the threshold distance.

Each time you decrease the threshold distance, remember, you will receive a First Correct Effort at that closer distance. Jackpot it accordingly, then move to a variable schedule of reinforcement.

The Compulsive Greeter & Threshold Distances

For dogs who are "over-friendly" and compulsive greeters (that is, most dogs!), you can determine the threshold distance based on the following: At what point does your dog: begin to look at the other dog? Start to wiggle and waggle around (before he begins to actually lunge at the other dog)?

1. As soon as your dog looks or orients toward you, Mark It & Feed It.

   After you have done this a few times from your current threshold distance, if your timing is adequate and you have begun at the correct distance, your dog will begin to glance at the other dog, then quickly glance or orient toward you briefly BEFORE he zeroes in on (starts fixating on) or reacts to the other dog. IT IS IMPERATIVE that you catch this quick glance he gives you the first 2 or 3 times with a Jackpot.

2. Next you will observe your dog glancing at the other dog, then quickly looking back to you for advice – Mark & Feed that behaviour and encourage your dog to maintain involvement with you. At this point, many dogs will begin to ignore the other dog and choose you to be the object of fascination. Good job!
3. Now you may move about 2 steps closer. As soon as you move, as far as the dog is concerned, this exercise becomes a whole new ball game again. Repeat your Move-Away, Back-Away or Leave-It (whatever is most convenient) until you have the dog ignoring the other dog at this distance.
4. Now move about 2 steps closer. Continue with this until you have good behaviour from your dog at about a 6 foot distance from the other dog.

This is a difficult exercise, mostly because you need the other dog to be, at least initially, a stable, reliable, non-reactive dog to practice with. You can also get lots of practice out on walks with your dog. Do not hesitate to do so. However, in the initial stages, if your dog is over-reactive around other dogs, it is going to be very bad news if you meet loose dogs, or other over-reactive dogs whose owners have no idea how to control them.

Keep working on this regardless. It is not always a perfect world, and when working with my own dogs, I have often had to be in less than ideal situations, where it would have been much less hair-raising for me if I could have participated in a more predictable desensitization program. However, the real world always intervenes when you least would like it to (the phone always rings when you're in the bath tub and don't have the cordless with you...) and so, in many cases, when out walking your dog, you will have to do the best you can with the current situation. If your dog is a known fighter and has injured other dogs, you absolutely MUST walk your dog with a muzzle.

In an ideal world, this behaviour would not be taken out and used in public until it was picture-perfect. Unfortunately, this is usually impossible. Before a desensitization program such as this could be completed, you will have to take your dog to the veterinarian. Your dog must be exercised, which in most cases means walking on a leash at least some time. Control the setting events as much as you can. That means, choose the times you walk your dog and the areas you walk to prevent meeting loose dogs. Practice this protocol every chance you get to the best of your ability, and even under less-than-ideal conditions, you will get results with a normal dog. You will get results even with dogs who have some abnormality.

Remember to Utilize Calming Signals.

Once you are capable of obtaining and *keeping* your dog's attention in the presence of other dogs, you are well on your way to having more control over situations that are relatively normal and non-volatile. He may not yet be ready to have a dog run up and leap all over him, but you will be well on your way to a better companion and a better relationship with your dog.

In earlier sections, I extensively discussed the use of calming signals: how dogs perceive them, how to recognize when your dog is using them, and those that you can use yourself with your own dog to convey that you are not threatening him, and that this situation is not dangerous. Go back and review that section now, because success at the next Approximation depends on your ability to recognize, reinforce and use these signals to your advantage.

Raising Criteria: Person-to-Person Approaches

For this approach, you will pass by your helper and her dog, with the people between the dogs. The dogs are on the outside, with a 2-Person-Cushion between them.

Photo essay by Sam Ziegenmeyer.

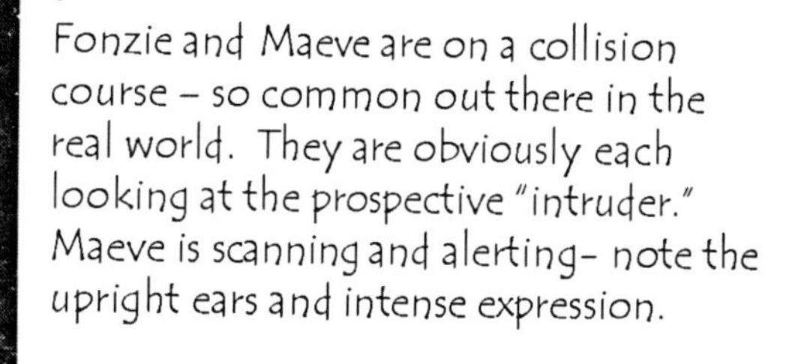

Fonzie and Maeve are on a collision course – so common out there in the real world. They are obviously each looking at the prospective "intruder." Maeve is scanning and alerting- note the upright ears and intense expression.

As the "intruders" get closer to each other, you can see Maeve lower her head and take on a more watchful attitude (slight guarding posture).

But then Maeve's behaviour modification (and Fonzie's, too) kicks in and she includes me. She begins to turn her head slightly toward me, as Fonzie looks to Lylenette. Training has triumphed and the spark has been deleted from this encounter just by the dogs looking away from each other. Both of these dogs are very assertive animals, so a head on meeting is inadvisable.

Dog Approaches #1 of 2

Voluntarily ignoring the other dog gets you a treat!

Once past the other dog, I stop and give Maeve a treat. This is necessary in the early stages of learning. Actually Maeve has been doing this for so long without a treat she looks a bit surprised when I deliver a cookie to her for behaviour she just considers a habit now. She has come a long way from the dog I brought into my home a few years ago.

Dog Approaches #2 of 2

Have your helper (with a non-reactive dog) face you and your dog from a distance of about 40 feet. This is to simulate another dog approaching you when you are on the sidewalk.

1. Predetermine and mark the middle – approximately that area where you would meet if you both held your ground (which you will not do!).
2. Simultaneously, begin walking toward each other.
3. Each person, from her respective side, will begin to arc away from the middle (and each other) by two or three steps, so there is a total of about 6 feet between you and your helper when you pass by each other. Encourage your dog to remain engaged with you and RM correct efforts. As soon as you are a couple of steps past the helper, stop and Mark It & Feed It.
4. If your dog becomes over-reactive, keep moving and, if necessary, break into a run and move quickly past the other dog. As soon as your dog orients and engages with you, Mark It & Feed It.

You will continue to do these passes over *many sessions*. When your dog remains calm at a large "arcing" distance, gradually reduce the size of the "arc." Do this until you can pass shoulder to shoulder with your helper while your dog remains non-reactive.

By arcing away from the oncoming dog/handler team, you are teaching your dog to do a polite and proper arced approach, which other dogs will perceive as non-threatening. By teaching this to your dog, at least on leash and with you present, he is learning to show deference to other dogs. This behaviour will also make the approaching dogs less reactive, therefore less likely to "set your dog off." This situation can very much become a case of "monkey see, monkey do." If you can keep your dog from becoming reactive, and, best case, to actually appear friendly, often you prevent the other dog from becoming reactive.

And, if he does not become reactive, neither will your dog. On the other hand, if one dog becomes threatening and reactive or defensive, most likely other dogs in the vicinity will mirror the reactive behaviour. You are beginning to actually handle other dogs in the environment. How very Sci-Fi!

Dog to Dog Approaches

You will repeat the above mise-en-scene exactly, except the passes will be with the dogs *next to each other* as you pass the other team, instead of the people next to each other. Do this many times, gradually moving the dogs closer, as their behaviour allows. Be sure to ARC as the dogs pass!

Dog approaches from behind

This exercise involves your helper passing with another dog from behind you.

- With you and your dog standing still, have your helper and his dog walk by you from behind. If your dog alerts on the other dog, immediately do a Move-Away.
- With your team walking, have the helper and dog walk from behind and pass you.

Challenges:

- Helper and dog run by you.
- Your team runs by the helper and his dog.

Raising Criteria:

The Fine Art of Butt-Sniffing

Even dogs who are "hot" (not dog friendly) should have coping skills adequate to handle an obviously non-threatening dog coming up and sniffing them very briefly. To work on this skill, your helper and her friendly, quiet dog will approach you with your dog, who is muzzled and on a Halti.

Before beginning this exercise, the dog-to-dog approaches outlined above should be no-brainers. Another dog approaching your dog, running up from behind, walking near him – all these should elicit calm behaviour from your dog

This step may take you weeks or months to accomplish if your dog is reactive. Take your

time! Do not place yourself, your dog, or someone else or their dog at risk!

You may have your dog in heel position or you can be standing in front of him. Of the two, facing your dog is a much easier position to control the dog from. The helper team circles with you and your dog in the middle, from a distance of maybe six feet. If you have done the preceding exercises, this should be a tolerable distance for your dog. If it is not, increase the circumference of the helper's circle. Mark & Feed all calm responses from your dog. If your dog becomes extremely reactive, have the helper team stop and stand still, with the helper person between her dog and you, and you can then do a move away exercise with your dog. As soon as your dog has calmed down, the helper team can begin to move again.

When you are observing calm behaviour from your dog, the helper team may decrease the circumference of the circle by taking one step in toward the middle and continuing on its circular path. The helper team must be able to be calm, and the dog used must be controllable. If there is any doubt about your helper and her dog, muzzle the helper dog also.

Muzzles make this exercise safe because this exercise can go to hell in a hand-basket very quickly.

Have the helper reverse direction and go the other way.

Decrease the circumference of the circle again. Practice with the helper team going both clockwise and counter-clockwise.

Repeat the above sequence until the helper team is circling at a distance of approximately 12 inches away from your dog. Ideally, your dog is remaining engaged with you, and will cease watching the other dog at a verbal cue from you: either "Leave It" or just saying his name. Better yet, your dog has opted to ignore the other dog entirely, only glancing at it occasionally. More Challenges:

- The helper team stands still nearby.
- The helper person can reach out and touch your dog.
- The helper dog can briefly (one second) sniff your dog's back (not face!).
- The helper dog can sniff your dog for 2 seconds. Work this up to 4 or 5 seconds.

At this point, if your dog is ignoring the other dog, great! If he is beginning to try to make a friendly overture to the other dog, you may permit VERY brief (one second or less) contact between the two dogs. At the one second mark or on a pre-designated signal from you, BOTH HANDLERS quickly, but CALMLY and simultaneously back away from each other, and, as you do so, make sure the dogs' heads are facing away from each other. I have seen many dogs become very reactive exactly at this juncture, if this situation is not carefully controlled.

As one dog sees the other moving away, the motion might cause him to lunge for the moving dog. If their heads are turned away from each other this cannot occur AND the dogs appear to be showing each other deference, even though, at this point, it may be totally controlled by the handler and the Halti.

In Closing...

Always keep Safety and Prevention as the first consideration. Your dog is your responsibility.

These exercises are required work. You are teaching your dog very important lessons about How To Stay Out Of Trouble. You are learning how to read the signals your dog and others are giving.

A large portion of our time in Resocialization class is spent doing a variety of dog approaches. These exercises are practiced until the human component of the team has a set of fluent and automatic responses to many different situations that might be encountered. The dogs are gaining fluency and automatic responses at the same time. These are the key to teaching your dog that non-reactive behaviour and calming signals can give them "control" of the environment, keeping it safe. The more this calm emotional state is practiced, the more it prevails. The more a calm emotional state prevails, the more hair-raising events are eschewed.

Photo essay by Joanne Weber.

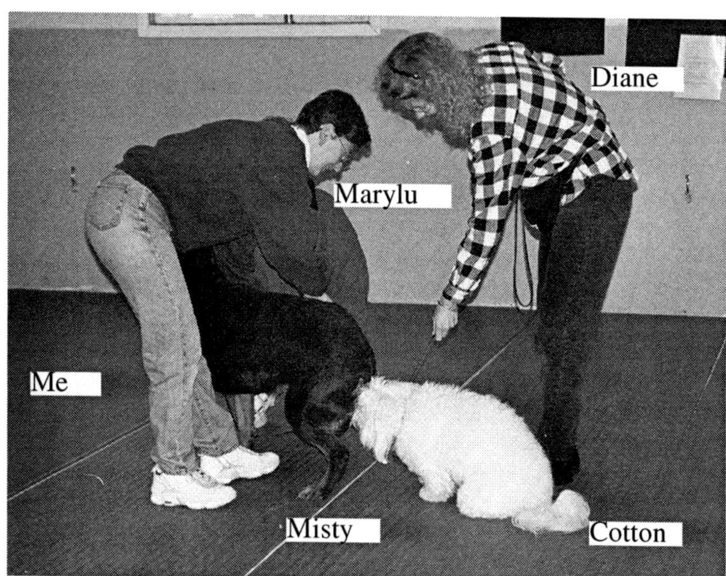

At first, heavy supervision is the name of the game, and the dog is allowed to make no judgments. This is because, in the past, these dogs have demonstrated that they have no ability to read other dogs, or have shown alarming or unfriendly behaviour. Misty obviously does not know quite how to act with this, her first close contact with a non-family dog in a very long time.

Above: Marylu (hidden behind me) has a muzzle and a Halti on Misty, and is holding the Halti, as shown on the right, to maximize control. I am steadying the dogs and want to be close in case one of the dogs begins to react, so I can move between them (placing myself at some risk...). Diane has Cotton on a short, but LOOSE leash, so she can quickly do a Back-Away, if the need arises. (Cotton is also wearing a Halti.)

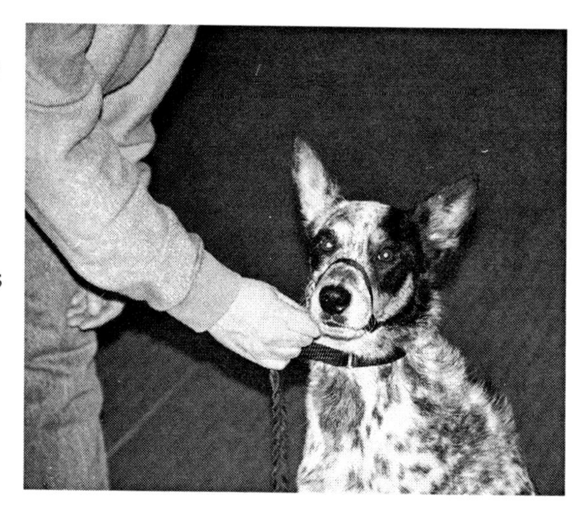

Right: This is a safe way to hold the Halti. Better yet, have a muzzle on the dog if there is ANY DOUBT that the dog might be reactive. Better safe than stitches!

The Fine Art Of Butt-Sniffing

Remember, if you get into too many situations that you just do not know how to handle, or your dog is becoming worse instead of better, it is time to stop and assess what is going on. Did your dog have all the prerequisite work necessary before beginning this phase of training? Are YOU handling yourself in a calm and controlled manner? I don't mean, are you nervous or afraid – of course you are to some degree. But the manner in which you control your stress will have a huge impact on the results you obtain with your dog. If you get in over your head, it may be time to seek professional help. Just screen the professional carefully – pay for a consult or for phone time so you can interview her. Ask if you can sit in on another lesson or attend a group class. If you sit in, note how the instructor handles disobedience. Does the instructor give clear directions to the handler? Is she patient, yet firm with the canines? Does the instructor make progress with the dogs she works with? Does the instructor explain to the students why she is using a certain procedure? If you ask, can the instructor explain to you why she used a certain technique?

51

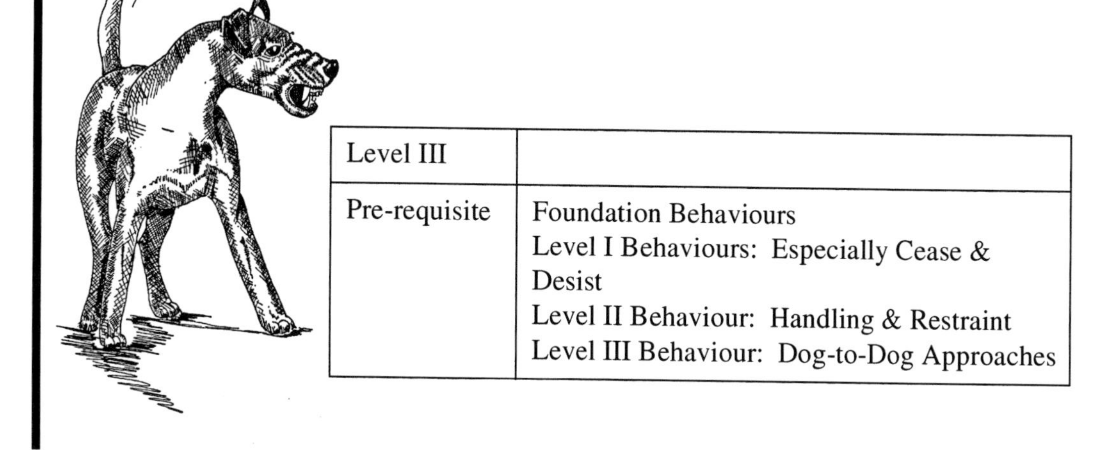

Level III	
Pre-requisite	Foundation Behaviours Level I Behaviours: Especially Cease & Desist Level II Behaviour: Handling & Restraint Level III Behaviour: Dog-to-Dog Approaches

LEASH AGGRESSION

Goal	Your dog will be able to walk around other dogs and walk up to other dogs without lunging toward them. A tight leash means "turn toward the handler," not "lunge toward the other dog."
What it teaches	Other dogs are not always available for play; they are not dangerous. Nor is it her business to run over and kick everybody's butt.

A tight leash can promote the dog perceiving the handler as restricting flight. This places the handler in the role of being part of the problem. Our goal is for the dog to see the handler as a team member, someone she can rely on as being the solution.

Many times I have had experienced dog trainers tell me, "Don't let your dog get a tight leash. It will promote aggression."

The tight leash is not really the problem. In one regard it is a symptom because the dog:
• Has never learned to pay attention.
• Has never learned to relinquish the environment in favor of the handler.
• Is uneducated about other coping mechanisms in lieu of being reactive.
• Is uncomfortable with restraint under certain conditions.

If a dog is lunging toward another animal in an excited state, guess what? The leash is tight! It is a symptom of the dog's over-reactive state. The best way to minimize this is to get and keep your dog's focus on you.

I know the tight leash is provocative, yet I have miserably failed, on occasion, to prevent my dogs from being in "tight leash" situations. Let's be realistic – situations come up and we all get slightly behind the power curve, especially before you learn to read your dog well. This results in a dog who is reactive or explosive. My own dogs, Breanna, Jynx, and Maeve, taught me that to be proactive means the difference between a dog who is amongst the living instead of sitting in an urn in my China Cabinet.

When a tight leash happens (and it will!), it is good to have a plan in place for curtailing over-reactive behaviour that is escalating. Of course, this protocol will also promote walking nicely on a loose leash and will prevent leash aggression from occurring.

Instead of thinking that I will always be able to maintain a loose leash, my approach to Leash Aggression involves teaching the dog that restricting flight distance (such as with a leash) does not mean the only option left is fight. The pragmatic approach is not to think that my dog will never experience a tight leash, but to teach the dog that, if she remains calm and non-reactive and uses calming signals, she can extricate herself from a volatile situation or prevent one from occurring. What I am teaching the dog is: if you are in a context that makes you feel uncomfortable, you can cope with your stress by remaining calm instead of panicking or escalating arousal. This calmer emotional state will gain you relief from discomfort better than defensive behaviour.

At first, you will do this by placing the dog in the context of having a slightly tight leash, and then use treats and prior training to teach her to be calm instead of resorting to defensive, assertive or fearful behaviour.

Obviously, the first time you bring your dog up to another dog and begin to work on the tight leash, you are operating under *very controlled* circumstances. This means the dog you are walking up to is stable. Your dog knows the prerequisite exercises well. Your dog is muzzled if she has shown any sort of extreme arousal or aggression toward other dogs. You have taught proper dog-to-dog approaches and you have a good Back-Away maneuver.

The Back-Away teaches the dog that tight leashes do not mean aggression must follow AND how to avoid the tight leash to begin with. After enough Back-Aways, your dog will begin to cue on your body language. Shifting your weight backwards becomes the cue to orient toward you, thus avoiding the tight leash.

By the time we are beginning to get the dogs close to each other in my Canine Resocialization classes, tight leashes are rare. The occasions that the leash is tightened have become a cue to orient toward the handler. Once this cue is habitual for your dog, tight leashes become a much less volatile situation for your dog. Slight tension on the leash becomes a cue for the dog to turn toward the handler.

If the dog does lunge toward anything, what do you do? Back-Away or Move-Away, of course. Then try again.

When I began working with my own dogs who had aggression problems, I found that, when I was in the midst of a volatile situation, there was no possible way I was going to be able to carry out some long, involved or physically controlling protocol. It is unnerving when you have a large, strong dog at the other end of your leash who is beginning to come unglued at the seams. (Although, a small terrier hell-bent on getting to something is not a piece of cake either.) There you stand, everyone in the world looking at you, and things begin to deteriorate very quickly. Because you are adrenalized by the situation also, you may not be thinking as logically as you normally do. I have been bitten breaking up dog fights and not even been sure which dog sent me to the emergency room for stitches. So, given all that, what I was seeking was something that had a high likelihood of working well and was easy to do. So easy that I could habituate myself to do the maneuver with few repetitions. Simple enough that I could carry out the steps when I was in the trenches under fire.

I began to think about what is really happening when my dog is focusing on another dog intensely (or, in the case of the terriers: a cat, a bird, a mouse, a rat, or a dog). I know, of course, that there are many chemical changes taking place in the animal, rendering her a slave to her limbic system. I knew from experience that food treats wouldn't pull my predacious dogs off prey, or my territorial dogs off whatever they felt was violating territory. So waving food treats around was an exercise in futility. Correcting dogs made them much more reactive and I saw that it would be quite easy to have the dog turn around and redirect aggression toward me. Tight leashes can cause aggression to be redirected toward the reachable target, and guess who was on the other end of the leash?

My decision was to treat this as a lack of attention, a failure to respond to a recall, or a failure to "Leave It." Once I had taken attention past the attention exercises and used it as an Anchoring exercise, taught an impeccable Cease & Desist exercise, and had a good Recall, I discovered that a Back-Away or Move-Away and Look-At-Me was the magic bullet. It filled the bill perfectly. It was easy to do. When under fire, I could manage it because all I had to remember, no matter what the circumstances, was: Back-Away From It, taking the dog with me and reinforcing her for coming toward me. The results were pretty incredible.

Better yet, the Back-Away was so simple that my clients, even the ones who got really flustered, had large dogs, and were not horribly experienced dog owners, could do this exercise when they were in a volatile situation (provided the dog was wearing a Halti, at least for the learning stages). They could remember it because they practiced it constantly and the rule is easy to remember: If my dog moves toward it, I move away from it and feed the dog when she comes toward me. If the dog refuses the food because of her stress and/or arousal level, I can at least use my established Reward Mark to mark the behaviour for the dog.

The other elegant feature about this exercise is that it works equally effectively for the overfriendly, overbearing dog, the dog who is going to take a snap at the other dog as soon as it gets close enough, the lunging dog, and the fearful dog.

Once you have done the Back-Away, you have also given yourself and your dog a slight reprieve so you can both take ten deep breaths and regroup.

The photo essay below is a simulation of a typical dog meeting. Whitney, the Pembroke Welsh Corgi, is an explosively reactive dog. She came to Pat as a rescue. She has dog-to-dog and dog-to-people aggression. Pat has put a lot of work into this dog and Whitney has made much improvement. Rix is the terrier mix. She is a "found" dog, rescued from the middle of the road on a foggy, cold morning – a flea-infested, terrified and exhausted puppy. Someone likely dumped her in the middle of the road. My kennel manager, Kathy, found her on her way to work one morning. Rix is well socialized, but she has a stability and intelligence that came with her. She is innately a savvy, sophisticated speaker.

This is extremely advanced work for a dog who has been aggressive, and may take a lot of work over a very long time to achieve. There are some dogs with whom this work would be so unsafe or stressful for the control dog that it would be impractical to do.

My goal with Whitney is not to get her ready to play at the dog park. It is to get her to the point that her owner can safely walk her down the street on a leash, or even through a crowded situation such as the annual rescue picnic that Pat likes to attend, or a dog class, without an incident.

I never, in my wildest dreams, when I started work with Breanna and (particularly) with Maeve, thought that I would be able to walk into a crowded dog class with my dogs off leash and have exuberant puppies and adolescents run up and jump into the faces of my dogs and have those other hapless dogs live. But it has happened. I didn't leave it to chance! I have done all of the protocols in this book, plus some, with my girls. I am still vigilant, but Maeve and

Breanna both are quite safe in all normal situations. If a dog walks up and challenges them in an assertive way, that is an entirely different matter. Both of these girls will happily and quickly react in that situation. So, they never get put in that situation. I am watchful, and keep careful track of the environment, and the dogs in it, to prevent mishaps. All the behaviour modification, and the alternative behaviours that result, buffer their reactivity, giving me that valuable five to ten seconds to intervene.

I was so proud of Maeve when I took her to the Detroit Kennel Club Show, which is an extremely large, crowded and stress-inducing environment, with many spectators. She conducted herself like a dog who has never had dog-to-dog and dog-to-human aggression. I did have one moment of near panic when a very ignorant (bless him, this guy didn't have a clue!) spectator walked right up into our personal space and attempted to take a toy out of her mouth so he could "play" with her. I was even paying attention, but this person acted so impulsively, I really didn't see this coming and it was as much a surprise to me as it was to Maeve. As he was reaching down toward her, I saw a moment of stillness, but before I could even react, Maeve immediately looked at me for advice, which gave me that valuable half-a-second to intervene. She did retain hold of her toy, instead of dropping it and disciplining this human. As he held on to the toy, she just sort of dragged him round with the toy so she could gain eye contact with me (as she began to feel aroused), just as I have taught her to do. It was a test I would have never asked of her, but I was quite glad she passed it with flying colors. I had proofed this situation with her by having known people take things from her.

Even though I am relentlessly proactive, this incident, and many others, are proof that you just cannot prepare for every eventuality. The more you have prepared for, of course, the better your chances are that the desired behaviour will "hold up under fire."

Incidents like this have made me a true believer in positive reinforcement and the protocols outlined in this book. The relationships I have built with my "difficult" dogs are deep and lasting and very close, very trusting. Again, I attribute much of this to these protocols. With my puppies who don't have problems, going through the steps of these protocols is still useful. By the end I really know what kind of dog I have on my hands, and, if there are any triggers that are going to set the dog off, at least I know what they are and can prepare and train for them.

We are simulating a normal encounter with dogs on slightly tight leashes – what usually happens in the real world, in spite of our best efforts. Whitney's discomfort shows with her body tension and upright, "short-in-body-length" posture.

She meets every dog figuring the best defense is a good offense. She is exactly the kind of dog who gets herself into trouble by over-reacting and causing the dog she is meeting to become defensive – all the ingredients required for a dandy little dog fight.

Tight Leash Approaches #1 of 4

Photo essay by Sam Ziegenmeyer.

Rix correctly reads Whitney as being somewhat of a jerk, with her unnecessarily unfriendly and assertive posture. I say unnecessary because Rix is CLEARLY NOT exhibiting anything but "Hi, how are you? I am a non-threatening character." Think of walking up to someone and saying a warm, "Hello, nice to meet you," and holding out your hand for a handshake. The other person reciprocates with a defensive "So What!" and glares at you.

Tight Leash Approaches #2 of 4

Rix is so savvy, so correct and so non-reactive that Whitney relaxes and begins to exhibit normal, friendly greeting behaviour. At first a bit rigidly accepting Rix mannerly sniffing her inguinal area...

Tight Leash Approaches #3 of 4

...then actually returning this normal, friendly behaviour. Rix is handling this situation with finesse. The wrong move will cause Whitney to react defensively.

Now is the time to gently interrupt the dogs: Both handlers Backing-Away, or getting their dogs to orient toward them simultaneously and then calmly moving away from each other.

Tight Leash Approaches #4 of 4

52

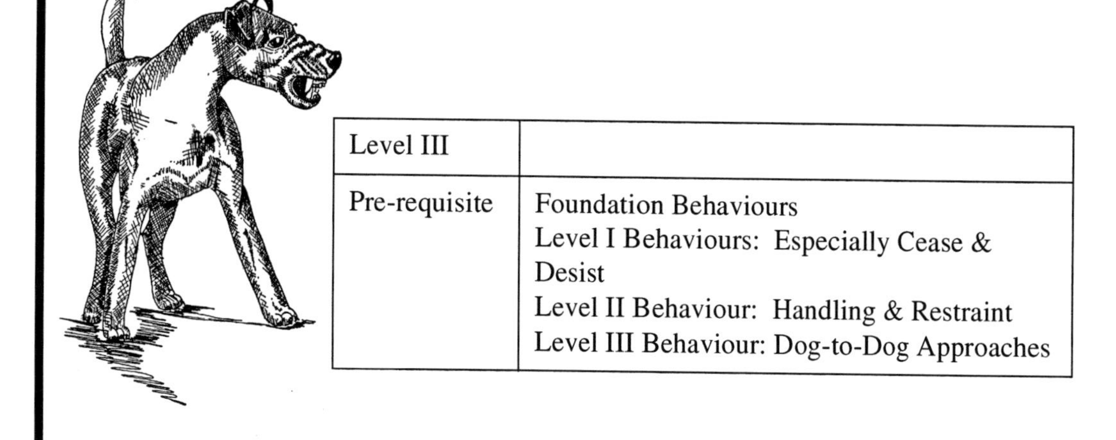

Level III	
Pre-requisite	Foundation Behaviours Level I Behaviours: Especially Cease & Desist Level II Behaviour: Handling & Restraint Level III Behaviour: Dog-to-Dog Approaches

ADVANCED WORK WITH DOG-TO-DOG APPROACHES

Goal	Your dog will allow other dogs to run loose in her vicinity without reacting inappropriately with extreme play behaviour, barking, lunging and growling, or by becoming so aroused she cannot pay attention to you. With reservations, this protocol may assist you with a dog who runs fences after other dogs, and overreacts to other dogs running outside her fenced area. Note, however, that these problems are primarily a management issue.
What it teaches	Other dogs are not always available for play, they are not dangerous, nor is it your dog's business to run over and kick everybody's butt.

The "chase" situation incites a very primitive prey reaction in many dogs. When you add the limiting restraint of a leash, their frustration level can go up. This means that, with some dogs, you see their eyes glaze over and they check right out, responding to any sort of physical correction (like a jerk on a pinch or choke collar) with amazing pain tolerance. The jerks on the collar will only make the dog more chemically reactive and pain tolerant.

If the dog who is fired-up by a prey object gets loose, she may, in her zeal to obtain the "prey" and to get release from her frustration, treat the first animal she comes to as her "dart-board." If "prey" is the primary motivation, you may observe this dog running a silent missile-like approach directly to her targeted prey. If another dog reaches the prey-object first (dog, squirrel, ball, frisbee), the first dog will quickly transfer all of her predacious actions to the other dog. If she decides that the "prey" *is* the other dog, the same silent approach will be aimed directly toward the other dog.

If frustration is the motivator, the dog will most likely charge the other dog and use vocalizations: barking, growling, and snarling directed at the other dog, whom she will tackle. If the other dog totally folds, this may be the end of the interaction, allowing you a chance to intervene. If the other dog becomes defensive or reactive, you will have a dandy little dog fight on your hands with a high probability that there will be injury to one or both animals.

The other great frustration-creator is a visible barrier like a fence, or, these days, even an invisible barrier such as an electronic containment system.

Fence Running

If a dog is left in a situation where she is fenced and other dogs are fenced adjacent to her, the situation is extremely volatile for many different reasons (depending on the dog). The dogs run the fence, but are prevented from interacting normally. I am not promoting no fences and dogs running free, I am just pointing out that dogs enclosed in fences need supervision and monitoring. Dogs find this circumstance very irritating and/or very stimulating, depending on the dog's basic temperament. Some dogs barely react to this situation at all, but a high percentage certainly will. If your dog is one of these, do not ignore his frustration level. This is primarily a management issue. This protocol may be of some help in this context, but you must certainly manage this situation to alleviate the frustration for the dog.

Dogs who are in a multi-dog or outdoor kennel are also prone to developing frustration because of the stimulation and the fact that they are impeded from interacting (in a friendly or unfriendly way) with the dogs they see. Just as a matter of course it is wise to avoid kenneling dogs straight across from each other. I have seen many dogs develop an active dislike for each other, fueled by being kenneled across from each other, invoking a lot of eye contact and visual stimulation that causes high arousal levels. A normally friendly dog may be stressed in this environment, which exacerbates the frustration. Dogs, when confined as is necessary in our world, can feel defensive. The symptom of this unease erupts as aggression.

My kennel has three-foot aisles between the kennel runs, so if dogs are out and take a dislike to the animal in the run next to them, the worst they can do is call each other names through the fence. They cannot actually get hold of each other through the fence. Dogs here are outside with compatible dogs only. If discord exists between two animals I have them out at separate times so their animosity does not increase by running the fence, barking and snarling at each other. Inside the kennel, if a dog is sensitive to it, his visual stimulation is kept at a minimum by blocking the view of dogs he is irritated by. If the crates are next to each other, a thin piece of wood or aluminum can be slid between the crates, or, if the kennel runs are chain link, you can bolt aluminum barriers to block vision. Maeve and Breanna are always kenneled so that they cannot see each other. They can be next to Rylie, my Border Collie, or Zasu or many other dogs, but not each other. If I maintain this simple rule, I reduce the animosity between Maeve and Bree immensely. If I am there to supervise, they are fine. I can even have them loose in the room with me, but I wouldn't want to leave the room even for a moment, because they truly detest each other.

It is important that dogs are managed carefully in fence/kennel/tie-out situations to minimize the occurrence of provocative situations. If dogs have indulged in fence-fighting with an adjacent dog, be extremely careful about letting them together "to settle it amongst themselves," as I have so often heard prescribed. If you catch the situation prior to frank aggression, you might still be able to resolve it. However, if there have been any vocalizations, charging or posturing through the fence, once the dogs do gain access to each other, they may well unleash all of their built-up frustration that is associated with each other *on* each other.

I am not a believer of allowing dogs to "settle" differences amongst themselves. This is, of course, highly dependent on the individual dogs involved. But certainly, if I have two socially inept animals who have had previous altercations, there is nothing that leads me to believe they will somehow develop the social conventions and language sophistication required to resolve the conflict peacefully.

For dogs who are fence-running and fighting through crates or kennels, you will get some improvement with this protocol – perhaps great improvement. My concern is that the improvement will be under a narrow band of circumstances, with one of the requirements being your presence. Remember: this is not a cure, just one of many components that will help with problem behaviour. Every small improvement contributes to overall improvement in the dog who is presenting with aggression.

Teaching the dogs to just "hang out" and relax in one another's presence. For some dogs, this is very difficult because, as soon as another dog moves, they tend to become reactive. This can be because a dog is uneasy if she is not constantly "controlling" the environment (low frustration threshold, anxiety). Sometimes it is because movement stimulates a dog to respond.

Advanced Dog Approaches Near Leashed Dogs

If your dog is fence running, you will work with your dog *inside* the fenced area and have the stimulation occurring from outside the fence. You will teach your dog to react to this environmental stimulation by coming to the middle of the yard, or another suitable area: one that is away from the direct stimulation. You are teaching your dog to come to you for help instead of running the fence.

Maeve, the premier fence runner (her eyes used to glaze over and she would have happily sifted anything through the fence that she could get hold of), has responded very well to this protocol. When I am present she doesn't even glance at dogs running fences anymore. Much to my surprise, she has generalized this behaviour and is much less reactive in most fence/kennel situations and non-reactive in some of them. After three years of work, she and Bree can be in runs nearby (but not touching), and they will both mind their manners. This will hold true right up to the point that something very stimulating occurs – for instance, a cat or strange dog running up to the fence. Both dogs might begin by being reactive about the "intruder," but would soon transfer this frustration onto each other if allowed to do so. Because I know this would happen, I closely supervise all such situations so we don't have any backsliding. I have worked long and hard to get these girls to be around each other. So, even in these cases that look really good, remember: MANAGEMENT is the key.

Equipment

For these exercises a Halti and leash are to be worn. The dog should also be wearing his martingale collar. Whether your dog wears a muzzle for these exercises depends on your dog – is he a young, wild uneducated dog? A dog who is becoming dangerously reactive who may redirect aggression toward you? What will this dog do if he does reach the other dogs? Don't know for sure? Then, you'd best add a muzzle to your equipment list for this exercise. Just as in the dog-to-dog approaches, once the dog is well under control, non-reactive, and relaxed, it may be okay to try these exercises without a muzzle for those dogs who must start out wearing one. However, you must be alert to any signs of body tension, stress or discomfort by the dog and be able to safely move away from the other team and without any aggressive incidents. This means you must have an excellent "come when called" behaviour and an excellent Leave-It behaviour.

PREPARATIONS

When we are working with dogs here at the training center, we begin by putting some of my dogs out in a fence to play. They are dogs I can guarantee will run around and bark like idiots. This is exactly the situation that drives many dogs crazy when they are on leash: other dogs in their vision running loose and perhaps even chasing balls or frisbees.

CAUTION: You need this to be an environment that is very safe and under control – there must be a safe sturdy fence that the enclosed dogs cannot get out of. It is absolutely necessary that your equipment is in good condition and properly fitted to the dog. Think ahead. 1. If the dog you are working gets loose and runs to the fence, and the other dogs run up, and a fight starts between the dogs on either side of the fence, what is your plan? 2. What if redirected aggression between the dogs together within the fence occurs? How are you going to handle this?

For the first scenario, make sure you have the proper equipment on the working dog, and that you will not be frightened to the point of immobility or overpowered by the dog. Ideally, a second person will be available to assist you. Have a baby gate handy near the fence where you will be working, because if, in the worst case scenario, the dogs do begin an argument through the fence, someone can get hold of the working dog's leash and pull him back and the other person can thrust the baby gate between the working dog and the fence to "herd" him back away from the fence. Also, before you begin this exercise, if you have followed the guidelines and protocols properly, you should have a high degree of control and be able to interrupt the working dog, even when he is in an aroused state. It might not be a "pretty," responsive and easy-to-do interruption, but backing away from the situation and cueing the dog to pay attention (using Name Recognition, Leave It, etc.) should help. You may need to back 60 to 100 feet away before you get a response from the dog, but it should be attainable if you have done your homework.

For scenario number 2, choose the dogs for inside the fence very wisely. I use my dogs because I know their reactions and that they have very excellent response to Name Recognition and Leave It. Zasu is great for this exercise because she will for sure chase her large white horse-stall ball and bark like an idiot for hours, yet she will not be over-reactive with the dogs outside the fence. The rest of the dogs I use for this are super-socialized dogs that have great language and are savvy around other dogs. They "keep their heads" and do not over-react in mildly volatile situations such as this. They will ignore, or at least remain non-reactive to (definitely an installed or learned behaviour!) anything short of a direct attack. I am 99.9% certain that amongst the dogs I am using, no fights will break out that I cannot walk in and silence with a word.

Session #1.
X = the Threshold Distance determined. In this case: 60′.
The Approach would begin at a distance beyond which the dog becomes reactive. At each new threshold distance, the dog is asked to exhibit several known behaviours on cue. Once some progress is made, end that session.

BEFORE ADVANCING DOG MUST EXHIBIT RELAXED BEHAVIOUR & BE ABLE TO RESPOND TO A VARIETY OF KNOWN COMMANDS AT DISTANCE X.

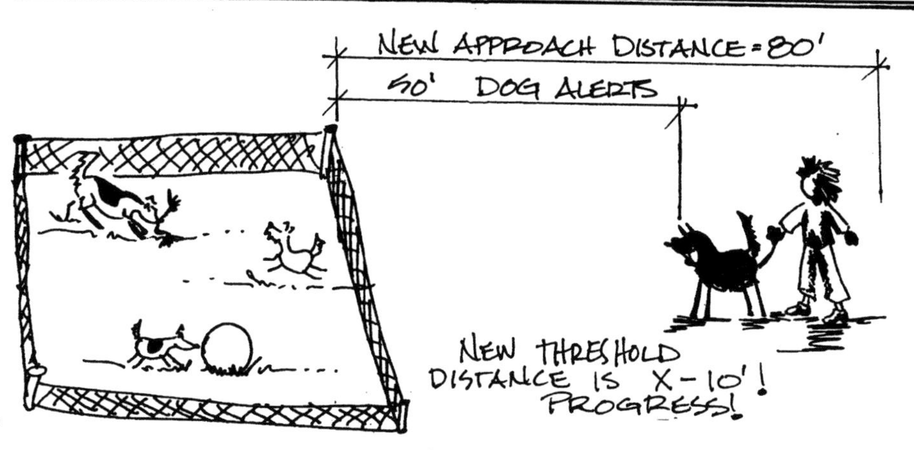

Session #2
Begin the new approach at a distance greater than X. In this case, 80′ to 100′ would be a good choice.
You will be doing a series of approaches, each one treated as a Trial. Several Trials in a row would make up a Session.

Dog Approaches & Threshold Distances

It may be necessary to have three persons. One would be inside the fence to monitor that group of dogs and have them chase a ball or frisbee, so they are moving around and playing, simulating a situation the working dog might encounter in the real world. The second person would be monitoring both the working dog and, according to what the working dog might need, shouting directions to the helper inside the fence, like "Have the dogs quiet for a minute," "Okay, throw the ball now," etc. This person is also the extra who is there in case things start to go to hell in a hand-basket, which you will avoid if you are prepared and proactive! The third person is the handler on the working dog – you! You are carrying out the approximations with your dog.

Data learns to look away from the other dogs, even though they are moving and, therefore, very provocative. Dogs who "explode" around other dogs have found it a successful strategy to gain personal space. That is Data's "old strategy." Data has learned to trust Lori, knowing that she will help him through the rough patches. As a result, he walks near the loose, barking and running dogs and, instead of exploding, remains anchored on Lori.

Advanced Dog Approaches Near "Loose" Dogs

APPROXIMATION #1

Have the dogs in the fence already out there as you bring the working dog by the fence. The first item on the list is to determine the threshold of the working dog. At what point does the dog alert? This is the first distance to begin your work. As soon as the dog alerts, quickly back away from the dogs in the fence, reinforcing your dog with a RM as soon as she turns away from the fenced dogs. Continue to encourage her toward you as you keep back-pedaling for another 5 feet or so. As your dog reaches you, another RM, a treat, and a little street party are in order.

Now it is a matter of continuing to repeat the above behaviour as many times as required, until, AT THE THRESHOLD DISTANCE, your dog is able to remain attentive to you. She may glance at the other dogs but will not commit to going to them, instead remaining committed to be involved with you.

It is an excellent idea to use your Eye Contact Anchor at this distance. You will find that, the more aroused your dog is, the more intensely she will stare through you, using YOU as the venue to remain grounded and under control.

You may choose to halt the lesson here. The deal with this exercise is that you must obtain calm, controlled behaviour at this distance BEFORE YOU STOP THE EXERCISE for this session.

To summarize:

1. Find the threshold distance at which your dog Alerts.
2. Obtain calm, reasonably relaxed behaviour at this distance. Your dog should be able to give you eye-contact and perform known behaviours on cue at this distance.
3. You must remain in this area long enough for the above to occur, and better yet, long enough for the dog to become relaxed in this context and at this distance. This may be five minutes or an hour or more.
4. You may begin another trial by advancing two to five steps closer, or at a distance that the dog begins to Alert again. If your dog adapted quickly (within five minutes) to the last distance you tried, you might try another trial. However, it is actually best to end on the initial success and end this session here and now.
5. When you end this session, remove the dog from the area, or at least retreat to a distance greater than you have just been working.
6. Begin the next session. How soon should the next session be? Five minutes or ten minutes is okay if you are up for it, although I encourage you not to push your luck. If you push the dog too far too fast, you will sabotage your efforts. 24 hours or more is a good time frame. Two days is fine. The next session may not be until a week hence.

Approximation # 2 & Beyond

The next session begins with doing known behaviours at a distance greater than the threshold you last worked at. Now move to the last distance where you had acceptable behaviour at the end of the last session. Obtain known behaviours and look for relaxed behaviour to reinforce.

NOTE: You may see spontaneous recovery of the behaviour when you begin your new session. Don't be alarmed at this – expect it. If it doesn't occur, you may say a little heartfelt prayer and continue on. Each time you do see the spontaneous recovery, in a normal, adaptable dog, you should be able to observe the following pattern: Over several repetitions of practice, when (not if) the spontaneous recovery occurs it is less intense, of shorter duration, and it occurs less frequently.

If you do not keep written notes of threshold distances, the amount of time that it took for your dog to relax and respond to known cues at this distance, and other pertinent information, you will not be able to keep accurate track of progress or lack thereof. So write stuff down!!!

Now move to a distance at which your dog begins to Alert. This may be one step or it may be ten steps closer.

You are to obtain the same non-response, or at least a much less reactive state, where the dog can still function and maintain attention on you and is still able to exhibit behaviours on cue as soon as you request them. Try "Look," "Sit," "Down," "Shake," "Roll-over," or any other known, familiar cue.

In this fashion, you will move closer and closer to the dogs running within the fence. Once you are up to the fence, a whole new situation develops. Your dog is going to be close to the other dogs, but still not allowed to interact with them. She may find this frustrating. This is an excellent exercise in impulse control. After all, it is not always appropriate for your dog to interact with other dogs. That is just the way life is. For dogs who are showing aggression toward other dogs, it may not ever be possible for them to run and play with large groups of dogs.

With the completion of this exercise, however, you and your dog have made huge steps forward toward being able to safely maneuver through the neighborhood for a calm walk. I have many clients who are relieved to reach this stage. They had been using several management strategies: they walk their dogs at 4 or 5 AM (boy, are they devoted!); they walk, but are terrified; they walk and worry; they have quit walking the dog altogether because they just cannot handle the dog.

Once your dog can deal calmly with the situation and still function and respond to known cues, you can try some advanced dog-to-dog leash approaches. The dogs in the photo essay below that I have on leash are my own and are safe. They are sophisticated communicators and relatively non-reactive. I am deliberately allowing my dogs to behave like heathens (out at the end of the leash, in front of me, and straining toward the approaching dogs) because many of the dogs my clients meet out on the street act like heathens. This is a safe setting to practice meeting other dogs who are "out of control" on the daily neighborhood walk.

This work should only be undertaken after your dog has completed all of the other protocols in this book AND if you have appropriate "helper" dogs.

As always, if in doubt – muzzle your dog.

REMEMBER! A successful trial (and by extension, session) is one in which NOTHING HAPPENS! Yes, No Reaction is exactly what we are looking for. Reinforcing all behaviour other than reactivity is a start, then work up to reinforcing looking at you, paying attention, calming signals, etc. The people in the resocialization class will vouch for that. We pray each week for boredom as we do the work!

In the following photo essay, each of the dogs with the handlers on the left is in their 4th Re-socialization Class. That is in addition to private consults with each. Time-wise, this means we have been working these dogs for about six months, class after class. The handlers and dogs have made great strides forward, but there will be more work to do. For these dogs, there will always be work to do. Age, past experiences, handler skill level, handler commitment – all play a part in the prognosis and results. My prognosis on all these dogs is good to excellent because of the increased skill level and commitment of the handlers, in addition to improved management skills.

Cotton above, has been "mainstreamed" into an agility class. He is much less reactive, even if dogs are running around him and bouncing up into his face.

Advanced On-Leash Approaches #1 of 2

Lori helps Data with a lure and moves along at a relaxed, but quick, pace. Data tends to "guard" his owner. He is a rescue and has had some traumatic dog-to-dog experiences. He handles this well; note his relaxed and confident body language, even though I am allowing my dogs to leap toward him and continue to invade his personal space.

Misty wears a muzzle for extra safety. She is big and can be reactive, although she is much improved. Misty is handling this situation very sensibly even though these unknown dogs are crowding her. Marylu watches closely for signs of tension.

Advanced On-Leash Approaches #2 of 2

These are great prevention exercises and the friendly but inexperienced dog will readily respond. For our "special" dogs who are already presenting with aggression, we go very slowly and take our time.

Dogs who are already presenting with over-reactivity and frank aggression will always require some work and, at the very least, close monitoring, lest they fall back into their "old ways."

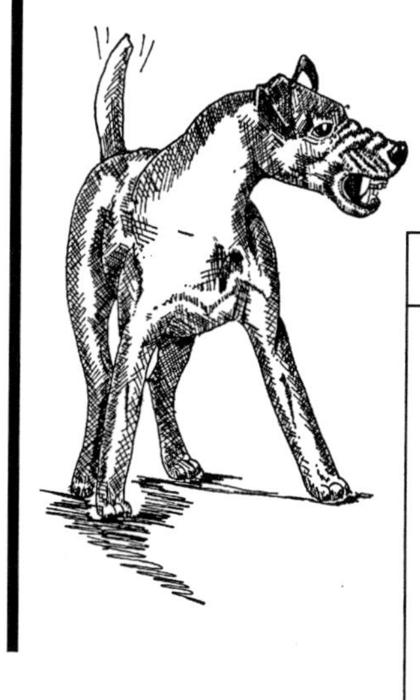

Level III	
Pre-requisite	Foundation Behaviours All Level I Behaviours Handling & Restraint protocol Yielding & Husbandry protocol Helpful will be: • Dog-to-Dog Approaches • Leash Aggressio • Advanced work with Dog-to-Dog Approaches

AGGRESSION DIRECTED TOWARD A CANINE HOUSEMATE

Aggression between dogs who are housemates is one of the most difficult problems to solve. The dogs are together all the time, so they get endless practice with the agonistic behaviour and little relief from each other. Some or all of the dogs involved are contributing to the problem. This means that you will need to retrain more than one dog at a time, as well as constantly manage the environment to prevent further fighting. It is a daunting task.

Why Are They Fighting?

My worst experiences with housemate aggression have involved already having mature dogs on territory and bringing in another mature adult of the same sex. Whether dogs or bitches, if the animals are intact, the situation is exponentially worse. If you have had a group of adult dogs getting along already, and you bring in an intact animal, you may create problems. If you bring in a bitch who is intact and comes into heat, plan on a rumble.

There can also be trouble when you have a Critical Mass of dogs. I have had dogs and bitches of varying ages, some intact, some altered. (The only reason I keep an intact animal is because I am showing it in the breed ring.) These have all been reasonably well-socialized animals, some of them purchased as pups, some rescues brought in as young adolescents or adults. With four or five dogs, everything goes pretty smoothly. Because many of the animals were normal and stable, I have even had reasonably good luck with numbers six and seven. But I begin to see cracks around the edges at that point. And by the time you get eight or nine, with a couple of males and several females, you may get the dogs separating into two or even three groups. At that point you are asking several "packs" to run in a very small territory – your home. This is a recipe for aggression! If you bring any dogs who have not been well socialized or are reactive into such a large group, there is big trouble ahead.

In most cases of interdog aggression, the aggression does not develop overnight, even though it appears that way to the humans involved. I very seldom had altercations, other than mild getting-to-know-each-other stuff, in the first couple of weeks after bringing in a new dog. So, just about when the human is patting himself on the back about how clever he is, the dogs are revving up for some serious business. In my experience, the two-to-six-week period after arrival is crucial when bringing new adult dogs onto territory. If the new dog you bring in is a puppy, you probably won't see problems (if any arise) until the puppy reaches 18 to 24 months of age. If you do see trouble prior to this, the dogs are telling you how very stressed they are by the environmental change.

Adding a new member to the household is not the only vulnerable time. Every time you add *or subtract* a member, the group dynamics alter drastically. So, you may have a situation similar to one I had: I was running three boys – one castrated and extremely sensible, one intact and sensible, one intact and pushy. By the time the youngest male was twelve months old, I castrated his father. So now I had two sensible castrated males and one intact male I was showing in the breed ring (whom I was encouraging to act with bravado so he "showed well"). With them I was running four girls, all spayed. When the oldest male "crossed over the Rainbow Bridge" at age fifteen, the two remaining boys, who had been just fine together for four years, started to gear up for a rumble. I could see it coming. If I had been complacent or non-observant at that time, I could have easily ended up with severe dog fights. In my house of terriers, that means a blood bath. We all kept reviewing our doggy manners lessons, and I managed to keep the household running reasonably smoothly. Unbeknownst to me, before his death, Sherman's presence (and he was a PRESENCE) had been keeping those boys toned down all along (with absolutely no violence whatsoever, I might add).

Besides such changes in the household makeup, dogs may be aggressive toward a canine housemate for a variety of other reasons. Common examples include:

- Competition for resources, including your attention. If a dog begins an agonistic display when another dog approaches you, it may well be a case of Resource Guarding. This is not as flattering as it can appear on the surface, because it is a form of possessive aggression. Your dog is preventing approach toward you just like she would toward a bone or favorite resting area or tasty tidbit – in other words, you are just another piece of rawhide!
- Status-related conflicts. Much interdog aggression involves housemates of the same sex, which makes sense if the conflict is originating over social status.
- A poor introduction to each other.
- One dog having established territory and resenting the other as an intruder.
- Redirected aggression. The dogs really want to go after the mailman or the dog next door, but are prevented from doing so and turn on each other in frustration.

Of course, more than one of these may be operating at the same time. In addition, the aggression may be learned with practice. Aggression toward a housemate might begin with Resource Guarding or some other reason, and then simply become routine because of the prior stimulus-response association. That is, the visual stimulus of the other dog becomes the CUE to begin conflict. This is a strong and persistent association.

Anatomy of a Dog Fight

Most people know what the later stages of an all-out dog fight look like. There is more to the fight than this final furious phase, though, and being able to recognize the *early warning signs* is rare. It is, however, critical for preventing an impending brawl.

Body Posture

Stress makes your dog more reactive – just like it does you. Watching carefully for signs of stress in your dog will allow you to *intervene early* to short circuit the tension that leads to physical violence.

Postures that often indicate that your dog is feeling *stress* are:
- Lip Licking (out of context).
- Pupil Dilation (out of context).
- Sniffing the ground (out of context).

Accelerating discomfort, which can spill over into *Agnostic Display*, may be indicated by some of the following:
- Urination.
- Excessive Salivation.
- Slinking postures.
- Rolling over on the back and retracting the lips – here, the animal is in severe conflict.
- Lowering or tucking of the tail.
- Ears pulled back horizontally.
- Piloerection reflex (hair standing up on the back of the neck, back and perhaps extending down the tail region).
- Growling.
- Snapping.
- Head and neck slightly lowered, looking up out of the "tops" of the eyes.
- Any sudden stillness. This often happens just prior to a Strike or Lunge culminating in a bite.

Again, the earlier you intervene when you see these behaviours, the more likely you are to prevent all-out aggression from following, which is obviously beneficial in the short run, but also in the long run, as you will be preventing further rehearsal of fighting.

Challenges (deliberate invitations for conflict) can begin with something as subtle as staring from across the room. Challenges can also be much more obvious than that! They may involve blocking access to a bed or crate, posturing in ritualized display with the classic T-position (head over the other dog's shoulders), or mounting behaviours. These challenges can then advance into a serious fight. The longer that challenges between dogs are allowed to last, the worse the fight potential becomes. So, intervene early! Challenges between dogs with a history of fighting rarely resolve in a safe manner all by themselves. Just like you would supervise unsociable toddlers in a sand box, so must you supervise your dogs' interactions.

Without intervention, the dog who is challenged will behave in one of three ways:
- Showing deference to the other dog by some manner of submissive display, such as: rolling over, urinating, muzzle licking, and relinquishing objects and locations. In short, he allows the other dog to always be first and have his own way.
- Choosing to escalate the agonistic display, thus winning or losing the challenge physically, to the apparent satisfaction of both animals concerned.
- Continuing the mutual challenge, with each dog being unwilling to concede and no clear outcome (from the dogs' perspective) as to status.

In both the second and third alternative, the situation may become quite dangerous for both humans and dogs. Even the first situation is unsafe in the long run, as circumstances may change in the future and lead the submissive dog to escalate the fights.

Remember, the goal here is to recognize stress, agonistic displays, and challenges and counter-challenges early, and *intervene*! **Refer to Foundation and Level I Protocols for intervention skills.**

Challenges (and fights) can differ in appearance and structure depending on the relationship between the dogs involved. For example, often there is same-sex conflict amongst canine housemates. In general, fights that are between two dogs of the same sex are more serious. Their challenges are also often extremely ritualized. The ritualization includes most or all of the behaviour one associates with a rank ordering display.

The dogs (males) tend to carry this posturing behaviour out a while. They may start with stares from across the room; approach each other stiff-legged from a distance; stand near and push on each other; put front legs on each other's shoulders. The entire sequence may be accompanied by low, throaty vocalizations. If one of the animals does not clearly capitulate at this juncture, both animals will escalate the agonistic display. At some point, both dogs will become very still. Then one will break the stillness and it becomes a free-for-all, knock-down, drag-out western-style saloon fight. However, these challenges can change over time: once this full blown fight has occurred a few times, the dogs may begin to go straight from staring across the room to running head-on at each other into physical battle.

The boys tend to drag all the ritual stuff out much longer than the girls. With my fox terriers, two people could get the boys apart using shoe-leather, broom handles, baby gates or whatever else that was handy to get between them. About half the time, the boys looked relieved to be broken up, and, although hot, would subside once we got them separated. Amongst experienced dog breeders and owners, bitch fights are the legendary ones, and my own experience bears this out. My own bitches tend to vocalize much less and cut to the chase. That is, they truncate the ritualized behaviour more abruptly, and are much more serious earlier into the altercation. The most serious fights I saw were totally silent, between two bitches who were housemates and had a long-standing feud brewing. The fighting style between female housemates can be chilling. There may be no warning beyond a split-second of eye-contact (which is merely their tacit agreement to begin, with no holds barred), with the remainder of the ritualized behaviour being abandoned. In these fights, the animals will often do throat bites, which are intended to be a hold until the other dog has suffocated to death. This may or may not be accompanied by shaking. If there is shaking, it is likely to occur at the beginning of the throat hold, which can cause massive damage, such as tearing the trachea loose. Sometimes one of the animals will obtain a throat-hold and just close her eyes and hang on waiting for her opponent to die. I had one bitch who, when she fought, always went for the other dog's eyes, which is a fighting style I typically associate more with cats. But it was an effective strategy, disabling her opponent quickly. The point here is that you need to be aware of the highly truncated challenge phase, as well as the immense danger involved, in such fights.

There is a high incidence of redirected aggression amongst dogs who no longer "trust" each other due to past conflict and fights. This is particularly true if the fights have culminated in injury to one or both dogs, even if the injury is minor. With redirected aggression, there may be very little warning (challenge phase).

So, if you have aggressive housemates, learn what their stress and their challenges look like. *These are the early stages of the fight.* Learn to recognize the earliest indications of when you must intervene and how much time you can expect to have before all hell breaks loose. Be prepared for how serious and dangerous these fights can become.

I have observed *two basic styles of fighting*. One is the bite and hold, often accompanied by shaking. The second is the jump in, bite, perhaps give a quick shake, back up, jump in, and bite again. The first type of fighting I associate most often with terriers. The second style I associate most with the rest of the canine world. This is not absolute, as it is certainly possible for any dog to fight in any manner that comes naturally to her at the time. If animals are allowed to rehearse behaviour, they will also learn "tricks" from those they fight with.

If the dogs are repeatedly lunging, biting and letting go, you can generally get something between them. The most favored option is something like a baby gate which might allow you enough time to steer one animal into another room and get a door shut between them. The least favored option here is yourself. Twice I have stepped between two dogs to save my dog from being bitten by someone else's, and each time I have taken the bite myself. Both times the other dog initiated the attack and I happened to see it coming and stepped between the dogs. I have, by doing this, been able to get my dog back and into a down, allowing me to get control of the other animal. This works okay with my GSD bitch, who, even under fire, will comply with cues. The compliance isn't pretty, but she will back off, teeth chattering uncontrollably, and lie down. This would not be so with the majority of my terrier bitches, who, when they are hot, are hot through and through, and do not even know who I am. In that case, I would need to get my terrier completely off the scene to keep her from escalating the conflict.

With bite-and-hold fighters, one can try to break the dogs off each other by inserting a thick piece of wood in each dog's jaws and prying them from each other. A breaking stick, which has one flattened end, works well since you can insert that end into the dog's mouth in the "thin" direction and then twist the stick so that the "thick" side pries the dog's mouth open. If you do not have a breaking stick, a screw-driver would work, but the risk of breaking teeth or damaging the dog's mouth would be much greater. Using ANYTHING other than your fingers or hands is the RULE. If you reach in between two dogs who are fighting, you may very well be bitten.

If the fight is fierce, and you are going to end up with a dead dog, make a judgment call and use whatever means is available to get the dogs apart. If you are alone, you will need to get one dog into another room (or tie one dog back to something, if possible, knowing that you are placing yourself at very great risk doing so).

Two of my Fox Terrier bitches got into an altercation one day long ago when I was home alone. It was the first serious dog fight I had witnessed. (Had I been more experienced, it could have been prevented!) They were in a bite-and-hold with each other. It was a typical, bite-and-never-let-go-till-you-die terrier battle. I was not physically strong enough to get them apart. Spraying pepper spray on them had served to make both of them fiercer. Trying to separate them with brute force failed. If I picked one up, I got them both and that, too, made them hold on to each other harder. Throwing water on them just got the floor wet and slippery with blood *and* water, and made it more difficult for me to maneuver without falling. In the end, after a fierce struggle to pry them apart, I left them to fight, fearing every second would be too late. I did the only thing I could think of: I filled the tub with water. I got them apart by holding them under water. Not pretty, and I was terrified I would drown them both. However, it was clear to me that if I didn't do something, I was going to have at least one dead dog. By the time I got the girls to the tub, Breanna was just holding on with her eyes closed and Jynx's tongue was hanging out, turning blue. Holding the girls under water allowed me to get Breanna off Jynx and toss her out of the room and get the door closed. Then we all got to go for emergency medical treatment. All of this began in a split second and lasted no longer than ten minutes.

Once dogs are fighting, keep in mind that you are now into damage control. There is no training opportunity here! The only goal, once the two dogs have begun an altercation, is to keep them from holding and/or shaking each other. Both intervening and not doing so is dangerous. Trying to keep them apart will only serve to stimulate the dogs into wanting each other more, but allowing them to get hold of each other will most certainly escalate the fighting. The holding, full-mouth bite is extremely punishing and can lead to suffocation. But the shaking that some dogs are so prone to can cause excessive amounts of tissue and organ damage. And the shaking is what tears the dog up, resulting in stitches.

If you have already had dog fights, or have seen enough signs to expect some, you need to have strategies and materials (baby gates, breaking sticks, doors and crates that can separate dogs, and so forth) ready. And, of course, a crucial strategy is to recognize the early warning signs and intervene then. An even better strategy is to manage the dogs to prevent challenges and fights from happening at all!

Management

If the animals involved are not *spayed or castrated*, that is my first recommendation. Sex hormones cause dogs to be more reactive and to remain in the reactive state for a longer period of time. Castration produces a greater than 60% reduction in aggression toward other dogs among males (Overall, 1997; Hopkins, et al, 1976). Spaying will also reduce interdog aggression among females. If the animals have been fighting for some time, you will also have learned behaviour and prior associations to deal with, but alteration will make all future behaviour modification easier.

Separate all dogs involved at ALL TIMES when not supervised. This means placing them in separate rooms, because you do not want to have antagonistic dogs staring each other down from their crates. When they are set free they will let loose on each other with all their frustration.

Minimize even supervised interactions between the dogs. Allowing them to groom each other or go out and urinate together (particularly males) can quickly escalate into a fight. Playing with toys with each other is forbidden. Anything that changes the environment can set off a fight – a doorbell ringing, a child entering the room, a person entering with food, another dog bringing in a toy. Even normal situations that are interrupted with a Sudden Environmental Contrast (SEC) are too volatile to expect the dogs to have good judgment.

Be aware that high-arousal situations will always be extremely volatile for these dogs. Examples may include feeding time, play with a favored toy, or someone coming to the door. Prevent those potentially explosive situations that you can. With those you cannot prevent, keep the dogs separated when they are likely to occur, and be ready to intervene in sudden explosions (again, see Foundation and Level I protocols for intervention strategies). Once the dogs are very well trained, down stays can be used to control them during high-arousal situations.

If you take one dog out for a walk or to work, crate them both on your return. The smartest thing to do in this instance is crate the "left" dog before you leave. Upon your return, both dogs will be in an aroused state which can quickly turn into redirected aggression.

Managing the dogs and the environment is essential with aggressive housemates. This cannot be emphasized enough. If you don't "like" crating dogs or separating them – get over it! You have to because, otherwise, things won't improve! "Managing" also involves constantly scrutinizing them during their supervised time together (if they proceed well enough in their training to be allowed such time together). Always, always supervise them when they are out together and be vigilant for signs of stress, agonistic displays or challenges that may precede fights. Intervene! Even break up and reward prolonged polite interactions to keep them from having bad ideas about each other again. This interrupts any increase in arousal levels and prevents reversions to "Lizard-Brain" behaviour. This also makes the dogs aware that you are "watching" them and that you are monitoring their interactions.

In addition to keeping antagonistic dogs separated as much as possible and reducing arousing situations, work the dogs through the following protocols to teach them new, better behaviours when they are out together.

Protocols for Housemate Aggression

What To Do and Not Do – Getting Started

One piece of advice you might have heard on how to handle interdog aggression is to choose a dominant dog and support his status over the other dog. This is a *very dangerous* strategy! If you are enforcing one dog's dominance, who is running the show: you or him? It better be you, because your dog is living in your world, and he cannot be expected to make human judgment calls. Anyway, do you *really* know which dog is dominant? People overestimate the degree to which they can read status among dogs. In reality, dog status is very fluid and contextual. Plus, it may be that both dogs are motivated temperamentally to be close to the same status level. In fact, this is the source of many prolonged status-related fights. So, in that case, whom would you support as the dominant dog?

Instead of trying to enforce one dog's dominance, make it clear to the dogs that they will both be *generously rewarded for displaying socially compatible behaviour:*

- Calming signals
- Ignoring each other
- "Sharing" your attention
- Remaining non-reactive with each other

Manage (see above section in this chapter) to minimize high arousal levels, and intervene to modify behaviour during high arousal levels when they do occur. Interrupt the dogs' interactions frequently, both to prevent challenges from starting, and to reward desirable behaviour when you see it.

Before getting started with protocols specific to housemate aggression, *be sure that the dogs involved are solid in their Foundation and Level I protocols.*

Teach a really good Sit & Remain Calm. Teach the Sit with all positives – no punishers (beyond a NRM or gentle pressure on the collar; no collar corrections made by jerking). What you are applying reinforcement to, here, is Sit AND RELAX and/or Down AND RELAX. Practice this Remain Calm behaviour in as many contexts as you possibly can. The goal here is not just to hold the Sit Stay, but to Sit and *Remain Calm.* How can you tell if the dog is calm? The dog will focus on the handler and the food. She will begin to look relaxed, and will cease rapid, hyperactive-looking movements. Her eyes will become softer, pupils less dilated. The tension will go out of her jaw. She will begin to ignore distractions and focus calmly on the handler.

You must have an EXTREMELY reliable response to several cues: Sit, Down, Stay, Come and Leave It are mandatory. It may take several months to install these behaviours, even if your dog already knows some obedience. You need reliable responses to these cues even if you give them suddenly and out of context. This is a skill that requires much practice. Let's take the context of you sitting in the living room watching television. You call your dog and cue her to Sit, Come, or Lie Down out of the clear blue sky. She may respond pretty well. But do you get an *immediate and reliable response*? In this situation, these cues are not preceded by the normal "routine" that your dog associates with working, such as when you gather up the leash and bait bag to prepare for a work session. Make it a point to practice getting a cued behaviour quickly and out of context several times a day, in many different locations, until the response to a cue becomes habit for your dog no matter what the setting is. A reliable response to these cues is necessary to the success of this program.

Once the dogs are reliable with the Foundation and Level I protocols and are reliable with the above cues, you can begin training them with protocols more specific to housemate aggression. Because, by definition, more than one dog is involved in housemate aggression (even if one dog is just being constantly attacked by the other, more aggressive dog), you will need to work with both dogs. Some protocols require you to work with both dogs at the same time, so a helper will be needed.

Under Controlled Circumstances – specifically, in this chapter, an environment in which you can control most variables and can reduce the incidence of Sudden Environmental Contrasts – the dogs must be able to be on leash around each other, and sit or lie down and stay in a variety of contexts around each other. Use your Sit (or Down) and Remain Calm, your Look, and your Leave It to begin to achieve this. Use Head collars to get both dogs under the control of verbal cues and muzzles if the extra safety is required.

As you are doing the behaviour modification protocols, be careful that you do not create situations where there is a lot of tension and conflict that can quickly explode into a dog fight. If the dogs are reactive and get fired up around treats, the two people handling the dogs on leash must keep the dogs' experiences around each other as upbeat as possible, while still keeping the dogs out of trouble.

Specific protocols

After achieving solid responses to Foundation and Level I protocols, the following protocols (covered earlier in the book) will be requisite:

- Common Sense Is Just Not That Common … Taking Advantage of Calming Signals
- Yielding & Husbandry Behaviours
- Handling & Restraint – Desensitization to Being Touched
- Relationships – A Program for Teaching Dogs that Humans Are Relevant!
- Dog-to-Dog Approaches

The Dog-to-Dog Approaches will require a second handler. Under Controlled Circumstances, practice dog approaches, with the goal of having the dogs acquire the *habit of Being Reinforced for Ignoring Each Other* in several different contexts. Practice the dog-to-dog approaches in a wide variety of contexts, *approximating up to* lots of distractions and arousing stimuli (e.g., sudden environmental contrasts, such as a new dog entering the training area or a doorbell ringing). Then, when you think you have this exercise down (your dogs are relatively immune to distractions and arousing situations around each other and they can sit side by side and remain calm) … keep practicing! Remember that these dogs have a history of fighting together. They have become cues to each other to fight. That option is always there in their behavioural repertoire. Even if you have great responses to these protocols and it looks like the old fighting response is gone, it is still "in there." Continual practicing of the new responses will keep these new better behaviours fresh and more likely to be accessed than the old fighting response.

Some new exercises that will help are:

1. Put both dogs in a sit near you. Pet one, and then feed that one. Then, feed the other one for tolerating your interactions with the first one. At first, this is best done with a second handler, but after the dogs become better at self-restraint, you can do this by yourself.
2. Sit on the sofa. Call the dogs over. Ask one (Dog 1) to Sit or Down. Make a fuss over Dog 2. Reward the sitting/downed Dog 1 for tolerance and remaining in place. Then reverse this: put Dog 2 in a sit or down, and make a big fuss over Dog 1. Reward Dog 2 for tolerance and staying. Again, you can do this by yourself if you have confidence that a brawl won't break out. Otherwise, use a second handler to keep an eye on the sitting/downed dog. This exercise is best practiced on-leash at first; advance to doing it off leash as the dogs exhibit good self-control.
3. Remember that if you take one for walk, crate the one left behind and also crate the walked dog on return. When things are calm for 5 to 15 minutes, get both dogs out and put them in sits and downs together for treats (never facing each other in a "conflict" position). Then allow them to interact, if you think that it is safe to do so at this point in training. Follow this advice when you work the dogs as well. Crate one dog, and work the other dog. Then trade, crating one and getting the other out to work. After a five to fifteen minute "rest" period, get the dogs out and carefully (this may require two handlers) work the dogs together. If you are using two handlers, work the dogs for a couple of minutes, and then switch dogs. Then have the dogs lie down, facing the same direction (not facing each other!). Reinforce both dogs for ignoring each other. Now you can give the dogs their end-working cue (refer to the protocol for RM/NRM & Release Cue).

These procedures give the dogs structure, explain to them what you are expecting in each other's presence, and manufacture pleasant experiences around each other.

How Trainers Thwart Their Own Progress

Dog owners often have incorrect assumptions and beliefs about their dogs which hinder their work on housemate aggression. These beliefs are usually examples of wishful thinking that stop people from recognizing how serious the problem is or lead them to mistakenly assume that the dogs cannot tolerate the required fixes.

One common false belief is that the dogs "should" love each other and get along – because they are "siblings" (or "pack mates"), or because "mommy" loves them both so much, or because they "know" that "mom" wants them to get along. People who fall into this trap are treating their dogs like human children and are assuming both that they "know" what we want and are motivated to give it to us simply because we want it. None of this is true. Dogs have no idea what we want until we train them. Even then, what they learn is what *behaviour* we want. They can perhaps learn to cease fighting, and maybe even learn to be calm and relaxed around each other, but they may never "love" the housemate they used to fight with.

Also, dogs have their own priorities, and are not motivated to give us what we want only because we want it. They can be trained to act in ways that we like and to refrain from behaviour we dislike when it is made worth their while to do so, but they are not motivated simply to please us. People who have these beliefs may also be assuming that dogs who live together are more likely to get along than dogs who are strangers, much like human siblings often do. But this is also not true. Just because the dogs are raised together, for example, does not mean they will "love" each other. There are all sorts of canine-specific reasons that dogs who live together might not get along: status conflicts, resource guarding, redirected aggression, learned fighting – things that are not readily applicable to human family members. Look at your dogs as *dogs* and realize that the things that motivate them are very different from the things that matter to humans. Just because your dogs love you does not mean that they will love other dogs in the household, nor does it mean they will act the way you want without training.

People often think, because they love their dogs or because their dogs are not aggressive with other dogs outside the home, that their dogs are "nice" dogs and "nice" dogs would not be fighting with their housemates. Sometimes this belief takes the form of minimizing the level of aggression occurring. "Sparky doesn't really mean it, he's just cranky/jealous/not used to the newcomer" or "Prince may be growling at Missy, but he won't actually bite her because he is a nice dog (and he has never bitten her or anyone else in the past)" or "It's just a little herding dog bite, not a real bite" are examples of this. Sometimes this belief manifests as disabling emotional disappointment and discouragement with the problem. "I just can't understand why Muffin would act like this when she knows I don't want her to and she is otherwise such a nice dog. I don't know what I can possibly do. It's not like she is one of those mean dogs." Sometimes people don't get the help they need because doing so "means" admitting that the dog is aggressive and they cannot tolerate that thought. Don't get bogged down in how "nice" your dog is. "Nice" and "not nice" are not concepts that are relevant to dogs who have conflicts with housemates. Remember that there are strong learned components to this aggression, as well as some strong instinctual components. Dogs are using aggression, not because they are not "nice," but because the aggression is:

- working for them to get them something they think they need (e.g., access to resources, status);
- working to keep something away they desperately want kept away (e.g., an aggressive housemate who would otherwise strike first);
- simply a result of the dogs' chemical arousal level being very high and their having learned to get release by turning on their housemates (as with redirected aggression).

This does not make the dogs "not nice." It only means that they have either not learned, or they do not have access to, better ways of handling their problems. Your job is to manage the environment so the stimuli to fight are minimized and to train the dogs to respond to these stimuli differently, without worrying about what their aggression "means" about their "niceness" or their deep psychological state.

A variation on the above theme occurs when people look at the protocols for this problem, especially the management requirements, and assume that the dog is too "nice" or too sensitive to tolerate them. Believing that you just cannot crate your dogs, or separate them, or interact with only one at a time, or "deprive" them of running loose in the backyard to run the fence for hours, or restrict their actions in any way necessary to stop the fighting is doing the dogs a great disservice. Usually it is the *people* involved who really cannot tolerate these things because of false beliefs about what dogs need. Dogs do not suffer from being crated or kept primarily indoors. And, believe me, if they are fighting, some of them, at least, will be grateful and relieved if you manage the environment to reduce the aggression! Separation, crating, and adding structure to their lives are all very tolerable to dogs, and will be welcomed by the dogs who are only reluctant participants in the aggression. Existing in a tension-filled, unpredictable, violent environment is very wearing on a dog. It is like being locked in the house with an abusive spouse 24 hours a day.

These obstructionist attitudes on the part of owners are very common, and very destructive. People just do not want to believe that their dogs are really causing as much damage to each other as they are (since "nice" dogs supposedly wouldn't). But dogs really can do tremendous damage to each other when there is frequent aggression, from both injuries and constant stress.

Many owners of aggressive dogs also do not want to buckle down and do what they need to do to fix things. The management prescriptions are *absolutely essential* for reducing housemate aggression, but they are the most resisted by people. Taking on the management prescriptions means greatly reorganizing the household and the amount of time and access the dogs have with each other and with you. Folks are not resistant to the effort involved, but to the fact that it means *admitting that their dogs really do have a serious problem that is evidenced by this tremendous lifestyle change.* They mistakenly think that this means admitting that their *dogs* are not "nice" or "good," when it really just means admitting that the *behaviour* is serious and difficult to modify and that it requires a lot of changes in the environmental structure to facilitate learning.

Being willing to make these management changes will determine the success or failure of getting the aggressive housemates to live together peaceably. I have had to severely manage my home environment (and relentlessly train these protocols) with Breanna, Maeve, and many of my other "projects." There was no way that I could kid myself about the level of aggression these dogs displayed: there have been near-deaths, stitches, and broken bones as a result of their fights. The terriers have breed predilections to this type of aggression, and Maeve came to me as a rescue dog, probably with learned aggression and poor socialization. But, all these dogs have been able to remain in my home and I rarely have an incident anymore, because I looked the problem square in the face, understood the canine dynamics involved, admitted immediately how serious and damaging it was, and did what was required to reorganize my household and train. These dogs *do not* interact with each other unsupervised (and rarely even when supervised), *are* kept crated when I am not around, *do not* have free access to high value resources, and have been highly trained to look at me *whenever* their arousal level starts to rise. Period!

This can be contrasted with some people who consult me for housemate aggression who resist the management prescriptions. A client I once had typifies this resistance. She had two male dogs: one resident dog and one acquired later as a puppy. Upon reaching that magic age of about 18 months, the younger dog began attacking the older dog (status-related aggression, in this case). The older dog tried to use calming signals and negotiation to stop the younger dog's attacks. But the younger dog ignored the signals and continued to attack. Since negotiation did not work, the older dog was forced to fight back. He had no other option than to fight. The owner was reluctant to crate her dogs (they would "hate" it), or to separate the dogs and restrict their access to her and each other, because they were "nice" dogs who should "know" that she loved them and didn't want them to fight. She thought it "should" work out that they get along simply because she wanted it so badly. The idea of separating her "babies" would make her teary. It truly *hurt her feelings* that the dogs did not like each other, and she could not bear to admit the full extent of the problem and take the necessary steps to manage the dogs' behaviour. She also failed to recognize early marginal behaviour for what it was, and ended up having to deal with extreme behaviour. The dogs' behaviour escalated into a deep-seated problem with a poor prognosis. Status-related attacks are very resistant to change. Plus, by this point, the older dog had learned that the only way to save himself was to fight back. In fact, what the older dog learned is that the owner was NOT going to protect him, and he was on his own to do whatever it took to save himself. He had become a "victim" in his own house, and behaved defensively, as his daily safety was no longer a given. The message the dogs were getting was: "You are on your own to duke it out and I don't care who wins or loses or how it occurs." This is the *opposite* of what the owner thought she was conveying to the dogs ("Please know that I love you and want you get along with each other"), but she was not realistic enough to give the dogs what they needed: separation and structure.

I cite this example not for its extremity, but rather because the fears and discomforts expressed are all too common. It is enormously difficult for people to admit that their dogs are dogs, not children (the "little people in fur suits" myth). People feel that dogs should understand what their owners want (without training and structure), and their feelings are hurt when dogs don't. Or, they feel that their dogs' behaviour reflects badly on them (which can be exacerbated by others' reactions to their "bad dogs"). It is even harder for people to make a huge shift in their understanding of the situation (that the dogs are just being *dogs*, albeit having learned some very undesirable behaviour requiring modification) while they are in the throes of being stressed by all of this scary fighting going on.

Housemate aggression requires clear-headedness about the seriousness of the problem, appreciating the dogs for what they are, and the toughness to make the needed changes in the household.

Summary

I am not going to candy-coat this. Aggression between housemates is one of the most difficult problems to fix. You must re-train two dogs at the same time. In addition to whatever problem initially caused the fighting (resource guarding, status conflicts, etc.), there has been a history of learned fighting and seeing each other as cues to aggression laid over top of that problem. These dogs are together all the time, continually "reminding" each other of that shared history. Plus, homes are huge sources of high arousal (toys, food, territory to guard, and so on) and sudden environmental contrasts that are difficult to control (doorbells ringing, squirrels appearing outside on the sidewalk, kids running in, etc.).

The dogs must be especially reliable in all the basic protocols, and several of the advanced protocols, as noted above. Plus, they must develop good habits around each other. This requires a *lot* of training, using a second handler in the later stages.

You need to learn to recognize the early signs of impending dog fights and learn how to intervene to curtail them. Also be prepared for those fights that do break out. Know how you will try to break it up, have several strategies available, and learn to stay focused on the task at hand. This last is hard to do, as it is terrifying to be in the midst of the primal violence of a dog fight. To this day, when anyone in my family even hears a dog growl, we are all on alert! Never do I get used to dogs fighting. It is horrifying each time, and the adrenaline dump makes me physically ill. What I strive for is to remain in control of my emotions and my body until the crisis is over. If other people are helping to break up the fight, try to give them clear directions about what you are doing (e.g., "I have Maeve. Get Breanna and put her in a crate.") Practice in your head, before a real fight, giving yourself and other people simple, direct instructions.

More than for any other problem, *management is crucial here*, and is at least as important as behaviour modification. Training is vital, but managing the environment allows the behaviour modification to occur. You must manage the environment to reduce arousal and sudden environmental contrast, *and* manage the dogs to keep them separate as much as possible and intervene early when necessary, *and* manage the other household members to make sure they can also do these things. This management is ongoing for the lifetime of the dogs involved! You must be sure that you are up to this task if you want to keep both dogs!

The prognosis for housemate aggression will vary, depending, in part, on the underlying reason the dogs are fighting. If you have two dogs in a persistent status-related battle, for example, you will be relying largely on management and have to face the fact that they may never co-exist peacefully. The dogs may learn to behave politely around each other under Controlled Circumstances, but will probably never behave well just being out together. In this situation, if the dogs were free-ranging (never something I would advise!), or left to their own devices (also inadvisable!), one dog would disperse or there would ensue a battle and one dog would be dead. Humans prevent this natural process from occurring, and therefore we must continually minimize the conflicts through management instead.

I manage my little pack at home very well, but even I have a tendency to become careless when I have not had a "Situation" for a long time. Every time I do get careless, some little incident occurs that reminds me that peace has a price, and that price is constant management. If housemate aggression is present between adult dogs, do not assume that those tendencies will ever go away. In many instances, the best that can be hoped for is that the dogs will choose to ignore each other.

You need to be ever watchful. Resist complacency when the dogs have "been good" for a month or a year. This problem is not one that you can put to bed. You can manage, minimize, modify. But you can *never* rest on your laurels!

Can it be done? Consider the family dynamics, and how you want to live your life. Consider the quality of life of the other people and canines in the home. How much danger are the humans in from these dogs? How much danger are the dogs to each other? Are there other pets at risk? How much tension is constantly present because of the dogs' dislike of each other? How severe are the dog fights? In my house full of terriers, for example, the fights are very dire indeed – especially when you add a mature, assertive GSD bitch who is very predacious to the mix. Broken bones, stitches, and death are potential results of fights among these dogs. Some of my clients, on the other hand, have dogs who make tremendous noise and have very frightening displays, but who do little damage when they actually fight. You *must* realistically appraise the risks you will be living with. *Resist sugar-coating this risk out of your affection for the dogs.*

See how the protocols and the management go. The relationship between you and your dog will be strengthened by the work. You will gain more reliable response to your cues over a variety of situations. Then look at whether the protocols are being successful with this problem and consider all other factors to help you come to a reasonable decision that is best for all concerned.

54

THERE ARE NO "RECIPES" TO MODIFY AGGRESSION

The protocols in this book were designed to take you step-by-step through the process of behaviour modification.

My clients and I have netted extremely good results from using these protocols. Most of these protocols were made for my clients to follow between visits. Others were developed specifically for use with groups of dogs, such as those in my Resocialization classes. These are all protocols that are useful over a wide variety of circumstances, and are pertinent to all dogs presenting with aggression, fear, anxiety, or over-reactivity. They will also *prevent* your dog from becoming a dog that accesses aggression.

It is important to keep in mind that these are NOT RECIPES. There is no such thing as a program that will work in one single way for every dog! These are meant to be guidelines, to aid you in treating your dog and to give you a starting place. Each dog will move through and understand some approximations very quickly, and others very slowly. People and dogs will learn tasks in their own manner and on their own time line. For some dogs, the approximations listed will be too large. This means that you will need to place intermediate steps in between the approximations I have identified for you.

How will you know if you need to do that? If your dog is struggling with a concept and is not performing as desired, there are technical reasons why. I cannot predict what problems you and your dog will encounter. However, one of the big problems dog trainers have is that they present the dog with too large a bite of information for that animal to process. If your dog has mastered one step, and you move to the next one, and he just cannot seem to "get it right," stop. Break the behaviour down into even smaller pieces of information. If moving one step away causes your dog to break his Sit Stay, just move one foot and put it back down and reinforce that. Now move both feet. Now try a half a step, and so on. It is amazing how "small" you can make an approximation.

Timing is another crucial component of behaviour modification. It is crucial that your feedback and information be given to the dog *very quickly*. You will have to learn to oscillate quickly between "Yes" (I liked that) and "Try Again" (not what I wanted). The Reward Mark/No Reward Mark System will provide you with a means of communication, but the timely manner in which it is given is up to you!

Another reason a dog does not advance is because the handler fails to raise criteria. Granted, if your dog has "already got a problem," raising criteria can be a very scary step for you. Safety of all involved must be the priority at all times.

But, given all that, if you never raise criteria, you simply will not advance beyond a given point.

As discussed previously, you may wish to place a time line on your protocol plan, and reassess your progress to determine if your goals are being met. You may need to extend your time line. If working with an aggressive dog, you may need to make a decision if extending the time line will produce appropriate improvement.

The owners who discover how much work this will be and decide it isn't worth their effort or "they don't have time," of course, will not net the kind of improvement the dedicated owners do. I am not saying these are bad people, I am just pointing out that this is an arena where effort and outcome are very dependant upon each other. The number of dogs who are extremely dysfunctional or have a serious neurological malfunction is small compared to the normal dogs who need management and behaviour modification or dogs who are real "do-able" even if some disorder is present.

You must determine how you are going to handle situations BEFORE they come up, so you can practice each one in low-arousal mode to prepare the dog to obey you when he is in high-arousal mode. You will use your list of "triggers" to determine what areas need work and apply a protocol to each and every one of them.

If your dog becomes more reactive, or more aggressive, over a 90 day time frame, or you are not seeing at least some progress over 30 days, you are misusing one of the techniques and may need to seek the help of a behaviour specialist. Your timing is off; the technique is not sufficient for the type and intensity of aggression your animal is presenting; you are lacking in sufficient technical skill (that just means you need some help until you master the technical skill); you are trying to mix philosophies and are confusing the dog; or any number of technical reasons why a training program needs a spot of help from someone who is experienced with the laws of learning, and, preferably, aggression as well.

As an alternative, if you really cannot find anyone to help you, have someone video-tape the training sessions. Watch the video multiple times and find your training errors. This is a great way to educate yourself!

Virtually all the dogs who have had committed owners who follow through with the protocols and remain proactive (do not become complacent) have netted improvements in their dog's behaviour using these protocols. Very occasionally, we need a 90% improvement and only get 25% in an area. Quite often these protocols produce amazing results, with 70-90% and sometimes 99.9% improvement. *Persistence and commitment are a big part of this success rate.* Reasonable expectations count, too.

My clients often surprise me with the results they get, as I tend to be conservative in my estimates of how much the dog will improve. Let's face it – my clients come to me with extremely challenging animals and nowhere near my experience level. (Read: they are not stupid enough to have been bitten as many times as I have....) Yet, they are committed and careful and eager to succeed and that alone – this handler attitude – makes a great difference.

A dog who presents with aggression is extremely unsettling, and some owners are not prepared emotionally to be able to deal with this manner of presentation in a calm and neutral way, which is imperative. Your attitude will have a huge effect on your dog and can verify or diffuse the situation for your dog. This is a learned behaviour for you. Your reactions will become calmer as YOU learn new coping strategies and have success with them.

You will, in many ways, follow the same path as your dog as you work through the protocols together. You and your dog will succeed in a big way by way of many small steps.

Appendices

CASE HISTORY EXAMPLES

Included in this chapter are a few case histories to provide you examples of behaviour problems and the protocols used to modify the behaviours. I have used some casual references (abbreviations and informal comments) for expediency, as these are actually taken from my clinical notes. Some, like using "vet" for veterinarian, I hope will be excused by my readers. These notes are taken, for the most part, unchanged from my files, so please also excuse my grammar and punctuation anomalies. I have jotted some additional notes for you, dear reader – thoughts that I considered might be interesting to you as you read through the case history.

Also, to preserve confidentiality, the names of the canine patients have been changed to an arbitrary choice, and the client's names and the names of the referring veterinarians have been omitted.

Please notice that, in most cases, the classification is not just one aggression classification, but often there are multiple issues to be addressed. Remember, I often withhold my final classification until I have placed the dog on a protocol program and carefully observed the response of the dog to the individual protocols.

All dogs should complete the Foundation Protocols. The Level I and Level II Protocols are also excellent for *all* dogs; however, dogs presenting with aggression might need to approach the protocols in a different order, spending more time on each step and doing so with great caution.

I believe in a "Scheduled Feed" and I believe there should be "no free food." Whether it is the dog's meal or treats, the dog should earn the food by following a command such as sit, down, shake hands, etc.

As you read through these case history examples, keep in mind that each dog is different and the level of response to stimuli is different.

Also, the protocols listed for each case history may not be complete. They do show you where we started, and so it may give you an idea where you could start if you had a similar problem. How the dog responds to the initial protocols and improves or regresses tells you in which direction to go next.

I have excerpted portions of case histories to illustrate a certain point. Therefore, these case histories are not meant for you to compare a dog you are working with and then go look at the solutions I used in that case history, then think you are done with the work. In the real world, each case history is different and the family dynamics in each situation are different. The case history is interesting for you to read and serves as a general example which will perhaps help to point you in a direction to begin work. Many of these clients have been working with me for months and years have obviously done extensive work, the extent of which is not evident in these short versions.

The following is a case history example of

LEARNED AGGRESSION, TERRITORIAL AGGRESSION.

HEAVEN ON ARF BEHAVIOUR COUNSELING
RE: Hound/Boxer-X, Female-spayed
DOB: ? 1997
NAME: Patty (name changed)

My initial consult with "Patty" was February 2000.

Past Medical History: Spayed. Unremarkable medical history, normal physical at the last veterinarian call.

Meds: Occasionally uses Benedryl for long trips to reduce nervous behaviour in the car per vet advice.

Environmental and Social History: This pet was a stray. The clients have owned the pet for one and a half years. There are two adults and two children (girl, age 11; boy, age 6) in household. There is another pet, a Basset bitch approximately 10 years old. The dog receives lots of exercise and plays well with the children. The clients are devoted to this dog.

Presenting Issues: The dog occasionally gets loose; slips her head-collar or charges out the front door and becomes very aggressive with people in the yard – particularly the mailman.

Will also charge and bark and become aggressive toward other dogs and people when she is being walked on her leash.

If people approach the house, Patty will bark and the clients have a hard time controlling her or getting her to quiet.

The precipitating incident happened in late January. The daughter was walking the dog and she slipped out of her collar. The dog charged the mailman very aggressively. He sprayed her with pepper spray and yelled at the daughter, threatening to call Animal Control. Earlier in the month, the son and his friend left the front door ajar and the dog ran out charging the mailman.

Classification: No overt abnormalities discovered. Learned aggression, Territorial aggression. Will be more definite when I see how she responds to the protocol.

The following list consists specifically of training and behaviour modification issues:
We are battling an excessive Reinforcement history for poor behaviour
Lack of Structure during the initial training sequence
Lack of Training in areas that would communicate to this dog what specific behaviour is expected in a given context
Lack of early experience and socialization

Management:

Dog is to drag a leash around the house, at least initially for control purposes.
Dog is not to be allowed access in any way to the front door, out of the front door, or anywhere near the mailman until more control is established.
Dog is to be in crate if the mailman comes while the owner is at work or not home
Addressed dog getting out of the head collar, modified the equipment (can be done with safety pin or a couple of stitches) to prevent the collar from slipping.
Scheduled feed.
Discussed fit of head collar and importance of using a safety pin or stitch to secure h.c. from slipping; also use two leashes, or a tie connecting collar to head-collar to prevent loose dog.

Behaviour Modification:

Apply positive reinforcement to appropriate behaviour.
Introduce client & dog to a Reward Mark/No Reward Mark Training System.
Introduce the client & dog to protocols that encompass three main areas of concern: involvement, impulse-control behaviours, and desist.
Practice the protocols for Friendly Greetings and Wait at the Door.
Desensitize to movement.

Recommendation: Would like to see this dog in 30 days.

Initial Conclusion: Patty is a very nice dog with relatively stable temperament. Her behaviour appears to have started at social maturity and has a very high learned component. I surmise that the dog will respond very readily to the program as the clients are conscientious and highly motivated. This makes the prognosis: good to excellent.

Recheck 3/03/00: When Patty is barking at the upstairs window, owner can now call & Patty complies right away. This was one of the settings where the dog was uncontrollable in the past. The scheduled feed is going well and the dog has lost some "extra" weight. Dog attending to owner better. Wife is doing the majority of the training. Overall, all is going well.

Continuing Protocol: Continue to practice all prior protocols, gradually introducing her to being outside or in the house when the mailman comes and being non-reactive, receiving R+ for doing so. Client was shown and provided information on what to do if the dog is reactive (relinquishment exercises).

August 01/ Resocialization class: dog improved dramatically during the 6 week session. Owner control markedly better. Will take a 2nd session.

Recheck 05/15/02: I took a walk through the neighbor with Patty and the owner. The dog started to become reactive around some people working on the sidewalk. I was able to show the owner exactly what to do in this circumstance. Soon the owner was able to control the dog as well as I could. Patty showed some fear reaction to people on the street. During our work session, I could see 90% improvement in the dog's reaction to meeting people. This is going to be an ongoing learning experience for Patty. I am confident that, over time with the owner's persistence, Patty will soon be maintaining a fairly non-reactive response to seeing people and dogs on the street when on a walk. I stressed the fact that the client must interrupt the reactive behaviour before it starts.

Conclusion: Prognosis remains excellent, with continued training. The client has taken several group classes at my training facility, including one six-week session of Resocialization class, in which the dog showed marked improvement in overall reactivity levels. Normal dog. This is a very nice dog and is learning to behave appropriately.

The following is a case history example of

PLAY AGGRESSION.

HEAVEN ON ARF BEHAVIOUR COUNSELING
RE: Patient Case #097-021
Welsh Terrier, bitch
DOB: 11-18-99
NAME: Maggy (name changed)

My initial consult with "Maggy" was June 2000.

Past Medical History: Unremarkable medical history, normal physical at the last veterinarian call.

Environmental and Social History: See case history notes. Placed with loving owners as puppy by reputable breeder. Stable temperament.

Presenting Issues: Aggressive behaviour toward owners. Bites them when they do not pay attention to her. Bites them occasionally when they try to take a toy away form her. Attention seeking constantly. Housebreaking issues, especially when owner's mother (who live with them) comes upstairs with her little Yorkie. After the mother leaves, Maggy urinates and defecates on the floor. Issues with Yorkie over rawhide bones but no injury to Yorkie. Maggy will not come when called.

The clients had taken her to puppy kindergarten (traditional training) and they disliked the training as it was "harsh" and made "her bite us more."

Bites daughter, guests and owners when they come in if they do not immediately pay attention to her. She also bites the clients when they play games with her. Behaviour is escalating.

Classification: Play aggression. Inappropriate defecation & urination behaviour. Marking behaviour. Learned aggression. Possessive aggression.

Management:
Be aware of resource guarding situations and control or eliminate them until more owner control is in place.
Dog drags a leash always.
Do not physically punish.
Scheduled feed.
No free lunch – dog earns food, treats, etc. by obeying a command (sit, down, etc.).

Behaviour Modification:

Desensitize to eye contact
Involvement
5-15 minutes basic obedience 2x daily
Halti head-collar
Scenting games to engage dog's mind and give her a job
Install RM/NRM (had RM)
On leash whenever visitors come over, until owners have verbal control
NO rough play until more training in place
Fetching games

Continued Behaviour Modification:
Handling & restraint
Recall
Polite greeting
Targeting (used to "distract" dog from biting when excited)
Desensitize to territory entry

Conclusion: There is no real pathology indicated; this is a normal dog that merely lacks education. The dog now accepts eye contact, restraint, sits, downs, stays and comes when called. The clients are exceptionally good at following the protocol to the letter and they are consistent. It was important to change the way the clients interacted with the dog and teach client about ignoring inappropriate behaviours or using neutral NRM and reinforcing appropriate behaviour. We placed many more limits on the dog's behaviour – this was a great help. I have seen these clients several times over the last year and the dog is wonderful now; a very sweet girl. She now fetches and the owners can easily control the attention-seeking behaviour, although it has much reduced on its own due to the structure. Dog has improved with guests, has to be on leash only occasionally now with guests. Owner's daughter has gotten a new puppy and the dogs love to play together and are very good together. They share toys, although this took some management initially.

The territorial marking behaviour ceased with management. The dog was diagnosed with a urinary tract infection, but that was much later on (this spring) and was not connected to the marking behaviour earlier. Because of education, the owners immediately knew when the inappropriate urination was NOT marking behaviour and took the dog to the veterinarian.

NOTE: After one year, the clients love their well-adjusted, well-behaved, social dog that comes when called.

The following is a case history example of

LEARNED AGGRESSION, TERRITORIAL AGGRESSION, BREED TENDENCIES

HEAVEN ON ARF BEHAVIOUR COUNSELING
RE: Chow Chow, Male
DOB: 2/2000
NAME: Jack (name changed)

My initial consult with "Jack" was June 2001.

Past Medical History: Altered at 6 months of age. Unremarkable medical history, normal physical at the last vet call.

Environmental and Social History: In home are two adults and an adult child who visits frequently. The dog was acquired at 6 weeks of age. Owners had a previous Chow who also had aggression issues. This breeder assured them that "her Chows were not aggressive." Started classes at local college and was advised the dog was too aggressive to attend a group class. The dog has a bite history – the dog was tied in the fenced back yard and was barking. A friend (that the dog knows) was visiting and he walked over to the dog, talking as he approached; he told the dog to "quiet down" in a friendly voice and then reached out to pet him. Dog immediately bit the friend on the hand resulting in 6-7 stitches. Later that night the friend returned and the dog was very friendly, licking his hand, etc.

The wife is clearly afraid of the dog. The husband handles the dog; both want to work with the dog.

Medications: Currently on heart worm preventative

Presenting Issues: Aggressive behaviour toward owners over being touched, groomed or guided by the collar. Aggression toward strangers and people dogs knows. Aggression toward children. Redirected aggression.

Classification: Learned aggression. Territorial aggression. Personal space issues (not a true "diagnosis," but a fact nonetheless). The personal space issues would commonly be called control conflict (dominance) aggression, but I classify dominance aggression as those dogs who are actually challenging owners over "control" issues, not something tangible like being touched. This dog's aggressive reactions are really because of lack of structure in the dog's environment and natural breed tendencies. Eye contact by humans/dogs causes reactivity in this animal. The dog is improving over space issues with the owners as they work with him, therefore I withhold classification of control-conflict aggression at this point. If the behaviour persists or worsens, I will rethink this.

Protocol Addressed

Management:

ALWAYS supervise around children
Dog to be muzzled around children
Dog is to be placed in no situation where he can practice aggression out in the yard where owners cannot give him feedback about his behaviour
Dog is to drag leash around until owners have verbal control

Do not physically punish

Scheduled feed

Behaviour Modification:

Self restraint

Desensitize to movement

Desensitize to eye involvement

5-15 minutes basic obedience 2x daily

Scenting games to engage dog's mind and give him a job

Install RM/NRM (had RM)

Conclusion: This dog allowed me to approach and pet him after I had been in the room with him & owners for about 55 minutes, although I wouldn't have pushed him. He would take treats from me. At first he is very reactive at any sudden environmental change (doors opening, etc.) and also with small changes – person moving around the room, etc. The owners have reinforced this behaviour inadvertently by not knowing how to handle him. They were recognizing that force and punishment exacerbated the behaviour seriously, so instead they were reassuring him.

Discussed with the clients the training program and the importance of "outlasting" the dog. When dog doesn't want to do something he immediately flings himself to the floor and begins biting the leash...which can transfer to the human if he continues to be thwarted (re-directed aggression) – temper tantrums.

The second visit I was able to approach the dog immediately, scratched him near the tail and pet his head.

He even accepted some mild verbal social disapproval from me and I was able to do a mild "sit" collar pull which he responded to favorably AND it was effective. Much better for owners already. Capitulating quickly to owner and less fussing and biting at owner's hands and leash. Owner working dog daily at the door, on leash with guests and using time outs for wild play and puppy mouthing behaviours. Owners are working hard on the collar touching behaviour and handling and restraint. The dog is still very irritated and becomes defensive with any sort of prolonged touching, but is tolerating more of it at a steady rate.

Owner continuing to work with me.

The following is a case history example of

POSSESSIVE AGGRESSION, PROTECTIVE AGGRESSION, LEARNED AGGRESSION.

HEAVEN ON ARF BEHAVIOUR COUNSELING
RE: Rottweiler, Male, Castrated
DOB: 1996
NAME: Mike (name changed)

My initial consult with "Mike" was February of 2000.

Past Medical History: Altered at 6 months of age. Unremarkable medical history, normal physical at the last veterinarian call.

Environmental and Social History: Obtained dog from breeder at 8 weeks old. Had older female dog at home, they get along fine. Had him with handler to show in conformation. While at a show, was attacked by a GSD. Owner claims that, since then, he has a fear of all large dogs, especially black ones. This was told to the owner by an animal communicator. Dog is Schutzhund III background in pedigree. Owners decided they wanted to do obedience work and found a trainer who had trained in Germany and had trained police dogs and was also involved with local search and rescue groups. Trainer believed in domination of the dog. Used collar corrections and alpha rolls on a regular basis and advised owners to do the same. These were private classes with one other dog and person sometimes. "Mike" was obedient, but "sassed" owners and trainer on occasion and didn't really show much improvement. After 3 or 4 months, owners decided to go to another trainer, as the "sassing" was getting worse and required more and more correction. Was fine in the conformation ring, never sassed handler and "turned on like a star." (Note: many conformation handlers use minimum correction and tons of food lure.) The next trainer used a prong collar, but did not believe in the alpha roll. This trainer recommended a "hang spin" to correct the "sassing" of the dog. The owners opted not to do this and left this trainer also.

The next trainer they found did positive reinforcement with clicker. The classes were group classes outside. This trainer would not get within 5 feet of the dog. The owners were ostracized because the dog was doing fairly well, *except* for occasional outbursts at the other dogs or the trainer. The owners were asked to work away from the group. They completed the 8 week course and never actually received any instructions on the clicker use.

The owners were very discouraged and worked with the dog at home with no distractions, but the "sassing" continued. A year latter they went to another group class at another training facility. Traditional training was used again with implementation of a choke collar. The owners tried an electric shock collar for the dog-dog aggression at the instructor's suggestion and this made the problem worse. The dog would always focus on one dog in the class and grumble at it throughout the class. The e-collar was discontinued. There was improvement (from being worse to just the usual bad) after they quit the e-collar. At this point, everyone told the owner that this dog was very aggressive. The owners got tired of the remarks and whispers at the classes – tired of the constant battle and fighting with the dog.

The owners took the dog to Doggie Camp where the dog finally got some positive reinforcement help. Myself and other trainers were not afraid of him and explained the use of the clicker to the owner. The dog improved drastically in a week, with other dogs being predicators of reinforcement. Chosen carefully, some stable dogs were enlisted to interact with this dog and all went fine.

Re-check: The owner brought "Mike" to my training facility. This dog was still resource guarding his person (the owner was not even aware this was happening), so he was getting endless "permission" from her to indulge in this behaviour. I could set the dog up to growl at me, OR to be friendly with me, just by using different body language. Pretty normal!! We worked endlessly for a week on eye-contact (desensitizing dog to direct eye contact from humans, which he perceived as threat behaviour – no surprise there, with all that traditional "roll & shake-em down" training). He would still focus on a dog and lock on and then lunge and bark at the dog(s) when meeting them, especially in "close-quarters." After a week of eye-contact and impulse control work, using back-aways the moment he locked on to another dog, he made great strides forward. The owner has continued working at home and is continuing to make progress, with the dog becoming less and less reactive. The owner's most recent communication stated: "The information we gained from you during camp and now reading your book is priceless…You have shown us the next step that we needed to take; the one that others did not know to show us." Nice for me to get a little R+ now and then....

Medications: Currently on Heart worm preventative

Presenting Issues: Aggressive behaviour towards owner, but limited to very slight growls. Dog is very reactive around other dogs, although has also behaved well around other dogs and has normal relationships with a number of dogs.

Classification: Possessive aggression. Learned aggression. Protective aggression.

NOTE: Lack of *positive* exposure to novel stimuli is at the root of the issue, also normal breed tendencies to guard objects (including owner) from other dogs and humans.

Management:

Do not physically punish.
Be aware of the environments you are taking the dog into.
Serious awareness on the part of the owner re: other dogs body language in area & of their own dog.
Scheduled feed.

Behaviour Modification:

Self restraint.
Desensitize to movement.
Desensitize to eye involvement.
5-15 minutes basic obedience 2x daily.
Halti head-collar, muzzle.
Desist.
Back away from ANY stimuli that the dog locks on to.
Over-correction (in the form of doggie push-ups) for over-reactive behaviour.
Educate owner about calming signals and apply R+ to proper use of them around other dogs and people.
Install RM/NRM (had RM).

Recheck Visit:

There is no pathology indicated; this dog responds normally over a variety of situations, especially when one takes into account the background of the dog.

It is most important that the owners continuously keep a management and structure program in place, with continued exposure to a wide variety of stimuli. The dog's behaviour is much improved with the client feeling much more confident about her ability to control Mike's behaviour. The incidents have reduced drastically.

This dog will always be a "strong" dog and a lot of dog to handle. The owner's skill level has increased dramatically. The dog's compliance level has gone up accordingly. This has become a very manageable situation.

The following is a case history example of

PREDATORY AGGRESSION.

HEAVEN ON ARF BEHAVIOUR COUNSELING
Rottweiler, Male, Castrated
DOB: 1994
NAME: Ralph (name changed)

My initial consult with "Ralph" was July of 2000.

Past Medical History: Altered at 6 months of age. Unremarkable medical history, normal physical at the last veterinarian call.

Environmental and Social History: Owner got as puppy. Lives rurally. Dog went to puppy classes, but has not been extensively socialized. Dog has not been around many children.

Presenting Issues: child safety (dog is good with older children, but reactive around younger children, under age 6 or 7). Grandchild, who is an infant, is coming to visit. Jumping up. Wants better control of dog's behaviour and dog to be gentle around baby. Dog goes crazy at the door.

Classification: Predatory behaviour inappropriately displayed. The rest is just a matter of obedience work and the dog finding the client relevant.

Protocol Addressed

Management:
ALWAYS supervise around children.
Muzzle around younger children, drag leash.
On leash around door and guests until have verbal control.
Scheduled feed.

Behaviour Modification:
Self-restraint.
Desensitize to movement.

Desensitize to eye involvement.

5-15 minutes basic obedience 2x daily.

Halti head-collar, muzzle.

Desist.

Over-correction (in the form of doggie push-ups) for over-reactive behaviour.

Install RM/NRM (had RM).

Long down stays – daily.

Dog must be relaxed BEFORE children approach and all safety steps are in place.

Recheck Visit in Home: Had pizza delivered and was able to put the dog through the doorbell behaviour. Dog is exuberant around adults but very friendly and sweet. Then had neighbor come over with 2 girls, age 3 and 9. Dog was okay with older girl. With Halti on dog, the 9 year old could approach and pet. The 3 year old child was approaching and the dog became tenser. I had them carefully and neutrally move the little 3 year old away as I moved the dog away, being careful to keep a distance of several feet. Suddenly, the little girl turned and ran up the stairs. The dog became extremely reactive. I was glad I had the Halti and muzzle on the dog, although I did manage to control him. After this, he would eye the little 3 year old and just would not give it up. So we could manage his behaviour, but every time the little girl moved, he would try to visually lock on to her. I was very concerned about this and notified the owner that he is unsafe around children and to always use all precautions.

This dog is excellent around adults, a quick leaner and very easy for me to handle in spite of his size, and normally was quite cooperative and attractive. But the stalking behaviour around the small child was very alarming. I counseled the owner to confine the dog around toddlers and infants, with no exceptions. He plays fine (according to owner) with her 7 year old grand daughter, but I still cautioned her about allowing them to be unsupervised.

Conclusion: There is no real pathology indicated; this dog responds normally over a variety of situations. It is most important that the owners continuously keep a management and structure program in place, with continued exposure to a wide variety of stimuli. Working around small children must be done will all safety precautions in place. That we have predatory aggression directed toward small children is alarming. I cautioned the client carefully and explained that modifying predatory aggression when it is directed toward small humans is risky and should be controlled by carefully managing the dog's environment very studiously and relentlessly.

This is very much a case of the dog never being around children and being excited, yet restrained, in their presence (not that you should let the dog go...). The dog has built a lot of frustration around this issue.

Recheck: The dog is doing very well with the lady's grand-daughter and has, so far, taken exception only to this one child. The client has moved out of the area so I will likely have limited contact with her now.

The following is a case history example of

TERRITORIAL AGGRESSION, LEARNED AGGRESSION, FEAR-BASED AGGRESSION.

HEAVEN ON ARF BEHAVIOUR COUNSELING
RE: Sheltie/Beagle mix – neutered male
DOB: Jan 2000.
NAME: Skip (name changed)
CLIENT: Name not disclosed

My initial consult with "Skip" was May 2001.

Past Medical History: Altered at 6 months of age. Unremarkable medical history, normal physical at the last veterinarian call.

Environmental and Social History: The family documented four significant and typical incidents, which are the total incidents of note that have occurred in this dog's life. "Skip" always alerts at the door by running to the door, becoming unruly and excited, exhibiting barking and growling. He quickly accepts adults within a few minutes, but he has had incidents with children. In three of the incidents (all of which occurred on the owner's property) the dog barked and growled at the children, but did not approach any closer than approximately 6 feet away from them. The owners, each time, managed to leash the dog and put him into a safe area. The following incident precipitated my visit in May 2001. The family had the dog locked in the bedroom from which he was accidentally released. The child was standing in the kitchen and the dog (frustrated from being locked up) charged down the hall and knocked the child down. The adults were all in shock and I assume there was a moment of confusion. The dog was taken out of the room and confined again. Upon examination, the child had a slight abrasion on her hand. It is not clear whether this was from the dog's toenails or his teeth. Since it was a single small mark with no bruising, my opinion is that it was caused from the dog's toenails. While this incident is extremely alarming, no bites have occurred.

Classification: Territorial Aggression, Learned Aggression, Fear-based Aggression.
The agonistic behaviour displays (barking, lunging, growling) are directed toward adult strangers, but only on their initial entry into the house. "Skip" quickly habituates to the presence of adults and then he is friendly; that is, he approaches them, or they can approach him, and he will then sniff and solicit attention in a normal manner. "Skip" also directs agonistic display, as above, toward children.

Management:

This dog is to be in NO CONTACT with children.
When visitors are in the house, this dog must be on a leash. If children are visiting he must be confined in a safe place. When outside, this dog must be supervised and confined or leashed so humans and dogs are safe.
Low protein dog food and much less of it.
Scheduled feed.
This dog must not receive any food, treats or attention for free, but must respond correctly to a request from a human (e.g., sit, down, etc.)
There is to be NO rough play with this dog by any family member.

Behaviour Modification:
Formal obedience sessions 2 to 3 times a day.
Desensitize to eye involvement – teach eye contact from humans i.e. a non-threatening gesture.
Desist.
Sit, self-restraint – dog must sit and relax for all attention.
Desensitize to a muzzle.
Desensitize to noises & activities centering around the door (Wait at Door).
Dog is to drag leash so that physical control is easier to manage at all time.
Dog fitted for a Halti head collar – to be worn for training and walks.
Dog to wear muzzle when with other than just the owners.
If children are encountered on walk, they are to be warned not to pet the dog and the dog should be taken away from the situation.

Discussed with the family the gravity of the situation, and the legal liability. We discussed their veterinarian's recommendation for euthanasia.

I worked with the dog and the family. The dog learns fairly quickly. His lack of early exposure to children is, in my opinion, at the root of this issue, coupled with the fact that, prior to this time, the family had not trained the dog to be under control in this situation. The owners are fully cognizant of this fact and are a caring family that just wants to get this situation corrected. The ultimate decision of whether to work with or euthanize this dog rests with the family. After discussing management and training techniques and demonstrating them to the family, then having the family members carry out the exercise, it was decided to re-evaluate the dog in June. Once the behaviour modification program is initiated and in place, the viability of keeping the dog safely will be better known. Until that time, the family has agreed that NO contact with children will be the rule.

On re-check, the dog is showing much improvement. He has now met with some children on walks and is accepting their pets quite normally. He is still closely monitored and kept on leash when children visit the home, and is given "short doses" of children, which helps a lot. Initially the dog was muzzled around children visiting and I advised them to continue this for the life of the dog as a preventative measure.

The following is a case history example of

FEAR BASED AGGRESSION, LEARNED AGGRESSION, GENERALIZED ANXIETY.

HEAVEN ON ARF BEHAVIOUR COUNSELING
RE: Wire Fox Terrier, Female, Spayed
DOB: approx. January to May of 1997
NAME: Star (name changed)

My initial consult with "Star" was January 1999.

Past Medical History: Spayed by Rescue League before placement. Unremarkable medical history, at time of consult. Just prior to June 1999 "Star" was treated at Veterinarian Clinic for pancreatitis.

Environmental and Social History: In the home are 2 adults and a Schnauzer mix. Got "Star" from an animal rescue. She was found wandering on November 1998; stray in extremely neglected condition. Owner got her December 1998 and the Veterinarian had approximated her age to be 18-24 months old at that time. The family has an invisible fence system. "Star" and Schnauzer sleep in bed with owners. "Star" began obedience class at the local pet store in January 1999, and she did great. I recommended that when they attended class they use no physical correction, and the instructor agreed. Clients have tried ignoring the undesired behaviour, leash corrections, frontal approaches, etc. All of these elicit defensive behaviour from the dog. The dogs were boarded in my kennel in February 1999. A synopsis of that visit: Slightly anxious, but not unusually high stress. No signs of aggression with me, three different kennel aides or my husband.

There was an appointment with me for follow-up on the behaviour modification protocol in March, but client cancelled appointment because "Star" was doing so well. About a month later, there was a phone contact; "Star" was calmer, still growling at husband occasionally but good once the husband got into the room. "Star" plays well with other dog. "Star" stays near wife all the time.

Diet: Science Diet Lite, after bout with pancreatitis – Science Diet WD for life.

Presenting Issues: When company is over she growls at them and will not approach the guests. She growls and snaps at husband, dog gets very upset when he enters the room. Dog is fine with the wife.

Classification 1/26/99: Fear-based aggression, Learned aggression, Generalized anxiety.
Lack of education and exposure to novel stimuli is at the root of the issue, at least the part that we will be able to modify. At the time of the initial consult, it is difficult to determine if the dog is misbehaving, uneducated, abnormal or (I suspect) all three. After the protocol has been followed for 30-90 days I will have much more information based on the response and adaptability of the dog. Generalized anxiety, if it does not abate, indicates a lack of ability to habituate, indicating definite abnormality.

Classification 5/25/99: Add to above diagnosis – Protective aggression.

Management:

Dog is to be placed in no situation where she can practice aggression.
Dog drags a leash always so clients can gain physical control.
Children not to be unattended with dog.
Do not physically punish.
Scheduled feed.

Initial Behaviour Modification:

Self restraint.
Desensitize to husband entering the room.
Desensitize to eye involvement.
5-15 minutes basic obedience 2x daily.
Install RM/NRM (had RM).

Discussed dog body language and response to individual programs at length. The key is to "get in ahead of" the aggressive behaviour by closely observing the dog and intervening by distracting the dog. Husband must become a predictor of reinforcement vs. the predictor of punishment and anxiety, the current paradigm. Wife is to stop giving the dog constant attention and only attend to the dog if she

is behaving appropriately. A head collar was fitted to the dog and I showed the clients how to use it. The dog is to be placed in a different room when husband initially comes home from work, when the environment is a bit calmer, and the SEC is past, then the husband can go get the dog and take her to the wife. While I was there, "Star" was extremely reactive to any movement by myself initially, but habituated somewhat before I left. She is anxious and tense and scanning much of the time.

Recheck Visit 5/25/99: "Star" snapped at a neighbor that she is somewhat familiar with (my thoughts: probably the neighbor's approach methodology). She sits on husband's lap for hours; sometimes she will nip him and then immediately lick him. She has weeks where she behaves normally, and then she has days where she withdraws from the family entirely, hiding behind the furniture (abnormal – lack of ability to habituate, paranoia). Wetting on the floor occasionally – owner thought out of spite (my thoughts: anxiety-discussed with client). Discussed re-homing dog. I advised impossible. If husband comes in the house or a room with wife not present, the dog is fine. Suggested I make an in-home visit, client will call for appointment.

Recheck 6/8/99: After brief hospitalization for pancreatitis, "Star" came home snarling worse (my thoughts: predictable – dog extremely stressed). They began physical discipline again (client understandably very frustrated) – again the dog became worse and is even more distant and withdrawn, even with wife. Urination in house increasing. We discussed euthanasia vs. medicating. The consensus was by 6/20 to try medication.

Conclusion: This is obviously a dog who is abnormal. The client will need to follow the behaviour and management protocol as well as a pharmacological protocol.

Recommendation for Pharmacological Protocol: I worked with the client's veterinarian and suggested the appropriate medications for this dog. Appropriate blood screening and urinalysis was done. The medication will help to reduce anxiety so "Star" can be calm enough to learn. (Specific medical information omitted.)

Plan: Get the dog started on medications. The client and I will meet to go over the protocol carefully, so I can ensure that the client is following the program exactly and that they are both capable of carrying out the program. Re-evaluate every 3 days; at the end of 90 days make a decision about discontinuing the meds temporarily as a diagnostic tool. If when the meds are discontinued, the behaviour deteriorates, it is probable that meds will need to be continued for the life of the pet.

On re-check the dog has improved to a level "livable" for these clients. Anxiety abated by 40-80% depending on context; aggression less & easier to interrupt. Improvement due primarily to management by client and clients consistent adherence to beh. mod. protocols. Did an additional house-call and dog is scanning less. Approaches by people on street are to be carefully controlled and made very reinforcing experiences. People may pet the dog if SHE approaches the person. Discussed stress and calming signals again extensively. The meds are helping the dog with her abnormal anxiety levels, and she is learning some new behaviours and the clients are working hard on the relax and leave it behaviours. Re-evaluation scheduled for 30-40 days.

The following is a discussion of a case history concerning

ABNORMAL BEHAVIOUR.

HEAVEN ON ARF BEHAVIOUR COUNSELING
RE: Labrador-mix, Male, Castrated
DOB: 1997
NAME: Sam (name changed)

I first saw this dog in February of 1998. I had actually seen him before the current owner (client) obtained him. A local member of a dog rescue group had gotten this dog and another littermate at approximately 2 weeks old. The rescue member kept the puppies until they were over 1 year old. They were kept in a multiple dog house with minimum problems either with people or other dogs. However, they did not socialize the dog to locations other than their country home. Many of the other dogs in the home were also rescues and may have had some inappropriate behaviour due to lack of socialization. The dogs were frequently in a yard without supervision, not that this is unusual, but does cause a "grey area" in regards to exactly what this dog may have learned from interacting with the other dogs. Behaviours learned at a VERY young age may be so ingrained it is difficult to distinguish between hard-wired and learned in some cases.

The new owners lived in the city for the first 3 years that they had this dog and they just moved to the country so they could have a fenced in back yard (2001). The clients are very sweet people and are quite devoted to their dogs. They had this Lab mix for 2 years before they obtained another rescue dog, a female Miniature Schnauzer, who came with some problem behaviours of her own, therefore exacerbating some of Sam's troubling behaviours. This meant another period of adjustment for the dog and the clients, which they have all weathered quite graciously.

The clients first brought this dog to me with severe separation anxiety, as well as aggression – especially around children and other dogs.

The clients were initially very permissive with both dogs, although they have, out of necessity, placed more limits on this dog's behaviour because of his many issues. It is very difficult for them to treat this dog as they should – consistently – because they are often very affectionate with him, and just go up to him giving him hugs and loads of love for no reason – i.e., free love. I give them much credit for altering their own natural behaviour patterns to make adjustments in Sam's behaviour.

In my opinion, this animal has abnormal learning patterns, constantly requiring re-teaching. Some of this was initially due to the laxity on the owners' part. They are really constantly trying and have become more aware of the dog's body language, etc. The owners keep the physical portion of the protocols in place but it is not in their nature to enforced strict guidelines for the dog.

The wife has brought the dog for private lesson for the last 7 months. Whenever we allow him to participate in a group class, the dog becomes extremely reactive and just cannot settle back down into a calm state. He is much less reactive with me, but he does "guard" the wife a lot, particularly in novel situations (e.g., visiting or when others visit, when they are on vacation and in a new location, etc.).

Any owner will always have a steep learning curve with this kind of dog – not always recognizing the really subtle signals of this guarding behaviour: she allows the dog to be out in front of her looking and sniffing. She feels that she has him under control because he is on the leash and close to her. What I see is the dog is out in front of her and feels this "position" or context gives him permission to "guard". The owners have improved in this area immensely and realize that marginal behaviour is significant.

Like other dogs I have worked with that present with this sort of anxiety-based "controlling" behaviour (but not control conflict aggression because it is not directed specifically toward his family), he actually does better with the separation anxiety while boarded in my kennel. This is easy to explain. For dogs that have panic attacks (separation anxiety) have to have someone they are abnormally super-attached or co-dependent on. Once I remove that person and the dog doesn't have access to her, the dog calms considerably. Also, the dog should never be placed in a situation where the rules are not absolutely black and white. Because I am controlling the dog's behaviour so rigidly, the dog can relax – there isn't any discussion. This means the dog makes no judgment calls – he can relax because he doesn't have to be "responsible" for anything other than his own responses. The schedule does not change much in the kennel. That means the dog can totally depend on certain events happening within certain time frames. For dogs who are "brittle" (little ability to "rebound" – they become easily stressed and recover from the stress reaction slowly, poorly, or not at all), living in a normally variable human environment becomes an increasingly tricky proposition. This is not a realistic way to live with a dog on a daily basis, however. Over time, with much work and dedication from the client, this dog has improved immeasurably at home. We have used a variety of techniques, including psychopharmacology which was helpful.

For dogs such as this one, the more control you exert over their behaviour, and the more rigid you make the rules, the more they relax. The problem, of course, is that the interaction (dog to human) can not be the same as with a normal pet; free love cannot be given.

Recently, we were "painting" with this dog. This involves putting a little "mitten" on the dog to hold the paint and having him target an easel with paper on it with his foot. I reached over to put the mitten on his foot and he did the open-mouth-with-all-his-teeth-out-lunge and hit me in the face. The owner naturally becomes rattled when these events happen and there is a lag time between the behaviour and the owner getting the dog to back away from the situation, or to show disapproval of the behaviour. With a dog like this, this very slight latency makes quite a difference. I gave him some verbal disapproval and then had him do the doggy push-up exercise. I waited a minute, then picked his foot up again. He repeated the lunge/snap/contact. I had him repeat the doggy push up exercise. I waited a few minutes for sympathetic nervous signs to abate a bit, and then we tried again. The dog was tense, but accepted the handling. It is notable that, without the owner present, I can clip the dog's toenails and handle him everywhere. When the owner is present, the dog has a lot more at stake, and some guarding behaviour or "I have someone here to back me up" behaviour occurs.

He has been on a variety of anti-anxiety meds. When he is taken off of them, he does have much more trouble focusing on learning and remembering tasks, and his separation anxiety gets worse. Getting the second dog has relieved the separation anxiety considerably.

This dog, when aroused, has a very difficult time returning to normal, calm behaviour. There are obviously faulty "switches" in there – when the dog receives an adrenal dump due to arousal either he gets this "huge" dump like the switch turns on but is very slow to turn off OR the switch turns on/off, on/

off, on/off and gets stuck in that cycle for a very long time, not allowing the dog to return to normal physiologically. Observable are a variety of symptoms: dilated pupils that don't return to normal for a long time after arousal, increased respiration, sweating paws, etc.

I stress to the clients to keep these protocols in place as consistently as they can and to really manage the dog's behaviour. The clients get into trouble every time they "pretend" (inadvertently) that this dog is a normal dog. This dog is not normal. The commitment level of these clients is extraordinary, and they are good dog parents – doing the "hard" stuff (the stuff that is emotionally difficult to do because they love the dog, like no free love) because it is in the dog's best interest in the long run.

One of the most difficult ongoing challenges is the dog's reactivity levels. They remain intense under low stimuli.

The Foundation and Level I behaviours have helped this dog immensely. Structure and placing limits on the dog's behaviour are imperative and help to keep him manageable and comfortable, even though he protests this a bit.

This dog continues a pharmacological protocol in addition to behaviour modification and this will be the lifestyle for this family for the life of the dog. He is a very sweet and affectionate with his family and with people that he knows well. The family has done such a good job with much of the behaviour modification that the dog presents almost as a normal dog in many circumstances now.

Protocols for this dog have included:
Protocols for Separation Anxiety
Pharmacological Protocol
Foundation & Level I Protocols
Dog-to-Dog approaches
Handling & Restraint Protocol
Basic Obedience, emphasis on Come When Called
Protocols for possession issues

The following is a case history example of

CONTROL CONFLICT AGGRESSION, POSSESSIVE AGGRESSION, ABNORMAL BEHAVIOUR.

HEAVEN ON ARF BEHAVIOUR COUNSELING
RE: Yellow Labrador Retriever, Male, Castrated
DOB: 1995
NAME: Sunny (name changed)

My initial consult with "Sunny" was February 1996.

Past Medical History: Altered at 6 months of age. Unremarkable medical history, normal physical at the last veterinarian call.

Environmental and Social History: In the home are 2 adults. "Sunny" was obtained at 5 weeks and had had one home. He was a friendly, but overbearing, puppy. The dog is crated and also has access to fenced- in yard. Pup was socialized and his owner took him to puppy class. She did everything she was told to do by the training instructor. The husband occasionally got extremely frustrated with the dog and did alpha rolls with him before coming to our first appointment. The dog presented with increasing aggression and unruly behaviour as he got older. He snaps suddenly at guests and at the owners. When younger he would pick up objects and, even though he understood "drop-it," he would consume any item the owner tried to take from him. To date, he has had to have socks removed surgically.

When someone tries to control him, he will assume a guarding posture and threaten owners or others who try to get him to respond to a command he doesn't wish to obey.

Separation anxiety (due to lack of ability to control the owners).

When he becomes excited, it takes him an abnormally long time to recover from an adrenal "dump."

Has bitten owner(s) and threatened me many times. Bites – level 1 & 2 (do not require stitches or emergency room care).

Diet: Purina Pro Plan

Meds: Currently on heart worm preventative

Presenting Issues: Aggressive Behaviour toward owners. Unruly behaviour, dog is difficult to control.

Classification: Learned aggression. Control Conflict aggression. Separation anxiety. Possessive aggression. Pica.

Management:

ALWAYS supervise around child.
Muzzle if around children.
Dog drags leash always.
Dog is to be placed in no situation where he can practice aggression.
Scheduled feed.
Do not physically punish.

Behaviour Modification:

Self-restraint
Desensitize to movement
Desensitize to eye contact
Involvement
5-15 minutes basic obedience 2x daily
Halti head-collar and muzzle
Scenting games to engage dog's mind and give him a job

Desist
Restraint
Install RM/NRM

Continued Behaviour Modification:
Polite greeting
Desensitize to territorial entry

Conclusion: There is pathology indicated; this dog responds abnormally over a variety of situations. Over a seven-year period, we have discussed euthanization many times, however the owners concluded each discussion with the decision to work with the dog. The dog is not horribly dangerous, but is definitely a liability. If the management and training is relaxed for a day or two, the dog immediately reverts back to guarding objects obsessively and growling at owners when they touch his head.

It is most important that the owners continuously keep management and structure program in place. There are frequent training regressions because of abnormal learning patterns. The dog does quite well in the kennel because of the absolutely rigid structure imposed on him when he stays with me. He handles quite well for me, but you cannot be normal with him (as a normal person would treat a pet). Every interaction must include obedience and yielding behaviours must be constantly reinforced. Coercion makes the dog violent and the reverberations from any coercion used last for days. At the same time, it is important that every time someone interacts with the dog, he is placed in a situation where he must obey the command. Therefore, Halti collar and leash are invaluable tools.

The dog was euthanized in the summer of 2001. The owners became worn out from living with the abnormal behaviours of this dog, The behaviour would improve temporarily, but then the dog would be placed in a slightly different context and he would become reactive. This decision was difficult for them to make, but they had my support. At this point he had bitten the owners and had also threatened guests. The liability issue was beginning to loom large for them.

GLOSSARY

abnormal

Deviating from what is normal; maladaptive or dysfunctional behaviour. Activity that demonstrates dysfunction.

antecedent

Any occurrence or event that precedes or happens prior to a behaviour.

approximations

When teaching your dog a new behaviour, it is often easier to communicate when the terminal response (goal or "finished" behaviour) is broken down into baby-steps or "approximations". See shaping.

associative learning

To associate means to connect or join together in thought. The events immediately surrounding your dog's behaviour, or events occurring during the behaviour, become the information the dog relies on to make decisions about future behaviour in this context.

attention word

An attention word is a cue to remind your dog to direct his attention to you (e.g., "watch me," "focus," "look," etc.).

aversive

Any event, context, or circumstance that causes avoidance behavior. An aversive event is a stimulus that would suppress a behaviour that precedes it or a stimulus that would increase a behaviour, where that behaviour would terminate the aversive.

back-chaining

Back-chaining or back-training is a specific method of linking separate behaviours into one behaviour sequence. Back-chaining involves developing a series of responses in reverse order. In this way, one can develop a complex series of behaviours by teaching the last one first. See chaining.

behaviour

Any observable response or act. Anything that one does in response to a stimuli that is overt (externally observable).

behaviour modification protocol

A protocol is the plan of a scientific experiment or treatment. A behaviour modification protocol refers to the specific, methodical principals (approximations or steps) one would follow to change a particular pattern of behaviour or set of behaviours.

behaviour sequences

When you link several behaviours together to make a continuous series of behaviours, you are creating a behaviour sequence. The individual behaviours would follow one after the other to form a complete sequence or terminal response. Almost any task you ask your dog to perform consists of several separate behaviours that are linked together and performed in a pattern.

bridge

A synonym for reward mark. See Reward Mark.

canis/canids

Carnivorous mammals of the family Canidae, which includes wolves, dogs, fox, coyotes, and jackals.

chain

A series of behaviours that occurs in a fixed pattern. Over time, an individual behaviour in the series becomes a cue or stimulus to perform the next behaviour in the series. In the same manner, each behaviour, excepting the first one, becomes a conditioned reinforcer for the behaviour preceding it. See Behaviour Sequence.

classical conditioning

A specific type of learning in which respondent behaviour is brought under the control of a stimulus or event that was previously unknown or unnoticed. Classical conditioning connects a conditioned stimulus with an unconditioned response (reflex).

clicker

A small training tool, usually made of plastic with a metal tab, that makes a "click-click" sound which is a clearly notable reward mark for our dogs, cats, horses, and other animals.

conditioned reinforcer

An event or stimulus that becomes reinforcing through learning. This event/stimulus is not reinforcing until it is paired with other events that are already known reinforcers. The best way to obtain a conditioned reinforcer is to pair your stimulus (a specific word or clicker) with food, which is a primary reinforcer. See also reward mark, secondary reinforcer, bridge.

conditioned response

Also known as CR. A response that is brought about by a specific cue or context after classical conditioning has taken place. The CR is exactly the same response as the Unconditioned Response (UCR) and is reflexive (not voluntary). For a conditioned response to occur, a conditioned stimulus (CS) is paired with an unconditioned stimulus (UCS). After a period of time, the conditioned response is apparent in the presence of the CS, even when the UCS is not present. (See classical conditioning.)

conditioned stimulus

Also known as CS. A previously neutral (unknown or unnoticed) stimulus which the dog learns to associate as being a predictor of another stimulus. (See classical conditioning.)

conflict resolution

Conflict resolution requires coming to terms with a specific disagreement so that all parties involved can amicably behave in a fashion that works for all. The task is upon humans, when dealing with animals, to resolve the conflict in a peaceful and non-confrontational manner.

consequent events

An event that logically or naturally follows behaviour. A result or effect of behaviour.

context

The specific pattern of conditions (settings, events) surrounding a behaviour.

contingency relationship

The relationship between a behaviour and the antecedent (events that precede the behaviour) or the consequences (events that follow the behaviour).

contingent events

Events that can be linked directly to the specific behaviour. For instance, contingent delivery of a reinforcer would indicate that the positive reinforcement is given only in the presence of a specific behaviour.

cue

Any antecedent event. A means of communicating with your dog to obtain a desired behaviour. May be verbal or a signal (e.g., the word "down" or pointing to the floor). There are also environmental cues.

discrimination

Responding differently in the presence of different antecedent events or cues.

display

behaviour patterns that are species-specific and have a specific message.

fading

The process of removing, in a methodical and gradual manner, additional prompts and/or physical guidance and extra cues from the antecedents required to elicit the behaviour. See also prompts.

fear

Fear is a very primal emotion. Fear can be so intense as to prevent learning all together. According to Webster's, "fear" is specifically: A feeling of alarm or disquiet caused by the expectation of danger, pain, or disaster. To feel anxious or apprehensive about a situation or context. Please note the "expectation." What may not look fear-inducing to you certainly may look fear-inducing to your dog, or another human, for that matter.

first events

First events are significant because of the effect they have on memory. First events are often remembered with great clarity. Make certain that your dog is getting the "first impression" that you want him to have. You don't get a second chance to make a first impression!

First correct effort

The very first time a dog exhibits a behaviour as desired OR takes a step in the right direction toward your terminal response is a Notable Event! First correct efforts should receive extra or jackpotted reinforcement in order to accelerate the acquisition of behaviour and the learning process.

generalization

Generalization is the ability to transfer a behaviour intact from one context to another, in the presence of a consistent antecedent.

inter-command discrimination

The ability to tell the difference between cues and therefore respond correctly in the presence of different cues. In other words, the dog has made the connection – he knows which cue belongs to which behaviour.

latency

Latency, in technical terms, is "latent period," which means the interval of time that occurs between a stimulus and a response. If you give your dog a cue (stimulus), the latency is the time it takes the dog to respond with a behaviour. Once your dog has responded to your cue, it is your job to respond with an appropriate consequence. How quickly you respond is also defined as latency. Latency should be a small time increment! In fact, for consequences, the recommended time frame is during the behaviour or within 1/2 second.

learned behaviours

An acquired wisdom, knowledge, or skill. Learned behaviours are attained through life experiences.

Learned behaviours are those an organism will repeat due to perceived favorable consequences.

leave it (desist)

A cue which predicts for the dog that he will not be allowed access to an item at that time. (Refer to the Desist protocol chapter for a detailed discussion.)

magnet

Anything your dog is currently attracted to (e.g.,. a squirrel, a toy, food, another dog, etc.). This magnet may be the technical reason that you are not getting compliance to a cue. So the magnet is a "competing reinforcer."

manufactured behaviour

The definition of "manufactured" in Webster's dictionary is "to make ... a raw material into a finished product." When dog trainers discuss this term, we specifically mean: A behaviour not naturally offered up by your dog, which must be obtained somehow so it can be reinforced so it will occur again. You, the trainer, elicit behaviour from your dog by using lures, prompts, physical guiding, and other methods of shaping. In short, the trainer manufactures a response so that he has the opportunity to apply positive reinforcement.

memory markers

Memory is the capability to retain and recall past experiences. A memory marker is an event or cue that aids in the retention of an experience so that it is easier for the organism to recall a specific behaviour.

negative punishment

The removal of an item that the dog wants to have, the results of that action being a decrease in the frequency of that particular response.

negative reinforcement

The removal of an aversive event, resulting in an increase in the frequency of that particular response. The desirable response should serve as a switch to "turn off" the aversive event.

neutral tone

Communication to your dog without expressing emotion (happiness, anger, impatience). This tone is used to convey information without clouding the learning process with excess emotion that is confusing for the dog.

no

Most overused word in training communication between human and dog. Should only be used when it expresses unacceptable behaviour that you "never" want to see again.

no reward mark

NRM. This is presented to the dog as information, not some huge emotional affair. A NRM is a Consequent event that has been paired with an aversive event. Specifically, for our purposes, the removal of a primary reinforcement. A NRM tells the dog: You will not be "paid" for that behaviour.

operant behaviour

Offered, voluntary behaviour that is directly controlled by the consequences contingent on that behaviour.

operant conditioning

A specific type of learning in which voluntary behaviour is modified, installed or altered by manipulating the consequences. This is an all-important lesson – the consequences are a direct result of (contingent on) the behaviour.

P+, P-

An abbreviation for positive punishment, negative punishment, respectively.

paradigm

An individual's belief system or perception of a given set of circumstances.

pilo-erector

Reflexive behaviour observable in domestic dogs (and other species) in response to being startled, alarmed or uneasy or uncertain. Most commonly observed as the hair rising along the shoulder area, but can extend all the way along the back and include the hair on the tail, as well (think of a Halloween cat without the arched back).

positive punishment

An aversive event that decreases the frequency of a behaviour.

positive reinforcement

Positive reinforcement is a desirable consequence (event or stimulus, e.g., cookie) that increases the frequency of a behaviour. Positive reinforcers are something the trainee desires. Positive reinforcement is the delivery of the desired item to the dog.

primary reinforcers

Required for survival. Food, water, air. Sex is listed in some literature; other behaviorists feel that sex should not be included as a primary reinforcer. My choice from this list is food – it is the simplest and most humane to control and manipulate. When we are discussing primary reinforcers in dog training, the general understanding amongst dog trainers is that we are discussing food.

prompts

Antecedent events that aid in initiating a response. An additional cue that helps elicit a specific response. Gestures, lures, and additional cues all serve as prompts. See also fading.

protocol

In Webster's New Collegiate Dictionary, it means: the plan of a scientific experiment or treatment. To a behaviourist, a protocol is the map or plan of a behaviour modification program. The protocol describes the program in a step-by-step manner, relying upon successive approximation as a core technique. The protocol is used by the behaviourist to outline the big picture and the details. It is also used by the client as a guideline.

punishment

Punishment DECREASES behaviour. Application of an aversive event or removal of an reinforcing event, with the result being that there is a decrease in the frequency of the target behaviour. Punishment causes avoidance behaviour and can encourage aggression in specific circumstances.

R+, R-

Positive reinforcement, negative reinforcement, respectively.

ready

Can be used as a cue word to indicate a "clock-in" (you are working) cue to the dog. "Ready" means that opportunity for reinforcement is now available – In Jean Donaldson's terms, "The bar is open."

reinforcement

Reinforcement INCREASES behaviour. Adding an event or stimulus that the dog wants to have happen again, or removal of an aversive event, the results being that there is an increase in the frequency of the target behaviour.

reinforcement history

Each behaviour will have a history of reinforcement and other consequences. Each dog will have an accumulation of experiences that he has had in this context, or with this cue or behaviour. This accumulation of experiences is called the reinforcement history.

reinforcement schedules

The rules or guidelines one uses to determine how many and which responses will receive how many and which reinforcers. Basically, there are four types: fixed ratio, fixed interval, variable ratio, and variable interval. Ratio refers to how many reinforcers per behaviour are given. Interval refers to how often the positive reinforcement is given. An intermittent schedule refers to a type of variable schedule in which only some occurrences of a behaviour are positively reinforced, usually only the "best efforts."

When developing a behaviour, a fixed schedule (1 behaviour = 1 R+) is the rule. To maintain behaviour that your dog already knows, a variable schedule (variable ratio, variable interval, and intermittent schedule with reinforcement variety) is the schedule to use. To obtain specific kinds of responses, differential reinforcement schedules are used.

release word

A cue to communicate to your dog that the exercise (or behaviour) has ended. For example, when you no longer require your dog to remain in a down stay, you cue him with a release word that the exercise has ended. This is a "clock-out" (work is over) cue.

response

A reaction of the dog to a specific stimulus.

respondent behaviour

In some of the technical literature, respondent behaviour is referred to as specifically involved with an autonomic response (behaviour directly related to the responses of smooth muscles and glands – reflexive behaviour). This would refer one to using the term in relation to classical conditioning only. However, the term respondent behaviour is used by some authors in a much broader sense and may be applied to include skeletal responses as well. In some of the current literature, it is accepted that respondent behaviour may be occurring on a reflexive or operant level – therefore a *broad definition* would be: behaviour that is elicited by a stimulus. It aids clarity to define the response in terms of the stimuli that reliably produce them. Is the behaviour emitted (conditional reflexes) or elicited (operant behaviour). Respondent *conditioning* itself is specifically discussed in terms of classical conditioning.

reward mark

RM. A reward mark is a precise way to communicate to your dog that you like the behaviour he is offering you, and wish to have it remembered and repeated. A verbal "yes" or "good" and/or a clicker are commonly used.

salient

An event or stimulus that is conspicuous or most noticed by the dog.

satiation

Too much of a good thing! Satiation occurs when a reinforcer temporarily loses its effectiveness because the trainee is gratified to the point that the reinforcer is no longer desirable to him. This is a good reason to use a variety of reinforcers. Your primary reinforcer (food) is tiny and varied and a desired treat by the dog. This will help avoid satiation. Training in short sessions also helps, although this is quite variable for the dog and the level of sophistication of the dog's training and age.

setting events

Those events that refer to context, conditions, or other situations that will have an effect on the antecedent-behaviour-consequence relationship. Setting events are all of those components that surround a behaviour, and therefore may influence the response of the animal.

shaping

Developing a behaviour toward a terminal response (end goal), specifically using successive approximation as the technique to get there. (See also: successive approximation.)

spoil

For our purposes in dog training, this term means to prevent direct access or prevent access to the dog reinforcing himself. If you drop food on the floor and you tell your dog to "leave it," and he attempts to get it, you must stop or "spoil" his opportunity of eating the food and thus rewarding himself by eating the food. If the dog is able to eat the food, he has just learned that "leave it" is optional!

spontaneous recovery

Recovery of a behaviour that had disappeared. A behaviour that had entered an extinction phase but has returned. When the behaviour returns it may appear in the same form or it may be of more or less intensity.

stress

A mental, emotional, and physical reaction to distress. Stress can prevent learning. (Often a dog under much stress will not be interested in food.) Stress occurs on a "chemical" level (changes in the neurotransmitter system) which is observable via sympathetic nervous system changes (e.g., respiratory, cardiac) and observable as behaviour changes. Stress is always present in the environment to some degree and your dog must be taught to deal with it.

successive approximation

Successive approximation is the process of breaking the end goal behaviour down into many tiny steps or "approximations." Your dog learns to sit, then sit stay, then sit stay at a distance, before he learns sit-stay out of sight. (See also: shaping.)

target behaviour

The behaviour you are currently trying to install, modify, or shape.

terminal response

The final behaviour or behaviour sequence that you want to get when you have applied training and, specifically, shaping. A terminal response is the end or final result of shaping behaviour. The end goal. The finished masterpiece.

Thorndike's Law of Effect

states that responses are made more probable by some consequences and less probable by other consequences. That is, the behaviour you observe is based on past consequences.

threshold

The intensity below which a mental or physical stimulus cannot be perceived and produces no response.

timing

Timing identifies the lapse of time that occurs between the dog offering a behaviour or response and the trainer's response to the behaviour: the quicker the better. Remember the 1/2 second rule!

training treats

Any quickly edible food delicacy used as a primary reinforcer. Treats must be very tiny! Use a variety of treats to keep your dog's interest.

unconditioned response

Also known as UCR. A response that is evoked by a stimulus that need not be taught nor learned. We don't have to "learn" that food and water make us salivate – that response is innate. If you put your hand on a hot stove burner, you will immediately remove it. Unconditioned responses may also be called unconditioned reflexes.

unconditioned stimulus

Also known as UCS. It is unique in that it causes a consistent response each time by the dog, with no prior training or conditioning. (See classical conditioning.)

under training

Probably the number one reason that you get non-compliance from your dog. Under training is not enough training in enough different circumstances: too few repetitions, not enough trials, inadequate number of locations, etc. The dog will not properly generalize the behaviour.

RESOURCES

Assess-a-Hand™ and **books by Sue Sternberg:**
Rondout Valley Kennels
Sue Sternberg
4628 Rt. 209
Accord, NY
(914) 687.7619

As complete a collection of **Dog Books and Videos** as you will find anywhere; great customer service; some training aids:
Dogwise
701B Poplar
Box 2778]
Wenatchee, WA 98807-2778
1.800.776.2665
1.509.663.9115
www.dogwise.com

Halti Head Collars:
Care-a-lot Pets
800.343.7680
In Virginia 757.460.9771
www.carealotpets.com

Martingale Collars, cotton & leather training leads, & great environmental enrichment toys:
Premier
800.933.5595

Great Leather Tug Toys:
www.Eurosportk-9.com

SUGGESTED READING AND VIEWING MATERIAL

Other great materials are listed in the References section.

Broitman, Virginia. *Take A Bow ... Wow! 2.* (Video).

Broitman, Virginia & Lippman, Sherri. *Take A Bow ... Wow!* (Video).

Dunbar, Ian. *Fighting & Biting.* (Video).

Miller, Pat. (2001). *The Power of Positive Dog Training*. NY: Hungry Minds.

O'Heare, James (2001). *The Canine Aggression Workbook.* Ontario: Gentle Solutions. (A book that I wish would have been out a bit sooner, actually, as I was done with this manuscript by the time I got to read it.)

Tellington-Jones, Linda: anything on *Tellington TTouch,* especially videos.

SEMINARS - AND THANKS

I have attended several seminars that have shaped my own training techniques. I have taken exercises from them, extrapolated them, perhaps changed them, and certainly put them in my own words. But these people shaped my ideas and/or sparked my imagination and got me thinking. I would like to thank the following people for their seminars:

- Karen Pryor, 1995, Operant Conditioning.
- Jean Donaldson, 1996, Operant Conditioning; Aggression.
- Suzanne Clothier, 1997, Aggression.
- Turid Rugaas, 1999, Calming Signals; Aggression.
- Patty Ruzzo, 1994, 1996, 1997, Obedience.
- Patty Ruzzo, Leslie Nelson, & Ted Turner, 1996, Operant Conditioning; Obedience; Aggression; Management.
- Chris Bach, 1998, Obedience.
- Sue Sternberg, 1999, Shelter Dogs and Evaluation.
- Cornell University, 1999, Solving Canine Behaviour Problems. Conversations with Dr. Ellen Lindell were particularly helpful.

REFERENCES

Adams, H. Richard (Ed.). (1995). *Veterinary Pharmacology and Therapeutics* (7th ed.). Ames, IA: Iowa State University Press.

Aloff, Brenda. (2001). *Positive Reinforcement: Training Dogs in the Real World.* Neptune City, NJ: T.F.H. Publications, Inc.

Burch, Mary R. & Bailey, Jon S. (1999). *How Dogs Learn.* New York: Howell Book House.

Campbell, William. (1975). *Behavior Problems in Dogs.* Santa Barbara: American Veterinary Publications.

Catania, A. Charles. (1992). *Learning* (3rd ed.). Englewood Cliffs, NJ: Prentice Hall.

Chance, Paul. (1994). *Learning and Behavior.* Pacific Grove, CA: Brooks/Cole Publishing.

Clothier, Suzanne. (1996). *Body Posture & Emotions: Shifting Shapes, Shifting Minds.* Stanton, NJ: Flying Dog Press.

Clothier, Suzanne. (1996). *Self Control.* Stanton, NJ: Flying Dog Press.

Dodman, Nicholas H. & Shuster, Louis (Eds.). (1998). *Psychopharmacology of Animal Behaviour Disorders.* Malden, MA: Blackwell Science, Inc.

Donaldson, Jean. (1996). *The Culture Clash.* Berkeley: James & Kenneth Publishers.

Guyton, Arthur C. (1976). *Textbook of Medical Physiology* (5th ed.). Philadelphia: W. B. Saunders Company.

Hopkins, S,G., Schubert, T.A., & Hart, B.L. (1976). "Castration of Adult Male Dogs: Effects on Roaming, Aggression, Urine Spraying, and Mounting." *JAVMA* 168:1108-1110.

Jecs, Dawn. (1995). *Choose to Heel* (1st ed., Book #1). Copyright and published by the author.

Lindsay, Steven R. (2000). *Handbook of Applied Dog Behavior And Training, Volume One, Adaptation and Learning.* Ames, IA: Iowa State University Press.

Martin, Garry & Pear, Joseph. (1996). *Behaviour Modification: What It Is and How To Do It.* Upper Saddle River, NJ: Prentice Hall.

McLennan, Bardi. (1993). *Dogs and Kids: Parenting Tips.* New York: Howell Book House.

Mitchell, Lana. (1997). *Click! For Success.* Hillsboro, OR: Lana Mitchell.

Nelson, Leslie, Pivar, Gail & the staff of Tails-U-Win™. (1997). *Management Magic.* Manchester, CT: Tails-U-Win.

Odendaal, J. S. J. (1997). *A Diagnostic Classification Of Problem Behavior In Dogs and Cats.* Philadelphia: W. B. Saunders Company.

Overall, Karen L. (1997). *Clinical Behavioral Medicine For Small Animals.* St. Louis, MO: Mosby-Year Book, Inc.

Pryor, Karen. (1985). *Don't Shoot the Dog!* New York: Bantam Books.

Pryor, Karen. (1997). *Clicker Magic* (Video).

Rugaas, Turid. (1997). *On Talking Terms With Dogs: Calming Signals.* Hawaii: Legacy By Mail, Inc.

Scott, John Paul & Fuller, John L. (1965). *Genetics and the Social Behavior of the Dog.* Chicago: The University of Chicago Press.

Sidman, Murray. (1989). *Coercion and its Fallout.* Boston: Authors Cooperative, Inc.

Spector, Morgan. (1999). *Clicker Training for Obedience.* Waltham, MA: Sunshine Books.

Sternberg, Sue. (No date given). *Environmentally Cued Training That Transfers.* NY: Rondout Valley Kennels.

Sternberg, Sue. (No date given). *Preventing Possessiveness In Shelter Dogs.* NY: Rondout Valley Kennels.

Tellington-Jones, Linda & Hood, Robyn. (1994). *The Tellington TTouch for...Dogs & Puppies: Step-By-Step. La Quinta,* CA: Thane Marketing International.

Weston, David. (1990). *Dog Training: The Gentle Modern Method.* New York: Howell Book House.

Weston, David and Ruth. (1997). *Your Ideal Dog: Teach Your Best Friends to Be a Perfect Companion.* New York: Howell Book House.

Index

A

acquisition 133
- establish A-B-C connection 135
- learning stage 133

alert 364
alerting
- and verbal cues 265
- example of in case history 396
- photo of 227, 344, 347
- threshold distance 364
- timing 345

alpha roll
- example in a case history 392, 403
- philosophy regarding 304

anchoring
- and tight leashes 355

antecedent 129
appropriate behavour 26
approximation 381
approximations
- raising criterion. See also successive approximations. 198

aquisition
- fixed schedules 136

arc
- dog approaches 349

arousal levels
- evaluating 117

assess-a-hand 334
- and restraint 306
- food bowl exercises 338
- resource for 415
- use with guarding objects 183

association 125
autonomic nervous system 147
- emotional response 147
- list of associated behaviour 101

B

behaviour 129
behaviour as an experiment 132
behavioural topography 32
brittle 41, 401
- stress 40

C

calming signals 42, 49
- and play behaviour 81
- around other dogs 346
- dog parks 89
- leash aggression 354
- list of 54

castration 36, 37
challenge
- why challenge? Involvement protocol 241

challenges
- definition 137
- definition of 281
- overview of OC 129

chess players 84
choosing playmates 83
classical conditioning 147
- and switching 148
- in a nutshell 126

classification
- Lack of socialization - interspecies 97

classifications
- accurate classification 114
- Control Conflict Aggression 99
- Dog-to-Dog Aggression 102
- Excessive Breed Tendencies or the lack of these 97
- Fear Aggression 101
- Human Selection for Aggression in Dogs 98
- Idiopathic Aggression 102
- Lack of socialization - intraspecies 96
- Learned Aggression 103
- Maternal Aggression 103
- Neophobia 104
- Pain-related aggression 104
- Play Aggression 105
- Predatory Aggression 107
- Redirected Aggression 111
- Territorial Aggression 112
- Using Classification as an accurate Descriptor 113

clocked in/clocked out 222
communication system 128
conflict
- maladaptive response 119

confrontations
- reminders 33

consequences 129
- acquisition stage 135
- contingent on behaviour 179

contingency 134
contraindicated 67

correction
  traditonal definition vs. mine 244
counter-conditioning 126, 146
cross-over dogs 131
cue 129
  adding the cue 133
  discrimination 130
  overview of OC 129
  pitfalls of adding too early 236

D

damage control 48
default to the environment 265
diagnostics vs. classification 115
differential reinforcement
  behaviour selection 145
  DRA 145
  DRE 145
  DRO 145, 146
differential reinforcement schedules 145
differential reinforcment
  DRI 145
displacement activities
  list of 54
distance decreasing signals
  list of 66
dominance
  ethologist definition 30
dominant
  and deference programs 177
  human attitudes and aggression 208
  in traditional dog training 30
  insecure animals 49
  play with humans 73
duration 137

E

effort vs. outcome 382
Einstein-brain 41
end working cue 222
engrams 287
entrapment 116
establish communication 130
establishing a pattern 134
expectations 211
extinction
  as a Tool 140
extinction burst 141

F

feedback
  overview of OC 129
fence fighting 360
fence running 361
first correct effort
  and variable ratio 135
  DRO 146
  pop quiz 250
first correct efforts
  and hazard pay 136
fixed schedule
  definition 133
flooding 143
  differs from desensitization 145
  example 144
fluency 80, 187
  variable schedules 136
food treats and human paradigms 129
foundation protocols
  and a master plan 213
frequency 137
frustration
  and confusion 325
  and greeting behaviour 285
  causes of 116
functional & task analysis 210

G

generalizing behaviour
  and reinforcement schedules 137
genetics
  and factors that influence aggression 35
graffiti painters 84
greeting ceremony 25, 88
guideline for classes 39

H

habituation
  and flooding 144
handling & restraint protocol
  and a master plan 213
hardening (a response) 242
hard-wired 25
hazard pay 136, 218
  and weeding behaviour 136
help vs. draw a line in the sand 260
hidden agenda 48
hit list 211

hormones
    as factors that influence aggression 36
humping 85
husbandry behaviours 301
    advanced 321
    basic, acquistion of 320

I

in context behaviour 26
inappropriate aggression 27
incorrect responses 137
indications that dogs are in Play Mode 82
intensity 137
intention behaviour
    Stays 257
intermittent reinforcement
    creating variable schedule 135

J

jack-pot 321

L

labeling
    problems inherent with 113
labels
    classification of aggression 93
Lassie myths and aggression 208
latency 401
learned aggression
    and factors that influence aggression 34
level I protocol
    and a master plan 213
limited hold 253
lizard-brain 41

M

magnet 265
maintain behaviour
    variable schedules 135
maintaining behaviour 135
maintenance of behaviour
    variable schedules 137
management 138
    operant conditioning 128
    overview of OC 129
manufacturing behaviour
    voluntary response 133
marginal 74
marginal behaviour 141
marking territory 54
missed associations 134, 190
multiple-home dog 39
muzzles and human attitudes 169

N

nail clipping
    and come when called 200
    as a husbandry behaviour (how to) 321
native language
    acquiring sophisticated language 80
    and play behaviour 80
    avoiding aggression 43
    ritualized behaviour patterns 33
navigation plan 207
no 138
no reward mark
    and intention behaviour on Stays 258
    For extensive discussion see protocol
        "RM/NRM & Release Cue. 131
no reward mark (and challenges) 242
normal behaviour 26
normal vs. abnormal
    classifying behaviour 94
novel stimuli
    risk for problems 38

O

offered behaviour
    operant conditioning 127
operant conditioning 147
    laws of learning 127
out-of-context behaviour
    used as signals 55
over-correction 393
    technique explained 270
owner attitude
    and outcome 208
    confrontation 208
    deer caught in the headlights 208
    sink or swim 208

P

physical correction
    and "cross-over" dogs 131
physiological changes
    emotional state 41
piloerector reflex 61

play and the older dog 85
playbBehaviour
  list of 80
pop quiz 250
positive punishment 153
positive reinforcement
  and the concept of "permissive" 139
posturing 82, 360
predatory drift
  play aggression 106
  predatory aggression 108
predictor of punishment
  and greeting behaviour 35
  and social tension 49
predictor of reinforcement
  and greeting behaviour 35
premack principle 182
preparing to begin a protocol
  "What To Have Ready" 249
pre-requisites 137
prey sequence 35
primary reinforcement 130
pro-active
  and SEC 205
problem solve 212
prognosis
  and the practitioner 95
  in a case history 387
prognosis (rating system) 95
punishment
  effect on discrimination 264
punishment cycle 118
puppy kindergarten 38
puppy kindergarten class 84
puppy play-groups 84

R

rank order 30, 85
  control conflict aggression 99
  lack of socialization 96
reassurance
  effect on dog 280
recall
  and play groups 85
recovery time 226
  and stress 41
reflexive behaviour
  as observable behaviour 127
rehearsal 118
rehearsing
  and incorrect responses in training 137
reinforcement schedules
  patterns 133
reinforcement variety 135
reinforcers 129
release cue 222
relevant
  scheduled feed 175
reminder antecedent 254
repetition
  and reliabile behaviour 178
resilient 41
retreat
  used as reinforcement 279
review sessions 239
reward mark
  For extensive discussion see protocol
    "RM/NRM & Release Cue." 130
risky behaviour 141
risky or marginal behaviour
  and a master plan 212
RM
  overview of OC 130
RM/NRM
  example of use 132
role-playing and dog games 87
rule of sevens 38
rules for puppy play-groups 84

S

safe vs. dangerous 264
salient 218
session 239
setting events 211
  and a master plan 212
shaping 137
  operant conditioning 127, 128
shaping. See also Successive Approximation.
signs of trouble
  play behaviour 83
social development periods
  as factors that influence aggression 37
social time-out 181
socialization
  and fear 324
socializing
  how long 38
spay 36
spontaneous recovery 127, 365
  and extinction 142

in the abnormal vs. normal dog 94
station
targeting 290
stimulus 125
stimulus control 27
adding the cue 235
and end-work cue 221
how to obtain it 129
overview of operant conditioning 129
stimulus gradient 143
strategic retreat
how to 327
street party 267
stress
allergy analogy 40
stress and fear
as factors that influence aggression 39
submissive 30, 40, 48, 81, 88
punishment 67
tail 71
submissive urination 67, 120
successive approximation 137
switch
and Sit or Down behaviours 257
switching
and arousal levels 119
and impulse control 248
and using Sit or Down as a vehicle 249
limbic vs. pre-frontal cortex 41
operant vs. classical conditioning 148
photo essay using prey object 274
systematic desensitization 142

T

teaching a behaviour
overview 129
territorial aggression 284
Thorndike's Law of Effect 127
threshold
and calming signals 278
bite 36
bite threshold 343
determining a... 345
determining for dog to dog approaches 345
distance and approximations 365
record keeping 365
worksheets 212
zen Sit/Down 255
tight leash
and Halti 164
leash aggression 353
timing 130
and use of food 129
contingency 134
fear aggression 101
intervention 52
is everything 198
the real "t" word... 130
use in behaviour modification 381
topography 48, 51, 235
and hidden agenda 48
training treats. See also food treats. 130
trial 239
trigger 49, 126
listing precursors 211
protocol choice 212, 382

U

uneducated dog 25

V

vacuum activity 94
Variable 136
variable interval 135
variable ratio 135
variable schedule
and variable behaviour 136
creating a variable schedule 135
definition 133
verbal cue
syntax 250

W

weed out undesirable behaviour 136
window of expectation
and approximations 138

Y

yielding
display (Distance Decreasing Signal) 66

About The Author

BRENDA ALOFF is a professional dog trainer specializing in problem behaviour. A large part of her practice consists of dogs who have been referred to her when traditional training techniques have failed. In addition to working with owners on re-socialization fearful and aggressive dogs, Brenda also teaches puppy socialization, fundamental to competition obedience, conformation, tracking, back-packing, musical freestyle, and agility classes at Heaven On Arf Behaviour and Training Center, in Midland Michigan.

Brenda's childhood love was training and showing horses. She has taken this knowledge about working with large, potentially dangerous animals and applied it to training dogs with problem behaviours. Her first Smooth Fox Terrier sparked culture shock and a fascination in dog behaviour.

Unsatisfied with the results of "traditional" dog training, Brenda studied marine mammal training, exotic animal training and learned about wolf pack behaviour. Working with a steady inflow of rescue dogs that required rehabilitation, many of them with aggression problems, as well as personal dogs who were aggressive, made Brenda particularly interested in aggression. Puzzled by the lack of answers in dog lore and literature, and because "traditional" dog training techniques did not offer the tools needed to deal with aggressive dogs, in particular, she became an expert in behaviour modification and positive reinforcement training. Brenda's understanding of Learning Theory, canine language and social systems provides dog owners with effective means of communicating with their dogs and modifying their behaviour.

Brenda lives in an old farmhouse with her husband, Steve (robotics and software), and her daughter, Abbey (seventeen and currently into creative writing). They currently live with: Maeve, a rescue German Shepherd Dog; Rylie, a Border Collie; and Brenda's beloved Smooth Fox Terrors (no typo!), Breanna, Punch and Zasu (aka Zoomer).

Brenda's first book, *Positive Reinforcement: Training Dogs in the Real World*, was published in 2000. In 2001, this book was a finalist for the prestigious Dog Writers Association of America Award. She has also authored several magazine articles on dog training, produced a television program about canine behaviour, and been a guest on radio talk shows dealing with canine issues. She is a member of Association of Pet Dog Trainers (APDT), The National Association of Dog Obedience Instructors (NADOI), Trainers Forum, and several other breed and training organizations.

Brenda travels all over the United States, giving talks on canine aggression and learning theory, from short lectures to intensive weekend workshops. People also travel long distances to spend a week in Midland, and do a week of private and group sessions with dogs who have aggression problems.

Photo by Joanne Weber.

Zasu, Brenda & Rylie. 2002.